BARRON'S
PRACTICE EXERCISES FOR THE
TOEFL®

TEST OF ENGLISH AS A FOREIGN LANGUAGE

7TH EDITION

Pamela J. Sharpe, Ph.D.
The Ohio State University

BARRON'S

To my students
with best wishes for success on the
TOEFL and after the TOEFL

All inquiries should be addressed to:
Barron's Educational Series, Inc.
250 Wireless Boulevard
Hauppauge, New York 11788
www.barronseduc.com

ISBN: 978-0-7641-4566-7 (book)

ISBN: 978-1-4380-7033-9 (book & listening CD)

ISSN: 1935-8512

PRINTED IN THE UNITED STATES OF AMERICA
9 8 7 6 5 4 3

10%
POST-CONSUMER
WASTE
Paper contains a minimum
of 10% post-consumer
waste (PCW). Paper used
in this book was derived
from certified, sustainable
forestlands.

Contents

IMPORTANT NOTE

If your version of this book does not contain audio CDs, you can test yourself by using the scripts that appear in Chapter 7, beginning on page 299.

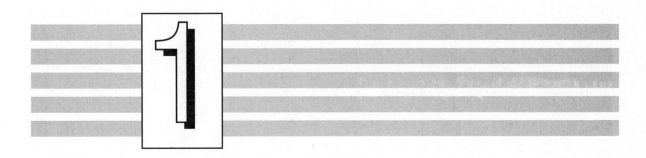

PLAN FOR SUCCESS

Introduction

The TOEFL examination is currently administered at test sites around the world in two different formats: the Paper-Based TOEFL (PBT) and the Internet-Based TOEFL (iBT®). Similar language proficiency skills are tested on both formats, but they are tested in different ways.

Paper-Based TOEFL (PBT)

The PBT is a pencil and paper test that is offered for two purposes. One purpose of the PBT is for placement and progress evaluations. Colleges or other institutions use the PBT to test their students. The scores are not valid outside of the place where they are administered, but the college or institution accepts the PBT that they administer as an official score. This PBT is also called an Institutional TOEFL. The other purpose of the PBT is to supplement the official Internet-Based TOEFL in areas where Internet-based testing is not possible. The scores are usually valid outside of the place where they are administered. This PBT is also called a Supplemental TOEFL.

The Paper-Based TOEFL has three parts: Listening Comprehension, Structure and Written Expression, and Reading. In addition, the Test of Written English (TWE) is an essay that is required to provide a writing score. The PBT is a linear test, which means that everyone who takes the TOEFL during the same administration will see and answer the same questions. The total score is based on a scale of 310–677.

Internet-Based TOEFL (iBT®)

The Internet-Based TOEFL (iBT®) is a computer-assisted test that was introduced in September 2005 worldwide. The Internet-Based TOEFL (iBT®) was initially referred to as the CBT2 and as the Next Generation TOEFL.

The iBT® has four parts: Listening, Speaking, Reading, and Writing. The Speaking Section was already introduced in 2003 as the TOEFL Academic Speaking Test (TAST). On the four-part iBT®, most of the questions are independent, but some of the questions are integrated. For example, you may be asked to listen to a lecture or read a text, and then speak or write a response. The total score is based on a scale of 0–120.

This book offers practice for both formats of the TOEFL. This book will help you succeed on any TOEFL examination that you take.

Advice for Success on the TOEFL

Develop a Positive Attitude

To succeed on the TOEFL, begin with a positive attitude, learn what to expect on the test, use your time well to prepare, and gain experience by reviewing English and practicing test items. Here is some specific advice.

Visualize

"Imagination is the beginning of creation. You imagine what you desire. You will what you imagine. And, at last, you create what you will."—George Bernard Shaw

To *visualize* means to see a picture of something in your mind. Spend one minute visualizing your success before each study session. Close your eyes and see what you want to happen. See yourself sitting at the TOEFL administration, visualize that you are relaxed, moving through the test confidently, completing it within the time limits. Now you are viewing the computer screen with your range of scores. See the score that you want on the computer screen. See yourself smiling. Now picture yourself achieving the goal that motivated you to take the TOEFL. If you are a student, see yourself on a university campus, going to class. If you are in the medical profession, see yourself working in a hospital. See your success. Enjoy your visualizations.

Affirm

"People become really quite remarkable when they start thinking that they can do things. When they believe in themselves, they have the first secret of success."—Norman Vincent Peale

To *affirm* means to have a positive conversation with yourself. Say in words what you have visualized. Spend 30 seconds repeating affirmations. For example, you might say, "I am confident."

This affirmation is from the current edition of *Barron's TOEFL iBT® 13th Edition*:

"I know more today than I did yesterday.
I am preparing.
I will succeed."

Formulate a Plan

Inform

"As a general rule, the most successful man in life is the one who has the best information."
—Benjamin Disraeli

To *inform* means to provide information. You need to know what to expect on the TOEFL. If you are informed, you will not be surprised and confused on the day of the exam. Visit the official TOEFL web site at *www.toefl.org*. Download the *TOEFL Bulletin of Information* from the site, or order it by mail. Be sure to download the format that you intend to take—Paper-Based or the Internet-Based (iBT®) TOEFL. If you have also purchased the current edition of *Barron's TOEFL iBT®*, read chapter one, "Questions and Answers About the TOEFL." Study the charts on the following pages for a summary and comparison of the different TOEFL exams.

THE TWO TOEFL FORMATS

	Paper-Based TOEFL (PBT)	*Internet-Based TOEFL (iBT®)*
Tutorial	NO questions	NO questions
Listening	50 questions	33–34 questions
Speaking	NO questions	6 questions
Listening/Speaking	NO questions	Included
Structure	40 questions	NO questions
Reading	50 questions	36–39 questions
Reading/Speaking	NO questions	Included
Writing	1 question	2 questions
Listening/Writing	NO questions	Included
Reading/Writing	NO questions	Included
TIME	2 hours	4 hours

Note: The actual times will vary in accordance with the time the supervisor completes the preliminary work and begins the actual test. On the TOEFL, the exact time for the test will vary from one person to another. This is a good estimate.

Quick Comparison—Listening

PAPER-BASED TOEFL AND INTERNET-BASED TOEFL (iBT®)

Paper-Based TOEFL	*Internet-Based TOEFL*
Three types of questions are presented in three separate parts. Part A has short conversations; Part B has long conversations and class discussions; Part C has mini-talks and lectures.	Two types of questions are presented in six sets. Each set has one long conversation and two lectures.
The talks and lectures are about 2 minutes long.	The lectures are about 5 minutes long.
Everyone taking the TOEFL answers the same questions.	Everyone taking the same form of the TOEFL answers the same questions.
There are no pictures or visual cues.	Each conversation and lecture begins with a picture to provide orientation. There are several pictures and visual cues with lectures.
You hear the questions, but they are not written out for you to read.	The questions are written out on the computer screen for you to read while you hear them.
Everyone taking the TOEFL proceeds at the same pace. You cannot pause the tape.	You may control the pace by choosing when to begin the next conversation or lecture.
The section is timed. At the end of the tape, you must have completed the section.	The section is timed. A clock on the screen shows the time remaining for you to complete the section.
You may not replay any of the conversations or lectures.	You may not replay any of the conversations or lectures.
All of the questions are multiple-choice.	Most of the questions are multiple-choice, but some of the questions have special directions.
Every question has only one answer. You answer on a paper Answer Sheet, filling in ovals marked Ⓐ, Ⓑ, Ⓒ, and Ⓓ.	Some of the questions have two or more answers. You click on the screen in the oval that corresponds to the answer you have chosen, or you follow the directions on the screen.
You can return to previous questions, erase, and change answers on your Answer Sheet.	You cannot return to previous questions. You can change your answer before you click on **OK**. After you click on **OK**, you cannot go back.
You may NOT take notes.	You may take notes while you listen to the conversations and lectures.

Quick Comparison—Speaking

PAPER-BASED TOEFL AND INTERNET-BASED TOEFL (iBT®)

Paper-Based TOEFL

There is NO Speaking Section.

Internet-Based TOEFL

Three types of questions are presented in six sets. The first two sets have a general question; other sets have questions about campus and academic topics.

After you see and hear the general questions, you will have 15 seconds to prepare your answers and 45 seconds to record them.

After you hear the campus and academic questions, you will have 20–30 seconds to prepare each answer and 60 seconds to record it.

Quick Comparison—Structure

PAPER-BASED TOEFL AND INTERNET-BASED TOEFL (iBT®)

Paper-Based TOEFL

Two types of questions are presented in separate parts. Part A has incomplete sentences, and Part B has sentences with underlined words and phrases.

All of the questions are multiple-choice.

Everyone taking the TOEFL answers the same questions.

Every question has only one answer.

You have twenty-five minutes to complete the section.

You answer on a paper Answer Sheet, filling in ovals marked Ⓐ, Ⓑ, Ⓒ, and Ⓓ.

You can return to previous questions, erase, and change answers on your Answer Sheet.

The score on the Structure Section is not combined with the score on the essay in the Test of Written English (TWE).

Internet-Based TOEFL

There is NO Structure Section.

Quick Comparison—Reading

PAPER-BASED TOEFL AND INTERNET-BASED TOEFL (iBT®)

Paper-Based TOEFL

There are five reading passages with an average of ten questions after each passage.

The passages are about 250–300 words in length.

Everyone taking the TOEFL answers the same questions.

There are no pictures or visual cues.

All of the questions are multiple-choice.

Every question has only one answer.

You answer on a paper Answer Sheet, filling in ovals marked Ⓐ, Ⓑ, Ⓒ, and Ⓓ.

You can return to previous passages and questions, erase, and change answers on your Answer Sheet.

There is NO glossary.

You may not take notes.

Internet-Based TOEFL

There are three reading passages with an average of 12–13 questions after each passage.

The passages are about 700–800 words in length.

You will answer the same questions as others who take the same form of the test.

There may be pictures in the text and visuals that refer to the content of the reading passage.

Most of the questions are multiple-choice, but some of the questions have special directions.

Some of the questions have two or more answers.

You click on the screen in the oval that corresponds to the answer you have chosen, or you follow the directions on the screen.

You can return to previous questions, change answers, and answer questions you have left blank in the same part, but you cannot return to passages in a previous part.

There may be a glossary of technical terms.

You may take notes while you read.

Quick Comparison—Writing

PAPER-BASED TOEFL AND INTERNET-BASED TOEFL (iBT®)

Paper-Based TOEFL

The essay, also called the Test of Written English (TWE), is offered five times each year. You must select a TOEFL test date when the TWE is scheduled if you need an essay score.

When you register for the TOEFL on one of the dates when the TWE is offered, you are registered for the TWE at no additional cost.

There is only one topic for each essay.

Everyone taking the TOEFL writes an essay about the same topic.

You do not know any of the topics for the essay before the test administration.

Most of the topics ask you to agree or disagree with a statement or to express an opinion.

The topics are very general and do not require any specialized knowledge of the subject to answer them.

You have 30 minutes to complete the essay.

You handwrite your essay on paper provided in the test materials.

You have one page to organize your essay. This page is not graded.

Your essay will not be scored for neatness, but the readers must be able to understand what you have written.

You should write about 300 words, or three to five short paragraphs.

A scale from 1 to 5 is used to grade the essay. The scale is explained on page 453.

The score is reported separately from the TOEFL score. It is not included in the computation of the total TOEFL score and does not affect your score on the multiple-choice TOEFL.

Internet-Based TOEFL

The Writing Section is required. It includes two essays.

When you register for the TOEFL, you are registered for the Writing Section at no additional cost.

There are two topics. The second topic is based on both a lecture and a reading passage.

Everyone taking the same form of the TOEFL will write about the same topics.

At this point, no writing topics have been published; however, the essay topics previously published for the Computer-Based TOEFL are good practice for the general-topic essay. Visit *www.toefl.org.*

The topic for the independent writing task asks you to agree or disagree with a statement or to express an opinion. The integrated task refers to topics from a lecture and a reading passage.

The independent topics are very general and do not require any specialized knowledge of the subject to answer them. Technical words are explained in the text or in a glossary for the integrated topics.

You have 30 minutes to complete the independent writing task. You have 20 minutes to complete the writing sample that refers to both a lecture and a reading.

You should type your writing samples on the computer. If this is not possible, you can ask for special accommodations.

You have paper to take notes and organize your writing. Your notes and outlines are not graded.

Your essays will not be scored for neatness, but the readers must be able to understand what you have written.

You should write 300–350 words for the independent writing task, 150–225 words for the integrated writing sample.

A scale from 0 to 5 is used to grade writing samples. The scales are explained in Chapter 9.

The score is reported as a Writing Section score.

Three Study Plans

Schedule

To *schedule* means to plan your time. If you plan your time and follow a schedule, you will be able to review and study everything in this book before you take the TOEFL. For help in preparing your schedule, choose one of the study plans outlined below. Then, stay on schedule.

"Diligence is the Mother of Good Luck."—Benjamin Franklin

The Best Study Plan

If you have time to do all of the exercises in this book, that is the best study plan. All of the exercises will help you prepare for the Paper-Based TOEFL (PBT) and the Internet-Based TOEFL (iBT®).

Alternative Study Plan One

If you have limited time, you can select only those exercises that correspond to the TOEFL format that you intend to take. This will give you specific experience with the type of items that are found on the test you plan to take.

Alternative Study Plan Two

If you have already taken the TOEFL, you will know which section or sections are the most difficult for you. Even if you have not taken the TOEFL, you probably know your strong and weak points. You can select only those exercises that correspond to the TOEFL section in which you need to improve. Choose from Listening, Speaking, Structure, Reading, or Writing. This will give you specific experience with the types of items that are the most challenging for you.

Use the following list of exercises to keep a record of your work. Make a check mark beside each exercise when you complete it.

	Paper-Based TOEFL	Internet-Based TOEFL		Paper-Based TOEFL	Internet-Based TOEFL
			LISTENING EXERCISES		
Exercise 1	❑		Exercise 16	❑	
Exercise 2	❑		Exercise 17	❑	
Exercise 3	❑		Exercise 18	❑	❑
Exercise 4	❑		Exercise 19	❑	
Exercise 5	❑		Exercise 20		❑
Exercise 6	❑		Exercise 21		❑
Exercise 7	❑		Exercise 22	❑	❑
Exercise 8	❑		Exercise 23		❑
Exercise 9	❑		Exercise 24	❑	
Exercise 10	❑		Exercise 25	❑	
Exercise 11	❑		Exercise 26		❑
Exercise 12	❑		Exercise 27	❑	
Exercise 13	❑	❑	Exercise 28	❑	
Exercise 14	❑		Exercise 29		
Exercise 15	❑	❑	Exercise 30		❑

	Paper-Based TOEFL	Internet-Based TOEFL		Paper-Based TOEFL	Internet-Based TOEFL
SPEAKING EXERCISES					
Exercise 31		❏	Exercise 36		❏
Exercise 32		❏	Exercise 37		❏
Exercise 33		❏	Exercise 38		❏
Exercise 34		❏	Exercise 39		❏
Exercise 35		❏	Exercise 40		❏
STRUCTURE EXERCISES					
Exercise 41	❏		Exercise 49	❏	
Exercise 42	❏		Exercise 50	❏	
Exercise 43	❏		Exercise 51	❏	
Exercise 44	❏		Exercise 52	❏	
Exercise 45	❏		Exercise 53	❏	
Exercise 46	❏		Exercise 54	❏	
Exercise 47	❏		Exercise 55	❏	
Exercise 48	❏				
READING EXERCISES					
Exercise 56	❏		Exercise 71	❏	
Exercise 57	❏		Exercise 72		❏
Exercise 58	❏		Exercise 73		❏
Exercise 59	❏		Exercise 74	❏	
Exercise 60		❏	Exercise 75	❏	
Exercise 61		❏	Exercise 76		❏
Exercise 62	❏		Exercise 77		❏
Exercise 63	❏		Exercise 78	❏	
Exercise 64		❏	Exercise 79	❏	
Exercise 65		❏	Exercise 80		❏
Exercise 66	❏		Exercise 81		❏
Exercise 67	❏		Exercise 82	❏	
Exercise 68		❏	Exercise 83	❏	
Exercise 69		❏	Exercise 84		❏
Exercise 70	❏		Exercise 85		❏
WRITING EXERCISES					
Exercise 86	❏	❏	Exercise 94		❏
Exercise 87	❏	❏	Exercise 95		❏
Exercise 88	❏	❏	Exercise 96		❏
Exercise 89	❏	❏	Exercise 97		❏
Exercise 90	❏	❏	Exercise 98		❏
Exercise 91	❏	❏	Exercise 99		❏
Exercise 92		❏	Exercise 100		❏
Exercise 93		❏			

MODEL TEST

Paper-Based TOEFL	Internet-Based TOEFL
❏	❏

Review

"To climb steep hills requires a slow pace at first."—William Shakespeare

To *review* is to study something that you have studied before. To succeed on the TOEFL, you must have studied English already. It is not possible to achieve an excellent score if you are just beginning to study English. However, it is possible to make a higher score by reviewing what you have already studied, especially when you concentrate on the type of English that appears most often on the TOEFL. For an extensive review of every section of the TOEFL, you can use the current edition of *Barron's TOEFL iBT®*.

Practice

"Practice makes perfect."—Anonymous

Practice is very important in order to succeed on the TOEFL. By practicing exercises that simulate the items on the TOEFL exam, you gain valuable experience. Because you understand the directions for each section, you know what to do on the official TOEFL without trying to figure it out under the stress of an actual test. You can learn test strategies as well—how to manage your time on each section, how to eliminate possible answer choices, and when to guess.

Work through the practice exercises in this book systematically, using the study plan that you have selected. Spend time practicing every day for at least an hour instead of sitting down to review once a week for seven hours. Even though you are studying for the same amount of time, research shows that shorter sessions every day produce better results on the test. Refer to the Explanatory Answers in Chapter 7 for each exercise. By studying the explanations, you will begin to understand the way that good test takers think. Why is the answer correct? Is it like other questions you have seen before? Can you explain the answer to someone else? This will help you to answer the test items correctly when you take the official TOEFL.

Do you need more review and practice? Select the resources you need from the Barron's web site, *www.barronseduc.com.*

Evaluate

"Nothing great was ever achieved without enthusiasm."—Ralph Waldo Emerson

Estimating your score before you take the TOEFL is important because the test is costly. You will want to take it at the point when you have the best opportunity to succeed. Use the answer keys on pages 505 for the Paper-Based TOEFL and 559 for the Internet-Based TOEFL, respectively, for your final practice test. Then estimate your score using the charts and rubrics in Chapter 9. By scoring your practice test, you will know whether you should register to take the official TOEFL or continue to prepare. Whatever you do, go forward with enthusiasm. Best wishes.

Dr. Pamela Sharpe
www.teflprep.com

2

PRACTICE EXERCISES
FOR LISTENING

IMPORTANT NOTE

If your version of this book does not contain audio CDs, you can test yourself by using the scripts that appear in Chapter 7, beginning on page 299.

Listening Section

The Listening Section of the TOEFL tests your ability to understand spoken English as it is heard in North America. This section is included in the Paper-Based TOEFL and the Internet-Based TOEFL. The section is different for each of the TOEFL formats.

Paper-Based TOEFL (PBT)

There are 50 questions in three parts on the Listening Section of the Paper-Based TOEFL. The conversations, talks, and questions are presented only one time. You may not take notes. The topics are both general and academic. The questions are all multiple-choice with four possible answer choices. The section takes about 40 minutes to complete.

In Part 1, you will hear short conversations between two people. After each conversation, you will hear one question. Choose the best answer choice from four possible answers. Refer to Exercise 9 to see examples.

In Part 2, you will hear long conversations between two people. After each conversation, you will hear several questions. After every question, choose the best answer choice from four possible answers. Refer to Exercise 16 to see examples.

In Part 3, you will hear short talks by one person. After each talk, you will hear several questions. After every question, choose the best answer choice from four possible answers. Refer to Exercise 24 to see examples.

Internet-Based TOEFL (iBT®)

There are usually 33 or 34 questions in two parts on the Listening Section of the iBT® TOEFL. The conversations, talks, and lectures are presented only one time. You may take notes. The topics are all academic. The questions are either multiple-choice with four possible answer choices or computer-assisted with special directions on the screen. It takes 20 minutes to complete the questions. The time for the conversations, talks, and lectures is not included in the 20-minute estimate.

There are two types of tasks included in the Listening Section: independent listening tasks and integrated listening tasks.

In the independent listening tasks, you will hear long conversations, class discussions, and lectures in an academic setting. They include natural pauses, and they are presented at a normal rate for native speakers. You may take notes. After each conversation, discussion, or lecture, you will hear several questions. After every multiple-choice question, choose the best answer choice from four possible answers. After every computer-assisted question, follow the special directions on the screen to complete the answer. Refer to Exercise 30 to see examples.

In the integrated listening tasks, you will hear and respond to long conversations, class discussions, and lectures in an academic setting. The language includes natural pauses and is presented at a normal rate for native speakers. You may take notes. After each conversation, discussion, or lecture, you will hear a question that requires you to respond by speaking or writing. Refer to Exercises 39 (Lecture) and 92 (Writing) to see examples.

EXERCISE 1: Dialogues—Topics

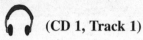 **(CD 1, Track 1)**

In some dialogues in the Listening Section on the Paper-Based TOEFL, you will be asked to iden-tify the main topic from among several secondary subjects in the conversations. Choose the best answer.

1. What are the man and woman talking about?
    Ⓐ A health club.
    Ⓑ A class.
    Ⓒ A game.
    Ⓓ A dentist.

2. What are these two people most probably discussing?
    Ⓐ Food and grocery items.
    Ⓑ Gasoline prices.
    Ⓒ Weights and measures.
    Ⓓ Money.

3. What are the two people talking about?
    Ⓐ A vacation.
    Ⓑ The mail.
    Ⓒ The newspaper.
    Ⓓ The office.

4. What are the two people discussing?
    Ⓐ A new doctor.
    Ⓑ A party they attended.
    Ⓒ Their friend Mary.
    Ⓓ A graduate program.

5. What are the man and the woman discussing?
    Ⓐ An exchange program.
    Ⓑ The man's trip to England.
    Ⓒ The man's illness.
    Ⓓ Their friend Nancy.

6. What are the man and woman talking about?
    Ⓐ The professor's lecture.
    Ⓑ The woman's children.
    Ⓒ The chairs they are sitting in.
    Ⓓ The size of the lecture room.

7. What are the two people discussing?
    Ⓐ The woman's computer.
    Ⓑ The woman's paper.
    Ⓒ The man's hometown.
    Ⓓ The man's job.

8. What are the two people talking about?
    Ⓐ The campus.
    Ⓑ Registration week.
    Ⓒ The parking situation.
    Ⓓ The woman's class.

9. What are the man and the woman discussing?
    Ⓐ The professor, Dr. Smith.
    Ⓑ The lab reports.
    Ⓒ The attendance policy.
    Ⓓ The teaching assistant.

10. What are the man and the woman talking about?
    Ⓐ The chemistry department.
    Ⓑ The woman's house.
    Ⓒ The man's employer.
    Ⓓ Having lunch on campus.

Refer to pages 299–300 for the Explanatory Answers.

EXERCISE 2: Dialogues—Details

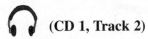 **(CD 1, Track 2)**

In some dialogues in the Listening Section on the Paper-Based TOEFL, you will be asked to remember details that are directly stated. Choose the best answer.

1. What is the man's problem?
   Ⓐ He is tired.
   Ⓑ He is drunk.
   Ⓒ He is thirsty.
   Ⓓ He is busy.

2. How does the woman want to pay?
   Ⓐ She wants to pay by check.
   Ⓑ She prefers to use a credit card.
   Ⓒ She has cash.
   Ⓓ She will need a loan.

3. Why did Sharon stop seeing the man?
   Ⓐ He was too short.
   Ⓑ She didn't know him very well.
   Ⓒ The expensive gift made her uncomfortable.
   Ⓓ The man never gave her gifts.

4. Why did the man look through the woman's purse?
   Ⓐ He thought she was a thief.
   Ⓑ He wanted to secure it for her.
   Ⓒ His job was to check everyone's belongings.
   Ⓓ He was looking for a standard size.

5. What does the woman want the man to do?
   Ⓐ Study with her.
   Ⓑ Help her on the test.
   Ⓒ Take a break.
   Ⓓ Lend her his notebook.

6. Who is driving Steve's car?
   Ⓐ Steve's girlfriend.
   Ⓑ Steve's sister.
   Ⓒ Steve.
   Ⓓ Mary Anne.

7. Why won't the door open?
   Ⓐ The door is locked.
   Ⓑ The woman doesn't have the right key.
   Ⓒ The door is stuck.
   Ⓓ The doorknob is broken.

8. What does the man want to do?
   Ⓐ Check the calculators.
   Ⓑ Use a calculator to do his test.
   Ⓒ Purchase a calculator.
   Ⓓ Borrow a calculator.

9. What is the woman's advice?
   Ⓐ She thinks the man should pay the bills.
   Ⓑ She thinks the man should ask his family for help.
   Ⓒ She thinks the man should contact his roommate's family for money.
   Ⓓ She thinks the man should leave.

10. How will the woman help the man?
    Ⓐ By filling out forms.
    Ⓑ By filing his taxes.
    Ⓒ By advising him about student loans.
    Ⓓ By completing his application.

Refer to pages 301–302 for the Explanatory Answers.

EXERCISE 3: Dialogues—Selections

 (CD 1, Track 3)

In some dialogues in the Listening Section on the Paper-Based TOEFL, you will be asked to select the correct detail from among several similar alternatives, all of which have been mentioned in different contexts in the conversation. Choose the best answer.

1. What is the relationship between Jack and the man?
   - Ⓐ They are brothers.
   - Ⓑ They are good friends.
   - Ⓒ They are cousins.
   - Ⓓ They are classmates.

2. What does the woman suggest?
   - Ⓐ That the man live with Frank and Geoff.
   - Ⓑ That the man ask Geoff to be his roommate.
   - Ⓒ That the man and Steve be roommates.
   - Ⓓ That the man share a room with Frank.

3. What grade did the woman receive?
   - Ⓐ She earned an *A*.
   - Ⓑ She received a *B*.
   - Ⓒ Her grade was *C*.
   - Ⓓ She got a *D* or *F*.

4. What advice does the woman give the man?
   - Ⓐ Buy the computer at a discount store.
   - Ⓑ Put an ad in the newspaper for a computer.
   - Ⓒ Go to a computer store to buy the computer.
   - Ⓓ Buy the computer at the university as part of a special offer.

5. Why didn't the woman receive a grade for the course?
   - Ⓐ She didn't pay her fees.
   - Ⓑ She didn't register for the class.
   - Ⓒ She didn't attend the class.
   - Ⓓ She didn't have her name on the roster.

6. What size will the man probably bring?
   - Ⓐ He will probably bring her a size 5½.
   - Ⓑ He will probably bring her a size 6.
   - Ⓒ He will probably bring her a size 7.
   - Ⓓ He will probably bring her a size 7½.

7. What does the man suspect?
   - Ⓐ The woman needs new glasses.
   - Ⓑ The woman has high blood pressure.
   - Ⓒ The woman has serious headaches.
   - Ⓓ The woman is suffering from stress.

8. For which class must the woman begin to prepare?
   - Ⓐ She must begin writing a paper for her history class.
   - Ⓑ She must start writing up her laboratory assignments for her chemistry class.
   - Ⓒ She must begin studying for her English examination.
   - Ⓓ She must begin studying for her French examination.

9. Where does the man live?
   - Ⓐ In New York.
   - Ⓑ In Boston.
   - Ⓒ In Michigan.
   - Ⓓ In Washington.

10. Which gear needs to be fixed?
    - Ⓐ First gear.
    - Ⓑ Second gear.
    - Ⓒ Reverse.
    - Ⓓ Drive.

Refer to pages 303–304 for the Explanatory Answers.

EXERCISE 4: Dialogues—Reversals

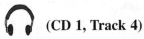 (CD 1, Track 4)

In some dialogues in the Listening Section on the Paper-Based TOEFL, you will be asked to iden-tify the speaker's final choice or decision after a change of opinion. Choose the best answer.

1. How will the woman get to the airport?
   - Ⓐ She will get a ride with the man.
   - Ⓑ She will ride the airport shuttle.
   - Ⓒ She will drive her car.
   - Ⓓ She will rent a car.

2. What does the woman want to eat?
   - Ⓐ She would like eggs and potatoes.
   - Ⓑ She wants eggs and pancakes.
   - Ⓒ She wants to eat potato pancakes.
   - Ⓓ Pancakes is what she would like to eat.

3. How many boxes of cookies did the man order?
   - Ⓐ The man bought one box of cookies.
   - Ⓑ The man ordered four boxes of cookies.
   - Ⓒ He purchased five boxes of cookies.
   - Ⓓ He did not order any cookies this year.

4. What is the correct area code for the woman?
   - Ⓐ The number is 6-9-1.
   - Ⓑ The area code is 1-9-6.
   - Ⓒ 9-1-6 is the area code.
   - Ⓓ 6-1-9 is the correct number.

5. How much per copy will the woman pay?
   - Ⓐ She will pay eight cents per page.
   - Ⓑ The price is ten cents a copy.
   - Ⓒ She owes fifteen cents per copy.
   - Ⓓ Twenty cents per page is the price.

6. How much will the woman pay?
   - Ⓐ One dollar a minute.
   - Ⓑ One dollar a page.
   - Ⓒ Two dollars and fifty cents a minute.
   - Ⓓ Two dollars and fifty cents a page.

7. What does the woman want to do?
   - Ⓐ See a documentary.
   - Ⓑ Change the channel.
   - Ⓒ Watch television.
   - Ⓓ Go to a movie.

8. What does the man want the woman to do?
   - Ⓐ He wants all twenty-dollar bills.
   - Ⓑ He wants all fifty-dollar bills.
   - Ⓒ He wants all large bills.
   - Ⓓ He wants some twenty- and some fifty-dollar bills.

9. Where will the man and woman eat lunch?
   - Ⓐ The Country Kitchen.
   - Ⓑ The Country Home.
   - Ⓒ The Old House.
   - Ⓓ The Old Kitchen.

10. When will the man be home?
    - Ⓐ He will be home at six o'clock.
    - Ⓑ He will not be home late.
    - Ⓒ He will be home a little after seven o'clock.
    - Ⓓ He will be home earlier than usual.

Refer to pages 305–306 for the Explanatory Answers.

EXERCISE 5: Dialogues—Idioms

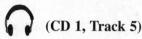 **(CD 1, Track 5)**

In some dialogues in the Listening Section on the Paper-Based TOEFL, you will be asked to paraphrase idiomatic expressions. Choose the best answer.

1. What does the woman mean?
   - Ⓐ She does not think that the man is serious.
   - Ⓑ She thinks that the man is going to take her to Florida.
   - Ⓒ She thinks that the man has a good idea.
   - Ⓓ She thinks that the man does not have any money.

2. What does the woman mean?
   - Ⓐ She needs one more semester.
   - Ⓑ She needs a hundred dollars.
   - Ⓒ The increase will be difficult for her.
   - Ⓓ The paper is not dependable.

3. What did the man do?
   - Ⓐ He has left the lecture.
   - Ⓑ He has used his last piece of paper.
   - Ⓒ He has said good-bye to the woman.
   - Ⓓ He has finished giving the lecture.

4. How does the man feel about the test?
   - Ⓐ He feels that the test was fair.
   - Ⓑ He agrees with the woman about the test.
   - Ⓒ He does not want the woman to tease him about the test.
   - Ⓓ He is not worried about the test.

5. What does the woman mean?
   - Ⓐ The man does not pay attention.
   - Ⓑ The man is very honest.
   - Ⓒ The man has gone away.
   - Ⓓ The man needs to repeat.

6. On what do the speakers agree?
   - Ⓐ The sign has Mickey Mouse on it.
   - Ⓑ They do not believe the sign.
   - Ⓒ The course is very easy.
   - Ⓓ They did not register for the course.

7. What does the woman mean?
   - Ⓐ She does not want the man to come for her.
   - Ⓑ She thinks that the man is a bother.
   - Ⓒ She does not want to go to class.
   - Ⓓ She accepts the man's offer.

8. What does the man mean?
   - Ⓐ The man likes ice cream.
   - Ⓑ The man will tell the woman later whether he wants ice cream.
   - Ⓒ The man does not want to say whether he likes ice cream.
   - Ⓓ The man will get some ice cream for the woman.

9. What does the woman mean?
   - Ⓐ She is glad Joan is moving.
   - Ⓑ She does not believe that Joan will move.
   - Ⓒ She saw Joan move.
   - Ⓓ She believes Joan is moving because she saw her.

10. What does the man mean?
   - Ⓐ He is angry with the woman.
   - Ⓑ He wants to talk with the woman.
   - Ⓒ It was a bad day for the man.
   - Ⓓ He does not know what day it is.

Refer to pages 306–308 for the Explanatory Answers.

EXERCISE 6: Dialogues—Emotions

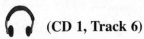 **(CD 1, Track 6)**

In some dialogues in the Listening Section on the Paper-Based TOEFL, you will be asked to draw conclusions about the feelings or emotions expressed by the speakers. Words and phrases as well as the tone of voice of speakers in the conversation will provide information for your conclusions. Choose the best answer.

1. How does the man feel?
   - Ⓐ He is worried.
   - Ⓑ He is happy.
   - Ⓒ He feels confident.
   - Ⓓ He feels tired.

2. How did the man feel about the movie?
   - Ⓐ He thought it was a very unrealistic movie.
   - Ⓑ He was impressed with the movie.
   - Ⓒ He agreed with the woman about the movie.
   - Ⓓ He liked the movie because it was a fairy tale.

3. How does the woman feel about the TOEFL?
   - Ⓐ She does not know whether she did well.
   - Ⓑ She thinks that she improved her score.
   - Ⓒ She believes that she scored about 490.
   - Ⓓ She is concerned about the reading comprehension.

4. How does the woman feel about the man?
   - Ⓐ She believes that he is having a bad day.
   - Ⓑ She does not like the man.
   - Ⓒ She thinks that he never pays attention.
   - Ⓓ She likes to help the man every day.

5. How does the man feel about Rick?
   - Ⓐ He forgot who he was.
   - Ⓑ He thinks that Rick and Lucy will forget to come.
   - Ⓒ He likes Rick, but not Lucy.
   - Ⓓ He does not want to invite them.

6. What is the man's reaction to the news?
   - Ⓐ He is surprised.
   - Ⓑ He is confused.
   - Ⓒ He does not agree.
   - Ⓓ He does not want to know.

7. How does the man feel about the assignments?
   - Ⓐ He does not care.
   - Ⓑ He does not like the lab assistant.
   - Ⓒ He does not like the grading system.
   - Ⓓ He does not agree with the woman.

8. What best describes the man's opinion of Terry?
   - Ⓐ He feels protective of Terry.
   - Ⓑ The man is supportive.
   - Ⓒ He has his doubts about Terry.
   - Ⓓ He feels hostile toward Terry.

9. How does the man feel about the review session?
   - Ⓐ He wants to go, but he won't.
   - Ⓑ He does not want to go, but he will.
   - Ⓒ He wants to go, and he will.
   - Ⓓ He does not want to go, and he won't.

10. How does the man feel about Janine?
    - Ⓐ He thinks Janine would be difficult to live with.
    - Ⓑ He thinks Janine and the woman will like living together.
    - Ⓒ He thinks it would be better to live with Janine than with Carol.
    - Ⓓ He thinks that Janine and Carol should live together.

Refer to pages 308–310 for the Explanatory Answers.

EXERCISE 7: Dialogues—Suggestions

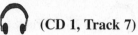 **(CD 1, Track 7)**

In some dialogues in the Listening Section on the Paper-Based TOEFL, you will be asked to recognize a suggestion. Words and phrases such as "you should" or "why don't you" or "why not" introduce a suggestion. Choose the best answer.

1. What does the man suggest that the woman do?
   - Ⓐ Buy dinner.
   - Ⓑ Pay for part of the dinner.
   - Ⓒ Tip the waiter after dinner.
   - Ⓓ Prepare the dinner.

2. What does the man suggest that the woman do?
   - Ⓐ Return later.
   - Ⓑ Telephone the security guard.
   - Ⓒ Stay at the dorm.
   - Ⓓ Look for the key.

3. What does the woman suggest that the man do?
   - Ⓐ Find another bathroom.
   - Ⓑ Use the bathroom in the main lobby.
   - Ⓒ Ask the custodian to unlock the bathroom.
   - Ⓓ Go to another building to locate a bathroom.

4. What does the man suggest that the woman do?
   - Ⓐ Get in line behind him.
   - Ⓑ Take a number.
   - Ⓒ Come back later.
   - Ⓓ Go to the end of the line.

5. What does the woman suggest that the man do?
   - Ⓐ Go to another bank.
   - Ⓑ Open an account with the bank.
   - Ⓒ Cash his check.
   - Ⓓ Make out the check for twenty dollars.

6. What does the woman suggest that the man do?
   - Ⓐ Pick her up at 11:35 A.M.
   - Ⓑ Wait for her at the airport.
   - Ⓒ Wait for her to call him.
   - Ⓓ Call the airport for the schedule.

7. What does the man suggest that the woman do?
   - Ⓐ Refer to the syllabus.
   - Ⓑ Go to Dr. Watson's office.
   - Ⓒ See Dr. Watson at 2:00 P.M.
   - Ⓓ Ask someone else.

8. What does the man suggest that they do?
   - Ⓐ Stay home.
   - Ⓑ Go out after dinner.
   - Ⓒ Find a baby sitter.
   - Ⓓ Take the children out to dinner.

9. What does the woman suggest that the man do?
   - Ⓐ Ask for an extension.
   - Ⓑ Use the interlibrary loan.
   - Ⓒ Look for references in the library.
   - Ⓓ Try the Internet.

10. What does the woman suggest that the man do?
   - Ⓐ Buy a larger wallet.
   - Ⓑ Keep the cards in his book bag.
   - Ⓒ Carry fewer cards.
   - Ⓓ Organize the cards.

Refer to pages 310–312 for the Explanatory Answers.

EXERCISE 8: Dialogues—Assumptions

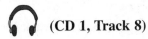 **(CD 1, Track 8)**

In some dialogues in the Listening Section on the Paper-Based TOEFL, you must be able to recognize remarks that register surprise, and draw conclusions about the assumptions that the speaker may have made. Choose the best answer.

1. What had the man assumed about the test?
   - Ⓐ The test would not be timed.
   - Ⓑ The test could be taken home to complete.
   - Ⓒ He would be able to use his book during the test.
   - Ⓓ He would have to study very hard for the test.

2. What had the man assumed?
   - Ⓐ The woman would not receive her deposit.
   - Ⓑ The old apartment was not safe.
   - Ⓒ The new apartment would require a deposit.
   - Ⓓ The woman would not move.

3. What had the man assumed about the woman?
   - Ⓐ She would not have lunch.
   - Ⓑ She would not start dating Phil again.
   - Ⓒ She would have lunch with him.
   - Ⓓ She would have to go before lunch.

4. What had the man assumed about the woman's daughter?
   - Ⓐ She was younger.
   - Ⓑ She was having a birthday party.
   - Ⓒ She was joking with him.
   - Ⓓ She would invite him to her house.

5. What had the woman assumed about the presentation?
   - Ⓐ There would not be any handouts.
   - Ⓑ Anne would finish the handouts.
   - Ⓒ Anne would not make the presentation.
   - Ⓓ The presentation had already been made.

6. What had the woman assumed about the health center?
   - Ⓐ The health center was in the student services building.
   - Ⓑ The health center was in the union.
   - Ⓒ The health center was on North Campus.
   - Ⓓ The health center was not on campus.

7. What had the man assumed about Bill?
   - Ⓐ Bill did not do much traveling.
   - Ⓑ Bill did not take the class.
   - Ⓒ Bill did not read novels.
   - Ⓓ Bill did not like to read.

8. What had the woman assumed about John?
   - Ⓐ He was serious about becoming a doctor.
   - Ⓑ He was not serious about changing majors.
   - Ⓒ He was serious about going into the family business.
   - Ⓓ He was not serious about applying for the business program.

9. What had the woman assumed about Mr. Brown?
   - Ⓐ He would be late getting to the lab.
   - Ⓑ He would be in the lab working.
   - Ⓒ He would not set up the equipment.
   - Ⓓ He would not have time to set up the equipment.

10. What had the woman assumed about Dr. Peterson?
   - Ⓐ She would not meet with their study group.
   - Ⓑ She would not give them an outline of the book.
   - Ⓒ She would not give them a break.
   - Ⓓ She would not let them use the book.

Refer to pages 312–314 for the Explanatory Answers.

EXERCISE 9: Dialogues—Predictions

🎧 (CD 1, Track 9)

In some dialogues in the Listening Section on the Paper-Based TOEFL, you will be asked to make predictions about the future activities of the speakers. Your prediction should be based on evidence in the conversation from which you can draw a logical conclusion. Choose the best answer.

1. What will the man probably do?
   Ⓐ He will probably leave.
   Ⓑ He will probably order the size orange juice they have.
   Ⓒ He will probably not have any orange juice.
   Ⓓ He will probably have orange juice instead of hot tea.

2. What will the woman probably do?
   Ⓐ Go to the kitchen to study.
   Ⓑ Go to her chemistry class.
   Ⓒ Go to the library to look for her book.
   Ⓓ Go to the table to eat.

3. What will the woman probably do?
   Ⓐ Call London about the charges.
   Ⓑ Accept the charges for the call.
   Ⓒ Refuse the call from London.
   Ⓓ Charge the call to someone in London.

4. What will the man probably do?
   Ⓐ Ask the woman to make a copy for him.
   Ⓑ Go across the street to make a copy.
   Ⓒ Ask the woman for directions to the building.
   Ⓓ Take his copies to the other building.

5. What will the woman probably do?
   Ⓐ Join the club.
   Ⓑ Pay five dollars for a video.
   Ⓒ Rent ten videos.
   Ⓓ Go to the video store.

6. What does the man probably want to do?
   Ⓐ Get directions.
   Ⓑ Make a call.
   Ⓒ Make a reservation.
   Ⓓ Talk to the woman.

7. What will the woman probably do?
   Ⓐ Walk to the mall.
   Ⓑ Get on the bus.
   Ⓒ Cross the street to wait for the bus.
   Ⓓ Take a taxi to the mall.

8. What will the woman probably do?
   Ⓐ Leave at once.
   Ⓑ Call the highway patrol.
   Ⓒ Go home with the man.
   Ⓓ Drive carefully.

9. What will the man do?
   Ⓐ Take the delivery to the university.
   Ⓑ Refuse to make the delivery to the woman.
   Ⓒ Make the delivery to the woman if she is close to the university.
   Ⓓ Deliver to a main location three miles from the university where the woman can pick it up.

10. What will the man probably do?
    Ⓐ Wait twenty minutes to be seated.
    Ⓑ Wait five minutes to be seated.
    Ⓒ Go right in to be seated.
    Ⓓ Go outside while he waits to be seated.

Refer to pages 314–316 for the Explanatory Answers.

EXERCISE 10: Dialogues—Implications

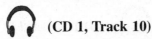

(CD 1, Track 10)

In some dialogues in the Listening Section on the Paper-Based TOEFL, you will be asked to draw general conclusions about the speakers or the situation. Words and phrases and the tone of voice of speakers in the conversation will provide information for your conclusions. Choose the best answer.

1. What does the man imply?
   Ⓐ He will not use the book.
   Ⓑ He will use the book in the library for two hours.
   Ⓒ He will check the book out before closing.
   Ⓓ He will reserve the book.

2. What does the man imply?
   Ⓐ The woman cannot get a soda.
   Ⓑ He will go downstairs to get the woman a soda.
   Ⓒ The woman should go downstairs to get a soda.
   Ⓓ He does not know where to get a soda.

3. What do we know about the woman?
   Ⓐ She thought she had applied to the right school.
   Ⓑ She attends an American university now.
   Ⓒ She does not have to take the TOEFL.
   Ⓓ She graduated from an American high school.

4. What did the man mean?
   Ⓐ The woman was in line for a long time.
   Ⓑ The man was in line longer than the woman.
   Ⓒ The man registered quickly.
   Ⓓ The woman did not register.

5. What does the man prefer to do?
   Ⓐ He prefers staying at home because he doesn't like to travel.
   Ⓑ He prefers taking a plane because the bus is too slow.
   Ⓒ He prefers taking a bus because the plane makes him nervous.
   Ⓓ He prefers traveling with the woman.

6. Where does this conversation most likely take place?
   Ⓐ On a reservation.
   Ⓑ At a party.
   Ⓒ At a restaurant.
   Ⓓ In a bakery.

7. What conclusion does the man want us to draw from his statement?
   Ⓐ Sally is serious about Bob.
   Ⓑ Bob is serious about Sally.
   Ⓒ Sally is not serious about Bob.
   Ⓓ Bob is not serious about Sally.

8. What are these people most probably discussing?
   Ⓐ Weights and measurements.
   Ⓑ Political systems.
   Ⓒ Employment.
   Ⓓ Money.

9. What does the man think about Jane?
   Ⓐ She will go away.
   Ⓑ She will be sorry.
   Ⓒ She will not quit her job.
   Ⓓ She will not buy him a present.

10. What do we learn about Betty from this conversation?
   Ⓐ She does not like plays.
   Ⓑ She went to see the play with the man and woman.
   Ⓒ She had not planned to attend the play.
   Ⓓ She was not at the play.

Refer to pages 316–318 for the Explanatory Answers.

EXERCISE 11: Dialogues—Problems

 (CD 1, Track 11)

In some dialogues in the Listening Section on the Paper-Based TOEFL, you will be asked to identify the problem that the speakers are discussing. This may be more difficult because different aspects of the problem may be included in the conversation. Choose the best answer.

1. What is the man's problem?
   - Ⓐ He does not have a checking account.
   - Ⓑ He does not have any checks.
   - Ⓒ He does not have the money to pay his rent.
   - Ⓓ There is a line at the cashier's window.

2. What is the woman's problem?
   - Ⓐ She does not like to live alone.
   - Ⓑ Her roommate will be moving out.
   - Ⓒ She wants to get married.
   - Ⓓ She does not have any messages.

3. What is the man's problem?
   - Ⓐ He needs his advisor to sign the registration form.
   - Ⓑ He does not have an academic advisor.
   - Ⓒ He does not know how to register for next semester.
   - Ⓓ He can't find his registration.

4. What is the woman's problem?
   - Ⓐ She does not have a car.
   - Ⓑ She needs a ride.
   - Ⓒ She is late to class.
   - Ⓓ She has to go shopping.

5. What is the problem that the man and woman are talking about?
   - Ⓐ They don't have a good book for their class.
   - Ⓑ They don't like Professor Jones.
   - Ⓒ The professor changed the book this semester.
   - Ⓓ Books are very expensive.

6. What is the woman's problem?
   - Ⓐ She has to wait for the telephone to be installed.
   - Ⓑ She does not have a telephone.
   - Ⓒ She has already seen the movie.
   - Ⓓ She cannot go to the movie because she has company.

7. What is the man's problem?
   - Ⓐ He has gained weight.
   - Ⓑ The sweatshirt is too big.
   - Ⓒ He does not have the receipt.
   - Ⓓ The clerk cannot authorize exchanges.

8. What is the woman's problem?
   - Ⓐ She needs child care that is closer to the university.
   - Ⓑ She needs someone to take care of her children while she is in class.
   - Ⓒ She needs the man to help her more with the children.
   - Ⓓ She needs to spend more time with the children.

9. What is the man's problem?
   - Ⓐ He does not like his job.
   - Ⓑ He wants to work more hours.
   - Ⓒ He cannot change jobs.
   - Ⓓ He needs to spend more time studying.

10. What is the woman's problem?
   - Ⓐ She needs to get more sleep.
   - Ⓑ She is starting to feel sick.
   - Ⓒ She did not finish her papers and projects.
   - Ⓓ She is tired of schoolwork.

Refer to pages 318–320 for the Explanatory Answers.

EXERCISE 12: Conversations—Friends on Campus

 (CD 1, Track 12)

In some conversations in the Listening Section on the Paper-Based TOEFL, you will be asked to recall information exchanged in conversations among friends in a variety of settings on campus. Choose the best answer.

Conversation One

1. What is the main topic of this conversation?
   - Ⓐ The man's graduation.
   - Ⓑ The couple's engagement.
   - Ⓒ The man's smoking.
   - Ⓓ The man's stress.

2. What does the woman suggest?
   - Ⓐ That the man rethink their plans.
   - Ⓑ That the man see a family doctor.
   - Ⓒ That the man see a psychiatrist.
   - Ⓓ That the man concentrate on his studies.

3. What does the man promise to do?
   - Ⓐ Get a patch to help him stop smoking.
   - Ⓑ Stop smoking immediately on his own.
   - Ⓒ Smoke less than usual for the next week.
   - Ⓓ Think about the woman's suggestions.

4. How does the man feel about the woman's decision?
   - Ⓐ Patient.
   - Ⓑ Surprised.
   - Ⓒ Worried.
   - Ⓓ Irritated.

5. What can we infer about the woman?
   - Ⓐ She has stopped smoking.
   - Ⓑ She does not want to get married to the man.
   - Ⓒ She has asked the man to quit smoking many times.
   - Ⓓ She is not in love with the man.

Conversation Two

1. What prompted this conversation?
   - Ⓐ Bill got hungry.
   - Ⓑ John noticed the time.
   - Ⓒ John had an exam.
   - Ⓓ John decided to go home.

2. Why is John studying?
   - Ⓐ He has a test that night.
   - Ⓑ He plans to go home for the weekend.
   - Ⓒ He has not studied during the semester.
   - Ⓓ He is helping his friend.

3. When will the cafeteria close?
   - Ⓐ At six o'clock.
   - Ⓑ At six-thirty.
   - Ⓒ Over the weekend.
   - Ⓓ On Monday.

4. What does Bill want John to do?
   - Ⓐ Bill wants John to study with him in the dormitory.
   - Ⓑ Bill wants John to go home with him for the weekend.
   - Ⓒ Bill wants John to let him know if he orders a pizza.
   - Ⓓ Bill wants John to find out what is being served in the cafeteria.

5. What will Bill most probably do now?
   - Ⓐ Continue studying.
   - Ⓑ Go to the cafeteria.
   - Ⓒ Cook dinner at home.
   - Ⓓ Eat pizza.

Refer to pages 320–322 for the Explanatory Answers.

EXERCISE 13: Conversations—Friends on Campus

 (CD 1, Track 13)

In some conversations in the Listening Section on the Internet-Based TOEFL, you will be asked to recall information exchanged in conversations among friends in a variety of settings on campus. The conversations will include natural pauses and will be at a normal rate for a conversation between native speakers. Choose the best answer.

Conversation One

1. What do the speakers mainly discuss?
   Ⓐ The use of photographs in painting.
   Ⓑ A TV program about Norman Rockwell.
   Ⓒ *The Saturday Evening Post* magazine.
   Ⓓ Exhibits of art at the library.

2. How did Rockwell paint such interesting faces?
   Ⓐ He imagined them.
   Ⓑ He used magazine covers.
   Ⓒ He hired models.
   Ⓓ He read stories.

3. What do we know about Rockwell?
   Ⓐ He was a prolific painter.
   Ⓑ He was an eccentric person.
   Ⓒ He was an avid reader.
   Ⓓ He was a good teacher.

4. What do the students plan to do for extra credit?
   Ⓐ Watch a video on reserve at the college library.
   Ⓑ Write a proposal to bring an art exhibit to the library.
   Ⓒ Take photographs of models like Norman Rockwell did.
   Ⓓ Submit a video of a TV program and photos of an exhibit.

5. Listen again to part of the conversation. Then answer the question.
   "Anyway, you know what I like most . . . about Rockwell?" "What?"

   Why does the woman say this:
   "Anyway, you know what I like most . . . about Rockwell?"
   Ⓐ She is checking to see whether the man was listening.
   Ⓑ She is trying to keep the man involved in the conversation.
   Ⓒ She is repeating part of an earlier conversation.
   Ⓓ She is telling the man that he has been talking too much.

6. What will the couple probably do?
   Ⓐ They will probably go to the exhibit.
   Ⓑ They will probably see the special on television.
   Ⓒ They will probably turn off the TV.
   Ⓓ They will probably go to Miami.

Refer to pages 322–325 for the Explanatory Answers.

Conversation Two

1. What are the students mainly discussing?
   - Ⓐ Taking notes.
   - Ⓑ Studying for a test.
   - Ⓒ The woman's grades.
   - Ⓓ The reading assignments.

2. Why does Bill mention colonial art?
   - Ⓐ It was an example of a question from the handouts.
   - Ⓑ It was an example of a question he had missed on the midterm.
   - Ⓒ It was an example of a topic that he had in his notes.
   - Ⓓ It was an example of a topic in the textbook assignments.

3. How does Linda usually study for a test?
   - Ⓐ She takes notes from the book.
   - Ⓑ She rewrites her class notes.
   - Ⓒ She makes handouts.
   - Ⓓ She rereads the highlights.

4. What kind of student is Linda?
   - Ⓐ She tries to get Bs.
   - Ⓑ She is an average student.
   - Ⓒ She is often absent.
   - Ⓓ She usually receives an A.

5. Listen again to part of the conversation. Then answer the question.
   "You . . . rewrite them?" "Yeah, I do."
   "You rewrite all of your notes?"

   Why does the man say this:
   "You rewrite all of your notes?"
   - Ⓐ He doesn't understand.
   - Ⓑ He is expressing surprise.
   - Ⓒ He made a joke.
   - Ⓓ He is asking for help.

6. What will Bill probably do?
   - Ⓐ He will borrow Linda's class notes.
   - Ⓑ He will rewrite all his class notes.
   - Ⓒ He will take notes from the textbook.
   - Ⓓ He will organize his lecture notes.

Refer to pages 325–327 for the Explanatory Answers.

EXERCISE 14: Conversations—Campus Personnel/Students

 (CD 1, Track 14)

In some conversations in the Listening Section on the Paper-Based TOEFL, you will be asked to recall information from conversations between personnel and students in a variety of settings on campus. Choose the best answer.

Conversation One

1. What do the speakers mainly discuss?
   - Ⓐ A sick friend.
   - Ⓑ A math class.
   - Ⓒ School policy.
   - Ⓓ The man's test.

2. Why can't the woman give Terry Young's test to the man?
   - Ⓐ It is against the law.
   - Ⓑ The man is not a member of Terry's family.
   - Ⓒ The woman cannot find the test.
   - Ⓓ Terry was too sick to take the test.

3. What is the man's last name?
   - Ⓐ Young.
   - Ⓑ Purcell.
   - Ⓒ Raleigh.
   - Ⓓ Kelly.

4. How does the woman feel about the policy?
   - Ⓐ She agrees with it.
   - Ⓑ She thinks it is odd.
   - Ⓒ She does not enforce it.
   - Ⓓ She is angry about it.

5. What will the man most probably do?
   - Ⓐ Call his friend.
   - Ⓑ Go to the office to get his test.
   - Ⓒ Send the woman a letter.
   - Ⓓ Take the test later.

Conversation Two

1. What is the purpose of this conversation?
   - Ⓐ To register the student for classes.
   - Ⓑ To register the student for placement tests.
   - Ⓒ To help the student change his major field of study.
   - Ⓓ To advise the student about the orientation to engineering program.

2. How many classes does the woman advise the man to take?
   - Ⓐ Two.
   - Ⓑ Five.
   - Ⓒ Three.
   - Ⓓ Seventeen.

3. What does the man need to be admitted to the examination?
   - Ⓐ A driver's license.
   - Ⓑ A permission slip.
   - Ⓒ A registration card.
   - Ⓓ Nothing.

4. What does the woman suggest?
   - Ⓐ The man should return Friday afternoon.
   - Ⓑ The man should complete his registration now.
   - Ⓒ The man should take five classes.
   - Ⓓ The man should schedule the Math 130 class.

5. What do we know about the student?
   - Ⓐ He is majoring in mathematics.
   - Ⓑ He has never taken a chemistry course.
   - Ⓒ He is a freshman.
   - Ⓓ He does not like his advisor.

Refer to pages 327–329 for the Explanatory Answers.

EXERCISE 15: Conversations—Campus Personnel/Students

 (CD 2, Track 1)

In some conversations in the Listening Section on the Internet-Based TOEFL, you will be asked to recall information from conversations between personnel and students in a variety of settings on campus. The conversations will include natural pauses and will be at a normal rate for a conversation between native speakers. Choose the best answer.

Conversation One

1. What is the purpose of this conversation?
   - Ⓐ The woman is asking the man's opinion of Professor Hendrix.
   - Ⓑ The woman is buying books for a college course.
   - Ⓒ The man is training the woman to work in the bookstore.
   - Ⓓ The man is helping the woman with her packages.

2. Why didn't the woman use her roommate's book?
   - Ⓐ She was taking the course with a different professor.
   - Ⓑ The professor was using a different book.
   - Ⓒ The book had a lot of marks in it.
   - Ⓓ Her roommate had already sold the book.

3. According to the man, what is the problem with using an older edition?
   - Ⓐ The instructor refers to different page numbers.
   - Ⓑ It is usually very marked up from use.
   - Ⓒ The professor doesn't order them.
   - Ⓓ They aren't much cheaper than the new edition.

4. Why does the woman buy the style manual?
   - Ⓐ The manual is required.
   - Ⓑ The price is not expensive.
   - Ⓒ The instructor will refer to it.
   - Ⓓ The man found one.

5. Listen again to part of the conversation. Then answer the question.
   "I don't think uh . . . Hendrix changed the order this semester." "Wouldn't you know? My roommate sold all her books at the end of the term."

   Why does the woman say this:
   "Wouldn't you know?"
   - Ⓐ She is asking the man if he knows what her roommate did.
   - Ⓑ She is confirming that the man knows her roommate.
   - Ⓒ She is commenting about her bad luck.
   - Ⓓ She is trying to get the man to laugh.

6. What can we infer about the woman?
   - Ⓐ She is happy with her purchase.
   - Ⓑ She is friends with the man.
   - Ⓒ She is an A student.
   - Ⓓ She is angry with her roommate.

Refer to pages 329–332 for the Explanatory Answers.

Conversation Two

1. What is the main topic of this conversation?
   Ⓐ The Internet.
   Ⓑ Research methods online.
   Ⓒ The school home page.
   Ⓓ Library computer terminals.

2. What is *Oasis*?
   Ⓐ The on-line library catalog.
   Ⓑ The name of the school.
   Ⓒ A Web site for books.
   Ⓓ The password for Netlibrary.

3. How does the man set up an account for Netlibrary?
   Ⓐ He tells his password to the librarian.
   Ⓑ He logs in on his home computer.
   Ⓒ He uses the computer in the library.
   Ⓓ He does it by telephoning the library.

4. How does the man pay for Netlibrary?
   Ⓐ There is a one-time fee.
   Ⓑ He will be charged every month.
   Ⓒ The service is free for students.
   Ⓓ He pays a fee per book.

5. Listen again to part of the conversation. Then answer the question.
   "Let me see if I've got this. Oasis is exactly like the catalog for the library here at school, and so uh . . . I can find . . . all the books and materials that are on the shelves, but they . . . I can't see them."

   Why does the man say this:
   "Let me see if I've got this."
   Ⓐ To check whether he has understood the woman.
   Ⓑ To look for something he has lost at school.
   Ⓒ To ask the woman to show him some books.
   Ⓓ To find out if he has a job at the library.

6. What will the man probably do now?
   Ⓐ Go back to his apartment.
   Ⓑ Open an account.
   Ⓒ Use Netlibrary.
   Ⓓ Ask the librarian for help.

Refer to pages 332–334 for the Explanatory Answers.

EXERCISE 16: Conversations—Service Personnel/Students

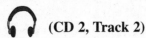 **(CD 2, Track 2)**

In some conversations in the Listening Section on the Paper-Based TOEFL, you will be asked to recall information exchanged in conversations between service personnel and students in a variety of settings off campus. Choose the best answer.

Conversation One

1. What prompted the conversation?
   - Ⓐ The man wants to place a classified ad in the newspaper.
   - Ⓑ The woman wants to find an apartment close to school.
   - Ⓒ The man wants to pay for a newspaper subscription.
   - Ⓓ The woman wants to fill out an application for employment.

2. What does the man want to sell?
   - Ⓐ Furniture.
   - Ⓑ Books.
   - Ⓒ Garden supplies.
   - Ⓓ An apartment.

3. What is the man's last name?
   - Ⓐ Martin.
   - Ⓑ Martyn.
   - Ⓒ Wynn.
   - Ⓓ Wartin.

4. How will the man pay?
   - Ⓐ He will pay by check.
   - Ⓑ He will have the amount billed to his home address.
   - Ⓒ He will give the woman cash.
   - Ⓓ He will come back to pay when he is billed.

5. Why does the man decide to revise what he has written?
   - Ⓐ To make it clearer to understand.
   - Ⓑ To make it longer to read.
   - Ⓒ To make it cheaper to print.
   - Ⓓ To make it easier to use.

Conversation Two

1. What is the purpose of the conversation?
   - Ⓐ To help the woman make a purchase.
   - Ⓑ To request the woman's identification.
   - Ⓒ To show the woman how to make out a check.
   - Ⓓ To register the woman for a course at City College.

2. What is meant by the term *cash*?
   - Ⓐ Money.
   - Ⓑ Money or credit cards.
   - Ⓒ Credit cards or checks.
   - Ⓓ Checks or money.

3. How does the woman pay for her purchase?
   - Ⓐ Credit card.
   - Ⓑ Money.
   - Ⓒ Debit card.
   - Ⓓ Check.

4. What did the woman use as identification?
   - Ⓐ She used her student ID card and a charge card.
   - Ⓑ She used her credit card.
   - Ⓒ She used her driver's license and her student ID card.
   - Ⓓ She used her telephone number and her student ID card.

5. Who is the man in this conversation?
   - Ⓐ A clerk.
   - Ⓑ The woman's husband.
   - Ⓒ A police officer.
   - Ⓓ A bank teller.

Refer to pages 334–336 for the Explanatory Answers.

EXERCISE 17: Conversations—Professors/Students

 (CD 2, Track 3)

In some conversations in the Listening Section on the Paper-Based TOEFL, you will be asked to recall information exchanged in conversations between professors and students in a variety of settings on campus. Choose the best answer.

Conversation One

1. What is the main subject of the conversation?
   - Ⓐ The man's last appointment.
   - Ⓑ Professor Irwin's office hours.
   - Ⓒ Student advisement during registration.
   - Ⓓ The man's health problems.

2. When is the man's new appointment scheduled?
   - Ⓐ Tuesday at two o'clock.
   - Ⓑ Thursday at two o'clock.
   - Ⓒ This afternoon at three o'clock.
   - Ⓓ Now.

3. What should the man have done about his first appointment?
   - Ⓐ He should have made an appointment.
   - Ⓑ He should have called to cancel his appointment.
   - Ⓒ He should have come for his appointment.
   - Ⓓ He should have stayed at home until he was well.

4. What is the man's excuse?
   - Ⓐ He wasn't well.
   - Ⓑ He was out of town.
   - Ⓒ He didn't know what to do.
   - Ⓓ He forgot the time.

5. What word best describes Professor Irwin's attitude toward the student?
   - Ⓐ Uninterested.
   - Ⓑ Apologetic.
   - Ⓒ Sick.
   - Ⓓ Annoyed.

Conversation Two

1. What is the woman's main purpose in this conversation?
   - Ⓐ To take her final exam.
   - Ⓑ To apologize to the professor.
   - Ⓒ To change the date of her exam.
   - Ⓓ To schedule her flight.

2. Why does the woman have a problem?
   - Ⓐ She is taking too many classes.
   - Ⓑ She lives too far from her family.
   - Ⓒ She made an error when she scheduled her trip.
   - Ⓓ She did not do well on her final exam.

3. On what day is the exam scheduled?
   - Ⓐ Monday.
   - Ⓑ Tuesday.
   - Ⓒ Wednesday.
   - Ⓓ Thursday.

4. What does the professor decide to do?
   - Ⓐ Allow the woman to repeat the exam.
   - Ⓑ Reschedule the woman's exam for another day.
   - Ⓒ Let the woman skip the final exam.
   - Ⓓ Give the woman a grade of incomplete.

5. When does this conversation most probably take place?
   - Ⓐ In March.
   - Ⓑ In May.
   - Ⓒ In November.
   - Ⓓ In December.

Refer to pages 336–338 for the Explanatory Answers.

EXERCISE 18: Conversations—Professors/Students

 (CD 2, Track 4)

In some conversations in the Listening Section on the Internet-Based TOEFL, you will be asked to recall information exchanged in conversations between professors and students in a variety of settings on campus. The conversations will include natural pauses and will be at a normal rate for a conversation between native speakers. Choose the best answer.

Conversation One

1. What is the main topic of this conversation?
   - Ⓐ The man's health.
   - Ⓑ The makeup test.
   - Ⓒ The man's classes.
   - Ⓓ The course syllabus.

2. Why did the man need to take the test?
   - Ⓐ He was absent when the test was given in class.
   - Ⓑ He will have to miss class on the day of the test.
   - Ⓒ He is taking an independent-study course.
   - Ⓓ He has to complete a placement test to take the class.

3. What kind of test will the man take?
   - Ⓐ True-false.
   - Ⓑ Multiple-choice.
   - Ⓒ Essay.
   - Ⓓ Oral recitation.

4. How long does he have to complete the test?
   - Ⓐ 10 minutes.
   - Ⓑ 45 minutes.
   - Ⓒ 50 minutes.
   - Ⓓ 1 hour.

5. Listen again to part of the conversation. Then answer the question.
   "Fifty minutes, which is just about the same amount of time you would have had in class. But, knowing you, I think you'll probably finish long before that."

   Why does the professor say this:
   "But, knowing you, I think you'll probably finish long before that."
   - Ⓐ To tell the student to finish the test as quickly as possible.
   - Ⓑ To give the student self-confidence for the test.
   - Ⓒ To let the student have more time to complete the test.
   - Ⓓ To find out how long the student needs to finish the test.

6. What can we assume about the man?
   - Ⓐ He is not a serious student.
   - Ⓑ He is still sick.
   - Ⓒ He has a syllabus.
   - Ⓓ He is prepared for the test.

Refer to pages 338–340 for the Explanatory Answers.

Conversation Two

1. What is the purpose of this conversation?
   - Ⓐ The woman's grade in biology.
   - Ⓑ The woman's major field of study.
   - Ⓒ The woman's workload.
   - Ⓓ The woman's lab reports.

2. What does Marge mean when she says she is "over her head"?
   - Ⓐ She does not understand the biology class.
   - Ⓑ She does not have time to complete the assignments.
   - Ⓒ She does not like the class because of the lab.
   - Ⓓ She is not majoring in biology for premed.

3. Why does Marge want to drop the biology class?
   - Ⓐ It is not her favorite class.
   - Ⓑ Her grades in the class are low.
   - Ⓒ She would not mind taking it again.
   - Ⓓ She does not like the professor.

4. Why does Marge need the professor's signature?
   - Ⓐ She wants to take an exam instead of attending the class.
   - Ⓑ She would like to withdraw from the professor's biology class.
   - Ⓒ She needs an excused absence from the laboratory sessions.
   - Ⓓ She has to notify her advisor that she is failing the class.

5. Listen again to part of the conversation. Then answer the question.
   "I see . . . Well, have you considered taking an incomplete?"

   Why does the professor say this:
   "Well, have you considered taking an incomplete?"
   - Ⓐ He is finding out about the student's academic record.
   - Ⓑ He is asking whether the student can finish the class.
   - Ⓒ He is making a suggestion for the student to think about.
   - Ⓓ He is trying to understand the student's problem.

6. Why does Dr. Jones want Marge to write a memo to her advisor?
   - Ⓐ So that she will not register for so many hours again.
   - Ⓑ So that her advisor will know that she failed the class.
   - Ⓒ So that Marge will complete the course in January.
   - Ⓓ So that the advisor will fill out the paperwork.

Refer to pages 340–342 for the Explanatory Answers.

EXERCISE 19: Consultations—Professors/Students

 (CD 2, Track 5)

In some consultations in the Listening Section on the Paper-Based TOEFL, you will be asked to recall information from conversations between professors and students about classroom content or policies. Choose the best answer.

Consultation One

1. What is the purpose of this consultation?
   - Ⓐ To discuss the results of the lab experiment.
   - Ⓑ To answer the students' questions about the lab experiment.
   - Ⓒ To explain the method of collection by water displacement.
   - Ⓓ To prepare the students to do the lab experiment.

2. What was deposited on the bottom of the gas bottle?
   - Ⓐ Magnesium.
   - Ⓑ Limestone.
   - Ⓒ Carbon.
   - Ⓓ Water.

3. What caused the deposits?
   - Ⓐ The hydrochloric acid broke the carbon bonds in the carbon dioxide.
   - Ⓑ The magnesium oxide broke the carbon-oxygen bonds in the carbon dioxide.
   - Ⓒ The burning magnesium broke the carbon-oxygen bonds in the carbon dioxide.
   - Ⓓ The gas collection method broke the carbon-oxygen bonds in the carbon dioxide.

4. Where does this consultation take place?
   - Ⓐ In the lab.
   - Ⓑ In the classroom.
   - Ⓒ In the hallway.
   - Ⓓ In Professor Smith's office.

5. What can we infer from this consultation?
   - Ⓐ Bob does not get along with his lab partner.
   - Ⓑ The students performed the experiment correctly.
   - Ⓒ The students had problems, and could not complete the lab experiment.
   - Ⓓ There was a fire in the lab during the experiment.

Consultation Two

1. What prompted the consultation?
   - Ⓐ The students did not understand the course requirements.
   - Ⓑ The students wanted to do a research paper instead of a final exam.
   - Ⓒ The professor changed the requirements for the course.
   - Ⓓ The professor offered to listen to the students' suggestions for the course.

2. What kind of research paper has Dr. Anderson assigned?
   - Ⓐ A report.
   - Ⓑ A book review.
   - Ⓒ An original study.
   - Ⓓ A five-page composition.

3. What kind of examination has Dr. Anderson prepared?
   - Ⓐ An essay examination.
   - Ⓑ An objective examination.
   - Ⓒ An open-book examination.
   - Ⓓ A take-home examination.

4. Which option do the students choose?
   - Ⓐ A lecture series.
   - Ⓑ A paper.
   - Ⓒ A reading list.
   - Ⓓ An examination.

5. Based upon the consultation, which course does Dr. Anderson most probably teach?
   - Ⓐ English 355.
   - Ⓑ Psychology 201.
   - Ⓒ Political Science 400.
   - Ⓓ Chemistry 370.

Refer to pages 342–345 for the Explanatory Answers.

EXERCISE 20: Consultations—Professors/Students

 (CD 2, Track 6)

In some consultations in the Listening Section on the Internet-Based TOEFL, you will be asked to recall information from consultations between professors and students about classroom content or policies. The interactions will include natural pauses and will be at a normal rate for a conversation between native speakers. Choose the best answer for multiple-choice questions. For computer-assisted questions, follow the directions on screen.

Consultation One

1. What is the purpose of the consultation?
   - Ⓐ Larry has some questions before the quiz.
   - Ⓑ Larry wants to know more about Hawaii.
   - Ⓒ Larry is concerned about his grade on the last quiz.
   - Ⓓ Larry is asking for help because he missed the lecture.

2. What is the main topic of this consultation?
   - Ⓐ Topography.
   - Ⓑ Volcanoes.
   - Ⓒ Hawaii.
   - Ⓓ Hot spots.

3. What is the altitude of Hawaii?
   - Ⓐ 400–500 meters.
   - Ⓑ 4,500 meters.
   - Ⓒ 5,500 meters.
   - Ⓓ 10,000 meters.

4. What does the professor say about the newest Hawaiian island?
   - Ⓐ It has not yet been given an official scientific name.
   - Ⓑ It will appear in 10–40 years according to estimates.
   - Ⓒ It is already a few feet above sea level when the ocean is calm.
   - Ⓓ It will already be very high when it appears above the water.

5. Listen again to part of the conversation. Then answer the question.
   "Of course, we won't actually see it above the surface of the ocean for another ten to forty thousand years, and you and I won't see it at all . . . but uh . . . we are observing it closely as it continues to build under water."

   Why does the professor say this:
   ". . . and you and I won't see it at all . . ."
   - Ⓐ He is sad that he won't see it.
   - Ⓑ He is giving a concrete example.
   - Ⓒ He is making a little joke.
   - Ⓓ He is disagreeing with the student.

6. Put the following events in order to explain how island chains are formed. Click on a choice. Then click on the number in the sequence.
   - Ⓐ Lithospheric plates move over the hot spot, carrying the island with them.
   - Ⓑ Active volcanoes in a hot spot erupt to build the first island.
   - Ⓒ Island building occurs in a second place close to the first island.
   - Ⓓ The plates move again while the hot spot remains in place.

1.
2.
3.
4.

Refer to pages 345–347 for the Explanatory Answers.

Consultation Two

1. What is Ronda's problem?
   - Ⓐ She does not have a topic for her term paper.
   - Ⓑ The topic that she has selected is too broad.
   - Ⓒ The professor does not like the topic for her paper.
   - Ⓓ She cannot find information about the topic she has chosen.

2. How long should the paper be?
   - Ⓐ Five pages.
   - Ⓑ Ten to twelve pages.
   - Ⓒ Fifteen to twenty pages.
   - Ⓓ Twenty-five pages.

3. What does Dr. Gilbert suggest?
   - Ⓐ Ronda should choose a different topic for her paper.
   - Ⓑ Ronda should use the resources that he has given her.
   - Ⓒ Ronda should talk with him again after she has a title.
   - Ⓓ Ronda should show him her first draft in class tomorrow.

4. Where did Ronda's family live five years ago?
   - Ⓐ Italy.
   - Ⓑ Spain.
   - Ⓒ France.
   - Ⓓ England.

5. Listen again to part of the conversation. Then answer the question.
   "Hi, Dr. Gilbert. Are you busy?" "Just getting organized for my class."

   Why does the student ask this:
   "Are you busy?"
   - Ⓐ She wonders what Dr. Gilbert is doing.
   - Ⓑ She is chatting with Dr. Gilbert.
   - Ⓒ She is interrupting Dr. Gilbert politely.
   - Ⓓ She would like to help Dr. Gilbert.

6. What will Ronda most probably do?
   - Ⓐ Write her paper about the Hall of Mirrors.
   - Ⓑ Try to find more sources for her term paper.
   - Ⓒ Change her topic to some other period of art.
   - Ⓓ Revise her second draft to make it longer.

Refer to pages 347–350 for the Explanatory Answers.

EXERCISE 21: Group Discussions—Students

 (CD 2, Track 7)

In some group discussions in the Listening Section on the Internet-Based TOEFL, you will be asked to understand interactions among three or more students about a variety of classroom and content topics. The discussions will include natural pauses, and will be at a normal rate for a conversation between native speakers. Choose the best answer.

Discussion One

1. What is the main purpose of this study group?
   - Ⓐ To prepare for a test.
   - Ⓑ To create a presentation.
   - Ⓒ To compare answers from a quiz.
   - Ⓓ To exchange lecture notes.

2. Who has identified an *ideal bureaucracy*?
   - Ⓐ Rosenberg.
   - Ⓑ Weber.
   - Ⓒ Graham.
   - Ⓓ Bensman.

3. Which law states that people advance until they reach a position in which they are less likely to succeed?
   - Ⓐ Weber's law.
   - Ⓑ Parkinson's law.
   - Ⓒ The Rosenberg principle.
   - Ⓓ The Peter principle.

4. Which topic will probably appear as an essay question?
   - Ⓐ Contrast the Peter principle and Parkinson's law.
   - Ⓑ Contrast formal and informal organizations.
   - Ⓒ Summarize the Bensman and Rosenberg study.
   - Ⓓ Summarize the characteristics in Weber's bureaucracy.

5. Listen again to part of the discussion. Then answer the question.
   "You got that right. He's gone over that definition at the beginning of almost every class since the last test."

   Why does the man say this:
   "He's gone over that definition at the beginning of almost every class since the last test."
   - Ⓐ He is confirming that the woman has answered the question correctly.
   - Ⓑ He is suggesting that the woman repeat the answer to the question.
   - Ⓒ He is ridiculing the woman because she should know the answer.
   - Ⓓ He is emphasizing that the question will be on the next test.

6. What can we assume about Dr. Graham?
   - Ⓐ He gives objective tests.
   - Ⓑ He requires study groups.
   - Ⓒ He teaches business.
   - Ⓓ He appreciates creativity.

Refer to pages 350–352 for the Explanatory Answers.

Discussion Two

1. What is the purpose of this study group?
   Ⓐ To help each other review for a test.
   Ⓑ To rehearse their group presentation.
   Ⓒ To compare their lecture notes and handouts.
   Ⓓ To encourage and motivate each other.

2. What do the letters in the SQ3R method represent?
   Ⓐ A new way to take notes.
   Ⓑ A short name for the survey method.
   Ⓒ The five steps in the reading process.
   Ⓓ Different ways to study for exams.

3. What does the word *survey* mean?
   Ⓐ To take the first step.
   Ⓑ To summarize.
   Ⓒ To ask questions.
   Ⓓ To look quickly.

4. What will the group do at the end of the presentation?
   Ⓐ Answer questions.
   Ⓑ Read from the textbook.
   Ⓒ Hand out a survey.
   Ⓓ Demonstrate the method.

5. Listen again to part of the discussion. Then answer the question.
   "At this point, you don't stop to write . . . sorry . . . I mean, read complete sentences. Just look at the important divisions of the material."

   Why does the man say this:
   ". . . sorry . . . I mean, read complete sentences."
   Ⓐ He noticed that he was speaking too fast.
   Ⓑ He forgot to read something to the group.
   Ⓒ He corrected something he had said.
   Ⓓ He was giving directions politely.

6. Who is probably the group leader?
   Ⓐ Carl.
   Ⓑ Joan.
   Ⓒ Phil.
   Ⓓ Martha.

Refer to pages 352–355 for the Explanatory Answers.

EXERCISE 22: Class Clarifications—Professor/Students

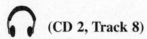 **(CD 2, Track 8)**

In some talks in the Listening Section on the Paper-Based TOEFL, you will be asked to recall information exchanged between professors and students in announcements and explanations that might be heard at the beginning or end of a college class. Choose the best answer.

Talk One

1. What is the purpose of the announcement?
   - Ⓐ To give an overview of the course.
   - Ⓑ To explain how to prepare for the test.
   - Ⓒ To cover the material from the textbooks.
   - Ⓓ To assist students with their lab assignments.

2. On the test, how much will the multiple-choice questions count?
   - Ⓐ Ten percent.
   - Ⓑ Twenty-five percent.
   - Ⓒ Forty percent.
   - Ⓓ Fifty percent.

3. For what percentage of the total grade will the test count?
   - Ⓐ Ten percent.
   - Ⓑ Twenty-five percent.
   - Ⓒ Forty percent.
   - Ⓓ Fifty percent.

4. What does the speaker say about math problems?
   - Ⓐ The students should not review their notes.
   - Ⓑ There won't be any math problems on the test.
   - Ⓒ There will be fifty math problems on the test.
   - Ⓓ The math formulas will not be necessary for the test.

5. In which class would this announcement occur?
   - Ⓐ An English class.
   - Ⓑ A history class.
   - Ⓒ A chemistry class.
   - Ⓓ A foreign language class.

Talk Two

1. What is the main topic of this talk?
   - Ⓐ The difference between plagiarism and legitimate writing strategies.
   - Ⓑ The penalties for plagiarism.
   - Ⓒ The use of quotations in term papers.
   - Ⓓ The requirement for a term paper on plagiarism.

2. What is *plagiarizing*?
   - Ⓐ Using your own ideas.
   - Ⓑ Quoting someone's exact words and citing the source.
   - Ⓒ Enclosing someone's exact words in quotation marks.
   - Ⓓ Copying ideas without citing the source.

3. What are two legitimate writing strategies?
   - Ⓐ Paraphrasing and plagiarizing.
   - Ⓑ Quoting and plagiarizing.
   - Ⓒ Paraphrasing and quoting.
   - Ⓓ Copying and paraphrasing.

4. What will happen to a student who plagiarizes on the term paper?
   - Ⓐ He will receive a lower grade.
   - Ⓑ He will be asked to repeat the course.
   - Ⓒ He will be asked to rewrite the paper.
   - Ⓓ He will fail the course.

5. Who is the speaker?
   - Ⓐ A writer.
   - Ⓑ A student.
   - Ⓒ A librarian.
   - Ⓓ A teacher.

Refer to pages 355–357 for the Explanatory Answers.

EXERCISE 23: Class Clarifications—Professors/Students

 (CD 3, Track 1)

In some talks in the Listening Section on the Internet-Based TOEFL, you will be asked to recall information exchanged between professors and students in announcements and explanations that might be heard at the beginning or end of a college class. The clarifications will include natural pauses, and will be at a normal rate for a conversation between native speakers. Choose the best answer.

Talk One

1. What is the main purpose of this talk?
   A   To discuss incomplete grades.
   B   To arrange for makeup exams.
   C   To explain course policies and procedures.
   D   To give an overview of the course content.

2. What is the speaker's policy for late assignments?
   A   He will allow the students one day after the due date before marking them down.
   B   He will not accept late assignments.
   C   He will subtract one letter from the grade for each day that the paper is late.
   D   He will excuse students who are ill.

3. What is the professor's attendance policy?
   A   He calls the roll before every session.
   B   He does not take attendance in class.
   C   He has each student check in after class.
   D   He uses a seating chart to take attendance.

4. What is the procedure for a student to receive a grade of incomplete?
   A   The student must submit a request form explaining why the incomplete is necessary.
   B   The student must call the speaker to explain.
   C   The student must arrange for the incomplete within one week of the final exam.
   D   The student must register to take the course again.

5. Listen again to part of the lecture. Then answer the question.
   "Remember that attendance is 10 percent . . . sorry . . . 15 percent of the grade, which usually makes the difference between an A and a B, or a B and a C."

   Why does the professor say this:
   "Remember that attendance is 10 percent . . . sorry . . . 15 percent of the grade . . ."
   A   He is acknowledging that his policy is unpopular.
   B   He is announcing a change in policy.
   C   He is correcting an error that he made.
   D   He is reminding students to attend.

6. What can we infer about the speaker?
   A   He is not very organized.
   B   He does not like his students.
   C   He does not mind if his students call him at home.
   D   He does not give many exams.

Refer to pages 357–358 for the Explanatory Answers.

Talk Two

1. What is the purpose of this talk?
   - Ⓐ The professor is announcing the grades for the group project.
   - Ⓑ The students are asking questions about the group project.
   - Ⓒ The professor is explaining how he will grade the group project.
   - Ⓓ The students are protesting their grades on the group project.

2. How will the written report be graded?
   - Ⓐ Each individual will receive a separate grade.
   - Ⓑ The same grade will be given to every member of the group.
   - Ⓒ The professor will give three grades for the report.
   - Ⓓ Three grades will be averaged for the evaluation of the report.

3. How will the final grade be calculated for each student?
   - Ⓐ The professor will average the grades of each member of the group.
   - Ⓑ Two group grades and one individual grade will be averaged.
   - Ⓒ The self-evaluation for each member of the group will be averaged.
   - Ⓓ The grades of all three groups will be averaged.

4. How will the professor know what each individual has contributed?
   - Ⓐ He will supervise each student closely.
   - Ⓑ He will rely on each individual to report.
   - Ⓒ The group will verify a report by each member.
   - Ⓓ The group leader will report each member's work.

5. Listen again to a part of the talk. Then answer the question.
   "How do you divide the work? Well, uh, . . . in the past, some of my students have actually divided the report into sections, and each group member does . . . has written one of the sections."

   Why does the professor ask this: "How do you divide the work?"
   - Ⓐ He wants to know how the students are approaching the project.
   - Ⓑ He does not understand what the students are doing.
   - Ⓒ He asks a question in order to provide an answer for the students.
   - Ⓓ He disapproves of the way that the students organized the work.

6. Why does the professor most probably use such a complicated grading system?
   - Ⓐ He is trying to be fair.
   - Ⓑ He has used it before.
   - Ⓒ He does not like to evaluate.
   - Ⓓ He can explain it easily.

Refer to pages 358–360 for the Explanatory Answers.

EXERCISE 24: General Talks—Professor

 (CD 3, Track 2)

In some talks in the Listening Section on the Paper-Based TOEFL, you will be asked to understand content similar to that of general interest topics that might be heard on a radio program. Choose the best answer.

Talk One

1. What is the main topic of this talk?
   - Ⓐ The American eagle as a symbol on coins.
   - Ⓑ The history of gold coins in the United States.
   - Ⓒ The United States Mint.
   - Ⓓ The value to collectors of gold coins.

2. What was the value of the original gold eagle?
   - Ⓐ $20.00.
   - Ⓑ $10.00.
   - Ⓒ $5.00.
   - Ⓓ $2.50.

3. What was the value of silver to gold in 1792?
   - Ⓐ Fifteen to one.
   - Ⓑ Fifteen and a quarter to one.
   - Ⓒ Fifteen and three quarters to one.
   - Ⓓ Fifteen to three.

4. What happened after the law of 1834?
   - Ⓐ The Great Depression occurred.
   - Ⓑ The size of gold coins was reduced.
   - Ⓒ All gold coins were turned in to the government.
   - Ⓓ The collecting of gold was severely reduced.

5. What are the restrictions on collecting gold coins today?
   - Ⓐ Gold coins may be imported without restrictions.
   - Ⓑ Gold coins may be collected but not exported.
   - Ⓒ There are few restrictions on the collection of gold coins.
   - Ⓓ Only certain kinds of gold coins may be purchased and sold.

Talk Two

1. What kind of music is associated with Stephen Foster?
   - Ⓐ Sentimental tunes.
   - Ⓑ Plantation songs.
   - Ⓒ Hymns for churches.
   - Ⓓ Serious society music.

2. Which piece was the most successful song written by an American?
   - Ⓐ "Open Thy Lattice, Love."
   - Ⓑ "Oh, Susanna."
   - Ⓒ "Old Folks at Home."
   - Ⓓ "Beautiful Dreamer."

3. Why did Stephen Foster withhold his name from the cover to some of his sheet music?
   - Ⓐ He was too young to publish music at that time.
   - Ⓑ His name was not yet very well known.
   - Ⓒ He knew that some songs would not be approved by high society.
   - Ⓓ He reserved his name for his most popular music.

4. What best describes Stephen Foster's most popular songs?
   - Ⓐ Easy to remember.
   - Ⓑ Written for the piano.
   - Ⓒ Appropriate for society events.
   - Ⓓ Very serious.

5. What do we know about Stephen Foster?
   - Ⓐ He wrote many songs during his career.
   - Ⓑ Only a few of his songs were popular.
   - Ⓒ He was not successful in his lifetime.
   - Ⓓ He wrote most of his music for children.

Refer to pages 360–363 for the Explanatory Answers.

EXERCISE 25: Content Lectures—Professor

 (CD 3, Track 3)

In some talks in the Listening Section on the Paper-Based TOEFL, you will be asked to understand academic content similar to that of short lectures that might be heard in a college classroom. Choose the best answer for multiple-choice questions.

Talk One

1. What is the main subject of this lecture?
   - Ⓐ Heredity.
   - Ⓑ Environment.
   - Ⓒ Birth order.
   - Ⓓ Motivation.

2. What should the students know before they hear this lecture?
   - Ⓐ Birth order may influence personality.
   - Ⓑ Heredity and environment play a role in the development of the personality.
   - Ⓒ There is research on birth order at the University of Texas at Arlington.
   - Ⓓ Firstborn children and only children have similar personalities.

3. Which one of the people would probably be the most comfortable interacting with a member of the opposite sex?
   - Ⓐ A man with younger sisters.
   - Ⓑ A man with older sisters.
   - Ⓒ A woman with younger sisters.
   - Ⓓ A woman with older sisters.

4. What personality trait will firstborn children probably exhibit?
   - Ⓐ Likable.
   - Ⓑ Ambitious.
   - Ⓒ Sociable.
   - Ⓓ Talkative.

5. According to the research, what might be the dominant personality trait of the youngest child?
   - Ⓐ Charming.
   - Ⓑ Shy.
   - Ⓒ Motivated.
   - Ⓓ Happy.

Talk Two

1. What is the main focus of this talk?
   - Ⓐ The Knickerbocker School.
   - Ⓑ The character of Natty Bumppo.
   - Ⓒ The *Leatherstocking Tales*.
   - Ⓓ Writers for the *New York Evening Post*.

2. What are the *Leatherstocking Tales*?
   - Ⓐ Stories by Washington Irving.
   - Ⓑ Five novels about frontier life.
   - Ⓒ Serials in the *New York Evening Post*.
   - Ⓓ Poems by the Knickerbocker group.

3. What kind of character is Natty Bumppo?
   - Ⓐ A frontier hero.
   - Ⓑ An inept settler on the frontier.
   - Ⓒ The son of an Indian chief.
   - Ⓓ The last member of his tribe.

4. Who was one of the most important members of the Knickerbocker School?
   - Ⓐ Rip Van Winkle.
   - Ⓑ Washington Irving.
   - Ⓒ Forrest Mohican.
   - Ⓓ Diedrich Knickerbocker.

5. Which of the following best describes James Fenimore Cooper?
   - Ⓐ Author, the *Leatherstocking Tales*.
   - Ⓑ Author, "The Legend of Sleepy Hollow."
   - Ⓒ Editor, the *New York Evening Post*.
   - Ⓓ Professor, the Knickerbocker School.

Refer to pages 363–365 for the Explanatory Answers.

EXERCISE 26: Content Lectures—Professor

 (CD 3, Track 4)

In some talks in the Listening Section on the Internet-Based TOEFL, you will be asked to understand academic content similar to that of short lectures that might be heard in a college classroom. The lectures will include natural pauses, and will be at a normal rate for a talk by a native speaker. Choose the best answer for multiple-choice questions. For computer-assisted questions, follow the directions on screen.

Talk One

1. What is the main topic of this lecture?
   - (A) Popcorn.
   - (B) Radiometric dating.
   - (C) Carbon-14.
   - (D) Geological formations.

2. What is the definition of a *half-life*?
   - (A) The average time it takes for half of a group to decay.
   - (B) Half the time it takes for a group to decay.
   - (C) Half an hour for an individual nucleus to decay.
   - (D) Half of the carbon present in a living organism.

3. Why does the professor mention popcorn?
   - (A) Because it was an example in the textbook.
   - (B) Because he is using popcorn in a laboratory demonstration.
   - (C) Because popcorn is a good analogy for half-lives.
   - (D) Because popcorn is a carbon-based life form.

4. What do we know about carbon-14?
   - (A) It is the only accurate isotope for radiometric dating.
   - (B) It represents most of the carbon in living things.
   - (C) It has a half-life of almost 50 billion years.
   - (D) It is used to estimate the age of carbon-based life forms.

5. Listen again to part of the lecture. Then answer the question.
   "So what about rocks that are millions or even billions of years old? Well, the same process can be applied, but we have to use isotopes that have longer half-lives."

   Why does the professor ask this question:
   "So what about rocks that are millions or even billions of years old?"
   - (A) He is preparing to suggest an answer to the question that he has just asked.
   - (B) He is trying to encourage the students to answer a difficult question.
   - (C) He is expressing doubt about the concept that he has been discussing.
   - (D) He is probing to see whether the students have understood the lecture so far.

6. Which of the following would NOT be dated using carbon-14?
   - (A) A fossilized shellfish.
   - (B) An animal skull.
   - (C) A dead tree.
   - (D) A giant crystal.

Refer to pages 365–368 for the Explanatory Answers.

Talk Two

1. What is this lecture mainly about?
   - (A) Ancient cities.
   - (B) Three types of cities.
   - (C) City planning.
   - (D) Urban sprawl.

2. What feature of ancient cities appears throughout most of the world?
   - (A) Walls and fortifications.
   - (B) A central marketplace.
   - (C) Plazas and parks.
   - (D) A pattern of square blocks.

3. When were symmetrical streets with circular patterns introduced?
   - (A) During Roman colonization.
   - (B) During the Renaissance.
   - (C) During the Industrial Revolution.
   - (D) During the Modern Era.

4. What was the problem for city planners during the Industrial Revolution?
   Click on the 2 best answers.
   - [A] Housing for immigrants from the countryside.
   - [B] Inadequate sanitation services for the population.
   - [C] Reconstruction of cities devastated by war.
   - [D] The growth of sprawling suburban areas.

5. Listen again to a part of the lecture. Then answer the question.
   "I know I went over that rather quickly, but . . . I advise you to refer to the three types of cities in your book. It's an important concept."

   Why did the professor say this:
   ". . . I advise you to refer to the three types of cities in your book"?
   - (A) She wants the students to spend more time reading their books.
   - (B) She did not have time to talk about the concept in depth.
   - (C) She is going to read some important information to the students.
   - (D) She wants the students to prepare for the next class.

6. Classify each of these cities by matching them with their type.
   Click on a city. Then click on the empty box in the correct column.
   - (A) Singapore
   - (B) Mexico City
   - (C) Los Angeles

Decentralized	Centralized	Densely populated

Refer to pages 368–370 for the Explanatory Answers.

EXERCISE 27: Interactive Lectures—Professor/Students

 (CD 3, Track 5)

In some talks in the Listening Section on the Paper-Based TOEFL, you will be asked to understand academic content similar to that of short lectures that might be heard in a college classroom. Both the professor and the students will be contributing to the class. Choose the best answer.

Talk One

1. What do the speakers mainly discuss?
   Ⓐ Admissions standards at the University of Michigan.
   Ⓑ The use of standardized tests for college admissions.
   Ⓒ The TOEFL (Test of English as a Foreign Language).
   Ⓓ Evaluation without standardized tests.

2. What is Paul's opinion about the TOEFL and the Michigan Test?
   Ⓐ He believes that the tests are good.
   Ⓑ He believes that the required test scores are too low.
   Ⓒ He believes that they are more important than academic preparation.
   Ⓓ He believes that the tests should not be used.

3. What does Sally say about the admissions officers?
   Ⓐ They don't always use the TOEFL and the Michigan Test scores correctly.
   Ⓑ They look at transcripts instead of scores.
   Ⓒ They should insist on a rigid cut-off score.
   Ⓓ They are looking for an appropriate alternative.

4. How does the professor handle the disagreement?
   Ⓐ He agrees with Sally.
   Ⓑ He restates both opinions.
   Ⓒ He asks the class to vote.
   Ⓓ He disagrees with both students.

5. Where did this discussion most probably take place?
   Ⓐ In a college classroom.
   Ⓑ At the Office of International Services.
   Ⓒ In the cafeteria.
   Ⓓ At a party.

Talk Two

1. What do the speakers mainly discuss?
   Ⓐ Making friends in a foreign country.
   Ⓑ Spanish and French.
   Ⓒ Foreign TV, radio, and other media.
   Ⓓ Learning a foreign language.

2. Why does Professor Baker begin the discussion by calling on Betty?
   Ⓐ Because she is not a shy person.
   Ⓑ Because she studied languages in high school.
   Ⓒ Because she knows several languages.
   Ⓓ Because she agrees with him.

3. What helped Betty most in learning Spanish?
   Ⓐ The language laboratory.
   Ⓑ Travel in other countries.
   Ⓒ Studying in high school.
   Ⓓ Going to movies and watching TV.

4. What is Professor Baker's opinion?
   Ⓐ He believes that it is a good idea to do all of the things that Betty and Bill suggested.
   Ⓑ He agrees with Betty's idea for learning languages.
   Ⓒ He believes that going to class is the best way to learn.
   Ⓓ He believes that it is ideal to live in a country where the language is spoken.

5. How can we best describe Professor Baker?
   Ⓐ He is not very knowledgeable.
   Ⓑ He is respectful of his students.
   Ⓒ He has a very formal manner in class.
   Ⓓ He has traveled extensively.

Refer to pages 370–373 for the Explanatory Answers.

EXERCISE 28: Interactive Lectures—Professor/Students

 (CD 3, Track 6)

In some talks in the Listening Section on the Internet-Based TOEFL, you will be asked to understand academic content similar to that of short lectures that might be heard in a college classroom. The lectures will include natural pauses, and will be at a normal rate for a conversation between native speakers. Both the professor and the students will be contributing to the class. Choose the best answer for multiple-choice questions. For computer-assisted questions, follow the directions on screen.

Talk One

1. What is this session mainly about?
   - Ⓐ Pop artists of the 1960s.
   - Ⓑ Andy Warhol's art.
   - Ⓒ Portraits of famous people.
   - Ⓓ The use of color in Pop Art.

2. According to the lecturer, why did Warhol paint objects in the environment?
   - Ⓐ He was once a commercial artist.
   - Ⓑ He was a very logical person.
   - Ⓒ He used the objects in his daily routine.
   - Ⓓ He was tired of painting landscapes.

3. Whose faces did Warhol paint?
   Click on the 2 best answers.
   - Ａ Marilyn Monroe.
   - Ｂ Elvis Presley.
   - Ｃ John Kennedy.
   - Ｄ Andy Warhol.

4. What problem does Tom mention?
   - Ⓐ The colors that Pop artists used were grotesque.
   - Ⓑ The paintings were used as commercial advertisements.
   - Ⓒ The paintings were too large for private collectors.
   - Ⓓ The subjects might not be of interest in the future.

5. Listen again to a part of the lecture. Then answer the question.
   "I mean, years from now, will . . . will anyone be eating Campbell's soup, or drinking Coca-Cola, or really, for that matter, uh . . . will anyone remember Marilyn Monroe?" "Interesting observation. So, Tom, you're saying that since Pop Art . . . since it depends on the popular culture, which by its very nature is uh . . . transient, you're asking . . . will the subject matter of the Pop Art movement doom its artists to . . . to temporary recognition?"

   Why did the professor say this:
   "So, Tom, you're saying that since Pop Art . . . since it depends on the popular culture, which by its very nature is uh . . . transient, you're asking . . . will the subject matter of the Pop Art movement doom its artists to . . . to temporary recognition?"
   - Ⓐ He asks the student to repeat his idea because it is interesting.
   - Ⓑ He disagrees with the student's statement about Pop Art.
   - Ⓒ He asks the student another question to continue the discussion.
   - Ⓓ He restates the student's comment to refine and clarify it.

6. Click on the drawing that is done in the Andy Warhol style.

Refer to pages 373–375 for the Explanatory Answers.

Talk Two

1. What is the main topic of today's lecture?
   - Ⓐ The climax association.
   - Ⓑ Pioneer plants.
   - Ⓒ A forest fire.
   - Ⓓ A disturbance in the balance of nature.

2. How does the scientific community view the theory of a stable climax community?
   - Ⓐ They no longer support it.
   - Ⓑ They were never interested in it.
   - Ⓒ They named it *dynamic equilibrium*.
   - Ⓓ They proposed it to replace *polyclimax*.

3. According to the lecturer, why is pioneer life important?
   - Ⓐ It prepares the environment for the forms that will replace it.
   - Ⓑ It is a stable environment that remains undisturbed in spite of conditions.
   - Ⓒ It assures that plants, animals, and minerals are replaced by exactly the same flora and fauna.
   - Ⓓ It is the only life that will ever be able to grow in areas where the balance of nature has been disturbed.

4. What is Dr. Green's opinion of a *controlled burn*?
   - Ⓐ He agrees with using a *cool fire* to control wildfires.
   - Ⓑ He disagrees with the author of the textbook they are using.
   - Ⓒ He thinks that using a *controlled burn* is the only reasonable opinion.
   - Ⓓ He does not think that fire-prevention strategies influence forest fires.

5. Listen again to part of the lecture. Then answer the question.
   "That is, a series of transitional life forms successively appears, preparing the environment for the forms that will replace them." "Excuse me, Dr. Green, would that be what the book refers to as *ecological succession*?"

   Why did the student ask this question: "Excuse me, Dr. Green, would that be what the book refers to as *ecological succession*?"
   - Ⓐ Because the book is difficult to understand.
   - Ⓑ Because he is trying to relate the lecture to the book.
   - Ⓒ Because Dr. Green's lecture was not very clear.
   - Ⓓ Because he wants to interrupt Dr. Green.

6. The professor describes the process of ecological succession that occurs after the balance of nature has been disturbed. Summarize the process by putting the events in order.
   Click on a sentence. Then click on the space where it belongs.
   - Ⓐ Pioneer flora and fauna appear.
   - Ⓑ The climax association occurs.
   - Ⓒ More stable plant and animal life is established.
   - Ⓓ Other forms of temporary plants and animals replace the early ones.

1
2
3
4

Refer to pages 375–377 for the Explanatory Answers.

EXERCISE 29: Visual Lectures—Professor/Student

 (CD 3, Track 7)

In some talks in the Listening Section on the Paper-Based TOEFL, you will be asked to understand academic content similar to that of short lectures that might be heard in a college classroom. Drawings, charts, or other visuals will support the lecture. Choose the best answer for multiple-choice questions.

Talk One

1. What is the main purpose of this lecture?
   Ⓐ The life of Louis Tiffany.
   Ⓑ The work of Louis Tiffany.
   Ⓒ The Art Nouveau movement.
   Ⓓ *Favrile* glass art objects.

2. What characterized Tiffany's jewelry?
   Ⓐ Iridescent glass.
   Ⓑ Precious stones.
   Ⓒ Traditional styles.
   Ⓓ Floral designs.

3. How did Tiffany help aspiring artists?
   Ⓐ He was a teacher.
   Ⓑ He founded a school.
   Ⓒ He provided scholarships.
   Ⓓ He sold their work in his shop.

4. For which interior design was Tiffany NOT commissioned?
   Ⓐ A glass curtain at the National Theater in Mexico.
   Ⓑ The altar in the Cathedral of Saint John the Divine.
   Ⓒ The reception rooms in the White House.
   Ⓓ Exclusive stores on Fifth Avenue in Manhattan.

5. Select the example of a Tiffany *favrile* design. Choose the letter of the drawing that was described in the lecture.

Refer to pages 377–379 for the Explanatory Answers.

Talk Two

1. What is the lecture mainly about?
   - ⓐ The structure of the cactus.
   - ⓑ Extreme climates.
   - ⓒ Water storage in cactus plants.
   - ⓓ The nutritive functions of leaves.

2. What is assumed about cactus plants millions of years ago?
   - ⓐ They were probably much larger.
   - ⓑ They probably had leaves like other plants.
   - ⓒ They probably grew underground.
   - ⓓ They probably had fruit as well as flowers.

3. According to the lecturer, why have cacti developed spines and needles?
   - ⓐ They grew closer to the surface.
   - ⓑ They could absorb water more quickly.
   - ⓒ They protected the plant from animals.
   - ⓓ They supported beautiful blossoms.

4. Where is the nutritive function of the cactus carried out?
   - ⓐ Leaves.
   - ⓑ Blossoms.
   - ⓒ Stems.
   - ⓓ Roots.

5. Select the Saguaro cactus from among the choices pictured.
   Choose the letter of the drawing that was described in the lecture.
   - ⓐ
   - ⓑ
   - ⓒ

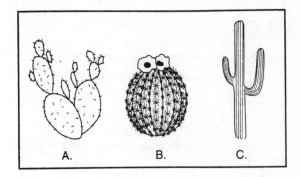

A.   B.   C.

Refer to pages 379–380 for the Explanatory Answers.

EXERCISE 30: Visual Lectures—Professors/Students

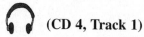 **(CD 4, Track 1)**

In some talks in the Listening Section on the Internet-Based TOEFL, you will be asked to understand academic content similar to that of short lectures that might be heard in a college classroom. The lectures will include natural pauses, and will be at a normal rate for a talk by a native speaker. Drawings, charts, or other visuals will support the lecture. Choose the best answer for multiple-choice questions. For computer-assisted questions, follow the directions on screen.

Talk One

1. What is the main purpose of this lecture?
   Ⓐ To make arrangements for the field trip.
   Ⓑ To introduce the students to some common petroglyphs.
   Ⓒ To discuss legends from the Hohokam culture.
   Ⓓ To classify the different clans in Hohokam culture.

2. What are *petroglyphs*?
   Ⓐ An early alphabet.
   Ⓑ Art on rocks.
   Ⓒ Anthropologists.
   Ⓓ Religious ceremonies.

3. How are anthropologists able to interpret the symbols?
   Click on the 2 best answers.
   Ⓐ Early inhabitants left a history.
   Ⓑ The descendants of early people know the stories.
   Ⓒ Some of the symbols are common to many cultures.
   Ⓓ The symbols are pictures that represent objects.

4. What might be represented by a *zoomorph*?
   Click on the 2 best answers.
   Ⓐ A religious ceremony.
   Ⓑ The history of a successful hunt.
   Ⓒ The name of a family clan.
   Ⓓ The symbol of a group of spirits.

5. Listen again to part of the lecture. Then answer the question.
   "But, um . . . why were they carved in the first place? For a variety of reasons really. . . ."

   Why did the professor say this:
   "But, um . . . why were they carved in the first place?"
   Ⓐ To emphasize the importance of the carvings.
   Ⓑ To ask a question that she will answer.
   Ⓒ To check on students' comprehension.
   Ⓓ To begin a discussion among the students.

6. Click on the petroglyph that is a spiritual symbol of life.

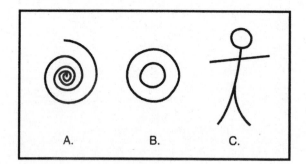

Refer to pages 380–383 for the Explanatory Answers.

Talk Two

1. What is the main purpose of this lecture?
   - Ⓐ To contrast short-period and long-period comets.
   - Ⓑ To discuss the structure and nature of comets.
   - Ⓒ To explain the orbit of planets.
   - Ⓓ To predict the probability of collisions between planets and comets.

2. What causes the tail of a comet to point away from the Sun?
   - Ⓐ The orbit of the comet.
   - Ⓑ The solar wind.
   - Ⓒ The coma of the comet.
   - Ⓓ The cloud that lies beyond Pluto.

3. What is the difference between a short-period comet and a long-period comet?
   - Ⓐ The shape of their orbits.
   - Ⓑ The size of their tails.
   - Ⓒ The probability that they will collide with planets.
   - Ⓓ The time they take to orbit the Sun.

4. What is *capture*?
   - Ⓐ The gravitational pull of a planet permanently attracts a comet.
   - Ⓑ A long-period comet is converted into a short-period comet.
   - Ⓒ The orbits of planets and comets intersect at one point.
   - Ⓓ The impact of comets on planets and moons causes craters.

5. Listen again to a part of the lecture. Then answer the question.
   "Comets are small bodies from the outer solar system that are characterized by gaseous emissions and consist of a solid nucleus, a cloudy atmosphere, which is called the *coma*, and a tail. Let me say that again. Comets are small bodies from the outer solar system that are characterized by gaseous emissions and consist of a solid nucleus, a cloudy atmosphere, which is called the *coma*, and a tail."

   Why does the professor say this:

   "Let me say that again."
   - Ⓐ He wants the students to write down the definition.
   - Ⓑ He did not say it correctly the first time.
   - Ⓒ He does not think that students are paying attention.
   - Ⓓ He believes in class participation.

6. Click on the orbit of a comet.

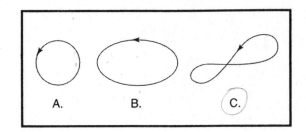

A.   B.   C.

Refer to pages 383–386 for the Explanatory Answers.

3

PRACTICE EXERCISES
FOR SPEAKING

Speaking Section

The Speaking Section of the TOEFL tests your ability to speak in English about a variety of general and academic topics. The Speaking Section is not included in the Paper-Based TOEFL. It is included only in the Internet-Based TOEFL. This section was formerly referred to as the TOEFL Academic Speaking Test (TAST).

Internet-Based TOEFL

There are usually six questions on the Speaking Section of the iBT®. The topics are both general and academic. There are two types of tasks included in the Speaking Section: two independent speaking tasks and four integrated speaking tasks. The questions are presented only one time. You may take notes.

In the independent speaking tasks, you will hear questions about familiar topics. You can use your personal experience and general knowledge to answer. After each question, you have 15 seconds to prepare your answer, and 45 seconds to record it. Refer to Exercise 31 to see examples.

In the integrated speaking tasks, you will hear a lecture, read a passage, or hear a lecture and read a related passage about a campus situation or an academic topic. You may take notes to prepare your answer. After each lecture or reading passage, you will hear a question that requires you to respond by speaking. You will have 20–30 seconds to prepare your answer, and 60 seconds to record it. Refer to Exercise 34 to see examples.

Be sure to use the audio to listen to the directions.

EXERCISE 31: General Topics—Personal Experiences

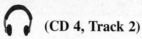 **(CD 4, Track 2)**

In Task 1 of the Speaking Section on the Internet-Based TOEFL, you will be asked to talk about a personal experience. You have 15 seconds to prepare after you have heard the question. Then, you have 45 seconds to record your answer.

Topic One

Question:

What are the qualities that you look for in a best friend? Describe a friend, and explain what influences you to choose this person as a best friend. Be sure to include specific details and examples in your answer.

Preparation Time: 15 seconds
Recording Time: 45 seconds

Notes

Refer to pages 388–389 for the Example Answer.

Topic Two

Question:
How do you like to spend your leisure time? Choose an activity and explain why you enjoy participating in it. Be sure to include specific details and examples in your answer.

Preparation Time: 15 seconds
Recording Time: 45 seconds

Notes

Refer to page 389 for the Example Answer.

EXERCISE 32: General Topics—Opinions

🎧 (CD 4, Track 3)

In Task 2 of the Speaking Section on the Internet-Based TOEFL, you will be asked to make a choice and defend your opinion. You have 15 seconds to prepare after you have heard the question. Then, you have 45 seconds to record your answer.

Topic One

Question:

Some teachers encourage competition among their students. Others help students learn how to collaborate and study in groups. Which approach do you think is better for learning and why do you think so? Be sure to use specific reasons and examples to support your opinion.

Preparation Time: 15 seconds
Recording Time: 45 seconds

Notes

Refer to page 390 for the Example Answer.

Topic Two

Question:
Some people cope with stress by exercising. Others talk with family or friends. How do you handle stressful situations? Be sure to use specific reasons and examples to support your opinion.

Preparation Time: 15 seconds
Recording Time: 45 seconds

Notes

Refer to page 391 for the Example Answer.

EXERCISE 33: Campus Situations—Connections

🎧 (CD 4, Track 4)

In Task 3 of the Speaking Section on the Internet-Based TOEFL, you will be asked to make a connection between a short reading passage and a talk. You have 30 seconds to prepare after you have read the passage and heard the talk. Then, you have 60 seconds to record your answer.

Topic One

Reading Time: 45 seconds

Accelerated Bachelor's Program

City College currently requires all bachelor's degree students to complete their degrees by fulfilling the course requirements in a four-year program plan. A three-year bachelor's degree program is being proposed to allow selected students to accelerate their programs, completing their degrees in three-fourths the time. If there is sufficient interest, the program will be offered to students in forty major fields of study. Classes will be limited to twenty students as compared with over one hundred in the large lecture classes for students enrolled in the four-year program. To find out whether you qualify for this opportunity, contact an advisor in the Millennium Program Office in the Old Main Building.

Now listen to a talk on the same topic.

Question:
The student expresses her opinion about the college's plans for an accelerated three-year degree program. Summarize her opinion and the reasons she gives for having that opinion.

Preparation Time: 30 seconds
Recording Time: 60 seconds

Notes

Refer to pages 393–394 for the Example Answer.

Topic Two

Reading Time: 45 seconds

Notice concerning dorm closing

State University is considering a proposal to close all but one of the dormitories over spring break. The Office of University Research reports that only 10 percent of the dorm students maintain their residence on campus over the break, whereas the other 90 percent go home or leave for vacations. The cost of keeping all of the dorms open is difficult to justify; however, Norman Hall would offer a temporary living situation for those students who chose to remain on campus. This proposal will be discussed at a public meeting in the Little Theater at 7 P.M. on January 10.

Now listen to a talk on the same topic.

Question:
The student expresses his opinion about the proposal for closing the dorms over spring break. Summarize his opinion and the reasons he gives for having that opinion.

Preparation Time: 30 seconds
Recording Time: 60 seconds

Notes

Refer to pages 394–395 for the Example Answer.

EXERCISE 34: Campus Situations—More Connections

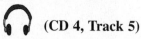 **(CD 4, Track 5)**

In Task 3 of the Speaking Section on the Internet-Based TOEFL, you will be asked to make a connection between a short reading passage and a conversation. You have 30 seconds to prepare after you have read the passage and heard the conversation. Then, you have 60 seconds to record your answer.

Topic One

Reading Time: 45 seconds

Registration hours shortened

The hours for on-site registration at City College have traditionally been from 7 A.M. to 7 P.M. Monday through Friday the week before classes. However, since many students have been taking advantage of on-line registration, next term registration week will be shortened to three days, starting at 7 A.M. the Wednesday before classes begin and ending at 7 P.M. on Friday. Late registration during the first two days of classes will not be affected. Both on-site and on-line registration wil! be open for late scheduling and drop-add scheduling as usual on the first Monday and Tuesday of the semester.

Now listen to a conversation on the same topic.

Question:
The man expresses his opinion about the changes in the registration procedure. Report his opinion and explain the reasons that he gives for having that opinion.

Preparation Time: 30 seconds
Recording Time: 60 seconds

Notes

Refer to pages 395–396 for the Example Answer.

Topic Two

Reading Time: 45 seconds

<u>Notice concerning the fall career fair</u>

Over 100 representatives from business and industry will be participating in the annual career fair on Saturday, October 7, including high-level officers from a number of international companies. Booths and exhibits will be set up in the college auditorium between 9 A.M. and 3 P.M. To take full advantage of this opportunity, bring copies of your resume and transcripts with you to the fair. Representatives will be collecting applications so that they can contact students to arrange interviews. Most of the representatives will return to campus next month to complete the screening process, although some companies have announced that they will interview immediately after the exhibits are closed on Saturday.

Now listen to a conversation on the same topic.

Question:
The woman expresses her opinion about the career fair. Report her opinion and explain the reasons that she gives for having that opinion.

Preparation Time: 30 seconds
Recording Time: 60 seconds

Notes

Refer to pages 396–398 for the Example Answer.

EXERCISE 35: Academic Content—Connections

🎧 (CD 4, Track 6)

In Task 4 of the Speaking Section on the Internet-Based TOEFL, you will be asked to make a connection between a short reading passage and a lecture. In most of these items, you will be required to relate an example to a general concept. You have 30 seconds to prepare after you have read the passage and heard the lecture. Then, you have 60 seconds to record your answer.

Topic One

Reading Time: 45 seconds

A Village

A traditional village is self-contained, which means that within the village, facilities for daily life such as sleeping, eating, health care, and social activities are constructed. Furthermore, nearly all the essential supplies of goods and services are stored within the confines of the village, although one village may trade with another to secure certain items. In addition, the residents of the village interact closely with each other and have common goals and interests that are reflected in their activities. Finally, it is said the outward appearance of a village expresses the essence of who the inhabitants believe themselves to be.

Now listen to part of a lecture on the same topic.

Question:
Refer to Thomas Jefferson's definition of a college campus presented in the lecture, and explain how the information in the anthropology text supported Jefferson's view.

Preparation Time: 30 seconds
Recording Time: 60 seconds

Notes

Refer to pages 398–399 for the Example Answer.

Topic Two

Reading Time: 45 seconds

Entrepreneurs

Numerous studies of small-business owners in the United States reveal that about 50 percent of them come from poor or lower middle-class families. Most begin their working life early and are already employed full time by the age of 18. Most have already established their businesses by the age of 30. In general, they tend to display three characteristics, including a strong desire for independence, a high level of initiative, and the ability to react quickly to take advantage of an opportunity. Another interesting characteristic is the fact that so many successful small-business owners establish their businesses as a result of a coincidence rather than by following a business plan.

Now listen to part of a lecture on the same topic.

Question:
Referring to both the lecture and the reading passage, explain why the experience of Levi Strauss is typical of small-business owners.

Preparation Time: 30 seconds
Recording Time: 60 seconds

Notes

Refer to pages 399–400 for the Example Answer.

EXERCISE 36: Academic Content—More Connections

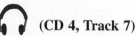 **(CD 4, Track 7)**

In Task 4 of the Speaking Section on the Internet-Based TOEFL, you will be asked to make a connection between a short reading passage and a lecture. In most of these items, you will be required to relate an example to a general concept. You have 30 seconds to prepare after you have read the passage and heard the lecture. Then, you have 60 seconds to record your answer.

Topic One

Reading Time: 45 seconds

Color

Color is light, a form of energy that travels in waves. Light waves emanate from a source, as for example, from a candle, a light bulb, or the Sun. In all of these sources of light there are many different wavelengths, measured from crest to crest in nanometers or millimicrons. All visible colors are contained in white or colorless light. When passed through a prism, a beam of white light is refracted into separate bands of colors, each with its own wavelength that differs from that of any other color. These are the colors of the visible spectrum which we occasionally see in nature as a rainbow.

Now listen to part of a lecture on the same topic.

Question:
Referring to both the lecture and the reading passage, explain why the sky is blue.

Preparation Time: 30 seconds
Recording Time: 60 seconds

Notes

Refer to pages 400–402 for the Example Answer.

Topic Two

Reading Time: 45 seconds

Polio

Polio is a virus that is spread by drinking water from sources contaminated by sewage, as for example, when local water supplies are not properly treated and the population uses contaminated water from the kitchen faucet for drinking or cooking. Polio is also occasionally spread from one person to another, especially among children whose hands may have been in contact with the virus. In any case, the polio virus enters the mouth and passes into the digestive tract where the cells lining the intestine are infected. It is then carried through the intestine and released into the sewage system to begin the cycle again.

Now listen to part of a lecture on the same topic.

Question:
Referring to both the lecture and the reading passage, explain how polio is spread and why the more developed societies tend to suffer more serious epidemics.

Preparation Time: 30 seconds
Recording Time: 60 seconds

Notes

Refer to pages 402–403 for the Example Answer.

EXERCISE 37: Campus Situations—Problems

(CD 4, Track 8)

In Task 5 of the Speaking Section on the Internet-Based TOEFL, you will be asked to listen to a conversation, describe the problem that the speakers are discussing, and evaluate the alternatives. You have 20 seconds to prepare after you have heard the conversation. Then, you have 60 seconds to record your answer.

Topic One

Question:
Describe the man's problem and the two suggestions that the woman makes about how to handle it. What do you think the man should do, and why?

Preparation Time: 20 seconds
Recording Time: 60 seconds

Notes

Refer to pages 403–404 for the Example Answer.

Topic Two

Question:
Describe the woman's problem and the three suggestions that the man makes about how to handle it. What do you think the woman should do, and why?

Preparation Time: 20 seconds
Recording Time: 60 seconds

Notes

Refer to pages 404–406 for the Example Answer.

EXERCISE 38: Campus Situations—More Problems

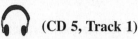 **(CD 5, Track 1)**

In Task 5 of the Speaking Section on the Internet-Based TOEFL, you will be asked to listen to a conversation, describe the problem that the speakers are discussing, and evaluate the alternatives. You have 20 seconds to prepare after you have heard the conversation. Then, you have 60 seconds to record your answer.

Topic One

Question:
Describe the woman's problem and the two suggestions that the man makes about how to handle it. What do you think the woman should do, and why?

Preparation Time: 20 seconds
Recording Time: 60 seconds

Notes

Refer to pages 406–407 for the Example Answer.

Topic Two

Question:
Describe the man's problem and the two suggestions that the woman makes about how to handle it. What do you think the man should do, and why?

Preparation Time: 20 seconds
Recording Time: 60 seconds

Notes

Refer to pages 407–408 for the Example Answer.

EXERCISE 39: Academic Content—Summaries

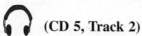 (CD 5, Track 2)

In Task 6 of the Speaking Section on the Internet-Based TOEFL, you will be asked to summarize the main points in a short lecture. In most of these summaries, you will be required to explain a term or a concept. You have 20 seconds to prepare after you have heard the lecture. Then, you have 60 seconds to record your answer.

Topic One

Question:

Referring to the main points and examples from the lecture, describe the two general groups of flowering plants. Then explain the problem for classification that the professor presents.

Preparation Time: 20 seconds
Recording Time: 60 seconds

Notes

Refer to pages 408–410 for the Example Answer.

Topic Two

Question:
Referring to the main points and examples from the lecture, describe the two types of bridge construction presented by the professor. Then explain the specific advantages and disadvantages of each type.

Preparation Time: 20 seconds
Recording Time: 60 seconds

Notes

Refer to pages 410–411 for the Example Answer.

EXERCISE 40: Academic Content—More Summaries

 (CD 5, Track 3)

In Task 6 of the Speaking Section on the Internet-Based TOEFL, you will be asked to summarize the main points in a short lecture. In most of these summaries, you will be required to explain a term or a concept. You have 20 seconds to prepare after you have heard the lecture. Then, you have 60 seconds to record your answer.

Topic One

Question:
Referring to the main points and examples from the lecture, describe the three basic functions of the liver presented by the professor.

Preparation Time: 20 seconds
Recording Time: 60 seconds

Notes

Refer to pages 411–413 for the Example Answer.

<u>Topic Two</u>

Question:
Referring to the main points and examples from the lecture, describe two types of research correlations that the professor presents. Then explain causality.

Preparation Time: 20 seconds
Recording Time: 60 seconds

Notes

Refer to pages 413–414 for the Example Answer.

PRACTICE EXERCISES
FOR STRUCTURE

Structure Section

The Structure Section of the TOEFL tests your ability to recognize standard written English as it is used in North America. The Structure Section is included in the Paper-Based TOEFL, but it is not included as a separate section in the Internet-Based TOEFL.

Paper-Based TOEFL (PBT)

There are 40 questions in two parts on the Structure Section of the Paper-Based TOEFL. The questions are all multiple-choice with four possible answer choices. The section takes 25 minutes to complete. The Structure Section is scored separately from the Test of Written English (TWE) in the Paper-Based TOEFL.

In Part 1, you will see 15 incomplete sentences. The questions are all multiple-choice with four possible answer choices. Choose the best answer choice from four possible answers to complete the sentence. Refer to Exercise 55 to see examples.

In Part 2, you will see 25 incorrect sentences with four underlined words or phrases marked (A), (B), (C), and (D). Choose the one word or phrase that must be changed to correct the sentence. Refer to Exercise 55 to see examples.

EXERCISE 41: Sentences—Verbs

In some sentences in the Structure Section on the Paper-Based TOEFL, you will be asked to identify the correct verb. In fact, most of the sentences in the Structure Section are verb problems. A verb is a word or phrase that expresses action or condition. A verb can be classified as transitive or intransitive according to whether it requires a complement; it can be classified further according to the kind of complement it requires, including not only nouns, pronouns, adjectives, and adverbs, but also *-ing* forms or infinitives. Choose the correct answer in the incomplete sentences. Choose the incorrect word or phrase in the underlined choices.

1. Almost everyone fails _____ the driver's test on the first try.
   A passing
   B to have passed
   C to pass
   D in passing

2. When the silkworm gets through to lay its
        A   B C

   eggs, it dies.
       D

3. If endangered species _____ saved, rain forests must be protected.
   A are to be
   B be
   C can be
   D will be

4. The average spoken sentence in conversational English takes 2.5 seconds _____.
   A for to complete
   B completing
   C to complete
   D by completing

5. Only twenty years ago, most doctors agreed _____ truthful with their terminally ill patients, a trend that has reversed itself in modern medical practice.
   A don't to be
   B not to be
   C we shouldn't been
   D not to been

6. William Torrey Harris was one of the first educators interested _____ a logical progression of topics in the school curriculum.
   A in establishing
   B for establishing
   C establishing
   D to establish

7. North American Indian tribes used sign language _____ with tribes that spoke a different language or dialect.
   A to communicating
   B for communicate
   C to communicate
   D for communicated

8. Art tends to be _____ more after the death of the artist, but most literary works tend to decrease in value when the writer dies.
   A price
   B worthy
   C worth
   D value

9. Adult eagles let their offspring _____ nests near their original nesting area.
   A build
   B builds
   C building
   D to build

10. A barometer is a device with a sealed metal
         A   B

    chamber designed to reading the changes
                       C

    in the pressure of air in the atmosphere.
                     D

11. If a person does not have an attorney, the court _____ one.
    Ⓐ will appoint
    Ⓑ appointed
    Ⓒ would appoint
    Ⓓ appointing

12. Since lightning was probably significant in the formation of life, understanding it
    _____Ⓐ
    might help us to understanding life itself.
    ___Ⓑ___   ___Ⓒ___   ___Ⓓ___

13. Iowa _____ of flat-topped hills erected by the ancient Mound Builder people as temples and burial sites.
    Ⓐ with a larger number
    Ⓑ has a large number
    Ⓒ having a large number
    Ⓓ a large number

14. If the oxygen supply in the atmosphere was
    _____Ⓐ_____Ⓑ
    not replenished by plants, it would soon be
    _____Ⓒ
    exhausted.
    __Ⓓ__

15. _____ the eight Ivy League schools are among the most prestigious colleges in the United States.
    Ⓐ It is generally accepted that
    Ⓑ That it is accepted
    Ⓒ Accepting that it is
    Ⓓ That is accepted

16. The Girl Scouts, which was found by
    _____Ⓐ
    Juliette Gordon Low in 1912, has grown to
    _____Ⓑ_____Ⓒ
    a current membership of more than three
    _____Ⓓ
    million girls.

17. To relieve pain caused by severe burns, prevent infection, and treat for shock, _____ immediate steps.
    Ⓐ taking
    Ⓑ to take
    Ⓒ taken
    Ⓓ take

18. If gasoline vapor _____ with air, combustion will occur.
    Ⓐ mixed
    Ⓑ had mixed
    Ⓒ mixes
    Ⓓ mixture

19. Vermont, commonly known as the Green Mountain State, refused _____ until 1791.
    Ⓐ to join the Union
    Ⓑ joining the Union
    Ⓒ the joining of the Union
    Ⓓ join the Union

20. Air constricted between the vocal chords makes them _____, producing sounds.
    Ⓐ to vibrate
    Ⓑ vibrating
    Ⓒ vibrate
    Ⓓ the vibration

Refer to pages 415–416 for the Explanatory Answers.

EXERCISE 42: Sentences—Auxiliary Verbs

In some sentences in the Structure Section on the Paper-Based TOEFL, you will be asked to select the correct auxiliary verb. An auxiliary verb is a verb that accompanies the main verb and makes distinctions in the meaning of the main verb. Some examples of auxiliary verbs are BE, HAVE, or a modal. Choose the correct answer in the incomplete sentences. Choose the incorrect word or phrase in the underlined choices.

1. On the average, a healthy heart _____ to pump five tablespoons of blood with every beat.
   Ⓐ must
   Ⓑ ought
   Ⓒ can
   Ⓓ should

2. It is generally believed that Thomas
   _____
        Ⓐ
   Jefferson was the one who had researched

   and wrote the *Declaration of Independence*
       Ⓑ
   during the months prior to its signing
                                  Ⓒ
   in July 1776.
      Ⓓ

3. In general, by the second year of production, the price of a new piece of technology _____ significantly.
   Ⓐ will decreased
   Ⓑ has decreased
   Ⓒ will have decreased
   Ⓓ will has decreased

4. Although some higher structures
              _____
                    Ⓐ
   have been build in New York City, none
   _____
       Ⓑ
   characterizes the skyline better than the
   _____   _____
       Ⓒ   Ⓓ
   Empire State Building.

5. Research in genetics and DNA having had a
                             _____
                               Ⓐ
   profound influence on the direction of
   _____   __
      Ⓑ   Ⓒ
   treatment for a large number of diseases.
                  _____
                       Ⓓ

6. Bones composed chiefly of calcium,
   ____ _____ _____
    Ⓐ   Ⓑ   Ⓒ
   phosphorous, and a fibrous substance

   known as collagen.
   _____
      Ⓓ

7. A cure for juvenile diabetes _____ until more funds are allocated to basic research.
   Ⓐ won't develop
   Ⓑ aren't developing
   Ⓒ don't develop
   Ⓓ won't be developed

8. During the past decade, twenty million
   _____
     Ⓐ
   college graduates spended more than fifty
                      _____ _____
                         Ⓑ   Ⓒ
   billion dollars in ten-year student loans.
                      _____
                         Ⓓ

9. Civil engineers had better _____ steel supports in concrete structures built on unstable geophysical sites.
   Ⓐ include
   Ⓑ including
   Ⓒ inclusion
   Ⓓ included

10. There is no limit to the diversity to be
              __
              Ⓐ
    finding in the cultures of people
    _____   _____   _____
       Ⓑ   Ⓒ   Ⓓ
    throughout the world.

11. The cones of pine trees _____ two or three years to reach maturity.
    Ⓐ to take
    Ⓑ taking
    Ⓒ may take
    Ⓓ takes

12. The government requires that a census taken
    (A)

    every ten years so that accurate statistics
    (B)   (C)

    may be compiled.
    (D)

13. It is important that cancer is diagnosed and
    (A)   (B)

    treated as early as possible in order
    (C)

    to assure a successful cure.
    (D)

14. Although the scientific community had
    hoped that the field of transplantation
    _____, the shortage of organ donors has
    curtailed research.
    (A) progress
    (B) had progressed
    (C) would progress
    (D) progressing

15. Before railroad lines were extended from
    (A)   (B)

    Missouri to New Mexico, millions of

    dollars in trade was used to be carried over
    (C)

    the Santa Fe Trail by wheeled wagons.
    (D)

16. Based on a decline in vehicular deaths

    during the past decade, seat belts, air bags,

    baby seats, and other safety features in
    (A)

    newer automobiles must be save lives.
    (B)   (C) (D)

17. The gold used in jewelry is not
    (A)

    strong enough unless it be alloyed.
    (B)   (C)(D)

18. Even without strong wings, the ostrich has
    survived because it _____ at high speeds
    to escape predators.
    (A) to run
    (B) can run
    (C) running
    (D) run

19. General damage that been caused
    (A)

    by aphids or pollution is sometimes
    (B)   (C)

    known as blight.
    (D)

20. Fred Astaire is said to had been
    (A)   (B)

    the most popular dancer of his time, but he
    (C)

    was also a talented actor, singer, and
    (D)

    choreographer.

Refer to page 416 for the Explanatory Answers.

EXERCISE 43: Sentences—Nouns

In some sentences in the Structure Section on the Paper-Based TOEFL, you will be asked to identify the correct noun. A noun is a word that names persons, objects, and ideas. There are two basic classifications of nouns in English: count nouns and noncount nouns. Count nouns are those that can be made plural by -s, -es, or an irregular form. They are used in agreement with either singular or plural verbs. Noncount nouns are those that cannot be made plural in these ways. They are used in agreement with singular verbs. It is necessary to know whether a noun is count or noncount to maintain verb agreement and to choose correct adjective modifiers. Choose the correct answer in the incomplete sentences. Choose the incorrect word or phrase in the underlined choices.

1. The understanding electricity depends on a
   (A)   (B)   (C)
   knowledge of atoms and the subatomic

   particles of which they are composed.
                                 (D)

2. The cost of delivering mails is estimated
      (A)   (B)
   at 600 percent more for mass mailing
                                (C)
   campaigns using the U.S. Post Office as
   compared with e-mail advertising.
                            (D)

3. The two main _____ are permanent
   magnets and electromagnets.
   (A) kinds of magnets
   (B) kind of magnets
   (C) kind magnets
   (D) kinds magnets

4. When water is frozen, it becomes _____.
   (A) ice
   (B) ices
   (C) the ice
   (D) an ice

5. _____ can live to be more than fifteen
   years old.
   (A) That it is dogs
   (B) That dogs
   (C) Dogs that
   (D) Dogs

6. One of the most distinctive plant found in
               (A)   (B)   (C)
   the desert is the Saguaro cactus.
                   (D)

7. In the fall, most trees lose _____, which
   have, by then, turned from green to gold
   and orange.
   (A) their leaf
   (B) their leaves
   (C) the leaf
   (D) the leafs

8. Doctors have concluded that in addition to
   regular exercise, a diet rich in _____ is
   good for the heart.
   (A) fruits and vegetable
   (B) a fruit and vegetable
   (C) the fruits and vegetables
   (D) fruit and vegetables

9. A thunder usually follows lightning by five
      (A)   (B)
   seconds for every mile between the flash
                (C)   (D)
   and the observer.

10. Canada stretches from the Atlantic Ocean
    to the Pacific Ocean, and covers _____ of
    almost four million square miles.
    (A) a area
    (B) an area
    (C) the area
    (D) area

11. During the early nineteenth century, _____
    were hunted for their pelts.
    (A) a beaver
    (B) beavers
    (C) the beaver
    (D) that beavers

12. The stories of Dr. Seuss have been enjoyed
    Ⓐ   Ⓑ
    by millions of childrens.
    Ⓒ   Ⓓ

13. Collections of simple and functional
    Ⓐ
    Shaker furniture can be seen in museum
          Ⓑ   Ⓒ   Ⓓ
    throughout the United States.

14. The decathlon is a two-day
                      Ⓐ
    athletic competition which consists of
        Ⓑ   Ⓒ
    ten types track and field events.
    Ⓓ

15. _____ designs on a wall, also called
    graffiti, has become associated with gang
    activity in many neighborhoods.
    Ⓐ Spraying of
    Ⓑ The spraying of
    Ⓒ Spray the
    Ⓓ Sprays

16. _____ by the author John Grisham are
    frequently on the best seller list.
    Ⓐ The novel
    Ⓑ Novels
    Ⓒ A novel
    Ⓓ Some novel

17. _____ have made communication faster
    and easier through the use of e-mail and
    the Internet is widely recognized.
    Ⓐ It is that computers
    Ⓑ That it is computers
    Ⓒ Computers that
    Ⓓ That computers

18. Provide pensions for retired persons is
    Ⓐ   Ⓑ   Ⓒ
    the primary function of the social security
                      Ⓓ
    system.

19. New equipments for medical diagnosis
            Ⓐ
    have made many formerly unpleasant
        Ⓑ   Ⓒ
    procedures quite painless.
    Ⓓ

20. Termites can do _____ to the wood in
    homes before they are detected.
    Ⓐ an extensive damage
    Ⓑ extensive damages
    Ⓒ the extensive damage
    Ⓓ extensive damage

Refer to pages 416–417 for the Explanatory Answers.

EXERCISE 44: Sentences—Pronouns

In some sentences in the Structure Section on the Paper-Based TOEFL, you will be asked to identify the correct pronoun. A pronoun is a word that can be used instead of a noun, usually to avoid repeating the noun. A pronoun may be singular or plural; masculine, feminine, or neuter; and first, second, or third person to agree with the noun to which it refers. A pronoun may be used as the subject of a sentence or a clause or as the object of a sentence, a clause, or a preposition. In English, pronouns are also used to express possessives and reflexives. Choose the correct answer in the incomplete sentences. Choose the incorrect word or phrase in the underlined choices.

1. The crime rate has begun to decline in New York City due to efforts on the part of both government and private citizens to curb _____.
   Ⓐ them
   Ⓑ him
   Ⓒ its
   Ⓓ it

2. Sloths spend <u>most</u> of <u>its</u> time hanging upside
   　　　　　Ⓐ　　Ⓑ
   down from trees and <u>feeding</u> on leaves and
   　　　　　　　　　　Ⓒ
   <u>fruit</u>.
   Ⓓ

3. When the European settlers came
   <u>in the seventeenth century</u>, the newcomers
   　　　　　Ⓐ
   began a systematic effort <u>to push</u> the Native
   　　　　　　　　　　　　Ⓑ
   Americans into the wilderness and to take
   <u>their</u> land <u>from their</u>.
   　Ⓒ　　　　Ⓓ

4. Seals can _____ because they have a thick layer of blubber under their fur.
   Ⓐ keep them warm
   Ⓑ keep themselves warm
   Ⓒ they keep warm
   Ⓓ keep their warm

5. After Dr. Werner Arber <u>discovered</u>
   　　　　　　　　　　　Ⓐ
   restriction enzymes, Drs. Daniel Nathan,
   Hamilton Smith, and <u>him</u> <u>were awarded</u> the
   　　　　　　　　　Ⓑ　　Ⓒ
   Nobel Prize for <u>their</u> research in that field.
   　　　　　　　　Ⓓ

6. There <u>are</u> <u>not</u> <u>many</u> people <u>which</u> adapt
   　　Ⓐ　　Ⓑ　　　　　　Ⓒ
   to a new culture without <u>feeling</u> some
   　　　　　　　　　　　　Ⓓ
   disorientation at first.

7. In order for people who speak different languages to engage in trade _____, they often develop a simplified language called *pidgin*.
   Ⓐ with each the other
   Ⓑ with each to the other
   Ⓒ with each another
   Ⓓ with each other

8. Those of us <u>who</u> have a family history of
   　　　　　　Ⓐ
   heart disease <u>should make</u> <u>yearly</u>
   　　　　　　　Ⓑ　　　　Ⓒ
   appointments with <u>their</u> doctors.
   　　　　　　　　　Ⓓ

9. Domestic cats often show loyalty to their owners by leaving freshly killed prey such as birds for _____ to find.
   Ⓐ they
   Ⓑ he
   Ⓒ them
   Ⓓ their

10. The United States and Canada have many trade agreements that benefit _____.
   Ⓐ one the other
   Ⓑ other
   Ⓒ other one
   Ⓓ each other

11. George Herman Ruth, <u>which</u> was <u>better</u>
                 ⓐ   ⓑ

    known as Babe Ruth, <u>began</u> his baseball
        ⓒ   ⓓ

    career in 1914 with the Baltimore Orioles.

12. The constellation Orion is easily
    recognized by _____ three vertical stars.
    ⓐ your
    ⓑ its
    ⓒ their
    ⓓ her

13. <u>The first</u> full-length animated movie, *Snow*
       ⓐ

    White, <u>was produced</u> by Walt Disney <u>whom</u>
           ⓑ   ⓒ

    creative genius also inspired <u>such</u> animated
                          ⓓ

    classics as *Bambi* and *Cinderella*.

14. Wolves, which are known to travel in
    packs, both provide for and defend _____
    through group cooperation.
    ⓐ himself
    ⓑ themselves
    ⓒ itself
    ⓓ theirselves

15. Although orchids give the appearance of
    being very fragile, they are actually very
    hardy plants _____ indoors during the
    winter months.
    ⓐ which may be grown
    ⓑ what may grow
    ⓒ who may be grow
    ⓓ where may be growing

16. Hyperactivity in children may result from
    _____ some food additives.
    ⓐ their eating
    ⓑ they eat
    ⓒ to eat
    ⓓ them eating

17. In <u>advanced</u> stages of anorexia, <u>the patient</u> is
         ⓐ   ⓑ

    unable <u>to feed</u> <u>themself</u>.
          ⓒ   ⓓ

18. <u>It is documented</u> that Custer <u>led</u> his troops
          ⓐ   ⓑ

    into a ravine near the Little Big Horn, where

    a huge army of Sioux Indians <u>was waiting</u>
                                ⓒ

    <u>for they</u>.
      ⓓ

19. The sea horse is unique <u>among fish</u> <u>because</u>
                         ⓐ   ⓑ

    the female deposits <u>their eggs</u> in a pouch
                     ⓒ

    that the male carries until the small sea

    horses <u>are hatched</u>.
          ⓓ

20. Hawkeye was a character _____ James
    Fenimore Cooper created for *The Last of
    the Mohicans*.
    ⓐ who
    ⓑ whom
    ⓒ which
    ⓓ whose

Refer to pages 417–418 for the Explanatory Answers.

EXERCISE 45: Sentences—Modifiers

In some sentences in the Structure Section on the Paper-Based TOEFL, you will be asked to identify the correct modifier. A modifier can be an adjective or an adjectival phrase that describes a noun or an *-ing* form. A modifier can also be an adverb or an adverbial phrase that adds information about the verb, adjective, or another verb. Adjectives do not change form to agree with the nouns or *-ing* forms that they describe, but some adjectives are used only with count nouns and others are used only with noncount nouns. Choose the correct answer in the incomplete sentences. Choose the incorrect word or phrase in the underlined choices.

1. The data on the winter migration patterns of the monarch butterfly is very _____.
   (A) interested
   (B) interest
   (C) interesting
   (D) of interest

2. There are more potatoes cultivated than any
   (A) _____ (B) _____
   the other vegetable crop worldwide.
   (C) _____ (D) _____

3. Marian Anderson, recognized both in the

   U.S. and in Europe as a real great
   (A) _____ (B) _____
   vocalist, was the first black singer to appear
   (C) (D)
   with the Metropolitan Opera Company.

4. The New England states have had _____ serious earthquakes since the Ice Age.
   (A) none
   (B) not any
   (C) not
   (D) no

5. _____ orangutans live alone.
   (A) Near all
   (B) Almost all
   (C) The all
   (D) The most all

6. Some hybrid flowers retain the fragrant scent of the nonhybrid, and _____ are bred without fragrance.
   (A) anothers
   (B) the other
   (C) some other
   (D) others

7. At the core of a star, temperatures and
   (A)
   pressures are so great as particles collide and
   (B)
   connect in a process called fusion.
   (C) (D)

8. The Cartwheel Galaxy is 500 million
   (A)
   light year away from Earth.
   (B) (C) (D)

9. According to a recent survey, _____ doctors do not have a personal physician.
   (A) a large amount of
   (B) large amount of
   (C) a large number of
   (D) large number of

10. Because none of food is as nutritious for a
    (A) (B)
    baby as its mother's milk, many women are
    (C) (D)
    returning to the practice of breast feeding.

11. John F. Kennedy was the youngest president of the United States, and _____ to be assassinated.
    (A) the fourth
    (B) fourth
    (C) four
    (D) the four

12. Euthanasia, the practice of assisting the

    death of a person suffering from an
    (A)
    incurable disease, is such a controversial

    issue as it is illegal in most countries.
    (B) (C) (D)

13. _____ in the world export diamonds.
   Ⓐ Only little nations
   Ⓑ Only few nations
   Ⓒ Only a little nations
   Ⓓ Only a few nations

14. Uranus is just _____ to be seen on a clear night with the naked eye.
   Ⓐ bright enough
   Ⓑ enough brightly
   Ⓒ as enough bright
   Ⓓ bright as enough

15. The conversations on the TOEFL

   will be spoken just one time; therefore, you
   _____
   　　　　Ⓐ

   must listen very careful in order
   　　　　　　　Ⓑ

   to understand what the speakers have said.
   _____ ____
   　　Ⓒ　　　　 Ⓓ

16. Gold, silver, and copper coins are often

   alloyed with harder metals to make
   　　　　　Ⓐ　　　　　 Ⓑ

   them hard as enough to withstand wear.
   ____ ____ _____
   　Ⓒ　　 Ⓓ

17. _____ like McDonald's and Kentucky Fried Chicken have used franchising to extend their sales internationally.
   Ⓐ Chain's restaurants
   Ⓑ Chains restaurants
   Ⓒ Chain restaurant
   Ⓓ Chain restaurants

18. Thirty-six years after his first flight, at the age of 77, John Glenn proved that he was not _____ to return to his role as an astronaut.
   Ⓐ so old
   Ⓑ too old
   Ⓒ oldest
   Ⓓ very older

19. _____ that is known as Art Deco culminated in the exhibits and expositions at the World's Fair in 1939.
   Ⓐ The art
   Ⓑ Arts
   Ⓒ An art
   Ⓓ Artist

20. The brightest body in the constellation Hydra, Alphard is only _____.
   Ⓐ a second-magnitude star
   Ⓑ a magnitude second star
   Ⓒ a star of the magnitude second
   Ⓓ a second magnitudes star

Refer to pages 418–419 for the Explanatory Answers.

EXERCISE 46: Sentences—Comparatives

In some sentences in the Structure Section on the Paper-Based TOEFL, you will be asked to identify the correct comparative. A comparative can be a word or phrase that expresses similarity or difference. A comparative can also be a word ending like -er or -est that expresses a degree of comparison with adjectives and adverbs. Choose the correct answer in the incomplete sentences. Choose the incorrect word or phrase in the underlined choices.

1. Tuition at an American university runs
   _____ thirty-five thousand dollars a
   semester.
   Ⓐ so high as
   Ⓑ as high to
   Ⓒ as high as
   Ⓓ as high than

2. Alligators are about the same color than
            Ⓐ   Ⓑ
   crocodiles, although the adults may be
                         Ⓒ
   slightly darker with broader heads and
   blunter noses.
   Ⓓ

3. DVDs provide images of best quality
        Ⓐ   Ⓑ
   than those of either television signals or
      Ⓒ   Ⓓ
   video tapes.

4. The cost of a thirty-second commercial on
   a network television station is _____ for
   most businesses.
   Ⓐ so much
   Ⓑ much
   Ⓒ very much
   Ⓓ much too much

5. The New York City subway system is
                  Ⓐ
   the most longest underground railroad
       Ⓑ   Ⓒ
   operating in the world.
   Ⓓ

6. School children in the same grade in
                  Ⓐ
   American schools are usually the same old
          Ⓑ   Ⓒ   Ⓓ
   as their classmates.

7. The seed heads of teasel plants raise the
   nap on coarse tweed cloth _____ than do
   the machine tools invented to replace them.
   Ⓐ more efficiently
   Ⓑ efficiently
   Ⓒ more efficient
   Ⓓ most efficient

8. Benjamin Franklin was the editor of
                  Ⓐ
   the larger newspaper in the colonies, a
     Ⓑ
   diplomatic representative to France and later
   to England, and the inventor of many useful
            Ⓒ   Ⓓ
   devices.

9. The standard for cleanliness in the area
   where a microchip is manufactured is
    Ⓐ   Ⓑ   Ⓒ
   same that of an operating room in a hospital.
   Ⓓ

10. The North American robin is only _____
    the European and African robins.
    Ⓐ half big
    Ⓑ as big half
    Ⓒ half as big as
    Ⓓ big by half

11. Mountain bikes differ ordinary bicycles in
                Ⓐ
    that they have ten or more gears, a
       Ⓑ
    more rugged frame, and wider treads on
      Ⓒ   Ⓓ
    the tires.

12. As a rule, the more rapid the heart rate,
        Ⓐ   Ⓑ   Ⓒ
    faster the pulse.
    Ⓓ

13. In U.S. law, a misdemeanor is a crime that is _____ a felony, and usually carries a term of imprisonment of less than one year for most offenses.
    - Ⓐ lesser than
    - Ⓑ less severe than
    - Ⓒ less than severe
    - Ⓓ severely lesser

14. Although both are mammals, the early stages of development on the part of placentals differ from _____.
    - Ⓐ marsupials
    - Ⓑ that of marsupials
    - Ⓒ those of marsupials
    - Ⓓ those marsupials

15. Eli Whitney's cotton gin enabled the cotton producers of the early nineteenth century to increase their production by _____ times the amount produced prior to the invention.
    - Ⓐ more fifty
    - Ⓑ more as fifty
    - Ⓒ more than fifty
    - Ⓓ most than fifty

16. _____ 250,000 species of fossils have been discovered in both organized, scientific searches and by sheer accident.
    - Ⓐ As much as
    - Ⓑ As many as
    - Ⓒ As many
    - Ⓓ Many as

17. The North's abundance of industry and commercial wealth proved to be a greater advantage _____ in determining the outcome of the Civil War.
    - Ⓐ than originally thought
    - Ⓑ that originally thought
    - Ⓒ as originally thought
    - Ⓓ originally thought

18. The Woodstock Music and Art Fair of 1969 captured the essence of the counterculture movement of the 1960s _____.
    - Ⓐ most than any of other events
    - Ⓑ best that any other event
    - Ⓒ than any other events
    - Ⓓ better than any other event

19. Alike her friend and fellow impressionist
        Ⓐ
    artist, Edgar Degas, Mary Cassatt used
        Ⓑ   Ⓒ
    brush strokes and colors in new and

    different ways.
        Ⓓ

20. A dancer, while always graceful and precise in her movements, trains _____ any other athlete.
    - Ⓐ as strenuously
    - Ⓑ more strenuously as
    - Ⓒ as strenuously as
    - Ⓓ as strenuously that

Refer to pages 419–420 for the Explanatory Answers.

EXERCISE 47: Sentences—Connectors

In some sentences in the Structure Section of the Paper-Based TOEFL, you will be asked to identify the correct connector. A connector is a word or phrase that joins words, phrases, or clauses. A connector expresses relationships between the words, phrases, and clauses that it joins. Some common relationships are cause and result, contradiction, substitution, addition, exception, example, and purpose. Choose the correct answer in the incomplete sentences. Choose the incorrect word or phrase in the underlined choices.

1. It is not clear how much students learn _____ television classes without supervision and monitoring.
   ⓐ for watching
   ⓑ from watching
   ⓒ by watch
   ⓓ to watch

2. In spite of the fact that 85 percent of all societies allow the men to take more than one wife, most prefer monogamy _____ polygamy.
   ⓐ than
   ⓑ to
   ⓒ for
   ⓓ that

3. Some metals <u>such</u> gold, silver, copper, and
             ⓐ   ⓑ
   tin occur <u>naturally</u>, and are easy <u>to work</u>.
             ⓒ   ⓓ

4. Stained glass becomes even more beautiful when it _____ because the corrosion diffuses light.
   ⓐ will age
   ⓑ ages
   ⓒ are aging
   ⓓ aged

5. All of the senses _____ smell must pass through intermediate gateways to be processed before they are registered in the brain.
   ⓐ until
   ⓑ but
   ⓒ to
   ⓓ for

6. <u>Because</u> the expense of traditional fuels
      ⓐ
   and the concern that <u>they</u> <u>might run out</u>,
                    ⓑ   ⓒ
   many countries <u>have been investigating</u>
                  ⓓ
   alternative sources of power.

7. The lights and appliances in most homes use alternating current _____.
   ⓐ instead direct current
   ⓑ instead of direct current
   ⓒ that instead direct current
   ⓓ for direct current instead

8. Only seventeen <u>on</u> one hundred
              ⓐ
   business calls <u>get through</u> to the correct
           ⓑ   ⓒ
   person on <u>the first</u> attempt.
           ⓓ

9. More murders are reported _____ December in the United States than during any other month.
   ⓐ on
   ⓑ in
   ⓒ at
   ⓓ for

10. The tendency to develop cancer, even in high-risk individuals, can be decreased _____ the amount of fruit and vegetables in the diet.
    ⓐ to increase
    ⓑ for increase
    ⓒ for increasing
    ⓓ by increasing

11. The concept of lift in aerodynamics refers to
    $\underline{\text{A}}$

    the relationship among the increased speed
    $\underline{\text{B}}$ $\underline{\text{C}}$

    of air over the top of a wing and the higher

    pressure of the slower air underneath.
    $\underline{\text{D}}$

12. If one of the participants in a conversation
    wonders _____, no real communication
    has taken place.
    - Ⓐ what said the other person
    - Ⓑ what the other person said
    - Ⓒ what did the other person say
    - Ⓓ what was the other person saying

13. A prism is used to refract light so as it
    $\underline{\text{A}}$ $\underline{\text{B}}$ $\underline{\text{C}}$

    spreads out in a continuous spectrum

    of colors.
    $\underline{\text{D}}$

14. Nuclear power plants are still supported
    $\underline{\text{A}}$

    by the society of Professional Engineers
    $\underline{\text{B}}$

    in spite unfortunate accidents like the
    $\underline{\text{C}}$

    one at Three Mile Island.
    $\underline{\text{D}}$

15. Neptune is an extremely cold planet, and
    _____.
    - Ⓐ so does Uranus
    - Ⓑ so has Uranus
    - Ⓒ so is Uranus
    - Ⓓ so Uranus

16. Deserts are often formed _____ they are
    cut off from rain-bearing winds by the
    surrounding mountain ranges.
    - Ⓐ because
    - Ⓑ in spite of
    - Ⓒ so
    - Ⓓ due to

17. There are many beautifully preserved
    historic buildings _____.
    - Ⓐ in Beacon Street in Boston
    - Ⓑ in Beacon Street at Boston
    - Ⓒ on Beacon Street in Boston
    - Ⓓ at Beacon Street at Boston

18. _____ the original document, the U.S.
    Constitution contains ten amendments
    called the Bill of Rights.
    - Ⓐ Beside
    - Ⓑ Besides
    - Ⓒ In addition
    - Ⓓ Also

19. National parks include not only
    $\underline{\text{A}}$

    the most scenic places in the nation but
    $\underline{\text{B}}$ $\underline{\text{C}}$

    places distinguished for their historic or
    $\underline{\text{D}}$

    scientific interest.

20. Cooking oil made from corn does not
    become saturated when heated, and _____.
    - Ⓐ neither oil made from soy
    - Ⓑ oil made from soy does either
    - Ⓒ neither does oil made from soy
    - Ⓓ oil made from soy either

Refer to pages 420–421 for the Explanatory Answers.

EXERCISE 48: Sentences—Sentences and Clauses

In some sentences in the Structure Section of the Paper-Based TOEFL, you will be asked to distinguish between a sentence, also called a main or independent clause, and a subordinate or dependent clause that is attached to a sentence. Choose the correct answer in the incomplete sentences. Choose the incorrect word or phrase in the underlined choices.

1. Some ancient units such as the day, the foot, and the pound, _____ today.
   Ⓐ are still in use
   Ⓑ that are still in use
   Ⓒ which are in use still
   Ⓓ still in use

2. Paper money _____ by the Continental Congress in order to finance the American Revolution.
   Ⓐ which was issued
   Ⓑ was issuing
   Ⓒ issued
   Ⓓ was issued

3. The plastic arts, mainly sculpture and
   Ⓐ   Ⓑ
   ceramics, that are produced
            Ⓒ
   by modeling or molding the materials into
            Ⓓ
   interesting shapes.

4. The Scholastic Aptitude Test (SAT) _____ by high school students as a requirement for admission to many colleges.
   Ⓐ which is taken
   Ⓑ is taken
   Ⓒ taken
   Ⓓ is taking

5. Ocean currents that help transfer heat from
   Ⓐ   Ⓑ
   the equator to the poles, thereby creating
                                    Ⓒ
   a more balanced global environment.
      Ⓓ

6. Camp David _____ the official country home of the U.S. presidents.
   Ⓐ that is
   Ⓑ that it is
   Ⓒ it is
   Ⓓ is

7. Gas and dust that stream away from a comet
   Ⓐ   Ⓑ
   forming one or more tails that may extend
      Ⓒ   Ⓓ
   for millions of miles.

8. The Northwest Ordinances which regulated
                            Ⓐ
   the sale and settlement of land between the
                                    Ⓑ
   Great Lakes and the Mississippi River,

   territories still occupied
                  Ⓒ
   by American Indian nations.
      Ⓓ

9. _____ considered strong and reliable, and is favored by investors who are interested in security.
   Ⓐ That blue chip stock
   Ⓑ Blue chip stock is
   Ⓒ It is blue chip stock
   Ⓓ Which is blue chip stock

10. Most botanists have observed _____ a period of dormancy, even when conditions may be favorable for growth.
    Ⓐ that seeds exhibiting
    Ⓑ that seeds exhibit
    Ⓒ seeds that exhibiting
    Ⓓ seeds that they exhibit

11. La Guardia Airport in New York City _____ for Fiorello La Guardia, one of New York's most popular mayors.
    Ⓐ which is named
    Ⓑ named
    Ⓒ which named
    Ⓓ is named

12. In a meritocracy, intelligence and ability
   _____ more than social position or wealth.
   Ⓐ which value
   Ⓑ that are valued
   Ⓒ valuing
   Ⓓ are valued

13. The larva of the boll weevil, which it feeds
                     Ⓐ   Ⓑ
   on the immature pods of the cotton plant,
                              Ⓒ
   often destroying an entire crop.
            Ⓓ

14. Of all the lawsuits in the world, _____ in
   U.S. courts.
   Ⓐ filed 95 percent of them
   Ⓑ 95 percent of them are filed
   Ⓒ that filed are 95 percent of them
   Ⓓ which of them 95 percent are filed

15. "Chicago" is a poem _____ in praise of
   one of the busiest industrial centers in the
   U.S.
   Ⓐ which by Carl Sandburg
   Ⓑ which was written by Carl Sandburg
   Ⓒ was written by Carl Sandburg
   Ⓓ Carl Sandburg who wrote it

16. _____ are kept as pets in almost every
   country in the world.
   Ⓐ Cats and dogs which
   Ⓑ Which cats and dogs
   Ⓒ Cats and dogs
   Ⓓ That cats and dogs

17. By studying the fossils of pollen, which
         Ⓐ   Ⓑ
   extremely resistant to decay, researchers

   can gain useful information about the
      Ⓒ   Ⓓ
   vegetation of the past.

18. The PTA _____ parents and teachers who
   support the school by fund-raising and
   other activities.
   Ⓐ it is a group of
   Ⓑ that is a group of
   Ⓒ which group of
   Ⓓ is a group of

19. The attribution of human characteristics to
         Ⓐ
   animals or inanimate objects appears in the
                                    Ⓑ
   mythologies of many cultures is a literary
                     Ⓒ
   device called anthropomorphism.
          Ⓓ

20. The jet stream _____ usually occurs at
   about thirty-five to sixty degrees latitude.
   Ⓐ a narrow band of wind that
   Ⓑ is a narrow band of wind that
   Ⓒ a narrow band of wind
   Ⓓ it is a narrow band of wind that

Refer to pages 421–422 for the Explanatory Answers.

EXERCISE 49: Sentences—Point of View

In some sentences in the Structure Section of the Paper-Based TOEFL, you will be asked to identify errors in point of view. Point of view is the relationship between the verb in the main clause of a sentence and other verbs, or between the verbs in a sentence and the adverbs that express time. Choose the correct answer in the incomplete sentences. Choose the incorrect word or phrase in the underlined choices.

1. Although there are approximately 120
             Ⓐ   Ⓑ
   intensive language institutes in the United
                         Ⓒ
   States in 1970, there are more than

   four times as many now.
            Ⓓ

2. Cartographers cannot make an accurate map

   because the political situation in many

   areas changes so rapidly that they were not
               Ⓐ   Ⓑ
   able to draw the boundaries correctly.
          Ⓒ   Ⓓ

3. Although Emily Dickinson publishes only
                        Ⓐ   Ⓑ
   three of her verses before she died, today

   there are more than one thousand of her
       Ⓒ   Ⓓ
   poems printed in many important

   collections.

4. Dew usually disappeared by seven o'clock
          Ⓐ   Ⓑ   Ⓒ
   in the morning when the sun comes up.
           Ⓓ

5. Before the 1800s, when William Young
   made different shoes for right and left feet,
   shoes _____ on either foot.
   Ⓐ can wear
   Ⓑ are wearing
   Ⓒ could be worn
   Ⓓ worn

6. Seven months before the stock market
                           Ⓐ
   crashed in 1929, President Hoover said that
          Ⓑ
   the economy of the nation is secure.
                      Ⓒ   Ⓓ

7. In the Middle Ages, the word
   "masterpiece" referred to a work that
   _____ by a journeyman in order to qualify
   as a master artisan.
   Ⓐ completed
   Ⓑ is completed
   Ⓒ was completed
   Ⓓ complete

8. Most archaeologists agree that humans
      Ⓐ
   are living in the area around Philadelphia
       Ⓑ
   for about twelve thousand years.
     Ⓒ   Ⓓ

9. Although we once thought that Saturn has
                                Ⓐ
   only seven rings, we now know that it
                               Ⓑ
   has hundreds of rings extending for
                      Ⓒ
   thousands of miles.
           Ⓓ

10. Before his death in 1943, in an effort to
    encourage less dependence on one crop by
    the South, George Washington Carver
    _____ for developing hundreds of
    industrial uses for peanuts and sweet
    potatoes.
    Ⓐ has responsibility
    Ⓑ were responsibility
    Ⓒ is responsible
    Ⓓ was responsible

11. The Greek historian Herodotus reported
    that one hundred thousand men _____ for
    twenty years to build the Great Pyramid at
    Gizeh.
    Ⓐ employ
    Ⓑ employed
    Ⓒ are employed
    Ⓓ were employed

12. In 1975, according to the National Center
                 Ⓐ
    for Health Statistics, the average life

    expectancy for people born during that
                            Ⓑ   Ⓒ
    year is only 72.4 years.
         Ⓓ

13. Champlain founded a base at Port Royal
                 Ⓐ
    in 1605, and builds a fort at Quebec three
         Ⓑ   Ⓒ   Ⓓ
    years later.

14. According to the Congressional Record,
       Ⓐ
    almost one third of all new laws in 1991
                        Ⓑ

    are passed to celebrate some day, week, or
      Ⓒ   Ⓓ
    month for a special interest group's

    purposes, such as Music Week.

15. The first significant engagement of the
       Ⓐ
    American Revolution occurs
                         Ⓑ
    on June 17, 1775, and has been referred to
          Ⓒ   Ⓓ
    as the Battle of Bunker Hill.

16. Evolutionary changes in the speech organs
    probably _____ the development of
    language in humanoids.
    Ⓐ to contribute
    Ⓑ contribute to
    Ⓒ contribution to
    Ⓓ contributed to

17. Originally, the purpose of a sampler is
       Ⓐ   Ⓑ
    to record complex stitches so that they
       Ⓒ   Ⓓ
    could be duplicated later.

18. Before he died, Armand Hammer _____
    an extraordinarily diverse business empire,
    including interests in oil, livestock, cattle,
    grain, and art.
    Ⓐ established
    Ⓑ establishing
    Ⓒ establishes
    Ⓓ establish

19. Many ancient cultures begin their spiritual
    Ⓐ   Ⓑ   Ⓒ
    life by worshipping the Sun.
        Ⓓ

20. People under forty years old cannot
    remember when _____ without a computer
    terminal.
    Ⓐ they have to work
    Ⓑ they had to work
    Ⓒ their working
    Ⓓ working

Refer to pages 422–423 for the Explanatory Answers.

EXERCISE 50: Sentences—Agreement

In some sentences in the Structure Section of the Paper-Based TOEFL, you will be asked to identify errors in agreement. Agreement is the relationship between a subject and verb or between a pronoun and noun, or between a pronoun and another pronoun. To agree, a subject and verb must both be singular or both be plural. To agree, a pronoun and the noun or pronoun to which it refers must both be singular or plural and both be masculine or feminine or neuter. Choose the correct answer in the incomplete sentences. Choose the incorrect word or phrase in the underlined choices.

1. Both a term paper and a final exam is often
   ⒶⒷ
   required for a college class.
   ⒸⒹ

2. The popularity of soccer in the United States

   were increased significantly by the playing
   ⒶⒷⒸ
   of the World Cup in cities throughout the

   country in 1994.
   Ⓓ

3. How many musical notes of the 11,000
   tones that the human ear can distinguish
   _____ in the musical scale?
   Ⓐ it is
   Ⓑ is it
   Ⓒ there are
   Ⓓ are there

4. Not one in a hundred seeds develop into a
   ⒶⒷⒸ
   healthy plant, even under laboratory
   Ⓓ
   conditions.

5. Nine of every ten people in the world
   _____ in the country in which they were
   born.
   Ⓐ living
   Ⓑ they are living
   Ⓒ lives
   Ⓓ live

6. Benjamin Franklin strongly objected to the
   ⒶⒷ
   eagle's being chosen as the national bird

   because of their predatory nature.
   ⒸⒹ

7. In order to grow well, the Blue Spruce,
   Ⓐ
   like other pine trees, require a temperate
   ⒷⒸⒹ
   climate.

8. Few airports in the United States is as
   Ⓐ
   modern as that of Atlanta.
   ⒷⒸⒹ

9. In the ocean, _____ more salt in the
   deeper water.
   Ⓐ is there
   Ⓑ it may be
   Ⓒ there is
   Ⓓ it is

10. Work on improving industrial disposal
    Ⓐ
    methods were begun in the early 1970s,
    Ⓑ
    shortly after the Clean Air bill was passed
    Ⓒ
    by Congress.
    Ⓓ

11. The average temperature of rocks on the
    surface of the earth _____ 55 degrees F.
    Ⓐ be
    Ⓑ are
    Ⓒ is
    Ⓓ been

12. The officials of the Board of Elections asked

    that each voter present their registration card
    ⒶⒷ
    and a valid Texas driver's license before
    Ⓒ
    receiving a ballot.
    Ⓓ

13. If one has a special medical condition such
    ⒶA

    as diabetes, epilepsy, or allergy, it is

    advisable that they carry some kind of
                  ⒷB ⒸC

    identification in order to avoid being given
                                    ⒹD

    improper medication in an emergency.

14. A large percentage of federal employees

    are participating in an experimental
    ⒶA

    four-day work week aimed at curbing
    ⒷB ⒸC

    gasoline consumption and pollution, two of

    the most urgent problems facing cities today.
                      ⒹD

15. A mature grove of Aspen trees often
    _____ that supports numerous trunks.
    ⒶA have a single system of roots
    ⒷB has a single root system
    ⒸC make a single system from roots
    ⒹD making a single roots system

16. One-cent coins issued in the United States
              ⒶA   ⒷB

    since 1982 is 96 percent zinc.
    ⒸC   ⒹD

17. According to a team of scientists, there are
    ⒶA   ⒷB   ⒸC

    evidence that Mount Everest is still rising.
                                        ⒹD

18. The urinary system, including both the
    ⒶA   ⒷB

    bladder and the kidneys, are contained in
    ⒸC   ⒹD

    the cavities of the trunk.

19. The smallest flying dinosaurs _____ of a
    robin.
    ⒶA about the size
    ⒷB was about the size
    ⒸC were about the size
    ⒹD have been about the size

20. In the 1920s, Art Deco, known for plastic
    ⒶA   ⒷB

    and chrome-plated objects, were very
        ⒸC   ⒹD

    popular.

Refer to pages 423–424 for the Explanatory Answers.

EXERCISE 51: Sentences—Introductory Verbal Modifiers

In some sentences in the Structure Section of the Paper-Based TOEFL, you will be asked to identify errors in introductory verbal modifiers and the subjects that they modify. Introductory verbal modifiers are *-ing* forms, participles, and infinitives. A phrase with an introductory verbal modifier occurs at the beginning of a sentence and is followed by a comma. The subject modified by an introductory verbal modifier must follow the comma. If the correct subject does not follow the comma, then the meaning of the sentence is changed. Often the changed meaning is not logical. Choose the correct answer in the incomplete sentences. Choose the incorrect word or phrase in the underlined choices.

1. After finishing *Roots*, the one-hundred-year
   (A)   (B)
   history of an African-American family,

   the Nobel Prize committee awarded author
                              (C)
   Alex Haley a special citation for literary
                              (D)
   excellence.

2. A competitive sport, gymnasts perform
   (A)
   before officials who must use their judgment
                   (B)
   along with their knowledge of the rules
          (C)
   to determine the relative skill of each
   (D)
   participant.

3. To remove stains from permanent press
                   (A)
   clothing, carefully soaking in cold water
            (B)
   before washing with a regular detergent.
         (C)   (D)

4. An abstract painter and pioneer of
   Surrealism, _____ and symbolic images.
   (A) Miro's works are characterized by
       bright colors
   (B) the works of Miro are characterized by
       bright colors
   (C) Miro is famous for works
       characterized by bright colors
   (D) bright colors characterize the works of
       Miro

5. Found in Tanzania by Mary Leakey, some
                   (A)
   archeologists estimated that the

   three-million-year-old fossils were the oldest
              (B)   (C)
   human remains to be discovered.
                      (D)

6. Originally having been buried in Spain,
   (A)   (B)   (C)
   and later moved to Santo Domingo

   in the Dominican Republic,

   Columbus's final resting place is in
                      (D)
   Andalucia, Spain.

7. One of the largest hotels on Earth, _____.
   (A) the MGM Grand has 91 elevators and
       5005 rooms
   (B) there are 91 elevators and 5005 rooms
       in the MGM Grand
   (C) 91 elevators and 5005 rooms are in the
       MGM Grand
   (D) it is the MGM Grand that has 91
       elevators and 5005 rooms

8. Written by Neil Simon,
         (A)
   New York audiences received the new play
                      (B)
   enthusiastically at the world premiere
        (C)
   Saturday evening.
        (D)

9. To prevent cavities,
   dental floss should be used daily after
        (A)   (B)
   brushing one's teeth.
   (C)   (D)

10. While researching the problem of violent

    crime, the Senate committee's discovery
    _____
    A

    that handguns were used to commit 64
    _____   _____
    B   C

    percent of all murders in the United States.
    _____
    D

11. One of the world's greatest rivers, _____.
    - Ⓐ one third of North America is linked
      by the water of the Mississippi
    - Ⓑ the Mississippi links one third of North
      America by water
    - Ⓒ North America is linked by the
      Mississippi in one third of the water
    - Ⓓ the water is linked in North America
      by one third of the Mississippi

12. After reviewing the curriculum, several
    _____   _____
    A   B

    significant changes were made by the
    _____
    C

    faculty in traditional business programs at
    __
    D

    Harvard University.

13. Having hit more home runs in his career
    ___
    A

    than any other player in the history of
    ____ _____
    B   C

    baseball, Hank Aaron's record is famous.
    _____
    D

14. Banned in the U.S., the effect of
    _____
    A

    fluorocarbons continues at a level that could
    _____
    B

    eventually damage the ozone layer, and
    _____
    C

    bring about such serious results as high risk
    ____
    D

    of skin cancer and global climate changes.

15. While trying to build a tunnel through the
    Blue Ridge Mountains, _____.
    - Ⓐ coal was discovered by workmen at
      the construction site
    - Ⓑ workmen discovered coal at the
      construction site
    - Ⓒ the construction site was where coal
      was discovered by workmen
    - Ⓓ it was the construction site where
      workmen discovered coal

16. To avoid jet lag, many doctors recommend
    _____
    A

    that their patients begin adjusting one week
    _____
    B

    before departure time by shifting one hour
    _____
    C

    each day toward the new time schedule.
    _____
    D

17. Traditionally named for women,
    _____ _____
    A   B

    Bob was chosen as the first male name for a
    _____   _____
    C   D

    hurricane.

18. Published by Penguin Press almost eighty
    years ago, _____ offered to the public.
    - Ⓐ Ernest Hemingway wrote *A Farewell
      to Arms* as the first paperback book
    - Ⓑ *A Farewell to Arms* was the first
      paperback book by Ernest Hemingway
      that it was
    - Ⓒ Ernest Hemingway's book *A Farewell
      to Arms* was the first paperback book
    - Ⓓ it was *A Farewell to Arms* that was the
      first paperback by Ernest Hemingway

19. Born in 1892, _____ while he wrote the
    poems and plays that made him famous.
    - Ⓐ the Library of Congress is where
      Archibald MacLeish worked as a
      librarian
    - Ⓑ Archibald MacLeish worked as a
      librarian at the Library of Congress
    - Ⓒ a librarian at the Library of Congress,
      Archibald MacLeish worked
    - Ⓓ at the Library of Congress, Archibald
      MacLeish worked as a librarian

20. Founded in 1919, students and teachers who
    _____   ___
    A   B

    are interested in spending several months

    abroad may benefit from educational
    _____
    C

    programs administered by the Institute
    _____
    D

    for International Education.

Refer to pages 424–425 for the Explanatory Answers.

EXERCISE 52: Sentences—Parallel Structure

In some sentences in the Structure Section of the Paper-Based TOEFL, you will be asked to identify errors in parallel structure. Parallel structure is the use of the same grammatical structures for related ideas of equal importance. Related ideas of equal importance often occur in the form of a list. Sometimes related ideas of equal importance are connected by conjunctions, such as *and*, *but*, and *or*. Choose the correct answer in the incomplete sentences. Choose the incorrect word or phrase in the underlined choices.

1. Country music is not only popular in the
   Ⓐ   Ⓑ   Ⓒ Ⓓ
   United States but also abroad.

2. To control quality and making decisions
                Ⓐ
   about production are among the many
   Ⓑ   Ⓒ   Ⓓ
   responsibilities of an industrial engineer.

3. Most of the Cajun French who live in
   Louisiana can neither read _____ the
   French variety that they speak fluently.
   Ⓐ nor they write
   Ⓑ nor write
   Ⓒ or writing
   Ⓓ neither write

4. The six main parts of a business letter are
       Ⓐ   Ⓑ   Ⓒ
   the address, the inside address, the

   salutation, the body, the closing, and

   signing your name.
   Ⓓ

5. Microwaves are used for cooking,
   telecommunications, and _____.
   Ⓐ to diagnose medically
   Ⓑ medical diagnosing
   Ⓒ diagnosed medically
   Ⓓ medical diagnosis

6. To read literature and being introduced to a
                Ⓐ   Ⓑ
   different culture are two excellent
           Ⓒ
   reasons for studying a foreign language.
         Ⓓ

7. Ice skating and to go skiing are popular
           Ⓐ   Ⓑ
   winter sports in the northern United States.
     Ⓒ   Ⓓ

8. To treat minor diarrhea, drink plenty of
   Ⓐ
   liquids, especially tea, water, and carbonated

   beverages, eat soup, yogurt, salty crackers,
             Ⓑ
   and bananas, and avoiding milk, butter,
               Ⓒ
   eggs, and meat for twenty-four hours.
          Ⓓ

9. A vacuum will neither conduct heat nor
   _____.
   Ⓐ transmit sound waves
   Ⓑ transmitting sound waves
   Ⓒ sound waves are transmitted
   Ⓓ the transmission of sound waves

10. The Smithsonian Institute is famous because
    it contains such interesting exhibits as the
    flag that was raised over Fort McHenry
            Ⓐ
    in 1812, the airplane that the Wright
        Ⓑ
    brothers built for their first flight at Kitty
          Ⓒ
    Hawk, and there are the gowns worn by
             Ⓓ
    every first lady since Martha Washington.

11. In order to become a law, a bill
        Ⓐ
    must be passed not only by the Senate but
        Ⓑ   Ⓒ
    also the House of Representatives.
             Ⓓ

12. The color of a star depends on the heat and

    _____.

    Ⓐ how much energy produced
    Ⓑ the energy it produces
    Ⓒ production of the energy
    Ⓓ producing energy

13. The cloverleaf is a common engineering

    design for expressways that permits traffic
                                 ‾‾‾‾‾‾‾
                                    Ⓐ

    between two intersecting highways to move
    ‾‾‾‾‾‾‾   ‾‾‾‾‾‾‾
      Ⓑ   Ⓒ

    more safely, efficiently, and with ease.
                                  ‾‾‾‾‾‾‾‾‾
                                     Ⓓ

14. A new product should be judged not by the
                  ‾‾‾‾‾‾‾‾‾‾‾‾‾‾‾
                        Ⓐ

    promises made in commercials and
                                  ‾‾‾
                                   Ⓑ

    advertisements, but also by the results
                   ‾‾‾‾‾‾‾‾
                      Ⓒ

    demonstrated in actual use.
    ‾‾‾‾‾‾‾‾‾‾‾‾
         Ⓓ

15. The artisans of the southwestern United
    States are famous for their beautiful art
    work, especially handmade jewelry cast
    from silver, carved from stones, or _____
    with beads and feathers.
    Ⓐ decorations
    Ⓑ decorating
    Ⓒ decorated
    Ⓓ decorate

16. Snakes stick out their tongues, move them
    ‾‾‾‾‾‾   ‾‾‾‾‾
     Ⓐ   Ⓑ

    around, and also they retract them
                  ‾‾‾‾‾‾‾‾‾
                      Ⓒ

    quickly to pick up odor molecules that aid in
            ‾‾‾‾‾‾‾‾‾‾
                Ⓓ

    detecting direction.

17. Thought by some to be the first labor party,
    ‾‾‾‾‾‾‾   ‾‾‾‾‾
       Ⓐ   Ⓑ

    the Workingman's Party struggled not

    only for better working conditions also for
                                      ‾‾‾‾
                                       Ⓒ

    public schools for all children.
                        ‾‾‾‾‾‾‾‾‾‾‾
                             Ⓓ

18. The cerebellum's main functions are
                     ‾‾‾‾‾‾‾‾‾‾‾‾‾‾ ‾‾‾
                           Ⓐ   Ⓑ

    the maintenance of posture and move the
    ‾‾‾‾‾‾‾‾‾‾‾‾‾‾‾‾‾   ‾‾‾‾
            Ⓒ   Ⓓ

    body.

19. The Cabinet consists of secretaries of
    departments who report to the president,
    give him advice, and _____ decisions.
    Ⓐ helping him making
    Ⓑ helping him make
    Ⓒ help him making
    Ⓓ help him make

20. Increasing involvement in agriculture

    by large corporations has resulted in
    ‾‾‾‾‾‾‾‾‾‾‾‾‾‾‾‾‾‾‾‾ ‾‾‾‾‾‾‾‾‾‾‾‾
             Ⓐ   Ⓑ

    what is known as agribusiness—that is,
        ‾‾‾‾‾‾‾‾‾‾‾
             Ⓒ

    agriculture with business techniques,

    including heavy capitalization,

    specialization of production, and to control
                                     ‾‾‾‾‾‾‾‾‾‾
                                         Ⓓ

    all stages of the operation.

Refer to pages 425–426 for the Explanatory Answers.

EXERCISE 53: Sentences—Redundancy

In some sentences in the Structure Section of the Paper-Based TOEFL, you will be asked to identify errors in redundancy. Redundancy is the unnecessary repetition of words and phrases. Choose the correct answer in the incomplete sentences. Choose the incorrect word or phrase in the underlined choices.

1. Some international students <u>use</u> a digital
   (A)
   recorder <u>to make</u> recordings of their classes
   (B)
   <u>so that</u> they can repeat the lectures <u>again</u>.
   (C)   (D)

2. Blood plasma <u>it</u> is the transportation system
   (A)
   for <u>all</u> of the <u>widely</u> separated organs in
   (B)   (C)
   the <u>human body</u>.
   (D)

3. Whereas a gas expands _____ in all
   directions, a vapor remains somewhat more
   concentrated.
   (A) in a uniform manner
   (B) uniformly
   (C) uniformly in manner
   (D) uniform

4. <u>Appointed</u> by the General Assembly <u>for</u> five
   (A)   (B)
   years, the Secretary-General of the United
   Nations <u>must act</u> <u>in an impartial manner</u>
           (C)   (D)
   toward all members.

5. Humans <u>who</u> lived thousands of years <u>ago</u>,
           (A)   (B)
   long before alphabets were devised, <u>they</u>
                                        (C)
   used pictures to record events and
   <u>to communicate ideas</u>.
        (D)

6. If one does not pick up <u>the</u> dry cleaning
                           (A)
   within thirty days, the management is not
            (B)
   obligated to <u>return</u> it <u>back</u>.
                (C)   (D)

7. That witches cause disasters and
   misfortunes _____ among the colonists in
   Salem, Massachusetts.
   (A) it was widely believed
   (B) was widely believed
   (C) was believed in a wide way
   (D) they widely believed

8. The southern part of the United States has
   ideal conditions <u>for raising</u> cotton because
                     (A)
   the climate is sufficiently warm <u>enough</u>
                                     (B)
   <u>to allow</u> a <u>six-month growing period</u>.
    (C)   (D)

9. People <u>who are</u> competitive <u>in nature</u> are
           (A)   (B)
   more likely <u>to suffer</u> from the effects of
                (C)
   stress <u>on their health</u>.
          (D)

10. International law <u>is</u> made up of the rules and
                      (A)
    customs <u>that</u> <u>they</u> deal with the relationships
             (B)   (C)
    <u>between</u> different nations and the citizens of
     (D)
    different nations.

11. Found in and near the Mohave Desert,
    _____ has a limited habitat.
    (A) is the Joshua tree that it
    (B) it is the Joshua tree
    (C) the Joshua tree
    (D) the Joshua tree it

12. Traditionally, the South has been mostly Democrat _____, while the North has been divided between Democrats and Republicans.
    Ⓐ in the politics
    Ⓑ politically
    Ⓒ politics-wise
    Ⓓ in a political way

13. It was Isadora Duncan who was responsible
       Ⓐ   Ⓑ
    for many of the new innovations that have
                  Ⓒ
    made modern dance different from classical
                  Ⓓ
    ballet.

14. *Little House on the Prairie*, a successful

    television program, was adapted from a

    series of books by a young pioneer woman
     Ⓐ

    whose life was similar to that of the
      Ⓑ   Ⓒ

    character called by name Laura.
           Ⓓ

15. In recent years great advances forward have
      Ⓐ   Ⓑ Ⓒ

    been made in the field of genetic research.
                  Ⓓ

16. Today the United States is one of the few
                Ⓐ

    countries in the Western Hemisphere that

    it has laws providing for the death penalty.
    ⒷⒸ   Ⓓ

17. According to recent geological research,
       Ⓐ

    the climate of the states along the Canadian
        Ⓑ

    border is changing with rapidity.
        Ⓒ   Ⓓ

18. Digital clocks, however precise, _____ because the earth's rotation changes slightly over the year.
    Ⓐ they cannot be perfectly accurate
    Ⓑ cannot be perfectly accurate
    Ⓒ not perfectly accurate
    Ⓓ not be perfectly accurate

19. Natural gas often occurs _____ petroleum in the minute pores of rocks such as sandstone and limestone.
    Ⓐ both together with
    Ⓑ both together
    Ⓒ with
    Ⓓ both with

20. World hunger it is one of the most urgent
           ⒶⒷ   Ⓒ

    problems that we face today.
          Ⓓ

Refer to page 427 for the Explanatory Answers.

EXERCISE 54: Sentences—Word Choice

In some sentences in the Structure Section of the Paper-Based TOEFL, you will be asked to identify errors in word choice. Word choice is the selection of words that express the exact meaning of an idea. Sometimes it is necessary to make a choice between words that are very similar in appearance but very different in meaning. Choose the correct answer in the incomplete sentences. Choose the incorrect word or phrase in the underlined choices.

1. According to the Pythagorean theorem, the
   (A)

   sum of the squares of the two sides

   of a triangle is equal as the square of the
   (B)   (C)   (D)

   hypotenuse.

2. The flag over the White House is risen
   (A)   (B)

   at dawn every day by a color guard from the
   (C)   (D)

   United States armed forces.

3. Commercials on the educational television

   network are generally shorter comparing
   (A)   (B)   (C)

   those on other networks.
   (D)

4. The Pilgrims _____ seven thousand
   dollars at 43 percent interest to make their
   journey in 1620.
   (A) lent
   (B) borrowing
   (C) to lend
   (D) borrowed

5. The Food and Drug Administration does not

   declare a drug a carcinogen until it has
   (A)

   been proven conclusively that the effects in
   (B)   (C)

   rats can be generalized for human beings.
   (D)

6. In some states, the law allows drivers to turn
   (A)

   right at a red light, but in other states,
   (B)

   the law does not leave them do it.
   (C)   (D)

7. The effective of a project on the general
   (A)

   population is difficult to measure unless a
   (B)

   statistician is employed to tabulate the
   (C)   (D)

   variables.

8. When a person is arrested, the cops must
   (A)

   let him make one telephone call.
   (B)(C)   (D)

9. Although blood _____ in urine and stool
   samples, it cannot always be detected
   without the aid of a microscope.
   (A) lets residue
   (B) leaves residue
   (C) residues
   (D) making residue

10. The audible range of frequencies for
    human beings _____ between 20 and
    20,000 Hz.
    (A) lies
    (B) lays
    (C) lying
    (D) laying

11. If the owner of a bar suspicions that
    (A)

    someone's identification is not valid, he can
    (B)

    refuse to serve the order.
    (C)   (D)

12. The condition of menkind has been
    (A)   (B)

    improved by recent technological advances.
    (C)   (D)

13. _____ mammals, once weaned, do not routinely drink milk.
    Ⓐ As a whole,
    Ⓑ As whole,
    Ⓒ Wholly,
    Ⓓ On a whole,

14. The classify of plants begins with those
    ___Ⓐ___   ___Ⓑ___
    having the simplest structure, and progresses
    to include the most highly organized forms
                    _____Ⓒ_____
    in four divisions called phylums.
                      ___Ⓓ___

15. With the develop of a cheap process
              ___Ⓐ___
    for desalination, 97 percent of
    ___Ⓑ___
    the Earth's water will become available
    _____Ⓒ_____ _____Ⓓ_____
    for freshwater purposes.

16. People with exceptionally high intelligence quotients may not be the best employees since they _____ unless the job is constantly changing.
    Ⓐ become bored of work
    Ⓑ are becoming boring in work
    Ⓒ become bored with their work
    Ⓓ work becoming bored

17. An understand of calculus is essential
    ___Ⓐ___   Ⓑ
    to the study of engineering.
    ___Ⓒ___   ___Ⓓ___

18. Henry Wadsworth Longfellow not only
    wrote poems and stories but also presided
                            __Ⓐ__ ___Ⓑ___
    the modern language department at Harvard
    University for more than eighteen years.
             __Ⓒ__ ___Ⓓ___

19. In cold weather, growers place wind machines _____ the groves to keep the air circulating and to warm up the citrus crops.
    Ⓐ near to
    Ⓑ near of
    Ⓒ next to
    Ⓓ nearly

20. Almost all life depends to chemical
    ___Ⓐ___   __Ⓑ__
    reactions with oxygen to produce energy.
                        ___Ⓒ___ ___Ⓓ___

Refer to pages 427–428 for the Explanatory Answers.

EXERCISE 55: Sentences—Comprehensive Structures

In the Structure Section of the Paper-Based TOEFL, the items will be organized into two parts—completion sentences and correction sentences. The test will include a comprehensive selection of structures. This exercise is an example of the Paper-Based TOEFL format. Choose the correct answer in the incomplete sentences. Choose the incorrect word or phrase in the underlined choices.

Part 1

1. In simple animals, _____ reflex movement or involuntary response to stimuli.
   - Ⓐ behavior mostly
   - Ⓑ most is behavior
   - Ⓒ most behavior is
   - Ⓓ the most behavior

2. Although the weather in Martha's Vineyard isn't _____ to have a year-round tourist season, it has become a favorite summer resort.
   - Ⓐ goodly enough
   - Ⓑ good enough
   - Ⓒ good as enough
   - Ⓓ enough good

3. According to the wave theory, _____ population of the Americas may have been the result of a number of separate migrations.
   - Ⓐ the
   - Ⓑ their
   - Ⓒ that
   - Ⓓ whose

4. It is presumed that rules governing the sharing of food influenced _____ that the earliest cultures evolved.
   - Ⓐ that the way
   - Ⓑ is the way
   - Ⓒ the way
   - Ⓓ which way

5. Calculus, _____ elegant and economical symbolic system, can reduce complex problems to simple terms.
   - Ⓐ it is an
   - Ⓑ that an
   - Ⓒ an
   - Ⓓ is an

6. Until recently, Canada did not require that U.S. citizens obtain passports to enter the country, and _____.
   - Ⓐ Mexico did neither
   - Ⓑ Mexico didn't either
   - Ⓒ neither Mexico did
   - Ⓓ either did Mexico

7. The poet _____ just beginning to be recognized as an important influence at the time of his death.
   - Ⓐ being Walt Whitman
   - Ⓑ who was Walt Whitman
   - Ⓒ Walt Whitman
   - Ⓓ Walt Whitman was

8. _____ the formation of the Sun, the planets, and other stars began with the condensation of an interstellar cloud.
   - Ⓐ It accepted that
   - Ⓑ Accepted that
   - Ⓒ It is accepted that
   - Ⓓ That is accepted

9. As a general rule, the standard of living _____ by the average output of each person in society.
   - Ⓐ is fixed
   - Ⓑ fixed
   - Ⓒ has fixed
   - Ⓓ fixes

10. The *Consumer Price Index* lists _____.
    - Ⓐ how much costs every car
    - Ⓑ how much does every car cost
    - Ⓒ how much every car costs
    - Ⓓ how much are every car cost

11. The Ford Theater where Lincoln was shot
    _____.
    Ⓐ must restore
    Ⓑ must be restoring
    Ⓒ must have been restored
    Ⓓ must restored

12. Fast-food restaurants have become popular
    because many working people want

    _____.
    Ⓐ to eat quickly and cheaply
    Ⓑ eating quickly and cheaply
    Ⓒ eat quickly and cheaply
    Ⓓ the eat quickly and cheaply

13. After seeing the movie *Centennial*, _____.
    Ⓐ the book was read by many people
    Ⓑ the book made many people want to
       read it
    Ⓒ many people wanted to read the book
    Ⓓ the reading of the book interested
       many people

14. _____, Carl Sandburg is also well-known
    for his multivolume biography of Lincoln.
    Ⓐ An eminent American poet
    Ⓑ He is an eminent American poet
    Ⓒ An eminent American poet who is
    Ⓓ Despite an eminent American poet

15. The examiner made us _____ our
    identification in order to be admitted to the
    test center.
    Ⓐ showing
    Ⓑ show
    Ⓒ showed
    Ⓓ to show

Part 2

16. A swarm of locusts is responsible the
                                   Ⓐ
    consumption of enough plant material
                      Ⓑ
    to feed a million and a half people.
       Ⓒ   Ⓓ

17. Oyster farming has been practice in most
              Ⓐ   Ⓑ   Ⓒ
    parts of the world for many years.
                      Ⓓ

18. Those of us who smoke should have
       Ⓐ   Ⓑ
    their lungs x-rayed regularly.
       Ⓒ   Ⓓ

19. After the team of geologists had drawn

    diagrams in their notebooks and wrote
                  Ⓐ   Ⓑ
    explanations of the formations which they
                                   Ⓒ
    had observed, they returned to their

    campsite to compare notes.
              Ⓓ

20. If Robert Kennedy would have lived
                      Ⓐ
    a little longer, he probably would have
                  Ⓑ   Ⓒ
    won the election.
     Ⓓ

21. It was Shirley Temple Black which
    Ⓐ   Ⓑ
    represented her country in the United
       Ⓒ
    Nations and later became an ambassador.
                  Ⓓ

22. The prices at chain stores are as
                  Ⓐ   Ⓑ
    reasonable, if not more reasonable, as those
               Ⓒ   Ⓓ
    at discount stores.

23. It is extremely important for an engineer
    Ⓐ   Ⓑ   Ⓒ
    to know to use up-to-date computer
       Ⓓ
    programs.

24. <u>Historically</u> <u>there</u> <u>has been</u> <u>only</u> two major
    (A)   (B)   (C)   (D)
    factions in the Republican Party—the
    liberals and the conservatives.

25. Whitman wrote *Leaves of Grass* as a
    tribute to the Civil War soldiers who
    <u>had laid</u> on the battlefields and <u>whom</u> he
      (A)   (B)
    <u>had seen</u> <u>while serving</u> as an army nurse.
      (C)   (D)

26. One of the first and <u>ultimately</u> the most
                              (A)
    important <u>purposeful</u> of a reservoir is
                  (B)
    <u>to control</u> <u>flooding</u>.
       (C)   (D)

27. <u>The Chinese</u> were the first and <u>large</u> ethnic
        (A)   (B)
    group <u>to work</u> on the construction of <u>the</u>
            (C)   (D)
    transcontinental railroad system.

28. The range of plant life on a mountainside
    <u>is</u> <u>a</u> results of <u>differences</u> in temperature
    (A) (B)   (C)
    and precipitation at <u>varying</u> altitudes.
                            (D)

29. <u>Even</u> a professional psychologist may have
      (A)
    difficulty talking <u>calm</u> and logically <u>about</u>
                          (B)   (C)
    <u>his own</u> problems.
       (D)

30. The more the relative humidity reading
    <u>rises</u>, the <u>worst</u> the heat <u>affects</u> <u>us</u>.
      (A)   (B)   (C)   (D)

31. Because correlations are not <u>causes</u>,
                                    (A)
    statistical data <u>which are</u> <u>extremely</u> easy
                        (B)   (C)
    <u>to misuse</u>.
       (D)

32. Lectures <u>for</u> the week of March 22–26
                (A)
    <u>will include</u> the <u>following</u>: The Causes of
         (B)   (C)
    the Civil War, The Economy of the South,
    Battle Strategies, and <u>The Assassinate</u>
                                (D)
    Lincoln.

33. <u>Despite of</u> <u>many</u> attempts <u>to introduce</u> a
        (A)   (B)   (C)
    universal language, notably Esperanto and
    Idiom Neutral, the effort has met with very
    <u>little</u> success.
      (D)

34. <u>As</u> every <u>other</u> nation, the United States
    (A)   (B)
    <u>used to define</u> <u>its</u> unit of currency, the
         (C)   (D)
    dollar, in terms of the gold standard.

35. It is necessary that one <u>met</u> with a judge
                               (A)
    <u>before signing</u> the <u>final papers</u>
         (B)   (C)
    <u>for a divorce</u>.
       (D)

36. <u>Until recently</u>, women were <u>forbidden</u>
         (A)   (B)
    <u>by law</u> <u>from owning</u> property.
       (C)   (D)

37. <u>According to</u> the graduate catalog, student
         (A)
    housing <u>is</u> <u>more cheaper</u> <u>than</u> housing off
              (B)   (C)   (D)
    campus.

38. John Dewey thought that children
    <u>will learn</u> <u>better</u> through participating in
         (A)   (B)
    experiences <u>rather</u> than through <u>listening to</u>
                    (C)   (D)
    lectures.

39. In England as early as the twelfth century,
    <u>A</u>   <u>B</u>   <u>C</u>

    young boys enjoyed to play football.
    <u>D</u>

40. Some methods to prevent soil erosion are
    <u>A</u>   <u>B</u>   <u>C</u>

    plowing parallel with the slopes of hills,

    to plant trees on unproductive land, and
    <u>D</u>

    rotating crops.

Refer to pages 428–430 for the Explanatory Answers.

5

PRACTICE EXERCISES
FOR READING

Reading Section

The Reading Section of the TOEFL tests your ability to understand written English as it is presented in textbooks and other academic materials in North America. This section is included in the Paper-Based TOEFL and the Internet-Based Computer-Based TOEFL. The section is different for each of the TOEFL formats.

Paper-Based TOEFL (PBT)

There are 50 questions in five or six reading passages on the Reading Section of the Paper-Based TOEFL. You may not take notes or write in your test book. The topics are both general and academic. The questions are all multiple-choice with four possible answer choices. The section takes about 55 minutes to complete. Refer to Exercise 56 to see examples.

Internet-Based TOEFL

There are between 36 and 39 questions on the Reading Section of the iBT®. You may take notes as you read. The topics are all academic. The comprehension questions are either multiple-choice with four possible answer choices or computer-assisted with special directions on the screen. It takes 25 minutes to complete the reading and to answer 12 or 13 comprehension questions for each of the three reading passages.

There are two types of tasks included in the Reading Section: three independent reading tasks and two integrated reading tasks.

In the independent reading tasks, you will read academic texts about 800 words long. After each passage, you will answer 12 or 13 comprehension questions. After every multiple-choice question, choose the best answer choice from four possible answers. After every computer-assisted question, follow the special directions on the screen to complete the answer. Refer to Exercise 69 to see examples.

In the integrated reading tasks, you will read and respond to academic passages. After each passage, you will read a question that requires you to respond by speaking or writing. Refer to Exercise 97 to see examples.

EXERCISE 56: Narration/Sequence—Popular Culture

In some questions in the Reading Section on the Paper-Based TOEFL, you will be asked to recall and relate information and content from narration or sequence passages about popular culture. Choose the best answer.

Basketball

Although he created the game of basketball at the YMCA in Springfield, Massachusetts, Dr. James A. Naismith was a Canadian. Working as a physical education instructor at the International
Line YMCA, now Springfield College, Dr. Naismith noticed a lack of
5   interest in exercise among students during the wintertime. The New England winters were fierce, and the students balked at participating in outdoor activities. Naismith determined that a fast-moving game that could be played indoors would fill a void after the baseball and football seasons had ended.
10   First he attempted to adapt outdoor games such as soccer and rugby to indoor play, but he soon found them unsuitable for confined areas. Finally, he determined that he would have to invent a game.

In December of 1891, Dr. Naismith hung two old peach baskets at either end of the gymnasium at the school, and, using a soccer ball
15   and nine players on each side, organized the first basketball game. The early rules allowed three points for each basket and made running with the ball a violation. Every time a goal was made, someone had to climb a ladder to retrieve the ball.

Nevertheless, the game became popular. In less than a year,
20   basketball was being played in both the United States and Canada. Five years later, a championship tournament was staged in New York City, which was won by the Brooklyn Central YMCA.

The teams had already been reduced to seven players, and five became standard in the 1897 season. When basketball was introduced
25   as a demonstration sport in the 1904 Olympic Games in St. Louis, it quickly spread throughout the world. In 1906, a metal hoop was used for the first time to replace the basket, but the name basketball has remained.

1. What does this passage mainly discuss?
   - Ⓐ The Olympic Games in St. Louis in 1904
   - Ⓑ The development of basketball
   - Ⓒ The YMCA athletic program
   - Ⓓ Dr. James Naismith

2. When was the first demonstration game of basketball held during the Olympics?
   - Ⓐ 1891
   - Ⓑ 1892
   - Ⓒ 1897
   - Ⓓ 1904

3. The phrase "balked at" in line 6 could best be replaced by
   - Ⓐ resisted
   - Ⓑ enjoyed
   - Ⓒ excelled at
   - Ⓓ were exhausted by

4. The word "fierce" in line 6 is closest in meaning to
   - Ⓐ long
   - Ⓑ boring
   - Ⓒ extreme
   - Ⓓ dark

5. The word "them" in line 11 refers to
   - Ⓐ indoors
   - Ⓑ seasons
   - Ⓒ games
   - Ⓓ areas

6. Where in the passage does the author discuss the first basketball championship tournament?
   - Ⓐ Lines 10–12
   - Ⓑ Lines 13–15
   - Ⓒ Lines 21–22
   - Ⓓ Lines 24–26

7. What does the author mean by the statement in lines 24–26: "When basketball was introduced as a demonstration sport in the 1904 Olympic Games in St. Louis, it quickly spread throughout the world"?
   - Ⓐ Basketball was not considered an Olympic sport at the St. Louis games.
   - Ⓑ Basketball became popular worldwide after its introduction at the Olympic Games in St. Louis.
   - Ⓒ Basketball players from many countries competed in the Olympic Games in St. Louis.
   - Ⓓ Basketball was one of the most popular sports at the Olympic Games in St. Louis.

8. Why did Naismith decide to invent basketball?
   - Ⓐ He did not like soccer or rugby.
   - Ⓑ He was tired of baseball and football.
   - Ⓒ He wanted his students to exercise during the winter.
   - Ⓓ He could not convince his students to play indoors.

9. The author mentions all of the following as typical of the early game of basketball EXCEPT
   - Ⓐ three points were scored for every basket
   - Ⓑ running with the ball was not a foul
   - Ⓒ nine players were on a team
   - Ⓓ the ball had to be retrieved from the basket after each score

10. It can be inferred from the passage that the original baskets
    - Ⓐ were not placed very high
    - Ⓑ had a metal rim
    - Ⓒ did not have a hole in the bottom
    - Ⓓ were hung on the same side

Refer to page 431 for the Explanatory Answers.

EXERCISE 57: Definition/Illustration—Popular Culture

In some questions in the Reading Section on the Paper-Based TOEFL, you will be asked to recall and relate information and content from definition or illustration passages about popular culture. Choose the best answer.

Mickey Mouse

Mickey Mouse was not Walt Disney's first successful cartoon creation, but he is certainly his most famous one. It was on a cross-country train trip from New York to California in 1927 that Disney
Line   first drew the mouse with the big ears. Supposedly, he took his
5   inspiration from the tame field mice that used to scamper into his old studio in Kansas City. No one is quite sure why he dressed the mouse in the now-familiar shorts with two buttons and gave him the yellow shoes. But we do know that Disney had intended to call him Mortimer until his wife Lillian intervened and christened him Mickey
10   Mouse.

Capitalizing on the interest in Charles Lindbergh, Disney planned Mickey's debut in the short cartoon Plane Crazy, with Minnie as a co-star. In the third short cartoon, *Steamboat Willie*, Mickey was whistling and singing through the miracle of the modern soundtrack.
15   By the 1930s Mickey's image had circled the globe. He was a superstar at the height of his career.

Although he has received a few minor changes throughout his lifetime, most notably the addition of white gloves and the alterations to achieve the rounder forms of a more childish body, he has
20   remained true to his nature since those first cartoons. Mickey is appealing because he is nice. He may get into trouble, but he takes it on the chin with a grin. He is both good-natured and resourceful. Perhaps that was Disney's own image of himself. Why else would he have insisted on doing Mickey's voice in all the cartoons for twenty
25   years? When interviewed, he would say. "There is a lot of the mouse in me." And that mouse has remained one of the most pervasive images in American popular culture.

1. Which of the following is the main topic of the passage?
   Ⓐ The image of Mickey Mouse
   Ⓑ The life of Walt Disney
   Ⓒ The history of cartoons
   Ⓓ The definition of American culture

2. What distinguished *Steamboat Willie* from earlier cartoons?
   Ⓐ Better color
   Ⓑ A sound track
   Ⓒ Minnie Mouse as co-star
   Ⓓ The longer format

3. The word "pervasive" in line 26 could best be replaced by
   Ⓐ well loved
   Ⓑ widespread
   Ⓒ often copied
   Ⓓ expensive to buy

4. The word "appealing" in line 21 is closest in meaning to
   Ⓐ attractive
   Ⓑ famous
   Ⓒ exceptional
   Ⓓ distinguishable

5. The word "those" in line 20 refers to
   Ⓐ cartoons
   Ⓑ forms
   Ⓒ gloves
   Ⓓ changes

6. Where in the passage does the author relate how Mickey got his name?
   Ⓐ Lines 8–10
   Ⓑ Lines 11–13
   Ⓒ Lines 15–16
   Ⓓ Lines 17–20

7. What does the author mean by the statement in lines 17–20: "Although he has received a few minor changes throughout his lifetime, most notably the addition of white gloves and the alterations to achieve the rounder forms of a more childish body, he has remained true to his nature since those first cartoons"?
   Ⓐ The current version of Mickey Mouse is different in every way from the early cartoons.
   Ⓑ The original Mickey Mouse was one of the first cartoon characters.
   Ⓒ In the first cartoons, Mickey Mouse looked more like a child.
   Ⓓ The personality of Mickey Mouse has not changed over the years.

8. What did Disney mean when he said, "There is a lot of the mouse in me?"
   Ⓐ He was proud of the mouse that he created.
   Ⓑ He knew that the mouse would be a famous creation.
   Ⓒ He created the mouse with many of his own qualities.
   Ⓓ He had worked very hard to create the mouse.

9. The first image of Mickey Mouse is described as all of the following EXCEPT
   Ⓐ he was dressed in shorts with two buttons
   Ⓑ he had big ears
   Ⓒ he wore yellow shoes
   Ⓓ he was wearing white gloves

10. The paragraph following the passage most probably discusses
    Ⓐ the history of cartoons
    Ⓑ other images in popular culture
    Ⓒ Walt Disney's childhood
    Ⓓ the voices of cartoon characters

Refer to pages 431–432 for the Explanatory Answers.

EXERCISE 58: Narration/Sequence—Social Sciences

In some questions in the Reading Section on the Paper-Based TOEFL, you will be asked to recall and relate information and content from narration or sequence passages in various fields of study. Choose the best answer for multiple-choice questions.

Federal Policies for Native Peoples

Federal policy toward the Native Americans has a long history of inconsistency, reversal, and failure. In the late 1700s, the United States government owned and operated factories, exchanging manufactured goods for furs and horses with the hope that mutual satisfaction with trade would result in peace between Native Americans and the rush of settlers who were moving west. At the same time, the government supported missionary groups in their efforts to build churches, schools, and model farms for those tribes that permitted them to live in their midst.

By the 1800s, federal negotiators were trying to convince many tribes to sell their land and move out of the line of frontier expansion, a policy that culminated in the forced expulsion of the major Southeastern tribes to the west. Over protests by Congress and the Supreme Court, President Andrew Jackson ordered the Native Americans to be removed to what is now Oklahoma. On the forced march, which the Cherokee Nation refers to as the "Trail of Tears," many Native Americans died of disease, exposure, and hunger.

By the end of the 1800s, the government had discovered that some of the land allocated as permanent reservations for the Native Americans contained valuable resources. Congress passed the Dawes Severalty Act, and for the next forty years Indian agents and missionaries attempted to destroy the tribal system by separating the members. It was during this time that the government boarding schools were established to educate Native American youth outside of the home environment.

Under the Indian Reorganization Act of 1934, scattered tribes were encouraged to reorganize their tribal governments. Anti-Indian sentiment resurfaced only ten years later, and by the 1950s relocation centers to move Native Americans from the reservations to urban areas were established.

Today, government policies are unclear. Many officials want to remove the federal government completely from Native American governance. Others believe that the government should support Native American efforts to maintain their culture. Not surprisingly, the Native Americans themselves are ambivalent about the role of the federal government in their affairs.

1. What is the author's main point?
   Ⓐ Government policies for Native Americans have not changed many times during the past three hundred years.
   Ⓑ Today government officials are in agreement about their role in Native-American affairs.
   Ⓒ The federal government has been inconsistent and unclear in its policies for Native Americans.
   Ⓓ The Indian Reorganization Act was a failure.

2. What was involved in the "Trail of Tears"?
   Ⓐ Native-American children were separated from their families and sent to boarding schools.
   Ⓑ Native-American families living in the Southeast were forced to move to Oklahoma.
   Ⓒ Native-American families were resettled on reservations.
   Ⓓ Native Americans were moved from reservations to cities.

3. The word "ambivalent" in line 35 refers to
   Ⓐ exhibiting suspicion
   Ⓑ experiencing contradictory feelings
   Ⓒ expressing concern
   Ⓓ demonstrating opposition

4. The word "culminated" in line 12 is closest in meaning to
   Ⓐ ended
   Ⓑ failed
   Ⓒ belonged
   Ⓓ caused

5. The word "them" in line 9 refers to
   Ⓐ missionary groups
   Ⓑ efforts
   Ⓒ model farms
   Ⓓ tribes

6. Where in the passage does the author refer to the congressional act that allowed Native-American students to be sent to boarding schools?
   Ⓐ Lines 6–9
   Ⓑ Lines 13–15
   Ⓒ Lines 20–25
   Ⓓ Lines 26–30

7. What does the author mean by the statement in lines 13–15: "Over protests by Congress and the Supreme Court, President Andrew Jackson ordered the Native Americans to be removed to what is now Oklahoma?"
   Ⓐ Oklahoma objected to the president's order to move Native Americans to their state.
   Ⓑ The Native Americans had to move to Oklahoma because Congress and the Supreme Court objected to the president's order.
   Ⓒ The president ordered the Native Americans in Oklahoma to move despite opposition by Congress and the Supreme Court.
   Ⓓ Despite objections by Congress and the Supreme Court, Native Americans were forced to move to Oklahoma by the president.

8. Why did Congress pass the Dawes Severalty Act?
   Ⓐ Because the government agencies wanted to exploit the resources on reservations
   Ⓑ Because missionaries wanted to convert the Native Americans to Christianity
   Ⓒ Because teachers wanted to set up schools for Native Americans in urban areas
   Ⓓ Because officials on the reservations wanted to preserve Native-American culture

9. Native American policies are described as all of the following EXCEPT
   Ⓐ inconsistent
   Ⓑ destructive
   Ⓒ permanent
   Ⓓ unclear

10. The paragraph following the passage most probably discusses
    Ⓐ the Native-American point of view regarding government policies today
    Ⓑ the efforts by Native Americans to maintain their culture
    Ⓒ the results of the reservation system
    Ⓓ the intertribal councils that Native Americans have established

Refer to page 432 for the Explanatory Answers.

EXERCISE 59: Narration/Sequence—Arts/Architecture

In some questions in the Reading Section on the Paper-Based TOEFL or the Computer-Based TOEFL, you will be asked to recall and relate information and content from narration or sequence passages in various fields of study. Choose the best answer for multiple-choice questions.

Eugene O'Neill

Universally acclaimed as America's greatest playwright, Eugene O'Neill was born in 1888 in the heart of the theater district in New York City. As the son of an actor he had early exposure to the world
Line of the theater. He attended Princeton University briefly in 1906, but
5 returned to New York to work in a variety of jobs before joining the crew of a freighter as a seaman. Upon returning from voyages to South Africa and South America, he was hospitalized for six months to recuperate from tuberculosis. While he was recovering, he determined to write a play about his adventures on the sea.

10 　　He went to Harvard, where he wrote the one-act *Bound East for Cardiff*. It was produced in 1916 on Cape Cod by the Provincetown Players, an experimental theater group that was later to settle in the famous Greenwich Village theater district in New York City. The Players produced several more of his one-acts in the years between
15 1916–1920. With the full-length play *Beyond the Horizon*, produced on Broadway in 1920, O'Neill's success was assured. The play won the Pulitzer Prize for the best play of the year. O'Neill was to be awarded the prize again in 1922, 1928, and 1957 for *Anna Christie*, *Strange Interlude*, and *Long Day's Journey Into Night*. Although he
20 did not receive the Pulitzer Prize for it, *Mourning Becomes Electra*, produced in 1931, is arguably his most lasting contribution to the American theater. In 1936, he was awarded the Nobel Prize for literature.

O'Neill's plays, forty-five in all, cover a wide range of dramatic
25 subjects, but several themes emerge, including the ambivalence of family relationships, the struggle between the sexes, the conflict between spiritual and material desires, and the vision of modern man as a victim of uncontrollable circumstances. Most of O'Neill's characters are seeking meaning in their lives. According to his
30 biographers, most of the characters were portraits of himself and his family. In a sense, his work chronicled his life.

1. This passage is a summary of O'Neill's
   - Ⓐ work
   - Ⓑ life
   - Ⓒ work and life
   - Ⓓ family

2. How many times was O'Neill awarded the Pulitzer Prize?
   - Ⓐ One
   - Ⓑ Three
   - Ⓒ Four
   - Ⓓ Five

3. The word "briefly" in line 4 is closest in meaning to
   - Ⓐ seriously
   - Ⓑ for a short time
   - Ⓒ on scholarship
   - Ⓓ without enthusiasm

4. The word "struggle" in line 26 is closest in meaning to
   - Ⓐ influence
   - Ⓑ conflict
   - Ⓒ appreciation
   - Ⓓ denial

5. The word "it" in line 20 refers to
   - Ⓐ Harvard
   - Ⓑ one-act play
   - Ⓒ theater group
   - Ⓓ theater district

6. Where in the passage does the author indicate the reason for O'Neill's hospitalization?
   - Ⓐ Lines 3–4
   - Ⓑ Lines 6–8
   - Ⓒ Lines 10–13
   - Ⓓ Lines 16–19

7. What does the author mean by the statement in lines 29–31: "According to his biographers, most of the characters were portraits of himself and his family"?
   - Ⓐ He used his family and his own experiences in his plays.
   - Ⓑ His biography contained stories about him and his family.
   - Ⓒ He had paintings of himself and members of his family.
   - Ⓓ His biographers took pictures of him with his family.

8. According to the passage, which of O'Neill's plays was most important to the American theater?
   - Ⓐ *Anna Christie*
   - Ⓑ *Beyond the Horizon*
   - Ⓒ *Long Day's Journey Into Night*
   - Ⓓ *Mourning Becomes Electra*

9. The author mentions all of the following as themes for O'Neill's plays EXCEPT
   - Ⓐ life in college
   - Ⓑ adventures at sea
   - Ⓒ family life
   - Ⓓ relationships between men and women

10. We can infer from information in the passage that O'Neill's plays were not
    - Ⓐ controversial
    - Ⓑ autobiographical
    - Ⓒ optimistic
    - Ⓓ popular

Refer to page 433 for the Explanatory Answers.

EXERCISE 60: Narration/Sequence—Humanities/Business

In some questions in the Reading Section on the Internet-Based TOEFL, you will be asked to recall and relate information and content from narration or sequence passages found in college textbooks. Choose the best answer for multiple-choice questions. For computer-assisted questions, follow the directions on the screen.

The Print Revolution

For more than five thousand years, from the dawn of civilization in Mesopotamia and Egypt, people in the West wrote by hand. Imperial decrees, sacred scriptures, commercial transactions, private letters—all required the skills of a select group of scribes, clerks, or monks. In Korea and China, however, mechanical printing using carved wooden blocks had been introduced by A.D. 750. Moveable type, using characters made of baked clay, was invented in China in the eleventh century. But the Chinese continued to prefer block printing well into the modern period. Written Chinese consists of thousands of ideographic characters. The labor of creating, organizing, and setting so many different bits of type made it much simpler to cut individual pages from a single wooden block. European languages, which can be written with fewer than a hundred characters, were much better adapted to printing with moveable, reusable type.

It appears that the Mongol armies brought examples of Chinese printing—the Venetian Marco Polo described seeing paper money during his travels—to western Asia and Europe at the end of the thirteenth century. In the early fourteenth century, Europeans began using block printing techniques to produce religious images, short prayers, and even decks of playing cards. As with Chinese printing, European block printing was a slow and expensive process for printing large numbers of varied texts. The print revolution had to wait another century, until the innovations of the German goldsmith Johann Gutenberg (ca. 1399–1468).

Gutenberg drew on his knowledge of metallurgy to devise a lead-tin-copper alloy that could be cast into durable, reusable type. His crucial invention was a type mold consisting of a flat strip of metal—stamped in the same way a coin is minted, leaving the impression of a single letter—inserted in the bottom of a rectangular brass box held together by screws. Molten metal was poured into it, producing a single piece of type. An experienced type founder could produce up to six hundred pieces of type a day. No wooden-block carver could have approached that rate. To solve the remaining problems, Gutenberg adapted the screw press commonly used to produce linen, paper, and wine to make a printing press. He followed the example of Flemish painters by adding linseed oil to the ink to make it thick enough to adhere uniformly to the metal type.

In 1455, the Gutenberg Bible was published in Mainz, Germany—but not by Gutenberg. After years of costly experimentation, Gutenberg was forced to turn over his equipment and newly printed

Bibles to his partner and creditor, the wealthy merchant and moneylender Johann Fust.

The new technology, which enabled printers to create a thousand or more copies in a single print run, was highly efficient. Simple printed school texts cost only a quarter of the price of hand-copied texts. The leading bookseller in the university town of Bologna managed to stock ten thousand copies of texts, treatises, and commentaries. By 1500, even street singers sold printed copies of their songs.

Gutenberg's invention was revolutionary because, for the first time, the same information and ideas were available throughout Europe at virtually the same time. The great Venetian printer Aldus Manutius (1450–1515) produced over 120,000 volumes, many in the new, smaller, easily portable "octavo" format—about 6 by 9 inches. Books from the Aldine Press and other humanistic publishers played a decisive role in spreading humanism to parts of Europe where manuscript books were difficult to acquire.

Moreover, book owning was no longer the exclusive preserve of scholars. This was all the more true because printers included on their lists works in vernacular languages, not just the ancient classics. The very popularity of printed vernacular texts affected language. William Caxton (1422–1492), for example, began printing books in English in 1472. His pioneering work helped standardize modern English, just as the publication of Martin Luther's German translation of the Bible in 1522 would standardize modern German. The advent of printing had other far-reaching consequences: it promoted the increase of literacy throughout Europe.

By the eighteenth century, printed books had changed the nature of popular culture. Myths, folk songs, and popular histories were traditionally passed by word of mouth, often changing in the telling to fit the time and place. Once they appeared in print, they could no longer be performed and refashioned, only recited. Printing not only changed the way information was transmitted but also changed the character of the information itself.

·The Print Revolution (Question References)

Paragraph 1   For more than five thousand years, from the dawn of civilization in Mesopotamia and Egypt, people in the West wrote by hand. Imperial decrees, sacred scriptures, commercial transactions, private letters—all required the skills of a select group of scribes, clerks, or monks. In Korea and China, however, mechanical printing using carved wooden blocks had been introduced by A.D. 750. Moveable type, using characters made of baked clay, was invented in China in the eleventh century. But the Chinese continued to prefer block printing well into the modern period. Written Chinese consists of thousands of ideographic characters. The labor of creating, organizing, and setting so many different bits of type made it much simpler to cut individual pages from a single wooden block. European languages, which can be written with fewer than a hundred characters, were much better adapted to printing with moveable, reusable type.

2   It appears that the Mongol armies brought examples of Chinese printing—the Venetian Marco Polo described seeing paper money during his travels—to western Asia and Europe at the end of the thirteenth century. In the early fourteenth century, Europeans began using block printing techniques to produce religious images, short prayers, and even decks of playing cards. As with Chinese printing, European block printing was a slow and expensive process for printing large numbers of varied texts. The print revolution had to wait another century, until the innovations of the German goldsmith Johann Gutenberg (ca. 1399–1468).

3   Gutenberg drew on his knowledge of metallurgy to devise a lead-tin-copper alloy that could be cast into durable, reusable type. His crucial invention was a type mold consisting of a flat strip of metal—stamped in the same way a coin is minted, leaving the impression of a single letter—inserted in the bottom of a rectangular brass box held together by screws. Molten metal was poured into it, producing a single piece of type. An experienced type founder could produce up to six hundred pieces of type a day. No wooden-block carver could have approached that rate. ⟦A⟧ To solve the remaining problems, Gutenberg adapted the screw press commonly used to produce linen, paper, and wine to make a printing press. ⟦B⟧ He followed the example of Flemish painters by adding linseed oil to the ink to make it thick enough to adhere uniformly to the metal type.

4   In 1455, the Gutenberg Bible was published in Mainz, Germany—but not by Gutenberg. After years of costly experimentation, Gutenberg was forced to turn over his equipment and newly printed Bibles to his partner and creditor, the wealthy merchant and moneylender Johann Fust. ⟦C⟧

5   The new technology, which enabled printers to create a thousand or more copies in a single print run, was highly efficient. Simple printed school texts cost only a quarter of the price of hand-copied texts. The leading bookseller in the university town of Bologna managed to stock ten thousand copies of texts, treatises, and commentaries. By 1500, even street singers sold printed copies of their songs. ⟦D⟧

6   Gutenberg's invention was revolutionary because, for the first time, the same information and ideas were available throughout Europe at virtually the same time. The great Venetian printer Aldus Manutius (1450–1515) produced over 120,000 volumes, many in the new, smaller, easily portable "octavo" format—about 6 by 9 inches. Books from the Aldine Press and other humanistic publishers played a decisive role in spreading humanism to parts of Europe where manuscript books were difficult to acquire.

7   Moreover, book owning was no longer the exclusive preserve of scholars. This was all the more true because printers included on their lists works in vernacular languages, not just the ancient classics. The very popularity of printed vernacular texts affected language. William Caxton (1422–1492), for example, began printing books in English in 1472. His pioneering work helped standardize modern English, just as the publication of Martin Luther's German translation of the Bible in 1522 would standardize modern German. The advent of printing had other far-reaching consequences: it promoted the increase of literacy throughout Europe.

8   By the eighteenth century, printed books had changed the nature of popular culture. Myths, folk songs, and popular histories were traditionally passed by word of mouth, often changing in the telling to fit the time and place. Once they appeared in print, they could no longer be performed and refashioned, only recited. Printing not only changed the way information was transmitted but also changed the character of the information itself.

1. With which of the following topics is the passage primarily concerned?
   - Ⓐ A comparison of religious and humanistic publications
   - Ⓑ A history of the printing process worldwide
   - Ⓒ An account of Gutenberg's inventions
   - Ⓓ The effects of books on the history of Europe

2. How was popular culture affected by printing?
   - Ⓐ The oral tradition required editing of printed documents.
   - Ⓑ Stories and songs changed less often.
   - Ⓒ More folk histories were preserved.
   - Ⓓ Traditional performers became more popular.

3. The word crucial in the passage is closest in meaning to
   - Ⓐ totally new
   - Ⓑ very significant
   - Ⓒ greatly debated
   - Ⓓ highly complex

4. The word character in the passage is closest in meaning to
   - Ⓐ popularity
   - Ⓑ nature
   - Ⓒ truth
   - Ⓓ difficulty

5. The word it in the passage refers to
   Ⓐ box
   Ⓑ letter
   Ⓒ impression
   Ⓓ coin

6. According to paragraph 6, how did Europeans learn about block printing?
   Ⓐ They saw examples that were brought from China by explorers and soldiers.
   Ⓑ A German goldsmith invented it at the beginning of the fifteenth century.
   Ⓒ It was first devised in Europe in order to print paper money.
   Ⓓ The Egyptians used the blocks for documents that the Europeans received.

7. Which of the sentences below best expresses the information in the highlighted statement in the passage? The other choices change the meaning or leave out important information.
   Ⓐ Scholars owned more books than other people.
   Ⓑ Scholars were not the only people who could own books.
   Ⓒ Scholars preserved books for use by other people.
   Ⓓ Scholars owned some exclusive books.

8. The author mentions all of the following advantages of the print revolution EXCEPT
   Ⓐ the standardization of English
   Ⓑ the advancement of literacy
   Ⓒ the dissemination of humanism
   Ⓓ the restoration of manuscripts

9. It can be inferred that Gutenberg
   Ⓐ had probably traveled to China and western Asia
   Ⓑ did not live to see his invention succeed
   Ⓒ was a painter before he became an inventor
   Ⓓ worked for a long time to perfect his printing process

10. Four squares (☐) indicate where the following sentence can be added to the passage.

    Although he did not receive the financial remuneration that he deserved, history has recorded his name among the most influential inventors of all time.

    Where would the sentence best fit into the passage?
    Ⓐ
    Ⓑ
    Ⓒ
    Ⓓ

11. Complete the table below by matching each of the places with the important event that corresponds to it. One of the answer choices will NOT be used.
    Ⓐ Germany
    Ⓑ Egypt
    Ⓒ Italy
    Ⓓ China
    Ⓔ France
    Ⓕ England
    Ⓖ Korea

• Scribes began to copy manuscripts.
• Block printing was devised.
•
• The Gutenberg Bible was published. A
• Smaller books were popularized.
• Native-language books appeared.

12. Complete a summary of the passage by selecting THREE answer choices that express the most important ideas. The other three sentences do not belong in the summary because they express ideas that are not in the passage or they do not refer to the major ideas. *This question is worth 2 points.*

Printing not only changed the way information was transmitted but also changed the character of the information itself.

Ⓐ Gutenberg devised reusable type for European languages to replace the block printing that was more appropriate for Asian languages.

Ⓑ Information and ideas were made available throughout Europe to a large number of people at virtually the same time.

Ⓒ A new format for books made them more portable and easier for people to handle.

Ⓓ Block printing continued to be used to print paper money in most of the European countries.

Ⓔ Many changes in literacy and vernacular languages occurred as a result of the printing press.

Ⓕ Gutenberg did not realize much from his invention because he had accumulated debts in order to pay for his experiments.

Refer to pages 433–434 for the Explanatory Answers.

EXERCISE 61: Narration/Sequence—Natural Sciences

In some questions in the Reading Section on the Internet-Based TOEFL, you will be asked to recall and relate information and content from narration or sequence passages found in college textbooks. Choose the best answer for multiple-choice questions. For computer-assisted questions, follow the directions on the screen.

Glacial Movement

Like all minerals, ice has specific properties of hardness, color, melting point (quite low in the case of ice), and brittleness. We know the properties of ice best from those brittle little cubes in the freezer. But glacial ice has different properties, depending on its location in a glacier. In a glacier's depths, glacial ice behaves in a plastic manner, distorting and flowing in response to weight and pressure from above and the degree of slope below. In contrast, the glacier's upper portion is more like the everyday ice we know, quite brittle.

A glacier's rate of flow ranges from almost nothing to a kilometer or two per year on a steep slope. The rate of snow accumulation in the formation area is critical to the pace of glacial movement.

Glaciers are not rigid blocks that simply slide downhill. The greatest movement within a valley's glacier occurs *internally*, below the rigid surface layer, where the underlying zone moves plastically forward. At the same time, the base creeps and slides along, varying its speed with temperature and the presence of any lubricating water or saturated sediment beneath the ice. This *basal slip* usually is much slower than the internal plastic flow of the glacier, so the upper portion of the glacier flows ahead of the lower portion. The difference in speed stretches the glacier's brittle surface ice.

In addition, the pressure may vary in response to unevenness in the landscape beneath the ice. Basal ice may be melted by compression at one moment, only to refreeze later. This process is called *ice regelation*, meaning to refreeze or re-gel. Regelation is important because it facilitates downslope movement and because the process incorporates rock debris into the glacier. Consequently, a glacier's basal ice layer, which can extend tens of meters above its base, has a much greater debris content than the ice above.

A flowing glacier can develop vertical cracks known as **crevasses**. Crevasses result from friction with valley walls, or tension from stretching as the glacier passes over convex slopes, or compression as the glacier passes over concave slopes. Traversing a glacier, whether an alpine glacier or an ice sheet, is dangerous because a thin veneer of snow sometimes masks the presence of a crevasse.

Glacier Surges. Although glaciers flow plastically and predictably most of the time, some will lurch forward with little or no warning in a **glacier surge**. A surge is not quite as abrupt as it sounds; in glacial terms, a surge can be tens of meters per day. The Jakobshavn Glacier in Greenland, for example, is known to move between 7 and 12 km (4.3 and 7.5 mi) a year.

In the spring of 1986, Hubbard Glacier and its tributary Valerie Glacier surged across the mouth of Russell Fjord in Alaska, cutting it off from contact with Yukutat Bay. This area, the St. Elias Mountain Range in southeastern Alaska, is fed by annual snowfall that averages more than 850 cm (335 in.) a year, so the surge event had been predicted. But the rapidity of the surge was surprising. The glacier's movement exceeded 34 m (112 ft) per day during the peak surge, an enormous increase over its normal rate of 15 cm (6 in.) per day.

The exact cause of such a glacier surge is being studied. Some surge events result from a buildup of water pressure under the glacier, sometimes enough to actually float the glacier slightly, detaching it from its bed, during the surge. As a surge begins, icequakes are detectable, and ice faults are visible. Surges can occur in dry conditions as well, as the glacier plucks (picks up) rock from its bed and moves forward. Another cause of glacier surges is the presence of a water-saturated layer of sediment, a so-called *soft bed*, beneath the glacier. This is a deformable layer that cannot resist the tremendous sheer stress produced by the moving ice of the glacier. Scientists examining cores taken from several ice streams now accelerating through the West Antarctic Ice Sheet think they have identified this cause—although water pressure is still important.

Glacial Movement (Question References)

Paragraph 1   Like all minerals, ice has specific properties of hardness, color, melting point (quite low in the case of ice), and brittleness. We know the properties of ice best from those brittle little cubes in the freezer. But glacial ice has different properties, depending on its location in a glacier. In a glacier's depths, glacial ice behaves in a plastic manner, distorting and flowing in response to weight and pressure from above and the degree of slope below. In contrast, the glacier's upper portion is more like the everyday ice we know, quite brittle.

2   A glacier's rate of flow ranges from almost nothing to a kilometer or two per year on a steep slope. [A] The rate of snow accumulation in the formation area is critical to the pace of glacial movement. [B]

3   Glaciers are not rigid blocks that simply slide downhill. [C] The greatest movement within a valley's glacier occurs *internally*, below the rigid surface layer, where the underlying zone moves plastically forward. [D] At the same time, the base creeps and slides along, varying its speed with temperature and the presence of any lubricating water or saturated sediment beneath the ice. This *basal slip* usually is much slower than the internal plastic flow of the glacier, so the upper portion of the glacier flows ahead of the lower portion. The difference in speed stretches the glacier's brittle surface ice.

4   In addition, the pressure may vary in response to unevenness in the landscape beneath the ice. Basal ice may be melted by compression at one moment, only to refreeze later. This process is called *ice regelation*, meaning to refreeze or re-gel. Regelation is important because it facilitates downslope movement and because the process incorporates rock debris into the glacier. Consequently, a glacier's basal ice layer, which can extend tens of meters above its base, has a much greater debris content than the ice above.

5   A flowing glacier can develop vertical cracks known as **crevasses**. Crevasses result from friction with valley walls, or tension from stretching as the glacier passes over convex slopes, or compression as the glacier passes over concave slopes. Traversing a glacier, whether an alpine glacier or an ice sheet, is dangerous because a thin veneer of snow sometimes masks the presence of a crevasse.

6   **Glacier Surges.** Although glaciers flow plastically and predictably most of the time, some will lurch forward with little or no warning in a **glacier surge**. A surge is not quite as abrupt as it sounds; in glacial terms, a surge can be tens of meters per day. The Jakobshavn Glacier in Greenland, for example, is known to move between 7 and 12 km (4.3 and 7.5 mi) a year.

7   In the spring of 1986, Hubbard Glacier and its tributary Valerie Glacier surged across the mouth of Russell Fjord in Alaska, cutting it off from contact with Yukutat Bay. This area, the St. Elias Mountain Range in southeastern Alaska, is fed by annual snowfall that averages more than 850 cm (335 in.) a year, so the surge event had been predicted. But the rapidity of the surge was surprising. The glacier's movement exceeded 34 m (112 ft) per day during the peak surge, an enormous increase over its normal rate of 15 cm (6 in.) per day.

8   The exact cause of such a glacier surge is being studied. Some surge events result from a buildup of water pressure under the glacier, sometimes enough to actually float the glacier slightly, detaching it from its bed, during the surge. As a surge begins, icequakes are detectable, and ice faults are visible. Surges can occur in dry conditions as well, as the glacier plucks (picks up) rock from its bed and moves forward. Another cause of glacier surges is the presence of a water-saturated layer of sediment, a so-called *soft bed*, beneath the glacier. This is a deformable layer that cannot resist the tremendous sheer stress produced by the moving ice of the glacier. Scientists examining cores taken from several ice streams now accelerating through the West Antarctic Ice Sheet think they have identified this cause—although water pressure is still important.

1. With which of the following topics is the passage primarily concerned?
   Ⓐ Glacial surges
   Ⓑ Crevasses
   Ⓒ Ice regelation
   Ⓓ Movement of glaciers

2. In which part of the glacier is the most debris concentrated?
   Ⓐ The basal ice layer in the glacier
   Ⓑ The crevasses that develop in the glacier
   Ⓒ The brittle surface ice of the glacier
   Ⓓ The soft bed beneath the glacier

3. The word brittle in the passage is closest in meaning to
   Ⓐ common
   Ⓑ fragile
   Ⓒ soft
   Ⓓ shiny

4. The word abrupt in the passage is closest in meaning to
   Ⓐ unexpected
   Ⓑ lengthy
   Ⓒ destructive
   Ⓓ simple

5. The word its in the passage refers to
   Ⓐ properties
   Ⓑ glacial ice
   Ⓒ cubes
   Ⓓ minerals

6. According to paragraph 8, why do glacial surges usually occur?
   Ⓐ Heavy snow pushes the glacier forward.
   Ⓑ Water pressure under the glacier causes the ice to float.
   Ⓒ Dry rock and dirt that is packed under the glacier moves.
   Ⓓ Earthquakes under the ice sheet pick up the glacier.

7. Which of the sentences below best expresses the information in the highlighted statement in the passage? The other choices change the meaning or leave out important information.
   A) Glaciers in different locations have distinct properties.
   B) The properties of ice vary according to its location in the glacier.
   C) The ice in glaciers has different properties from other types of ice.
   D) The factor that determines the properties of glaciers is the ice.

8. The author mentions all of the following characteristics of glaciers EXCEPT
   A) glaciers are a major source of fresh water
   B) glacial ice has all the properties of a mineral
   C) ice flows below the surface of a glacier
   D) a crust of snow often forms on top of the glacier

9. It can be inferred from this passage that
   A) glaciers normally move very slowly
   B) ice regelation does not affect glacial movement
   C) all glacial surges are caused by icequakes
   D) Alaska has more glaciers than Greenland

10. Four squares (□) indicate where the following sentence can be added to the passage.

   In other words, the heavier the snowfall, the faster the glacier moves.

   Where would the sentence best fit into the passage?
   [A]
   [B]
   [C]
   [D]

11. Complete the table below by identifying each of the answer choices as a characteristic of *basal slip*, *regelation*, or *glacier surge*. Three of the answer choices will not be used.
   A) Basal ice refreezes, thereby incorporating debris into the glacier.
   B) The debris in a glacier is deposited in front of the melting ice.
   C) A glacier may become detached from the bed, floating slightly.
   D) The color of the ice changes somewhat as the glacier moves.
   E) The lower part of the glacier moves more slowly than the upper part.
   F) Stretching or compressing can cause vertical cracks in the ice.
   G) A difference in the speed of the top layer and the interior ice stretches the surface ice.
   H) Compression may temporarily melt the basal ice.
   I) As the process begins, icequakes are often detected.

Basal slip	Regelation	Glacier surge
•	•	•
•	•	•

12. Complete a summary of the passage by selecting THREE answer choices that express the most important ideas. The other three sentences do not belong in the summary because they express ideas that are not in the passage or they do not refer to the major ideas. *This question is worth 2 points*.

How do glaciers move?

Ⓐ A glacial surge can occur unpredictably, moving the ice sheet more abruptly than usual.

Ⓑ A thin layer of snow can sometimes hide the presence of a potentially dangerous crevasse.

Ⓒ Below the surface of a glacier, the ice flows, thereby moving the glacier forward.

Ⓓ Hubbard Glacier in Alaska experienced a sudden and very rapid surge in 1986.

Ⓔ Snow accumulation, temperature, water, or sediment beneath the ice can affect the rate of the movement.

Ⓕ The movement of a glacier is usually so slow that it must be studied over a long period of time.

Refer to pages 434–435 for the Explanatory Answers.

EXERCISE 62: Definition/Illustration—Humanities/Business

In some questions in the Reading Section on the Paper-Based TOEFL, you will be asked to recall and relate information and content from definition or illustration passages about various fields of study. Choose the best answer for multiple-choice questions.

The Canadian Government

Canada is a democracy organized as a constitutional monarchy with a parliamentary system of government modeled after that of Great Britain. The official head of state in Canada is Queen Elizabeth
Line II of Britain, who is also Queen of Canada. The governor-general is
5   the queen's personal representative in Canada and the official head of the Canadian parliament, although with very limited powers.

The federal parliament in Canada consists of the House of Commons and the Senate. The actual head of government is the prime minister, who is responsible for choosing a cabinet. The
10   cabinet consists of a group of ministers of varied expertise who serve with the support of the House of Commons. They are responsible for most legislation, and have the sole power to prepare and introduce bills that provide for the expenditure of public funds or taxation. The system is referred to as responsible government, which means that
15   cabinet members sit in the parliament and are directly responsible to it, holding power only as long as a majority of the House of Commons shows confidence by voting with them. If a cabinet is defeated in the House of Commons on a motion of censure or a vote of no confidence, the cabinet must either resign, in which case the
20   governor-general will ask the leader of the opposition to form a new cabinet, or a new election may be called.

The Canadian Senate has 104 members, appointed by the governor-general on the advice of the prime minister. Their actual function is advisory, although they may make minor changes in bills and no bill
25   may become a law without being passed by the Senate. Senators hold office until age seventy-five unless they are absent from two consecutive sessions of parliament. The real power, however, resides in the House of Commons, the members of which are elected directly by the voters. The seats are allocated on the basis of population, and there
30   are about 300 constituencies. By custom, almost all members of the cabinet must be members of the House of Commons or, if not already members, must win seats within a reasonable time.

General elections must be held at the end of every five years, but they may be conducted whenever issues require it, and most
35   parliaments are dissolved before the end of the five-year term. When a government loses its majority support in a general election, a change of government occurs.

Although major and minor political parties were not created by law, they are recognized by law in Canada. The party that wins the
40   largest number of seats in a general election forms the government, and its leader becomes the prime minister. The second largest party becomes the official opposition, and its leader is recognized as the leader of the opposition. In this way, the people are assured of an effective alternative government should they become displeased with
45   the one in power.

1. What does this passage mainly discuss?
   Ⓐ Political parties in Canada
   Ⓑ The Canadian election process
   Ⓒ The Canadian system of government
   Ⓓ The powers of parliament in Canada

2. When does a change of government occur in Canada?
   Ⓐ When the governor-general decides to appoint a new government
   Ⓑ When the voters do not return majority support for the government in a general election
   Ⓒ When the prime minister advises the governor-general to appoint a new government
   Ⓓ When the House of Commons votes for a new government

3. The word "dissolved" in line 35 could best be replaced by
   Ⓐ approved
   Ⓑ evaluated
   Ⓒ reorganized
   Ⓓ dismissed

4. The word "varied" in line 10 is closest in meaning to
   Ⓐ little
   Ⓑ different
   Ⓒ good
   Ⓓ steady

5. The word "it" in line 16 refers to
   Ⓐ majority
   Ⓑ parliament
   Ⓒ cabinet
   Ⓓ system

6. Where in the passage does the author indicate whose responsibility it is to choose the cabinet in Canada?
   Ⓐ Lines 4–6
   Ⓑ Lines 8–9
   Ⓒ Lines 11–13
   Ⓓ Lines 27–29

7. What does the author mean by the statement in lines 1–3: "Canada is a constitutional monarchy with a . . . parliamentary system of government modeled after that of Great Britain"?
   Ⓐ Whereas Canada has a constitutional form of government, Great Britain has a parliamentary system.
   Ⓑ Canada and Great Britain both have model systems of government.
   Ⓒ Great Britain and Canada have very similar systems of government.
   Ⓓ Canada's parliament has adopted Great Britain's constitution.

8. What is the role of political parties in Canada?
   Ⓐ Until they become powerful, they are not legally recognized.
   Ⓑ Although they serve unofficial functions, they are not very important.
   Ⓒ If they win a majority of seats, their leader becomes prime minister.
   Ⓓ Because they are not elected, they offer the government opposing views.

9. The governor-general is described as all of the following EXCEPT
   Ⓐ the official head of parliament
   Ⓑ the head of government
   Ⓒ the queen's representative in Canada
   Ⓓ the official who appoints the Senate

10. It can be inferred from the passage that the voters in Canada
   Ⓐ choose the prime minister and the cabinet
   Ⓑ do not usually vote in general elections
   Ⓒ allow their representatives to vote on their behalf
   Ⓓ determine when a change of government should occur

Refer to pages 435–436 for the Explanatory Answers.

EXERCISE 63: Definition/Illustration—Natural Sciences

In some questions in the Reading Section on the Paper-Based TOEFL, you will be asked to recall and relate information and content from definition or illustration passages about various fields of study. Choose the best answer for multiple-choice questions.

Hydrogen

Hydrogen is the most common element in the universe and was perhaps the first to form. It is among the ten most common elements on Earth as well and one of the most useful for industrial purposes.
Line   Under normal conditions of temperature, hydrogen is a gas.
5   Designated as H, hydrogen is the first element in the periodic table because it contains only one proton. Hydrogen can combine with a large number of other elements, forming more compounds than any of the others. Pure hydrogen seldom occurs naturally, but it exists in most organic compounds, that is, compounds that contain carbon,
10   which account for a very large number of compounds. Moreover, hydrogen is found in inorganic compounds. For example, when hydrogen burns in the presence of oxygen, it forms water.

The lightest and simplest of the elements, hydrogen has several properties that make it valuable for many industries. It releases more
15   heat per unit of weight than any other fuel. In rocket engines, tons of hydrogen and oxygen are burned, and hydrogen is used with oxygen for welding torches that produce temperatures as high as 4,000 degrees F and can be used in cutting steel. Fuel cells to generate electricity operate on hydrogen and oxygen.
20   Hydrogen also serves to prevent metals from tarnishing during heat treatments by removing the oxygen from them. Although it would be difficult to remove the oxygen by itself, hydrogen readily combines with oxygen to form water, which can be heated to steam and easily removed. Furthermore, hydrogen is one of the coolest
25   refrigerants. It does not become a liquid until it reaches temperatures of –425 degrees F. Pure hydrogen gas is used in large electric generators to cool the coils.

Future uses of hydrogen include fuel for cars, boats, planes, and other forms of transportation that currently require petroleum
30   products. These fuels would be lighter, a distinct advantage in the aerospace industry, and they would also be cleaner, thereby reducing pollution in the atmosphere.

Hydrogen is also useful in the food industry for a process known as hydrogenation. Products such as margarine and cooking oils are
35   changed from liquids to semisolids by combining hydrogen with their molecules. Soap manufacturers also use hydrogen for this purpose.

In addition, in the chemical industry, hydrogen is used to produce ammonia, gasoline, methyl alcohol, and many other important products.

1. What is the author's main purpose in the passage?
   Ⓐ To explain the industrial uses of hydrogen
   Ⓑ To describe the origin of hydrogen in the universe
   Ⓒ To discuss the process of hydrogenation
   Ⓓ To give examples of how hydrogen and oxygen combine

2. How can hydrogen be used to cut steel?
   Ⓐ By cooling the steel to a very low temperature
   Ⓑ By cooling the hydrogen with oxygen to a very low temperature
   Ⓒ By heating the steel to a very high temperature
   Ⓓ By heating the hydrogen with oxygen to a very high temperature

3. The word "readily" in line 22 could best be replaced by
   Ⓐ completely
   Ⓑ slowly
   Ⓒ usually
   Ⓓ easily

4. The word "combining" in line 35 is closest in meaning to
   Ⓐ trying
   Ⓑ changing
   Ⓒ finding
   Ⓓ adding

5. The word "them" in line 21 refers to
   Ⓐ fuel cells
   Ⓑ metals
   Ⓒ treatments
   Ⓓ products

6. Where in the passage does the author explain why hydrogen is used as a refrigerant?
   Ⓐ Lines 8–10
   Ⓑ Lines 15–18
   Ⓒ Lines 20–21
   Ⓓ Lines 24–26

7. What does the author mean by the statement in lines 21–24: "Although it would be difficult to remove the oxygen by itself, hydrogen readily combines with oxygen to form water, which can be heated to steam and easily removed"?
   Ⓐ It is easy to form steam by heating water.
   Ⓑ Water can be made by combining hydrogen and oxygen.
   Ⓒ Hydrogen cannot be separated from oxygen because it is too difficult.
   Ⓓ Oxygen is removed by combining it with hydrogen and heating it.

8. How does hydrogen generally occur?
   Ⓐ It is freely available in nature.
   Ⓑ It is contained in many compounds.
   Ⓒ It is often found in pure form.
   Ⓓ It is released during hydrogenation.

9. The author mentions all of the following as uses for hydrogen EXCEPT
   Ⓐ to remove tarnish from metals
   Ⓑ to produce fuels such as gasoline and methyl alcohol
   Ⓒ to operate fuel cells that generate electricity
   Ⓓ to change solid foods to liquids

10. It can be inferred from the passage that hydrogen
    Ⓐ is too dangerous to be used for industrial purposes
    Ⓑ has many purposes in a variety of industries
    Ⓒ has limited industrial uses because of its dangerous properties
    Ⓓ is used in many industries for basically the same purpose

Refer to page 436 for the Explanatory Answers.

EXERCISE 64: Definition/Illustration—Social Sciences

In some questions in the Reading Section on the Internet-Based TOEFL, you will be asked to recall and relate information and content from definition or illustration passages found in college textbooks. Choose the best answer for multiple-choice questions. For computer-assisted questions, follow the directions on the screen.

The McDonaldization of Society

Sometimes the problems and peculiarities of bureaucracy can have effects on the total society. Such has been the case with what George Ritzer (1996) has called the *McDonaldization of society*, a term coined from the well-known fast-food chain. Ritzer noticed that the principles that characterize fast-food organizations are increasingly coming to dominate more and more aspects of U.S. society, indeed, of societies around the world. "McDonaldization" refers to the increasing and ubiquitous presence of the fast-food model in most of the organizations that shape daily life: work, travel, leisure, shopping, health care, education, and politics have all become subject to McDonaldization. Each of these industries is based on a principle of high and efficient productivity, based on a highly rational social organization, with workers employed at low pay, but customers experiencing ease, convenience, and familiarity.

Ritzer argues that McDonald's has been such a successful model of business organization that other industries have adopted the same organizational characteristics, so much so that their nicknames associate them with the McDonald's chain: McPaper for *USA Today*, McChild for child-care chains like Kinder-Care, McDoctor for the drive-in clinics that deal quickly and efficiently with minor health and dental problems.

Ritzer identifies four dimensions of the McDonaldization process: efficiency, calculability, predictability, and control.
1. **Efficiency** means that things move from start to completion in a streamlined path. Steps in the production of a hamburger are regulated so that each hamburger is made exactly the same way— hardly characteristic of a home-cooked meal. Business can be even more efficient if the customer does the work once done by an employee. In fast-food restaurants, the claim that you can "have it your way" really means that you assemble your own sandwich or salad.

2. **Calculability** means that there is an emphasis on the quantitative aspects of products sold—size, cost, and the time it takes to get the product. At McDonald's, branch managers must account for the number of cubic inches of ketchup used per day; likewise, ice cream scoopers in chain stores measure out predetermined and exact amounts of ice cream, unless machines do it for them. Workers are carefully supervised to record how long it takes them to complete a transaction; every bit of food and drink is closely monitored by computer, and everything has to be accounted for.

3. Predictability is the assurance that products will be exactly the same, no matter when or where they are purchased. Eat an Egg McMuffin in New York, and it will taste just the same as an Egg McMuffin in Los Angeles or Paris!

4. Control is the primary organizational principle that lies behind McDonaldization. People's behavior, both customers and workers alike, is reduced to a series of machinelike actions. Ultimately, efficient technologies replace much of the work that humans once did. At one national credit card chain, managers routinely listen in on telephone calls being handled by service workers; in other settings, computers might monitor the speed with which workers handle a particular function. Sensors on drink machines can actually cut off the liquid flow to ensure that each drink is exactly the same size.

McDonaldization clearly brings many benefits. There is a greater availability of goods and services to a wide proportion of the population, instantaneous service and convenience to a public with less free time, predictability and familiarity in the goods bought and sold, and standardization of pricing and uniform quality of goods sold, to name a few. However, this increasingly rational system of goods and services also spawns irrationalities. Ritzer argues that, as we become more dependent on the familiar and taken for granted, there is the danger of dehumanization. People lose their creativity, and there is little concern with the quality of goods and services, thereby disrupting something fundamentally human—the capacity for error, surprise, and imagination. Even with increasing globalization and the opportunities it provides to expose ourselves to diverse ways of life, McDonaldization has come to characterize other societies, too. The tourist can travel to the other side of the world and taste the familiar Chicken McNuggets or a Dunkin' Donut!

The McDonaldization of Society (Question References)

Paragraph 1   Sometimes the problems and peculiarities of bureaucracy can have effects on the total society. Such has been the case with what George Ritzer (1996) has called the *McDonaldization of society*, a term coined from the well-known fast-food chain. Ritzer noticed that the principles that characterize fast-food organizations are increasingly coming to dominate more and more aspects of U.S. society, indeed, of societies around the world. "McDonaldization" refers to the increasing and ubiquitous presence of the fast-food model in most of the organizations that shape daily life: work, travel, leisure, shopping, health care, education, and politics have all become subject to McDonaldization. Each of these industries is based on a principle of high and efficient productivity, based on a highly rational social organization, with workers employed at low pay, but customers experiencing ease, convenience, and familiarity.

2   Ritzer argues that McDonald's has been such a successful model of business organization that other industries have adopted the same organizational characteristics, so much so that their nicknames associate them with the McDonald's chain: McPaper for *USA Today*, McChild for child-care chains like Kinder-Care, McDoctor for the drive-in clinics that deal quickly and efficiently with minor health and dental problems.

3   Ritzer identifies four dimensions of the McDonaldization process: efficiency, calculability, predictability, and control.
1. Efficiency means that things move from start to completion in a streamlined path. Steps in the production of a hamburger are regulated so that each hamburger is made exactly the same way— hardly characteristic of a home-cooked meal. Business can be even more efficient if the customer does the work once done by an employee. In fast-food restaurants, the claim that you can "have it your way" really means that you assemble your own sandwich or salad.

4   **2. Calculability** means that there is an emphasis on the quantitative aspects of products sold—size, cost, and the time it takes to get the product. At McDonald's, branch managers must account for the number of cubic inches of ketchup used per day; likewise, ice cream scoopers in chain stores measure out predetermined and exact amounts of ice cream, unless machines do it for them. Workers are carefully supervised to record how long it takes them to complete a transaction; every bit of food and drink is closely monitored by computer, and everything has to be accounted for. [A]

5   **3.** [B]**Predictability** is the assurance that products will be exactly the same, no matter when or where they are purchased. Eat an Egg McMuffin in New York, and it will taste just the same as an Egg McMuffin in Los Angeles or Paris! [C]

6   **4. Control** is the primary organizational principle that lies behind McDonaldization. [D] People's behavior, both customers and workers alike, is reduced to a series of machinelike actions. Ultimately, efficient technologies replace much of the work that humans once did. At one national credit card chain, managers routinely listen in on telephone calls being handled by service workers; in other settings, computers might monitor the speed with which workers handle a particular function. Sensors on drink machines can actually cut off the liquid flow to ensure that each drink is exactly the same size.

7   McDonaldization clearly brings many benefits. There is a greater availability of goods and services to a wide proportion of the population, instantaneous service and convenience to a public with less free time, predictability and familiarity in the goods bought and sold, and standardization of pricing and uniform quality of goods sold, to name a few. However, this increasingly rational system of goods and services also spawns irrationalities. Ritzer argues that, as we become more dependent on the familiar and taken for granted, there is the danger of dehumanization. People lose their creativity, and there is little concern with the quality of goods and services, thereby disrupting something fundamentally human—the capacity for error, surprise, and imagination. Even with increasing globalization and the opportunities it provides to expose ourselves to diverse ways of life, McDonaldization has come to characterize other societies, too. The tourist can travel to the other side of the world and taste the familiar Chicken McNuggets or a Dunkin' Donut!

1. Which of the following best expresses the main idea of the passage?
   - Ⓐ McDonald's has developed a very efficient business plan for global chains.
   - Ⓑ The McDonald's organization is being copied in many aspects of society.
   - Ⓒ George Ritzer has outlined the benefits of the McDonald's process.
   - Ⓓ Many societies around the world now have McDonald's as well as local restaurants.

2. What is *calculability*?
   - Ⓐ Efficient steps in the production of goods
   - Ⓑ Similarity of all products at diverse locations
   - Ⓒ Replacement of people by new technologies
   - Ⓓ Precise inventories of and use of supplies

3. The phrase subject to in the passage is closest in meaning to
   - Ⓐ influenced by
   - Ⓑ studied by
   - Ⓒ eliminated by
   - Ⓓ purchased by

4. The word capacity in the passage is closest in meaning to
   - Ⓐ patience
   - Ⓑ potential
   - Ⓒ pleasure
   - Ⓓ pattern

5. The word them in the passage refers to
   Ⓐ characteristics
   Ⓑ nicknames
   Ⓒ industries
   Ⓓ chains

6. According to the passage, which is the most important dimension of McDonaldization?
   Ⓐ Control
   Ⓑ Efficiency
   Ⓒ Calculability
   Ⓓ Predictability

7. Which of the sentences below best expresses the information in the highlighted statement in the passage? The other choices change the meaning or leave out important information.
   Ⓐ Employees get the work done efficiently for customers.
   Ⓑ Customers work with employees in an efficient business.
   Ⓒ Customers are responsible for work that employees used to do.
   Ⓓ Employees do the work once for customers in an efficient business.

8. The author mentions all of the following as benefits of McDonaldization EXCEPT
   Ⓐ wider access to goods and services
   Ⓑ more exposure to diverse products
   Ⓒ greater convenience for the consumer
   Ⓓ highly standardized prices for products

9. It can be inferred from this passage that Ritzer
   Ⓐ does not support the McDonaldization of world societies
   Ⓑ does not understand the term McDonaldization as it is used here
   Ⓒ has developed organizational principles for the McDonald's chain
   Ⓓ has consulted with international companies to help them use McDonald's plan

10. Four squares (☐) indicate where the following sentence can be added to the passage.

    It is virtually impossible to tell the difference.

    Where would the sentence best fit into the passage?
    Ⓐ
    Ⓑ
    Ⓒ
    Ⓓ

11. Complete the table below by matching each of the answer choices with one of the four dimensions of the McDonaldization process. One of the answer choices will not be used.
    Ⓐ Machines measure exact quantities of each ingredient.
    Ⓑ Customer service calls are monitored by supervisors.
    Ⓒ Prices are determined by the value of the local currency.
    Ⓓ All of the supplies must be carefully inventoried.
    Ⓔ Every sandwich is the same in every McDonald's.
    Ⓕ Customers prepare their own salads at the salad bar.

Efficiency	•
Calculability	•
	•
Predictability	•
Control	•

12. Complete a summary of the passage by selecting THREE answer choices that express the most important ideas. The other three sentences do not belong in the summary because they express ideas that are not in the passage or they do not refer to the major ideas. *This question is worth 2 points*.

Bureaucracy can have widespread effects.

Ⓐ Tourists who travel to Paris or Los Angeles can eat at the same chain restaurants and order the same food.

Ⓑ The principles developed for the fast-food industry are being used in many aspects of society.

Ⓒ McDonald's model includes efficient production, accountability, uniform products, and control.

Ⓓ McPaper is used as a nickname for the nation's newspaper, *USA Today*.

Ⓔ Ritzer has called the process described in the passage "McDonaldization."

Ⓕ The purpose of the McDonald's business model was to dominate many other organizations in society.

Refer to pages 436–437 for the Explanatory Answers.

EXERCISE 65: Definition/Illustration—Arts/Architecture

In some questions in the Reading Section on the Internet-Based TOEFL, you will be asked to recall and relate information and content from definition or illustration passages found in college textbooks. Choose the best answer for multiple-choice questions. For computer-assisted questions, follow the directions on the screen.

The Audible Frequency Spectrum

Every musical culture of the world uses only a certain number of frequencies from the audible spectrum. Few cultures use the same selection of pitches, and few approach the entire gamut of frequencies.

Most cultures, however, make use of the *octave*. An octave is an acoustic and scientific relationship between two pitches, one of which vibrates twice as fast as the other and thus sounds higher. But the higher pitch also sounds the "same" as the lower pitch; in fact, it duplicates the lower pitch but in a higher *register*, which can be defined as a specific segment of the audible frequency spectrum.

If a string produces C when it's plucked, it will sound C an octave higher if it's divided in half. If either half is divided again in half, yet another C, an octave higher, is sounded. This phenomenon can also be used to demonstrate how octaves and frequency coordinate. If the original string vibrates at 16 Hz, each half vibrates at 32 Hz, and each of their halves vibrates at 64 Hz, and so on. If the entire audible frequency spectrum is similarly divided, there are ten octaves.

How do we get the term *octave*? This term has to do with how European-based music divides the octave into constituent pitches. Although most cultures of the world recognize the octave (calling it by different names) and use it in their music, the similarity often ends there. How the octave is divided is unique to each culture. Remember that this eight-part structure is unique to Western music. Other musical cultures do not necessarily divide pitches within an octave the way we do. Not surprisingly, each culture labels pitches differently. We name ours with seven letters—A, B, C, D, E, F, and G.

In European-based music, the octave represents an eight-pitch structure, but if you count the number of white *and* black piano keys in an octave, you will count thirteen. These thirteen keys represent the smallest divisions of the octave in the Western tradition. These divisions, called *half steps*, occur between two adjacent keys: from a white key to a black key and vice versa or, where there is no intervening black key, from a white key to a white key. There are *twelve* half steps in an octave.

Dividing the octave into more than twelve half steps results in smaller distances between pitches than are found in Western music. Some cultures, such as that of Bali (Indonesia), use fewer pitches with wider distance between them; others use more pitches—twenty-two in Indian music, twenty-four in Arabic music.

When two half steps are added together, they equal a whole step, represented on the piano by two keys separated by an intervening key. Whole steps occur between two white keys, two black keys, and in some cases, a black key and a white key. Half steps and whole steps are examples of what are called *intervals*—specifiable distances between two pitches.

Because our tuning system uses only seven letter names but divides the octave into twelve tones (the thirteenth is an octave of the first tone), pitch names are modified for tones between those identified by letter name only. To refer to a pitch one half step higher than a particular pitch, we use the designation *sharp* (#). Thus, the black key to the right of C is C#. To refer to a pitch one half step lower, we use the designation *flat* (♭). Thus, the black key to the left of D is D♭.

We have just given two names to the same key. We say that C sharp and D flat are *enharmonic* because they sound the same but have different names. But all pitches, not just those of the black keys, have at least two enharmonic designations. This is because "sharp" and "flat" can apply to any pitch. Thus, C is enharmonic to B sharp, because "sharp" simply means a pitch is raised a half step. Similarly, E is enharmonic to F flat. Remember that a sharp or flat is not necessarily a black key.

The terms we have learned—pitch, octave, interval, half step, whole step, enharmonic, and related terms—are basic to any discussion of melody. They refer to the constituent parts of melody and are therefore fundamental to understanding its qualities, which we will discuss next.

The Audible Frequency Spectrum (Question References)

Paragraph 1   Every musical culture of the world uses only a certain number of frequencies from the audible spectrum. Few cultures use the same selection of pitches, and few approach the entire gamut of frequencies.

2   Most cultures, however, make use of the *octave*. An octave is an acoustic and scientific relationship between two pitches, one of which vibrates twice as fast as the other and thus sounds higher. But the higher pitch also sounds the "same" as the lower pitch; in fact, it duplicates the lower pitch but in a higher *register*, which can be defined as a specific segment of the audible frequency spectrum.

3   ⬛A If a string produces C when it's plucked, it will sound C an octave higher if it's divided in half. If either half is divided again in half, yet another C, an octave higher, is sounded.⬛B This phenomenon can also be used to demonstrate how octaves and frequency coordinate. If the original string vibrates at 16 Hz, each half vibrates at 32 Hz, and each of their halves vibrates at 64 Hz, and so on. If the entire audible frequency spectrum is similarly divided, there are ten octaves.⬛C

4   How do we get the term *octave*? This term has to do with how European-based music divides the octave into constituent pitches.⬛D Although most cultures of the world recognize the octave (calling it by different names) and use it in their music, the similarity often ends there. How the octave is divided is unique to each culture. Remember that this eight-part structure is unique to Western music. Other musical cultures do not necessarily divide pitches within an octave the way we do. Not surprisingly, each culture labels pitches differently. We name ours with seven letters—A, B, C, D, E, F, and G.

5   In European-based music, the octave represents an eight-pitch structure, but if you count the number of white *and* black piano keys in an octave, you will count thirteen. These thirteen keys represent the smallest divisions of the octave in the Western tradition. These divisions, called *half steps*, occur between two adjacent keys: from a white key to a black key and vice versa or, where there is no intervening black key, from a white key to a white key. There are *twelve* half steps in an octave.

6   Dividing the octave into more than twelve half steps results in smaller distances between pitches than are found in Western music. Some cultures, such as that of Bali (Indonesia), use fewer pitches with wider distance between them; others use more pitches—twenty-two in Indian music, twenty-four in Arabic music.

7   When two half steps are added together, they equal a whole step, represented on the piano by two keys separated by an intervening key. Whole steps occur between two white keys, two black keys, and in some cases, a black key and a white key. Half steps and whole steps are examples of what are called *intervals*—specifiable distances between two pitches.

8   Because our tuning system uses only seven letter names but divides the octave into twelve tones (the thirteenth is an octave of the first tone), pitch names are modified for tones between those identified by letter name only. To refer to a pitch one half step higher

than a particular pitch, we use the designation *sharp* (#). Thus, the black key to the right of C is C#. To refer to a pitch one half step lower, we use the designation *flat* (♭). Thus, the black key to the left of D is D ♭.

9   We have just given two names to the same key. We say that C sharp and D flat are *enharmonic* because they sound the same but have different names. But all pitches, not just those of the black keys, have at least two enharmonic designations. This is because "sharp" and "flat" can apply to any pitch. Thus, C is enharmonic to B sharp, because "sharp" simply means a pitch is raised a half step. Similarly, E is enharmonic to F flat. Remember that a sharp or flat is not necessarily a black key.

10   The terms we have learned—pitch, octave, interval, half step, whole step, enharmonic, and related terms—are basic to any discussion of melody. They refer to the constituent parts of melody and are therefore fundamental to understanding its qualities, which we will discuss next.

1. With which of the following topics is the passage primarily concerned?
    - Ⓐ A comparison of music education across cultures
    - Ⓑ A definition of the audible spectrum
    - Ⓒ A discussion of the octave in Western music
    - Ⓓ The qualities of melody in music

2. How many pitches are in an octave in Western music?
    - Ⓐ Seven
    - Ⓑ Eight
    - Ⓒ Twelve
    - Ⓓ Thirteen

3. The word particular in the passage is closest in meaning to
    - Ⓐ previous
    - Ⓑ specific
    - Ⓒ changed
    - Ⓓ neutral

4. The word adjacent in the passage is closest in meaning to
    - Ⓐ beside each other
    - Ⓑ like each other
    - Ⓒ without each other
    - Ⓓ despite each other

5. The word that in the passage refers to
   Ⓐ half steps
   Ⓑ smaller distances
   Ⓒ fewer pitches
   Ⓓ some cultures

6. According to paragraph 7, the term *intervals* means
   Ⓐ the distance between two pitches
   Ⓑ a specific segment of the frequency system
   Ⓒ a vibration twice as fast as another
   Ⓓ the same sound with a different name

7. Which of the sentences below best expresses the information in the highlighted statement in the passage? The other choices change the meaning or leave out important information.
   Ⓐ Two or more enharmonic designations are assigned to every pitch.
   Ⓑ Only black keys have more than one enharmonic designation.
   Ⓒ Some keys have less than two enharmonic designations.
   Ⓓ The pitches are designated by the enharmonic keys.

8. The author mentions all of the following characteristics of the European octave EXCEPT
   Ⓐ seven letters
   Ⓑ twelve half steps
   Ⓒ thirteen keys
   Ⓓ ten frequencies

9. It can be inferred that the author will continue this discussion by
   Ⓐ reviewing the previously defined terms
   Ⓑ listing the constituent parts of melody
   Ⓒ explaining the qualities of melody
   Ⓓ comparing melodies of various cultures

10. Four squares (□) indicate where the following sentence can be added to the passage.

    Thus, in the European tradition, all the keys marked C are octaves or multiples of octaves.

    Where would the sentence best fit into the passage?
    Ⓐ ,
    Ⓑ
    Ⓒ
    Ⓓ

11. Complete the table below by classifying each of the answer choices as characteristic of Western music or the non-Western music of other cultures. Two of the answer choices will not be used because they were not mentioned in the passage.
    Ⓐ There are eight pitches in each octave.
    Ⓑ Twenty-four pitches are customary.
    Ⓒ Letter names for the pitches begin with A.
    Ⓓ Four to six tones make up the scale.
    Ⓔ More than twelve half steps are typical.
    Ⓕ The octave is divided into five intervals.
    Ⓖ Thirteen piano keys represent the octave.

Western Music	Non-Western Music
•	•
•	•
•	

12. Complete a summary of the passage by selecting THREE answer choices that express the most important ideas. The other three sentences do not belong in the summary because they express ideas that are not in the passage or they do not refer to the major ideas. *This question is worth 2 points.*

The audible frequency spectrum offers a large selection of pitches.

Ⓐ C is enharmonic to a B sharp because "sharp" means the pitch is raised a half step.

Ⓑ In European music, there are eight pitches and thirteen keys to represent the octave.

Ⓒ The first seven letters in the alphabet are used to label pitches in Western music.

Ⓓ Almost every culture relies on the concept of the octave, although it may be called by a different name.

Ⓔ The octave can be divided into more or fewer pitches depending on the distance between them.

Ⓕ The progression of a melody is more important in non-Western music than harmony.

Refer to pages 437–438 for the Explanatory Answers.

EXERCISE 66: Classification—Humanities/Business

In some questions in the Reading Section on the Paper-Based TOEFL, you will be asked to recall and relate information and content from classification passages about various fields of study. Choose the best answer for multiple-choice questions.

Competition

Rivalry among businesses and service industries is called competition. This feature of a market economy encourages businesses to improve their goods and services, keep their prices
Line affordable, and offer new products to attract more buyers.
5   There are four basic types of competition in business that form a continuum from *pure competition* through *monopolistic competition* and *oligopoly* to *monopoly*. (See diagram). At one end of the continuum, pure competition results when every company has a similar product. Companies that deal in commodities such as
10 wheat or corn are often involved in pure competition. In *pure competition*, it is often the ease and efficiency of distribution that influences purchase.

    In contrast, in *monopolistic competition*, several companies may compete for the sale of items that may be substituted. The classic
15 example of monopolistic competition is coffee and tea. If the price of one is perceived as too high, consumers may begin to purchase the other. Coupons and other discounts are often used as part of a marketing strategy to influence sales.

    Oligopoly occurs when a few companies dominate the sales of a
20 product or service. For example, only five airline carriers control more than 70 percent of all ticket sales in the United States. In oligopoly, serious competition is not considered desirable because it would result in reduced revenue for every company in the group. Although price wars do occur, in which all companies offer
25 substantial savings to customers, a somewhat similar tendency to raise prices simultaneously is also usual.

    Finally, *monopoly* occurs when only one firm sells the product. Some monopolies have been tolerated for producers of goods and services that have been considered basic or essential, including
30 electricity and water. In these cases, it is government control, rather than competition, that protects and influences sales. The following chart represents the competition continuum.

Most	Competition	Least
Pure——————Monopolistic—Oligopoly—Monopoly		
competition competition		

1. Which of the following would be a better title for the passage?
   Ⓐ Monopolies
   Ⓑ The Commodity Market
   Ⓒ The Competition Continuum
   Ⓓ The Best Type of Competition

2. An example of a product in monopolistic competition is
   Ⓐ corn
   Ⓑ electricity
   Ⓒ airline tickets
   Ⓓ coffee

3. The word "tolerated" in line 28 could best be replaced by
   Ⓐ permitted
   Ⓑ reserved
   Ⓒ criticized
   Ⓓ devised

4. The word "dominate" in line 19 is closest in meaning to
   Ⓐ evaluate
   Ⓑ control
   Ⓒ modify
   Ⓓ oppose

5. The word "it" in line 22 refers to
   Ⓐ competition
   Ⓑ group
   Ⓒ company
   Ⓓ revenue

6. Where in the passage does the author explain pure competition?
   Ⓐ Lines 7–12
   Ⓑ Lines 13–15
   Ⓒ Lines 19–21
   Ⓓ Lines 27–30

7. What does the author mean by the statement in lines 24–26: "Although price wars do occur, in which all companies offer substantial savings to customers, a somewhat similar tendency to raise prices simultaneously is also usual"?
   Ⓐ It is not unusual for all companies to increase prices at the same time.
   Ⓑ It is common for companies to compete for customers by lowering prices.
   Ⓒ Customers may lose money when companies have price wars.
   Ⓓ Prices are lower during price wars, but they are usually higher afterward.

8. Which type of competition is subject to the greatest government control?
   Ⓐ Monopolies
   Ⓑ Oligopolies
   Ⓒ Monopolistic competition
   Ⓓ Pure competition

9. The author mentions all of the following as characteristic of monopoly EXCEPT
   Ⓐ the use of coupons or other discounts
   Ⓑ government control
   Ⓒ basic or essential services
   Ⓓ only one firm

10. It can be inferred that this passage was first printed in
    Ⓐ a business textbook
    Ⓑ a government document
    Ⓒ an airline brochure
    Ⓓ a newspaper

Refer to page 438 for the Explanatory Answers.

EXERCISE 67: Classification—Social Sciences

In some questions in the Reading Section on the Paper-Based TOEFL, you will be asked to recall and relate information and content from classification passages about various fields of study. Choose the best answer for multiple-choice questions.

Sleep Cycles

Whether one is awake or asleep, the brain emits electrical waves. These waves occur in predictable sleep cycles that can be measured with an electroencephalograph, known more commonly as an EEG.

Line
5
During wakefulness, the waves are recorded at about ten small waves per second, but with the onset of sleep, the waves become larger and slower. The largest, slowest waves occur during the first three hours of sleep when mental activity slows down but does not stop. In fact, if awakened from slow-wave sleep, a person can often remember vague thoughts that occurred during that period of sleep, but the

10
sleeper does not generally dream. Referred to as NREM or non-REM sleep, it is characterized by large, slow waves.

During sleep, intervals of small, fast waves also occur in patterns similar to those experienced while awake. The eyes move rapidly, and it appears to the observer that the sleeper is watching some

15
event. Sleepers who are awakened during this rapid-eye-movement sleep will often recall the details of dreams they have been having. Sleep of this kind is called dreaming sleep or rapid-eye-movement sleep, also known as REM sleep. REM sleep is emotionally charged. The heart beats irregularly, and blood pressure may be elevated. In

20
contrast, the body is so still that the dreamer may appear to be paralyzed.

In a period of eight hours, most sleepers experience from three to five instances of REM sleep. Each instance lasts from five to thirty minutes with an interval of at least ninety minutes between each one.

25
Later instances of REM sleep are usually of longer duration than are instances earlier in the eight-hour period.

Since people who suffer sleep deprivation experience fatigue, irritability, and loss of concentration, we must conclude that sleep is essential because in some way it regenerates the brain and the

30
nervous system. NREM sleep increases after physical exertion, whereas REM sleep tends to increase after a stressful day. Studies suggest that non-REM sleep may be especially helpful in restoring muscle control, whereas REM sleep may be more important in revitalizing mental activity. It appears that both kinds of sleep are

35
necessary, and the recuperation of sleep of one kind will not compensate for a lack of the other kind of sleep.

1. What is the author's main purpose in the passage?
   - Ⓐ To describe REM sleep
   - Ⓑ To explain sleep deprivation
   - Ⓒ To discuss the two types of sleep
   - Ⓓ To recommend an increase in the number of hours of sleep

2. How many times per night do most sleepers experience REM sleep?
   - Ⓐ Eight
   - Ⓑ Three to five
   - Ⓒ Five to thirty
   - Ⓓ Ninety

3. The word "vague" in line 9 could best be replaced by
   - Ⓐ familiar
   - Ⓑ indefinite
   - Ⓒ unpleasant
   - Ⓓ detailed

4. The word "essential" in line 29 is closest in meaning to
   - Ⓐ planned
   - Ⓑ natural
   - Ⓒ interesting
   - Ⓓ necessary

5. The word "it" in line 29 refers to
   - Ⓐ deprivation
   - Ⓑ the brain
   - Ⓒ sleep
   - Ⓓ concentration

6. Where in the passage does the author explain why sleep is essential?
   - Ⓐ Lines 4–6
   - Ⓑ Lines 7–10
   - Ⓒ Lines 18–21
   - Ⓓ Lines 27–30

7. What does the author mean by the statement in lines 31–34: "Studies suggest that non-REM sleep may be especially helpful in restoring muscle control, whereas REM sleep may be more important in revitalizing mental activity"?
   - Ⓐ REM sleep is more important than slow-wave sleep for all types of activities.
   - Ⓑ Mental and physical activities require both kinds of sleep.
   - Ⓒ Slow-wave sleep, also called REM sleep, restores mental activity.
   - Ⓓ Physical activity is supported by slow-wave sleep, but mental activity is supported by REM sleep.

8. Which response is NOT typical of REM sleep?
   - Ⓐ Irregular heartbeat
   - Ⓑ Dreams and visions
   - Ⓒ Movements in arms and legs
   - Ⓓ Higher blood pressure

9. The author mentions all the following as characteristics of REM sleep EXCEPT
   - Ⓐ vague thoughts
   - Ⓑ smaller brain waves
   - Ⓒ eye movements
   - Ⓓ dreams

10. It can be inferred from the passage that students who are writing term papers
    - Ⓐ require slow-wave sleep to increase mental activity
    - Ⓑ can stay up all night working and recover the sleep they need by sleeping for a few hours the next afternoon
    - Ⓒ need REM sleep to restore mental functioning
    - Ⓓ do not need as much sleep because of the heightened brain waves involved in creative activity

Refer to pages 438–439 for the Explanatory Answers.

EXERCISE 68: Classification—Arts/Architecture

In some questions in the Reading Section on the Internet-Based TOEFL, you will be asked to recall and relate information and content from classification passages found in college textbooks. Choose the best answer for multiple-choice questions. For computer-assisted questions, follow the directions on the screen.

Classical Architecture

There are three different types or styles of order (column) in Greek architecture: Doric, Ionic and Corinthian. The relative proportions of base, shaft and capital varied in the different types of order. The Romans adapted the Greek orders for their own purposes, but in general Roman orders were lighter, and more heavily decorated.

Doric

The Doric order is the most massive of the three. It is the only style in which the column has no base and the shaft is placed directly on the platform. The shaft itself is grooved and the grooves meet in a sharp edge. The capital can be described as a *plain convex moulding.* The architrave can be plain or decorated with intermittent rows of small triangular carvings. The frieze is decorated with a series of tablets with vertical flutings, alternating with square spaces which were either left plain or decorated with relief carvings.

Ionic

In the Ionic order, the shaft is taller and more slender. The grooves on the shaft are separated by flat bands. Occasionally the shafts are replaced by female figures (caryatids). According to legend, they represent the women from an ancient tribe whom the Greeks captured and enslaved. The capital has two sets of spirals, rather like a roll of paper with its ends curled towards each other. The architrave is made up of three horizontal planes, each projecting slightly beyond the one below. The frieze can be plain or sculptured. The cornice in the Ionic order is often decorated with rows of small blocks, which look like teeth and are called **dentals.**

Corinthian

The Corinthian order is similar to the Ionic. The main difference is in the capital, which is much more richly decorated. A Corinthian capital is like an inverted bell. Some of them are decorated with acanthus leaves surmounted by four symmetrical scrolls. In others, lotus or palm leaves replace the scrolls.

Mathematical Rules in Greek Architecture

The Greeks never used more than one style for the whole of a building. The only exception to this rule was to have one order for the exterior and another for the interior. As a result it is relatively easy to decide the style of any Greek building, even one in ruins, by looking at a capital, a segment of a column or part of an entablature.

All the measurements used by the architects, such as the height of a column, were expressed in multiples of the diameter at the base of the shaft. Each order had its own rules concerning the size of its component parts. For example, the height of a Doric column is between four and six times the diameter of its base. The height of an Ionic column is nine times, and the height of a Corinthian column is ten times the diameter of its base. Similar rules governed even the smallest component of a building.

The system had many advantages. One was that while only a man of great talent could build a masterpiece, even a mediocre architect, working within the rules, could produce a passable result.

Although little of ancient Greek architecture remains in its original form, its influence has been enormous. The ancient Greeks took their styles to the lands which they colonized—for example Sicily and much of the Mediterranean littoral—and when Greece itself became a Roman colony in the second century B.C., the Romans happily adopted the styles of what they instinctively recognized as fine art. Greek influence on Roman architecture was profound, particularly after Greece became a Roman province in the second century B.C. Many of Rome's outstanding buildings were indeed built by Greeks.

Roman Orders

The Romans had five different styles or orders. Three were borrowed directly from the Greeks: Doric—the plainest and sturdiest; Ionic—with fluted capitals; and Corinthian—in which the capital is decorated with acanthus leaves. This last order was the most popular among the Romans.

The two styles which the Romans added were Tuscan—an even simpler form of Doric, and Composite—a richer form of Corinthian. In Roman buildings of more than one story, the orders were placed one above the other and usually in a prescribed sequence. The lowest would be the Doric, above it the Ionic, and above that the Corinthian.

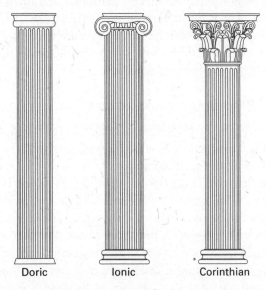

Doric   Ionic   Corinthian

Glossary

architrave: a base support for a column

capital: the feature on top of a column

shaft: the column between the base and the capital

Classical Architecture (Question References)

Paragraph 1   There are three different types or styles of order (column) in Greek architecture: Doric, Ionic and Corinthian. [A] The relative proportions of base, shaft and capital varied in the different types of order. [B] The Romans adapted the Greek orders for their own purposes, but in general Roman orders were lighter, and more heavily decorated. [C]

Doric

2   [D] The Doric order is the most massive of the three. It is the only style in which the column has no base and the shaft is placed directly on the platform. The shaft itself is grooved and the grooves meet in a sharp edge. The capital can be described as a *plain convex moulding.* The architrave can be plain or decorated with intermittent rows of small triangular carvings. The frieze is decorated with a series of tablets with vertical flutings, alternating with square spaces which were either left plain or decorated with relief carvings.

Ionic

3   In the Ionic order, the shaft is taller and more slender. The grooves on the shaft are separated by flat bands. Occasionally the shafts are replaced by female figures (caryatids). According to legend, they represent the women from an ancient tribe whom the Greeks captured and enslaved. The capital has two sets of spirals, rather like a roll of paper with its ends curled towards each other. The architrave is made up of three horizontal planes, each projecting slightly beyond the one below. The frieze can be plain or sculptured. The cornice in the Ionic order is often decorated with rows of small blocks, which look like teeth and are called **dentals**.

Corinthian

4   The Corinthian order is similar to the Ionic. The main difference is in the capital, which is much more richly decorated. A Corinthian capital is like an inverted bell. Some of them are decorated with acanthus leaves surmounted by four symmetrical scrolls. In others, lotus or palm leaves replace the scrolls.

Mathematical Rules in Greek Architecture

5   The Greeks never used more than one style for the whole of a building. The only exception to this rule was to have one order for the exterior and another for the interior. As a result it is relatively easy to decide the style of any Greek building, even one in ruins, by looking at a capital, a segment of a column or part of an entablature.

6   All the measurements used by the architects, such as the height of a column, were expressed in multiples of the diameter at the base of the shaft. Each order had its own rules concerning the size of its component parts. For example, the height of a Doric column is between four and six times the diameter of its base. The height of an Ionic column is nine times, and the height of a Corinthian column is

ten times the diameter of its base. Similar rules governed even the smallest component of a building.

7   The system had many advantages. One was that while only a man of great talent could build a masterpiece, even a mediocre architect, working within the rules, could produce a passable result.

8   Although little of ancient Greek architecture remains in its original form, its influence has been enormous. The ancient Greeks took their styles to the lands which they colonized—for example Sicily and much of the Mediterranean littoral—and when Greece itself became a Roman colony in the second century B.C., the Romans happily adopted the styles of what they instinctively recognized as fine art. Greek influence on Roman architecture was profound, particularly after Greece became a Roman province in the second century B.C. Many of Rome's outstanding buildings were indeed built by Greeks.

Roman Orders

9   The Romans had five different styles or orders. Three were borrowed directly from the Greeks: Doric—the plainest and sturdiest; Ionic—with fluted capitals; and Corinthian—in which the capital is decorated with acanthus leaves. This last order was the most popular among the Romans.

10   The two styles which the Romans added were Tuscan—an even simpler form of Doric, and Composite—a richer form of Corinthian. In Roman buildings of more than one story, the orders were placed one above the other and usually in a prescribed sequence. The lowest would be the Doric, above it the Ionic, and above that the Corinthian.

1. What does this passage mainly discuss?
   - (A) Classical columns in architecture
   - (B) Greek influence on Roman columns
   - (C) Mathematical rules for columns
   - (D) Fine art in ancient buildings

2. What is the rule for the height of a Corinthian column?
   - (A) Six times the diameter of the base
   - (B) Nine times the diameter of the base
   - (C) Ten times the diameter of the base
   - (D) Twelve times the diameter of the base

3. The word passable in the passage is closest in meaning to
   - (A) recognized
   - (B) similar
   - (C) satisfactory
   - (D) correct

4. The word enormous in the passage is closest in meaning to
   - (A) very good
   - (B) very large
   - (C) very beautiful
   - (D) very strong

5. The word another in the passage refers to
   - Ⓐ exterior
   - Ⓑ order
   - Ⓒ rule
   - Ⓓ exception

6. According to paragraph 10, which new orders did the Romans add to the architectural styles of the Greeks?

   Click on 2 answers.
   - Ⓐ Doric
   - Ⓑ Composite
   - Ⓒ Tuscan
   - Ⓓ Corinthian

7. Which of the sentences below best expresses the information in the highlighted statement in the passage? The other choices change the meaning or leave out important information.
   - Ⓐ Buildings were designed with several styles.
   - Ⓑ The styles in a building complimented it.
   - Ⓒ Only one style was used in each building.
   - Ⓓ There is one style of Greek architecture.

8. The author mentioned all of the following characteristics of the Corinthian order EXCEPT
   - Ⓐ It was the Greek style that the Romans preferred.
   - Ⓑ It included a heavily decorated capital.
   - Ⓒ It was a design that first appeared in Corinth.
   - Ⓓ It was often used as the top story above the Doric and Ionic.

9. It can be inferred from the mathematical rules that
   - Ⓐ the Ionic column is the heaviest
   - Ⓑ the Corinthian column is the slimmest
   - Ⓒ the Doric column is the tallest
   - Ⓓ the Tuscan column is the most ornate

10. Four squares (☐) indicate where the following sentence can be added to the passage.

    Both the Greek and the Roman orders have inspired a number of classical revivals, and many examples are evident in modern buildings.

    Where would the sentence best fit into the passage?
    - Ⓐ
    - Ⓑ
    - Ⓒ
    - Ⓓ

11. Complete the table below by classifying each of the answer choices under the order to which it refers. One of the answer choices will not be used.
    - Ⓐ Various leaves and scrolls decorate the column.
    - Ⓑ The column is often painted in bright colors.
    - Ⓒ A column without a base, it sits on the platform.
    - Ⓓ The largest, widest style of the Greek columns.
    - Ⓔ The column is nine times as high as the diameter of the base.
    - Ⓕ Female figures are sometimes substituted for the shaft.
    - Ⓖ Four symmetrical scrolls grace the column.

Doric	Ionic	Corinthian
•	•	•
•	•	•

12. Complete a summary of the passage by selecting THREE answer choices that express the most important ideas. The other three sentences do not belong in the summary because they express ideas that are not in the passage or they do not refer to the major ideas. *This question is worth 2 points.*

Classical styles have exercised a great influence on architecture.

Ⓐ The Doric, Ionic, and Corinthian orders can be distinguished by the style of their columns.

Ⓑ It is possible to determine the style of a Greek building by looking at a ruin.

Ⓒ Roman architects supplemented the Greek orders with two more, the Tuscan and the Composite.

Ⓓ The Egyptians had also used several types of columns to construct and decorate buildings.

Ⓔ The sturdy Doric order is used as a foundation for large, multi-story buildings.

Ⓕ Greek architecture had rules concerning the relative size of component parts in a structure.

Refer to pages 439–440 for the Explanatory Answers.

EXERCISE 69: Classification—Natural Sciences

In some questions in the Reading Section on the Internet-Based TOEFL, you will be asked to recall and relate information and content from classification passages found in college textbooks. Choose the best answer for multiple-choice questions. For computer-assisted questions, follow the directions on the screen.

Galaxies

Astronomers classify galaxies into three major categories.

Spiral Galaxies

Like the Milky Way, other spiral galaxies also have a thin disk extending outward from a central *bulge* (Figure 1). The bulge itself merges smoothly into a *halo* that can extend to a radius of over 100,000 light-years. Together, the bulge and halo of a spiral galaxy make up its **spheroidal component**, so named because of its rounded shape. Although no clear boundary divides the pieces of the spheroidal component, astronomers usually consider stars within 10,000 light-years of the center to be members of the bulge and those outside this radius to be members of the halo.

The **disk component** of a spiral galaxy slices directly through the halo and bulge. The disk of a large spiral galaxy like the Milky Way can extend 50,000 light-years or more from the center. The disks of all spiral galaxies contain an *interstellar medium* of gas and dust, but the amounts and proportions of the interstellar medium in molecular, atomic, and ionized forms differ from one spiral galaxy to the next. Spiral galaxies with large bulges generally have less interstellar gas and dust than those with small bulges.

Not all galaxies with disks are standard spiral galaxies. Some spiral galaxies appear to have a straight bar of stars cutting across the center, with spiral arms curling away from the ends of the bar. Such galaxies are known as *barred spiral galaxies*.

Other galaxies have disks but do not appear to have spiral arms. These are called *lenticular galaxies* because they look lens-shaped when seen edge-on (*lenticular* means "lens-shaped"). Although they look like spiral galaxies without arms, *lenticular* galaxies might more appropriately be considered an intermediate class between spirals and ellipticals because they tend to have less cool gas than normal spirals, but more than ellipticals.

Among large galaxies in the universe, most (75% to 85%) are spiral or lenticular. (Spiral and lenticular galaxies are much rarer among small galaxies.) Spiral galaxies are often found in loose collections of several galaxies, called **groups**, that extend over a few million light-years. Our Local Group is one example, with two large spirals: the Milky Way and the Great Galaxy in Andromeda. Lenticular galaxies are particularly common in **clusters** of galaxies, which can contain hundreds and sometimes thousands of galaxies, extending over more than 10 million light-years.

Elliptical Galaxies

The major difference between elliptical and spiral galaxies is that ellipticals lack a significant disk component (Figure 2). Thus, an elliptical galaxy has only a spheroidal component and looks much like the bulge and halo of a spiral galaxy. (In fact, elliptical galaxies are sometimes called *spheroidal galaxies*). Most of the interstellar medium in large elliptical galaxies consists of low-density, hot x-ray, emitting gas like the gas in bubbles and superbubbles in the

Milky Way. Elliptical galaxies usually contain very little dust or cool gas, although they are not completely devoid of either. Some have relatively small and cold gaseous disks rotating at their centers; these disks might be the remnants of a collision with a spiral galaxy.

Elliptical galaxies appear to be more social than spiral galaxies: They are much more common in clusters of galaxies than outside clusters. Elliptical galaxies make up about half the large galaxies in the central regions of clusters, while they represent only a small minority (about 15%) of the large galaxies found outside clusters. However, ellipticals are more common among small galaxies. Particularly small elliptical galaxies with less than a billion stars, called **dwarf elliptical galaxies**, are often found near larger spiral galaxies. At least 10 dwarf elliptical galaxies belong to the Local Group.

Irregular Galaxies

A small percentage of the large galaxies we see nearby fall into neither of the two major categories. This *irregular* class of galaxies is a miscellaneous class, encompassing small galaxies such as the Magellanic Clouds and "peculiar" galaxies that appear to be in disarray. (Figure 3). These blobby star systems are usually white and dusty, like the disks of spirals. Telescopic observations probing deep into the universe show that distant galaxies are more likely to be irregular in shape than those nearby. Because the light of more distant galaxies was emitted longer ago in the past, these observations tell us that irregular galaxies were more common when the universe was younger.

Figure 1

Figure 2

Figure 3

Glossary

bulge: central part of a spiral galaxy in the shape of a football

disk: part of a spiral galaxy in the shape of a disk

halo: region around the disk of a spiral galaxy

Galaxies (Question References)

Paragraph 1   Astronomers classify galaxies into three major categories.

Spiral Galaxies

2   Like the Milky Way, other spiral galaxies also have a thin disk extending outward from a central *bulge* (Figure 1). The bulge itself merges smoothly into a *halo* that can extend to a radius of over 100,000 light-years. Together, the bulge and halo of a spiral galaxy make up its **spheroidal component**, so named because of its rounded shape. Although no clear boundary divides the pieces of the spheroidal component, astronomers usually consider stars within 10,000 light-years of the center to be members of the bulge and those outside this radius to be members of the halo.

3   The **disk component** of a spiral galaxy slices directly through the halo and bulge. The disk of a large spiral galaxy like the Milky Way can extend 50,000 light-years or more from the center. The disks of all spiral galaxies contain an *interstellar medium* of gas and dust, but the amounts and proportions of the interstellar medium in molecular, atomic, and ionized forms differ from one spiral galaxy to the next. Spiral galaxies with large bulges generally have less interstellar gas and dust than those with small bulges.

4   Not all galaxies with disks are standard spiral galaxies. Some spiral galaxies appear to have a straight bar of stars cutting across the center, with spiral arms curling away from the ends of the bar. Such galaxies are known as *barred spiral galaxies*.

5   Other galaxies have disks but do not appear to have spiral arms. These are called *lenticular galaxies* because they look lens-shaped when seen edge-on (*lenticular* means "lens-shaped"). Although they look like spiral galaxies without arms, *lenticular* galaxies might more appropriately be considered an intermediate class between spirals and ellipticals because they tend to have less cool gas than normal spirals, but more than ellipticals.

6   Among large galaxies in the universe, most (75% to 85%) are spiral or lenticular. (Spiral and lenticular galaxies are much rarer among small galaxies.) Spiral galaxies are often found in loose collections of several galaxies, called **groups**, that extend over a few million light-years. Our Local Group is one example, with two large spirals: the Milky Way and the Great Galaxy in Andromeda. Lenticular galaxies are particularly common in **clusters** of galaxies, which can contain hundreds and sometimes thousands of galaxies, extending over more than 10 million light-years.

Elliptical Galaxies

7   The major difference between elliptical and spiral galaxies is that ellipticals lack a significant disk component (Figure 2). Thus, an elliptical galaxy has only a spheroidal component and looks much like the bulge and halo of a spiral galaxy. (In fact, elliptical galaxies are sometimes called *spheroidal galaxies*). Most of the interstellar medium in large elliptical galaxies consists of low-density, hot x-ray, emitting gas like the gas in bubbles and superbubbles in the Milky Way. Elliptical galaxies usually contain very little dust or cool gas, although they are not completely devoid of either. Some have relatively small and cold gaseous disks rotating at their centers; these disks might be the remnants of a collision with a spiral galaxy.

8   Elliptical galaxies appear to be more social than spiral galaxies: They are much more common in clusters of galaxies than outside clusters. ☐A☐ Elliptical galaxies make up about half the large galaxies in the central regions of clusters, while they represent only a small minority (about 15%) of the large galaxies found outside clusters. ☐B☐ However, ellipticals are more common among small galaxies. ☐C☐ Particularly small elliptical galaxies with less than a billion stars, called **dwarf elliptical galaxies**, are often found near larger spiral galaxies. At least 10 dwarf elliptical galaxies belong to the Local Group. ☐D☐

Irregular Galaxies

9   A small percentage of the large galaxies we see nearby fall into neither of the two major categories. This *irregular* class of galaxies is a miscellaneous class, encompassing small galaxies such as the Magellanic Clouds and "peculiar" galaxies that appear to be in disarray. (Figure 3). These blobby star systems are usually white and dusty, like the disks of spirals. Telescopic observations probing deep into the universe show that distant galaxies are more likely to be irregular in shape than those nearby. Because the light of more distant galaxies was emitted longer ago in the past, these observations tell us that irregular galaxies were more common when the universe was younger.

1. What does this passage mainly discuss?
   - Ⓐ The major components of spiral galaxies
   - Ⓑ The most important types of galaxies
   - Ⓒ The Milky Way and the Andromeda galaxies
   - Ⓓ Measuring galaxies in light-years

2. What distinguishes a spiral galaxy from an elliptical galaxy?
   - Ⓐ Elliptical galaxies have a much larger halo.
   - Ⓑ Elliptical galaxies have more dust and cool gas.
   - Ⓒ Spiral galaxies are more irregularly shaped.
   - Ⓓ Spiral galaxies have a more prominent disk.

3. The word devoid in the passage is closest in meaning to
   - Ⓐ hidden
   - Ⓑ empty
   - Ⓒ dense
   - Ⓓ bright

4. The word remnants in the passage is closest in meaning to
   - Ⓐ remains
   - Ⓑ origin
   - Ⓒ damage
   - Ⓓ evidence

5. The word either in the passage refers to
   Ⓐ bubbles or superbubbles
   Ⓑ elliptical or spheroidal galaxies
   Ⓒ dust or cool gas
   Ⓓ small or cold disks

6. According to paragraph 5, *lenticular galaxies*
   Ⓐ look like spiral galaxies without arms
   Ⓑ consist of a bulge and a halo in a spiral galaxy
   Ⓒ appear to have a bar of stars across the center
   Ⓓ are in the shape of a white spiral disk

7. Which of the sentences below best expresses the information in the highlighted statement in the passage? The other choices change the meaning or leave out important information.
   Ⓐ Spiral galaxies with small bulges have more gas and dust.
   Ⓑ Spiral galaxies have more gas and dust in their bulges.
   Ⓒ There is less gas and dust in a spiral galaxy with a small bulge.
   Ⓓ Gas and dust collect in the bulges of the large spiral galaxies.

8. Irregular galaxies are described as all of the following EXCEPT
   Ⓐ very white and dusty like the Magellanic Clouds
   Ⓑ older than most of the other types of galaxies
   Ⓒ similar to the disks of a spiral galaxy
   Ⓓ an intermediate class between spirals and ellipticals

9. It can be inferred from the passage that
   Ⓐ astronomers do not agree on the classifications of galaxies
   Ⓑ galaxies always collect together in clusters
   Ⓒ the Milky Way is a typical spiral galaxy
   Ⓓ most halos extend to about 100,000 light-years

10. Four squares (☐) indicate where the following sentence can be added to the passage.

    A good example of a dwarf elliptical galaxy is Leo I in the Local Group.

    Where would the sentence best fit into the passage?
    Ⓐ
    Ⓑ
    Ⓒ
    Ⓓ

11. Complete the table below by classifying each of the answer choices as a *spiral*, *elliptical*, or *irregular* galaxy. Two of the answer choices will NOT be used.
    Ⓐ Less gas or dust is found.
    Ⓑ A disk component is prominent.
    Ⓒ More radiation is noted.
    Ⓓ The stars are older.
    Ⓔ Their atmosphere is slightly blue.
    Ⓕ The Milky Way is an example.
    Ⓖ They are often found in large clusters.
    Ⓗ A miscellaneous class of galaxies.

Spiral	Elliptical	Irregular
•	•	•
•	•	•

12. Complete a summary of the passage by selecting THREE answer choices that express the most important ideas. The other three sentences do not belong in the summary because they express ideas that are not in the passage or they do not refer to the major ideas. *This question is worth 2 points*.

Astronomers classify galaxies into three major categories.

Ⓐ Although stars of all ages can be found in the Milky Way, young galaxies are located at great distances from Earth.

Ⓑ An irregular galaxy is attributed to a miscellaneous category that does not fit into either of the two major types of galaxies.

Ⓒ Dwarf galaxies are very small elliptical galaxies with fewer than one billion stars in them.

Ⓓ Spiral galaxies have a bulge and halo in the spheroidal component and a separate disk component.

Ⓔ Elliptical galaxies have a spheroidal component, but they do not have a disk component.

Ⓕ Clusters of galaxies may include hundreds or even thousands of individual galaxies.

Refer to pages 440–441 for the Explanatory Answers.

EXERCISE 70: Comparison/Contrast—Humanities/Business

In some questions in the Reading Section on the Paper-Based TOEFL, you will be asked to recall and relate information and content from comparison or contrast passages about various fields of study. Choose the best answer for multiple-choice questions.

Levels of Vocabulary

Most languages have several levels of vocabulary that may be used by the same speakers. In English, at least three have been identified and described.

Line
5   Standard usage includes those words and expressions understood, used, and accepted by a majority of the speakers of a language in any situation regardless of the level of formality. As such, these words and expressions are well defined and listed in standard dictionaries. Colloquialisms, on the other hand, are familiar words and idioms that are understood by almost all speakers of a language and used in
10   informal speech or writing, but not considered acceptable for more formal situations. Almost all idiomatic expressions are colloquial language. Slang, however, refers to words and expressions understood by a large number of speakers but not accepted as appropriate formal usage by the majority. Colloquial expressions and
15   even slang may be found in standard dictionaries but will be so identified. Both colloquial usage and slang are more common in speech than in writing.

    Colloquial speech often passes into standard speech. Some slang also passes into standard speech, but other slang expressions enjoy
20   momentary popularity followed by obscurity. In some cases, the majority never accepts certain slang phrases but nevertheless retains them in their collective memories. Every generation seems to require its own set of words to describe familiar objects and events.

    It has been pointed out by a number of linguists that three
25   cultural conditions are necessary for the creation of a large body of slang expressions. First, the introduction and acceptance of new objects and situations in the society; second, a diverse population with a large number of subgroups; third, association among the subgroups and the majority population.
30   Finally, it is worth noting that the terms "standard," "colloquial," and "slang" exist only as abstract labels for scholars who study language. Only a tiny number of the speakers of any language will be aware that they are using colloquial or slang expressions. Most speakers of English will, during appropriate situations, select and use
35   all three types of expressions.

1. Which of the following is the main topic of the passage?
   - (A) Standard speech
   - (B) Idiomatic phrases
   - (C) Different types of vocabulary
   - (D) Dictionary usage

2. How is slang defined by the author?
   - (A) Words and phrases accepted by the majority for formal usage
   - (B) Words and phrases understood by the majority but not found in standard dictionaries
   - (C) Words and phrases that are understood by a restricted group of speakers
   - (D) Words and phrases understood by a large number of speakers but not accepted as formal usage

3. The word "obscurity" in line 20 could best be replaced by
   - (A) disappearance
   - (B) influence
   - (C) qualification
   - (D) tolerance

4. The word "appropriate" in line 14 is closest in meaning to
   - (A) old
   - (B) large
   - (C) correct
   - (D) important

5. The word "them" in line 22 refers to
   - (A) words
   - (B) slang phrases
   - (C) memories
   - (D) the majority

6. Where in the passage does the author explain where colloquial language and slang are most commonly used?
   - (A) Lines 4–6
   - (B) Lines 16–17
   - (C) Lines 24–26
   - (D) Lines 33–35

7. What does the author mean by the statement in lines 8–11: "Colloquialisms, on the other hand, are familiar words and idioms that are understood by almost all speakers of a language and used in informal speech or writing, but not considered acceptable for more formal situations"?
   - (A) Familiar words and phrases are found in both speech and writing in formal settings.
   - (B) Familiar situations that are experienced by most people are called colloquialisms.
   - (C) Informal language contains colloquialisms, which are not found in more formal language.
   - (D) Most of the speakers of a language can use both formal and informal speech in appropriate situations.

8. Which of the following is true of standard usage?
   - (A) It can be used in formal or informal settings.
   - (B) It is limited to written language.
   - (C) It is only understood by the upper classes.
   - (D) It is constantly changing.

9. The author mentions all of the following as requirements for slang expressions to be created EXCEPT
   - (A) new situations
   - (B) a new generation
   - (C) interaction among diverse groups
   - (D) a number of linguists

10. It can be inferred from the passage that the author
    - (A) does not approve of either slang or colloquial speech in any situation
    - (B) approves of colloquial speech in some situations, but not slang
    - (C) approves of slang and colloquial speech in appropriate situations
    - (D) does not approve of colloquial usage in writing

Refer to page 441 for the Explanatory Answers.

EXERCISE 71: Comparison/Contrast—Arts/Architecture

In some questions in the Reading Section on the Paper-Based TOEFL, you will be asked to recall and relate information and content from comparison or contrast passages about various fields of study. Choose the best answer for multiple-choice questions.

The New Photography

In order to establish photography as art, members of the
Aesthetic Movement modeled their work on classical paintings, even
copying the subjects and poses popularized by artists of the Classical
Line   Period. As the movement gained in popularity, photographers made
5   a clear distinction between the elegant, artistic photography that
conformed to the aesthetic standard used for paintings and the
work of more realistic photographers that was beginning to appear.
Since they were cloudy because of the gum bichromate plate that
allowed for manual intervention, the aesthetic prints were easily
10   distinguished from the more modern prints, which came to be called
straightforward photographs. In contrast, the straightforward
photographers produced images that were sharp and clear. Whereas
the proponents of the Aesthetic movement continued to hand color
their photographs, adding details and textures to conform to the art
15   of printmakers, the philosophy that surrounded the new photography
rejected manipulation of either the subject matter or the print. The
subjects included nature in its undisturbed state and people in
everyday situations.
A number of major exhibitions and the formation of photographic
20   clubs during the late nineteenth century provided the impetus for the
Photo-Secession Movement. Founded by Alfred Steiglitz in New
York City in 1902, Photo-Secession had as its proposition the
promotion of straightforward photography through exhibits and
publications. One of the publications, *Camera Work*, has been
25   recognized among the most beautiful journals ever produced. By
the 1920s, the mechanical precision that had once been criticized
as a defect by members of the Aesthetic Movement had become a
hallmark of modern photography. Chiefly through the efforts of
Steiglitz, modern photography had seceded from painting and
30   emerged as a legitimate art form. In summary, the Aesthetic
Movement rejected reality for beauty, but the Photo-Secessionists
embraced realism as even more beautiful.

1. Which of the following would be an
   alternative title for the passage?
   Ⓐ The Photo-Secession Movement
   Ⓑ The Aesthetic Movement
   Ⓒ Alfred Steiglitz
   Ⓓ Photography as Art

2. How can earlier photographs be
   distinguished from more modern
   photographs?
   Ⓐ They were not the same color.
   Ⓑ They were not as clear.
   Ⓒ They did not look like paintings.
   Ⓓ They were not retouched.

3. The word "defect" in line 27 is closest in
   meaning to
   Ⓐ disturbance
   Ⓑ ideal
   Ⓒ requirement
   Ⓓ imperfection

4. The word "chiefly" in line 28 is closest in
   meaning to
   Ⓐ only
   Ⓑ mostly
   Ⓒ rarely
   Ⓓ likely

5. The word "they" in line 8 refers to
   Ⓐ paintings
   Ⓑ aesthetic prints
   Ⓒ modern prints
   Ⓓ straightforward photographs

6. Where in the passage does the author
   identify the subjects that modern
   photographers used?
   Ⓐ Lines 4–7
   Ⓑ Lines 16–18
   Ⓒ Lines 25–28
   Ⓓ Lines 30–32

7. What does the author mean by the
   statement in lines 25–28: "By the 1920s,
   the mechanical precision that had once
   been criticized asa defect by members of
   the Aesthetic Movement had become a
   hallmark of modern photography"?
   Ⓐ The defect of the Aesthetic Movement
      was eliminated by the mechanical
      precision of later photographers.
   Ⓑ Later photographers used mechanical
      precision in spite of criticism by earlier
      photographers in the Aesthetic
      Movement.
   Ⓒ The modern photographers used
      hallmarks, unlike the photographers of
      the earlier Aesthetic Movement.
   Ⓓ Mechanical precision was a defect that
      later photographers eliminated from
      their work.

8. What is NOT true of *Camera Work*?
   Ⓐ It is considered among the most
      attractive magazines.
   Ⓑ It encouraged members of the
      Aesthetic Movement.
   Ⓒ It was promoted by Alfred Steiglitz.
   Ⓓ It was a vehicle for realistic beauty.

9. The Photo-Secession Movement is
   described as including all of the following
   EXCEPT
   Ⓐ straightforward photographs
   Ⓑ mechanical precision
   Ⓒ sharp, clear images
   Ⓓ manipulation of prints

10. It can be inferred from the passage that the
    author
    Ⓐ knew Alfred Steiglitz personally
    Ⓑ was not interested in Alfred Steiglitz
    Ⓒ disagreed with Alfred Steiglitz
    Ⓓ admired Alfred Steiglitz

Refer to pages 441–442 for the Explanatory Answers.

EXERCISE 72: Comparison/Contrast—Social Sciences

In some questions in the Reading Section on the Internet-Based TOEFL, you will be asked to recall and relate information and content from comparison or contrast passages found in college textbooks. Choose the best answer for multiple-choice questions. For computer-assisted questions, follow the directions on the screen.

Functionalism

Many North American psychologists were uncomfortable with the strict structuralist approach advocated by European psychologists. Whereas structuralists tended to focus exclusively on the *content* of immediate experience, dissecting the mind into parts, North American psychologists worried more about the *function* of immediate experience. What is the purpose of the mental operations that underlie immediate experience? How are the components of mind used to achieve this end? Because of the emphasis on function rather than content, this school of thought became generally known as functionalism (Angell, 1903; Dewey, 1896; James, 1890).

Functionalists such as William James (1842–1910) and James Rowland Angell (1869–1949) were convinced that it was impossible to understand a whole like the mind by simply looking at its parts—that would be like trying to understand a house by analyzing the underlying bricks and mortar (James, 1884). It is necessary to first understand the goal—what specifically is being attempted by the mental operation? Then you can try to decipher how the individual parts work together to achieve that goal. For example, to understand how memory works, you must first consider its purpose—what specific kinds of problems do our memory systems help us solve as we work our way through the day?

Darwin's ideas about evolution through natural selection were extremely influential in the development of functionalism. If you want to analyze the color markings on a butterfly's wings, a Darwinian theorist would argue, you must ask how those markings help the butterfly survive, or at least reproduce. Similarly, when analyzing the operations and processes of mind, a functionalist would argue, you need to understand the adaptive value of those operations—how do they help people solve the problems they face?

Functionalism had a liberalizing effect on the development of psychology in North America. It greatly expanded the acceptable range of topics. For example, it became fashionable to study how an organism interacts with its environment, which led to an early emphasis on learning (Thorndike, 1898) and to the study of individual differences. Later, some functionalists turned their attention to applied issues, such as how people solve practical problems in industry and in educational settings (Taylor, 1911). To a functionalist, almost any aspect of behavior was considered fair game for study, and psychology boomed in North America.

Psychology changed even more radically in the first two decades of the twentieth century. Although functionalism and structuralism clearly differed in their emphases, both still considered the fundamental problem in psychology to be understanding immediate conscious experience. The great functionalist William James is well known for his superb analysis of consciousness, which he compared to a flowing and ever-changing stream. Around 1900, the technique of introspection—looking inward to observe one's own mind—remained the dominant method of analysis in the tool kit of the experimental psychologist.

Behaviorism

Not all psychologists were convinced that self-observation could produce valid scientific results. By definition, self-observations are personal, so it is difficult to determine whether the knowledge gained is accurate or representative of all people. It was also recognized that introspection might change the mental operations being observed. If you are concentrating intently on documenting the elements of a banana, you experience "banana" in an atypical way—not as something to eat, but rather as a complex collection of sensations. Introspection also limited the range of populations and topics that could be covered—it is difficult to ask someone with a severe mental disorder, for example, to introspect systematically on his or her condition (Marx & Cronan-Hillix, 1987).

Therefore, around 1910, psychologists began to question the usefulness of studying immediate conscious experience. Increasingly, the focus shifted toward the study of observable behavior. The intellectual leader of this new movement was a young professor at Johns Hopkins University named John B. Watson (1878–1958). Watson was convinced that psychology must discard all references to consciousness or mental events, because such events cannot be publicly observed and therefore fall outside of the proper domain of science. Observable behavior should be the proper subject matter of psychology; consequently, the task for the scientific researcher should be to discover how changes in the environment can lead to changes in measurable behavior. Because its entire emphasis was on behavior, Watson called this new approach **behaviorism** (Watson, 1913, 1919).

Behaviorism had an enormous impact on the development of psychology, particularly in North America. Remember: The psychology of Wundt and James was the psychology of mind and immediate experience. Yet by the second and third decades of the twentieth century, references to consciousness had largely vanished from the psychological vocabulary, as had the technique of systematic introspection. Researchers now concerned themselves with measuring behavior, especially in animals, and noting how carefully controlled laboratory experiences could change behavior (Skinner, 1938; Hull, 1943). Influential psychologists such as B. F. Skinner (1904–1990) offered repeated demonstrations of the practical value of the behaviorist approach. Skinner discovered the principles of behavior modification—how actions are changed by reinforcement and nonreinforcement—that are now widely used in mental hospitals, schools, and the workplace (Skinner, 1969).

The behaviorist approach dominated psychology for decades. However, many psychologists have returned to the study of mental events (but with a healthy insistence on defining those events in observational terms). Behaviorism continues to be influential in modern psychology, but it no longer commands the dominant position that it once held.

Functionalism (Question References)

Paragraph 1   Many North American psychologists were uncomfortable with the strict structuralist approach advocated by European psychologists. Whereas structuralists tended to focus exclusively on the *content* of immediate experience, dissecting the mind into parts, North American psychologists worried more about the *function* of immediate experience. What is the purpose of the mental operations that underlie immediate experience? How are the components of mind used to achieve this end? Because of the emphasis on function rather than content, this school of thought became generally known as functionalism (Angell, 1903; Dewey, 1896; James, 1890).

2   Functionalists such as William James (1842–1910) and James Rowland Angell (1869–1949) were convinced that it was impossible to understand a whole like the mind by simply looking at its parts— that would be like trying to understand a house by analyzing the underlying bricks and mortar (James, 1884). It is necessary to first understand the goal—what specifically is being attempted by the mental operation? Then you can try to decipher how the individual parts work together to achieve that goal. For example, to understand how memory works, you must first consider its purpose—what specific kinds of problems do our memory systems help us solve as we work our way through the day?

3   Darwin's ideas about evolution through natural selection were extremely influential in the development of functionalism. If you want to analyze the color markings on a butterfly's wings, a Darwinian theorist would argue, you must ask how those markings help the butterfly survive, or at least reproduce. Similarly, when analyzing the operations and processes of mind, a functionalist would argue, you need to understand the adaptive value of those operations—how do they help people solve the problems they face?

4   Functionalism had a liberalizing effect on the development of psychology in North America. It greatly expanded the acceptable range of topics. For example, it became fashionable to study how an organism interacts with its environment, which led to an early emphasis on learning (Thorndike, 1898) and to the study of individual differences. Later, some functionalists turned their attention to applied issues, such as how people solve practical problems in industry and in educational settings (Taylor, 1911). To a functionalist, almost any aspect of behavior was considered fair game for study, and psychology boomed in North America.

5   Psychology changed even more radically in the first two decades of the twentieth century. Although functionalism and structuralism clearly differed in their emphases, both still considered the fundamental problem in psychology to be understanding immediate conscious experience. The great functionalist William James is well known for his superb analysis of consciousness, which he compared to a flowing and ever-changing stream. Around 1900, the technique of introspection—looking inward to observe one's own mind— remained the dominant method of analysis in the tool kit of the experimental psychologist.

Behaviorism

6   Not all psychologists were convinced that self-observation could produce valid scientific results. [A] By definition, self-observations are personal, so it is difficult to determine whether the knowledge gained is accurate or representative of all people. It was also recognized that introspection might change the mental operations being observed. [B] If you are concentrating intently on documenting the elements of a banana, you experience "banana" in an atypical way–not as something to eat, but rather as a complex collection of sensations. Introspection also limited the range of populations and topics that could be covered—it is difficult to ask someone with a severe mental disorder, for example, to introspect systematically on his or her condition (Marx & Cronan-Hillix, 1987).

7   Therefore, around 1910, psychologists began to question the usefulness of studying immediate conscious experience. [C] Increasingly, the focus shifted toward the study of observable behavior. [D] The intellectual leader of this new movement was a young professor at Johns Hopkins University named John B. Watson (1878–1958). Watson was convinced that psychology must discard all references to consciousness or mental events, because such events cannot be publicly observed and therefore fall outside of the proper domain of science. Observable behavior should be the proper subject matter of psychology; consequently, the task for the scientific researcher should be to discover how changes in the environment can lead to changes in measurable behavior. Because its entire emphasis was on behavior, Watson called this new approach **behaviorism** (Watson, 1913, 1919).

8   Behaviorism had an enormous impact on the development of psychology, particularly in North America. Remember: The psychology of Wundt and James was the psychology of mind and immediate experience. Yet by the second and third decades of the twentieth century, references to consciousness had largely vanished from the psychological vocabulary, as had the technique of systematic introspection. Researchers now concerned themselves with measuring behavior, especially in animals, and noting how carefully controlled laboratory experiences could change behavior (Skinner, 1938; Hull, 1943). Influential psychologists such as B. F. Skinner (1904–1990) offered repeated demonstrations of the practical value of the behaviorist approach. Skinner discovered the principles of behavior modification—how actions are changed by reinforcement and nonreinforcement—that are now widely used in mental hospitals, schools, and the workplace (Skinner, 1969).

9   The behaviorist approach dominated psychology for decades. However, many psychologists have returned to the study of mental events (but with a healthy insistence on defining those events in observational terms). Behaviorism continues to be influential in modern psychology, but it no longer commands the dominant position that it once held.

1. With which of the following topics is the passage primarily concerned?
   - Ⓐ Modern psychological approaches
   - Ⓑ Experimental psychological methods
   - Ⓒ The function of behavior in psychology
   - Ⓓ The influence of evolution in psychology

2. Which of the psychologists studied the purpose of experience?
   - Ⓐ Evolutionists
   - Ⓑ Behaviorists
   - Ⓒ Structuralists
   - Ⓓ Functionalists

3. The word atypical in the passage is closest in meaning to
   - Ⓐ not acceptable
   - Ⓑ not orderly
   - Ⓒ not new
   - Ⓓ not usual

4. The word expanded in the passage is closest in meaning to
   - Ⓐ determined
   - Ⓑ demonstrated
   - Ⓒ enlarged
   - Ⓓ sustained

5. The word its in the passage refers to
   - Ⓐ changes
   - Ⓑ environment
   - Ⓒ task
   - Ⓓ behaviorism

6. In paragraph 6, what does the author say about self-observation?
   - Ⓐ It should be the primary method for psychology.
   - Ⓑ It may not provide accurate data.
   - Ⓒ It is useful for the study of abnormal psychology.
   - Ⓓ It is best to document the experience.

7. Which of the sentences below best expresses the information in the highlighted statement in the passage? The other choices change the meaning or leave out important information.
   - Ⓐ Although behaviorism is still respected, it is not the primary approach in modern psychology.
   - Ⓑ The influence of behaviorism is still as prominent as ever in modern psychology.
   - Ⓒ In spite of its former position of importance, behaviorism has lost respect in modern psychology.
   - Ⓓ Behaviorism has dominated modern psychology longer than any other approach.

8. The author mentions all of the following methods of analysis EXCEPT
   - Ⓐ psychoanalysis
   - Ⓑ behavior modification
   - Ⓒ problem solving
   - Ⓓ introspection

9. It can be inferred that the previous page in the textbook was a summary of
   - Ⓐ structuralism in Europe
   - Ⓑ North American psychologists
   - Ⓒ Charles Darwin's theory
   - Ⓓ recent trends in psychology

10. Four squares (☐) indicate where the following sentence can be added to the passage.

    The most obvious problem with the method is that it is simply not possible to replicate the experiments scientifically.

    Where would the sentence best fit into the passage?
    - Ⓐ
    - Ⓑ
    - Ⓒ
    - Ⓓ

11. Complete the table below by classifying each of the answer choices as representative of *functionalism* or *behaviorism*. One of the answer choices will NOT be used.
    - Ⓐ The purpose of mental operations must be understood.
    - Ⓑ Introspection is not a valid, scientific method.
    - Ⓒ The main concern is analysis of conscious experience.
    - Ⓓ Self-observation is one of the primary tools.
    - Ⓔ Humanistic views form the basis for the theory.
    - Ⓕ Changes in the environment cause modifications in activity.

Functionalism	Behaviorism
•	•
•	•
•	

12. Complete a summary of the passage by selecting THREE answer choices that express the most important ideas. The other three sentences do not belong in the summary because they express ideas that are not in the passage or they do not refer to the major ideas. *This question is worth 2 points.*

    Several theories were influential in the history of psychology.
    - Ⓐ Skinner developed behavior modification using positive and negative reinforcement.
    - Ⓑ Behaviorists advocated the study of observable, measurable behaviors.
    - Ⓒ Structuralism analyzed the content of experience by looking at the discrete parts.
    - Ⓓ Darwin's theory of evolution supported the proponents of functional psychology.
    - Ⓔ Humanism emphasized self-awareness and individual responsibility.
    - Ⓕ A functional approach considered the purpose of the mental operations in experience.

Refer to pages 442–443 for the Explanatory Answers.

EXERCISE 73: Comparison/Contrast—Natural Sciences

In some questions in the Reading Section on the Internet-Based TOEFL, you will be asked to recall and relate information and content from comparison or contrast passages found in college textbooks. Choose the best answer for multiple-choice questions. For computer-assisted questions, follow the directions on the screen.

Engineering and Science

To better understand what engineers do, let's contrast the roles of engineers with those of the closely related field of the scientist. Many students approach both fields for similar reasons; they were good at math and science in high school. While this is a prerequisite for both fields, it is not a sufficient discriminator to determine which is the right career for a given individual.

The main difference between the engineer and the scientist is in the object of each one's work. The scientist searches for answers to technological questions to obtain a knowledge of why a phenomenon occurs. The engineer also searches for answers to technological questions, but always with an application in mind.

Theodore Von Karman, one of the pioneers of America's aerospace industry, said "Scientists explore what is; engineers create what has not been." (Paul Wright, *Intro to Engineering*).

In general, science is about discovering things or acquiring new knowledge. Scientists are always asking, "Why?" They are interested in advancing the knowledge base that we have in a specific area. The answers they seek may be of an abstract nature, such as understanding the beginning of the universe, or more practical, such as the reaction of a virus to a new drug.

The engineer also asks, "Why?" but it is because of a problem which is preventing a product or service from being produced. The engineer is always thinking about the application when asking why. The engineer becomes concerned with issues such as the demand for a product, the cost of producing the product, the impact on society and the environment of the product.

Scientists and engineers work in many of the same fields and industries but have different roles. Here are some examples:

- Scientists study the planets in our solar system to understand them; engineers study the planets so they can design a spacecraft to operate in the environment of that planet.
- Scientists study atomic structure to understand the nature of matter; engineers study the atomic structure in order to build smaller and faster microprocessors.
- Scientists study the human neurological system to understand the progression of neurological diseases; engineers study the human neurological system to design artificial limbs.
- Scientists create new chemical compounds in a laboratory; engineers create processes to mass-produce new chemical compounds for consumers.

• Scientists study the movement of tectonic plates to understand and predict earthquakes; engineers study the movement of tectonic plates to design safer buildings.

The Engineer and the Engineering Technologist

Another profession closely related to engineering is engineering technology. Engineering technology and engineering have similarities, yet there are differences; they have different career opportunities. ABET, which accredits engineering technology programs as well as engineering programs, defines engineering technology as follows: *Engineering technology is that part of the technological field which requires the application of scientific and engineering knowledge and methods combined with technical skills in support of engineering activities; it lies in the occupational spectrum between the craftsman and engineering at the end of the spectrum closest to the engineer.*

Technologists work with existing technology to produce goods for society. Technology students spend time in their curricula working with actual machines and equipment that are used in the jobs they will accept after graduation. By doing this, technologists are equipped to be productive in their occupation from the first day of work.

Both engineers and technologists apply technology for the betterment of society. The main difference between the two fields is that the engineer is able to create new technology through research, design and development. Rather than being trained to use specific machines or processes, engineering students study additional mathematics and engineering science subjects. This equips engineers to use these tools to advance the state of the art in their field and move technology forward.

There are areas where engineers and engineering technologists perform very similar jobs. For example, in manufacturing settings, engineers and technologists are employed as supervisors of assembly line workers. Also, in technical service fields both are hired to work as technical support personnel supporting equipment purchased by customers. However, most opportunities are different for engineering and engineering technology graduates.

Engineering and Science (Question References)

Paragraph 1   To better understand what engineers do, let's contrast the roles of engineers with those of the closely related field of the scientist. Many students approach both fields for similar reasons; they were good at math and science in high school. [A] While this is a prerequisite for both fields, it is not a sufficient discriminator to determine which is the right career for a given individual.

2   [B] The main difference between the engineer and the scientist is in the object of each one's work. The scientist searches for answers to technological questions to obtain a knowledge of why a phenomenon occurs. [C] The engineer also searches for answers to technological questions, but always with an application in mind. [D]

3   Theodore Von Karman, one of the pioneers of America's aerospace industry, said "Scientists explore what is; engineers create what has not been." (Paul Wright, *Intro to Engineering*).

4   In general, science is about discovering things or acquiring new knowledge. Scientists are always asking, "Why?" They are interested in advancing the knowledge base that we have in a specific area. The answers they seek may be of an abstract nature, such as understanding the beginning of the universe, or more practical, such as the reaction of a virus to a new drug.

5   The engineer also asks, "Why?" but it is because of a problem which is preventing a product or service from being produced. The engineer is always thinking about the application when asking why. The engineer becomes concerned with issues such as the demand for a product, the cost of producing the product, the impact on society and the environment of the product.

6   Scientists and engineers work in many of the same fields and industries but have different roles. Here are some examples:

- Scientists study the planets in our solar system to understand them; engineers study the planets so they can design a spacecraft to operate in the environment of that planet.
- Scientists study atomic structure to understand the nature of matter; engineers study the atomic structure in order to build smaller and faster microprocessors.
- Scientists study the human neurological system to understand the progression of neurological diseases; engineers study the human neurological system to design artificial limbs.
- Scientists create new chemical compounds in a laboratory; engineers create processes to mass-produce new chemical compounds for consumers.
- Scientists study the movement of tectonic plates to understand and predict earthquakes; engineers study the movement of tectonic plates to design safer buildings.

The Engineer and the Engineering Technologist

7   Another profession closely related to engineering is engineering technology. Engineering technology and engineering have similarities, yet there are differences; they have different career opportunities. ABET, which accredits engineering technology programs as well as engineering programs, defines engineering technology as follows: *Engineering technology is that part of the technological field which requires the application of scientific and engineering knowledge and methods combined with technical skills in support of engineering activities; it lies in the occupational spectrum between the craftsman and engineering at the end of the spectrum closest to the engineer.*

8   Technologists work with existing technology to produce goods for society. Technology students spend time in their curricula working with actual machines and equipment that are used in the jobs they will accept after graduation. By doing this, technologists are equipped to be productive in their occupation from the first day of work.

9   Both engineers and technologists apply technology for the betterment of society. The main difference between the two fields is that the engineer is able to create new technology through research, design and development. Rather than being trained to use specific machines or processes, engineering students study additional mathematics and engineering science subjects. This equips engineers to use these tools to advance the state of the art in their field and move technology forward.

10   There are areas where engineers and engineering technologists perform very similar jobs. For example, in manufacturing settings, engineers and technologists are employed as supervisors of assembly line workers. Also, in technical service fields both are hired to work as technical support personnel supporting equipment purchased by customers. However, most opportunities are different for engineering and engineering technology graduates.

1. With which of the following topics is the passage primarily concerned?
   Ⓐ A scientific definition of engineering
   Ⓑ A comparison of careers in science and engineering
   Ⓒ A classification of the types of engineering
   Ⓓ An example of technology in engineering

2. What kind of work do engineering technologists perform?
   Ⓐ They engage in basic technological research.
   Ⓑ They apply research to create technology.
   Ⓒ They make new products, using the latest technology.
   Ⓓ They use technological advances in tools and machines.

3. The word roles in the passage is closest in meaning to
   Ⓐ training
   Ⓑ ideas
   Ⓒ problems
   Ⓓ positions

4. The word phenomenon in the passage is closest in meaning to
   Ⓐ hazard
   Ⓑ system
   Ⓒ occurrence
   Ⓓ triumph

5. The word them in the passage refers to
   Ⓐ scientists
   Ⓑ planets
   Ⓒ engineers
   Ⓓ solar system

6. How does the author define *engineering technology* in paragraph 7?
   Ⓐ He uses the definition in a textbook.
   Ⓑ He defines the term in his own words.
   Ⓒ He quotes from a professional organization.
   Ⓓ He reads a definition from an engineering professor.

7. Which of the sentences below best expresses the information in the highlighted statement in the passage? The other choices change the meaning or leave out important information.
   Ⓐ Engineering science subjects and math are less important than training on machinery for engineering students.
   Ⓑ Training to use equipment is part of the students' curriculum, along with math and engineering courses.
   Ⓒ Engineering students take higher math and engineering science instead of engaging in hands-on training.
   Ⓓ Additional math and engineering science courses are required before training on machinery.

8. The author mentions all of the following in reference to a career in engineering EXCEPT
   Ⓐ engineers try to solve practical problems
   Ⓑ engineers apply scientific knowledge
   Ⓒ engineers are hired to teach technologists
   Ⓓ engineers consider production costs

9. It can be inferred that this passage would be published in
   Ⓐ a mathematics textbook at the college level
   Ⓑ an orientation book for engineering students
   Ⓒ a workbook in an advanced science course
   Ⓓ an engineering technology textbook

10. Four squares (□) indicate where the following sentence can be added to the passage.

    In order to make a good choice, it is necessary to understand what scientists and engineers do on the job.

    Where would the sentence best fit into the passage?
    Ⓐ
    Ⓑ
    Ⓒ
    Ⓓ

11. Complete the table below by matching each of the answer choices with the career to which it refers. All of the choices will be used.
    Ⓐ They study the movement of tectonic plates to predict earthquakes.
    Ⓑ They use the latest equipment to monitor changes in patterns.
    Ⓒ They design buildings that will withstand the stresses of earthquakes.
    Ⓓ They create models to build faster computers.
    Ⓔ They study each of the parts to repair computers.
    Ⓕ They propose theories of atomic structures for computer application.

Scientist	Engineer	Technologist
•	•	•
•	•	•

12. Complete a summary of the passage by selecting THREE answer choices that express the most important ideas. The other three sentences do not belong in the summary because they express ideas that are not in the passage or they do not refer to the major ideas. *This question is worth 2 points*.

What are the roles of various technology professionals?

Ⓐ An engineer seeks the answers to technological questions to create new technology.

Ⓑ Engineers and technicians provide customer support for technical equipment.

Ⓒ A scientist is involved in basic research to advance scientific knowledge.

Ⓓ Many students who excel in math and science are attracted to engineering fields.

Ⓔ Technicians use skills to accomplish work with existing equipment.

Ⓕ The engineer often works with managers in an office instead of in a laboratory setting.

Refer to pages 443–444 for the Explanatory Answers.

EXERCISE 74: Cause/Effect—Natural Sciences

In some questions in the Reading Section on the Paper-Based TOEFL, you will be asked to recall and relate information and content from cause-and-effect passages about various fields of study. Choose the best answer for multiple-choice questions.

Bioluminescence

Light from a living plant or animal is called bioluminescence, or cold light, to distinguish it from incandescence, or heat-generating light. Life forms could not produce incandescent light without being
Line burned. Their light is produced by chemicals combining in such a
5 way that little or no measurable heat is produced, and the life forms generating it are unharmed. Although bioluminescence is a relatively complicated process, it can be reduced to simple terms. Living light occurs when luciferin and oxygen combine in the presence of luciferase. In a few cases, fireflies the most common, an additional
10 compound called ATP is required.

The earliest recorded experiments with bioluminescence in the late 1800s are attributed to Raphael Dubois, who extracted a luminous fluid from a clam, observing that it continued to glow in the test tube for several minutes. He named the substance *luciferin*,
15 which means "the bearer of light." In further research, Dubois discovered that several chemicals were required for bioluminescence to occur. In his notes, it was recorded that a second important substance, which he called *luciferase*, was always present. In later studies of small, luminous sea creatures, Newton Harvey concluded
20 that *luciferin* was composed of carbon, hydrogen, and oxygen, which are the building blocks of all living cells. He also proved that there are a variety of *luciferins* and *luciferases*, specific to the plants and animals that produce them.

Much remains unknown, but many scientists who are studying
25 bioluminescence now believe that the origin of the phenomenon may be traced to a time when there was no oxygen in the Earth's atmosphere. When oxygen was gradually introduced into the atmosphere, it was actually poisonous to life forms. Plants and animals produced light to use up the oxygen in a gradual but
30 necessary adaptation. It is speculated that millions of years ago, all life may have produced light to survive. As the millennia passed, life forms on Earth became tolerant of, and finally dependent on oxygen, and the adaptation that produced bioluminescence was no longer necessary, but some primitive plants and animals continued to
35 use the light for new functions such as mating or attracting prey.

1. Which of the following is the main topic of the passage?
   Ⓐ Cold light
   Ⓑ Luciferase
   Ⓒ Primitive plants and animals
   Ⓓ Earth's atmosphere

2. According to the author, why has bioluminescence continued in modern plants and animals?
   Ⓐ For survival
   Ⓑ For mating or attracting prey
   Ⓒ For producing heat
   Ⓓ For burning excess oxygen

3. The word "primitive" in line 34 is closest in meaning to
   Ⓐ very old
   Ⓑ very large
   Ⓒ very important
   Ⓓ very common

4. The word "relatively" in line 6 is opposite in meaning to
   Ⓐ comparatively
   Ⓑ moderately
   Ⓒ exclusively
   Ⓓ partially

5. The word "it" in line 2 refers to
   Ⓐ a plant
   Ⓑ an animal
   Ⓒ bioluminescence
   Ⓓ incadescence

6. Where in the passage does the author explain how living light occurs?
   Ⓐ Lines 1–3
   Ⓑ Lines 7–9
   Ⓒ Lines 11–14
   Ⓓ Lines 18–21

7. What does the author mean by the statement in lines 4–6: "Their light is produced by chemicals combining in such a way that little or no measurable heat is produced and the life forms generating it are unharmed"?
   Ⓐ Chemicals combine to produce light without heat.
   Ⓑ The combination of chemicals produces more heat than light.
   Ⓒ The chemicals that produce heat and light cannot be measured.
   Ⓓ Heat and light are measured by chemicals.

8. What is true about *luciferin*?
   Ⓐ It was recently discovered.
   Ⓑ It was found to be poisonous.
   Ⓒ It occurs in the absence of *luciferase*.
   Ⓓ It produces light in animals.

9. Bioluminescence is described as all of the following EXCEPT
   Ⓐ a complex chemical process
   Ⓑ an adaptation of early plants and animals to the environment
   Ⓒ a form of cold light
   Ⓓ a poisonous substance

10. The paragraph following the passage most probably discusses
    Ⓐ incandescence in prehistoric plants and animals
    Ⓑ incandescence in modern plants and animals
    Ⓒ bioluminescence in prehistoric plants and animals
    Ⓓ bioluminescence in modern plants and animals

Refer to page 444 for the Explanatory Answers.

EXERCISE 75: Cause/Effect — Social Sciences

In some questions in the Reading Section on the Paper-Based TOEFL, you will be asked to recall and relate information and content from cause-and-effect passages about various fields of study. Choose the best answer for multiple-choice questions.

Why Are Americans Getting Older?

In 2000, persons sixty-five years and over already represented 13 percent of the total population in America, and by 2025, there will be 59 million elderly Americans, representing 21 percent of the population
Line of the United States. Furthermore, the percentage of the population over
5 age eighty-five will increase from about 1 percent currently to 5 percent in 2050. This population trend has been referred to as the graying of America.

To explain this demographic change, we must look to three factors. Fertility, mortality, and immigration in large part influence
10 all demographic trends and the graying of America is no exception. The large number of children born after World War II will increase the pool of elderly between 2010 and 2030. The "baby boom" will have become the "senior boom" sixty-five years later as this large segment of the population ages.

15 Although the increase in the birth rate is the most dramatic factor, the decline in the death rate is also significant. Medical advances have influenced life expectancy. Antibiotics and drug therapies as well as new surgical techniques have made a significant contribution. In addition, technological devices for diagnosis and treatment have saved and
20 extended lives. For example, whereas only 40 percent of those Americans born in 1900 had a life expectancy of sixty-five, in the year 2000, 80 percent reached the classic retirement age. The average male life span in 2000 was 71.4 years and increased to 73.3 by 2005. Among females, the life span increased from 78.3 years in 2000 to 81.3 years by 2005
25 (see chart).

In addition, immigration has contributed to the increasing number of elderly. After World War I, a massive immigration of young adults of child-bearing age occurred. Because the customs and traditions of the immigrants encouraged large families, and birth rates among this
30 specialized population were very high, their children, now among the elderly, are currently a significant segment of the older population.

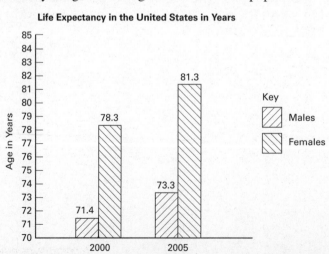

Life Expectancy in the United States in Years

1. Which of the following would be an
    alternative title for the passage?
    Ⓐ The Graying of America
    Ⓑ Immigration Patterns in America
    Ⓒ Trends in Life Expectancy
    Ⓓ Baby Boomers

2. The average life expectancy for an
    American woman in 2000 was
    Ⓐ 71.4 years
    Ⓑ 73.3 years
    Ⓒ 78.3 years
    Ⓓ 81.3 years

3. The word "pool" in line 11 refers to
    Ⓐ a group of people
    Ⓑ a general direction
    Ⓒ a negative attitude
    Ⓓ an increase in influence

4. The word "trends" in line 10 is closest in
    meaning to
    Ⓐ many questions
    Ⓑ small mistakes
    Ⓒ final conclusions
    Ⓓ general directions

5. The word "their" in line 30 refers to
    Ⓐ families
    Ⓑ elderly
    Ⓒ immigrants
    Ⓓ birth rates

6. Where in the passage does the author
    explain what has influenced life
    expectancy?
    Ⓐ Lines 12–14
    Ⓑ Lines 16–20
    Ⓒ Lines 22–25
    Ⓓ Lines 26–28

7. What does the author mean by the
    statement in lines 15–16: "Although the
    birth rate is the most dramatic factor, the
    decline in the death rate is also
    significant"?
    Ⓐ Both the increase in births and the
       decrease in deaths are significant.
    Ⓑ The higher number of births is less
       significant than the decrease in deaths.
    Ⓒ Lower birth rates and higher death
       rates have had dramatic results.
    Ⓓ A significant change in the number of
       births has balanced the change in the
       death rates.

8. When will the number of elderly people
    exceed 20 percent of the population?
    Ⓐ 2010
    Ⓑ 2020
    Ⓒ 2025
    Ⓓ 2030

9. The authors mentions all of the following
    as factors that have influenced population
    trends EXCEPT
    Ⓐ the "baby boom" after World War II
    Ⓑ the immigration after World War I
    Ⓒ the improvements in health care
    Ⓓ the decline in the birth rate among
       young Americans

10. It can be inferred from the passage that the
    word "gray" is a reference to
    Ⓐ the hair color typical of older people
    Ⓑ the last name of the person who has
       studied the population trends
    Ⓒ the diversity of colors in the
       population that mix to make gray
    Ⓓ the dismal outlook for the future
       because of population trends

Refer to pages 444–445 for the Explanatory Answers.

EXERCISE 76: Cause/Effect—Arts/Architecture

In some questions in the Reading Section on the Internet-Based TOEFL, you will be asked to recall and relate information and content from cause-and-effect passages found in college textbooks. Choose the best answer for multiple-choice questions. For computer-assisted questions, follow the directions on the screen.

The Art of Healing

Taking part in music and art classes is a well-established form of therapy. It can benefit patients socially, emotionally and physically. But researchers at the Chelsea and Westminster Hospital in England are exploring a different premise—that simply pleasing the eyes and the ears will help people recover. It's not a new idea. Back in 1860, Florence Nightingale wrote in her *Notes on Nursing* that brightly colored flowers and art helped patients recover more quickly. "This is no fancy. People say the effect is all on the mind. It is no such thing. The effect is on the body too." But the truth is that no one knows exactly why patients who listen to music or see paintings should recover quicker, or how to maximize the effect. That's what the new research is hoping to show.

Over the years, a trickle of results has suggested a link between the arts and well-being. But there have been few strictly controlled randomized trials like those that test the effectiveness of a new drug. One classic American study, which shows that architecture can affect recovery times and that patients do respond to their surroundings, is nearly 20 years old. It looked at 46 people who had had their gall bladders removed. Half of them were kept in hospital rooms with a pleasant view over some trees. The other half had rooms looking out onto a brick wall. The patients who had a room with a view needed smaller doses of painkillers on average and left the hospital almost a day earlier: a 10 percent shorter hospital stay than those faced with the brick wall (*Science*, vol 224, p 420). But it isn't so clear whether looking at pleasing pictures will have the same kind of effect.

More research has been done on the effect of music, and in 2002, David Evans of the Royal Adelaide Hospital in South Australia reanalyzed data from 19 earlier studies. He concluded that music was a cheap and effective way of relieving patients' anxiety (*Journal of Advanced Nursing*, vol 37, p 8). Some of the studies seemed to suggest that music could also lower blood pressure and reduce the need for painkillers. But these studies were too small to tell for sure.

At the Chelsea and Westminster, they have analyzed the results from studies of nearly 300 patients so far, and they are turning up some interesting effects. "For the first time, we have established physical and biological evidence for the influence of art on healthcare," says Rosalia Lelchuk Staricoff, who heads the hospital's research team.

The three-year research program began in 1999. The first phase established that 80 percent of patients in the hospital found art and music helped distract them from their medical problems and raised their spirits. Then in June 2000, the research moved up a gear when the King's Fund, a British charitable foundation, put up £70,000 to measure the clinical effect. The final stages of the research won't be made public for a while, but "the results so far are almost all positive," says Staricoff.

One of the early studies looked at cancer patients who were being given chemotherapy at the hospital. Many were anxious about their treatment and depressed about the possible outcome. "If you can relieve stress then it can help patients to make the most of the time they have to live," says Debbie Fenlon of Cancer Research UK.

But Fenlon thinks that easing anxiety and depression has physical effects, too. For example, it relieves pain and reduces nausea from chemotherapy. "If you're tense, you're more likely to feel pain. It's a fairly straightforward physical thing," she says. Although the effect is controversial, she thinks that reducing anxiety and depression could spur the body's immune system to fight cancer, too.

The 83 patients in this study were divided into three groups. One group listened to a 45-minute performance by live musicians during their treatment. A second group was treated in a room that had a selection of pictures hung on the walls. These were changed every week so that patients wouldn't see the same ones week after week. Finally, a control group was treated in a standard hospital ward, without any music or art.

Staricoff and her colleague Jane Duncan used a standard psychological questionnaire to assess anxiety and clinical depression in the patients. They found that both the paintings and the music lowered depression by about a third. However, music was more effective at lowering anxiety than art. On average, the art group had an anxiety score that was 18 percent lower, and the music group had a score 32 percent lower than the controls.

Is it trivial to worry about what's hanging on ward walls when there are bed and staff shortages and growing waiting lists to deal with? Staricoff hopes their work will convince funding bodies otherwise. After all, if music or paintings can take the place of a course of antidepressants, it has to be better for everyone.

The Art of Healing (Question References)

Paragraph 1 Taking part in music and art classes is a well-established form of therapy. It can benefit patients socially, emotionally and physically. But researchers at the Chelsea and Westminster Hospital in England are exploring a different premise—that simply pleasing the eyes and the ears will help people recover. It's not a new idea. Back in 1860, Florence Nightingale wrote in her *Notes on Nursing* that brightly colored flowers and art helped patients recover more quickly. "This is no fancy. People say the effect is all on the mind. It is no such thing. The effect is on the body too." But the truth is that no one knows exactly why patients who listen to music or see paintings should recover quicker, or how to maximize the effect. That's what the new research is hoping to show.

2 Over the years, a trickle of results has suggested a link between the arts and well-being. But there have been few strictly controlled randomized trials like those that test the effectiveness of a new drug. One classic American study, which shows that architecture can affect recovery times and that patients do respond to their surroundings, is nearly 20 years old. It looked at 46 people who had had their gall bladders removed. Half of them were kept in hospital rooms with a pleasant view over some trees. The other half had rooms looking out onto a brick wall. The patients who had a room with a view needed smaller doses of painkillers on average and left the hospital almost a day earlier: a 10 percent shorter hospital stay than those faced with the brick wall (*Science*, vol 224, p 420). But it isn't so clear whether looking at pleasing pictures will have the same kind of effect.

3 More research has been done on the effect of music, and in 2002, David Evans of the Royal Adelaide Hospital in South Australia reanalyzed data from 19 earlier studies. He concluded that music was a cheap and effective way of relieving patients' anxiety (*Journal of Advanced Nursing*, vol 37, p 8). Some of the studies seemed to suggest that music could also lower blood pressure and reduce the need for painkillers. But these studies were too small to tell for sure.

4 At the Chelsea and Westminster, they have analyzed the results from studies of nearly 300 patients so far, and they are turning up some interesting effects. "For the first time, we have established physical and biological evidence for the influence of art on healthcare," says Rosalia Lelchuk Staricoff, who heads the hospital's research team.

5 The three-year research program began in 1999. The first phase established that 80 percent of patients in the hospital found art and music helped distract them from their medical problems and raised their spirits. Then in June 2000, the research moved up a gear when the King's Fund, a British charitable foundation, put up £70,000 to measure the clinical effect. The final stages of the research won't be made public for a while, but "the results so far are almost all positive," says Staricoff.

6 One of the early studies looked at cancer patients who were being given chemotherapy at the hospital. Many were anxious about their treatment and depressed about the possible outcome. "If you can relieve stress then it can help patients to make the most of the time they have to live," says Debbie Fenlon of Cancer Research UK.

7   But Fenlon thinks that easing anxiety and depression has
physical effects, too. For example, it relieves pain and reduces
nausea from chemotherapy. "If you're tense, you're more likely to
feel pain. It's a fairly straightforward physical thing," she says.
Although the effect is controversial, she thinks that reducing anxiety
and depression could spur the body's immune system to fight cancer,
too.

8   The 83 patients in this study were divided into three groups. One
group listened to a 45-minute performance by live musicians during
their treatment. A second group was treated in a room that had a
selection of pictures hung on the walls. These were changed every
week so that patients wouldn't see the same ones week after week.
Finally, a control group was treated in a standard hospital ward,
without any music or art.

9   Staricoff and her colleague Jane Duncan used a standard
psychological questionnaire to assess anxiety and clinical depression
in the patients. They found that both the paintings and the music
lowered depression by about a third. [A] However, music was more
effective at lowering anxiety than art. [B] On average, the art group
had an anxiety score that was 18 percent lower, and the music group
had a score 32 percent lower than the controls. [C]

10   Is it trivial to worry about what's hanging on ward walls when
there are bed and staff shortages and growing waiting lists to deal
with? [D] Staricoff hopes their work will convince funding bodies
otherwise. After all, if music or paintings can take the place of a
course of antidepressants, it has to be better for everyone.

1. What is the main idea in this passage?
   Ⓐ Cancer patients respond positively to
   music during chemotherapy.
   Ⓑ Music and art classes are excellent
   forms of therapy for patients.
   Ⓒ Music and art in the hospital
   environment contribute to patient
   recovery.
   Ⓓ Research is being carried out at
   hospitals in England, the U.S., and
   Australia.

2. How did Staricoff and Duncan determine
   levels of anxiety and depression in their
   test subjects?
   Ⓐ By testing their blood pressures often
   Ⓑ By interviewing them in the hospital
   Ⓒ By using a psychological questionnaire
   Ⓓ By measuring their intake of
   antidepressants

3. The word trivial in the passage is closest in
   meaning to
   Ⓐ outmoded
   Ⓑ insignificant
   Ⓒ disputed
   Ⓓ extravagant

4. The word controversial in the passage is
   closest in meaning to
   Ⓐ having advantages
   Ⓑ causing disagreement
   Ⓒ doing damage
   Ⓓ making improvements

5. The word ones in the passage refers to
   Ⓐ patients
   Ⓑ pictures
   Ⓒ musicians
   Ⓓ walls

6. According to paragraph 8, how was the control group treated?
   Ⓐ With a questionnaire
   Ⓑ With a musical performance
   Ⓒ Without music or art
   Ⓓ Without changing the art

7. Which of the sentences below best expresses the information in the highlighted statement in the passage? The other choices change the meaning or leave out important information.
   Ⓐ Pain causes you to feel like you are tense.
   Ⓑ The more pain you have, the greater the tension.
   Ⓒ Tension increases the tendency to feel pain.
   Ⓓ When you are very tense, it is painful.

8. The author mentions all of the following as advantages of art and music in the hospital environment, EXCEPT
   Ⓐ most hospital staff have a higher level of job satisfaction
   Ⓑ the patients in some studies leave the hospital sooner
   Ⓒ some researchers believe the immune system is stimulated
   Ⓓ fewer pain medications are required by some patients

9. It can be inferred that
   Ⓐ the author is skeptical of the research results
   Ⓑ the researchers expect the final results to be positive
   Ⓒ there is very little funding for the current study
   Ⓓ the patients are not aware that they are in a study

10. Four squares (□) indicate where the following sentence can be added to the passage.

    The researchers have also gathered results from four additional studies in the antenatal clinic and the orthopedic unit, three of which were very promising.

    Where would the sentence best fit into the passage?
    Ａ
    Ｂ
    Ｃ
    Ｄ

11. Complete the table below by classifying each of the answer choices under the research study to which it refers. One of the answer choices will NOT be used.
    Ⓐ Patients with a pleasant view recovered sooner.
    Ⓑ Music relieved anxiety in 19 studies.
    Ⓒ Music and art diminished depression by one-third.
    Ⓓ The nausea from chemotherapy may have been reduced.
    Ⓔ Surgical patients required fewer doses of pain medication.
    Ⓕ Participating in art and music classes lowered blood pressure.
    Ⓖ Anxiety was alleviated by 18–32 percent.
    Ⓗ Music appeared to lower blood pressure in a few small studies.

Royal Adelaide study in Southern Australia	• •
Chelsea and Westminster study in the UK	• • •
Classic hospital study in the United States	• •

12. Complete a summary of the passage by selecting THREE answer choices that express the most important ideas. The other three sentences do not belong in the summary because they express ideas that are not in the passage or they do not refer to the major ideas. *This question is worth 2 points.*

    How do the arts relate to healing?
    Ⓐ The current Chelsea and Westminster studies are verifying the positive effect of the arts on healing.
    Ⓑ Historically, several studies have suggested a relationship between health and the arts.
    Ⓒ Music was more effective than art in lowering anxiety among cancer patients.
    Ⓓ Florence Nightingale noticed that art influenced her patients' recovery.
    Ⓔ The first phase of the Chelsea and Westminster studies established that art and music had a positive effect on attitudes.
    Ⓕ Additional funding will be required to continue longitudinal studies in England.

Refer to page 445 for the Explanatory Answers.

EXERCISE 77: Cause/Effect—Social Sciences

In some questions in the Reading Section on the Internet-Based TOEFL, you will be asked to recall and relate information and content from cause-and-effect passages found in college textbooks. Choose the best answer for multiple-choice questions. For computer-assisted questions, follow the directions on the screen.

The Dust Bowl

An ecological and economic disaster of unprecedented proportions struck the southern Great Plains in the mid 1930s. The region had suffered several drought years in the early 1930s. Such dry spells occurred regularly in roughly twenty-year cycles. But this time the parched earth became swept up in violent dust storms the likes of which had never been seen before. The dust storms were largely the consequence of years of stripping the landscape of its natural vegetation. During World War I, wheat fetched record-high prices on the world market, and for the next twenty years Great Plains farmers had turned the region into a vast wheat factory.

The wide flatlands of the Great Plains were especially suited to mechanized farming, and gasoline-powered tractors, disc plows, and harvester-thresher combines increased productivity enormously. Back in 1830 it had taken some fifty-eight hours of labor to bring an acre of wheat to the granary; in much of the Great Plains a hundred years later it required less than three hours. As wheat prices fell in the 1920s, farmers broke still more land to make up the difference with increased production. Great Plains farmers had created an ecological time bomb that exploded when drought returned in the early 1930s. With native buffalo grass destroyed for the sake of wheat growing, there was nothing left to prevent soil erosion. Dust storms blew away tens of millions of acres of rich topsoil, and thousands of farm families left the region. Those who stayed suffered deep economic and psychological losses from the calamity. The hardest-hit regions were western Kansas, eastern Colorado, western Oklahoma, the Texas Panhandle, and eastern New Mexico. It was the calamity in this southern part of the Great Plains that prompted a Denver journalist to coin the phrase "Dust Bowl."

Black blizzards of dust a mile and a half high rolled across the landscape, darkening the sky and whipping the earth into great drifts of dust that settled over hundreds of miles. Dust storms made it difficult for humans and livestock to breathe and destroyed crops and trees over vast areas. Dust storms turned day into night, terrifying those caught in them. "Dust pneumonia" and other respiratory infections afflicted thousands, and many travelers found themselves stranded in automobiles and trains unable to move. The worst storms occurred in the early spring of 1935.

Several federal agencies intervened directly to relieve the distress. Many thousands of Great Plains farm families were given direct emergency relief by the Resettlement Administration. Other federal assistance included crop and seed loans, moratoriums on loan payments, and temporary jobs with the Works Progress

Administration. In most Great Plains counties, from one-fifth to one-third of the families applied for relief; in the hardest-hit communities as many as 90 percent of the families received direct government aid. The Agricultural Adjustment Administration paid wheat farmers millions of dollars not to grow what they could not sell and encouraged the diversion of acreage from soil-depleting crops like wheat to soil-enriching crops such as sorghum.

To reduce the pressure from grazing cattle on the remaining grasslands, the Drought Relief Service of the Department of Agriculture purchased more than 8 million head of cattle in 1934 and 1935. For a brief time, the federal government was the largest cattle owner in the world. This agency also lent ranchers money to feed their remaining cattle. The Taylor Grazing Act of 1934 brought stock grazing on 8 million acres of public domain lands under federal management.

The federal government also pursued longer-range policies designed to alter land-use patterns, reverse soil erosion, and nourish the return of grasslands. The Department of Agriculture, under Secretary Henry A. Wallace, sought to change farming practices. The spearhead for this effort was the Soil Conservation Service (SCS), which conducted research into controlling wind and water erosion, set up demonstration projects, and offered technical assistance, supplies, and equipment to farmers engaged in conservation work on farms and ranches. The SCS pumped additional federal funds into the Great Plains and created a new rural organization, the soil conservation district, which administered conservation regulations locally.

By 1940 the acreage subject to blowing in the Dust Bowl area of the southern Plains had been reduced from roughly 50 million acres to less than 4 million acres. In the face of the Dust Bowl disaster, New Deal farm policies had restricted market forces in agriculture. But the return of regular rainfall and the outbreak of World War II led many farmers to abandon the techniques that the SCS had taught them to accept. Wheat farming expanded and farms grew as farmers once again pursued commercial agriculture with little concern for its long-term effects on the land.

The Dust Bowl (Question References)

Paragraph 1   An ecological and economic disaster of unprecedented proportions struck the southern Great Plains in the mid 1930s. The region had suffered several drought years in the early 1930s. Such dry spells occurred regularly in roughly twenty-year cycles. But this time the parched earth became swept up in violent dust storms the likes of which had never been seen before. The dust storms were largely the consequence of years of stripping the landscape of its natural vegetation. During World War I, wheat fetched record-high prices on the world market, and for the next twenty years Great Plains farmers had turned the region into a vast wheat factory.

2   The wide flatlands of the Great Plains were especially suited to mechanized farming, and gasoline-powered tractors, disc plows, and harvester-thresher combines increased productivity enormously. Back in 1830 it had taken some fifty-eight hours of labor to bring an acre of wheat to the granary; in much of the Great Plains a hundred years later it required less than three hours. As wheat prices fell in the 1920s, farmers broke still more land to make up the difference with increased production. Great Plains farmers had created an ecological time bomb that exploded when drought returned in the early 1930s. [A] With native buffalo grass destroyed for the sake of wheat growing, there was nothing left to prevent soil erosion. [B] Dust storms blew away tens of millions of acres of rich topsoil, and thousands of farm families left the region. Those who stayed suffered deep economic and psychological losses from the calamity. [C] The hardest-hit regions were western Kansas, eastern Colorado, western Oklahoma, the Texas Panhandle, and eastern New Mexico. [D] It was the calamity in this southern part of the Great Plains that prompted a Denver journalist to coin the phrase "Dust Bowl."

3   Black blizzards of dust a mile and a half high rolled across the landscape, darkening the sky and whipping the earth into great drifts of dust that settled over hundreds of miles. Dust storms made it difficult for humans and livestock to breathe and destroyed crops and trees over vast areas. Dust storms turned day into night, terrifying those caught in them. "Dust pneumonia" and other respiratory infections afflicted thousands, and many travelers found themselves stranded in automobiles and trains unable to move. The worst storms occurred in the early spring of 1935.

4   Several federal agencies intervened directly to relieve the distress. Many thousands of Great Plains farm families were given direct emergency relief by the Resettlement Administration. Other federal assistance included crop and seed loans, moratoriums on loan payments, and temporary jobs with the Works Progress Administration. In most Great Plains counties, from one-fifth to one-third of the families applied for relief; in the hardest-hit communities as many as 90 percent of the families received direct government aid. The Agricultural Adjustment Administration paid wheat farmers millions of dollars not to grow what they could not sell and encouraged the diversion of acreage from soil-depleting crops like wheat to soil-enriching crops such as sorghum.

5   To reduce the pressure from grazing cattle on the remaining grasslands, the Drought Relief Service of the Department of

Agriculture purchased more than 8 million head of cattle in 1934 and 1935. For a brief time, the federal government was the largest cattle owner in the world. This agency also lent ranchers money to feed their remaining cattle. The Taylor Grazing Act of 1934 brought stock grazing on 8 million acres of public domain lands under federal management.

6   The federal government also pursued longer-range policies designed to alter land-use patterns, reverse soil erosion, and nourish the return of grasslands. The Department of Agriculture, under Secretary Henry A. Wallace, sought to change farming practices. The spearhead for this effort was the Soil Conservation Service (SCS), which conducted research into controlling wind and water erosion, set up demonstration projects, and offered technical assistance, supplies, and equipment to farmers engaged in conservation work on farms and ranches. The SCS pumped additional federal funds into the Great Plains and created a new rural organization, the soil conservation district, which administered conservation regulations locally.

7   By 1940 the acreage subject to blowing in the Dust Bowl area of the southern Plains had been reduced from roughly 50 million acres to less than 4 million acres. In the face of the Dust Bowl disaster, New Deal farm policies had restricted market forces in agriculture. But the return of regular rainfall and the outbreak of World War II led many farmers to abandon the techniques that the SCS had taught them to accept. Wheat farming expanded and farms grew as farmers once again pursued commercial agriculture with little concern for its long-term effects on the land.

1. What is the main idea in this passage?
   - Ⓐ The Dust Bowl was named by a journalist in Denver.
   - Ⓑ Ranchers and farmers competed for land in the Dust Bowl.
   - Ⓒ Conservation policies never succeeded in the Dust Bowl.
   - Ⓓ Farming practices in the Dust Bowl resulted in a disaster.

2. How many acres were affected by the erosion at the height of the storms?
   - Ⓐ 50 million
   - Ⓑ 10 million
   - Ⓒ 8 million
   - Ⓓ 4 million

3. The word calamity in the passage is closest in meaning to
   - Ⓐ situation
   - Ⓑ disaster
   - Ⓒ storm
   - Ⓓ region

4. The word alter in the passage is closest in meaning to
   - Ⓐ expand
   - Ⓑ predict
   - Ⓒ notice
   - Ⓓ modify

5. The word them in the passage refers to
   - Ⓐ farmers
   - Ⓑ techniques
   - Ⓒ farms
   - Ⓓ policies

6. According to paragraph 7, which of the following practices did farmers use after World War II?
   - Ⓐ New Deal farm policies
   - Ⓑ The SCS techniques
   - Ⓒ Cattle grazing on farmland
   - Ⓓ Commercial methods

7. Which of the sentences below best expresses the information in the highlighted statement in the passage? The other choices change the meaning or leave out important information.
   - Ⓐ Planting sorghum with wheat saved the government millions of dollars in subsidies.
   - Ⓑ The government subsidized crops that contributed to the regeneration of the soil.
   - Ⓒ Farmers sold their wheat crops to the government for a large subsidy.
   - Ⓓ The soil was depleted because the government had subsidized wheat crops.

8. The author mentions all of the following government relief programs EXCEPT
   - Ⓐ technical support for farmers in soil conservation techniques
   - Ⓑ loans to ranchers for the purchase of cattle feed
   - Ⓒ temporary employment in the Works Progress Administration
   - Ⓓ the purchase of homesteads that had been abandoned

9. It can be inferred from the passage that
   - Ⓐ ranchers caused the Dust Bowl by grazing too many buffalo on the grasslands
   - Ⓑ the Dust Bowl was brought to an end by World War II
   - Ⓒ the Great Plains is a wheat-producing region in the United States
   - Ⓓ all the homesteaders had to abandon their farms during the Dust Bowl

10. Four squares (☐) indicate where the following sentence can be added to the passage.

    A contemporary newspaper account describes dust blowing in through closed doors and windows, destroying possessions and making provisions inedible.

    Where would the sentence best fit into the passage?
    - Ⓐ
    - Ⓑ
    - Ⓒ
    - Ⓓ

11. Complete the table below by classifying each of the answer choices as either one of the causes of the Dust Bowl or one of the solutions to the problem. One of the answer choices will NOT be used.

   Ⓐ Wind storms
   Ⓑ Soil Conservation Service
   Ⓒ Transportation costs
   Ⓓ High prices for wheat
   Ⓔ Sorghum crops
   Ⓕ Government policies
   Ⓖ Less natural vegetation
   Ⓗ Subsidies for farmers

Causes	• • •
Solutions	• • • •

12. Complete a summary of the passage by selecting THREE answer choices that express the most important ideas. The other three sentences do not belong in the summary because they express ideas that are not in the passage or they do not refer to the major ideas. *This question is worth 2 points.*

   In the 1930s, an ecological and economic disaster struck the Great Plains.
   Ⓐ The federal government became the largest cattle owner in the world.
   Ⓑ Federal agencies intervened to assist farmers and ranchers in the Great Plains.
   Ⓒ Many farmers and homesteaders left the Great Plains during the worst drought.
   Ⓓ The Works Progress Administration built bridges, roads, and public structures.
   Ⓔ Farmers plowed under the natural vegetation in order to grow wheat.
   Ⓕ Soil erosion and dust storms combined to create the Dust Bowl.

Refer to page 446 for the Explanatory Answers.

EXERCISE 78: Persuasion/Justification—Natural Sciences

In some questions in the Reading Section on the Paper-Based TOEFL, you will be asked to recall and relate information and content from persuasion or justification passages about various fields of study. Choose the best answer for multiple-choice questions.

Endangered Species

There are three valid arguments to support the preservation of endangered species. An aesthetic justification contends that biodiversity contributes to the quality of life because many of the

Line endangered plants and animals are particularly appreciated for their

5 unique physical beauty. The aesthetic role of nature in all its diverse forms is reflected in the art and literature of every culture, attaining symbolic status in the spiritual life of many groups. According to the proponents of the aesthetic argument, people need nature in all its diverse and beautiful forms as part of the experience of the world.

10 Another argument that has been put forward, especially by groups in the medical and pharmacological fields, is that of ecological self-interest. By preserving all species, we retain a balance of nature that is ultimately beneficial to humankind. Recent research on global ecosystems has been cited as evidence that every species

15 contributes important or even essential functions that may be necessary to the survival of our own species. Some advocates of the ecological argument contend that important chemical compounds derived from rare plants may contain the key to a cure for one of the diseases currently threatening human beings. If we do not protect

20 other species, then they cannot protect us.

Apart from human advantage in both the aesthetic and ecological arguments, the proponents of a moral justification contend that all species have the right to exist, a viewpoint stated in the United Nations World Charter for Nature, created in 1982. Furthermore, if

25 humankind views itself as the stewards of all the creatures on Earth, then it is incumbent upon human beings to protect them, and to ensure the continued existence of all species. Moral justification has been extended by a movement called "deep ecology," the members of which rank the biosphere higher than people because the

30 continuation of life depends on this larger perspective. To carry their argument to its logical conclusion, all choices must be made for the biosphere, not for people.

1. Which of the following is the main topic of the passage?
   Ⓐ The beauty of the world
   Ⓑ The quality of life
   Ⓒ The preservation of species
   Ⓓ The balance of nature

2. Which of the arguments supports animal rights?
   Ⓐ Aesthetic justification
   Ⓑ Ecological argument
   Ⓒ Self-interest argument
   Ⓓ Moral justification

3. The word "perspective" in line 30 could best be replaced by
   Ⓐ ideal
   Ⓑ event
   Ⓒ truth
   Ⓓ view

4. The word "unique" in line 5 is closest in meaning to
   Ⓐ strong
   Ⓑ new
   Ⓒ special
   Ⓓ active

5. The word "them" in line 26 refers to
   Ⓐ humankind
   Ⓑ stewards
   Ⓒ creatures
   Ⓓ human beings

6. Where in the passage does the author explain how rare species contribute to the health of the human species?
   Ⓐ Lines 2–5
   Ⓑ Lines 7–9
   Ⓒ Lines 16–19
   Ⓓ Lines 24–27

7. What does the author mean by the statement in lines 7–9: "According to the proponents of the aesthetic argument, people need nature in all its diverse and beautiful forms as part of the experience of the world"?
   Ⓐ The world is experienced by nature in various forms that are equally beautiful.
   Ⓑ People are naturally attracted to beautiful forms rather than to different ones.
   Ⓒ Nature is beautiful because it provides varied experiences for people.
   Ⓓ An appreciation of the Earth requires that people have an opportunity to enjoy the diversity and beauty of nature.

8. According to the passage, what do we know from research on global ecosystems?
   Ⓐ Nature is very diverse.
   Ⓑ A balance of nature is important.
   Ⓒ Humans have a responsibility to nature.
   Ⓓ Nature represents spiritual values.

9. The author mentions all of the following as justifications for the protection of endangered species EXCEPT
   Ⓐ the natural compounds needed for medicines
   Ⓑ the intrinsic value of the beauty of nature
   Ⓒ the control of pollution in the biosphere
   Ⓓ the right to life implied by their existence

10. It can be inferred from the passage that the author
   Ⓐ is a member of the "deep ecology" movement
   Ⓑ does not agree with ecological self-interest
   Ⓒ supports all of the arguments to protect species
   Ⓓ participated in drafting the Charter for Nature

Refer to pages 446–447 for the Explanatory Answers.

EXERCISE 79: Persuasion/Justification—Social Sciences

In some questions in the Reading Section on the Paper-Based TOEFL, you will be asked to recall and relate information and content from persuasion or justification passages about various fields of study. Choose the best answer for multiple-choice questions.

Prison Reform

In the United States today there are more than half a million criminals serving time in jails or prisons. Most prisoners are male high school dropouts between the ages of 18 and 29. Even more
Line　shocking is the fact that the number and rate of imprisonment has
5　more than doubled over the past twenty years, and the recidivism—that is, the rate for rearrest—is more than 60 percent.

Although the stated objective of the criminal justice system, on both federal and state levels, is to rehabilitate the inmates and reintegrate them into society, the system itself does not support such
10　a goal. Although most jails are located within the community, prisons are usually geographically or psychologically isolated and terribly overcrowded. Even in the more enlightened prisons, only one-third of the inmates have vocational training opportunities or work release options. Even fewer have access to qualified counselors,
15　psychologists, or social workers.

If prisons are indeed to achieve the goal of rehabilitating offenders, then the prisons themselves will have to change. First, they will have to be smaller, housing no more than five hundred prisoners. It has been shown that crowding in large facilities is not
20　conducive to behavior modification. Second, they will have to be built in or near population centers with community resources available for gradual reintegration into society. This must include social and psychological services. Finally, prison programs must be restructured to provide work release and vocational and academic
25　training for all inmates to prepare them with skills that carry over into their lives after release. In addition to parole terms and community supervised work release, successful models for such collaborative efforts between the criminal justice system and the community already exist in several hundred half-way houses
30　throughout the country where inmates complete their sentences while beginning to reestablish their lives as productive members of society. Studies suggest that imprisonment as it is currently administered must be viewed as punishment rather than reform. Until we approach the problem in terms of changing behaviors rather
35　than segregating offenders, prisoners who are released will probably return to a life of crime.

1. What is the author's main point?
    - Ⓐ Prisons must be restructured if they are to accomplish the goal of rehabilitation.
    - Ⓑ Goals for community collaboration have been successful.
    - Ⓒ Most of the criminals serving time in prison do not have goals.
    - Ⓓ The criminal justice system must establish a better goal.

2. According to the author, how many prisoners are offered training or work release?
    - Ⓐ None
    - Ⓑ $33\frac{1}{3}$ percent
    - Ⓒ 50 percent
    - Ⓓ 60 percent

3. The word "recidivism" in line 5 refers to
    - Ⓐ all people who are imprisoned
    - Ⓑ people who return to prison after release
    - Ⓒ people who drop out of high school
    - Ⓓ people who have been in prison for a long time

4. The word "options" in line 14 is closest in meaning to
    - Ⓐ exceptions
    - Ⓑ challenges
    - Ⓒ alternatives
    - Ⓓ benefits

5. The word "them" in line 9 refers to
    - Ⓐ prison systems
    - Ⓑ inmates
    - Ⓒ goals
    - Ⓓ levels

6. Where in the passage does the author explain the rate of imprisonment over the past twenty years?
    - Ⓐ Lines 1–2
    - Ⓑ Lines 3–6
    - Ⓒ Lines 7–10
    - Ⓓ Lines 12–14

7. What does the author mean by the statement in lines 7–10: "Although the stated objective of the criminal justice system, on both federal and state levels, is to rehabilitate the inmates and reintegrate them into society, the systems themselves do not support such a goal"?
    - Ⓐ Inmates in prisons do not participate in rehabilitation programs before they are reintegrated into society.
    - Ⓑ The goal of rehabilitation and reintegration into society is encouraged by the prison systems.
    - Ⓒ Prison systems do not promote rehabilitation and reintegration despite their goal.
    - Ⓓ Rehabilitation cannot be achieved by prisons without reintegration into society.

8. Why should prisons be built near towns or cities?
    - Ⓐ Prisoners benefit from family visitations.
    - Ⓑ Workers need to be close to their homes.
    - Ⓒ Reintegration programs require resources.
    - Ⓓ Prisons contribute to the economies.

9. The author mentions all the following as necessary to prison reform EXCEPT
    - Ⓐ newer buildings
    - Ⓑ smaller institutions
    - Ⓒ vocational training
    - Ⓓ collaboration with the community

10. The paragraph following this passage most probably discusses
    - Ⓐ the goals of most state and federal prisons
    - Ⓑ the cost of prison reform
    - Ⓒ examples of models for community collaboration
    - Ⓓ problems with the current criminal justice system

Refer to pages 447–448 for the Explanatory Answers.

EXERCISE 80: Persuasion/Justification—Humanities/Business

In some questions in the Reading Section on the Internet-Based TOEFL, you will be asked to recall and relate information and content from persuasion or justification passages found in college textbooks. Choose the best answer for multiple-choice questions. For computer-assisted questions, follow the directions on the screen.

Lexicostatistical Glottochronology

Lexicostatistical glottochronology is an approach, devised by the American linguists Morris Swadesh (1909–67) and Robert Lees (1922–) in the late 1940s, which determines the rate at which a language has changed, over the centuries. It aims to work out the length of time which has elapsed since two related languages (or two languages thought to be related) began to diverge. *Glottochronology* is the name of the study; *lexicostatistics* is the name of the technique it uses (but some authors use the two terms synonymously).

A sample of vocabulary is taken from the languages, using the basic word-list, and the number of similar words between the languages is counted, allowing for the effect of phonetic change. Thus, Italian *padre* and Portuguese *pai* would be accepted as equivalent, or *cognate*, words for "father," because the relationship is explicable, whereas there is no reasonable phonetic explanation which could relate either of these to, say, the Eskimo word for "father," *ataataq*. The word-list tries to avoid geographically or culturally biased words, such as the names of plants or animals, which would vary greatly from one part of the world to another.

Glottochronologists assume that the lower the number of vocabulary agreements between the two samples, the longer the languages have been separated. Two languages which have 60% vocabulary in common would be thought to have diverged longer ago than two languages which have 80% in common. Swadesh and Lees took several languages where the period of time-change is known, and worked out a correlation between the percentage of common vocabulary and the interval of time (or "time-depth") which has elapsed since they diverged (as in the case of the Romance languages, which have diverged from Latin since the early Christian era). They found that on average two languages would have 86% in common after 1,000 years of separation.

Working backwards, on this basis, they constructed a table of historical divergence. Using this kind of table, estimates have been given for the possible point of divergence of the languages in many of the world's families.

Criticisms

The approach is a controversial one for several reasons. The method itself has been attacked on the ground that it is impossible to construct a word-list that shows no cultural bias—*sun* and *moon*, for example, have great religious significance in some cultures. It is also argued that the rate of change may not be the same for all languages, and that far more known language histories would need to be analyzed before the 86% figure was truly convincing. The method becomes less definite the further back in history it goes, and the slightest of errors in the compilation of the word sample could result in great inaccuracy; for instance, after 70 centuries of divergence, there would be only 12% of cognates left, so that if just one cognate was misanalyzed, the result would be three centuries in error. There are all kinds of problems which arise relating to whether words from different languages are indeed "the same"—in meaning as well as in form. And often, not enough information is available about a language (especially for older states) for a complete sample to be drawn up.

Swadesh was fully aware of the limitations of the procedure. But he argued that there must be a balance between the forces which maintain uniformity in language and those which encourage fluctuation, and pointed out that it is possible to obtain ancillary evidence from the dating methods used in archaeology. Certainly the approach has generated many interesting hypotheses about early language states and the relative chronology of modern languages, and several scholars still use it in their work—if only because no alternative technique has been devised.

Glossary
cognate: words from two different languages that look or sound alike
phonetic: the sounds of speech

Lexicostatistical Glottochronology (Question References)

Paragraph 1   Lexicostatistical glottochronology is an approach, devised by the American linguists Morris Swadesh (1909–67) and Robert Lees (1922–) in the late 1940s, which determines the rate at which a language has changed, over the centuries. It aims to work out the length of time which has elapsed since two related languages (or two languages thought to be related) began to diverge. *Glottochronology* is the name of the study; *lexicostatistics* is the name of the technique it uses (but some authors use the two terms synonymously).

2   A sample of vocabulary is taken from the languages, using the basic word-list, and the number of similar words between the languages is counted, allowing for the effect of phonetic change. Thus, Italian *padre* and Portuguese *pai* would be accepted as equivalent, or *cognate*, words for "father," because the relationship is explicable, whereas there is no reasonable phonetic explanation which could relate either of these to, say, the Eskimo word for "father," *ataataq*. The word-list tries to avoid geographically or culturally biased words, such as the names of plants or animals, which would vary greatly from one part of the world to another.

3   Glottochronologists assume that the lower the number of vocabulary agreements between the two samples, the longer the languages have been separated. Two languages which have 60% vocabulary in common would be thought to have diverged longer ago than two languages which have 80% in common. Swadesh and Lees took several languages where the period of time-change is known, and worked out a correlation between the percentage of common vocabulary and the interval of time (or "time-depth") which has elapsed since they diverged (as in the case of the Romance languages, which have diverged from Latin since the early Christian era). They found that on average two languages would have 86% in common after 1,000 years of separation. [A]

4   Working backwards, on this basis, they constructed a table of historical divergence. [B] Using this kind of table, estimates have been given for the possible point of divergence of the languages in many of the world's families.

Criticisms

5   The approach is a controversial one for several reasons. [C] The method itself has been attacked on the ground that it is impossible to construct a word-list that shows no cultural bias—*sun* and *moon*, for example, have great religious significance in some cultures. [D] It is also argued that the rate of change may not be the same for all languages, and that far more known language histories would need to be analyzed before the 86% figure was truly convincing. The method becomes less definite the further back in history it goes, and the slightest of errors in the compilation of the word sample could result in great inaccuracy; for instance, after 70 centuries of divergence, there would be only 12% of cognates left, so that if just one cognate was misanalyzed, the result would be three centuries in error. There are all kinds of problems which arise relating to whether words from different languages are indeed "the same"—in meaning

as well as in form. And often, not enough information is available about a language (especially for older states) for a complete sample to be drawn up.

6   Swadesh was fully aware of the limitations of the procedure. But he argued that there must be a balance between the forces which maintain uniformity in language and those which encourage fluctuation, and pointed out that it is possible to obtain ancillary evidence from the dating methods used in archaeology. Certainly the approach has generated many interesting hypotheses about early language states and the relative chronology of modern languages, and several scholars still use it in their work—if only because no alternative technique has been devised.

1. Which of the following is the main topic of the passage?
   Ⓐ Cognate vocabulary word-lists
   Ⓑ Limitations of glottochronology
   Ⓒ Comparisons of Romance languages
   Ⓓ Historical divergence of related languages

2. How much common vocabulary could be expected after languages had been separated for 1000 years?
   Ⓐ 12 percent
   Ⓑ 60 percent
   Ⓒ 80 percent
   Ⓓ 86 percent

3. The word ancillary in the passage is closest in meaning to
   Ⓐ recent
   Ⓑ convincing
   Ⓒ additional
   Ⓓ organized

4. The word limitations in the passage is closest in meaning to
   Ⓐ weak points
   Ⓑ difficult instructions
   Ⓒ dangerous results
   Ⓓ brief conclusions

5. The word those in the passage refers to
   Ⓐ methods
   Ⓑ language
   Ⓒ limitations
   Ⓓ forces

6. According to paragraph 1, what is a definition of *lexicostatistical glottochronology*?
   Ⓐ A method to determine the relationship between two languages
   Ⓑ A technique that dates the age of a language
   Ⓒ An approach that verifies the spelling of related words
   Ⓓ A system that locates synonyms in a language

7. Which of the sentences below best expresses the information in the highlighted statement in the passage? The other choices change the meaning or leave out important information.
   Ⓐ Languages separated for a long time will have two samples of vocabulary that agree.
   Ⓑ Vocabulary in two samples will have fewer agreements because the languages are separated.
   Ⓒ Fewer vocabulary items will agree when languages have separated a long time ago.
   Ⓓ Longer words will tend to agree even when languages have been separated.

8. The author mentions all of the following as criticisms of the approach, EXCEPT
   Ⓐ some languages may change more rapidly than others
   Ⓑ small errors compound over time
   Ⓒ no alternative method is available
   Ⓓ word-lists may be culturally biased

9. It can be inferred from the passage that the author
   Ⓐ is not interested in glottochronology
   Ⓑ worked with linguists Swadesh and Lees
   Ⓒ uses glottochronology in his own research
   Ⓓ has a balanced view of the work by Swadesh and Lees

10. Four squares (☐) indicate where the following sentence can be added to the passage.

    The scale in years begins at 25,000 years ago and stops at 0 years ago, that is, the present.

    Where would the sentence best fit into the passage?
    Ⓐ
    Ⓑ ·
    Ⓒ
    Ⓓ

11. Complete the table below by classifying each of the answer choices as either an acceptable or a controversial word for the basic word-list. All answer choices will be used.
    Ⓐ Sun
    Ⓑ Father
    Ⓒ Pine tree
    Ⓓ Man
    Ⓔ Eye
    Ⓕ Deer
    Ⓖ Blueberry

Acceptable Word	Controversial Word
•	•
•	•
•	•
	•

12. Complete a summary of the passage by selecting THREE answer choices that express the most important ideas. The other three sentences do not belong in the summary because they express ideas that are not in the passage or they do not refer to the major ideas. *This question is worth 2 points*.

   Lexicostatistical glottochronology is a linguistic approach devised by Swadesh and Lees.

   Ⓐ A table provides estimates for the number of years of linguistic divergence.

   Ⓑ Evidence from archaeology can be used to date the language separation.

   Ⓒ The Italian word *padre* and Portuguese *pai* are accepted cognates.

   Ⓓ Samples of languages are compared using a carefully constructed word-list.

   Ⓔ Cognate words are counted, and a percentage of word agreements is calculated.

   Ⓕ The word-list includes 100 of the most common vocabulary words across cultures.

Refer to pages 448–449 for the Explanatory Answers.

EXERCISE 81: Persuasion/Justification—Arts/Architecture

In some questions in the Reading Section on the Internet-Based TOEFL, you will be asked to recall and relate information and content from persuasion or justification passages found in college textbooks. Choose the best answer for multiple-choice questions. For computer-assisted questions, follow the directions on the screen.

Looking at Art

Art communicates to us primarily through our eyes. We look at art, and we try to find some meaning in the experience. If we are to begin to think about art more seriously, we might do well to become more aware of the process of seeing itself. What is it to look?

Science tells us that seeing is a mode of perception, which is the recognition and interpretation of sensory data—in other words, how information comes in our eyes (ears, nose, taste buds, fingertips), and what we make of it. In visual perception our eyes take in information in the form of light patterns; the brain processes these patterns to give them meaning. The mechanics of perception work much the same way for everyone, yet in a given situation we do not all see the same things.

We can take great pleasure in merely looking at art, just as we take pleasure in the view of a distant mountain range or watching the sun set over the ocean. But art, unlike nature, is a human creation. It is one of the many ways we express ourselves and attempt to communicate. A work of art is the product of human intelligence, and we can meet it with our own intelligence on equal footing. This is where study comes in.

The understanding of process—the *how*—often contributes quite a lot to our appreciation of art. If you understand why painting in watercolor may be different from painting in oil, why clay responds differently to the artist's hands than does wood or glass, why a stone building has different structural needs than one made of poured concrete—you will have a richer appreciation of the artist's expression.

Knowing the place of a work of art in history—what went before and came after—can also deepen your understanding. Artists learn to make art by studying the achievements of the past and observing the efforts of their contemporaries. They adapt ideas to serve their own needs and then bequeath those ideas to future generations of artists. The more you know about this living current of artistic energy, the more interesting each work of art will become. For example, Matisse assumed that his audience would know that Venus was the ancient Roman goddess of love. But he also hoped that they would be familiar with one Venus in particular, a famous Greek statue known as the *Venus de Milo*. Knowing the Greek work deepens our pleasure in Matisse's version, for we see that in "carving" his Venus out of a sheet of white paper, he evokes the way a long-ago sculptor carved her out of a block of white marble.

An artist may create a specific work for any of a thousand reasons. An awareness of the *why* may give some insight as well. Looking at Van Gogh's *The Starry Night*, it might help you to know that Van Gogh was intrigued by the belief that people journeyed to a star after their death, and that there they continued their lives. "Just as we take the train to get to Tarascon or Rouen," he wrote in a letter, "we take death to reach a star." The tree that rises so dramatically in the foreground of the painting is a cypress, which has often served as a symbol of both death and eternal life. This knowledge might help you to understand why Van Gogh felt so strongly about the night sky, and what his painting might have meant to him.

But no matter how much you study, Van Gogh's painting will never mean for you exactly what it meant for him, nor should it. An artist's work grows from a lifetime of experiences, thoughts, and emotions; no one else can duplicate them exactly. Great works of art hold many meanings. The greatest of them seem to speak anew to each generation and to each attentive observer. The most important thing is that some works of art come to mean something for *you*, that your own experiences, thoughts, and emotions find a place in them, for then you will have made them live.

Looking at Art (Question References)

Paragraph 1   Art communicates to us primarily through our eyes. We look at art, and we try to find some meaning in the experience. If we are to begin to think about art more seriously, we might do well to become more aware of the process of seeing itself. What is it to look?

2   Science tells us that seeing is a mode of perception, which is the recognition and interpretation of sensory data—in other words, how information comes in our eyes (ears, nose, taste buds, fingertips), and what we make of it. In visual perception our eyes take in information in the form of light patterns; the brain processes these patterns to give them meaning. ⒶThe mechanics of perception work much the same way for everyone, yet in a given situation we do not all see the same things. Ⓑ

3   We can take great pleasure in merely looking at art, just as we take pleasure in the view of a distant mountain range or watching the sun set over the ocean. Ⓒ But art, unlike nature, is a human creation. It is one of the many ways we express ourselves and attempt to communicate. Ⓓ A work of art is the product of human intelligence, and we can meet it with our own intelligence on equal footing. This is where study comes in.

4   The understanding of process—the *how*—often contributes quite a lot to our appreciation of art. If you understand why painting in watercolor may be different from painting in oil, why clay responds differently to the artist's hands than does wood or glass, why a stone building has different structural needs than one made of poured concrete—you will have a richer appreciation of the artist's expression.

5   Knowing the place of a work of art in history—what went before and came after—can also deepen your understanding. Artists learn to make art by studying the achievements of the past and observing the efforts of their contemporaries. They adapt ideas to serve their own needs and then bequeath those ideas to future generations of artists. The more you know about this living current of artistic energy, the more interesting each work of art will become. For example, Matisse assumed that his audience would know that Venus was the ancient Roman goddess of love. But he also hoped that they would be familiar with one Venus in particular, a famous Greek statue known as the *Venus de Milo*. Knowing the Greek work deepens our pleasure in Matisse's version, for we see that in "carving" his Venus out of a sheet of white paper, he evokes the way a long-ago sculptor carved her out of a block of white marble.

6   An artist may create a specific work for any of a thousand reasons. An awareness of the *why* may give some insight as well. Looking at Van Gogh's *The Starry Night*, it might help you to know that Van Gogh was intrigued by the belief that people journeyed to a star after their death, and that there they continued their lives. "Just as we take the train to get to Tarascon or Rouen," he wrote in a letter, "we take death to reach a star." The tree that rises so dramatically in the foreground of the painting is a cypress, which has often served as a symbol of both death and eternal life. This knowledge might help you to understand why Van Gogh felt so

strongly about the night sky, and what his painting might have meant to him.

7   But no matter how much you study, Van Gogh's painting will never mean for you exactly what it meant for him, nor should it. An artist's work grows from a lifetime of experiences, thoughts, and emotions; no one else can duplicate them exactly. Great works of art hold many meanings. The greatest of them seem to speak anew to each generation and to each attentive observer. The most important thing is that some works of art come to mean something for *you*, that your own experiences, thoughts, and emotions find a place in them, for then you will have made them live.

1. What is the main topic of this passage?
   Ⓐ Visual perception of sensory material
   Ⓑ The historical context for artistic expression
   Ⓒ Studying Van Gogh's *The Starry Night*
   Ⓓ The appreciation of works of art

2. What did Matisse reinterpret?
   Ⓐ A story from mythology
   Ⓑ A painting by another artist
   Ⓒ An ancient sculpture
   Ⓓ A woman in history

3. The word bequeath in the passage is closest in meaning to
   Ⓐ make out
   Ⓑ pass on
   Ⓒ look over
   Ⓓ take in

4. The word intrigued in the passage is closest in meaning to
   Ⓐ very pleased
   Ⓑ very confused
   Ⓒ very interested
   Ⓓ very surprised

5. The word them in the passage refers to
   - Ⓐ each attentive observer
   - Ⓑ thoughts and emotions
   - Ⓒ a lifetime of experiences
   - Ⓓ great works of art

6. According to paragraph 2, the process of visual perception
   - Ⓐ is not the same for all people
   - Ⓑ begins with patterns of light
   - Ⓒ is not very scientific
   - Ⓓ requires other senses to function

7. Which of the sentences below best expresses the information in the highlighted statement in the passage? The other choices change the meaning or leave out important information.
   - Ⓐ We see images differently because of the mode of perception.
   - Ⓑ Although we see images differently, the mode of perception is similar.
   - Ⓒ Since the mode of perception is similar, we see images in the same way.
   - Ⓓ When the mode of perception is the same, we see the same images.

8. The author mentions all of the following ways to enhance the appreciation of art EXCEPT
   - Ⓐ understanding the artistic process
   - Ⓑ becoming familiar with the history
   - Ⓒ experiencing the art by copying
   - Ⓓ knowing about the life of the artist

9. Why might Van Gogh have painted a cypress in *The Starry Night*?
   - Ⓐ To symbolize the journey of life after death
   - Ⓑ To create a dramatic contrast with the sky
   - Ⓒ To place a strong image in the foreground
   - Ⓓ To include nature from his early experience

10. Four squares (□) indicate where the following sentence can be added to the passage.

    For example, one person may focus on the image while another person may experience the color.

    Where would the sentence best fit into the passage?
    - Ⓐ
    - Ⓑ
    - Ⓒ
    - Ⓓ

11. Complete the table below by classifying each of the answer choices under one of the ways to appreciate art. Two of the answer choices will NOT be used.
    - Ⓐ Knowing Van Gogh's belief in life among the stars
    - Ⓑ Identifying brain functions that process patterns of light
    - Ⓒ Understanding the difference between oil and watercolor
    - Ⓓ Adapting classical art to contemporary expression
    - Ⓔ Using the ears, nose, taste bud, and fingertips to perceive
    - Ⓕ Passing on ideas to the next generation of artists
    - Ⓖ Studying why there is a preference for building materials

Biography	History	Media
•	•	•
	•	•

12. Complete a summary of the passage by selecting THREE answer choices that express the most important ideas. The other three sentences do not belong in the summary because they express ideas that are not in the passage or they do not refer to the major ideas. *This question is worth 2 points.*

Art can be appreciated in various ways.

Ⓐ Van Gogh believed that people traveled to a star after death to continue living there.

Ⓑ Studying the historical context of the artist's life may contribute to art appreciation.

Ⓒ Works of art have many meanings that every individual interprets on a personal level.

Ⓓ Science defines perception as the recognition and interpretation of sensory data.

Ⓔ Sensory perception allows us to see art, but different people may see different things.

Ⓕ The title of a work of art can be the first clue to the artist's purpose.

Refer to page 449 for the Explanatory Answers.

EXERCISE 82: Problem/Solution—Arts/Architecture

In some questions in the Reading Section on the Paper-Based TOEFL, you will be asked to recall and relate information and content from problem-solution passages about various fields of study. Choose the best answer for multiple-choice questions.

The Art World

One of the major problems in the art world is how to distinguish and promote an artist. In effect, a market must be created for an artist to be successful. The practice of signing and numbering individual
Line prints was introduced by James Abbott McNeill Whistler, the
5 nineteenth-century artist best known for the painting of his mother, called "Arrangement in Grey and Black," but known to most of us as "Whistler's Mother." Whistler's brother-in-law, Sir Francis Seymour Haden, a less well-known artist, had speculated that collectors might find prints more attractive if they knew that there were only a limited
10 number of copies produced. By signing the work in pencil, an artist could guarantee and personalize each print.

As soon as Whistler and Haden began the practice of signing and numbering their prints, their work began to increase in value. When other artists noticed that the signed prints commanded higher prices,
15 they began copying the procedure.

Although most prints are signed on the right-hand side in the margin below the image, the placement of the signature is a matter of personal choice. Indeed, prints have been signed within the image, in any of the margins, or even on the reverse side of the print.
20 Wherever the artist elects to sign it, a signed print is still valued above an unsigned one, even in the same edition.

1. Which of the following would be a better
   title for the passage?
   Ⓐ Whistler's Mother
   Ⓑ Whistler's Greatest Works
   Ⓒ The Practice of Signing Prints
   Ⓓ Copying Limited Edition Prints

2. What made Whistler's work more
   valuable?
   Ⓐ His fame as an artist
   Ⓑ His painting of his mother
   Ⓒ His signature on the prints
   Ⓓ His brother-in-law's prints

3. The word "speculated" in line 8 could best
   the replaced by
   Ⓐ guessed
   Ⓑ noticed
   Ⓒ denied
   Ⓓ announced

4. The word "distinguish" in line 1 is closest
   in meaning to
   Ⓐ recognize differences
   Ⓑ make improvements
   Ⓒ allow exceptions
   Ⓓ accept changes

5. The word "it" in line 20 refers to
   Ⓐ the same edition
   Ⓑ the image
   Ⓒ the reverse side
   Ⓓ a print

6. Where in the passage does the author
   indicate where an artist's signature might
   be found on a work?
   Ⓐ Lines 10–11
   Ⓑ Lines 12–15
   Ⓒ Lines 16–19
   Ⓓ Lines 20–21

7. What does the author mean by the
   statement in lines 12–13: "As soon as
   Whistler and Haden began the practice of
   signing and numbering their prints, their
   work began to increase in value"?
   Ⓐ The prints that were signed and
      numbered were worth more.
   Ⓑ The signing and numbering of prints
      was not very popular.
   Ⓒ The signatures became more valuable
      than the prints.
   Ⓓ Many copies of the prints were made.

8. What was true about the painting of
   Whistler's mother?
   Ⓐ It was painted by Sir Francis Seymour
      Haden.
   Ⓑ Its title was "Arrangement in Grey and
      Black."
   Ⓒ It was not one of Whistler's best
      paintings.
   Ⓓ It was a completely new method of
      painting.

9. The author mentions all of the following as
   reasons why a collector prefers a signed
   print EXCEPT
   Ⓐ it guarantees the print's authenticity
   Ⓑ it makes the print more personal
   Ⓒ it encourages higher prices for the
      print
   Ⓓ it limits the number of copies of the
      print

10. It can be inferred from the passage that
    artists number their prints
    Ⓐ as an accounting procedure
    Ⓑ to guarantee a limited edition
    Ⓒ when the buyer requests it
    Ⓓ at the same place on each of the prints

Refer to pages 449–450 for the Explanatory Answers.

EXERCISE 83: Problem/Solution—Humanities/Business

In some questions in the Reading Section on the Paper-Based TOEFL, you will be asked to recall and relate information and content from problem-solution passages about various fields of study. Choose the best answer for multiple-choice questions.

Negotiation

The increase in international business and in foreign investment has created a need for executives with knowledge of foreign languages and skills in cross-cultural communication. Americans, *Line* however, have not been well trained in either area and, consequently,
5 have not enjoyed the same level of success in negotiation in an international arena as have their foreign counterparts.

Negotiating is the process of communicating back and forth for the purpose of reaching an agreement. It involves persuasion and compromise, but in order to participate in either one, the negotiators
10 must understand the ways in which people are persuaded and how compromise is reached within the culture of the negotiation.

In many international business negotiations abroad, Americans are perceived as wealthy and impersonal. It often appears to the foreign negotiator that the American represents a large multimillion-
15 dollar corporation that can afford to pay the price without bargaining further. The American negotiator's role becomes that of an impersonal purveyor of information and cash, an image that succeeds only in undermining the negotiation.

In studies of American negotiators abroad, several traits have
20 been identified that may serve to confirm this stereotypical perception, while subverting the negotiator's position. Two traits in particular that cause cross-cultural misunderstanding are directness and impatience on the part of the American negotiator. Furthermore, American negotiators often insist on realizing short-term goals.
25 Foreign negotiators, on the other hand, may value the relationship established between negotiators and may be willing to invest time in it for long-term benefits. In order to solidify the relationship, they may opt for indirect interactions without regard for the time involved in getting to know the other negotiator.
30 Clearly, perceptions and differences in values affect the outcomes of negotiations and the success of negotiators. For Americans to play a more effective role in international business negotiations, they must put forth more effort to improve cross-cultural understanding.

1. What is the author's main point?
   Ⓐ Negotiation is the process of reaching an agreement.
   Ⓑ Foreign languages are important for international business.
   Ⓒ Foreign perceptions of American negotiators are based on stereotypes.
   Ⓓ American negotiators need to learn more about other cultures.

2. According to the author, what is the purpose of negotiation?
   Ⓐ To undermine the other negotiator's position
   Ⓑ To communicate back and forth
   Ⓒ To reach an agreement
   Ⓓ To understand the culture of the negotiators

3. The word "persuaded" in line 10 is closest in meaning to
   Ⓐ respected
   Ⓑ accused
   Ⓒ informed
   Ⓓ convinced

4. The word "undermining" in line 18 is closest in meaning to
   Ⓐ making known
   Ⓑ making clear
   Ⓒ making brief
   Ⓓ making weak

5. The word "that" in line 16 refers to
   Ⓐ bargaining
   Ⓑ role
   Ⓒ corporation
   Ⓓ price

6. Where in the passage does the author indicate the two criteria necessary for negotiation?
   Ⓐ Lines 8–11
   Ⓑ Lines 12–13
   Ⓒ Lines 21–23
   Ⓓ Lines 25–27

7. What does the author mean by the statement in lines 3–6: "Americans, however, have not been well trained in either area and, consequently, have not enjoyed the same level of success in negotiation in an international arena as have their foreign counterparts"?
   Ⓐ Training is not available for Americans who must interact in international negotiations.
   Ⓑ Foreign businesspersons negotiate less effectively than Americans because of their training.
   Ⓒ Because their training is not as good, Americans are less successful as negotiators than their international counterparts.
   Ⓓ Foreign businesspersons do not like to negotiate with Americans, who are not well trained.

8. According to the passage, how can American businesspersons improve their negotiation skills?
   Ⓐ By living in a foreign culture
   Ⓑ By getting to know the negotiators
   Ⓒ By compromising more often
   Ⓓ By explaining the goals more clearly

9. The American negotiator is described as all of the following EXCEPT
   Ⓐ perceived by foreign negotiators as wealthy
   Ⓑ willing to invest time in relationships
   Ⓒ known for direct interactions
   Ⓓ interested in short-term goals

10. The paragraph following the passage most probably discusses
    Ⓐ ways to increase cross-cultural understanding
    Ⓑ traits that cause cross-cultural misunderstanding
    Ⓒ knowledge of foreign languages
    Ⓓ relationships between negotiators

Refer to pages 450–451 for the Explanatory Answers.

EXERCISE 84: Problem/Solution—Social Sciences

In some questions in the Reading Section on the Internet-Based TOEFL, you will be asked to recall and relate information and content from problem-solution passages found in college textbooks. Choose the best answer for multiple-choice questions. For computer-assisted questions, follow the directions on the screen.

School Children with Disabilities

Who Are Children with Disabilities?

Approximately 10 percent of all children in the United States receive special education or related services (Reschly, 1996). Within this group, a little more than half have a learning disability. Substantial percentages of children also have speech or language impairments (21 percent of those with disabilities), mental retardation (12 percent), and serious emotional disturbance (9 percent).

Educators now prefer to speak of "children with disabilities" rather than "disabled children" to emphasize the person, not the disability (Culatta and Tompkins, 1999). The term *handicapping condition* is still used to describe impediments to the learning and functioning of individuals with a disability that have been imposed by society. For example, when children who use a wheelchair do not have adequate access to a bathroom, transportation, and so on, this is referred to as a handicapping condition.

Learning Disabilities

Children with a learning disability (1) are of normal intelligence or above, (2) have difficulties in at least one academic area and usually several, and (3) have a difficulty that is not attributable to any other diagnosed problem or disorder. The global concept of learning disabilities includes problems in listening, concentrating, speaking, thinking.

About three times as many boys as girls are classified as having a learning disability (U.S. Department of Education, 1996). Among the explanations for this gender difference are a greater biological vulnerability of boys, as well as referral bias (boys are more likely than girls to be referred by teachers for treatment because of their disruptive, hyperactive behavior).

Educational Issues

The legal requirement that schools serve all children with a disability is fairly recent. Beginning in the mid 1960s to mid 1970s, legislatures, the federal courts, and the United States Congress laid down special educational rights for children with disabilities. Prior to that time, most children with a disability were either refused enrollment or inadequately served by schools. In 1975, *Public Law 94–142*, the Education for All Handicapped Children Act, required that all students with disabilities be given a free, appropriate public education and be provided the funding to help implement this education.

In 1990, *Public Law 94–142* was renamed the *Individuals with Disabilities Education Act (IDEA)*. The IDEA spells out broad mandates for services to all children with disabilities. These include evaluation and eligibility determination, appropriate education and the individualized education plan (IEP), and the least restrictive environment (LRE) (Martin, Martin, and Terman, 1996).

The IDEA requires that students with disabilities have an **individualized education plan (IEP)**, *a written statement that spells out a program specifically tailored for the student with a disability. In general, the IEP should be (1) related to the child's learning capacity; (2) specially constructed to meet the child's individual needs and not merely a copy of what is offered to other children, and (3) designed to provide educational benefits.*

Under the IDEA, a child with a disability must be educated in the **least restrictive environment (LRE)**. *This means a setting that is as similar as possible to the one in which children who do not have a disability are educated.* The provision of the IDEA has given a legal basis to making an effort to educate children with a disability in the regular classroom (Crockett and Kaufmann, 1999). The term used to describe the education of children with a disability in the regular classroom used to be *mainstreaming*. However, that term has been replaced by the term **inclusion**, *which means educating a child with special education needs full-time in the general school program.* Today, **mainstreaming** *means educating a student with special education needs partially in a special education classroom and partially in a regular classroom.*

Many legal changes regarding children with disabilities have been extremely positive. Compared with several decades ago, far more children today are receiving competent, specialized services. For many children, inclusion in the regular classroom, with modifications or supplemental services, is appropriate (Kochhar, West, and Taymans, 2000; Turnbull and others, 1999). However, some experts believe that separate programs may be more effective and appropriate for children with disabilities (Martin, Martin, and Terman, 1996). Best practices in service delivery to children who are disabled or at risk for disabilities are moving toward a family-focused or family-centered approach (Lynch and Hanson, 1993). This approach emphasizes the importance of partnerships between parents and disability professionals, and shared decision making in assessment, intervention, and evaluation. It also underscores the belief that services for children must be offered in the context of the entire family and that the entire family system is the partner and the client, not just the child (Lyytinen and others, 1994).

School Children with Disabilities (Question References)

Who Are Children with Disabilities?

Paragraph 1   Approximately 10 percent of all children in the United States receive special education or related services (Reschly, 1996). [A] Within this group, a little more than half have a learning disability. [B] Substantial percentages of children also have speech or language impairments (21 percent of those with disabilities), mental retardation (12 percent), and serious emotional disturbance (9 percent). [C]

2   Educators now prefer to speak of "children with disabilities" rather than "disabled children" to emphasize the person, not the disability [D] (Culatta and Tompkins, 1999). The term *handicapping condition* is still used to describe impediments to the learning and functioning of individuals with a disability that have been imposed by society. For example, when children who use a wheelchair do not have adequate access to a bathroom, transportation, and so on, this is referred to as a handicapping condition.

Learning Disabilities

3   Children with a learning disability (1) are of normal intelligence or above, (2) have difficulties in at least one academic area and usually several, and (3) have a difficulty that is not attributable to any other diagnosed problem or disorder. The global concept of learning disabilities includes problems in listening, concentrating, speaking, thinking.

4   About three times as many boys as girls are classified as having a learning disability (U.S. Department of Education, 1996). Among the explanations for this gender difference are a greater biological vulnerability of boys, as well as referral bias (boys are more likely than girls to be referred by teachers for treatment because of their disruptive, hyperactive behavior).

Educational Issues

5   The legal requirement that schools serve all children with a disability is fairly recent. Beginning in the mid 1960s to mid 1970s, legislatures, the federal courts, and the United States Congress laid down special educational rights for children with disabilities. Prior to that time, most children with a disability were either refused enrollment or inadequately served by schools. In 1975, *Public Law 94–142*, the Education for All Handicapped Children Act, required that all students with disabilities be given a free, appropriate public education and be provided the funding to help implement this education.

6   In 1990, *Public Law 94–142* was renamed the *Individuals with Disabilities Education Act (IDEA)*. The IDEA spells out broad mandates for services to all children with disabilities. These include evaluation and eligibility determination, appropriate education and the individualized education plan (IEP), and the least restrictive environment (LRE) (Martin, Martin, and Terman, 1996).

7   The IDEA requires that students with disabilities have an **individualized education plan (IEP),** *a written statement that spells* *out a program specifically tailored for the student with a disability. In general, the IEP should be (1) related to the child's learning capacity; (2) specially constructed to meet the child's individual needs and not merely a copy of what is offered to other children, and (3) designed to provide educational benefits.*

8   Under the IDEA, a child with a disability must be educated in the **least restrictive environment (LRE)**. *This means a setting that is as similar as possible to the one in which children who do not have a disability are educated.* The provision of the IDEA has given a legal basis to making an effort to educate children with a disability in the regular classroom (Crockett and Kaufmann, 1999). The term used to describe the education of children with a disability in the regular classroom used to be *mainstreaming*. However, that term has been replaced by the term **inclusion**, *which means educating a child with special education needs full-time in the general school program.* Today, **mainstreaming** *means educating a student with special education needs partially in a special education classroom and partially in a regular classroom.*

9   Many legal changes regarding children with disabilities have been extremely positive. Compared with several decades ago, far more children today are receiving competent, specialized services. For many children, inclusion in the regular classroom, with modifications or supplemental services, is appropriate (Kochhar, West, and Taymans, 2000; Turnbull and others, 1999). However, some experts believe that separate programs may be more effective and appropriate for children with disabilities (Martin, Martin, and Terman, 1996). Best practices in service delivery to children who are disabled or at risk for disabilities are moving toward a family-focused or family-centered approach (Lynch and Hanson, 1993). This approach emphasizes the importance of partnerships between parents and disability professionals, and shared decision making in assessment, intervention, and evaluation. It also underscores the belief that services for children must be offered in the context of the entire family and that the entire family system is the partner and the client, not just the child (Lyytinen and others, 1994).

1. What does this passage mainly discuss?
   - Ⓐ Mainstreaming for school children with disabilities
   - Ⓑ Providing educational services for children with disabilities
   - Ⓒ Identification of children with learning disabilities
   - Ⓓ Removing handicapping conditions in schools

2. What is the most current view of support programs for children with disabilities?
   - Ⓐ All children should be included in the regular classroom.
   - Ⓑ Parents and professionals should confer and make decisions.
   - Ⓒ Mainstreaming should be reinstituted.
   - Ⓓ Teachers should be trained to help children with disabilities.

3. The word broad in the passage is closest in meaning to
   - Ⓐ expensive
   - Ⓑ general
   - Ⓒ adequate
   - Ⓓ practical

4. The word disruptive in the passage refers to
   - Ⓐ finding fault
   - Ⓑ causing confusion
   - Ⓒ taking charge
   - Ⓓ getting lost

5. The word their in the passage refers to
   - Ⓐ boys
   - Ⓑ girls
   - Ⓒ teachers
   - Ⓓ behavior

6. According to paragraph 3, a child with a learning disability
   - Ⓐ always has problems in several school subjects
   - Ⓑ must be identified according to specific criteria
   - Ⓒ could find it challenging to concentrate
   - Ⓓ does not know how to read at grade level

7. Which of the sentences below best expresses the information in the highlighted statement in the passage? The other choices change the meaning or leave out important information.
   - Ⓐ Fewer children were receiving adequate services twenty years ago.
   - Ⓑ Children had to travel long distances to receive services twenty years ago.
   - Ⓒ Services for children have not improved much in twenty years time.
   - Ⓓ Children have been receiving special services for twenty years.

8. The IDEA legislation includes all the following EXCEPT
   - Ⓐ a legal basis for inclusion in the regular classroom
   - Ⓑ an individualized program requirement
   - Ⓒ special equipment for home schooling
   - Ⓓ specifications for eligibility and testing

9. It can be inferred from the passage that
   - Ⓐ most children with learning disabilities do not have normal intelligence
   - Ⓑ 5 percent of all children in the U.S. have some type of learning disability
   - Ⓒ handicapping conditions are more common than learning disabilities
   - Ⓓ disruptive or hyperactive behavior always accompanies a learning disability

10. Four squares (☐) indicate where the following sentence can be added to the passage.

    The most common problem that characterizes children with a learning disability involves reading.

    Where would the sentence best fit into the passage?
    - Ａ
    - Ｂ
    - Ｃ
    - Ｄ

11. Complete the table below by matching the definitions with the important terms from the passage. Two of the answer choices will NOT be used.
    - Ⓐ An educational program specifically prepared for a child with a disability
    - Ⓑ Full-time instruction for children with disabilities in the general school program
    - Ⓒ A test that is required by law for all children to determine eligibility
    - Ⓓ Funding to support the free public education of children with learning disabilities
    - Ⓔ A school setting that is as much like that of nondisabled children as possible
    - Ⓕ Obstructions in society that interfere with learning by children with disabilities
    - Ⓖ A law that includes regulations for services to all children with disabilities

Handicapping condition	•
LRE	•
Inclusion	•
IEP	•
IDEA	•

12. Complete a summary of the passage by selecting THREE answer choices that express the most important ideas. The other three sentences do not belong in the summary because they express ideas that are not in the passage or they are minor points that are not as important as the three major ideas. *This question is worth 2 points.*

10 percent of the children in the U.S. receive special education services.
- Ⓐ The fact that boys are more active than girls may account for the fact that their teachers refer them more often.
- Ⓑ Most children with learning disabilities can graduate from high school when they have an IEP.
- Ⓒ By law, children with disabilities must be served in public school settings.
- Ⓓ The best way to serve children with disabilities is to involve their families in the services.
- Ⓔ Children with learning disabilities score average or above average on intelligence tests.
- Ⓕ Most of the children with disabilities in the United States have learning disabilities.

Refer to pages 451–452 for the Explanatory Answers.

EXERCISE 85: Problem/Solution—Natural Sciences

In some questions in the Reading Section on the Internet-Based TOEFL, you will be asked to recall and relate information and content from problem-solution passages found in college textbooks. Choose the best answer for multiple-choice questions.

Resistance to Antibiotics

About 100 different antibiotics are currently available commercially in the United States. These antibiotics block the life cycle of bacteria that invade the human body. The first of these antibiotics, penicillin, works by blocking the molecules that construct the cell walls of particular bacteria. The bacteria, with incomplete cell walls, are not able to reproduce—in fact, they usually just explode as the rest of the cell goes about the process of mitosis.

When penicillin was introduced during World War II, it was truly a "miracle drug." Until that time, anyone who was cut or wounded stood a great risk of bacterial infection. Once penicillin became available, the situation changed. Not only wounded soldiers, but also children with ear infections, old people with pneumonia, and many others began to benefit from the ability to introduce molecules into the body that would block the growth of bacteria.

While humanity may have won that particular battle against bacteria, the war is far from over. The reason is that in any bacterial population, there are bound to be a few bacteria that, for one reason or another, are not affected by a particular antibiotic. For example, they may have a slightly differently shaped enzyme that builds cell walls, so that penicillin will not fit onto that particular shape of the enzyme. These bacteria will not be affected by that particular drug.

In fact, for that small group of resistant bacteria, the introduction of the antibiotic is a real godsend. It doesn't affect them, but it does wipe out all of their competition. They are thus free to multiply, and, over time, all of the bacteria will have whatever properties that made those individuals resistant.

Traditionally, medical scientists have dealt with this phenomenon by developing a large number of antibiotics, each of which intervenes in the bacterial life cycle in a slightly different way. Consequently, if you happen to have a bacterium that is resistant to one antibiotic, probably it will succumb to the action of another. You may, in fact, have had the experience of going to a doctor with an infection, being given an antibiotic, and then finding that it didn't work. In all likelihood, all your doctor had to do then was prescribe a different antibiotic and everything was fine.

The problem is that as time has passed, more and more bacteria have become resistant to more and more antibiotics. In fact, as of this writing, there is one strain of bacteria—a common hospital *Staphylococcus*—that is resistant to every commercially available antibiotic except one, and in 1996, a bacterium with lowered resistance to that last antibiotic appeared in Japan.

The appearance of drug-resistant bacteria is not particularly surprising; in fact, it probably should have been anticipated. Nevertheless, in the late 1980s, there was a general sense of complacency among scientists on the antibiotic question. Little profit was to be made by developing the one-hundred-and-first antibiotic. Drug companies concentrated their efforts on what seemed to be more useful and profitable areas. Because of this situation, a gap developed between the production of new antibiotics and the development of resistance among bacteria.

By the early 1990s, this gap was recognized—in fact, the problem was highlighted in several national news magazines. More companies returned to the task of developing new kinds of antibiotics, and as this book is being prepared, a number are undergoing clinical trials. By early in the twenty-first century, some of these new drugs will start to come on the market, and the problem will be "solved," at least for the moment. There may, however, be a gap in the early 2000s when it is quite possible that the old scourge of bacterial infection will once again threaten humanity.

Much current research and funding is being devoted to genetic diseases, which arise from one or more malfunctioning genes. A promising future technology, gene therapy involves replacing a defective gene with a healthy one. Additional research will focus on the processes by which cells repair the constant damage to DNA, but the computer design of new drugs, the development of new antibiotics, and techniques to combat bacteria should remain a top priority.

Resistance to Antibiotics (Question References)

Paragraph 1   About 100 different antibiotics are currently available commercially in the United States. These antibiotics block the life cycle of bacteria that invade the human body. The first of these antibiotics, penicillin, works by blocking the molecules that construct the cell walls of particular bacteria. The bacteria, with incomplete cell walls, are not able to reproduce—in fact, they usually just explode as the rest of the cell goes about the process of mitosis.

2   When penicillin was introduced during World War II, it was truly a "miracle drug." Until that time, anyone who was cut or wounded stood a great risk of bacterial infection. Once penicillin became available, the situation changed. Not only wounded soldiers, but also children with ear infections, old people with pneumonia, and many others began to benefit from the ability to introduce molecules into the body that would block the growth of bacteria.

3   While humanity may have won that particular battle against bacteria, the war is far from over. The reason is that in any bacterial population, there are bound to be a few bacteria that, for one reason or another, are not affected by a particular antibiotic. For example, they may have a slightly differently shaped enzyme that builds cell walls, so that penicillin will not fit onto that particular shape of the enzyme. These bacteria will not be affected by that particular drug.

4   In fact, for that small group of resistant bacteria, the introduction of the antibiotic is a real godsend. It doesn't affect them, but it does wipe out all of their competition. They are thus free to multiply, and, over time, all of the bacteria will have whatever properties that made those individuals resistant.

5   Traditionally, medical scientists have dealt with this phenomenon by developing a large number of antibiotics, each of which intervenes in the bacterial life cycle in a slightly different way. Consequently, if you happen to have a bacterium that is resistant to one antibiotic, probably it will succumb to the action of another. You may, in fact, have had the experience of going to a doctor with an infection, being given an antibiotic, and then finding that it didn't work. In all likelihood, all your doctor had to do then was prescribe a different antibiotic and everything was fine.

6   The problem is that as time has passed, more and more bacteria have become resistant to more and more antibiotics. In fact, as of this writing, there is one strain of bacteria—a common hospital *Staphylococcus*—that is resistant to every commercially available antibiotic except one, and in 1996, a bacterium with lowered resistance to that last antibiotic appeared in Japan.

7   The appearance of drug-resistant bacteria is not particularly surprising; in fact, it probably should have been anticipated. [A] Nevertheless, in the late 1980s, there was a general sense of complacency among scientists on the antibiotic question. Little profit was to be made by developing the one-hundred-and-first antibiotic. [B] Drug companies concentrated their efforts on what seemed to be more useful and profitable areas. Because of this situation, a gap developed between the production of new antibiotics and the development of resistance among bacteria.

8   By the early 1990s, this gap was recognized—in fact, the problem was highlighted in several national news magazines. [C] More companies returned to the task of developing new kinds of antibiotics, and as this book is being prepared, a number are undergoing clinical trials. [D] By early in the twenty-first century, some of these new drugs will start to come on the market, and the problem will be "solved," at least for the moment. There may, however, be a gap in the early 2000s when it is quite possible that the old scourge of bacterial infection will once again threaten humanity.

9   Much current research and funding is being devoted to genetic diseases, which arise from one or more malfunctioning genes. A promising future technology, gene therapy involves replacing a defective gene with a healthy one. Additional research will focus on the processes by which cells repair the constant damage to DNA, but the computer design of new drugs, the development of new antibiotics, and techniques to combat bacteria should remain a top priority.

1. Which of the following best expresses the main idea of this passage?
    Ⓐ The "miracle drug" penicillin
    Ⓑ Drug-resistant bacteria
    Ⓒ *Staphylococcus* infections
    Ⓓ Gene therapy treatments

2. How do antibiotics treat infections?
    Ⓐ They interfere with the reproductive cycle of bacteria.
    Ⓑ They construct cell walls to resist bacteria.
    Ⓒ They inject enzymes that explode in affected cells.
    Ⓓ They increase the mitosis of healthy cells.

3. The word complacency in the passage is closest in meaning to
    Ⓐ consensus of agreement
    Ⓑ fear of consequences
    Ⓒ lack of concern
    Ⓓ awareness of potential

4. The word anticipated in the passage is closest in meaning to
    Ⓐ predicted
    Ⓑ concealed
    Ⓒ investigated
    Ⓓ disregarded

5. The word them in the passage refers to
   Ⓐ whatever properties
   Ⓑ resistant bacteria
   Ⓒ their competition
   Ⓓ those individuals

6. According to paragraph 4, why do some bacteria benefit from antibiotics?
   Ⓐ The antibiotic eliminates competing bacteria, allowing resistant bacteria to reproduce.
   Ⓑ The resistant bacteria compete with the antibiotic, and the bacteria becomes stronger.
   Ⓒ The competition helps the resistant bacteria to multiply by reproducing with the resistant type.
   Ⓓ The properties of the antibiotic are acquired by the bacteria, making it resistant to the competition.

7. Which of the sentences below best expresses the information in the highlighted statement in the passage? The other choices change the meaning or leave out important informaiton.
   Ⓐ Some antibiotics affect a population of bacteria more efficiently than others.
   Ⓑ There are several reasons why some bacteria do not respond to most antibiotics.
   Ⓒ The effect of antibiotics on bacteria is to bind them together into one population.
   Ⓓ A small number of bacteria in any sample will probably be resistant to a specific antibiotic.

8. The author mentions all of the following reasons for drug resistant bacteria to appear EXCEPT
   Ⓐ there was not enough profit incentive for companies to continue developing new antibiotics
   Ⓑ statistically, some drug-resistant bacteria will occur naturally in any large population of bacteria
   Ⓒ the newer antibiotics were not as strong and effective as the original penicillin-based drugs
   Ⓓ competing bacteria are destroyed by antibiotics, allowing resistant bacteria to prosper

9. It can be inferred from the passage that
   Ⓐ research to develop new antibiotics will not be necessary in the future
   Ⓑ the scientific community was not surprised by the resistant strains of bacteria
   Ⓒ antibiotics are not very expensive when they are made available commercially
   Ⓓ it takes years for a new drug to be made available commercially for consumers

10. Four squares (□) indicate where the following sentence can be added to passage.

    There was a clear pattern of resistance in previously effective antibiotics that should have alerted the scientific community to the problem.

    Where would the sentence best fit into the passage?
    Ⓐ
    Ⓑ
    Ⓒ
    Ⓓ

11. Complete the table below by putting each of the answer choices in chronological order. One of the answer choices will NOT be used.
    Ⓐ Drug companies began developing new antibiotics again.
    Ⓑ Drug companies stopped developing new antibiotics because of profit margins.
    Ⓒ Some bacteria became resistant to the antibiotics.
    Ⓓ New types of antibiotics were developed to combat the resistant bacteria.
    Ⓔ When the first antibiotics were introduced, they were very effective.
    Ⓕ Genetic research solved the problem of bacterial resistance.

The sequence of events is as follows:
•
•
•
•
•

12. Complete a summary of the passage by selecting THREE answer choices that express the most important ideas. The other three sentences do not belong in the summary because they express ideas that are not in the passage or they are minor points that are not as important as the three major ideas. *This question is worth 2 points.*

    About 100 different antibiotics are currently available commercially in the U.S.
    Ⓐ Many strains of bacteria have become resistant to the antibiotics currently available.
    Ⓑ Funding for the production of new antibiotics has been allocated to drug companies.
    Ⓒ The first antibiotics were very effective in blocking the reproduction of bacteria.
    Ⓓ *Staphylococcus* can be treated with only one antibiotic because it is resistant to the rest.
    Ⓔ New antibiotics are being developed to combat bacteria that resist the older antibiotics.
    Ⓕ Most of the time, when you do not respond to one type of antibiotic, you can take another.

Refer to page 452 for the Explanatory Answers.

PRACTICE EXERCISES
FOR WRITING

Writing Section

The Writing Section of the TOEFL tests your ability to write in English on a variety of general and academic topics. This section is included in the Paper-Based TOEFL and the Internet-Based TOEFL. The section is different for each of the TOEFL formats.

Paper-Based TOEFL (PBT)

The Writing Section of the Paper-Based TOEFL is called the Test of Written English (TWE). There is one question on a general topic. You can use your personal experience and general knowledge to write an essay about the topic. The essay must be completed in 30 minutes. The score is calculated separately from the total score on the Paper-Based TOEFL. Refer to Exercise 86 to see examples.

Internet-Based TOEFL

There are usually two questions in two parts on the Writing Section of the iBT®. The topics are both general and academic. There are two types of tasks included in the Writing Section: one independent writing task and one integrated writing task.

In the independent writing task, you will see a question about a general topic. You can use your personal experience and common knowledge to answer. After the question, you have 30 minutes to prepare and write your essay. The essay should be between 300 and 350 words long. Refer to Exercise 91 to see examples.

In the integrated writing task, you will hear a lecture, read a passage, or hear a lecture and read a passage about an academic topic. You may take notes to prepare your answer. After each lecture, reading passage, or both, you will read a question that requires you to respond by writing. You will have 20 minutes to prepare and write the answer to the question. The answer should be between 150 and 225 words long. Refer to Exercise 92 and Exercise 97 to see examples.

EXERCISE 86: General Topics—Agree or Disagree

In some essays in the Writing Section on the Paper-Based TOEFL or the Internet-Based TOEFL, you will be asked to agree or disagree with a statement. First, spend 5 minutes thinking about the topic and making notes. Based on your notes, write an essay of 300–350 words. Complete it in 20 minutes. Then, use the last 5 minutes to read your essay and make corrections.

Topic One

Do you agree or disagree with the following statement? Smoking should not be permitted in restaurants, and state laws that prohibit it should be upheld. Use specific reasons and examples to support your opinion.

Notes

Use this space for essay notes only. Work done on this work sheet will **not** be scored.

Essay

Refer to page 454 for the Example Answer.

Topic Two

Do you agree or disagree with the following statement? All college students should be required to take classes outside of their major fields of study. Use specific reasons and examples to support your opinion.

Notes

Use this space for essay notes only. Work done on this work sheet will *not* be scored.

Essay

Refer to pages 454–455 for the Example Answer.

Topic Three

Do you agree or disagree with the following statement? The saying, "If at first you don't succeed, try, try again" means to continue working toward a goal in spite of difficulties. Use specific reasons and examples to support your opinion.

Notes

Use this space for essay notes only. Work done on this work sheet will *not* be scored.

Essay

Refer to pages 455–456 for the Example Answer.

EXERCISE 87: General Topics—Argue a Point of View

In some essays in the Writing Section on the Paper-Based TOEFL or the Internet-Based TOEFL, you will be asked to choose between two viewpoints and argue your point of view. First, spend 5 minutes thinking about the topic and making notes. Based on your notes, write an essay of 300–350 words. Complete it in 20 minutes. Then, use the last 5 minutes to read your essay and make corrections.

Topic Four

Some international students choose American roommates. Others choose roommates from their own countries. Compare the advantages of having an American roommate with the advantages of having a roommate from your country. Which kind of roommate would you prefer? Why? Use specific reasons and examples to support your opinion.

Notes

Use this space for essay notes only. Work done on this work sheet will *not* be scored.

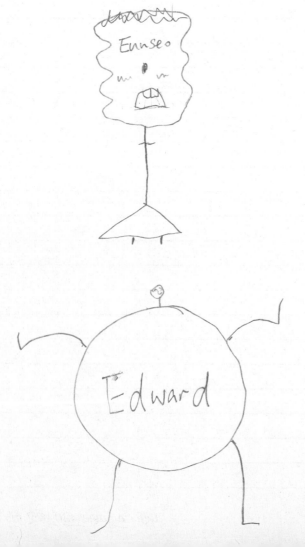

Essay

_____
_____
_____
_____
_____
_____
_____
_____
_____
_____
_____
_____
_____
_____
_____
_____
_____
_____
_____
_____
_____
_____
_____
_____
_____
_____
_____
_____
_____
_____
_____
_____

Refer to pages 456–457 for the Example Answer.

Topic Five

Some people want to attend a small college. Other people think that it is better to attend a large university. Which type of school do you prefer? Why? Use specific reasons and examples to support your opinion.

Notes

Use this space for essay notes only. Work done on this work sheet will *not* be scored.

<u>Essay</u>

Refer to pages 457–458 for the Example Answer.

Topic Six

Some students in the United States work while they are earning their degrees. Others receive support from their families. Which arrangement do you agree with? Why? Use specific reasons and examples to support your opinion.

Notes

Use this space for essay notes only. Work done on this work sheet will *not* be scored.

Essay

Refer to pages 458–459 for the Example Answer.

EXERCISE 88: General Topics—Describe Characteristics

In some essays in the Writing Section on the Paper-Based TOEFL or the Internet-Based TOEFL, you will be asked to describe the characteristics or qualities of a person. First, spend 5 minutes thinking about the topic and making notes. Based on your notes, write an essay of 300–350 words. Complete it in 20 minutes. Then, use the last 5 minutes to read your essay and make corrections.

Topic Seven

What are the important qualities of a good teacher? Use specific reasons and examples to explain why these qualities are important.

Notes

Use this space for essay notes only. Work done on this work sheet will *not* be scored.

Essay

Refer to pages 459–460 for the Example Answer.

EXERCISE 89: General Topics—Imagine a Situation

In some essays in the Writing Section on the Paper-Based TOEFL or the Internet-Based TOEFL, you will be asked to respond to an imaginary situation. First, spend 5 minutes thinking about the topic and making notes. Based on your notes, write an essay of 300–350 words. Complete it in 20 minutes. Then, use the last 5 minutes to read your essay and make corrections.

Topic Eight

If you could meet one important person during your stay in the United States, which person would you choose? Why? Use specific reasons and examples to explain your choice.

Notes

Use this space for essay notes only. Work done on this work sheet will **not** be scored.

Essay

Refer to page 460 for the Example Answer.

EXERCISE 90: General Topics—Support or Oppose

In some essays in the Writing Section on the Paper-Based TOEFL or the Internet-Based TOEFL, you will be asked to support or oppose a plan. First, spend 5 minutes thinking about the topic and making notes. Based on your notes, write an essay of 300–350 words. Complete it in 20 minutes. Then, use the last 5 minutes to ready your essay and make corrections.

Topic Nine

A group of business leaders plans to construct an airport in your community. Discuss the advantages and disadvantages. Do you support or oppose the airport? Why? Use specific reasons and examples to explain your position.

Notes

Use this space for essay notes only. Work done on this work sheet will *not* be scored.

Essay

Refer to page 461 for the Example Answer.

EXERCISE 91: General Topics—Defend a Choice

In some essays in the Writing Section on the Paper-Based TOEFL or the Internet-Based TOEFL, you will be asked to make a selection from among several options and defend your choice. First, spend 5 minutes thinking about the topic and making notes. Based on your notes, write an essay of 300–350 words. Complete it in 20 minutes. Then, use the last 5 minutes to read your essay and make corrections.

Topic Ten

Which of the inventions in the twentieth century has been the most significant for the world? Why? Use specific reasons and examples to support your choice.

Notes

Use this space for essay notes only. Work done on this work sheet will *not* be scored.

Essay

Refer to pages 461–462 for the Example Answer.

EXERCISE 92: Academic Topics—
Summaries of Textbooks and Lectures

In some essays in the Writing Section on the Internet-Based TOEFL, you will be asked to respond to a question from both a reading passage and a lecture. First, read the passage for Exercise 92 and take notes. Next, listen to the lecture and take notes. Based on your notes, write an essay of 150–225 words. Complete it in 15 minutes. Then, use the last 5 minutes to read your essay and make corrections.

Textbook Passage

In the 1950s, the field of sociology embraced consensus theory, or structural functionalism, which assumed that there were standard social norms and that deviant behavior could be defined objectively as the violation of those social norms. Deviance then was a particular form of behavior, and those people who engaged in deviant behavior could justifiably be identified as social deviants. Conversely, those around them in society would be considered normal. More recently, labeling theory has rejected this approach, claiming that deviance is not merely a form of behavior, but rather the label that is attached to that behavior. Labeling theory proposes that people who are labeled as having abnormal disorders may, in fact, be reflecting social expectations. In other words, the label becomes a self-fulfilling prophecy. In addition, it appears that the individuals who are labeled will probably conform their behavior to the label that they are assigned. Therefore, labeling theory requires consideration of the social context and the environment in which behaviors take place. Furthermore, it must be assumed that people who interact with those who are labeled will contribute to their behavior by providing an environment in which the deviant activity is encouraged.

Notes

Use this space for textbook notes only. Work done on this work sheet will *not* be scored.

<u>Lecture</u>

 (CD 5, Track 4)

Now listen to a professor's response to the textbook passage.

Notes

Use this space for lecture notes only. Work done on this work sheet will *not* be scored.

Writing Question:
   Summarize the main points presented in the reading, and explain how the information in the lecture provides a different perspective. You have 20 minutes to write 150–225 words.

Essay

_____

_____

_____

_____

_____

_____

_____

_____

_____

_____

_____

_____

_____

_____

_____

_____

_____

_____

_____

_____

_____

_____

_____

_____

_____

_____

_____

_____

_____

_____

_____

_____

_____

Refer to pages 464–465 for the Example Answer.

EXERCISE 93: Academic Topics— Summaries of Textbooks and Lectures

In some essays in the Writing Section on the Internet-Based TOEFL, you will be asked to respond to a question from both a reading passage and a lecture. First, read the passage for Exercise 93 and take notes. Next, listen to the lecture and take notes. Based on your notes, write an essay of 150–225 words. Complete it in 15 minutes. Then, use the last 5 minutes to read your essay and make corrections.

Textbook Passage

Because infants do not have communication skills that will allow them to state their preferences, the analysis of their perception requires studies that rely on inference. In a technique developed by Robert Fantz, an infant subject is simultaneously presented with two visual choices. The investigator then records how long the infant looks at each visual. By choosing to look at one visual longer than the other, the infant shows a preference. Viewed in isolation, one preference is not very convincing. However, Fantz hypothesized that by presenting the same choices a number of times, and changing their relative position with each presentation, the infant would track the same visual, and that would indicate a preference. In an experiment by Johnson and colleagues, babies were shown three visuals. One was a drawing of a human face with the eyes, nose, and mouth in the correct position; another was a drawing with the facial features scrambled. Perhaps the eyes were in a position where the mouth might ordinarily be drawn. A third visual was blank; that is, it had no features at all. Each visual was positioned over the infant's head, and then moved from one side to the other and back again. Researchers recorded the extent to which the infant tracked each visual with his or her head and eye movements. The result was that even babies as young as one day old preferred to look at the correctly drawn face rather than the scrambled face or the blank.

Notes

Use this space for textbook notes only. Work done on this work sheet will *not* be scored.

<u>Lecture</u>

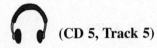 **(CD 5, Track 5)**

Now listen to a professor's response to the textbook passage.

Notes

Use this space for lecture notes only. Work done on this work sheet will *not* be scored.

Writing Question:

Summarize the main points presented in the reading, and explain how the information in the lecture provides a different perspective. You have 20 minutes to write 150–225 words.

Essay

Refer to pages 465–466 for the Example Answer.

EXERCISE 94: Academic Topics— Summaries of Textbooks and Lectures

In some essays in the Writing Section on the Internet-Based TOEFL, you will be asked to respond to a question from both a reading passage and a lecture. First, read the passage for Exercise 94 and take notes. Next, listen to the lecture and take notes. Based on your notes, write an essay of 150–225 words. Complete it in 15 minutes. Then, use the last 5 minutes to read your essay and make corrections.

Textbook Passage

Formal taxonomy, or the naming and classification of species and groups of species, had its origin in the 18th century when Linnaeus wrote an ambitious book called the *System of Nature* in which he attempted to organize all known life forms into a related system. The Linnaean system of classification for animals has two major characteristics. It requires a two-part name for each species and a hierarchical classification of those species into larger related groups. About one hundred years later, Darwin's *Origin of Species* introduced the concept of genealogy, or the relationships among species in the evolutionary chain. By comparing the anatomies of animals and by using fossil records, scientists were able to draw conclusions about common ancestors. Today, most biologists represent those relationships by constructing a tree with branches. Each branch point represents the place where two species diverge from a common ancestor. Some scientists use the older five-kingdom system, but many now use a three-domain system at the bottom of the tree. Continuing through the lower branches, we reach the classifications designated as orders, and above them, families. It is about at this level that the similarities become apparent. For example, marine forms in the Cetaceans order are supposed to be related because they have fish-shaped bodies, paddles for forelimbs, and no hind limbs, as well as a thick layer of blubber for insulation. Some examples of Cetaceans are whales, dolphins, and porpoises. But what about the common ancestor? Recently, the introduction of DNA testing has allowed us to draw conclusions based on hereditary relationships at the molecular level, rather than relying solely on physical similarities.

Notes

Use this space for textbook notes only. Work done on this work sheet will ***not*** be scored.

Lecture

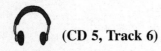 **(CD 5, Track 6)**

Now listen to a professor's response to the textbook passage.

Notes

Use this space for lecture notes only. Work done on this work sheet will ***not*** be scored.

Writing Question:
   Summarize the main points presented in the reading, and explain how the information in the lecture provides a different perspective. You have 20 minutes to write 150–225 words.

Essay

_____

_____

_____

_____

_____

_____

_____

_____

_____

_____

_____

_____

_____

_____

_____

_____

_____

_____

_____

_____

_____

_____

_____

_____

_____

_____

_____

_____

_____

Refer to pages 466–467 for the Example Answer.

EXERCISE 95: Academic Topics—
Summaries of Textbooks and Lectures

In some essays in the Writing Section on the Internet-Based TOEFL, you will be asked to respond to a question from both a reading passage and a lecture. First, read the passage for Exercise 95 and take notes. Next, listen to the lecture and take notes. Based on your notes, write an essay of 150–225 words. Complete it in 15 minutes. Then, use the last 5 minutes to read your essay and make corrections.

Textbook Passage

Emotional intelligence is the ability to monitor feelings and emotions, discriminate among those emotions, and use the information about them to guide thinking and behavior. Emotionally intelligent people can perceive and understand the emotions of others as well as those that they experience themselves. Specific measures include emotional awareness or being able to separate one's feelings from actions; managing emotions like anger instead of acting them out; reading the emotions of others and responding appropriately to them; and forming and maintaining successful relationships. People who receive high scores on emotional intelligence tests tend to be empathetic, good at managing their own emotional responses to situations, and skilled at resolving conflict.

Although this concept has been around for some time, Daniel Coleman popularized it with the publication of his book, *Emotional Intelligence.* According to Coleman, standardized intelligence tests do not predict competence and success in career and social settings as well as measures of emotional intelligence. Business and industry have been especially interested in research on emotional intelligence with a view to screening candidates for positions in their companies. Applicants with high academic qualifications have not always been successful in working with others, and many businesses that rely on teamwork are looking for new ways to locate and recruit team players.

It has been observed that most of these life skills were previously part of parenting, but the fact remains that many children are not prepared to respond in acceptable ways to situations in school, and less so in a wider social environment. Emotional intelligence is now thought to be so important to future success that some schools have instituted programs designed to help children with their emotional growth. A typical curriculum includes how to be a good listener; how to be assertive without being aggressive; how to cooperate, negotiate, and resolve conflicts; and how to take responsibility for decisions and follow through on commitments. Partly in response to the interest on the part of employers, a growing number of educators believe that these skills are as important, if not more important, than the traditional school subjects.

Notes

Use this space for textbook notes only. Work done on this work sheet will **not** be scored.

Lecture

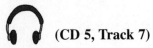 **(CD 5, Track 7)**

Now listen to a professor's response to the textbook passage.

Notes

Use this space for lecture notes only. Work done on this work sheet will ***not*** be scored.

Writing Question:

Summarize the main points presented in the reading, and explain how the information in the lecture provides a different perspective. You have 20 minutes to write 150–225 words.

Essay

_____

_____

_____

_____

_____

_____

_____

_____

_____

_____

_____

_____

_____

_____

_____

_____

_____

_____

_____

_____

_____

_____

_____

_____

_____

_____

_____

_____

_____

_____

_____

Refer to pages 467–468 for the Example Answer.

EXERCISE 96: Academic Topics— Summaries of Textbooks and Lectures

In some essays in the Writing Section on the Internet-Based TOEFL, you will be asked to respond to a question from both a reading passage and a lecture. First, read the passage for Exercise 96 and take notes. Next, listen to the lecture and take notes. Based on your notes, write an essay of 150–225 words. Complete it in 15 minutes. Then, use the last 5 minutes to read your essay and make corrections.

Textbook Passage

The coastal environment is also referred to as a *littoral zone*. The littoral zone includes both land and water, extending from the highest water line that appears on the land during a storm to the sea floor at the point where the water is too deep for the storm waves to stir the sediment. Under the ocean, the sea floor usually remains undisturbed at about 200 feet or 60 meters.

In general, the *coast* is a common name for the visible area that stretches from the ocean at high tide to the first major topographical change such as a mountain range or a forest. The point at which the sea and the land meet is called the *shoreline*, a specific line within the littoral zone, and the area that is also easily visible to the eye. The shoreline shifts, however, because of adjustments in sea level that occur with the changes in tides and storms.

Because of the changes in the level of the ocean, the entire littoral zone may naturally shift. For example, when the sea level rises, the land will disappear under the ocean, but when the sea level falls, new coastal areas are revealed. Time will also cause sea level to vary. Ocean currents, tidal changes, air and ocean temperatures, barometric pressure, ocean currents and waves, and even slight variations in gravity will result in changes in sea levels. Although a mean sea level (MSL) is calculated for a specific littoral zone, using the average tidal levels recorded every hour at a designated site, actual sea levels can vary quite a lot, and the term *sea level* tends to be very relative.

In the United States, there are about forty sites where sea levels are tracked. During the last century, sea levels have been rising at a rate of ten times the average. In addition, changes in the adjacent land have been occurring due to uplift or other underground activity, circumstances that also affect changes in the littoral zone. If there is volcanic activity, for instance, the zone may change suddenly and dramatically. On the other hand, erosion, which occurs very slowly, will also cause changes, but they will be recorded over a much longer period of time and may not be noticed except by those involved in researching littoral zones.

Notes

Use this space for textbook notes only. Work done on this work sheet will *not* be scored.

<u>Lecture</u>

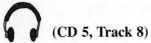 **(CD 5, Track 8)**

Now listen to a professor's response to the textbook passage.

Notes

Use this space for lecture notes only. Work done on this work sheet will *not* be scored.

Writing Question:
Summarize the main points presented in the reading, and explain how the information in the lecture provides a different perspective. You have 20 minutes to write 150–225 words.

Essay

_____

_____

_____

_____

_____

_____

_____

_____

_____

_____

_____

_____

_____

_____

_____

_____

_____

_____

_____

_____

_____

_____

_____

_____

_____

_____

_____

_____

_____

Refer to pages 468–469 for the Example Answer.

EXERCISE 97: Academic Topics—
Summaries of Textbooks and Lectures

In some essays in the Writing Section on the Internet-Based TOEFL, you will be asked to respond to a question from both a reading passage and a lecture. First, read the passage for Exercise 97 and take notes. Next, listen to the lecture and take notes. Based on your notes, write an essay of 150–225 words. Complete it in 15 minutes. Then, use the last 5 minutes to read your essay and make corrections.

Textbook Passage

The Pearl by John Steinbeck is the retelling of a legend about a fisherman who finds a huge pearl, realizes that the discovery is destroying his life, and returns the pearl to the sea. Some critics have pointed out that the author was committed to ecology, and that this book was really his statement about the dangers of creating an imbalance in the natural environment. When the fisherman throws the pearl back into the sea, he is restoring the natural order. In fact, Steinbeck was a member of an expedition to explore marine life along the Gulf of California when he heard the legend of the "pearl of the world." Other critics have suggested that Steinbeck's concern for the conditions of the working class was reflected in the relationships among the characters. The priest becomes interested in the poor fisherman's family after the pearl is found because he hopes to receive a donation that will enable him to improve his church. The doctor who has refused to treat the fisherman's baby in the past is solicitous when it becomes known that the fisherman has found a valuable pearl. An even more direct example of exploitation is the way that the pearl merchants take advantage of the fishermen in the village. It is true that the plight of the disenfranchised is a consistent theme in Steinbeck's work, including *Tortilla Flat*, *Of Mice and Men*, and *The Grapes of Wrath*. In *The Pearl*, however, the exploitation of a native culture by a colonial society elevates this theme from the individual to the societal level.

Notes

Use this page for textbook notes only. Work done on this work sheet will ***not*** be scored.

Lecture

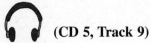 **(CD 5, Track 9)**

Now listen to a professor's response to the textbook passage.

Notes

Use this space for lecture notes only. Work done on this work sheet will *not* be scored.

Writing question:
    Summarize the main points presented in the reading, and explain how the information in the lecture provides a different perspective. You have 20 minutes to write 150–225 words.

Essay

_____

_____

_____

_____

_____

_____

_____

_____

_____

_____

_____

_____

_____

_____

_____

_____

_____

_____

_____

_____

_____

_____

_____

_____

_____

_____

_____

_____

_____

_____

_____

Refer to pages 470–471 for the Example Answer.

EXERCISE 98: Academic Topics— Summaries of Textbooks and Lectures

In some essays in the Writing Section on the Internet-Based TOEFL, you will be asked to respond to a question from both a reading passage and a lecture. First, read the passage for Exercise 98 and take notes. Next, listen to the lecture and take notes. Based on your notes, write an essay of 150–225 words. Complete it in 15 minutes. Then, use the last 5 minutes to read your essay and make corrections.

Textbook Passage

Social support refers to the help and comfort that is provided by other people or groups. Having a good friend or a support group to talk with can be a key factor in dealing with stress in a positive way. For those individuals who like to keep pets, the companionship of dogs, cats, and other animals has been found to be another significant form of social support.

In a study by Karen Allen, the findings confirmed that having a pet present significantly lowered the stress reaction in subjects who were required to complete a stressful task. Allen performed the study using female subjects who owned dogs. The subjects were divided into random groups. In the first group, the subjects were allowed to take a good friend with them into the room where the task would be done; in the second group, no support was provided in the room; in the third group, the subjects were allowed to take their dogs with them. During the task, which consisted of solving a very difficult math problem, a number of physiological reactions were measured, including blood pressure and heart rate. As expected, the presence of emotional support seemed to influence the level of stress. The group that was allowed to keep their dogs in the room showed significantly less stress as measured by their physiological reactions to the task, whereas the control group without emotional support had a higher stress level.

What was somewhat unexpected in the study was the negative response by subjects to having a good friend in the room. Rather than decreasing the stress level, the presence of a human actually seemed to cause the highest stress reaction. A typical response by a subject was a pulse rate below 80 with the dog present, about 100 when alone in the room, and more than 115 when the human friend was seated nearby. The conclusion suggested that having a pet may be a more effective way to lower stress than having a human companion. At a minimum, Allen proved that pets do provide very positive emotional support under conditions of stress.

Notes

Use this space for textbook notes only. Work done on this work sheet will ***not*** be scored.

Lecture

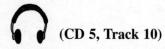 **(CD 5, Track 10)**

Now listen to a professor's response to the textbook passage.

Notes

Use this space for lecture notes only. Work done on this work sheet will *not* be scored.

Writing Question:

Summarize the main points of the study presented in the reading, and use the information in the lecture to explain the results. You have 20 minutes to write 150–225 words.

Essay

_____

_____

_____

_____

_____

_____

_____

_____

_____

_____

_____

_____

_____

_____

_____

_____

_____

_____

_____

_____

_____

_____

_____

_____

_____

_____

_____

_____

_____

_____

Refer to pages 471–472 for the Example Answer.

EXERCISE 99: Academic Topics—
Summaries of Textbooks and Lectures

In some essays in the Writing Section on the Internet-Based TOEFL, you will be asked to respond to a question from both a reading passage and a lecture. First, read the passage for Exercise 99 and take notes. Next, listen to the lecture and take notes. Based on your notes, write an essay of 150–225 words. Complete it in 15 minutes. Then, use the last 5 minutes to read your essay and make corrections.

Textbook Passage

Telecommuting is any of several types of computer communication between employees in their homes and their offices at a distance. For employees whose jobs involve sitting at a terminal or a word processor to enter data or type reports, the location of the computer is of no consequence. If the machine can communicate over telephone lines, when the work is completed, employees can dial the office computer at a distant site and transmit the material to their employers. A recent survey in *USA Today* estimates that there are approximately 8.7 million telecommuters, but although the numbers are rising annually, the trend does not appear to be as significant as predicted when *Business Week* published "The Portable Executive" as its cover story a few years ago. Why hasn't telecommuting become more popular?

Clearly, change simply takes time, but in addition, there has been active resistance on the part of many managers. These executives claim that supervising the telecommuters in a large work force scattered across the country would be too difficult, or, at least, systems for managing them are not yet developed, thereby complicating the manager's responsibilities.

It is also true that employees who are given the option of telecommuting are often reluctant to accept the opportunity. Many people feel that they need regular interaction with a group, and more than a few are concerned that they will not have the same consideration for advancement if they are not more visible in the office setting. Some people feel that even when a space in their homes is set aside as a work area, they never really get away from the office. Taking a minute to look at e-mail can expand into several hours if a problem is communicated in one of the messages.

Notes

Use this space for textbook notes only. Work done on this work sheet will ***not*** be scored.

Lecture

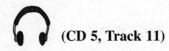 **(CD 5, Track 11)**

Now listen to a professor's response to the textbook passage.

Notes

Use this space for lecture notes only. Work done on this work sheet will *not* be scored.

Writing Question:

Summarize the main points presented in the reading, and explain how the information in the lecture provides a different perspective. You have 20 minutes to write 150–225 words.

Essay

_____

_____

_____

_____

_____

_____

_____

_____

_____

_____

_____

_____

_____

_____

_____

_____

_____

_____

_____

_____

_____

_____

_____

_____

_____

_____

_____

_____

_____

_____

_____

Refer to pages 472–473 for the Example Answer.

EXERCISE 100: Academic Topics— Summaries of Textbooks and Lectures

In some essays in the Writing Section on the Internet-Based TOEFL, you will be asked to respond to a question from both a reading passage and a lecture. First, read the passage for Exercise 100 and take notes. Next, listen to the lecture and take notes. Based on your notes, write an essay of 150–225 words. Complete it in 15 minutes. Then, use the last 5 minutes to read your essay and make corrections.

Textbook Passage

Anthropologists have studied how social bonds are created and maintained in a large number of cultures through systems of gift giving In fact, much of what has been learned about this complicated exchange has resulted from the attempts of anthropologists to give gifts to the people that they were studying either as a token of goodwill or in appreciation for their help. The response to the gift and the way that it was reciprocated offered insights into the social meaning of gifting.

In some cases, the gift was inspected and refused because it was viewed as a way of reflecting prestige on the anthropologist at the expense of the local person or group. In other cases, the gift was accepted but the value was questioned, as in one society that deprecated gifts in an effort to diminish the expectation for a large reciprocal offering. Anthropologists have discovered to their dismay that gifts can be used as a symbol of aggression, a strategy to humiliate or obligate the recipient, or even as a substitute for warfare.

The length of time that the recipient should wait to reciprocate a gift may also be a challenge to discern. In some societies, reciprocating a gift too soon is an indication that the friendship is not desired. In contrast, a delay in repayment signals a stronger relationship. Unfortunately, waiting too long to reciprocate can also be insulting in many societies. But how long is too long to wait?

One of the most complex systems of gift giving is the *kula* which is important to the culture that is found in a circle of islands near New Guinea. For the most part, kula gifts are limited to shell necklaces and armbands. When a necklace is received, it is expected that an armband will be given to the person initiating the kula. This reciprocal gift may be sent several months or even years after the necklace has been accepted. The value of a kula necklace is determined by the quality and rarity of the shells in it and by the association with a noteworthy person who may have possessed it during a previous exchange.

Notes

Use this space for textbook notes only. Work done on this work sheet will *not* be scored.

Lecture

 (CD 5, Track 12)

Now listen to a professor's response to the textbook passage.

Notes

Use this space for lecture notes only. Work done on this work sheet will *not* be scored.

Writing Question:

Compare the information about other cultures presented in the reading with the information about American culture presented in the lecture. You have 20 minutes to write 150–225 words.

Essay

_____

_____

_____

_____

_____

_____

_____

_____

_____

_____

_____

_____

_____

_____

_____

_____

_____

_____

_____

_____

_____

_____

_____

_____

_____

_____

_____

_____

_____

_____

_____

_____

_____

Refer to pages 473–474 for the Example Answer.

EXPLANATORY ANSWERS AND AUDIO SCRIPT FOR TOEFL PRACTICE EXERCISES

Listening

EXERCISE 1: Dialogues—Topics

🎧 (CD 1, Track 1)

Audio

1. Woman: The professor drilled and drilled until I couldn't stand it.

    Man: I heard he assigned a whole lot of exercises without explaining any of the grammar rules, too. I'm glad I went to the gym.

    Third Voice: What are the man and woman talking about?

Answer

(B) From the references to the *professor*, *assignments*, and *grammar rules*, it must be concluded that they are talking about a class. Choice (A) refers to the place the man went instead of to class. Choices (C) and (D) are not mentioned and may not be concluded from information in the conversation.

Audio

2. Man: They sell gas by the gallon here.

    Woman: Yes, and I see that the bulk food in the grocery store is sold in pounds and ounces.

    Third Voice: What are these two people most probably discussing?

Answer

(C) From the reference to *gallons*, *pounds*, and *ounces*, it must be concluded that the two people are talking about weights and measures. Choices (A), (B), and (D) are mentioned in reference to the main topic of discussion, "the English system of measurement."

Audio

3. Woman: You should have your mail held at the post office until you get back.

    Man: Good idea. I remembered to get the newspaper stopped, but I'd forgotten about that.

    Third Voice: What are these two people talking about?

Answer

(A) Since the man will be *gone*, it must be concluded that he is going on a trip. Choices (B), (C), and (D) are mentioned in reference to the main topic of discussion, "the man's vacation."

Audio

4. Man: Do you know how many students were accepted in the new doctoral program?

    Woman: Well, I saw Mary at the party last night, and she said that only six got in.

    Third Voice: What are the two people discussing?

Answer

(D) Since they are talking about the *new doctoral program*, it must be concluded that they are discussing a graduate program. Choices (B) and (C) are mentioned in reference to the main topic of discussion, "acceptance in the new doctoral program." Choice (A) is not mentioned and may not be concluded from information in the conversation.

Audio

5. Man: I applied for the exchange program to Europe this year but I couldn't go because I got sick.

    Woman: That's too bad. Nancy went to England last year, and she said it was really a great experience.

    Third Voice: What are the man and woman discussing?

Answer

(A) Since they are talking about the man's *application* for an *exchange program* to Europe, it must be concluded that they are discussing the exchange program. The place in choice (B) refers to Nancy's trip, not to the man's trip. Choice (C) is the reason that the man could not go on the exchange program, not the topic of conversation. Choice (D) refers to the friend who went on the exchange program last year.

Audio

6. Man: The chairs in that lecture room are really uncomfortable.
   Woman: You said it. They're so small that my children wouldn't even fit in them.
   Third Voice: What are the man and woman talking about?

Answer

(C) "The chairs in that lecture room are really uncomfortable." Choice (B) is mentioned in reference to the main topic of discussion, "the chairs." Choices (A) and (D) are not mentioned and may not be concluded from information in the conversation.

Audio

7. Woman: I've had it with my computer. I lost another paper when I tried to save it on a disk.
   Man: You have to do something about that. Why don't you try over at Computer World?
   Third Voice: What are the two people discussing?

Answer

(A) Since the woman mentions a *problem* with her *computer*, and the man offers a suggestion, it must be concluded that they are discussing the woman's computer. Choice (B) is mentioned in reference to the main topic of discussion, "the computer." Choices (C) and (D) are not mentioned and may not be concluded from information in the conversation.

Audio

8. Woman: I was late for class because I couldn't find a parking space.
   Man: It's because of registration week. I drove around for almost half an hour before I
                   found one this morning.
   Third Voice: What are the two people talking about?

Answer

(C) From the references to *parking space* and *driving around to find one* [a parking space], it must be concluded that they are talking about the parking situation. Choices (A), (B), and (D) are mentioned in reference to the main topic of discussion, the "parking situation."

Audio

9. Man: I really like Dr. Smith, but I can't say as much for her T.A.
   Woman: Sally? Oh, she's okay as long as you go to class and get the lab reports in on time.
   Third Voice: What are the man and woman discussing?

Answer

(D) A *T.A.* is a teaching assistant. Choices (A), (B), and (C) are mentioned in reference to the main topic of discussion, "the T.A., Sally."

Audio

10. Man: I used to bring my lunch to school when I was working in the Chemistry Department,
                   but now that I'm a full-time student I just eat at the Snack Bar.
    Woman: Me, too. It's too hard trying to get everyone ready in the morning at my house.
    Third Voice: What are the man and woman talking about?

Answer

(D) From the references to *bringing lunch to school* and eating *at the Snack Bar*, it must be concluded that they are talking about having lunch on campus. Choices (A), (B), and (C) are mentioned in reference to the main topic of discussion, "lunch on campus."

EXERCISE 2: Dialogues—Details

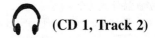

Audio

1. Woman: You look awful. Do you have a hangover?
   Man: No. I've been up all night finishing a paper. All I've had to drink is coffee.
   Third Voice: What is the man's problem?

Answer

(A) "I've been up all night finishing a paper." Choice (B) is not correct because all the man has had to drink is coffee. Choice (D) is not correct because the man has finished the paper. Choice (C) is not mentioned and may not be concluded from information in the conversation.

Audio

2. Woman: Can I use my credit card to pay my fees, or do I have to give you a check?
   Man: Your card is fine as long as your credit approval goes through.
   Third Voice: How does the woman want to pay?

Answer

(B) "Can I use my credit card . . . ?" Choice (A) refers to the alternative that the woman suggests, not to her preference. Choices (C) and (D) are not mentioned and may not be concluded from information in the conversation.

Audio

3. Woman: No wonder Sharon won't see you. She probably thought that such an expensive gift was inappropriate on such short acquaintance.
   Man: It certainly is different here. In my country, men are supposed to show women that they care for them by giving them jewelry.
   Third Voice: Why did Sharon stop seeing the man?

Answer

(C) "She probably thought that such an expensive gift was inappropriate on such short acquaintance." The word *short* in Choice (A) refers to the acquaintance, not to the man. Choice (B) is true, but it is not the reason Sharon stopped seeing the man. Choice (D) is not correct because the man gave Sharon an expensive gift.

Audio

4. Woman: Why do you need to check my purse? Do you think I stole something?
   Man: Not at all. This is a standard security procedure.
   Third Voice: Why did the man look through the woman's purse?

Answer

(C) "This is a standard security procedure." Choice (A) is not correct because the man denied that he suspected the woman of theft. The word *secure* in Choice (B) and the word *standard* in Choice (D) refer to a standard security procedure, not to securing a purse or to a standard size.

Audio

5. Woman: I lost my notebook. Could I borrow yours before the test?
   Man: I'm sorry. I'd like to help you, but I just can't. I have to take it with me to work so I can study on my breaks.
   Third Voice: What does the woman want the man to do?

Answer

(D) "Could I borrow yours [your notebook] before the test?" The word *study* in Choice (A) refers to the man's plan to study, not to the woman's request. The word *break* in Choice (C) refers to the man's breaks at work, not to the woman's request. Choice (B) is not mentioned and may not be concluded from information in the conversation.

Audio

6. Woman: That looks like Steve's car, but who is that girl driving it?
   Man: Oh, that's Steve's sister. I met her last night at Mary Anne's party.
   Third Voice: Who is driving Steve's car?

Answer

(B) "Oh, that's Steve's sister." Choice (C) refers to the owner of the car, not to the driver. Choice (D) refers to the person who had a party, not to the person driving. Choice (A) is not mentioned and may not be concluded from information in the conversation.

Audio

7. Woman: The door seems to be locked. Do I need a key for the bathroom?
   Man: No. Just push hard. It sticks a little.
   Third Voice: Why won't the door open?

Answer

(C) "It [the door] sticks a little." Choice (A) refers to the woman's original conclusion, not to the real reason that the door would not open. The word *key* in Choice (B) refers to the woman's question about a key, not to the reason that the door would not open. Choice (D) is not mentioned and may not be concluded from information in the conversation.

Audio

8. Man: Can we use our calculators on the test?
   Woman: Yes, if you bring them to me at the beginning of the test, I'll check them out and return them right away so you can use them.
   Third Voice: What does the man want to do?

Answer

(B) "Can we use our calculators on the test?" The word *check* in Choice (A) refers to the woman's offer to check the calculators, not to what the man wants to do. Choices (C) and (D) are not mentioned and may not be concluded from information in the conversation.

Audio

9. Man: My roommate left, and he didn't pay his share, so I'm stuck with all the rent and utilities for last month.
   Woman: That's not fair. You should call his family.
   Third Voice: What is the woman's advice?

Answer

(C) "You should call his [your roommate's] family." Choice (A) is not correct because the woman does not think it is fair for the man to be stuck with the bills. The word *family* in Choice (B) refers to the family of the roommate, not of the man. The word *leave* in Choice (D) refers to the roommate's leaving, not the man's leaving.

Audio

10. Man: I want to apply for a student loan, please.
    Woman: All right. Fill out these forms and bring in your income tax records from last year. Then I'll review your options with you.
    Third Voice: How will the woman help the man?

Answer

(C) "Then I'll review your options with you." Choices (A), (B), and (D) refer to instructions that the woman gives the man about what he is to do before their interview, not to the way that the woman will help the man at the interview.

EXERCISE 3: Dialogues—Selections

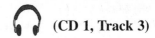 (CD 1, Track 3)

Audio

1. Woman: Is Jack your cousin?
    Man: No. He seems more like a brother, really, but we are just good friends.
    Third Voice: What is the relationship between Jack and the man?

Answer

(B) "... we are just good friends." Choice (A) refers to the way that the man feels about Jack, not to their actual relationship. Choice (C) refers to the woman's assumption, not to the relationship. Choice (D) is not mentioned and may not be concluded from information in the conversation.

Audio

2. Man: So I asked Frank if we could live together next semester, and he said that he was going to room with Geoff.
    Woman: Oh, that's too bad. Well, I know that Steve is looking for a roommate.
    Third Voice: What does the woman suggest?

Answer

(C) "Well, I know that Steve is looking for a roommate." Because the woman mentions that Steve is looking for a roommate, it may be concluded that she is suggesting that the man and Steve be roommates. Choice (A) is not correct because Frank responded to the man's offer by saying that he was going to live with Geoff. Choices (B) and (D) are not correct because Frank and Geoff plan to be roommates.

Audio

3. Man: What did you get on the calculus exam?
    Woman: A *C*. And I feel lucky to have it. Mike got a *B*, but almost everyone else got *D*s and *F*s.
    Third Voice: What grade did the woman receive?

Answer

(C) "A *C*." Choice (B) refers to Mike's grade, not to the woman's grade. Choice (D) refers to the grades received by almost everyone else. Choice (A) is not mentioned and may not be concluded from information in the conversation.

Audio

4. Man: Where can I buy a computer? It doesn't have to be the best on the market.
    Woman: Umhum. You could go to a computer store, or a discount store, but if I were you, I'd look into some of the special offers through the university. I saw something in the paper just last night.
    Third Voice: What advice does the woman give the man?

Answer

(D) "... if I were you, I'd look into some of the special offers through the university." Choices (A) and (C) refer to alternatives that the woman mentions, not to the advice she gives the man. The word *newspaper* in Choice (B) refers to an article about special offers, not to an ad for a computer.

Audio

5. Man: You didn't get your grades because your name isn't on the roster. Did you attend the class and take the exams?
    Woman: I certainly did. And I paid my fees, too.
    Third Voice: Why didn't the woman receive a grade for the course?

Answer

(D) "You didn't get your grades because your name isn't on the roster." Choice (A) is not correct because the woman paid her fees. Choice (C) is not correct because she attended class. Choice (B) is not mentioned and may not be concluded from information in the conversation.

Audio

6. Man: What size do you need?

    Woman: I'm not too sure. I wear a $5\frac{1}{2}$ or a 6 in Europe, and a 7 in Canada, but I think I need a $7\frac{1}{2}$ here.

    Third Voice: What size will the man probably bring?

Answer

(D) ". . . I think I need a $7\frac{1}{2}$ here." Choices (A) and (B) refer to the size that the woman takes in Europe, not to the size she needs here. Choice (C) refers to the size that the woman takes in Canada.

Audio

7. Woman: I have been having the worst headaches. I know some of it is stress, but I'm worried that I might have something more serious, like high blood pressure.

    Man: Well, we'll check that out, of course, but first, tell me the last time you had your glasses changed. It really sounds more like eye strain.

    Third Voice: What does the man suspect?

Answer

(A) ". . . tell me the last time you had your glasses changed. It really sounds more like eye strain." Choices (B), (C), and (D) refer to the concerns that the woman has about her health, not to the problem that the man suspects.

Audio

8. Man: Have you started writing your paper for history?

    Woman: Not yet. I'm still writing up my laboratory assignments for chemistry and studying for my midterms in English and French.

    Third Voice: For which class must the woman begin to prepare?

Answer

(A) "Have you started writing your paper for history?" "Not yet." Choices (B), (C), and (D) refer to assignments that she is doing now, not to an assignment she must begin.

Audio

9. Woman: Are you glad that you came to Washington?

    Man: Yes, indeed. I'd considered going to New York or Boston, but I've never regretted my decision.

    Third Voice: Where does the man live?

Answer

(D) "Are you glad that you came to Washington?" "Yes, indeed." Choices (A) and (B) refer to places the man considered before coming to Washington. Choice (C) is not mentioned and may not be concluded from information in the conversation.

Audio

10. Man: Something is wrong with second gear. It seems to run fine in reverse, and drive, but when I shift into second, the motor stalls out.

    Woman: I hope that it won't be too difficult to fix.

    Third Voice: Which gear needs to be fixed?

Answer

(B) "Something is wrong with second gear." Choices (C) and (D) refer to gears that run fine. Choice (A) is not mentioned and may not be concluded from information in the conversation.

Exercise 4: Dialogues—Reversals

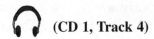 (CD 1, Track 4)

Audio

1. Man: Do you need a ride to the airport?
   Woman: Thanks, anyway. I thought I would, but I have my car back now.
   Third Voice: How will the woman get to the airport?

Answer

(C) ". . . I have my car back now." Choice (A) refers to the man's offer, and to the woman's first plan, not to the way that the woman will get to the airport. Choices (B) and (D) are not mentioned and may not be concluded from information in the conversation.

Audio

2. Man: Okay. What'll you have?
   Woman: Give me the eggs and potatoes. Oh, wait a minute. How about the eggs and pancakes?
   Third Voice: What does the woman want to eat?

Answer

(B) "How about the eggs and pancakes?" Choice (A) refers to the woman's choice before she changes her mind. Choice (D) refers to part of the woman's order, but leaves out the fact that she wants eggs, also. Choice (C) is not mentioned and may not be concluded from information in the passage.

Audio

3. Woman: How many boxes of Girl Scout cookies did you order?
   Man: Four, no, five.
   Third Voice: How many boxes of cookies did the man order?

Answer

(C) "Four, no five." Choice (B) refers to the man's first thought, not to his final statement about the number of boxes he ordered. Choices (A) and (D) are not correct because the man ordered five boxes of cookies.

Audio

4. Man: What is the area code from which you are calling?
   Woman: 6-9-1. Oops, that's not right. It's 6-1-9.
   Third Voice: What is the correct area code for the woman?

Answer

(D) "It's 6-1-9." Choice (A) refers to the woman's first response, before she corrects herself. Choices (B) and (C) are not mentioned and may not be concluded from information in the conversation.

Audio

5. Woman: I thought you said it was eight cents a copy.
   Man: I did, but it's ten cents a copy when you make fewer than twenty copies, and you have only fifteen.
   Third Voice: How much per copy will the woman pay?

Answer

(B) ". . . it's ten cents a copy when you make fewer than twenty copies, and you have only fifteen." Choice (A) refers to the price per page for twenty copies or more. The number in Choice (C) refers to the number of copies the woman has, not to the price per copy. The number in Choice (D) refers to the number of copies required for the lower price, not to the price per copy.

Audio

6. Woman: How much to send a one-page fax?
   Man: One dollar. Oh, wait a minute. This is an overseas transmission. That's two-fifty.
   Third Voice: How much will the woman pay?

Answer

(D) "That's $2.50." Choice (B) refers to the price of a one-page domestic fax, not to the overseas transmission that the woman wants to send. The per-minute prices in Choices (A) and (C) are not mentioned and may not be concluded from information in the conversation.

Audio

7. Man: Let me see. There's a documentary about wolves on Channel Three.
   Woman: That sounds pretty interesting, but I'd rather go to the movies.
   Third Voice: What does the woman want to do?

Answer

(D) "... I'd rather go to the movies." Choices (A) and (C) refer to the man's preference, not to the woman's preference. Choice (B) is not mentioned and may not be concluded from information in the passage.

Audio

8. Woman: Do you want large bills or twenties?
   Man: Give me twenties, please. Oh, wait, maybe I should take two fifties and the rest in twenties.
   Third Voice: What does the man want the woman to do?

Answer

(D) "... I should take two fifties and the rest in twenties." Choice (A) refers to the man's request before he changed his mind. Choices (B) and (C) are not correct because he asks for some twenties.

Audio

9. Man: Where shall we go for lunch? It's your turn to choose.
   Woman: How about The Country Kitchen, or better yet, The Old House. They have great salads.
   Third Voice: Where will the man and woman eat lunch?

Answer

(C) "... better yet, The Old House." Choice (A) refers to the woman's first suggestion before she changed her mind. Choices (B) and (D) are not mentioned and may not be concluded from information in the conversation.

Audio

10. Woman: Will you be home late again tonight?
    Man: I'm afraid so. But I should be able to get away by six, or let's say seven, just to be on the safe side.
    Third Voice: When will the man be home?

Answer

(C) "... let's say seven, just to be on the safe side." The time in Choice (A) refers to the man's first estimate, not to the man's final estimate. Choices (B) and (D) are not correct because the man acknowledged that he would be home late.

EXERCISE 5: Dialogues—Idioms   (CD 1, Track 5)

Audio

1. Man: Let's go to Florida on spring break.
   Woman: You're putting me on!
   Third Voice: What does the woman mean?

Answer

(A) "You're putting me on" is an idiomatic expression that means the speaker does not think the other person is serious. Choices (B), (C), and (D) are not paraphrases of the expression.

Audio

2. Man: Can you believe it? It says in the paper that tuition is going up another hundred dollars
                   a semester.
    Woman: That's just what I need.
    Third Voice: What does the woman mean?

Answer

(C) "That's just what I need" is an idiomatic expression that means the speaker will be inconvenienced.
Choices (A), (B), and (D) are not paraphrases of the expression.

Audio

3. Man: Can you let me borrow some paper? This lecture is so long that I've run out.
    Woman: Sure. Here you go.
    Third Voice: What did the man do?

Answer

(B) ". . . I've run out" is an idiomatic expression that means the speaker has used all of the supply.
Choices (A), (C), and (D) are not paraphrases of the expression.

Audio

4. Woman: That test was not what I studied for.
    Man: No joke. I hope I passed it.
    Third Voice: How does the man feel about the test?

Answer

(B) "No joke" is an idiomatic expression that means the speaker agrees with another person. Choices
(A), (C), and (D) are not paraphrases of the expression.

Audio

5. Man: What did you say?
    Woman: Honestly, Will. You're just not all there sometimes.
    Third Voice: What does the woman mean?

Answer

(A) "You're just not all there . . ." is an idiomatic expression that means the speaker does not believe
the other person is very attentive. Choices (B), (C), and (D) are not paraphrases of the expression.

Audio

6. Woman: I can't believe that I signed up for this class.
    Man: Neither can I. It is such a Mickey Mouse course.
    Third Voice: On what do the speakers agree?

Answer

(C) "Mickey Mouse" is an idiomatic expression that describes something easy or without substance.
Choices (A), (B), and (D) are not paraphrases of the expression.

Audio

7. Man: I'll pick you up after class.
    Woman: Don't bother.
    Third Voice: What does the woman mean?

Answer

(A) "Don't bother" is an idiomatic expression that means the speaker does not want the other person
to take action. Choices (B), (C), and (D) are not paraphrases of the expression.

Audio

8. Woman: Do you like ice cream?
    Man: I'll say!
    Third Voice: What does the man mean?

Answer

(A) "I'll say" is an idiomatic expression that means the speaker agrees with the other person. Choices (B), (C), and (D) are not paraphrases of the expression.

Audio

9. Man: Did you know that Joan is going to move back to Maine?
   Woman: I'll believe it when I see it.
   Third Voice: What does the woman mean?

Answer

(B) "I'll believe it when I see it" is an idiomatic expression that means the speaker is doubtful. Choices (A), (C), and (D) are not paraphrases of the expression.

Audio

10. Woman: How was your day?
    Man: Don't ask.
    Third Voice: What does the man mean?

Answer

(C) "Don't ask" is an idiomatic expression that means an emphatic no. Choices (A), (B), and (D) are not paraphrases of the expression.

EXERCISE 6: Dialogues—Emotions   (CD 1, Track 6)

Audio

1. Woman: Are you worried about getting a job after graduation?
   Man: No. I've had several good interviews, and I can always work for my dad for a while.
   Third Voice: How does the man feel?

Answer

(C) Since the man says that he has had several interviews, and that he can work for his father, and since his tone is confident, it may be concluded that he feels confident. Choice (A) is not correct because the man says he is not worried. Choices (B) and (D) are not mentioned and may not be concluded from information in the conversation.

Audio

2. Woman: That was a great movie!
   Man: Sure, if you like fairy tales.
   Third Voice: How did the man feel about the movie?

Answer

(A) Since the man compares the movie to fairy tales, and since his tone is sarcastic, it may be concluded that he thought it was a very unrealistic movie. Choices (B), (C), and (D) are not mentioned and may not be concluded from information in the conversation.

Audio

3. Man: Did you get your TOEFL scores yet?
   Woman: Not yet, but I think I got more than 500. I had 490 the first time I took it, and I know I did much better this time because I knew a lot about several of the reading comprehension passages.
   Third Voice: How does the woman feel about the TOEFL?

Answer

(B) Since the woman says she knows she did much better, it may be concluded that she thought she improved her score. Choice (A) is not correct because she knows she did much better. The number in Choice (C) refers to the score she received the first time, not this time. Choice (D) is not correct because she knew a lot about several of the reading comprehension passages.

Audio

4. Man: What page are we on? I'm just not with it today.

   Woman: Or any other day.

   Third Voice: How does the woman feel about the man?

Answer

(C) Since the woman says that the man is not *with it* any day, and since her tone is impatient, it may be concluded that she thinks he never pays attention. Choices (A), (B), and (D) are not mentioned and may not be concluded from information in the conversation.

Audio

5. Woman: If you invite Lucy, you'll have to ask Rick, too.

   Man: Forget it!

   Third Voice: How does the man feel about Rick?

Answer

(D) Since the man says to forget asking Rick, and since his tone is negative, it may be concluded that he does not want to invite them. Choice (C) is not correct because he does not want to invite Rick. Choices (A) and (B) are not mentioned and may not be concluded from information in the conversation.

Audio

6. Woman: I heard that Professor Saunders has retired.

   Man: What?

   Third Voice: What is the man's reaction to the news?

Answer

(A) Since the man says *what*, and since his tone is surprised, it may be concluded that the man is surprised by the news. Choices (B), (C), and (D) are not mentioned and may not be concluded from information in the conversation.

Audio

7. Woman: I don't care much for the way that our lab assistant grades our assignments.

   Man: Neither do I.

   Third Voice: How does the man feel about the assignments?

Answer

(C) Since the man agrees with the woman, it may be concluded that he does not like the grading system. Choice (A) misinterprets the idiom *to not care for*, which means "to not like." Choice (D) is not correct because he agrees with the woman. Choice (B) is not mentioned and may not be concluded from information in the conversation.

Audio

8. Woman: You are wrong about Terry.

   Man: If you say so.

   Third Voice: What best describes the man's opinion of Terry?

Answer

(C) Since the man agrees reluctantly, and since his tone is dubious, it may be concluded that he has his doubts about Terry. Choices (A), (B), and (D) are not mentioned and may not be concluded from information in the conversation.

Audio

9. Woman: I don't want to go to that review session.

   Man: Neither do I, but I think we should.

   Third Voice: How does the man feel about the review session?

Answer

(B) Since the man agrees with the woman when she says that she does not want to go to the review session, it may be concluded that he does not want to go. Since he says they should go, it may be concluded that he will go. Choices (A) and (C) are not correct because the man does not want to go. Choice (D) is not correct because he will go.

Audio

10. Woman: I was going to room with Carol, but when I got here, I had been assigned to live with Janine.
    Man: Bummer.
    Third Voice: How does the man feel about Janine?

Answer

(A) Since the man says *bummer*, and since his tone is sympathetic, it may be concluded that he thinks Janine would be difficult to live with. Choices (B) and (C) are not correct because the man thinks it is a bummer for the woman to have been assigned to live with Janine instead of with Carol. Choice (D) is not mentioned and may not be concluded from information in the conversation.

EXERCISE 7: Dialogues—Suggestions

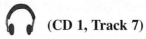 (CD 1, Track 7)

Audio

1. Woman: I'll leave the tip since you got dinner.
   Man: Okay. Five dollars is about 20 percent.
   Third Voice: What does the man suggest that the woman do?

Answer

(C) Since the man says "okay" when the woman offers to leave the tip, and he calculates the amount, it must be concluded that the woman will tip the waiter after dinner. Choice (A) refers to what the man, not the woman, will do. Choice (B) is not correct because the man will pay for dinner. Choice (D) is not correct because they are leaving a tip for a waiter in a restaurant.

Audio

2. Woman: Oh, no. We're locked out of the dorm. I didn't think it was that late.
   Man: Do you have a phone number for the security guard?
   Third Voice: What does the man suggest the woman do?

Answer

(B) Since the man asks whether the woman has a phone number for the security guard, it must be concluded that he suggests phoning the guard. Choices (A), (C), and (D) are not mentioned and may not be concluded from information in the conversation.

Audio

3. Man: All the bathrooms are locked.
   Woman: That's odd. Why don't you go down to the main lobby? I think I saw a custodian there when we came in.
   Third Voice: What does the woman suggest that the man do?

Answer

(C) Since the woman mentions that she saw a custodian in the main lobby, and suggests that the man "go down to the main lobby," it must be concluded that the custodian could unlock the bathroom for the man. Choice (B) is not correct because a custodian, not a bathroom, is in the main lobby. Choice (D) is not correct because the woman mentions the main lobby in the building they are in, not in another building. Choice (A) is not mentioned and may not be concluded from information in the conversation.

Audio

4. Woman: Are you in line here?
   Man: We all are. You need to take a number.
   Third Voice: What does the man suggest that the woman do?

Answer

(B) "You need to take a number." Choices (A), (C), and (D) are not mentioned and may not be concluded from information in the conversation.

Audio

5. Man: It's only twenty dollars.
   Woman: I know, but unless you have an account with us, we can't cash your check. There's a branch of your bank across the street.
   Third Voice: What does the woman suggest that the man do?

Answer

(A) Since the woman points out that there is a branch of the man's bank nearby, it must be concluded that she suggests he go to the other bank. Choice (C) is not correct because she cannot cash his check since he does not have an account at the bank. Choice (D) is not correct because the check is already made out for twenty dollars. Choice (B) is a possible solution to the problem, but it is not mentioned and may not be concluded from information in the conversation.

Audio

6. Man: I'll be glad to pick you up at the airport. What time does your plane arrive?
   Woman: Well, it's scheduled to be here at eleven thirty-five, but it might be late if the weather is bad out of Chicago. Why don't I call you when I get in?
   Third Voice: What does the woman suggest that the man do?

Answer

(C) "Why don't I call you when I get in?" Choice (A) refers to what the man offers to do, not to what the woman suggests. Choices (B) and (D) are not mentioned and may not be concluded from information in the conversation.

Audio

7. Woman: When does Dr. Watson have her office hours this semester?
   Man: I think her hours are from two to three o'clock every day. I'm not sure, but I know it's on the syllabus.
   Third Voice: What does the man suggest that the woman do?

Answer

(A) Since the man mentions that the hours are on the syllabus, it must be concluded that he wants the woman to refer to the syllabus. The time in Choice (C) refers to the man's recollection of the office hours, not to his suggestion. Choices (B) and (D) are not mentioned and may not be concluded from information in the conversation.

Audio

8. Woman: There won't be any kids at the dinner. Maybe we should stay at home.
   Man: Why don't we get a baby sitter? We could use an evening out.
   Third Voice: What does the man suggest that they do?

Answer

(C) "Why don't we get a baby sitter?" Choice (A) refers to what the woman, not the man suggests. Choices (B) and (D) are not mentioned and may not be concluded from information in the conversation.

Audio

9. Man: I've tried the interlibrary loan before, and it took too long for the material to get here.
   Woman: I'd just use the Internet then. You can probably find some similar references.
   Third Voice: What does the woman suggest that the man do?

Answer

(D) "I'd just use the Internet then." Choice (B) refers to the way that the man has done his research in the past, not to the woman's suggestion. Choices (A) and (C) are not mentioned and may not be concluded from information in the conversation.

Audio

10. Man: I don't like carrying a lot of cards in my wallet, but then I never have the one I need.
    Woman: You could put them in a card case and leave them in your book bag.
    Third Voice: What does the woman suggest that the man do?

Answer

(B) "You could put them in a card case and leave them in your book bag." Choices (A), (C), and (D) are not mentioned and may not be concluded from information in the conversation.

EXERCISE 8: Dialogues—Assumptions   (CD 1, Track 8)

Audio

1. Man: You mean this test isn't open book?
    Woman: Not this time.
    Third Voice: What had the man assumed about the test?

Answer

(C) Since the man is surprised that the test is not open book, it must be concluded that he assumed he could use his book during the test. Choice (B) refers to a take-home test, not an open book test. Choices (A) and (D) are not mentioned and may not be concluded from information in the conversation.

Audio

2. Woman: I just used the security deposit from my old apartment for a deposit on the new one.
    Man: So you did get your deposit back after all.
    Third Voice: What had the man assumed?

Answer

(A) Since the man is surprised that she got her deposit back, it must be concluded that he assumed she would not receive it. Choices (B), (C), and (D) are not mentioned and may not be concluded from information in the conversation.

Audio

3. Man: You mean you are going out with Phil again?
    Woman: Just for lunch.
    Third Voice: What had the man assumed about the woman?

Answer

(B) Since the man is surprised that the woman is going out with Phil again, it must be concluded that he assumed she would not start dating Phil again. Choice (C) refers to the woman's date with Phil, not with the man. Choices (A) and (D) are not mentioned and may not be concluded from information in the conversation.

Audio

4. Woman: My daughter's first birthday is Saturday. Why don't you come?
    Man: You don't mean it. She can't be a year old already.
    Third Voice: What had the man assumed about the woman's daughter?

Answer

(A) Since the man is surprised that the woman's daughter is one year old already, it must be concluded that he thought she was younger. Choice (B) refers to what the woman, not the man, says. Choices (C) and (D) are not mentioned and may not be concluded from information in the conversation.

Audio

5. Man: We're almost finished with the handouts for Anne.

   Woman: Anne is going to give the presentation for the group?

   Third Voice: What had the woman assumed about the presentation?

Answer

(C) Since the woman is surprised that Anne is going to make the presentation for the group, it must be concluded that she assumed Anne would not make the presentation. Choice (A) is not correct because they are almost finished with the handouts. Choices (B) and (D) are not mentioned and may not be concluded from information in the conversation.

Audio

6. Man: The health center is in the student services building, not in the union.

   Woman: No wonder I couldn't find it. Now I have to go all the way over to North Campus.

   Third Voice: What had the woman assumed about the health center?

Answer

(B) Since the man tells the woman that the health center is not in the union, it must be concluded that she thought it was there. Choice (A) is not correct because the woman went to the union, not to the student services building. Choice (C) refers to the place where the woman must go, not to where she had assumed the health center to be. Choice (D) is not mentioned and may not be concluded from information in the conversation.

Audio

7. Woman: I wanted to read *Saratoga Trunk* for my report in English class, but Bill had already asked for it.

   Man: Bill is reading a novel?

   Third Voice: What had the man assumed about Bill?

Answer

(C) Since the man is surprised that Bill is reading a novel, it must be concluded that the man assumed Bill did not read novels. Choices (A), (B), and (D) are not mentioned and may not be concluded from information in the conversation.

Audio

8. Woman: John must have been joking when he said he was going to drop out of the business program to apply for medical school.

   Man: I don't think so. He seemed very serious to me.

   Third Voice: What had the woman assumed about John?

Answer

(B) "John must have been joking." Choice (A) is not correct because the woman did not think the man would apply for medical school. Choice (D) is not correct because the man was already in the business program. Choice (C) is not mentioned and may not be concluded from information in the conversation.

Audio

9. Man: When we got there Mr. Brown was already in the lab getting the equipment set up.

   Woman: You mean he was on time?

   Third Voice: What had the woman assumed about Mr. Brown?

Answer

(A) Since the woman was surprised that Mr. Brown was on time, it must be concluded that she assumed he would be late. Choice (B) is not correct because she thought he would not be in the lab yet. Choices (C) and (D) are not mentioned and may not be concluded from information in the conversation.

Audio

10. Man: So we met with our study group during the break and we each took one part of the book to outline.

    Woman: Wait a minute. Dr. Peterson actually gave you a break?

    Third Voice: What had the woman assumed about Dr. Peterson?

Answer

(C) Since the woman was surprised that Dr. Peterson gave them a break, it must be concluded that she assumed Dr. Peterson would not give them a break. The *meeting*, the *outline*, and the *book* in Choices (A), (B), and (D) are activities of the study group, not Dr. Peterson.

EXERCISE 9: Dialogues—Predictions
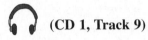 (CD 1, Track 9)

Audio

1. Man: I'll have hot tea and a large glass of orange juice.

   Woman: We only have one size orange juice. It's pretty big, though. About like that.

   Third Voice: What will the man probably do?

Answer

(B) Since the man has ordered a large orange juice, he will most probably accept the size orange juice they have. Choice (A) is less probable because they have the drink that he wants. Choice (C) is less probable because there is no reason for him to change his order because of the size glass available. Choice (D) is less probable because the hot tea was ordered in addition to the orange juice, not instead of it.

Audio

2. Woman: Have you seen my chemistry book?

   Man: It was on the kitchen table yesterday. Did you have it with you when you went to the library last night? Maybe you left it there.

   Third Voice: What will the woman probably do?

Answer

(C) Since the woman went to the library last night, and the man suggests that she might have left her book there, the woman will most probably go to the library to look for her book. Choices (A) and (D) are less probable because the kitchen and the table refer to the place where the book was yesterday, not to places where the woman will go to study or eat instead of looking for the lost book. Choice (B) is less probable because in the conversation *chemistry* refers to the book, not a class.

Audio

3. Man: You have a long distance call from London. Will you accept the charges?

   Woman: I don't know anyone in London.

   Third Voice: What will the woman probably do?

Answer

(C) Since the woman does not know anyone in London, she will most probably refuse the collect call. Choice (B) is less probable because she will probably not accept the charges. Choices (A) and (D) are less probable because she does not know anyone in London.

Audio

4. Man: Is there a copy machine in this building?

   Woman: No. But there is one in the building across the street.

   Third Voice: What will the man probably do?

Answer

(B) Since the man is looking for a copy machine, and the woman directs him to a building across the street, he will most probably go across the street to make a copy. Choice (A) is less probable because she does not have access to a copy machine. Choice (C) is less probable because the building is right across the street. Choice (D) is less probable because the man wants to make copies, but he does not have them now.

Audio

5. Man: Tuesdays you can rent two videos for the price of one. Wednesdays you can rent any video you want for ninety-nine cents. And every time you have rented a total of ten, you get one free. But you have to join the club, and that costs five dollars.

Woman: Okay. That sounds good to me.

Third Voice: What will the woman probably do?

Answer

(A) Since the woman says that the offer sounds good to her, she will most probably join the club. Choice (B) is less probable because the $5.00 refers to the cost of joining the club, not the price of a video. Choice (C) is less probable because the offer of one free video after renting ten is available after joining the club. Choice (D) is less probable because she is already in the video store.

Audio

6. Woman: How may I direct your call?

Man: Reservations, please.

Third Voice: What does the man probably want to do?

Answer

(C) Since the man asks for his call to be directed to reservations, he will most probably make a reservation. Choice (A) is less probable because his call, not he, is being directed. Choice (B) is less probable because he is already on the phone, making a call. Choice (D) is less probable because the woman is directing his call to someone else.

Audio

7. Woman: Is this where the bus to the mall stops?

Man: No. It's on the other side of the street.

Third Voice: What will the woman probably do?

Answer

(C) Since the woman asks where the bus will stop, she will most probably cross the street to wait for the bus. Choices (A) and (D) are less probable because she wants to take a bus. Choice (B) is less probable because the bus stop is on the other side of the street.

Audio

8. Woman: Did you drive in on I-17?

Man: Yes, and it was already starting to get slick. By now it should be really bad. You'd better call the highway patrol before you leave to make sure it's still open.

Third Voice: What will the woman probably do?

Answer

(B) Since the man suggests that the woman call the highway patrol, she will most probably call them. Choice (A) is less probable because the man suggests that she check with the highway patrol before leaving. Choices (C) and (D) are not mentioned and may not be concluded from the information.

Audio

9. Woman: Do you deliver?

Man: That depends. We do if you are within three miles of the university.

Third Voice: What will the man do?

Answer

(C) Since the man delivers within three miles of the university, he will most probably make the delivery to the woman if she is close to the university. Choice (A) is less probable because the woman has not indicated that she is at the university. Choice (B) is less probable because the woman may be within the delivery area. Choice (D) is not mentioned and may not be concluded from information in the conversation.

Audio

10. Woman: It will be about a twenty-minute wait if you want to sit indoors. We can seat you out-
                    doors on the patio in five minutes.
    Man: Okay. I don't have twenty minutes to wait.
    Third Voice: What will the man probably do?

Answer

(B) Since the man does not have twenty minutes to wait, he will most probably wait five minutes to be
seated outdoors on the patio. Choice (A) is less probable because the man says he does not have twenty
minutes to wait. Choice (C) is less probable because both sections have a waiting list. Choice (D) is
not mentioned and may not be concluded from the information in the conversation.

EXERCISE 10: Dialogues—Implications 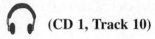 (CD 1, Track 10)

Audio

1. Woman: That book is on reserve, so you can't take it out of the library. You can use it here
                   for two hours, though. Or, you can wait until an hour before closing and check it out
                   until the library opens at eight in the morning.
   Man: Okay. I'll come back tonight.
   Third Voice: What does the man imply?

Answer

(C) Since the man says that he will come back tonight, he implies that he will check the book out before
closing. Choice (A) is less likely because he plans to return to the library. Choice (B) is less likely
because he leaves the library. Choice (D) is less likely because the book is already on reserve.

Audio

2. Woman: Do you know where I can get a soda?
   Man: Isn't there a machine downstairs?
   Third Voice: What does the man imply?

Answer

(C) Since the man says that there is a machine downstairs, he implies that the woman should go downstairs to get a soda. Choice (A) is less likely because there is a soda machine downstairs. Choice (B) is
less likely because he gives directions to the woman. Choice (D) is not correct because he gives directions to a soda machine.

Audio

3. Man: Why do *you* have to take the TOEFL? I thought if you graduated from an American
                   high school you didn't have to take it.
   Woman: I thought so, too. But the universities where I applied required a score even with an
                   American diploma.
   Third Voice: What do we know about the woman?

Answer

(D) Since the man expresses surprise that the woman will have to take the TOEFL, and mentions that
he thought those who graduated from an American high school were exempted from taking it, we know
that the woman graduated from an American high school. Choice (B) is less likely because she is making
application to American universities now. Choice (C) is not correct because she thought she would NOT
be required to take the TOEFL, but has been required to do so by the universities to which she applied.
Choice (A) is not mentioned and may not be concluded from information in the conversation.

Audio

4. Woman: How long did it take you to register? I was in line for two hours.
   Man: You were lucky.
   Third Voice: What did the man mean?

Answer

(B) Since the man says the woman was lucky to be in line for two hours, the man most probably means that he was in line longer than the woman. Choice (A) is true, but it is not what the man means by his comment. Choice (C) is not correct because the man thought the woman's two-hour wait was lucky compared to his. Choice (D) is not correct because it took the woman two hours to register.

Audio

5. Woman: If I were you, I would take a plane instead of a bus. It will take you forever to get there.
   Man: But flying makes me so nervous.
   Third Voice: What does the man prefer to do?

Answer

(C) Because the man offers an argument against taking a plane, it must be concluded that he prefers to take a bus. Choice (B) refers to the way that the woman, not the man, prefers to travel. Choices (A) and (D) are not mentioned and may not be concluded from information in the conversation.

Audio

6. Man: The name is Baker. We don't have a reservation, but we have time to wait.
   Woman: Party of four? It shouldn't be more than ten minutes, Mr. Baker. We'll call you when we have a table.
   Third Voice: Where does this conversation most likely take place?

Answer

(C) From the references to *reservation, party of four*, and *table*, it must be concluded that this conversation takes place in a restaurant. The word *reservation* in Choice (A) refers to a place saved, not to land owned by Native Americans. The word *party* in Choice (B) refers to a group, not an occasion. The word *Baker* in Choice (D) refers to a name, not to a place where bread and pastries are made.

Audio

7. Woman: Do you think that Bob is serious about Sally?
   Man: Well, I know this. I've never seen him go out so often with the same person.
   Third Voice: What conclusion does the man want us to draw from his statement?

Answer

(B) Because the man has never seen Bob go out so often with the same person, it must be concluded that Bob is serious about Sally. Choice (D) is not correct because Bob has never gone out so often with the same person. Choices (A) and (C) are not mentioned and may not be concluded from information in the conversation.

Audio

8. Woman: Whereas European nations have traditionally employed metric units such as meters and grams, the United States has employed English units such as feet and pounds.
   Man: Both systems are now in use in the U.S., though.
   Third Voice: What are these people most probably discussing?

Answer

(A) From the references to *metric units*, *meters*, *grams*, *feet*, and *pounds*, it must be concluded that the people are discussing weights and measurements. The phrase *European nations* in Choice (B) refers to the countries using the metric system, not to politics. The word *employ* in Choice (C) refers to use, not employment. The word *pounds* in Choice (D) refers to weight, not money.

Audio

9. Woman: Jane told me that she was going to quit her job. I'll certainly be sorry to see her go.
   Man: Oh, she always says that! I wouldn't buy her a going-away present if I were you.
   Third Voice: What does the man think about Jane?

Answer

(C) Because the man says that Jane always says she is going to quit her job, it must be concluded that he does not take her seriously. Choice (A) is not correct because the man does not believe Jane will quit. Choice (B) refers to the way that the woman, not Jane, feels. The word *present* in Choice (D) refers to a going-away present for Jane, not for the man.

Audio

10. Man: I wonder what happened to Betty Thompson? I don't see her anywhere.
    Woman: I don't know. She told me that she would be here at the play tonight.
    Third Voice: What do we learn about Betty from this conversation?

Answer

(D) Because they do not see her there, it must be concluded that Betty was not at the play. Choices (A) and (C) are not correct because she told the man she would be at the play. Choice (B) is not correct because the man and woman don't see her at the play.

EXERCISE 11: Dialogues—Problems

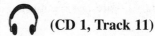 (CD 1, Track 11)

Audio

1. Man: Oh, no. I've run out of checks and the rent is due.
   Woman: Maybe you could get a cashier's check at the bank.
   Third Voice: What is the man's problem?

Answer

(B) "I've run out of checks. . . ." Choice (A) is not correct because the man has run out of checks. Choices (C) and (D) are not mentioned and may not be concluded from information in the conversation.

Audio

2. Woman: My roommate is getting married next month. I'd like to live by myself, but I really can't afford to.
   Man: Why don't you sign up on the message board in the housing office?
   Third Voice: What is the woman's problem?

Answer

(B) Since her roommate will be getting married, it must be concluded that she will be moving out. Choice (A) is not correct because she would like to live by herself, but can't afford to. Choices (C) and (D) are not mentioned and may not be concluded from information in the conversation.

Audio

3. Woman: What's the matter?
   Man: I can't register until I get my advisor's signature on my registration form, and, as usual, I can't find him.
   Third Voice: What is the man's problem?

Answer

(A) Since the man can't get registered without his advisor's signature on the registration form, it must be concluded that he needs his advisor to sign the form. Choice (B) is not correct because he is looking for his advisor. Choice (C) is not correct because he has the registration form. In Choice (D), it is his advisor, not his registration, that he can't find.

Audio

4. Woman: Can you give me a lift? My car's in the shop and I'm already late to work.

   Man: Sure. I'll drop you off on my way to class.

   Third Voice: What is the woman's problem?

Answer

(B) Since the woman asks for a lift, it must be concluded that she needs a ride. To give someone a "lift" is an idiomatic expression that means to give them a ride. Choice (A) is not correct because her car is in the shop. Choice (C) is not correct because she is late for work, not class. Choice (D) is not correct because she is going to work, not shopping. It is her car that is in the shop.

Audio

5. Woman: Great! Professor Jones is using a different book this semester. Now I'll have to buy a new one.

   Man: Me, too. My friend let me have a copy of the book he used last semester, but that won't do me any good now.

   Third Voice: What is the problem that the man and woman are talking about?

Answer

(C) "Professor Jones is using a different book this semester." Choices (A), (B), and (D) are not mentioned and may not be concluded from information in the conversation.

Audio

6. Woman: Sorry. I have to stay here until someone comes from the phone company to install my phone.

   Man: That's too bad. I wish you could go with us to the movie.

   Third Voice: What is the woman's problem?

Answer

(A) "I have to stay here until someone comes from the phone company to install my phone." Choice (B) is not correct because she is waiting for her phone to be installed. Choice (C) refers to the movie that the man and his friends are going to see, but it is not mentioned whether the woman has seen it already. The *company* in the conversation is the phone company, not visitors, as in Choice (D).

Audio

7. Man: Excuse me. I need to exchange this sweatshirt for a larger size, but I can't find the receipt.

   Woman: That's okay since it's an even exchange. Just take the size you want and give me that one.

   Third Voice: What is the man's problem?

Answer

(C) ". . . I can't find the receipt." Choice (B) is not correct because he needs a larger size because the sweatshirt is too small. Choice (D) is not correct because the clerk exchanges the sweatshirt. Choice (A) is not mentioned and may not be concluded from information in the conversation.

Audio

8. Woman: If the university had child care on campus, it would make my life a lot easier.

   Man: It really would. It must take a lot of time going back and forth to day care all the way across town.

   Third Voice: What is the woman's problem?

Answer

(A) Since child care on campus would make the woman's life easier, and we know that she is traveling across town, it must be concluded that she needs child care that is closer to the university. Choices (B), (C), and (D) are not mentioned and may not be concluded from information in the conversation.

Audio

9. Man: I need to get a different job. The one I have just doesn't give me enough hours anymore.

    Woman: Have you tried the library? They're always looking for help.

    Third Voice: What is the man's problem?

Answer

(B) "The one [job] I have just doesn't give me enough hours anymore." Choices (A), (C), and (D) are not mentioned and may not be concluded from information in the conversation.

Audio

10. Woman: I've been staying up until three and four in the morning trying to get all my papers and projects done. I'm exhausted.

    Man: Well, you can't do that for very long without getting sick.

    Third Voice: What is the woman's problem?

Answer

(A) Since the woman has been staying up late, and she says she is exhausted, it must be concluded that she needs to get more sleep. Choice (B) refers to the man's concern about her getting sick, not to how she feels now. Choice (C) is not correct because she is getting her papers and projects done. She says she feels tired, but being tired of school work is not mentioned and may not be concluded from information in the conversation.

EXERCISE 12: Conversations—Friends on Campus   (CD 1, Track 12)

Conversation One

Audio

Narrator: Listen to part of a conversation between two students on campus.

Man: We seem to be having this conversation over and over again.

Woman: You're right.

Man: Look, I know how you feel about my smoking. You don't have to tell me every day.

Woman: I'm sorry. I worry about you.

Man: I know. But work and school have me so stressed out. Maybe I'll be able to quit after I graduate.

Woman: Let's be honest. There's always going to be a reason not to. After you graduate, it's going to be hard to find a job, then there will be the stress from just starting a job, then there will be. . . .

Man: Okay, I get your point. It's just so hard. You don't really understand because you never smoked.

Woman: You need some help. Why don't you go to a doctor?

Man: You mean a psychiatrist.

Woman: No, I don't. I mean a general practitioner. Maybe you can get a patch, or . . . or some pills, well, I don't know, something to help you with the withdrawal. Because that's what it is.

Man: Really, I believe I can quit on my own. Just not right now. But I'll think about what you said. I will.

Woman: All right. I won't mention it for a week. Then I want to know your decision. Because if you don't get some help, I need to rethink our plans.

Man: You mean you'd break our engagement over this? I can't believe it!

Woman: I don't know. I love you, but I'm not sure I could accept everything that goes along with the smoking.

Audio

1. What is the main topic of this conversation?

Answer

(C) "Look, I know how you feel about my smoking. You don't have to tell me every day." Choices (A), (B), and (D) are mentioned in reference to the main topic of the conversation, "the man's smoking."

Audio

2. What does the woman suggest?

Answer

(B) "Why don't you go to a doctor? . . . I mean a general practitioner." Choice (A) is not correct because the woman, not the man, will rethink their plans. Choice (C) refers to the man's interpretation of the suggestion, not to what the woman suggests. Choice (D) refers to a source of stress, not to the woman's suggestion.

Audio

3. What does the man promise to do?

Answer

(D) "But I'll think about what you said." Choice (A) refers to a suggestion by the woman, not to a promise by the man. Choice (B) is not correct because the man says that he will quit, but ". . . not right now." Choice (C) is not mentioned and may not be concluded from information in the conversation.

Audio

4. How does the man feel about the woman's decision?

Answer

(B) "I can't believe it!" Choice (C) refers to the woman's feelings, not to those of the man. Choices (A) and (D) are not mentioned and may not be concluded from information in the conversation.

Audio

5. What can we infer about the woman?

Answer.

(C) Since the man says that the woman does not have to tell him how she feels about his smoking every day, it may be concluded that she has asked the man to quit smoking many times. Choice (B) is not correct because she is engaged. Choice (D) is not correct because she loves the man. Choice (A) is not correct because the woman has never smoked.

Conversation Two

Audio

Narrator: Listen to part of a conversation between two students in a college dormitory.

Bill: Want to go down to dinner, John? The line is going to close in about half an hour, and I'm hungry.

John: What time is it?

Bill: Six o'clock. You had better go now if you want to eat. They're serving fish cakes and baked potatoes.

John: I don't think I'll go.

Bill: Oh, come on. Get yourself a big salad if you don't want fish. The dessert will probably be good.

John: No, thanks Bill. I think that I'll keep studying for a while, and then maybe I'll order a pizza later.

Bill: Suit yourself. Do you have a test or something?

John: Yeah. It's not until Monday, but I want to go home this weekend.

Bill: Lucky you. Two days of home cooking.

John:	It sure beats the cafeteria at this place.
Bill:	True. Well, knock on my door if you decide to get that pizza later.
John:	Why? Aren't you going to eat either?
Bill:	Sure. But I'll be hungry again by ten.

Audio

1. What prompted this conversation?

Answer

(A) ". . . . I'm hungry." Choice (B) is not correct because Bill, not John, noticed the time. Choices (C) and (D) are true, but not the reasons for the conversation.

Audio

2. Why is John studying?

Answer

(B) "It's [the test is] not until Monday, but I want to go home this weekend." Choice (A) is not correct because the test is on Monday, not that night. Choices (C) and (D) are not mentioned and may not be concluded from information in the conversation.

Audio

3. When will the cafeteria close?

Answer

(B) Because the cafeteria is going to close in half an hour and it is six o'clock now, it must be concluded that the cafeteria closes thirty minutes later, or at six-thirty. Choice (A) refers to the time it is now, not to the time the cafeteria closes. Choice (C) refers to when John is going to go home. Choice (D) refers to when John has a test.

Audio

4. What does Bill want John to do?

Answer

(C) "Well, knock on my door if you decide to get that pizza later." Choice (D) is not correct because Bill tells John what is being served in the cafeteria. Choices (A) and (B) are not mentioned and may not be concluded from information in the conversation.

Audio

5. What will Bill most probably do now?

Answer

(B) Because Bill has asked John to join him for dinner in the cafeteria and John has refused, it must be concluded that Bill will go to the cafeteria by himself. Choice (A) refers to John, not to Bill. Choice (D) refers to a plan for later, not for now. Choice (C) is not mentioned and may not be concluded from information in this conversation.

EXERCISE 13: Conversations—Friends on Campus (CD 1, Track 13)

Conversation One

Audio

Narrator:	Listen to part of a conversation between two friends on campus.
Man:	Did you see that TV special on Norman Rockwell last night? You know, the one that Dr. Mitchell mentioned in class last Wednesday.
Woman:	Yeah, I did. I don't have a TV, but I went over to a friend's house. It was really good, wasn't it?
Man:	It sure was. I thought it was really interesting how he made . . . he developed the paintings in stages . . . starting with photographs. I'm glad Dr. Mitchell mentioned that in class or I . . . I mean, I might not have understood that part of the program as well.

Woman:	Unhuh. Unhuh. I thought that was interesting too. It never occurred to me that he would have actually employed, uh, models. I just assumed that he invented all those . . . those . . . wonderful characters. Then when Dr. Mitchell said that the characters were real . . . well.
Man:	I know. But it does make sense to use photographs of real people to solve as many of the, uh, the composition problems as . . . well, before starting to paint.
Woman:	Unhuh. True. The special really made that clear, didn't it?
Man:	It did. I liked the way they . . . they . . . interspersed recreations of the modeling scenes with . . . the actual Rockwells.
Woman:	Really. That was awesome. I'm sorry I didn't record it.
Man:	I *did*.
Woman:	Really?
Man:	Yeah. Would you . . . I mean, do you want to see it again?
Woman:	Sure. Hey, maybe we could do something for, um, extra credit.
Man:	That would be great. Let's talk to Dr. Mitchell about it.
Woman:	Okay. He said he was . . . open to extra-credit projects. Oh, but you probably don't need any extra credit.
Man:	Oh, yes I do. I don't do that well on tests, so. . . .
Woman:	Really, that's surprising. You're always the first to answer in class.
Man:	Sure . . . but the tests are essays, and I'm not . . . I mean, I'm not that good at writing.
Woman:	Okay then, let's do the extra credit.
Man:	Okay.
Woman:	Anyway, you know what I like most . . . about Rockwell?
Man:	What?
Woman:	Well, when you look at one of the magazine covers . . . which magazine was it?
Man:	*The Saturday Evening Post.*
Woman:	Right . . . well, you can just tell what the people are thinking and feeling. The picture really tells a story.
Man:	Yeah, I like that, too. And to think that he created . . . several hundred of those.
Woman:	Amazing. Of course, that was over a long period of time . . . wasn't it almost sixty years? But still. . . .
Man:	I'd like to see them when the exhibit comes to Miami.
Woman:	What exhibit?
Man:	The one they mentioned after the special.
Woman:	Oh, I must have turned it off before the announcement. I'd like to see it, too.
Man:	Maybe . . . we can work that into our extra-credit project . . . going to the exhibit . . . but, even if we can't, let's go.
Woman:	Okay. When is it?
Man:	Next week. And it's here on campus, so that's easy.
Woman:	Well, that gives us a couple of weeks before the end of the semester . . . to finish the extra credit.
Man:	What do you want to, uh, propose for it? Remember, I'm . . . I'm not great at writing.
Woman:	Well, you've already got the video, right?
Man:	Right.
Woman:	Then, why don't we submit the video and, uh, some photographs . . . of the exhibit. We could do a short introduction and maybe . . . I know, we could package it for the reserve desk at the library.
Man:	Great idea. That way people who didn't have a chance to see the video or, uh, go to the exhibit . . . they could see the material in the library.
Woman:	And the really good thing is that Dr. Mitchell can use it every semester for his class.
Man:	Wow! That's brilliant. He should like that. Now all we have to do is, uh, write the proposal for the extra credit.

Woman:	I'll do that. I really don't mind writing.
Man:	This is terrific. I can do the photos easily.
Woman:	I was counting on that. After all, you're the art major.
Man:	Oh . . . uh . . . just one thing. We'd better find out if I . . . if I can shoot photos at the exhibit. I mean sometimes they won't let you do that.
Woman:	Even for a class project?
Man:	Look, I don't know. But I'll find out who, uh, who to call for . . . for permission. Usually you can get permission if it isn't for, you know, profit.
Woman:	Perfect. Just let me know as soon as you can so I can get going on the proposal.

Audio

1. What do the speakers mainly discuss?

Answer

(B) "Did you see that TV special on Norman Rockwell last night?" Choices (A), (C), and (D) are mentioned in reference to the main topic of the conversation, "the TV program about Norman Rockwell."

Audio

2. How did Rockwell paint such interesting faces?

Answer

(C) "It never occurred to me that he would have actually employed . . . models. . . . But it does make sense to use photographs of real people. . . ." Choice (A) refers to the woman's assumption, not to Rockwell's method. Choice (B) refers to Rockwell's finished work, not to the source of the interesting faces. Choice (D) is not correct because the picture tells a story.

Audio

3. What do we know about Rockwell?

Answer

(A) "And to think that he [Rockwell] created several hundred of those [paintings]." Choices (B), (C), and (D) are not mentioned and may not be concluded from information in the conversation.

Audio

4. What do the students plan to do for extra credit?

Answer

(D) ". . . why don't we submit the video . . . and some photographs of the exhibit. . . ." Choice (A) is not correct because the video will not be at the reserve desk until the students package it. The exhibit in Choice (B) refers to the Rockwell exhibit that the students will see, not to an exhibit that they will bring to the library. The photographs in Choice (C) refer to the photographs that the man will take of the Rockwell exhibit, not to photographs of models.

Audio

5. Listen again to part of the conversation.
   Then answer the question.
   "Anyway, you know what I like most . . . about Rockwell?"
   "What?"
   Why does the woman say this:
   "Anyway, you know what I like most . . . about Rockwell?"

Answer

(B) Questions that ask whether the listener knows something are often used in conversations to encourage involvement. The response "What?" allows the speaker to continue. Choice (A) is not correct because the conversation is moving along, and both the man and the woman are participating. We know that the man is listening. Choice (C) is not correct because this is new information, not a repetition of previous information. Choice (D) is not mentioned and may not be concluded from information in the conversation.

Audio

6. What will the couple probably do?

Answer

(A) "I'd like to see it [the exhibit], too. Let's go." Choice (B) is not correct because they already saw the special. Choice (C) is not correct because the television special aired last night, not now. Choice (D) is not correct because they are in Miami now.

Conversation Two

Audio

Narrator: Listen to part of a conversation between two students on campus.

Bill: So, Linda . . . how are you going to study for the final?

Linda: Me? I'm going to use my notes mostly, I guess.

Bill: You mean you aren't going to, uh, read the book?

Linda: Oh, well yeah, I read the book, but I'm not going to spend that much time reviewing it. You know, I did that for the first couple of quizzes, but, uh, there were hardly any questions from the book on them at all. So well, I figured that, uh, the midterm wouldn't have that much from the book, either.

Bill: Well, you were right about that. Most of the questions *did* come from . . . from the notes.

Linda: From the notes, and, uh, well, there were some from the handouts, too.

Bill: Right. Remember that question about . . . what was it? . . . colonial art?

Linda: Colonial art? Oh, yeah . . . okay.

Bill: It was. . . .

Linda: . . . directly from the handout. But I had some notes on that, too.

Bill: Did you? I'm not sure I did. Maybe your notes are more detailed . . . are, uh, are . . . better than mine.

Linda: I don't know about that, but, I do try to write down everything I can in class, you know, then I put it . . . I organize it into headings afterward.

Bill: You . . . rewrite them?

Linda: Yeah, I do.

Bill: You rewrite all of your notes?

Linda: Yeah. It's part of my study plan.

Bill: That must take a lot of time.

Linda: Well, I guess so, but still, I find that I remember better when I write something down.

Bill: Hmmn. Okay.

Linda: And besides, when I get ready to study for the final, I can . . . I have everything in one place. Come to think of it . . . I think it, actually it probably saves me time.

Bill: Because you aren't organizing everything at the last minute for the tests?

Linda: Yeah, and I sort of remember more since I've already gone over it once.

Bill: Okay, okay . . . that sure makes sense, but, uh, but how do you find the time to do all that, uh, rewriting? I'm always behind as it is. I hardly have time to do the reading assignments.

Linda: But I think maybe you spend more time on the reading assignments than I do. I just skim over them before class. It probably doesn't take me more than, say . . . fifteen or twenty minutes max.

Bill: You're joking.

Linda: No, no, really.

Bill: Then you . . . must be a speed reader.

Linda: I read fairly fast, but remember, I'm just skimming.

Bill: Okay, but I'm not sure I know what, uh, what you mean by that . . . by skimming.

Linda: Well, I'm looking for the main ideas . . . before I listen to the lecture. So I pay a lot of attention to the headings . . . and, uh, any words that are in bold type. If there's a summary at the end of the chapter, you know . . . I read that more carefully.

Bill: Okay, okay. But do you, uh, highlight the book or . . . or underline anything?

Linda: Oh, maybe once in a while. But it's not how I . . . not the way I'm using the book really. I'm just getting some general background information so I can be . . . you know, a better listener in class.

Bill: Hmmn, now I see why you're going to use your notes for the final. By the way, what was . . . how did you do . . . on the midterm . . . using that system, I mean?

Linda: I got an A. Just barely, but an A anyway. I usually pull off an A, though. I have a scholarship, so you know how it is.

Bill: Okay, okay. I got a B. And I studied a lot for it. But I mostly went over the highlighted material in my book. And, uh, after I finished with that, I didn't have much time left to go over my notes.

Linda: Well, maybe you could start with the notes this time, and . . . you know, go over the book last.

Bill: No kidding. Thanks for the ideas, Linda. I guess it's too late to, uh, rewrite . . . all my notes for the final, but I sure plan to spend more time organizing and studying my notes than I do reviewing the book this time.

Linda: Oh, and another thing. I never miss a class . . . you know, since the notes are so important.

Bill: No problem. I'm always there, too.

Linda: I thought so, but anyway, good luck, Bill. If you get an A on the final, you can still get an A for the course.

Bill: I know. I'm going to try. Hey, thanks again. I, uh, I really appreciate your suggestions.

Audio

1. What are the students mainly discussing?

Answer

(B) ". . . how are you going to study for the final?" Choices (A), (C), and (D) are mentioned in reference to the main topic of the conversation, "studying for a test."

Audio

2. Why does Bill mention colonial art?

Answer

(A) "It [the question about colonial art] was . . . directly from the handout." Choice (C) is not correct because he is not sure that he had notes on colonial art. Choice (D) is not correct because the topic was on a handout, not in the book. Choice (B) is not mentioned and may not be concluded from information in this conversation.

Audio

3. How does Linda usually study for a test?

Answer

(B) "You . . . rewrite them [the notes]?" Choice (A) is not correct because Linda does not spend much time reviewing the book. The *handouts* in Choice (C) refer to material from the professor, not Linda. Choice (D) refers to the way that the man, not the woman, usually studies for a test.

Audio

4. What kind of student is Linda?

Answer

(D) "I usually pull off an A. . . ." The grade of B in Choice (A) refers to the grade that the man received on his midterm, not to the grade that the woman tries to get. Choice (B) is not correct because she is a scholarship student who usually pulls off an A. Choice (C) is not correct because she never misses a class.

Audio

5. Listen again to part of the conversation.
   Then answer the question.
   "You . . . rewrite them?"
   "Yeah, I do."
   "You rewrite all of your notes?"
   Why does the man say this:
   "You rewrite all of your notes?"

Answer

(B) Speakers often repeat something they have heard using a question intonation to express surprise. Choice (A) is not correct because the man is able to repeat what he has heard. Choice (C) is not correct because he is not using a humorous tone. Choice (D) is not correct because the man is asking for information and advice, not help.

Audio

6. What will Bill probably do?

Answer

(D) "I sure plan to spend more time . . . organizing and studying my notes. . . ." Choice (B) is not correct because it is too late to rewrite the notes for the final. Choice (C) is not correct because he is not going to spend as much time reviewing the book. Choice (A) is not mentioned and may not be concluded from information in this conversation.

EXERCISE 14: Conversations—Campus Personnel/Student 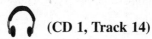 (CD 1, Track 14)

Conversation One

Audio

Narrator: Listen to part of a conversation between a student and a secretary on campus.

Man: Hello, Mrs. Kelly. I'd like to pick up my test, please.
Woman: Sure. Whose class are you in?
Man: Dr. Purcell's math class.
Woman: And your name?
Man: My last name is Raleigh. R-A-L-E-I-G-H.
Woman: That's right. Jim Raleigh. Here it is.
Man: Thank you. And Terry Young's test, too, please.
Woman: Oh, I'm sorry. I can't let you take someone else's test.
Man: He's sick, and he can't come in to get it. He's my roommate.
Woman: I understand. But the privacy act won't permit it.
Man: Really? Maybe you could call him.
Woman: Not even then. I can only give a test to the student whose name appears on it. I can't even give it to a family member.
Man: That's weird.
Woman: I think so, too, frankly, but that's the law.
Man: Okay. I'll tell Terry. Thanks anyway.
Woman: You're welcome. Tell him I'll just keep his test here until he feels better and can come in for it himself.
Man: Okay. I'll do that.
Woman: Have a nice day, Jim.
Man: You, too, Mrs. Kelly.

Audio

1. What do the speakers mainly discuss?
Answer
(C) "I can't let you take someone else's test . . . the privacy act won't permit it." Choices (A), (B), and (D) are mentioned in reference to the main topic of the conversation, "school policy."

Audio

2. Why can't the woman give Terry Young's test to the man?

Answer

(A) "I can only give a test to the student whose name appears on it . . . that's the law." Choice (B) is not correct because she can't even give it [the test] to a family member. Choice (D) is not correct because Jim wants to pick up the test that Terry took. Choice (C) is not mentioned and may not be concluded from information in the conversation.

Audio

3. What is the man's last name?

Answer

(C) "My last name is Raleigh." Choice (A) is the name of the man's friend. Choice (B) is the name of the professor. Choice (D) is the name of the secretary.

Audio

4. How does the woman feel about the policy?

Answer

(B) Because the man says that the policy is *weird* and the woman agrees with him, it must be concluded that the woman thinks that the policy is "odd." Choice (A) is not correct because she agrees with the man. Choice (C) is not correct because she will not give the man his roommate's test, thereby enforcing the policy. Choice (D) is not mentioned and may not be concluded from information in this conversation.

Audio

5. What will the man most probably do?

Answer

(A) "Okay. I'll tell Terry." Choice (B) is not correct because the man is in the office and has picked up his test. Choice (D) is not correct because the man has already taken the test. Choice (C) is not mentioned and may not be concluded from information in the conversation.

Conversation Two

Audio

Narrator: Listen to part of a conversation between a student and an advisor on campus.

Woman: I usually advise first-year engineering students to take mathematics, chemistry, and an introductory engineering course the first quarter.

Man: Oh. That's only three classes.

Woman: Yes. But I'm sure that you'll be busy. They're all five-hour courses, and you'll have to meet each class every day. The chemistry course has an additional two-hour laboratory.

Man: So that would be seventeen hours of class a week.

Woman: That's right.

Man: Okay. Which mathematics course do you think I should take?

Woman: Have you taken very much math in high school?

Man: Four years. I had algebra, geometry, trigonometry. . . .

Woman: Good. Then I suggest that you take the math placement test. It's offered this Friday at nine o'clock in the morning in Tower Auditorium.

Man: Do I need anything to be admitted? I mean a permission slip?

Woman: No. Just identification. A driver's license will be fine.

Man: Do I take a chemistry test too?

Woman: No. Chemistry 100 is designed for students who have never taken a chemistry course, and Chemistry 200 is for students who have had chemistry in high school.

Man: I've had two courses.

Woman: Then you should take Chemistry 200, Orientation to Engineering, and either Mathematics 130 or 135, depending on the results of your placement test. Come back Friday afternoon. I should have your score on the test by then and we can finish getting you registered.

Audio

1. What is the purpose of this conversation?

Answer

(A) ". . . I should have your score on the test by then and we can finish getting you registered." Choices (B) and (D) are mentioned as secondary themes that are used to develop the main purpose of the conversation, "to register the student for classes." Choice (C) is not mentioned and may not be concluded from information in the conversation.

Audio

2. How many classes does the woman advise the man to take?

Answer

(C) "That's only three classes." Choice (A) refers to the number of hours that the two-hour laboratory meets per week. Choice (B) refers to the number of hours that each five-hour class meets per week. Choice (D) refers to the total number of hours that the classes meet per week.

Audio

3. What does the man need to be admitted to the examination?

Answer

(A) "A driver's license will be fine." Choice (B) refers to the man's suggestion, not to what he needs. Choice (D) is not correct because the man needs identification to be admitted to the examination. Choice (C) is not mentioned and may not be concluded from information in the conversation.

Audio

4. What does the woman suggest?

Answer

(A) "Come back Friday afternoon." Choice (B) is not correct because the results of the placement test are needed before the advisor can finish the registration process. Choice (C) is not correct because the advisor says three classes will keep the man busy. Choice (D) is not correct because the advisor needs the results of a placement test before choosing between Mathematics 130 or 135.

Audio

5. What do we know about the student?

Answer

(C) Because the woman says that she advises first-year students, it must be concluded that the student is a first-year student, or a freshman. Choice (A) is not correct because he is an engineering student. Choice (B) is not correct because he has had two courses in chemistry. Choice (D) is not mentioned and may not be concluded from information in the conversation.

EXERCISE 15: Conversations—Campus Personnel/Students (CD 2, Track 1)

Conversation One

Audio

Narrator: Listen to part of a conversation between a student and a clerk at the campus bookstore.

Kathy: Excuse me. Do you work here?

Jim: Yes, I do. How can I help you?

Kathy: Oh, well, um, I'm looking for a book for . . . for English 100.

Jim: Okay. Textbooks are in the back of the store. Did you want a new book or a used book?

Kathy: . . . I, . . . uh . . . I don't know. Is there much difference . . . in the price, I mean?

Jim: Well, that depends. We price the used books based on the, uh, depending on their condition. But in general, you can probably save, I'd say, at least 40 percent.

Kathy: Oh, great. I'll do that then.

Jim:	Okay. These are the used books . . . uh . . . over here. Now, uh . . . which section did . . . are you signed up for? See, every instructor selects a book, so there are several different textbooks for each course. And English 100 is a core course, so there are, uh, a lot of sections.
Kathy:	I don't remember the number, but it meets at eight o'clock.
Jim:	In the morning? That sounds awful.
Kathy:	Really. I registered late.
Jim:	Do you know the instructor's name?
Kathy:	Yes, it's Henry . . . Henley . . . uh . . . .
Jim:	Hendrix?
Kathy:	That's it. Hendrix.
Jim:	Oh, well, that's not so bad, then. She's a good teacher. I wish I'd taken that class with her.
Kathy:	That's what I was . . . what I heard. My roommate had her last semester.
Jim:	Oh, then why don't you use your roommate's book? I don't think, uh, Hendrix changed the order this semester.
Kathy:	Wouldn't you know? My roommate sold all her books at the end of the term.
Jim:	Oh . . . so she sold the one for this course? Too bad. Well, this is the shelf . . . and you're looking for a book called, uh, *College Writing*. I think it's green, or maybe green and blue. There should be a fairly clean one here.
Kathy:	Thanks . . . Look, here's one . . . oh . . . but it's pretty marked up.
Jim:	Let's see it. Sometimes it actually helps to use someone else's highlighting, I mean, if you happen to get a . . . get an A student's book.
Kathy:	True, I see your point, but really, I'd really rather highlight it myself.
Jim:	Okay. That one didn't look like it belonged to an A student anyway. Hey, look at this. I don't think there's a mark in it . . . except for the name.
Kathy:	Wow! That's great.
Jim:	Wait . . . let's check on the edition.
Kathy:	The edition? Does that matter?
Jim:	Unhuh. It really does. Sometimes there's, uh, new information in a later edition, so that's why the professor . . . orders it. But the worst part is if the instructor is always referring to, say, page 50, and the information is on a different page in your edition, well, uh, it gets confusing.
Kathy:	Oh . . . anyway . . . this is the tenth edition.
Jim:	And you need, uh, the tenth edition. You really lucked out. The new one would have cost you at least thirty dollars, but this one's only fifteen.
Kathy:	Thanks.
Jim:	Wait a minute. See this? Right over here, over the shelf? It's a list of the books that Professor Hendrix ordered. And it looks like . . . yep . . . you have another book for that class. It's not required . . . but, uh, it's recommended.
Kathy:	So I don't have to buy it.
Jim:	No, it's up to you, but you . . . you'd better look . . . take a look at it . . . before you decide.
Kathy:	It looks like a handbook . . . or really, you know, a . . .
Jim:	. . . style manual.
Kathy:	Exactly.
Jim:	Well then, the instructor will probably want you to, you know, use the format and, uh, style in this book . . . for your essays.
Kathy:	I'd better get it then. Don't you think?
Jim:	I would.
Kathy:	How much is it?
Jim:	All of these are ten dollars but they're fairly clean . . . uh, because, uh, because people don't usually write in a handbook. I mean, it's more of a reference.
Kathy:	Well, I'll take one then. . . . . This one looks good.
Jim:	Okay . . . are you looking for anything else?
Kathy:	No. Just this. But I really appreciate your help. You saved me some money.

Jim: Glad it, uh, worked out for you. I'm a student too. I just work here part time, and, believe me, I understand the problem. Most of the textbooks are, uh, fifty or a hundred dollars. When you're taking, say, four classes, that really adds up.

Kathy: It sure does. Anyway, thanks again.

Jim: Sure.

Audio

1. What is the purpose of this conversation?

Answer

(B) ". . . I'm looking for a book for . . . English 100." Choice (A) is not correct because the man offers his opinion without being asked. Choices (C) and (D) are not mentioned and may not be concluded from information in this conversation.

Audio

2. Why didn't the woman use her roommate's book?

Answer

(D) "My roommate sold all her books at the end of the term." Choice (A) is not correct because her roommate had her [Dr. Hendrix] last semester. Choice (B) is not correct because Hendrix did not change the book order this semester. Choice (C) refers to a used book on the shelf, not to her roommate's book.

Audio

3. According to the man, what is the problem with using an older edition?

Answer

(A) ". . . the instructor is always referring to, say, page 50, and the information is on a different page in your edition. . . ." Choice (B) is not correct because many of the used books they are looking at do not have marks. Choice (C) is true, but it is not the problem that students have using an older edition. Choice (D) is not mentioned and may not be concluded from information in this conversation.

Audio

4. Why does the woman buy the style manual?

Answer

(C) ". . . the instructor will probably . . . want you to . . . use the format and, uh, style in this book. . . ." Choice (A) is not correct because the manual is recommended, but not required. Choice (B) is not correct because the woman asks the price after she decides to buy it. Choice (D) is true, but it is not the reason why she decides to buy the manual.

Audio

5. Listen again to part of the conversation.
   Then answer the question.
   "I don't think, uh, Hendrix changed the order this semester."
   "Wouldn't you know? My roommate sold all her books at the end of the term."
   Why does the woman say this:
   "Wouldn't you know?"

Answer

(C) The question is asked with an ironic tone, in a way that invites commiseration. Choice (A) is not correct because the woman tells the man what her roommate did. She doesn't ask him. Choice (B) is not correct because the roommate's name is not mentioned. Choice (D) is not correct because the woman is using an ironic tone, not a humorous tone.

Audio

6. What can we infer about the woman?

Answer

(A) "I really appreciate your help. . . . You saved me some money." Choice (B) is not correct because the woman greets the man formally, asking whether he works in the bookstore, and because they do not call each other by name. The *A student* in Choice (C) refers to a previous owner of a used book, not to the woman. Choice (D) is not correct because the woman does not complain about her roommate when she mentions that she sold her book.

Conversation Two

Audio

Narrator: Listen to part of a conversation between a student and a librarian.

Joe: Hi. Is it true that I can search the library catalog from home? I mean, from my home computer? One of my friends at the dorm told me I could, uh, do that, but I live off campus, so I wasn't sure whether it would work for me.

Librarian: You're talking about the Oasis catalog, which is the on-line library catalog system. Here. It's easier if I just show you at this computer terminal.

Joe: Okay. Thanks.

Librarian: See. First, you get online.

Joe: Oh, I get it. It's all through the Internet.

Librarian: Right. You click on a browser, then, uh, go to the library . . . the home page.

Joe: Wait, wait. The home page is, uh, *www.awu.org*.

Librarian: Right. See all those options? Oasis is what you want . . . for the catalog. So you click on that.

Joe: Okay . . . okay. Did you use a password or, uh, anything to get into it?

Librarian: No. All you need is an Internet connection. But if you actually want to look at the books. . . .

Joe: I can do that?

Librarian: Sure. You want to go to a different . . . a different web site though. Here. . . . First, enter *www.netlibrary.org*. . . . There. See? This site lets you access all the e-books in our system.

Joe: Oh, well, do you have many of those?

Librarian: Thousands. They're all part of our collection, but we . . . we store them electronically, which means we don't have to have all that shelf space anymore.

Joe: Sounds good.

Librarian: But if you want to access Netlibrary, then you'll need to . . . you'll need a user name and a password.

Joe: So, how do I . . . do I just set that up online from home?

Librarian: No. You have to set up the account here in the library. You can do that on this terminal, if you like.

Joe: Great. Then I can . . . I can see the books on screen from my apartment.

Librarian: You can view the books from any place you have access to the Internet. If you're out of town or you go somewhere on break, you can still use Netlibrary. Of course, we don't have all of our books online yet, but we're working on building the collection.

Joe: So can I go directly to Netlibrary to do a search, or um . . . do I have to go to . . . what do you call it . . . the Oasis catalog first?

Librarian: You can go right to the Netlibrary if you want. But that'll just show you the books and, uh, databases that are online. If you search Oasis, you'll have access to all of the books in print, I mean, the ones in the library, as well. Of course, you'll have to . . . to come into the library to check them out.

Joe: Let me see if I've got this. Oasis is exactly like the catalog for the library here at school, and so, uh, I can find all the books and materials that are on the shelves, but they . . . I can't see them.

Librarian: Right. But, if you want to go to Netlibrary after you use Oasis, then you can look for a particular resource . . . to see whether it's part of our on-line holdings. If it is, then you can just read it on your computer screen. . . . Look, you can enter a title or an author, or even a subject, and then you get a list of books. When you click on a title, you see the table of contents. You can read one chapter or the . . . the whole book if you want.

Joe: That is so great. Oh, one more thing. If I don't have time to read it all, do I just start over again next time, or, I mean, is there like an easy way to . . . to get back to my book?

Librarian: It's very easy. You just bookmark your place and click on your e-book when you go into the site next time. It'll open to the page you marked.

Joe: Well, I think the best thing for me to do is, uh, open an account, and then go back to my apartment, and start working with it.

Librarian: There's a help screen on the site, but if you get stuck, just call the library, and someone will walk you through it.

Joe: And, uh, how do I pay for this? Do I have a one-time fee or a monthly charge or what?

Librarian: No charge. It's part of the library system. You're a student here, so when you log in, you'll be asked to enter your student ID number after your user name, and then your password, and, uh, that's it. Here's the screen you need to open the account . . . I'm sure you'll like using Netlibrary. Everyone does.

Audio

1. What is the main topic of this conversation?

Answer

(B) Because they discuss the *on-line library catalog* and the *Netlibrary* service, it may be concluded that the main topic is research methods on the Internet. Choices (A), (C), and (D) are mentioned in reference to the main topic, "research methods online."

Audio

2. What is *Oasis*?

Answer

(A) ". . . the Oasis catalog, which is the on-line library catalog system." Choice (C) refers to Netlibrary, not to Oasis. The name of the school in Choice (B) and the password in Choice (D) are not mentioned and may not be concluded from information in the conversation.

Audio

3. How does the man set up an account?

Answer

(C) "But if you want to access Netlibrary. . . . You have to set up the account here in the library." Choice (A) is not correct because the man will not have a password until he sets up the account. Choice (B) refers to Oasis, not to Netlibrary. Choice (D) refers to how he should get help, not how he should set up the account.

Audio

4. How does the man pay for Netlibrary?

Answer

(C) "No charge. It's part of the library system." Choices (A) and (B) refer to the man's question about payment, not to the librarian's response. Choice (D) is not mentioned and may not be concluded from information in this conversation.

Audio

5. Listen again to part of the conversation.
   Then answer the question.
   "Let me see if I've got this. Oasis is exactly like the catalog for the library here at school, and so, uh, I can find all the books and materials that are on the shelves, but they . . . I can't see them."
   Why does the man say this:
   "Let me see if I've got this."

Answer

(A) The phrase *to get* something means "to understand" it. The man paraphrases the information as a comprehension check. Choices (B), (C), and (D) are not mentioned and may not be concluded from information in the conversation.

Audio

6. What will the man probably do now?

Answer

(B) Because the librarian directs him to the screen he needs to open the account, it may be concluded that he will open the account now. Choice (C) is not correct because he needs to open the account before using Netlibrary. Choice (A) is not correct because the man says the best thing to do is open an account, and then [after opening the account] go back to the apartment and start working with it. Choice (D) refers to the librarian's offer to help after he starts using Netlibrary, not now.

EXERCISE 16: Conversation—Service Personnel/Students 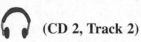 (CD 2, Track 2)

Conversation One

Audio

Narrator: Listen to part of a conversation between a student and a secretary at the newspaper office.

Man: I'd like to put an ad in the newspaper, please.

Woman: A classified ad?

Man: Yes. I want to sell my furniture. I'm moving.

Woman: I see. May I have your name, please?

Man: Bill Martyn.

Woman: M-A-R-T-I-N?

Man: Y-N

Woman: Okay. M-A-R-T-Y-N. And your address, Mr. Martyn?

Man: For the next few weeks I'll be at the Garden Apartments on Book Boulevard.

Woman: Is that where you want to be billed?

Man: No. I'll probably be gone before a bill could be sent. I'm just going to pay cash.

Woman: Okay. The rates are by the inch, not by the word. So, if you want to use abbreviations, that might save you some money.

Man: Oh, that's a good idea. I have everything written out here, but I'll just check it over before I give it to you. Maybe I can use some shorter words, too.

Woman: Okay. You can use that table over there to make your revisions. Just bring it back to me when you're ready.

Audio

1. What prompted the conversation?

Answer

(A) "I'd like to put an ad in the newspaper, please." Choices (B), (C), and (D) are not mentioned and may not be concluded from information in the conversation.

Audio

2. What does the man want to sell?

Answer

(A) "I want to sell my furniture." Choice (B) refers to the name of the boulevard where the man lives, not to what he is trying to sell. Choice (C) refers to the name of the apartment building where the man lives. Choice (D) is not mentioned and may not be concluded from information in the conversation.

Audio

3. What is the man's last name?

Answer

(B) "M-A-R-T-Y-N." Choice (A) refers to the spelling that the woman used, not to the correct spelling by the man himself. Choice (C) sounds like the last two letters that the man emphasized, not to the complete spelling. Choice (D) is a similar spelling, but it is not mentioned and may not be concluded from information in this conversation.

Audio

4. How will the man pay?

Answer

(C) "I'm just going to pay cash." Choice (A) refers to checking the wording of an ad, not to a method of payment. Choices (B) and (D) are not correct because the man does not wish to be billed.

Audio

5. Why does the man decide to revise what he has written?

Answer

(C) "So, if you want to use abbreviations, that might save you some money." Choice (B) is not correct because abbreviations make the ad shorter, not longer. Choices (A) and (D) are not mentioned and may not be concluded from information in the conversation.

Conversation Two

Audio

Narrator: Listen to part of a conversation between a student and a sales clerk at the Family Store.
Man: Will that be cash or charge? We also accept debit cards if they are on a local bank.
Woman: I want to pay by check if I may.
Man: Certainly. That's cash, then.
Woman: Cash?
Man: Yes. Both money and checks are considered cash. Only credit cards are charge.
Woman: Oh.
Man: Just make the check out to the Family Store.
Woman: Okay.
Man: And I'll need two pieces of identification. A driver's license and a major credit card.
Woman: Well, here's my driver's license. I don't have any charge cards, but I do have my student ID card from City College. Will that be all right?
Man: I think so. I need two numbers. Your student number is on the ID, isn't it?
Woman: Yes, it is. Do you need anything else?
Man: Just put your telephone number on the front of the check.
Woman: Okay.
Man: Good. Now let me give you your license, your ID, and your package. And thank you for shopping at the Family Store.
Woman: Thank *you*.

Audio

1. What is the purpose of the conversation?

Answer

(A) "And thank you for shopping at the Family Store." Choice (B) is a secondary theme used to develop the main theme of the conversation. Choice (C) refers to the fact that the clerk asks the woman to put her telephone number on the front of the check, not to his showing her how to write a check. Choice (D) refers to the woman's college ID, not to her registration at the college.

Audio

2. What is meant by the term *cash*?

Answer

(D) "Both money and checks are considered cash." Choice (A) is considered correct, but incomplete. Choices (B) and (C) are not correct because money and checks, not charge cards, are considered cash.

Audio

3. How does the woman pay for her purchase?

Answer

(D) "I want to pay by check . . .". Choice (A) refers to the man's explanation of the term *charge*, not to the way that the woman will pay. Choice (B) is not correct because the woman wants to pay by check. Choice (C) refers to an option that the man offers but the woman does not choose to use.

Audio

4. What did the woman use as identification?

Answer

(C) "Well, here's my driver's license. I don't have any charge cards, but I do have my student ID card from City College." Choice (A) is not correct because the woman doesn't have any charge cards. Choice (B) refers to identification that can be used, not to the identification that the woman actually uses. Choice (D) refers to the fact that she must put her telephone number on the front of the check, but it is not a piece of identification.

Audio

5. Who is the man in this conversation?

Answer

(A) Since the man thanks the woman for shopping at the Family Store, it may be concluded that he is a clerk. It is not as probable that the persons in Choices (B), (C), and (D) would help a woman with a purchase.

EXERCISE 17: Conversations—Professors/Students (CD 2, Track 3)

Conversation One

Audio

Narrator: Listen to part of a conversation between a student and a professor on campus.

Man: I'm really sorry, Professor Irwin. I was sick yesterday.

Woman: Look, I'm not upset that you couldn't keep the appointment, but it is common courtesy to call. You know that.

Man: Yes, I do.

Woman: During registration I have to see all my students, and sometimes they have to wait several days to get in. When someone doesn't show and doesn't call, that deprives someone else of an appointment time.

Man: You're right. I apologize. I didn't feel well, and I guess I just wasn't thinking straight at the time.

Woman: Okay, Apology accepted. Now, I suppose you need to set up another appointment.

Man: Yes, I do. Can you see me now if I wait?

Woman: No. I can see you at three o'clock this afternoon, or during my office hour on Tuesday or Thursday.

Man: Great. Your office hour is best. That's two o'clock, right?

Woman: That's right. Which day do you prefer?

Man: Tuesday.

Woman: Okay. Be there this time.

Man: I will be. Thanks a lot.

Audio

1. What is the main subject of the conversation?

Answer

(A) ". . . I'm not upset that you couldn't keep the appointment, but it is common courtesy to call." Choices (B), (C), and (D) are mentioned in reference to the main topic of the conversation, "the man's last appointment."

Audio

2. When is the man's new appointment scheduled?

Answer

(**A**) "That's two o'clock . . . Tuesday." Choices (B) and (C) refer to alternative times that the professor suggests, not to the time that the student chooses for the appointment. Choice (D) refers to the time that the student suggests.

Audio

3. What should the man have done about his first appointment?

Answer

(**B**) ". . . it is common courtesy to call." Choice (A) is not correct because he had an appointment that he did not keep. Choice (C) is not correct because the professor is not upset because he couldn't keep the appointment. Choice (D) is not mentioned and may not be concluded from information in the conversation.

Audio

4. What is the man's excuse?

Answer

(**A**) "I was sick yesterday." Choice (C) is not correct because the professor confirms, ". . . it is common courtesy to call. You know that," and the man responds, "Yes, I do [know that]." Choices (B) and (D) are not mentioned and may not be concluded from information in this conversation.

Audio

5. What word best describes Professor Irwin's attitude toward the student?

Answer

(**D**) From the tone of the conversation, it may be concluded that the professor is annoyed because the student did not call to cancel his appointment. Choice (B) refers to the student's attitude, not to that of the professor. Choices (A) and (C) are not mentioned and may not be concluded from information in the conversation.

Conversation Two

Audio

Narrator: Listen to part of a conversation between a student and a professor on campus.

Woman: Dr. Newbury, could I speak with you?

Man: Sure. Come on in.

Woman: I need to ask you to let me take the final early.

Man: May I ask why?

Woman: Yes. It's because I bought a ticket to go home for Christmas, and my flight leaves on Tuesday. That's the day before the exam.

Man: Yes, well, Penny, the exam schedule is printed in the registration materials. You had to know the dates. Why didn't you buy your ticket for the day after the exam?

Woman: Truthfully, I just made a mistake. And now, I've got a real problem because the ticket is non-refundable, and I can't afford to buy another one.

Man: Hmmn.

Woman: Dr. Newbury, I live too far away to get home for Thanksgiving and Spring Break like the other students do. This is my only chance to see my family during the school year. I'm sorry that it happened, but couldn't you make an exception this time? Or could you give me an incomplete and let me make it up next semester?

Man: Okay. Anyone can make a mistake. You can take the exam on Monday.

Woman: Thank you. I really appreciate this.

Audio

1. What is the woman's main purpose in this conversation?

Answer

(C) "I need to ask you to let me take the final early." Choices (A) and (B) are mentioned in reference to the main topic of the conversation, "a change in the date of the woman's exam." Choice (D) is not correct because the woman has already scheduled her flight.

Audio

2. Why does the woman have a problem?

Answer

(C) "Truthfully, I just made a mistake [scheduling the trip]." Choice (B) is true, but it is not the problem that is the concern of the conversation. Choice (D) is not correct because the woman has not yet taken the final exam. Choice (A) is not mentioned and may not be concluded from information in the conversation.

Audio

3. On what day is the exam scheduled?

Answer

(C) ". . . my flight leaves on Tuesday. That's the day before the exam." Choice (A) would be the day before the flight, not the day of the exam. Choice (B) refers to the day of the flight, not to the day of the exam. Choice (D) is not mentioned and may not be concluded from information in this conversation.

Audio

4. What does the professor decide to do?

Answer

(B) "You can take the exam on Monday." Choice (A) is not correct because the woman has not taken the exam yet. Choice (D) refers to the woman's suggestion, not to the professor's decision. Choice (C) is not mentioned and may not be concluded from information in the conversation.

Audio

5. When does this conversation most probably take place?

Answer

(D) Since the woman bought a ticket to go home for Christmas, and her flight leaves on Tuesday, it may be concluded that the conversation took place in December. Choices (A), (B), and (C) are not close enough to Christmas.

EXERCISE 18: Conversations—Professors/Students 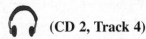 (CD 2, Track 4)

Conversation One

Audio

Narrator: Listen to part of a conversation between a student and a professor.

Jim: Dr. Stephens?

Stephens: Oh, hi Jim.

Jim: I'm a little early. About . . . ten minutes. Do you want me to come back later?

Stephens: No, no, not at all. Come on in.

Jim: Thanks.

Stephens: Have a seat. I want to talk with you a little bit . . . before you take the test. You realize that this won't be . . . it isn't the same test that everyone else took in class last Friday.

Jim: Yes, I know. I, uh, I noticed that policy on the syllabus.

Stephens: Good. I try to include everything on the syllabus, but . . . well . . . students don't always read a syllabus that carefully, so. . . . The test that I gave in class was mostly multiple-choice and true-false and, uh, with a few matching. In other words, it was an objective test.

Jim:	Okay.
Stephens:	The makeup is an essay test, with . . . uh . . . let's see, it has three questions on it. I occasionally give oral recitations instead of essays, but. . . .
Jim:	Oh, I'm glad it isn't an oral exam.
Stephens:	Good. In general, my makeup tests are . . . uh . . . let's say they're more difficult than the tests in class because . . . frankly, I want to discourage my students from using the makeup option.
Jim:	Okay . . . I understand, Dr. Stephens. I'm just glad to . . . to have an opportunity . . . to make it up. I was so sick last Friday, believe me, I couldn't have gotten a good grade on a test.
Stephens:	And . . . how are you now?
Jim:	A lot better, thanks. I went over to the health center instead of going to classes last Friday, and I got some medicine, uh, some antibiotics and some kind of decongestant. By Sunday, I was starting to . . . I was feeling better. You should have seen the waiting room over there. Anyway, I was lucky. My other classes meet on Tuesdays and Thursdays, and I have, uh, one independent study. . . . I didn't miss any other classes, I mean, just yours on Friday. . . . Too bad it was a test day, though.
Stephens:	Yes, well, when you finish this, you'll be all caught up.
Jim:	Mostly I still have a lot of reading to do in my other classes. That medicine just knocked me out, you know, so I slept a lot. Um, am I the only one taking a makeup?
Stephens:	You are. So, if you want to get started, you can just leave your books here. All you need to take with you is your pencil, and . . . just a second . . . I'll get your test. . . . Here you go.
Jim:	Thanks.
Stephens:	Why don't you take a look at it and, uh, I can answer any questions you have before you get started.
Jim:	Okay . . . okay . . . okay. Hmmn. It's pretty straightforward, Dr. Stephens. The only thing I can think of to ask is . . . how long you want . . . uh . . . how long the essays should be . . . for each question, I mean.
Stephens:	Well, the answer should be as long as it takes to respond to the question . . . but that doesn't help you much, does it? . . . I'd say you'd need, uh, two, or maybe three paragraphs, to develop each of the questions fully.
Jim:	Okay.
Stephens:	Anything else?
Jim:	Not that I can think of.
Stephens:	Okay, then. I'm going to . . . you can just leave your jacket and your backpack here. There's a conference room two doors down. And, uh, it should be quiet there. I'll show you where it is, and then when you finish, you can just bring your test back to me.
Jim:	You'll be . . . ?
Stephens:	I'll be in my office.
Jim:	Oh, Dr. Stephens. Sorry . . . I just thought of another question. How long do I have to finish?
Stephens:	Of course. I'm glad you asked. Fifty minutes, which is just about the same amount of time you would have had in class. But, knowing you, I think you'll probably finish long before that. Do you have a watch on?
Jim:	Yes.
Stephens:	Good. I don't think there's a clock in the conference room. In any case, if you haven't turned in the test by 1:45, I'll . . . I'll come to the room to collect it, okay?
Jim:	Okay. Well, thanks again . . . I appreciate this.
Stephens:	You're welcome, Jim. Good luck.

Audio

1. What is the main topic of this conversation?

Answer

(B) Because the purpose of the man's appointment is to take a makeup test, it is the main topic of conversation. Choices (A), (C), and (D) are mentioned in reference to the main topic, "the makeup test."

Audio

2. Why did the man need to take the test?

Answer

(A) ". . . I didn't miss any other classes, I mean, just yours on Friday . . . a test day . . . ." Choice (B) is not correct because he missed class in the past, not that he will miss class. Choice (C) is true, but he is not taking the test for the independent-study course. Choice (D) is not mentioned and may not be concluded from information in this conversation.

Audio

3. What kind of test will the man take?

Answer

(C) "The makeup is an essay test." Choices (A) and (B) refer to the test that the professor gave in class, not to the makeup test. Choice (D) refers to an option that the professor occasionally uses but not to this makeup test.

Audio

4. How long does he have to complete the test?

Answer

(C) "Fifty minutes, which is just about the same amount of time you would have had in class." Choice (A) refers to the amount of time early that Jim arrived. Choices (B) and (D) refer to the clock time, 1:45, when the test must be turned in.

Audio

5. Listen again to part of the conversation.

   Then answer the question.

   "Fifty minutes, which is just about the same amount of time you would have had in class. But, knowing you, I think you'll probably finish long before that."

   Why does the professor say this:

   "But, knowing you, I think you'll probably finish long before that."

Answer

(B) The professor expresses a positive opinion based on her knowledge of the student's abilities. The tone is encouraging, and should increase the student's self-confidence. Choices (A), (B), and (D) are not correct because the professor has already told him that he has fifty minutes to finish the test.

Audio

6. What can we assume about the man?

Answer

(C) "I noticed that policy on the syllabus." Choice (A) is not correct because Jim has read the syllabus and has arranged for a makeup test. Choice (B) is not correct because Jim is a lot better. Choice (D) is not mentioned and may not be concluded from information in this conversation.

Conversation Two

Audio

Narrator: Listen to part of a conversation between a student and a professor.

Marge: Dr. Jones?

Jones: Hi, Marge.

Marge: Hi . . . I was wondering whether I should . . . whether to make an appointment with you or, uh, whether I should come back while the secretary's here.

Jones: Do you have time to talk now? My two o'clock canceled, so . . . I'm free.

Marge: That'd be great.

Jones: What do you have on your mind?

Marge:	Well . . . I need your advice. Um . . . I like your class. I mean, it's my favorite one.
Jones:	I'm glad. Are you a biology major?
Marge:	Uh . . . premed, but biology is my emphasis.
Jones:	Good. And, I'm looking at my grade book, and, uh, you have a B+ in the class. . . . You could probably pull that up to an A before the end of the semester.
Marge:	I know I could [deep breath] if I had the time to study. But the problem is . . . well you see . . . I took six classes this semester . . . and that's okay. I can handle that. I've taken six classes before and I've done all right, but . . . but two of my classes are lab classes . . . so I have the labs and the lab assignments on top of the classes, and I'm . . . I'm really in over my head.
Jones:	I see. Labs do take a lot of time.
Marge:	They do, if you do them right. So . . . so, I thought, uh, if you'd sign, I mean, if you'd give me permission to drop your biology class, then I'd take it over again next semester.
Jones:	Well, it's very late in the semester to drop a course. You have only two weeks left before the final.
Marge:	I know. I can't do it without the professor's, I . . . I mean, without your signature. But I . . . I just don't see any other way.
Jones:	Marge, I'm sure you've thought this through, so . . . can you tell me why you decided to drop the biology class? You said it was your favorite class, and you're doing well in it . . . so, uh, I'm a little surprised that you didn't decide to, perhaps, drop another class instead.
Marge:	Oh, no. You see, I'll have to take the course that I drop over again . . . from the beginning I mean, next semester . . . and I really like biology . . . and I really like the way you teach it, so I thought . . . I wouldn't mind repeating it as much as, well, some of my other classes.
Jones:	I see . . . Well, have you considered taking an incomplete?
Marge:	Not really. I've never done that. I'm not even, uh, not sure what it means.
Jones:	Marge, what you would do is continue attending class, but . . . you wouldn't have to turn in your lab reports and take your final until next semester.
Marge:	Is . . . is that possible?
Jones:	Not always . . . but in this case, I'm willing to do it . . . with one condition.
Marge:	What's that?
Jones:	I want you to write a memo to your advisor explaining that the eighteen-hour schedule was too much . . . and, uh, that you have indicated to me that . . . that . . . you don't plan to take so many hours again. And, I'd like to have a copy of the memo for my file.
Marge:	Oh, Dr. Jones, I'd be glad to do that. I've really learned my limits this semester . . . I mean, I know . . . and, and . . . I don't ever plan to get myself in this mess again.
Jones:	Good. Then, I'll fill out the paperwork when I turn in my grades, and you'll see an *I* on your grade report. . . . And Marge, I should tell you that if you don't complete the requirements for the course by the end of next semester, then . . . you'll receive an F for the class.
Marge:	That won't happen. I'll finish my lab reports and study for the final over the break, and . . . if it's okay with you, I'll, uh, I'll just take the exam as soon as we get back . . . in January, I mean.
Jones:	That's a good plan.

Audio

1. What is the purpose of this conversation?

Answer

(C) Because the woman asks permission to drop a course in order to decrease her course load, it may be concluded that the purpose of the conversation is to talk about her workload. Choices (A), (B), and (D) are mentioned in reference to the main topic, "the workload."

Audio

2. What does Marge mean when she says she is "over her head"?

Answer

(B) "Labs do take a lot of time." The idiom *over one's head* means to be "overwhelmed." Choice (A) is not correct because the woman has a B+ and could have an A before the end of the semester. Choice (C) is not correct because it is her favorite class. Choice (D) is true because she has a premed major with a biology emphasis, but it is not the meaning of the phrase *over one's head*.

Audio

3. Why does Marge want to drop the biology class?

Answer

(C) "I thought I wouldn't mind repeating it [the biology class] . . . ." Choice (A) is not correct because she says biology is her favorite class. Choice (B) is not correct because she has a B+ in the grade book. Choice (D) is not correct because she likes the way the professor teaches the course.

Audio

4. Why does Marge need the professor's signature?

Answer

(B) "I can't do it [drop the class] without the professor's, I mean without your signature." Choice (A) is not correct because she has the professor's permission to take the exam at the beginning of next term, but she does not need the professor's signature. Choice (C) is not correct because she has not asked for excused absences. Choice (D) is not correct because she has a grade of B in the class.

Audio

5. Listen again to part of the conversation.
   Then answer the question.
   "I see. . . . Well, have you considered taking an incomplete?"
   Why does the professor say this:
   "Well, have you considered taking an incomplete?"

Answer

(C) Speakers often ask whether the listener has considered something as a way to make a suggestion without being too direct. Choice (A) is not correct because the consideration of an option would not provide information about the student's academic record. Choice (B) is not correct because the student has already told him that she cannot complete the work for the class. Choice (D) is not correct because the student has already explained the problem.

Audio

6. Why does Dr. Jones want Marge to write a memo to her advisor?

Answer

(A) Because the memo states that she will not "plan to take so many hours again," it may be concluded that the purpose of the memo is to prevent her advisor from allowing her to register for so many hours. Choice (B) refers to the grade that she will receive if she does not complete the course, not to the grade that she already has. Choice (D) is not mentioned and may not be concluded from information in this conversation.

EXERCISE 19: Consultations—Professors/Students 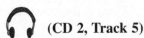 (CD 2, Track 5)

Consultation One

Audio

Narrator: Listen to part of a consultation in a professor's office.

Smith: You wanted to talk about the results of your laboratory experiment. Did you have any problems with it?

Bob: Yes, Professor Smith. We did.

Smith: And you two are lab partners?
Bob: Yes, we are.
Smith: Well, then, can you go over the procedure for me?
Anne: Sure. First we put ten grams of crushed limestone in a bottle.
Smith: Anything special about the bottle?
Bob: It was a gas-collecting bottle with a one-hole stopper and bent glass tubing.
Smith: Very good. So you put the limestone in a gas-collecting bottle. Then what?
Anne: Then we poured in ten milligrams of hydrochloric acid, put on the stopper, and collected a bottle of carbon dioxide.
Smith: Right. What was the method of collection?
Anne: Water displacement.
Smith: Good.
Anne: Then, we lit a magnesium ribbon and put it in the bottle of carbon dioxide.
Bob: And carbon deposits began to form on the bottom of the bottle. You see, we didn't have any problem with procedure . . .
Anne: Well, we had a little problem getting the magnesium ribbon to stay lit until we could get it into the bottle.
Bob: Okay. But we did it. The big problem was that we really didn't understand what happened. Did the magnesium combine with the oxygen in the carbon dioxide?
Smith: You have just answered your own question, Bob. The burning magnesium broke the carbon-oxygen bonds in the carbon dioxide, and then the oxygen combined with the magnesium to produce magnesium oxide.
Anne: And the carbon was freed to deposit itself on the bottle.
Smith: Exactly.

Audio

1. What is the purpose of this consultation?

Answer

(A) "Let's talk about the results of your laboratory experiment." Choices (B) and (C) are mentioned as secondary themes that are used to develop the main theme of the discussion, "the results of the lab experiment." Choice (D) is not correct because the students had already done the lab experiment.

Audio

2. What was deposited on the bottom of the gas bottle?

Answer

(C) "And carbon deposits began to form on the bottom of the bottle." Choice (A) refers to the ribbon that was lit, not to the deposits. Choice (B) refers to the material that was put in the bottle at the beginning of the experiment, not to what was deposited at the end. Choice (D) refers to the method of collection, water displacement.

Audio

3. What caused the deposits?

Answer

(C) "The burning magnesium broke the carbon-oxygen bonds in the carbon dioxide, and then the oxygen combined with the magnesium to produce magnesium oxide." Choices (A), (B), and (D) are not correct because burning magnesium broke the carbon-oxygen bonds.

Audio

4. Where does this consultation take place?

Answer

(D) "Listen to part of a consultation in a professor's office." The *lab* in Choice (A) refers to the place where the experiment took place, not to where the conversation is taking place. Choices (B) and (C) are not mentioned and may not be concluded from information in this consultation.

Audio

5. What can we infer from this consultation?

Answer

(B) Since the students are able to explain the procedures for the experiment, it may be concluded that they performed the experiment correctly. Choice (C) is not correct because in spite of a little problem, the students completed the experiment. Choice (D) refers to the fact that there is burning magnesium, not a fire in the lab. Choice (A) is not mentioned and may not be concluded from information in the discussion.

Consultation Two

Audio

Narrator: Listen to part of a consultation with a professor.

Tom: Dr. Anderson, could you please clarify the requirements for this course? Some of us are a little bit confused about the final examination.

Anderson: Oh? Well, you have two options in this course. You can either take a final examination or you can write a research paper instead.

Tom: Excuse me, Dr. Anderson. That's the point I need you to clarify. What kind of research paper did you have in mind? An original study? A report? A book review, perhaps?

Anderson: A report. A summary really, based upon a reading list of current research in the field.

Jane: How long should the reports be?

Anderson: Length is really not important. I should think that it would take at least ten pages in order to develop the topic, however.

Jane: And should we check the topic with you before we begin writing?

Anderson: You may, if you wish. But the only requirement is that it relate to current trends in United States foreign policy. Are you considering writing a paper, Jane?

Jane: I'm not sure. I think that I'd like to know a little bit more about the examination.

Anderson: All right. One hundred multiple-choice questions covering both the lectures and the outside readings.

Tom: Didn't you say that you would give us one hour for the examination?

Anderson: Yes, I did.

Tom: I'm going to do the paper, then.

Jane: Me too.

Audio

1. What prompted the consultation?

Answer

(A) "Dr. Anderson, could you please clarify the requirements for this course?" Choice (B) refers to Jane and Tom, not to all the students. Choice (C) is not correct because the professor is clarifying the requirements he has previously explained. Choice (D) is not mentioned and may not be concluded from information in the talk.

Audio

2. What kind of research paper has Dr. Anderson assigned?

Answer

(A) "What kind of research paper did you have in mind? An original study? A report? A book review, perhaps?" "A report." Choices (B) and (C) refer to options that the student, not the professor, mentions. Choice (D) is not mentioned and may not be concluded from information in the discussion.

Audio

3. What kind of examination has Dr. Anderson prepared?

Answer

(B) "One hundred multiple-choice questions covering both the lectures and the outside readings." From the reference to *multiple-choice* questions, it must be concluded that it is an objective test. Choices (A), (C), and (D) are not mentioned and may not be concluded from information in the discussion.

Audio

4. Which option do the students choose?

Answer

(B) When the man says, "I'm going to do the paper, then," the woman agrees. The *lectures* in Choice (A) refer to one source of the questions on the examination, not to the option that the students choose. Choice (C) refers to the *reading list* that will be required for the paper, not to a separate option. Choice (D) refers to the option that the students decide not to choose.

Audio

5. Based upon the consultation, which course does Dr. Anderson most probably teach?

Answer

(C) From the reference to current trends in *U.S. foreign policy*, it must be concluded that Dr. Anderson teaches political science. Choices (A), (B), and (D) are not mentioned and may not be concluded from information in the discussion.

EXERCISE 20: Consultations—Professors/Students

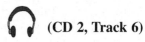 (CD 2, Track 6)

Consultation One

Audio

Narrator: Listen to part of a consultation between a student and a professor.

Larry: Hi, Professor Davidson.

Professor: Oh, hello, Larry.

Larry: Um . . . I know it's not your office hour right now, but I saw you, and I . . . I wondered if . . .

Professor: Sure, come in. What can I do for you?

Larry: I just want to check something out with you, uh, from the lecture on Wednesday. I want to get it straightened out before . . . before class tomorrow, because . . . uh, because . . .

Professor: . . . because it might be on the quiz.

Larry: Well, yes.

Professor: Okay. Fire away.

Larry: It's about hot spots. Under the ocean. I've got two questions. First, you said that hot spots appear to be fixed in place for . . . let's see . . . tens or even hundreds of millions of years . . . and, uh, they're stable even when the litho . . . litho . . . spheric plates move over them. And then you said that volcanic activity is stronger at hot spots.

Professor: Right so far.

Larry: Then, I have in my notes here . . . that in Hawaii . . . I think it was Hawaii because I have Iceland scratched out and Hawaii written in . . . so I think it was in Hawaii . . . where the hot spots have, uh, have active volcanoes under the ocean . . . and, uh, the volcanoes continue to erupt and . . . and . . . that builds the island.

Professor: Right again.

Larry: Now here's the part that gets confusing. I wrote this down, "The quantity of lava produced by hot-spot volcanoes is so large that such volcanoes are the tallest topographic features on Earth's surface."

Professor: Larry, that's exactly what I said in my lecture.

Larry: But then . . . this is what I can't figure out . . . I wrote that the, uh, mountains in Hawaii are only about 4,500 meters above sea level.

Professor: Oh, now I see your problem. The island actually rises 5,500 meters . . . that is . . . 5,500 meters from the sea floor to the surface of the ocean.

Larry: From the surface of the ocean. So, then . . . okay . . . I need to add 5,500 meters to the 4,500 to calculate the actual elevation from the surface of the planet . . . which is actually the ocean floor.

Professor: Exactly.

Larry: Well, that takes care of one of my questions.

Professor: Okay. What else do you have?

Larry: It's about hot spots again . . . the ones remaining in place as the uh . . . the uh . . . plate moves over them. What did you say about chains of islands? Like, well, like Hawaii, to use that example again.

Professor: Okay. Visualize a hot spot on the ocean floor. It doesn't move. But the plate moves over it, and the plate carries one of the Hawaiian Islands that the hot spot has created . . . away from the hot spot that formed it.

Larry: But uh . . . the hot spot is still active, so . . . so it's still building an undersea formation . . . that, I mean, the undersea formation . . . will, uh, become another island close to the first island. Okay. And then . . . the plate moves the second island away from the hot spot, so . . . so a chain of islands . . . that's how a chain is formed . . . from the same hot spot.

Professor: From the hot spot and the movement of the lithospheric plates.

Larry: The litho . . . litho . . .

Professor: The lithospheric plates . . . *Lithospheric* just means Earth's crust and the upper part of the mantle.

Larry: So this process is going on all the time.

Professor: It is. In fact, if volcanic activity continues at its present rate, another island may be appearing at the end of the Hawaiian chain.

Larry: Really?

Professor: We've given it a name already—Loihi. Of course, we won't actually see it above the surface of the ocean for another ten to forty thousand years, and you and I won't see it at all . . . but uh . . . we are observing it closely as it continues to build under water.

Larry: That is so cool.

Professor: It is, isn't it? And to get back to your original question, when Loihi is only a few feet above the water, it will already be a very significant topographical feature.

Larry: Because . . . because of the height it has reached . . . before breaking the surface.

Professor: Well said. You should do just fine on that quiz.

Audio

1. What is the purpose of the consultation?

Answer

(A) "I want to get it straightened out . . . because it might be on the quiz." Choice (B) is true, but the reason he wants to know is because it will probably be a quiz question. The *quiz* in Choice (C) refers to the next quiz, not to the last quiz. Choice (D) is not correct because Larry refers to the lecture on Wednesday.

Audio

2. What is the main topic of this consultation?

Answer

(D) "It's about hot spots." Choices (A), (B), and (C) are all mentioned in reference to the main topic, "hot spots."

Audio

3. What is the altitude of Hawaii?

(D) "So . . . I need to add 5,500 meters to the 4,500 to calculate the actual elevation from the surface of the planet . . . which is actually the ocean floor." Choice (A) sounds like 4,500 meters [forty-five hundred], which is the elevation above sea level, not the total altitude. Choice (B) is the elevation above sea level but does not include the elevation below the surface of the ocean. Choice (C) is the elevation below the surface of the ocean but does not include the elevation above sea level.

Audio

4. What does the professor say about the newest Hawaiian island?

Answer

(D) ". . . when Loihi is only a few feet above water, it will already be a very significant topographical feature." Choice (A) is not correct because the island is named Loihi. Choice (B) is not correct because it will appear in ten to forty thousand years. Choice (C) is not correct because it will not appear for ten to forty thousand years.

Audio

5. Listen again to part of the conversation.

   Then answer the question.

   "Of course, we won't actually see it above the surface of the ocean for another ten to forty thousand years . . . and you and I won't see it at all . . . but uh . . . we are observing it closely as it continues to build under water."

   Why does the professor say this:

   ". . . and you and I won't see it at all. . . ."

Answer

(C) Because the island will not appear for thousands of years, the professor makes a joke of the fact that they cannot expect to live long enough to see it. Choice (B) is not correct because the island is not visible yet and not well-known, and therefore, it is not a concrete example. Choice (D) is not correct because the student is asking questions, not presenting an argument. Choice (A) is not correct because it is not mentioned and may not be concluded from information in the consultation.

Audio

6. Put the following events in order to explain how island chains are formed.

Answer

(B) (A) (C) (D) ". . . the plate moves over it [the first island], and the plate carries one of the Hawaiian islands . . . away from the hot spot that formed it. . . . But . . . the hot spot is still active, . . . so it is still building . . . another island close to the first island."

Consultation Two

Audio

Narrator: Listen to part of a consultation between a student and a professor.

Ronda: Hi, Dr. Gilbert. Are you busy?

Gilbert: Just getting organized for my class.

Ronda: Oh. . . . Do you want me to come back later?

Gilbert: No, no. Come in. This is an open office hour. I was just working on some notes until someone showed up, so . . .

Ronda: Thanks. I wanted to talk about . . . about my term paper. I have a topic . . . but I'm not sure where to begin. I'm finding so many references, I, well, I couldn't possibly read them all.

Gilbert: Okay. What's the topic?

Ronda: The Baroque style.

Gilbert: The Baroque style?

Ronda: Yes, I really like the . . . the . . .

Gilbert: Opulence is the word usually associated with Baroque.

Ronda: I was thinking of "over the top," but opulence is even better. I'm attracted to it.

Gilbert: Well, that's good. You want to choose a topic you're interested in, or, uh, attracted to. But let's talk about the problem you're having. Ronda, it's no wonder that you are finding so much material. That topic is extremely broad. To really do it justice, you'd have to write a dissertation. Remember, your paper is supposed to be only ten to twelve pages long.

Ronda: Well, I haven't started writing yet. Do you think maybe I should choose another topic?

Gilbert: Another topic? No, I didn't say that. I said the topic was too broad. What you need to do is, uh, narrow it down. Look at, uh, one aspect of the Baroque style, perhaps architecture or painting or sculpture, or you could do some research on one artist and, uh, demonstrate . . . discuss how the Baroque style is . . . is reflected in the work. You could probably even narrow it down to one work by one artist and still have more than enough material for such a short paper.

Ronda: Oh, okay. Actually, that sounds really good. A lot more manageable. Thanks, Dr. Gilbert.

Gilbert: Wait a minute, Ronda. Let's talk a little more about the research you've been doing, and, uh, maybe we can find a topic.

Ronda: Really? That would be perfect. I have my research on my laptop, but . . .

Gilbert: Just talk to me about it.

Ronda: Okay. I started out with some general sources, and I . . . I found a lot on, uh, Bernini.

Gilbert: Umhum. That makes sense. Bernini was certainly at the center of the Baroque movement. But even that topic would be very broad since he was such a Renaissance man—hard to imagine someone who could be a sculptor, a painter, and an architect. I think he even wrote plays and composed music. So what else did you find?

Ronda: Well, I had a lot on Versailles. And, you know, the Hall of Mirrors. And the Spanish painters of the period.

Gilbert: Diego Velazquez.

Ronda: Unhuh . . . and, oh, did I mention Saint Peter's Cathedral in Rome?

Gilbert: So you have Italy, France, and Spain in your research.

Ronda: More than that. I've got some information on the Dutch Baroque, too . . . although I think it seems different from the rest somehow. Wasn't Rembrandt Dutch?

Gilbert: Right you are.

Ronda: So . . .

Gilbert: Hold on a minute, Ronda. Of everything you've read, what's the one person or building, or work of art, or fact that you found the most interesting?

Ronda: Let me see, well, probably . . . the architecture.

Gilbert: And which structure stands out in your mind?

Ronda: Oh, that's easy. Versailles. The inside though, not the outside, which to me has at least some classical influence. Don't you think so? It isn't as typical of Baroque as the magnificent rooms inside the palace.

Gilbert: I would agree with that.

Ronda: I . . . I actually saw Versailles when my family was living in Europe five years ago. My Dad was transferred to London, and . . . it was so great . . . we traveled a lot while we were there. The trains go everywhere, but you probably know that. I didn't get to Italy and Spain, though. I'd like to some day.

Gilbert: Well, let's see what we've accomplished. You started out with Baroque, which was very broad, then you said that you were interested in architecture . . . which limited the topic somewhat . . . and, uh, let's see . . . then you found one building.

Ronda: Versailles.

Gilbert: And, as I understood you, you eliminated the outside . . . the outside of Versailles . . . so your topic is much more narrow now . . . if you choose to write about the interior of Versailles. Frankly, that's still a major topic.

Ronda: Is it? So, do you think I should narrow it even more?

Gilbert: I do. Remember a ten-page paper is only a few thousand words. And, uh, I should think, uh, fifteen to twenty sources should be more than enough.

Ronda: Well then . . . how do I put this? Do you think I could . . . I could find enough to write about, I mean, if I just focused on the Hall of Mirrors? I think I have more than twenty sources about that in my list already.

Gilbert: I'm sure you could. In fact, you should probably think about an even more specific aspect of the Hall . . . something that would interest you. There has been a tremendous amount of research on it. Look, why don't you go back to your research files, and, uh, try to come up with a title? We can talk about it more after you do . . . after you have a title . . . and then, uh, I'll try to direct you to some specific resources if you don't have enough material already. How's that?

Ronda: That would be perfect. Maybe I can have it figured out . . . I mean, I'll try to have it by class tomorrow.

Audio

1. What is Ronda's problem?

Answer

(B) "That topic is extremely broad." Choice (A) is not correct because Ronda's topic is *the Baroque style*. Choice (D) is not correct because she is finding so many references that she can't read them all. Choice (C) is not mentioned and may not be concluded from information in this consultation.

Audio

2. How long should the paper be?

Answer

(B) "Remember, your paper is supposed to be only ten to twelve pages." The number in Choice (A) refers to how many years ago Ronda and her family lived in Europe. Choices (C) and (D) are not mentioned and may not be concluded from information in this consultation.

Audio

3. What does Dr. Gilbert suggest?

Answer

(C) ". . . try to come up with a title. We can talk about it more after you do. . . ." Choice (A) is not correct because the professor tells Ronda that he didn't say she should find another topic. Choice (B) refers to the offer to direct Ronda to specific *resources*, but he has not given her resources in the past. Choice (D) is not mentioned and may not be concluded from information in this consultation.

Audio

4. Where did Ronda's family live five years ago?

Answer

(D) "My Dad was transferred to London. . . ." Choices (A) and (B) refer to places she would like to visit some day, not to where she has lived. Choice (C) refers to a place she visited, not to where she has lived.

Audio

5. Listen again to part of the conversation.
    Then answer the question.
    "Hi, Dr. Gilbert. Are you busy?" "Just getting organized for my class."
    Why does the student ask this:
    "Are you busy?"

Answer

(C) Speakers who are interrupting someone in an office setting often ask the question, *Are you busy?* to give the other person the opportunity to postpone the conversation. Choice (A) is not correct because she asks a general question, but she does not ask for specific details. Choice (B) is not correct because she asks the question before she begins to chat. Choice (D) is not mentioned and may not be concluded from information in the conversation.

Audio

6. What will Ronda most probably do?

Answer

(A) ". . . do you think I could . . . find enough to write about I mean, if I just focused on the Hall of Mirrors?" "I'm sure you could." Choice (B) is not correct because she already has more than twenty sources. Choice (C) is not correct because the Hall of Mirrors is a topic in the Baroque period. Choice (D) is not correct because she has not started writing a draft yet.

EXERCISE 21: Group Discussions—Students 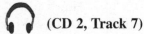 (CD 2, Track 7)

Discussion One

Audio

Narrator: Listen to part of a discussion among students in a study group.

Man: So . . . what do you think will be on the test?

Woman: I'll bet the first question will be: "Define the term *organization*." And Dr. Graham will want it . . . word for word. So, here it is, straight from the book, "An *organization* represents a specific type of social relationship or arrangement between persons, with either closed or limited admission, and regulations enforced by a person or group in a position of authority."

Man 2: You got that right. He's gone over that definition at the beginning of almost every class since the last test. And then, uh, let me see here, then . . . we'll probably have to compare *formal* and *informal* organizations. . . . So . . . this is the answer, guys, "A *formal organization* is characterized by formality . . . no surprise there . . . a hierarchy of ranked positions, and a complex division of labor, as well as a relatively large size." Okay. Now, want me to do *informal organizations*?

Woman: I'll do it. "An *informal organization* brings people together to explore a common interest."

Man: Okay. . . . Don't forget about *bureaucracies*.

Woman: Yeah, yeah. Besides the definition, what?

Man 2: I've got a lot on Weber's ideal type of bureaucracy.

Woman: You do? Hmmn. I don't remember anything about that.

Man 2: Here, let me read you some of my notes. It's called Weber's *ideal bureaucracy*. Maybe you'll remember something. I have a list of the characteristics: 1. Paid officials; 2. Benefits for career officials; 3. Salary increases, seniority rights and, uh, promotions by examination; 4. Hierarchical organization.

Woman: Oh, okay . . . sure. I have that. I just didn't have it . . . uh . . . identified . . . you know, as Weber's ideal bureaucracy.

Man 2: You've got them all then? All the characteristics?

Woman: Yeah. Yeah, I got them.

Man: Okay. We should probably be ready for the, uh, Bensman and . . . and . . . Rosenberg . . . the Bensman and Rosenberg study.

Woman: That's the one about advancement, right?

Man: Right. I have it, uh, summarized like . . . like this, "It's not *what* you know but *who* you know."

Woman: And how well you're liked by the right people.

Man: Bingo!

Man 2: Moving right along. Parkinson's Law has to be there. Here's what I have on that one, "In any bureaucratic organization, work expands to fill the time available for its completion."

Man: I always get that mixed up with the, uh, what's the other one? . . . you know, the Peter principle.

Woman:	No, listen . . . the Peter principle is "in any hierarchy, every employee tends to rise to his level of incompetence."
Man:	Okay . . . okay . . . so what does that mean, really?
Woman:	Look, let's say you're a great professor, and you get a promotion to, maybe, department chair . . . which is an administrative position, but you, uh, can't use your teaching skills in the administrative position, so you aren't as successful. You see, you got hired on the basis of skills that . . . skills that don't translate, I mean transfer to the next job.
Man:	So you don't get promoted again because you aren't doing such a great job, you know, as an administrator?
Woman:	Right. You've reached your . . . just a minute . . . I've got it right here . . . you've reached your level of incompetence.
Man 2:	Listen, the way that I keep them straight is to think Parkinson's law is about the work, and the Peter principle is about the people.
Man:	Hey, thanks. That's a good idea.
Woman:	Yeah. Do you think he'll include anything on leadership?
Man 2:	Maybe. If he does, he'll probably ask us about the . . . the, uh, two different types of leaders.
Woman:	Okay. Let me see if I can remember that. The *instrumental leader* is goal oriented and, uh, organizes the group by . . . by assigning, uh, tasks, and . . . and . . . the *expressive leader* is uh, more socially inclined . . . someone who works toward . . . oh wait, let me think. . . . The expressive leader works toward solidarity among group members by . . . by offering support.
Man 2:	I'm impressed. That's almost word for word from the lecture.
Woman:	Remember, Dr. Graham doesn't reward creativity. He's looking for the stuff he taught, uh, just like he taught it. Haven't you noticed how he grades the quizzes?
Man 2:	I know, I know. Just kidding.
Woman:	Okay. So, the short-answer questions will be "explain the Peter principle, state Parkinson's law, summarize the Bestman . . . I mean Bensman and Rosenberg study . . . Bensman and Rosenberg . . . and contrast formal and informal organizations." Anything else?
Man 2:	Compare the two types of leaders.
Woman:	Right. That leaves the . . . the . . . what's-his-name ideal bureaucracy for the essay.
Man:	Weber's ideal bureaucracy.
Woman:	Weber . . . Weber.
Man:	That should about do it, then. . . . I think we covered the most important points in the chapter, and the notes.
Man 2:	Now, all we have to do is review a little and, uh, we should be ready for it.

Audio

1. What is the main purpose of this study group?

Answer

(A) "So . . . what do you think will be on the test?" The *quiz* in choice (C) refers to a quiz that the professor has already graded, not to the purpose of this study group. The lecture *notes* in Choice (D) refer to the source of the important points that the group is discussing, not to the purpose of their study group. Choice (B) is not mentioned and may not be concluded from information in this discussion.

Audio

2. Who has identified an *ideal bureaucracy*?

Answer

(B) I've got a lot on *Weber's ideal type of bureaucracy*. Choices (A) and (D) refer to the Bensman and Rosenberg study about advancement, not to ideal bureaucracies. Choice (C) refers to the professor's name, not to the researcher who has identified an ideal bureaucracy.

Audio

3. Which law states that people advance until they reach a position in which they are less likely to succeed?

Answer

(D) "The Peter principle is 'in any hierarchy, every employee tends to rise to his level of incompetence.'" Choice (A) refers to the ideal type of bureaucracy. Choice (B) refers to the fact that work expands to fill the time available for its completion. Choice (C) refers to the Bensman and Rosenberg study about advancement.

Audio

4. Which topic will probably appear as an essay question?

Answer

(D) "That leaves the . . . ideal bureaucracy for the essay." Choices (B) and (C) refer to the short-answer questions, not to the essay. Choice (A) is not mentioned and may not be concluded from information in this discussion.

Audio

5. Listen again to part of the conversation.
   Then answer the question.
   "You got that right. He's gone over that definition at the beginning of almost every class since the last test."
   Why does the man say this:
   "He's gone over that definition at the beginning of almost every class since the last test."

Answer

(D) Because the man remembers that the professor has made repeated references to the definition, it may be concluded that he agrees with the woman's statement that the question will be on the next test. Choice (A) is not correct because the man is referring to the probability that the question will be on the test, not to the woman's answer to the question. Choice (B) is not correct because the man says, "You got that right," indicating that he has heard and agrees with the answer. Choice (C) is not correct because the man acknowledges that the woman knows the answer.

Audio

6. What can we assume about Dr. Graham?

Answer

(C) Because all the questions that the study group is reviewing are related to business, it may be concluded that Dr. Graham teaches business. Choice (A) is not correct because the study group is preparing for short-answer and essay questions. Choice (D) is not correct because the students agree that Dr. Graham does not reward creativity. Choice (B) is not mentioned and may not be concluded from information in the discussion.

Discussion Two

Audio

Narrator: Listen to part of a discussion among students who are working on a group project.

Joan: Okay, let's get going now that we're all here.

Carl: Okay.

Martha: Fine.

Joan: Just to remind everyone, we agreed to do our group presentation on the SQ3R study reading method, and since there are four of us in the group, all of you are going to take two of the steps in the method, and I'm . . . I'm going to say a few words to introduce the presentation . . . and then I'll summarize at the end, and . . . and, uh, finally, we can go over the handout.

Carl: Sounds good. Except I had only one step.

Joan: Right, Carl. Phil and Martha have two, though. And, uh, I mean, we said we'd all be ready to go through everything this time.

Martha: I think we all brought our scripts, Joan.

Joan: Okay. I'll start. This is it, "Today our group will show you how to use the study reading method known as SQ3R. The letters stand for, uh, five steps . . . in the reading process: *Survey*, *Question*, *Read*, *Review*, and *Recite*." Then I'll say, "Each of the steps should be done carefully and in the order that I mentioned."

Phil: . . . Is that it?

Joan: Yes. We only have ten minutes, Phil, and we want to spend I'd say . . . at least six or seven minutes going over the handout . . . so we have less than a minute for each step.

Phil: Okay. Well, after the introduction, it's my turn. And, uh, I'll say, "In all study reading, a *survey* should be the first step. *Survey* means 'to look quickly.' In study reading, you need to look quickly at titles, words in darker or larger print or italics, words with capital letters, illustrations, and charts. At this point, you don't stop to write . . . sorry . . . I mean, read complete sentences. Just look at the important divisions of the material. . . ."

Martha: Okay. I'm up next. "The second step is *question*. Try to form questions based on your survey. Use the question words *who*, *what*, *when*, *where*, *why*, and *how*."

Carl: . . . My turn? Let's see. "Now you're ready for the third step: *Read* . . . You'll be rereading the titles and important words that you looked at in the survey. But this time you'll read the examples and details as well. Sometimes it's useful to take notes while you read. Some readers prefer to underline important points, and it seems to be just as useful as note taking. What you should do, whether you take notes or underline, is to read actively. Think about what you're reading as a series of ideas, not just a sequence of words." . . . Go ahead, Phil.

Phil: Okay, uh, thanks. "The fourth step is *review*. Remember the questions that you wrote down before you read the material? You should be able to answer them now. You'll notice that some of the questions were treated in more detail in the reading. Concentrate on those. Also . . . also. . . ." Wait a minute. . . . I changed this part. "Also, review material that you didn't consider in your questions." . . . Martha?

Martha: Oh, uh sorry. "The last step is *recite*. Try to put the reading into your own words. Summarize it either in writing or orally."

Joan: . . . Done?

Martha: Yeah. That's it.

Joan: Okay. Now I'm going to just uh . . . summarize in one sentence. I'll say: "SQ3R—*survey*, *question*, *read*, *review*, and *recite*. Let me repeat that—SQ3R—*survey*, *question*, *read*, *review*, and *recite*." Then I'll say, "But to really understand the method, let's take a look at a reading passage, and try to use SQ3R." Then I'm going to um . . . pass out a passage from . . . from our textbook. I thought I'd use something in the next chapter because, uh, so most people probably wouldn't have read it yet.

Carl: That's a great idea.

Martha: Yeah. What's the next chapter on?

Joan: It's about motivation. There's a really good passage about intrinsic and extrinsic motivation.

Martha: What's that?

Joan: *Intrinsic motivation* is when you want to do something for your own reasons, and . . . but . . . *extrinsic motivation* is when you . . . have external rewards like, uh, money or something. That's really a simplistic explanation, but anyway, the passage isn't too long . . . and it has, uh . . . the headings are good, and a few words in bold type, and, uh . . . capital letters, so I think it should be perfect for the survey part.

Phil: Look. Here it is in the book . . . on page 351. . . . This does look good for our purposes.

Carl: So what are you thinking? Maybe just like have everyone look in their books?

Martha: I think we should copy the pages onto a handout. Everybody doesn't bring a book to class. I know, I don't. I just show up with my notebook.

Carl:	True.
Joan:	Well, it's easy enough to copy it. I'll do that.
Phil:	I know it'll be a little more work, but it would probably be good to, uh, summarize the SQ3R words . . . maybe at the top of the page.
Martha:	And it would be nice to have all of our names on it.
Joan:	Sure. No problem.

Audio

1. What is the purpose of this study group?

Answer

(B) ". . . We said we'd all be ready to go through [rehearse] everything this time." Choice (A) is not correct because they are working on a group project, not a test. Choice (D) may be true, but it is not the purpose of the group. Choice (C) is not mentioned and may not be concluded from information in this discussion.

Audio

2. What do the letters in the SQ3R method represent?

Answer

(C) ". . . SQ3R. The letters stand for five steps in the reading process . . ." Choices (A), (B), and (D) are not mentioned and may not be concluded from information in the statement.

Audio

3. What does the word *survey* mean?

Answer

(D) "*Survey* means 'to look quickly.'" The first step in Choice (A) refers to the order of the five steps that surveying occupies, not to the meaning of survey. Choice (B) refers to the last step *recite*, not survey. Choice (C) refers to the second step, *question*.

Audio

4. What will the group do at the end of the presentation?

Answer

(D) "Then I'll say, '. . . let's take a look at a reading passage and try to use SQ3R.'" Choice (B) may be part of the demonstration, but it is not clear whether they will read or the members of the class will do the SQ3R on their own. The *survey* in Choice (C) refers to one of the steps in the SQ3R method, not to a questionnaire. Choice (A) is logical but is not mentioned and may not be concluded from information in this discussion.

Audio

5. Listen again to part of the conversation.
   Then answer the question.
   "At this point, you don't stop to write . . . sorry . . . I mean, read complete sentences. Just look at the important divisions of the material."
   Why does the man say this:
   ". . . sorry . . . I mean, read complete sentences."

Answer

(C) Speakers occasionally need to correct a previous statement. In this case, the man apologizes for the error by saying "sorry" and provides the correct word. Choice (D) is not correct because he was apologizing, not giving directions. Choices (A) and (B) are not mentioned and may not be concluded from information in the passage.

Audio

6. Who is probably the group leader?

Answer

(B) Joan is probably the group leader because she calls the meeting to order, reminds everyone of the plan and the assignments, and proposes how they will demonstrate the method. The group members mentioned in Choices (A), (C), and (D) all contribute less than Joan.

EXERCISE 22: Class Clarifications—Professor/Students 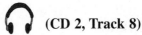 (CD 2, Track 8)

Talk One

Audio

Narrator: Listen to part of a talk by a college professor.

Professor:

Your test on Friday will cover material from both of your textbooks, my lecture notes, and your lab assignments. There will be fifty multiple-choice questions and five short answer essay questions. The multiple-choice will count half of your grade and the essay questions will count half of your grade.

I will tell you right now that there won't be any math problems, but that doesn't mean that you shouldn't review the formulas and know what they are used for.

I wouldn't bother much with the notes from my first lecture since that was an overview of the course, but you'll probably want to look at them when you study for the final.

Oh yes, this test represents twenty-five percent of your total grade for the semester. The lab reports are twenty-five percent, attendance ten, and your final forty.

Any questions?

Audio

1. What is the purpose of the announcement?

Answer

(B) "Your test on Friday will cover material from both of your textbooks, my lecture notes and your lab assignments." Choice (A) refers to the first lecture, not to this lecture. Choice (C) refers to the test on Friday. Choice (D) refers to the material to be tested, not to the purpose of the lecture.

Audio

2. On the test, how much will the multiple-choice questions count?

Answer

(D) "The multiple-choice will count half of your grade [on the test]." Choice (A) refers to the credit toward the final grade for attendance, not to the credit on the test for multiple-choice questions. Choice (B) refers to the credit toward the final grade for the test and for the lab report, not to the credit for the multiple-choice questions. Choice (C) refers to the credit toward the final grade for the final exam.

Audio

3. For what percentage of the total grade will the test count?

Answer

(B) "Oh yes, this test represents twenty-five percent of your total grade for the semester." Choice (A) refers to the credit toward the final grade for attendance, not for the test. Choice (C) refers to the credit toward the final grade for the final exam. Choice (D) refers to the credit on the test for the multiple-choice questions and for the essay questions.

Audio

4. What does the speaker say about math problems?

Answer

(B) "I will tell you right now that there won't be any math problems . . ." Choice (A) refers to the notes from the first lecture, not to all of the notes. Choice (C) is not correct because the speaker reveals that there will be no math problems on the test. Choice (D) is not correct because the speaker encourages students to review the formulas.

Audio

5. In which class would this announcement occur?

Answer

(C) "Your test on Friday will cover material from both of your textbooks, my lecture notes, and your lab assignments . . . there won't be any math problems, but that doesn't mean that you shouldn't review formulas . . ." Choices (A), (B), and (D) would be less likely to have *lab assignments* and *formulas*.

Talk Two

Audio

Narrator: Listen to part of a talk by a college professor.

Professor:

Before you start writing your term papers, I would like to clarify the differences among paraphrasing, quoting, and plagiarizing. All of these activities involve the use of someone else's ideas, but whereas paraphrasing and quoting are legitimate writing strategies, plagiarizing is a serious offense.

In your term papers, I expect you to paraphrase, that is, to summarize someone else's ideas in your own words. I also expect you to quote, that is to copy information from another source and enclose it in quotation marks in your paper.

When you paraphrase and quote, be sure to cite the source of your information. If you do not cite the source, then you are plagiarizing. You are stealing the ideas and using them as your own. If I discover that you have plagiarized on your term paper, you will receive a zero for the paper and an F for the course.

Audio

1. What is the main topic of this talk?

Answer

(A) "I would like to clarify the differences among paraphrasing, quoting [which are legitimate strategies], and plagiarizing." Choices (B) and (C) are mentioned as secondary themes that are used to develop the main theme of the talk, "the difference between plagiarism and legitimate writing strategies." Choice (D) is not mentioned and may not be concluded from information in the talk.

Audio

2. What is *plagiarizing*?

Answer

(D) "If you do not cite the source, then you are plagiarizing." Choices (B) and (C) refer to quoting, not to plagiarizing. Choice (A) is not mentioned and may not be concluded from information in the lecture.

Audio

3. What are two legitimate writing strategies?

Answer

(C) ". . . whereas paraphrasing and quoting are legitimate writing strategies . . ." Choices (A) and (B) are not correct because plagiarizing is not a legitimate writing strategy. Choice (D) is not correct because copying [without citing the source] is not a legitimate writing strategy.

Audio

4. What will happen to a student who plagiarizes on the term paper?

Answer

(D) "If I discover that you have plagiarized on your term paper, you will receive a zero for the paper and an F for the course." Choices (A), (B), and (C) are not mentioned as alternatives, and may not be concluded from information in the lecture.

Audio

5. Who is the speaker?

Answer

(D) Since the speaker is teaching the audience how to write a term paper, it may be concluded that the speaker is a teacher. Choices (A) and (B) refer to the audience, not to the speaker. Choice (C) is less probable because a librarian does not usually assign term papers.

EXERCISE 23: Class Clarifications—Professor/Students (CD 3, Track 1)

Talk One

Audio

Narrator: Listen to part of a talk by a college professor.

The first few pages of the syllabus are an outline of, uh, the topics for each session. As you can see, you'll be responsible for reading the material before you come to class so, uh, you'll have enough background to be able to . . . follow the lecture. For example, on September 3, when you come to class, you should already have read the first two chapters in the text, so, uh, we can discuss the history of psychology in that session. The following week, you should have a grasp of chapters three and four, so . . . so we can cover biology and the psychology of the brain. And so on.

Now, let's take a few minutes to look at the policies and procedures listed on page three of the course syllabus. Uh . . . refer to the section under assignments first, please. You'll notice that all assignments must be typewritten and submitted on the due date . . . in order for you to receive full credit and, uh, the grade for a late assignment will be lowered by one letter for each day past the due date.

Now, look at the section under examinations. As you see, all exams must be completed on the dates and times, uh, scheduled in the syllabus. If you must be absent . . . I mean for an exam, then try to call me to let me know what your problem is. My office phone is on the syllabus, and . . . and my home phone is listed in the telephone directory. Of course, e-mail is best, and you have my e-mail address on page one, uh, it's right under my name on the syllabus. A make-up exam must be arranged within one week of the scheduled date of the exam. And, I must warn you, the questions on the makeup will not be the same as the questions on the regular exam. In fact, I, uh, usually give multiple-choice tests, but I always give short answer tests for makeups. And, my students tell me . . . they say the makeups are quite a bit more difficult than the regularly scheduled exams.

Oh, yes, let's take a minute to clarify my attendance policy. I suggest that you come to class. I'll be assigning you a seat. . . . Yes, yes I know you'd rather choose your own seat, but, uh, this is a large class, and it would take up too much time to call the roll every session, so I'll just mark those people absent who aren't present in their seats by the time the class begins. Better late than never, but, uh, if you're late, you'd better check in with me after class so I can change my attendance records. Remember that attendance is 10 percent . . . sorry . . . 15 percent of the grade, which usually makes the difference between an A and a B, or a B and a C. Let's not even talk about Ds and Fs.

One more thing . . . if you need to request an incomplete, please remember that I only approve them for illness or for a serious personal problem, not just for a . . . because you ran out of time. And you must submit a request form with a signed statement of explanation to my office in order for your incomplete to be considered. Otherwise, you'll have to register and take the entire course over again to get credit.

Audio

1. What is the main purpose of this talk?

Answer

(C) "Let's take a few minutes to look at the policies and procedures listed on page three . . ." Choices (A) and (B) are mentioned as secondary themes that are used to develop the main purpose of the talk, "to explain course policies and procedures." Choice (D) is not mentioned and may not be concluded from information in the talk.

Audio

2. What is the speaker's policy for late assignments?

Answer

(C) "The grade for a late assignment will be lowered by one letter for each day past the due date." Choice (A) is not correct because assignments must be submitted on the due date for students to receive full credit. Choice (B) is not correct because grades for late assignments will be lowered. Choice (D) is not mentioned and may not be concluded from information in the talk.

Audio

3. What is the professor's attendance policy?

Answer

(D) "It would take up too much time to call the roll . . . so I will just mark those people absent who are not present in their seats . . ." Choice (A) is not correct because the professor says it would take too much time to call the roll. Choice (B) is not correct because he mentions his attendance records. Choice (C) is not correct because only students who are late should check in with the professor.

Audio

4. What is the procedure for a student to receive a grade of incomplete?

Answer

(A) ". . . you must submit a request form with a signed statement of explanation . . ." Choice (B) refers to the procedure for being absent from an exam, not to the procedure for an incomplete. Choice (C) refers to the procedure for a makeup exam. Choice (D) refers to the consequences of failing to comply with the procedure, not to the procedure itself.

Audio

5. Listen again to part of the talk.
   Then answer the question.
   "Better late than never, but, uh, if you're late, you'd better check in with me after class so I can change my attendance records. Remember that attendance is 10 percent . . . sorry . . . 15 percent of the grade, which usually makes the difference between an A and a B, or a B and a C."
   Why does the professor say this:
   "Remember that attendance is 10 percent . . . sorry . . . 15 percent of the grade . . ."

Answer

(C) Professors occasionally need to correct a previous statement. In this case, the professor apologizes for the error by saying "sorry" and provides the correct number. Choice (A) is not correct because he makes the statement without comment. Choice (B) is not correct because the correction is for a misstatement, but the policy is not changed. Choice (D) is not correct because he has already reminded students to attend.

Audio

6. What can we infer about the speaker?

Answer

(C) Because the professor announces that his ". . . home phone is listed in the telephone directory," it may be concluded that he does not mind receiving calls at home. Choice (A) is not correct because the syllabus is very detailed and organized. Choice (D) is not correct because he refers to a section under *examinations* on the syllabus. Although the professor appears to be strict, Choice (B) cannot be concluded from information in this talk.

Talk Two

Audio

Narrator: Listen to part of a class clarification by a professor.

Professor:

I've been getting quite a few e-mails with, uh, with questions about grading for the group projects so let me clarify that before we start class today. Each group has five members in it, except one group that . . . that has six. The group project includes a presentation and a written report. But I'll be giving you three grades and, uh, averaging them for a final grade on the project. First, I'll be grading the written report as a whole, and every member of the group will receive the same grade on the written report, so, uh, so it'll be to your benefit to divide the work and produce the best report you can. How do you divide the work? Well, uh, in the past, some of my students have actually divided the report into sections, and each group member does . . . has written one of the sections. That's certainly a possibility, especially for groups who may have a problem finding mutual meeting times. But, uh, some of the other groups have assigned tasks to the group members. For example, two members might do the research, two members might write the report, and another member might, uh, provide editing and . . . and formatting . . . of the final draft. In my experience, it's been difficult for a group of five or six people to write . . . to do the actual writing, line by line, but I have had a few groups do it that way. So, you can see that you have a lot of flexibility in . . . how to prepare the report. However, remember that everyone will receive the same grade for it.

That brings us to the second grade, which is a group grade for the presentation. Again, I suggest that you share the labor here. If you have a group member who's . . . artistic, you could . . . you could capitalize on that talent . . . maybe by having posters, overheads, or, uh, visuals as part of the presentation. If you have an excellent speaker . . . someone who likes presenting . . . that person might be responsible for . . . for the majority of the oral presentation. Another person who writes well but prefers not to speak could, uh, prepare the handout, if you choose to provide one. I think you see what I mean.

The best way to get a high grade is to play to the strength of every group member. I mean that you shouldn't ask someone to perform a task that is outside his or her unique ability. And remember, everyone has the potential to contribute something to the group. But, uh, about the grade . . . again . . . there will be one grade for the group presentation, and everyone will receive the same grade. The major problem for previous groups, and, uh, I'll alert you to it right now . . . is preparing too much material for the time frame. Remember, you have thirty minutes, and that might seem like a lot of time, but, uh, many groups haven't been able to complete their presentations, and of course, they have had points deducted because of it.

So what about the third grade? This is an individual grade based on your contribution to the group. I'll be asking you to prepare a list of your activities as a group member, and I . . . I'll be giving you a grade based on participation. Let me explain that a little more. Let's say that one group member has an impressive list. How will I know that it's, uh, accurate? Not that anyone in this class would exaggerate, but to be as fair as possible, your list will not be complete without . . . I'll be asking for the signatures of every group member, uh, verifying that your list is appropriate for the work you've done. Then, you see, I can evaluate your performance on an individual basis.

So, I'll have the three grades, and, uh, and I'll add them together and average them to give you a total grade. I've found that this system discourages hitchhikers. By that I mean, someone who belongs to the group but doesn't contribute to the group. Let's say I have a group member with a grade of A for the group report, a grade of . . . A for the group presentation, but a grade of D for the participation . . . then that student will have a B or, uh, even a C . . . for the final grade, whereas someone in the same group who has an A for participation will have an A for the final grade. I think that uh . . . makes the grading a little more fair.

Audio

1. What is the purpose of this talk?

Answer

(C) "I've been getting . . . questions about grading for the group projects . . . so let me clarify that. . . ." Choices (A) and (B) are not correct because the projects have not been graded yet. Choice (B) is not correct because the students are not participating in the clarification while the professor speaks.

Audio

2. How will the written report be graded?

Answer

(B) "...every member of the group will receive the same grade on the written report." Choice (A) refers to the grade for participation, not to the grade for the written report. Choices (C) and (D) refer to the way that the group project will be graded, not to the way that the written report will be graded.

Audio

3. How will the final grade be calculated for each student?

Answer

(B) "So, I'll have the three grades [two group grades and one individual grade], and, uh, I'll add them together and average them to give you a total grade." Choices (A), (C), and (D) are not mentioned as options for grading, and may not be concluded from information in the clarification.

Audio

4. How will the professor know what each individual has contributed?

Answer

(C) "I'll be asking you to prepare a list of your activities as a group member . . . [but] your list will not be complete without . . . the signatures of every group member, uh, verifying that your list is appropriate." Choice (B) is part of the procedure, but the verification is the way that the professor will know that the list is accurate. Choices (A) and (D) are not mentioned and may not be concluded from information in the clarification.

Audio

5. Listen again to part of the talk.
   Then answer the question
   "How do you divide the work? Well, uh, in the past, some of my students have actually divided the report into sections, and each group member does . . . has written one of the sections."
   Why does the professor ask this:
   "How do you divide the work?"

Answer

(C) Professors often ask and answer rhetorical questions. In this case, he is preparing to offer advice about dividing the work. Choices (A) and (B) are not correct because he does not pause long enough to invite student responses. Choice (D) is not correct because the students have not organized the work yet.

Audio

6. Why does the professor most probably use such a complicated grading system?

Answer

(A) "I think that uh . . . makes the grading a little more fair." Choice (B) is true, but it is not the reason that he is using the system. Choice (D) is not correct because the professor has been getting a lot of questions, and he is taking the time to answer them in class. Choice (C) is not mentioned and may not be concluded from information in this clarification.

EXERCISE 24: General Talks—Professor

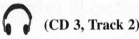 (CD 3, Track 2)

Talk One

Audio

Narrator: Listen to part of a lecture in a history class. The professor will discuss gold coins.
Professor:

In 1792, Congress passed an act authorizing the coinage of gold eagles valued at ten dollars, half eagles valued at five dollars, and quarter eagles valued at two dollars and fifty cents. These gold coins were standardized to silver on a fifteen to one ratio, that is, fifteen ounces of silver to one ounce of gold. Although the ratio was reasonable at the time that the bill was passed, by the turn of the century, the ratio in Europe had reached fifteen and three quarters to one, and the overvalued gold coins in the United States were either smuggled out of the country or melted down. Gold therefore disappeared from circulation until 1834 when a new law reduced the weight of gold pieces. Soon afterward, gold coins appeared in a smaller size and returned to circulation. The new interest and demand for gold encouraged the Mint to strike twenty-dollar double eagles and a smaller number of fifty-dollar gold coins.

The financial uncertainty during the Great Depression of 1929 encouraged hoarding of gold coins by individuals, a situation that became so serious that the government finally ordered all gold coins to be turned in. During the next several years, a number of amendments exempted certain kinds of gold coins and allowed limited collecting. Since then, the interest in collecting gold coins has increased, and the restrictions have decreased. Now, there are no restrictions regarding the export, import, purchase, sale, or collecting of gold coins in the United States.

Audio

1. What is the main topic of this talk?

Answer

(B) "By 1792, Congress passed an act authorizing the coinage of gold eagles . . . by the turn of the century . . . gold disappeared from circulation until 1834. . . . The financial uncertainty during the Great Depression . . . encouraged hoarding of gold. . . . Now, there are no restrictions. . . ." Choices (A), (C), and (D) are mentioned as secondary themes that are used to develop the main theme of the talk, "the history of gold coins in the United States."

Audio

2. What was the value of the original gold eagle?

Answer

(B) "In 1792, Congress passed an act authorizing the coinage of gold eagles valued at ten dollars, half eagles valued at five dollars, and quarter eagles valued at two dollars and fifty cents." Choice (C) refers to the half eagle, not to the gold eagle. Choice (D) refers to a quarter eagle, not to a gold eagle. Choice (A) refers to the double eagle that was minted later.

Audio

3. What was the value of silver to gold in 1792?

Answer

(A) "By 1792 . . . gold coins were standardized to silver on a fifteen to one ratio." Choice (C) refers to the value by the turn of the century or 1800. Choices (B) and (D) are not mentioned and may not be concluded from information in the talk.

Audio

4. What happened after the law of 1834?

Answer

(B) "Gold coins therefore disappeared from circulation until 1834 when a new law reduced the weight of gold pieces. Soon afterward, gold coins appeared in a smaller size. . . ." Choice (A) refers to 1929, not 1834. Choice (C) refers to 1929, the Great Depression. Choice (D) refers to the years following the Great Depression.

Audio

5. What are the restrictions on collecting gold coins today?

Answer

(A) "Now, there are no restrictions regarding the export, import, purchase, sale, or collecting of gold coins in the United States." Choice (B) is not correct because there are no restrictions on the export of gold coins. Choices (C) and (D) refer to the period after the Great Depression, not to today.

Talk Two

Audio

Narrator: Listen to part of a lecture in a music appreciation class. The professor is discussing the work of Stephen Foster.

Professor:

Stephen Foster was one of the most prolific song writers of his time, contributing more than 200 songs during his twenty-year career. His first attempt, when he was fourteen was a forgettable composition called the "Tioga Waltz," a melody for three flutes which debuted at a school exhibition. His first published piece appeared only three years later in 1844. It was called "Open Thy Lattice, Love," and it was rather typical of the sentimental tunes of the time. Still, it was a good effort for a seventeen-year-old composer.

But, it was minstrel music for which Foster will always be remembered. The songs of Southern black slaves in the pre-Civil War days evoked nostalgic themes, like the plantation era that was already fated to pass into history. His first successful piece, "Oh, Susanna," became popular throughout the world, and is still widely sung. "Camptown Races" followed with similar success. The most successful song written by an American to that date was Stephen Foster's "Old Folks at Home," which appeared in 1851. Some of you may recall it as "Way Down Upon the Swanee River," since it was also referred to by that title as well. In any case, an item in the *Musical World* of New York stressed the unprecedented sales. At a time when half of all the sheet music published was a total failure, and a sale of 5,000 copies was considered highly successful, "Old Folks at Home" sold nearly 100,000 copies. "Old Kentucky Home" which came out two years later, capitalized on the reputation that Foster was making for himself, and was also a huge seller.

Now what is interesting about the success of Stephen Foster is that he himself was ambivalent about it. Sometimes he hid his identity with pseudonyms, sometimes he requested that his name be withheld from the cover to the sheet music, and other times he insisted that his name be displayed. Out of the context of the times, none of this seems to make sense, but when we contrast the musical world of high society with that of the common people, it becomes clear. Stephen Foster's success came from writing "plantation songs" for popular entertainment. The music was easy to remember, very repetitious, and available to everyone in the popular music halls. But the music that was considered serious and appropriate for society events was quite different. Foster proved that he could write such music, and perhaps had some secret desire to succeed on those terms, but that type of music didn't enjoy the widespread popularity of the plantation melodies that we still recognize today. Most school children have heard "Jeannie with the Light Brown Hair" and "Beautiful Dreamer," but none would recognize the saccharine ballads and hymns that were considered by a genteel few his "better music."

Audio

1. What kind of music is associated with Stephen Foster?

Answer

(B) "Foster's success came from writing 'Plantation songs' for popular entertainment." Choice (A) refers to the type of music that was popular at the time. Choices (C) and (D) refer to the kind of music that Foster occasionally wrote, but that did not enjoy much success.

Audio

2. Which piece was the most successful song written by an American?

Answer

(C) "The most successful song written by an American to that date was Stephen Foster's 'Old Folks at Home'. . . ." Choice (A) refers to the first song that Foster published, not to the most successful song written. Choices (B) and (D) refer to popular songs, but not to the most successful song written by an American.

Audio

3. Why did Stephen Foster withhold his name from the cover to some of his sheet music?

Answer

(C) "...the music that was considered serious and appropriate for society events was quite different [from that written by Foster]." Choice (A) is not correct because he wrote for more than twenty years. Choice (B) is not correct because he was famous for his plantation songs. Choice (D) is not mentioned and may not be concluded from information in the lecture.

Audio

4. What best describes Stephen Foster's most popular songs?

Answer

(A) "The music was easy to remember, very repetitious, and available to everyone in the popular music halls." Choice (C) is not correct because his music was popular in the music halls, not at society events. Choice (D) is not correct because his most popular songs were not among the serious ballads and hymns that a few considered his "better music." Choice (B) is not mentioned and may not be concluded from information in the lecture.

Audio

5. What do we know about Stephen Foster?

Answer

(A) "Stephen Foster was one of the most prolific song writers of his time, contributing more than 200 songs during his twenty-two year career." Choice (B) is not correct because he wrote many popular songs, seven of which are mentioned in the passage. Choice (C) is not correct because "Oh Susanna" was his first successful piece, and other songs met with similar success. Choice (D) refers to the fact that most school children have heard his music, but it was not written specifically for children.

EXERCISE 25: Content Lectures—Professor (CD 3, Track 3)

Talk One

Audio

Narrator: Listen to part of a lecture in a psychology class. The professor will discuss heredity and environment.

Professor:

Good morning. I trust that you have all read the assignment and that we can proceed with today's lecture. As you know from your text, both heredity and environment play a role in the development of the personality.

In addition, research at the University of Texas at Arlington has shown that the order of one's birth in relationship to brothers and sisters may be a significant factor. Those born first tend to develop personality traits that make them domineering, ambitious, and highly motivated to achieve. And the same is true for only children. In contrast, children born later in the family tend to be more socially adept, likable, talkative individuals.

Also interesting in the research is the fact that a woman with older brothers and a man with older sisters seem to be able to interact more easily with the opposite sex. Having older opposite-sex siblings seems to be important in being able to establish social relationships with members of the opposite sex.

There is also some evidence that the youngest child may develop a very charming personality in order to be included in the activities of the older group. Of course, if the other children are no longer living at home, the youngest child is more likely to develop the characteristics of an only child.

Audio

1. What is the main subject of this lecture?

Answer

(C) "...research at the University of Texas at Arlington has shown that the order of one's birth in relationship to brothers and sisters may be a significant factor." Choices (A), (B), and (D) are mentioned as secondary subjects that are used to develop the main subject of the lecture, "birth order."

Audio

2. What should the students know before they hear this lecture?

Answer

(B) "As you know from your text, both heredity and environment play a role in the development of the personality." Choice (A) refers to the topic of the lecture, not to what students should know before the lecture. Choices (C) and (D) refer to the information in the lecture.

Audio

3. Which one of the people would probably be the most comfortable interacting with a member of the opposite sex?

Answer

(B) ". . . a woman with older brothers and a man with older sisters seem to be able to interact more easily with the opposite sex." Choice (A) is not correct because a man with older sisters is able to interact more easily. Choices (C) and (D) are not correct because a woman with older brothers is able to interact more easily.

Audio

4. What personality trait will firstborn children probably exhibit?

Answer

(B) "Those born first tend to develop personality traits that make them domineering, ambitious, and highly motivated to achieve." Choices (A), (C), and (D) refer to personality traits of children born later in the family.

Audio

5. According to the research, what might be the dominant personality trait of the youngest child?

Answer

(A) "Those born first tend to develop personality traits that make them . . . highly motivated . . . children born later . . . tend to be . . . talkative individuals . . . There is also some evidence that the youngest child may develop a very charming personality in order to be included. . . ."

Talk Two

Audio

Narrator: Listen to part of a lecture in an English literature class. The professor will be talking about American writers in the early nineteenth century.

Professor:

Today we will discuss the Knickerbocker School, which was a rather informal group of writers who met in New York City during the early 1800s. The name Knickerbocker—let me write that down for you—was a tribute to Diedrich Knickerbocker, a character created by one of their members, the writer Washington Irving.

At any one time, about twenty writers belonged to the group, including the three most important figures in early American literature—William Cullen Bryant, the editor of the *New York Evening Post*; Washington Irving, a well-known poet and story teller; and novelist, James Fenimore Cooper.

Although Irving gained recognition in Europe as America's first legitimate man of letters, and his stories "Rip Van Winkle" and "The Legend of Sleepy Hollow" were widely published as serials, it was James Fenimore Cooper who achieved success with subjects and settings that were typically American. Cooper created the frontier novel, with a hero who embodied the American frontier spirit. In the *Leatherstocking Tales*, five novels about frontier life, the affable old scout Natty Bumppo evolves into a philosopher and even, some say, an epic hero. Bumppo is a frontiersman who knows how to live close to nature and possesses all the skills necessary for a rugged pioneer existence, but he is also an observer of life. He sees that the settlers are a civilizing influence. He respects the social order that they create. But he also sees the thoughtless and sometimes selfish abuse of the natural environment.

The best of all the *Leatherstocking Tales* has to be *The Last of the Mohicans*, which, I believe at least some of you have seen on video. You may recall that the story recounts the conflict between the French and the English during the early years of independence, with Indians fighting on both sides. I personally feel that this represents some of Cooper's best writing, especially in those passages that recount the death of the Mohican chief's son in a noble attempt to avenge the murder of his love.

Of course, there were others who had membership in the Knickerbocker School, but if you are familiar with the three major writers that we have discussed today, you'll have a feel for early American literature.

Audio

1. What is the main focus of this talk?

Answer

(A) "Today we will discuss the Knickerbocker School. . . ." Choices (B), (C), and (D) are mentioned as secondary themes that are used to develop the main focus of the lecture, "the Knickerbocker School."

Audio

2. What are the *Leatherstocking Tales*?

Answer

(B) "In the *Leatherstocking Tales*, five novels about frontier life. . . ." Choice (A) refers to Natty Bumpo, the hero of the *Leatherstocking Tales*. Choices (C) and (D) refer to characters in the novels.

Audio

3. What kind of character is Natty Bumppo?

Answer

(A) ". . . Bumpo evolves into . . . an epic hero . . . a frontiersman who knows how to live close to nature. . . ." Choice (B) is not correct because Bumpo possesses all the skills necessary for a rugged pioneer existence. Choices (C) and (D) refer to other characters in the *Leatherstocking Tales*, not to Natty Bumpo.

Audio

4. Who was one of the most important members of the Knickerbocker School?

Answer

(B) ". . . the three most important figures in early American literature—William Cullen Bryant . . . Washington Irving . . . and . . . James Fenimore Cooper." Choice (A) refers to a character in a story by Washington Irving, not to a writer of the Knickerbocker School. Choice (C) refers to the Native American tribe in a story by James Fenimore Cooper. Choice (D) refers to the character, also created by Irving, for whom the group was named.

Audio

5. Which of the following best describes James Fenimore Cooper?

Answer

(A) "William Cullen Bryant, the editor of the *New York Evening Post* . . . Irving . . . [whose story] 'The Legend of Sleepy Hollow' was widely published . . . and James Fenimore Cooper . . . who embodied the American spirit in the *Leatherstocking Tales*. . . ."

EXERCISE 26: Content Lectures—Professor

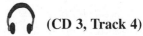 (CD 3, Track 4)

Talk One

Audio

Narrator: Listen to part of a lecture in a biology class.

Professor:

The concept of a half-life is mentioned in your textbook, but I'm going to take a few minutes to discuss it with you. The method is called *radiometric dating*. Okay. . . . Physicists use the term half-life to describe the average time it takes . . . for half of a group of radioactive isotopes to undergo decay.

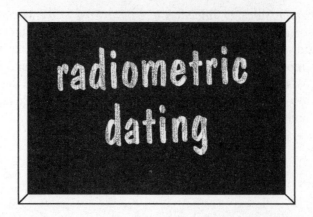

Trefil and Hazen have an excellent analogy. It's in the chapter assigned for next week. Okay. . . . They compare the group of isotopes to a batch of microwave popcorn. If you watch one kernel in the batch, it'll pop at a specific time, but all the kernels don't pop at the same time. And although you can't predict the exact time that the . . . the one kernel will pop, uh, you do know for how many minutes to set the microwave, because you can predict the amount of time necessary for the batch. Okay . . . to get back to the radioactive nuclei, some nuclei will decay immediately, while . . . while others will take much longer. The important thing is that . . . that the percentage of nuclei that decay in each second remains more or less constant. Okay . . . let's go back to that definition. Remember, a half-life is the average time that it takes for half of the group to undergo decay. So let's just use 100 nuclei as an example, and if . . . and if it takes thirty minutes for fifty of them to undergo radioactive decay, then the half-life of that nucleus is . . . thirty minutes. And if we continue observing for another thirty minutes, you'll have half of the fifty, or twenty-five . . . that have decayed, leaving you twenty five. Okay . . . and at the end of thirty more minutes, you'll have twelve or thirteen, and so on, and so on. But this is why the popcorn example that, uh, Trefil and Hazen came up with is so useful. If a nucleus has a half-life of thirty minutes, all the nuclei won't wait half an hour before they all begin to decay . . . they don't all decay at the same moment. Each one will decay at a different moment, like the popcorn. A half-life of thirty minutes means that, on the average, an individual nucleus will take thirty minutes to decay.

Okay, this is the interesting part. Since the half-life is relatively easy to measure, it's a very useful tool in determining the age of both . . . uh natural and man-made materials. The method is called *radiometric dating*, or since the isotope carbon-14 is the most commonly used nucleus, you may hear the term *carbon-14 dating*, but that isn't really accurate since many different isotopes can be used in the process, uh, not just carbon-14. Anyway, let's turn our attention to carbon to . . . uh . . . to see why the dating system is so effective and why carbon-14 is such a good choice for dating fossils.

Every living organism uses carbon. Right now you're using carbon from the food you ate earlier, and . . . and . . . through a series of complex processes, you're turning it into living tissue. Plants take in carbon dioxide from the air, so I think you can agree that carbon is essential to all living things. Okay, most of the carbon is carbon-12, probably close to 99 percent, and the other 1 percent is almost all carbon-13, but, uh, there's a minuscule amount of carbon-14 . . . that's the important one for the purposes of dating, because, uh, carbon-14 has a half-life of approximately . . . 5,700 years.

Now, remember that all living things are taking in carbon, all the time, including carbon-14, but at . . . at the point of death, the carbon begins to decay. In radiometric dating, we can determine the age of wood or bone or . . . or other materials that have once been alive by, uh, by measuring the carbon-14 that remains in comparison with the amount that we know must have been present when it was a living plant or animal. And . . . and . . . that's pretty exciting.

But, of course, carbon-14 can go back in time only about 50,000 years until the amount of carbon is so small that it's no longer a useful measure, uh, to date geological formations, like rocks and minerals. So . . . what about rocks that are millions or even billions of years old? Well, the same process can be applied, but we have to use isotopes that have longer half-lives. For example, uh, uh, for example, uranium-238 with a half-life of about 4.5 billion years . . . or . . . or even rubidium-87 with a half-life of almost 50 billion years. So, most of the dates that we'll refer to in this class will have been determined by the use of radiometric dating using carbon-14 since we'll be dealing with living organisms but, uh, but it's important for you to understand that the method has application in other sciences that don't treat carbon-based life forms. Okay. Any questions so far?

Audio
1. What is the main topic of this lecture?
Answer
(B) "The concept of a half-life is mentioned in your textbook, but I'm going to take a few minutes to discuss it with you. . . . The method is called *radiometric dating*. . . ." Choice (A) refers to an analogy that the professor uses to explain radiometric dating. Choice (C) is the most commonly used nucleus for radiometric dating, but it is not the correct term for the topic. Choice (D) is mentioned in reference to the main topic, "radiometric dating."

Audio
2. What is the definition of a *half-life*?
Answer
(A) "Physicists use the term half-life to describe the average time it takes . . . for half of a group of radioactive isotopes to undergo decay." Choices (B), (C), and (D) are not mentioned and may not be concluded from information in this talk.

Audio
3. Why does the professor mention popcorn?
Answer
(C) "Trefil and Hazen have an excellent analogy. . . . They compare the group of isotopes to a batch of microwave popcorn." Choice (A) is true but it is not the reason that the professor mentions it. Choices (B) and (D) are not mentioned and may not be concluded from information in this talk.

Audio
4. What do we know about carbon-14?
Answer
(D) "Every living organism uses carbon. . . . We can determine the age of . . . materials that have once been alive by, uh, measuring the carbon-14 that remains." Choice (A) is not correct because uranium-238 and rubidium-87 are also used in radiometric dating. Choice (B) is not correct because carbon-14 represents a very small percentage of the carbon in living things, compared with carbon-12 and carbon-13. Choice (C) is not correct because carbon-14 has a half-life of 5,700 years.

Audio
5. Listen again to part of the talk.
Then answer the question.
"So . . . what about rocks that are millions or even billions of years old? Well, the same process can be applied, but we have to use isotopes that have longer half-lives."
Why does the professor ask this question:
"So . . . what about rocks that are millions or even billions of years old?"
Answer
(A) professors often ask and answer rhetorical questions. In this case, he is asking a question and providing a response to extend the concept he has been discussing. Choices (B) and (D) are not correct because he does not pause long enough to invite student responses. Choice (C) is not correct because he extends the concept that he has been discussing by demonstrating how the process can be used with non-carbon-based elements.

Audio

6. Which of the following would NOT be dated using carbon-14?

Answer

(D) Choices (A), (B), and (C) are all carbon-based life forms, but Choice (D) is a geological formation that requires an isotope with a longer half-life, as, for example, uranium-238.

Talk Two

Audio

Narrator: Listen to a lecture in an anthropology class.

Professor:

Evidence of systematic planning, now called *city planning*, has been uncovered during archaeological excavations of ancient cities from as early as 3500 B.C. It isn't surprising is it . . . that the locations of these cities have revealed certain basic requirements for life in ancient times, including not only the necessities of water and arable land, but uh . . . but also the requirement of a strategic fortification against invaders.

By about 3000 B.C., cities along the Indus Valley had, uh, regular patterns of streets. Houses with shared walls were built around courtyards, with differences in, uh, the height of the house and, uh, the width of the street as an . . . an . . . as outward indications of social rank among inhabitants. At about the same time, in Pompeii, a central marketplace was already in evidence, with a regular pattern of streets and sidewalks extending out from the commercial area. Less than a thousand years later, Egyptian cities were being built with, uh, parallel streets. In contrast with the Greek cities on the mainland, colonial cities incorporated a . . . gridiron pattern for streets, and by that I mean a pattern of square blocks. Rome itself was somewhat hap . . . haphazard at the time, but again, Roman colonies and military camps were being built in gridiron patterns throughout what is, uh, now Europe. In China and Japan, a central commercial area was in evidence in cities from this time period. The marketplace, in fact, was . . . was the most universal feature of cities throughout uh . . . the ancient world.

Now, I'm going to skip ahead to the Middle Ages, which, was the second interesting historic period in city planning. About uh . . . the tenth century, heavily fortified garrisons were replaced by towns of a few thousand inhabitants. The towns were only about one square mile in size, and, uh, many were located in strategic areas near rivers or . . . or along the seacoast . . . where larger cities would later flourish. But, uh, in spite of the earlier examples of organized grid patterns from the Roman Empire, the streets in these small towns . . . the streets were narrow and winding, often projecting out in a . . . in an arbitrary way . . . from a public square that was, uh, often built around a church or a mosque. Gated walls usually surrounded the city, and a custom house for the collection of tolls was . . . it was almost always constructed on a conspicuous site.

Let me see. . . . Uh, that brings us to the Renaissance. The Renaissance began near the end of the Middle Ages and continued into the 1600s. It was a period in city planning in which huge plazas were erected to overcome the overcrowding of the earlier towns. In order to accommodate burgeoning populations . . . and, uh, new modes of transportation, cities were planned with wide boulevards, spacious parks, and . . . symmetrical, ordered streets. It is in this period that we start to see . . . intricate patterns of circles with diagonals radiating out like, uh . . . like the spokes in a wheel. And this was popular, especially in Europe.

Moving into the 1700s and 1800s, which roughly correspond to, uh, the Industrial Revolution, the . . . the towns that had been planned for 2,000 inhabitants became very overcrowded, as people moved into the urban areas for . . . rather, to work in factories. In North America and Europe, the streets that had been designed for pedestrians and horses were much too narrow, and sanitation, uh, became a major concern near the factories where workers were . . . were crowding into dirty, noisy neighborhoods. Although governments tried to regulate housing, in many cases proposing the separation of housing from industrial zones, uh, city planning could simply not keep pace with the migration of workers from, uh, rural areas to urban centers.

City planning in the nineteenth and twentieth centuries has been chiefly an . . . a response to the need to improve living conditions in, uh, overcrowded urban areas, and by that I mean not only a city but also, more recently, sprawling suburbs. The mass production of automobiles in . . . after World War I . . . made, uh, cars a viable means of transportation for . . . a larger segment of the population, and opened up areas beyond the immediate downtown for, uh . . . for, uh . . . residential use. The need for streets to accommodate more and more vehicles has been one of the modern-day challenges. And a movement called the "garden city plan," which was exported from Britain to the former colonies, . . . the plan called for public land and buildings to serve as a green belt, and this was an attempt to, uh, limit the urban sprawl that was . . . characteristic of this period. In Europe, after World War II, the reconstruction of cities devastated by bombing necessitated even more attention to the concept of city planning.

Do we still have a few minutes? Let's go to the modern period of, uh . . . of, uh . . . city planning. Today, there are three types of cities. The decentralized metropolitan city in . . . in developed nations with high automobile ownership, like metropolitan areas in the United States. And the centralized and heavily planned metro areas in European nations, Singapore, and Japan where, uh . . . land is limited and the high cost of . . . of fuel discourages suburban living. And densely populated cities in nations where automobile ownership is still out of reach for most people, like some areas in Latin America where we see new towns springing up on the fringes of cities almost overnight. I know I went over that rather quickly, but, uh, I advise you to refer to the three types of cities in your book. It's an important concept.

Audio
1. What is this lecture mainly about?
Answer
(C) "Evidence of systematic planning, now called *city planning*, has been uncovered during archaeological excavations of ancient cities from as early as 3500 B.C." Choices (A), (B), and (D) are mentioned as secondary themes that are used to develop the main theme of the lecture, "city planning."

Audio
2. What feature of ancient cities appears throughout most of the world?
Answer
(B) "The marketplace, in fact, was . . . the most universal feature of cities throughout . . . the ancient world." Choice (A) includes features of cities in the Middle Ages, not those in the ancient world. Choice (C) includes features of cities in the Renaissance. Choice (D) is a feature of colonial cities of the Roman and Greek Empires but not a feature throughout the world.

Audio
3. When were symmetrical streets with circular patterns introduced?
Answer
(B) "[During] the Renaissance . . . symmetrical, ordered streets [in] . . . intricate patterns of circles with diagonals radiation out." Choice (A) was noted for a gridiron pattern. Choice (C) was noted for narrow streets. Choice (D) was noted for urban sprawl.

Audio
4. What was the problem for city planners during the Industrial Revolution?
Answer
(A) (B) "the towns . . . became very overcrowded, as people moved into the urban areas to work in factories . . . and sanitation . . . became a major concern." Choices (C) and (D) refer to the nineteenth and twentieth centuries, not to the Industrial Revolution.

Audio

5. Listen again to part of the talk.

Then answer the question.

"I know I went over that rather quickly, but uh . . . I advise you to refer to the three types of cities in your book. It's an important concept."

Why does the professor say this:

"I advise you to refer to the three types of cities in your book."

Answer

(B) Because the professor says that she has gone over the material quickly, it may be concluded that she did not have time to talk about the concept in depth. Choice (C) is not correct because the students, not the teacher, will refer to their books. Choices (A) and (D) are not mentioned and may not be concluded from information in the passage.

Audio

6. Classify each of these cities, matching them with their type.

Answer

(A) Singapore is *Centralized*.

(B) Mexico City is *Densely populated*.

(C) Los Angeles is *Decentralized*.

EXERCISE 27: Interactive Lectures—Professor/Students 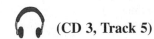 (CD 3, Track 5)

Talk One

Audio

Narrator: Listen to part of a discussion in an education class.

Sally: I'm sorry. I just don't agree with you at all.

Paul: Look. Take the example of an international student applying for university admission. If the student has a 550 on the TOEFL or an 80 on the Michigan Test, most admissions officers will accept the applicant. The student with a 547 or 79 won't be considered. The officer won't even look at transcripts.

Sally: Right. But I think that proves my point, not yours.

Paul: How?

Sally: Well, it's the admissions officer who decides *how* to use the test. The TOEFL and the Michigan are good English proficiency tests, but that's all they are. And English proficiency is necessary for success in an American university, but so are several other factors, including good academic preparation.

Paul: Good academic preparation is more important.

Sally: Maybe. I don't really know. But what I'm trying to explain to you is that admissions officers should use the proficiency test as one of many considerations, and as such, they really shouldn't insist on a rigid cut-off score like 550 or 80.

Ayers: Isn't this the basic disagreement: that Paul thinks the tests are bad in themselves, and Sally believes that the tests are good, but that many people don't use them for their intended purpose?

Paul: I don't agree with having the tests, Professor Ayers, and that's my position.

Sally: But Paul, what would you do to evaluate the English proficiency of a student ten thousand miles away without a standardized test?

Paul: I admit that's a big problem.

Sally: It sure is.

Ayers: Okay, class. For Wednesday, let's consider the problem of evaluation without standardized tests like the TOEFL, the SAT, GMAT, and GRE. Paul says that there ought to be an alternative. Sally doesn't seem to believe that there is an appropriate alternative. Please bring in your ideas and suggestions, and we'll discuss them.

Audio

1. What do the speakers mainly discuss?

Answer

(B) "The TOEFL and Michigan are good English proficiency tests [for college admissions]." Choice (A) refers to the name of a test, the Michigan Test, not to admissions standards at the University of Michigan. Choice (C) is mentioned as a secondary theme that is used to develop the main theme of the talk, "the use of standardized tests for college admissions." Choice (D) refers to the topic assigned for Wednesday, not to the main theme of the talk.

Audio

2. What is Paul's opinion about the TOEFL and the Michigan Test?

Answer

(D) "I don't agree with having the tests, Professor Ayers, and that's my position." Choice (A) refers to Sally's, not Paul's, opinion. Choices (B) and (C) are not mentioned and may not be concluded from information in the discussion.

Audio

3. What does Sally say about the admissions officers?

Answer

(A) ". . . Sally believes that the tests are good, but that many people don't use them for their intended purpose." Choice (C) refers to what the admissions officers do, not to what Sally believes they should do. Choices (B) and (D) refer to what Paul believes admissions officers should do, not to what they actually do.

Audio

4. How does the professor handle the disagreement?

Answer

(B) "Isn't this the basic disagreement: that Paul thinks the tests are bad in themselves, and Sally believes that the tests are good, but that many people don't use them for their intended purpose?" Choices (A) and (D) are not correct because Professor Ayers does not comment after he restates each student's position. Choice (C) is not mentioned and may not be concluded from information in this discussion.

Audio

5. Where did this discussion most probably take place?

Answer

(A) "Okay, class." From the reference to *class*, it must be concluded that this conversation took place in a classroom. Choices (B), (C), and (D) are not mentioned and may not be concluded from information in the discussion.

Talk Two

Audio

Narrator: Listen to part of a discussion in a linguistics class.

Baker: Since so many of you have asked me about how to learn a language, I thought it might be useful to take some class time today to discuss it. Betty, you speak several languages, don't you?

Betty: Yes, I speak Spanish and French.

Baker: And what helped you most in learning those languages?

Betty: What helped me most. . . . Well, I studied both languages in high school, and I'm still studying Spanish here at the university, but I think that travel has probably been the most help to me. You see, I've been lucky in that I've lived in Europe. Believe me, I didn't speak very well before I moved there.

Bill: You're right, Betty. After studying a language, practice is very useful. When you live in a country where the language is spoken, it's ideal. But, you know, sometimes it's difficult to make friends in a new place, even when the people are very friendly.

Betty: Yes, I know what you mean. Especially if you don't speak the language too well. I had some problems when I first moved to Europe.

Baker: And, of course, some people are shy.

Betty: That's true.

Bill: Professor Baker, whether or not I'm living in a country where the language is spoken, I always go to movies, and whenever I can, I watch TV or listen to the radio in the language I'm trying to learn.

Betty: Me too. And reading is another good way to learn. Books are good, but I think that newspapers and magazines are even better.

Baker: Probably the best way to learn is to combine all of these ideas: traveling, talking with people, going to movies, watching TV, listening to the radio, and reading books, newspapers and magazines. What do you think?

Betty: I agree with that, Professor Baker.

Bill: So do I. But I don't believe that it's possible to take advantage of practice opportunities without some knowledge of the language first.

Betty: Sure. First it's a good idea to study grammar, vocabulary . . .

Bill: . . . and listening, perhaps even reading.

Betty: Then practice is very, very helpful.

Audio

1. What do the speakers mainly discuss?

Answer

(D) "Since so many of you have asked me how to learn a language, I thought that it might be useful to take some class time to discuss it." Choices (A), (B), and (C) are mentioned as secondary themes that are used to develop the main theme of the talk, "learning a foreign language."

Audio

2. Why does Professor Baker begin the discussion by calling on Betty?

Answer

(C) "Betty, you speak several languages, don't you?" The shy person in Choice (A) is a reference to language learners, not to Betty. Choice (B) is true, but Betty mentions it after she is called on. Choice (D) is not mentioned and may not be concluded from information in this discussion.

Audio

3. What helped Betty most in learning Spanish?

Answer

(B) ". . . I think that travel has probably been the most helpful to me." Choice (C) refers to what Betty did before traveling. Choice (D) refers to what helped Bill, not Betty. Choice (A) is not mentioned and may not be concluded from information in the discussion.

Audio

4. What is Professor Baker's opinion?

Answer

(A) "Probably the best way to learn is to combine all of these ideas: traveling, talking with people, going to movies, watching TV, listening to the radio, and reading books, newspapers and magazines." Choice (B) is true, but incomplete. Choice (D) refers to Betty's opinion, not to Professor Baker's opinion. Choice (C) is not mentioned and may not be concluded from information in the discussion.

Audio

5. How can we best describe Professor Baker?

Answer

(B) Since Professor Baker encourages the students to express their opinions, it may be concluded that he is respectful of them. Choice (A) is not correct because Professor Baker rephrases the students' comments and combines them into a better answer. Choice (C) is not correct because the students interact informally without waiting to be called on. Choice (D) refers to Betty, not to Professor Baker.

EXERCISE 28: Interactive Lectures—Professor/Students 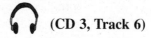 (CD 3, Track 6)

Talk One

Audio

Narrator: Listen to part of a seminar in an art class.

Stephens: Let me remind you that this is a seminar, so uh . . . I won't uh . . . I won't be lecturing. This is a discussion format, and that means that I expect you to respond to the reading assignments. No need to raise your hand. Just be moderately courteous about taking turns. Remember that uh . . . 30 percent of your grade is based on par . . . class participation. Okay? . . . Now, with that in mind, let's begin our discussion of Chapter 22 in the main textbook. What is *Pop Art*?

Julia: I'll start. Pop Art, as I understand it, was . . . a movement that began in, um, the early 60s when painters . . . I think it was mostly painters . . . began to use popular . . . I mean commercial objects . . . like bottles, comic strips, um . . . cigarette packages, and like that as . . . as subjects for their art.

Stephens: Okay. So I'll ask the obvious question: Why paint these objects . . . when they're everywhere?

Tom: Well, first, let me mention that, although there were several artists who were . . . part . . . who were associated with the Pop movement, it's uh . . . it's probably Andy Warhol whose paintings best represent it, and I uh . . . I believe Warhol had a response for that question. I think he said, "Everything is art. Everything is beautiful."

Stephens: Yes, he did say that. I'm glad you mentioned it. So let's focus on Warhol for a few minutes. There are some examples of his work on . . . let's see . . . on page 524 of your textbook . . . As you see, he painted enormous Campbell's soup cans, lines of Coca-Cola bottles, and rows of Martinson Coffee cans. Any ideas about these particular subjects?

Tom: Well, of course the story is that uh . . . that uh Warhol actually ate soup for lunch every day for twenty years, so when he decided to paint objects in the environment, then . . . then the soup can naturally came to mind. Do you think that's true, Dr. Stephens?

Stephens: Tom, it certainly is a widespread myth, but uh . . . probably closer to reality is the fact that Warhol was once a commercial artist and that it was a logical transition for him, personally, to paint products. He went from commercial ads to art, well, that gave expression to the same kinds of objects. But he painted people, too. Any thoughts on that?

Julia: Well, he painted faces, actually—huge images of the popular . . . the celebrities of the sixties. There were several of Marilyn Monroe and Elvis Presley.

Karen: And at least one of Jacqueline Kennedy. But . . . but I was thinking that they really weren't portraits in the strictest sense.

Stephens: That's interesting. What do you mean?

Karen: I'm not sure, but . . . besides the giant canvases . . . well . . . well the way that they were presented . . . it also had a commercial feel. I don't know . . . I'm not saying that too well.

Stephens: No, I think you're on to something. Do you mean perhaps that the people are commercialized in a sense, like a brand name?

Karen: Exactly. I think the book identified the subjects in the face series as um . . . as popular icons . . . that was it . . . of the 60s . . . so maybe their faces do have . . . commercial appeal.

Julia: Yes, and he wasn't always very . . . wasn't very flattering, was he?

Stephens: No, he wasn't. What did you think about the colors?

Julia: That's what I mean! Sometimes the colors are almost . . . psychedelic. Again, that's very retro . . . I mean . . . you know . . . very 60s.

Stephens: Let's go back to one of the Marilyn Monroe paintings in your book. Let me see . . . here it is. Turn to page 526. You can't see it very well here, but uh . . . on the original, the paint actually gives the impression of colored ink, and . . . and there's usually . . . often a black stencil over it, which produces a unique effect. See how the orange background contrasts with the yellow hair, and there's a pink and a . . . a purple tone on the face? Then there's this green eye shadow. And, to me, it looks like he stenciled the black over the . . . the flat surfaces of the face. It's not a lovely portrait. And the critics agreed with you, Julia. Some critics even called it grotesque. But uh . . . it is . . . absolutely original.

Tom: Original, but dated, don't you think? I mean, years from now, will . . . will anyone be eating Campbell's soup, or drinking Coca-Cola, or really, for that matter, uh . . . will anyone remember Marilyn Monroe?

Stephens: Interesting observation. So, Tom, you're saying that since Pop Art . . . since it depends on the popular culture, which by its very nature is uh . . . transient, you're asking . . . will the subject matter of the Pop Art movement doom its artists to . . . to temporary recognition?

Tom: Exactly. Which, I'm thinking, is really different from . . . well, unlike a painter who chooses to create landscapes, which don't change.

Audio

1. What is this session mainly about?

Answer

(B) "Although there were several artists who are associated with the Pop movement . . . it's . . . probably Andy Warhol whose paintings best represent it." Choices (A), (C), and (D) are mentioned as secondary themes that are used to develop the main theme of the lecture, "Andy Warhol's art."

Audio

2. According to the lecturer, why did Warhol paint objects in the environment?

Answer

(A) "Probably closer to reality is the fact that Warhol was once a commercial artist, and that it was a logical transition for him personally to go from commercial ads to art that gave expression to the same kinds of objects." Choice (C) refers to the story, rather than the fact. Choices (B) and (D) are not mentioned and may not be concluded from information in the lecture.

Audio

3. Whose faces did Warhol paint?

Answer

(A) (B) "There were several [faces] of Marilyn Monroe and Elvis Presley. . . ." Warhol also painted Jacqueline Kennedy, but John Kennedy in Choice (C) is not mentioned and may not be concluded from information in the lecture. There is also no mention of a self-portrait, as in Choice (D).

Audio

4. What problem does Tom mention?

Answer

(D) "The problem with Warhol is that unlike a painter who chooses to create landscapes, his subject matter is very dated. . . . Will the subject matter of the Pop Art movement doom its artists to temporary recognition?" Choices (A), (B), and (C) are not mentioned as problems.

Audio

5. Listen again to part of the talk.

Then answer the question.

"I mean, years from now, will . . . will anyone be eating Campbell's soup, or drinking Coca-Cola, or really, for that matter, uh . . . will anyone remember Marilyn Monroe?" "Interesting observation. So, Tom, you're saying that since Pop Art . . . since it depends on the popular culture, which by its very nature is, uh, transient, you're asking . . . will the subject matter of the Pop Art movement doom its artists to . . . to temporary recognition?"

Why does the professor say this:

"So, Tom, you're saying that since Pop Art . . . since it depends on the popular culture, which by its very nature is, uh, transient, you're asking . . . will the subject matter of the Pop Art movement doom its artists to . . . to temporary recognition?"

Answer

(D) Professors often restate a student's comment to improve or clarify it. In this case, Tom provides several examples, and Professor Stephens restates them by making a generalization. Choice (A) is not correct because it is the professor, not the student, who restates the comment. Choice (B) is not correct because the professor restates the student's idea without agreement or disagreement. Choice (C) is not correct because the professor restates the previous question. He does not answer the question.

Audio

6. Select a drawing that is done in the Andy Warhol style.

Answer

(C) The objects from the environment are typical of the subject matter in the Andy Warhol style. Choice (A) is a traditional portrait, unlike the huge faces that Warhol created. Choice (B) is a landscape, which does not represent popular culture.

Talk Two

Audio

Narrator: Listen to part of a lecture in an environmental science class. The professor is discussing the *web of life*.

Green: To review from yesterday's lecture, *ecology* is the study of organisms in relation to their environment. The total complex of relationships . . . is referred to as the *web of life*. Now, you'll remember that when the relationships don't change much from year to year . . . when they don't change, we observe a balance of nature. Today, we'll discuss what occurs when the balance of nature's disturbed, either . . . either by a geological change such as a change of climate . . . or . . . or a local agitation such as a fire, like the recent forest fire north of here. Now, after the balance of nature has been disturbed . . . when it's disturbed, a period of rehabilitation must occur. And the first life to appear has traditionally been called . . . pioneer flora and fauna. But, the pioneer life is temporary and soon replaced by other forms of life. In turn, these forms are . . . these forms are replaced by others. That is, a series of transitional life forms successively appears, preparing the environment for the forms that will replace them.

Mike: Excuse me, Dr. Green, would that be what the book refers to as *ecological succession*?

Green: It is. For example, after a forest fire, pioneer plants will appear, and . . . and they are usually herbs or ground cover. Now, soon they'll be replaced by shrubs. Shrubs will be replaced by trees. And so it goes in succession, which is where we get the term *ecological succession*. Now, until very recently, it was assumed that plants and animals would . . . form a climax community, and . . . and that's a final stage in the ecological succession, and that tended to be stable for a long time. So, in the case of the forest fire, when the appearance . . . when a permanent climax flora appeared, we would have assumed that the environment had finally stabilized in balance with the fauna, minerals, and water supply. And the theory was interesting, because a climax community . . . because it usually didn't have the same kinds of plants and animals as . . . as the community that had been prevalent before the balance of nature was disturbed. Now, what was essential to the concept of a climax was that . . . that the balance of nature permitted the community . . . to continue . . . in . . . in spite of other organic competition for the area. But the notion of a stable, symbiotically functioning community has been mostly abandoned by scientists. Currently, we believe that . . . that natural ecosystems are much too complex to be neatly organized into predictable stages with a final stable community. So what we can expect in the case of the fire is the . . . the emergence of patches of former landscapes, and probably . . . and these patches will be at different stages in the same local environment. Question?

Mike: So the patches are in different stages, and that would be . . . a *polyclimax* condition?

Green: That's exactly right, Mike. *Poly* means *many*, so *polyclimax* refers to adjoining ecosystems at different but mature stages. I believe it's explained as *dynamic equilibrium* in your text.

Mike: Thank you. That's very helpful.

Green: Janet?

Janet: Yes. I was wondering what your opinion was of that wildfire. You know, the one near here. In . . . in the book, it was mentioned that sometimes . . . that fire is now recognized . . . how did they say it? Fire is a natural part of uh . . . fire is a natural part of an ecosystem, and . . . and at least some experts have been quoted in news reports . . . that they feel fire-prevention strategies may have contributed to that disaster. So, um . . . do you agree with that?

Green: I do. That particular ecosystem had an enormous amount of undergrowth, and I think that it may have fueled the fire. Now, in my opinion, if we had purposely burned some of the undergrowth in what we call a *cool fire*, we would have removed the accumulation of brush that contributed to . . . to the destructive *hot fire* that destroyed more than . . . I think I read that it was 50,000 acres of wilderness . . . Yes?

Janet: Is a cool fire a controlled burn?

Green: Yes, it's referred to as a *controlled burn*. But back to your original question, I have to tell you that everyone wouldn't agree with my opinion. Critics call that policy the "let it burn" policy. Now, of course, many people have a . . . a . . . let's say a vested interest in fire suppression, because so many people have built their homes close to the natural environments, they don't want any fires started in their immediate vicinity. So, like your textbook indicates, it's a very controversial topic.

Audio
1. What is the main topic of today's lecture?
Answer
(D) "Today we will discuss what occurs when the balance of nature is disturbed, either by a geological change such as a change of climate, or a local agitation such as a fire." Choices (A), (B), and (C) are mentioned as secondary ideas that are used to develop the main idea, "a disturbance in the balance of nature."

Audio
2. How does the scientific community view the theory of a stable climax community?
Answer
(A) "But the notion of a stable, symbiotically functioning [climax] community has been mostly abandoned by scientists." Choice (B) is not correct because the professor says it was an interesting theory. Choice (C) refers to the terminology used in the textbook to describe the new theory, not the older stable climax theory. Choice (D) is not correct because it was *polyclimax* that replaced the stable climax theory.

Audio
3. According to the lecturer, why is pioneer life important?
Answer
(A) "The pioneer life is temporary and soon replaced by other forms of life . . . preparing the environment for the forms that will replace them." Choice (B) is not correct because it is temporary and soon replaced by other forms of life. Choices (C) and (D) are not correct because pioneer plants are replaced by shrubs and shrubs are replaced by trees.

Audio

4. What is Dr. Green's opinion of a *controlled burn*?

Answer

(A) "In my opinion, if we had purposely burned some of the undergrowth in what we call a *cool fire*, we would have removed the accumulation of brush that contributed to . . . to the destructive *hot fire* . . . It's [a cool fire] referred to as a *controlled burn*."

Choice (B) is not correct because the professor says he agrees with the book about fire-prevention strategies. Choice (C) is not correct because the professor admits that it is a very controversial topic and that everyone would not agree with his opinion. Choice (D) contradicts the fact the professor agrees with the news reports in which fire-prevention strategies were blamed for the disaster.

Audio

5. Listen again to part of the talk.

Then answer the question.

"That is, a series of transitional life forms successively appears, preparing the environment for the forms that will replace them."

"Excuse me, Dr. Green, would that be what the book refers to as *ecological succession?*"

Why did the student ask this question:

". . . would that be what the book refers to as *ecological succession?*"

Answer

(B) Professors encourage students to relate information from their textbooks to information in the lectures. In this case, the student is trying to understand the meaning of technical terms. Choice (D) is not correct because the student is polite and he asks a sincere question. Choices (A) and (C) are not mentioned and may not be concluded from information in the lecture.

Audio

6. The professor describes the process of *ecological succession* that occurs after the balance of nature has been disturbed. Summarize the process by putting the events in order.

Answer

(A) (D) (C) (B) "The first life to appear is called pioneer flora and fauna. The pioneer life is temporary and soon replaced by other forms of life . . . a series of transitional life forms successively appears. . . . The final stage . . . in transition tends to be stable. . . . It is called a *climax association*."

EXERCISE 29: Visual Lectures—Professor/Students   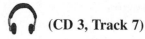 (CD 3, Track 7)

Talk One

Audio

Narrator: Listen to part of a lecture in an art class. The professor has been discussing the Art Nouveau school.

Professor:

By the last quarter of the nineteenth century, Louis Tiffany had begun experimenting with different methods of adding color to blown glass. Finally, he produced a unique, iridescent glass which he called Tiffany *favrile*. It was this glass that he shaped and pieced together with metals to form lamps, windows, and other objects of art. This is a typical example of a Tiffany lamp. Look at the way that the pieces are fitted together. You've probably seen one or a reproduction of one at one time or another.

From 1890 to about 1920, Tiffany's favrile glass became very popular throughout the world. It regained popularity in the 1960s, and is still prized by many glass collectors today.

In addition, Tiffany created floral jewelry that was considered very stylish at the turn of the century. Rebelling against current fashion that dictated the use of precious stones, Tiffany began working with new materials, creating symbolic, dramatic forms. As a member of the Art Nouveau movement, he tried to create new and unusual pieces, with delicate designs and curved lines.

Although his name is associated with glass and jewelry today, Tiffany was probably best known during his lifetime for the interior designs that he created. It was Tiffany who was commissioned to design the altar in the Cathedral of Saint John the Divine in New York City, and to redecorate the reception rooms in the White House during the administration of President Chester Arthur. The spectacular glass curtain at the National Theater in Mexico City was perhaps his crowning achievement.

His estate on Long Island was filled with beautiful furnishings and decorations, many of them designed by Tiffany, himself. When it was sold, the proceeds were transferred to the Louis Tiffany Foundation for Art Students to provide scholarships for aspiring artists. The jewelry store on Fifth Avenue in Manhattan that his father had founded, still bears the name Tiffany's, and it is still considered a highly fashionable shop for wealthy clientele.

Audio

1. What is the main purpose of this lecture?

Answer

(B) Since most of the information is about Louis Tiffany's work, it must be concluded that his work is the main purpose of the lecture. Choices (A), (C), and (D) are mentioned as secondary themes that are used to develop the main theme of the lecture, "the work of Louis Tiffany."

Audio

2. What characterized Tiffany's jewelry?

Answer

(D) ". . . Tiffany created floral jewelry . . . with delicate designs and curved lines." Choice (A) refers to the material Tiffany used in his lamps and windows. Choice (B) is not correct because Tiffany rebelled against the use of precious stones. Choice (C) is not correct because TIffany created new and unusual pieces, not traditional designs.

Audio

3. How did Tiffany help aspiring artists?

Answer

(C) ". . . the proceeds [from his estate] were transferred to the Louis Tiffany Foundation for Art Students to provide scholarships for aspiring artists." Choices (A), (B), and (D) are not mentioned and may not be concluded from information in the lecture.

Audio

4. For which interior design was Tiffany NOT commissioned?

Answer

(D) "It was Tiffany who was commissioned to design the altar in the Cathedral of Saint John the Divine . . . and to redecorate the reception rooms in the White House. . . . The spectacular glass curtain at the National Theater in Mexico City was perhaps his crowning achievement." Choice (D) refers to the area where Tiffany's father founded a jewelry store.

Audio

5. Select the example of a Tiffany *favrile* design.

Answer

(B) ". . . he produced a unique, iridescent glass which he called Tiffany *favrile*." Choice (B) is an example of Tiffany favrile glass. Choice (A) is an example of carved furniture, not favrile glass. Choice (C) is a piece of pottery, not favrile glass.

Talk Two

Audio

Narrator: Listen to part of a lecture in a botany class. The professor will discuss cacti.

Professor:

The cactus is one example of the way that plants adapt to extreme conditions of climate. A cactus like this one has the same basic structure as all other plants, but the function of leaves is carried out by the stems and branches of the plant.

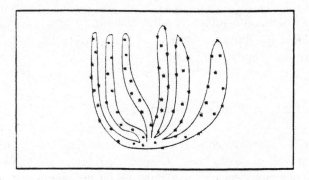

Here are some more examples of the most familiar cacti—the barrel, the Saguaro, and the prickly pear. As you see, they all have stems, branches, or spines, but no leaves. In spring, they may have beautiful blossoms.

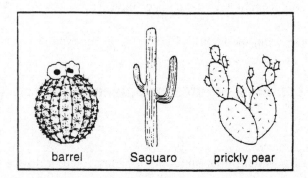

barrel   Saguaro   prickly pear

It is assumed that the predecessors of the modern cactus had leaves, but that during millions of years of changes in the climate, resulting in desert conditions, the cactus gradually adapted to the hotter, drier environment. The roots spread out and began to grow closer to the surface so that water could be absorbed more quickly. The roots and spongy or hollow stem of the cactus began to serve as a storage container for water, and the outer layer of the plant developed thick, waxy walls to prevent the water from draining out. Some varieties of cactus actually have ribbed folds that expand and contract depending on the volume of water stored inside the stem.

Although there are a few members of the cactus family that retain their leaves, in most cacti, they have evolved into spines, needles, or hairs to protect the plant in areas where little green vegetation is available for foraging animals. In cacti without leaves, the stems and branches carry out the nutritive functions that usually take place in the thin-leafed surfaces of other plants.

Audio

1. What is the lecture mainly about?

Answer

(A) "A cactus . . . has the same basic structure as all other plants . . ." Choices (B), (C), and (D) are mentioned as secondary ideas that are used to support the main idea of the lecture, "The structure of the cactus."

Audio

2. What is assumed about cactus plants millions of years ago?

Answer

(B) "It is assumed that the predecessors of the modern cactus had leaves, but . . . the cactus gradually adapted to the hotter, drier environment." Choices (A), (C), and (D) are not mentioned and may not be concluded from information in the lecture.

Audio

3. According to the lecturer, why have cacti developed spines and needles?

Answer

(C) ". . . leaves . . . have evolved into spines, needles or hairs to protect the plant in areas where little green vegetation is available for foraging animals." Choices (A), (B), and (D) are not mentioned as reasons why the cacti developed spines and needles.

Audio

4. Where is the nutritive function of the cactus carried out?

Answer

(C) "In cacti without leaves, the stems and branches carry out the nutritive functions that usually take place in the thin-leafed surfaces of other plants." Choice (A) refers to the place where the nutritive function of thin-leafed plants, not cacti, takes place. Choice (B) is not mentioned and may not be concluded from information in the lecture. Choice (D) refers to the place where water is stored.

Audio

5. Select the Saguaro cactus from among the choices pictured.

Answer

(C) As shown in the visuals from the lecture, Choice (A) is an example of a prickly pear. Choice (B) is an example of a barrel cactus.

EXERCISE 30: Visual Lectures—Professor/Students 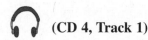 (CD 4, Track 1)

Talk One

Audio

Narrator: Listen to part of a lecture in an anthropology class. The professor is preparing the students for a field trip.

Professor:

Today the lecture's about petroglyphs, but before we begin, we . . . let's go over our plans for the field trip. As you'll remember, next week we'll be meeting in the parking lot of . . . the lot outside this building . . . at eight o'clock in the morning. The bus will be leaving by eight-fifteen so, um, we can be at the petroglyph site by ten o'clock. A heads up. Please wear comfortable shoes because we'll be doing quite a lot of walking. And the area at the site . . . it's laid out with paths . . . so we won't actually be doing any climbing. In fact, climbing on the rocks is against the law since, um, since the area's a protected site. But it's a rather long walk from the bus parking area over there to the site, and . . . and then we'll be walking the paths to view the petroglyphs, so you'll be glad you've got comfortable shoes on.

That said, let's begin our discussion of . . . petroglyphs. What are they? Well, the general definition's very broad, including any symbols that have been carved or . . . or hammered into rocks. The term "petroglyph" comes from two Greek words: *petro*, which means "rock," and *glyph*, which means "carving." But, um . . . why were they carved in the first place? For a variety of reasons really. Some petroglyphs simply appear to mark a trail or identify the presence of water or . . . or good hunting grounds, but many petroglyphs record important events in the history of the people, or they invoke some uh . . . magical presence in religious ceremonies.

The major culture in the area that we'll be exploring on our field trip is, uh, the Hohokam . . . who, uh, probably lived at the site from about A.D. 300 to A.D. 1450. Since there are no current inhabitants, it's . . . it's difficult to interpret the symbols on the rock art, but their modern descendants have, uh . . . the descendants of the Hohokam have provided some insights. In addition, uh, some of the symbolism is shared by many cultures and, therefore, we're able to . . . we can interpret a few of the symbols that we see there, um, either by researching other similar symbols or by relying on . . . interpretations by current cultural groups with, uh, with similar inscriptions.

Okay. There are four basic types of symbols common to the area we're going to explore . . . which I've drawn on the handout . . . the one I passed out at the beginning of class. So let's refer to the first drawing, which looks like this. As you can see, it's a figure of a person.

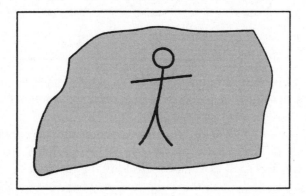

You'll see these on . . . on many of the rocks. Some of them have . . . illustrate activities that may have been . . . significant to the Hohokam. Drawings of this kind are called *anthropomorphs*.

The second set of symbols . . . and these are called *zoomorphs* . . . are animal figures. S . . . Some of the more common zoomorphs are deer, sheep, um . . . snakes, lizards, coyotes, and, um, birds . . . all of which are still found in the area. But besides the obvious allusion to a successful hunt or um . . . when they are drawn close to . . . close to other drawings, like a reference to a historic event, then these zoomorphs might also represent clans or family groups that are named for animals. Look at this deer.

Here's what I mean. It could be a reference to a family that . . . a family that had taken the deer as the symbol for their clan.

So . . . a third set of symbols—and again I am referring to the handout—these are various representations of circles, especially concentric circles. In most cultures, symbols like . . . like this . . . represent the sun, which usually figures, uh, prominently in religious ceremonies. Here are some . . . several examples.

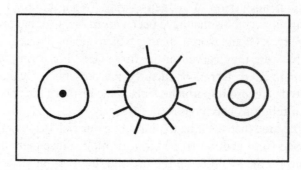

Finally, I want you to watch for spirals like these.

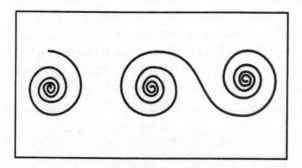

The spiral is thought to be related to water, which . . . which can symbolize life or migration, but more often is interpreted as a spiritual symbol. . . . Perhaps a representation of the emergence . . . of the first people from, uh, the spiritual world to this place.

Let me also mention that—when we go—you may see some crosses carved into some of the rocks, um, which are frankly very difficult to interpret. Some scholars believe that, um, the cross could . . . may represent the important stars such as Venus or the Morning Star, but . . . but other scholars remind us that many missionaries passed through the desert and may have carved the symbol of the cross on the rocks a thousand years or more after the . . . the original carvings were made. Which reminds me, just a word about the site that we're going to visit. . . . This entire area has a . . . highly significant spiritual meaning to the Native Americans, so . . . so I expect our group to treat it as a sacred place. You can bring a camera if you wish since there's no objection to our taking photographs, but we should be respectful. Any questions?

Audio
1. What is the main purpose of this lecture?
Answer
(B) "Today the lecture is about petroglyphs." Choices (A), (C), and (D) are mentioned as secondary themes that are used to develop the main purpose of the lecture, to introduce "common petroglyphs."

Audio
2. What are *petroglyphs*?
Answer
(B) ". . . the general definition [of petroglyphs] is very broad, including any symbols that have been carved or hammered into rocks." Choices (A), (C), and (D) are not mentioned in the definition of petroglyphs.

Audio

3. How are anthropologists able to interpret the symbols?

Answer

(B) (C) "Since there are no current inhabitants, it is difficult to interpret the symbols on the rock art, but their descendants have provided some insights. In addition, some of the symbolism is shared by many cultures . . ." Choice (A) is not probable because the lecturer does not mention it. Choice (D) is not correct because the petroglyphs sometimes represent ideas such as life or migration as well as clan names and spiritual symbols.

Audio

4. What might be represented by a *zoomorph*?

Answer

(B) (C) ". . . besides the obvious allusion to a successful hunt or, when shown with other drawings, the reference to an historic event, these zoomorphs might also represent clans or family groups of the same name." Choices (A) and (D) are not mentioned in reference to zoomorphs.

Audio

5. Listen again to part of the talk.
    Then answer the question.
    "But, um . . . why were they carved in the first place? For a variety of reasons really. Some petroglyphs simply appear to mark a trail or identify the presence of water or . . . or good hunting grounds, but many petroglyphs record important events in the history of the people, or they invoke some, uh, magical presence in religious ceremonies."
    Why did the professor say this: "But, um . . . why were they carved in the first place?"

Answer

(B) Professors often ask and answer rhetorical questions. In this case, she is asking a question that she answers in the following statement. Choices (C) and (D) are not correct because she continues her lecture without pausing long enough to invite student responses. Choice (A) is not mentioned and may not be concluded from information in the lecture.

Audio

6. Select the petroglyph that is a spiritual symbol of life.

Answer

(A) "The spiral is thought to be related to water, which can symbolize life . . ." Choice (B) is the symbol for the sun, which figures prominently in religious ceremonies. Choice (C) is an anthropomorph, which is a figure of a person.

Talk Two

Audio

Narrator: Listen to part of a lecture in an astronomy class. The professor will discuss comets.

Professor:
    Comets are small bodies from the outer solar system that are characterized by gaseous emissions and consist of a solid nucleus, a cloudy atmosphere, which is called the *coma*, and a tail. Let me say that again. Comets are small bodies from the outer solar system that are characterized by gaseous emissions and consist of a solid nucleus, a cloudy atmosphere, which is called the *coma*, and a tail. This is an example of a typical comet.

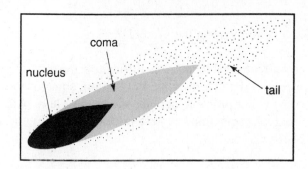

You can't really see it in this diagram, but, uh, the nucleus is made of ice with rocks and dust particles encrusted in it. When it's far from the Sun, the nucleus of a comet may be completely frozen, and most are quite small. But, as . . . as a comet approaches the sun, some of the ice on the surface vaporizes, and, uh, the gas and dust particles that were embedded in the ice of the nucleus . . . are released and blown back by the solar wind . . . and that's what forms a hydrogen atmosphere, and, uh, the tail of the comet. It's important to note that the tails of comets always point away from the Sun because, uh, the solar wind pushes them . . . pushes them back.

Most comets have a nucleus . . . that is less than, say, a body ten miles in diameter, but the comas can extend out nearly one million miles. And . . . and some exceptional tails have been known to trail 100 million miles behind their comets.

We classify comets as, uh, either short-period comets or long-period comets, depending on how long they take to orbit the Sun. And you may want to write this down. Short-period comets require fewer than 200 years, whereas long-period comets need more than 200 years. . . . The key number there is 200 years. So, when you do the math, you see that, uh, short-period comets tend to recur often enough to be . . . well, anticipated by the scientific community. For example, Edmund Halley used Newton's law of gravitation to . . . to calculate a comet's seventy-six year orbit and predicted that it would return in 1758. When it appeared on schedule, the comet was named Halley's comet, and as many of you know, it passed near Earth on schedule in 1986, and, uh, when we add 76 years, we should see it again in 2061. Well, maybe *you* will even if I don't.

A little more on, uh, on short-period comets. They're nearer the Sun, so consequently, they're heated and . . . and lose their ice by a process called sublimation. So, their supply of gas may be depleted after only a few hundred revolutions . . . leaving them without . . . devoid of the coma and tail . . . and all but invisible. But, let me back up a minute. What I'm really saying is that, uh, the gaseous envelope burns up, leaving only a nucleus, which is virtually impossible to see.

As far as we can tell, the short-period comets have their origin in a belt of comets that . . . that lies just beyond the orbit of Pluto. And, uh, since they are constantly burning up, in maybe less than a million years, all of the short-period comets . . . that's the short-period comets we're talking about now . . . they would have disappeared if it hadn't been for something called *capture*, a process whereby the planets, especially Jupiter, attract comets that have originated further away, replacing those that are, uh, that are decaying, and maintaining the population of the short-period group at, uh, at a more or less stable level. By the way, capture doesn't usually occur on the first pass, but may happen after many passes. And . . . and eventually, the comets that have been captured . . . they detach themselves and start moving toward the Sun, like other short-period comets.

Okay, let's just touch on the long-period comets now. We think that the long-period comets come from a cloud of comets one thousand times further away than Pluto. One thousand times. Consequently, they may be seen only once in . . . in recorded history. It's also worth thinking about that . . . that most of these comets travel in, uh, elongated orbits that . . . that cross the circular orbits of the planets. Thus, the possibility of collision does exist at the points where the orbits intersect. Here. . . . Look at this drawing, which . . . which shows the orbits of four planets with several comets intersecting them. See what I mean? Where they cross?

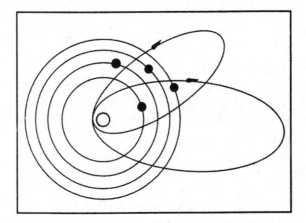

Oh, yes, another interesting point. Some of the craters on the satellites of, uh, of the outer planets . . . are probably evidence of past cometary collisions. In fact, the *Galileo* spacecraft on its way to Jupiter got some fantastic photographs of impacts on Jupiter's right side. And . . . and . . . even the craters on Earth's moon could have been caused by comets.

Audio
1. What is the main purpose of this lecture?
Answer
(B) Most of the information in the lecture is about the structure and nature of comets. Choices (A), (C), and (D) are mentioned as secondary themes that are used to develop the two main themes of the lecture, "the structure and the nature of comets."

Audio
2. What causes the tail of a comet to point away from the Sun?
Answer
(B) "The tails of comets always point away from the Sun because the solar wind pushes them back." Choice (A) refers to the way that we classify comets, not to the reason that the tail points away from the Sun. Choice (C) refers to the cloudy atmosphere that projects out from the nucleus. Choice (D) refers to the origin of comets, not to the reason the tails of comets point away from the Sun.

Audio
3. What is the difference between a short-period comet and a long-period comet?
Answer
(D) "We classify comets as either short-period comets or long-period comets, depending on how long they take to orbit the Sun." Choice (A) refers to the difference between comets and planets, not to the difference between types of comets. Choices (B) and (C) are not mentioned as factors that differentiate between comets.

Audio
4. What is *capture*?
Answer
(B) ". . . *capture*, a process whereby the planets . . . attract comets that have originated further away [long-period], replacing those [short-period] that are decaying." Choice (A) is not correct because the comets eventually detach themselves. Choices (C) and (D) are occasionally true, but neither is a definition of *capture*.

Audio

5. Listen again to part of a talk.

    Then answer the question.

    "Comets are small bodies from the outer solar system that are characterized by gaseous emissions and consist of a solid nucleus, a cloudy atmosphere, which is called the *coma*, and a tail. Let me say that again. Comets are small bodies from the outer solar system that are characterized by gaseous emissions, and consist of a solid nucleus, a cloudy atmosphere, which is called the *coma*, and a tail."

    Why does the man say this:

    "Let me say that again."

Answer

(A) Professors often tell students that they are repeating information as a signal for them to write it down. Choice (B) is not correct because he repeats it in exactly the same words. Choice (C) is not correct because he does not suggest that students pay attention. He simply repeats a definition. Choice (D) is not correct because students are not interacting with the professor in class.

Audio

6. Identify the orbit of a comet.

Answer

(B) "Most comets travel in elongated orbits that cross the circular orbits of the planets." Choice (A) refers to the orbit of a planet, not a comet. Choice (C) is not mentioned and may not be concluded from information in the lecture.

Evaluation of Speaking—General Topics

Talks on general topics can be evaluated by referring to the checklist printed below and the rubric on page 566. Examples of level 4 talks for Exercises 31–32 follow.

NO ⇨ ⇨ ⇨ YES
0   1   2   3   4

- ✓ The talk answers the topic question.

- ✓ The point of view or position is clear.

- ✓ The talk is direct and well-organized.

- ✓ The sentences are logically connected to each other.

- ✓ Details and examples support the main idea.

- ✓ The speaker expresses complete thoughts.

- ✓ The meaning is easy for the listener to comprehend.

- ✓ A wide range of vocabulary is used.

- ✓ There are only minor errors in grammar and idioms.

- ✓ The talk is within a range of 100–150 words.

Speaking

Narrator 2: This is the script for the speaking exercises. During each exercise, you will respond to a speaking question. You may take notes as you listen. The reading passages and the questions are printed in the book, but most of the directions will be spoken.

EXERCISE 31: General Topics—Personal Experiences (CD 4, Track 2)

Topic One

Audio

Narrator 2:

Exercise 31, Topic One. Listen for a question about a familiar topic. After you hear the question, you have 15 seconds to prepare and 45 seconds to record your answer.

Narrator 1:

What are the qualities that you look for in a best friend? Describe a friend, and explain what influences you to choose this person as a best friend. Be sure to include specific details and examples in your answer.

Narrator 2:

Please prepare your answer after the beep.

Beep

[Preparation Time: 15 seconds]

Narrator 2:

Please begin speaking after the beep.

Beep

[Recording Time: 45 seconds]

Example Notes

best friend
   neighbor
   grade school
qualities
   high moral values—honest + reliable
   same interests—reading + music
reason
   help each other
   spend time together

Example Speaking Answer

My best friend's also my neighbor so we've known each other since we were in grade school. The qualities that I like in her are . . . high moral values and also we like to do the same things. Her family's taught her to be honest and reliable. Um . . . so I trust her because I know that she'll tell the truth, and . . . and she'll be there for me. Also, we both like to read and we enjoy music, so we have a good time going to bookstores and concerts or . . . or just listening to music. Um . . . the reason that I think these qualities are important is because . . . best friends should help each other and enjoy spending time together, and a person with good values can . . . you can trust to help you, and if you have common interests, you'll enjoy doing the same things.

Beep

Topic Two

Audio
Narrator 2:
Exercise 31, Topic Two. Listen for a question about a familiar topic. After you hear the question, you have 15 seconds to prepare and 45 seconds to record your answer.

Narrator 1:
How do you like to spend your leisure time? Choose an activity and explain why you enjoy participating in it. Be sure to include specific details and examples in your answer.

Narrator 2:
Please prepare your answer after the beep.

Beep

[Preparation Time: 15 seconds]

Narrator 2:
Please begin speaking after the beep.

Beep

[Recording Time: 45 seconds]

Example Notes
volleyball
   exercise
   interact with friends
     healthy way
     team—travel
   scholarship

Example Speaking Answer
One of the activities that I enjoy the most is playing volleyball. Um . . . I like it because it . . . it gives me the opportunity to get exercise, uh, and to interact with my friends . . . in a healthy way. Um . . . I like to be part of a team, and sometimes we travel to other cities, uh, to compete. And this gives my friends and me a chance to see other places and meet new people. But, um, the reason that I'm spending so much of my leisure time playing volleyball is because I'm a good player, and, um, I hope that I can improve my game enough to earn a volleyball scholarship from a college. My coach says I have a good chance if I work hard.

Beep

EXERCISE 32: General Topics—Opinions

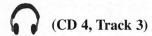 (CD 4, Track 3)

Topic One

Audio

Narrator 2:

Exercise 32, Topic One. Listen for a question that asks your opinion about a familiar topic. After you hear the question, you have 15 seconds to prepare and 45 seconds to record your answer.

Narrator 1:

Some teachers encourage competition among their students. Others help students learn how to collaborate and study in groups. Which approach do you think is better for learning and why do you think so? Be sure to use specific reasons and examples to support your opinion.

Narrator 2:

Please prepare your answer after the beep.

Beep

[Preparation Time: 15 seconds]

Narrator 2:

Please begin speaking after the beep.

Beep

[Recording Time: 45 seconds]

Example Notes

Teachers should help students collaborate because
    employment—teams and committees
    biographies—successful people collaborate
    business and industry—win-win situation

Example Speaking Answer

I think teachers should help students learn how to study in groups because after students leave school, they'll have to rely on collaboration in order to succeed. Um . . . teams and committees get the job done in most employment settings. There are very few positions in which the responsibility and the credit for a project belong to one individual. In the biographies of successful people, they . . . it's clear that they owe their success to others, and . . . and that they've had to collaborate in order to achieve it. And, competition implies that, uh, someone must lose in order for another to win, and the current thinking in business and industry is to try to work out a win-win situation, and that means that all parties have to collaborate.

Beep

Topic Two

Audio

Narrator 2:

Exercise 32, Topic Two. Listen for a question that asks your opinion about a familiar topic. After you hear the question, you have 15 seconds to prepare and 45 seconds to record your answer.

Narrator 1:

Some people cope with stress by exercising. Others talk with family or friends. How do you handle stressful situations? Be sure to use specific reasons and examples to support your opinion.

Narrator 2:

Please prepare your answer after the beep.

Beep

[Preparation Time: 15 seconds]

Narrator 2:

Please begin speaking after the beep.

Beep

[Recording Time: 45 seconds]

Example Notes

cope—depending on why I'm upset
   situation I can do something about—talk + express feelings
   part of life—long walks
      rhythm + fresh air
      clear mind + calm down

Example Speaking Answer

I use several methods to cope with stress depending on why I'm feeling upset. If it's a situation I can do something about, I try to talk with the people involved. For example, when I'm angry with my friend, I'll tell him so, um . . . and I'll try to resolve the problem with him directly. I feel better—less stressed—when I express my feelings. But sometimes stressful things happen that you can't really do much about. For example, when I have a lot to do at school, it's just part of life. So, when that happens, then I take long walks. I'm not sure whether it's the rhythm of the walking or maybe the fresh air, but I do know that it always helps me clear my mind and calm down so, uh, I can go back to the stressful situation again, without feeling so out of control.

Beep

Evaluation of Speaking—Campus and Academic Topics

Talks on campus and academic topics can be evaluated by referring to the checklist printed below and the rubric on page 566. Examples of Level 4 talks for Exercises 33–40 follow.

NO ⇨ ⇨ ⇨ YES
0   1   2   3   4

✓ The talk answers the topic question.

✓ There are only minor inaccuracies in the content.

✓ The talk is direct and well-organized.

✓ The sentences are logically connected to each other.

✓ Details and examples support the main idea.

✓ The speaker expresses complete thoughts.

✓ The meaning is easy for the listener to comprehend.

✓ A wide range of vocabulary is used.

✓ The speaker paraphrases, using his or her own words.

✓ The speaker credits the lecturer with wording when necessary.

✓ There are only minor errors in grammar and idioms.

✓ The talk is within a range of 100–150 words.

EXERCISE 33: Campus Situations—Connections

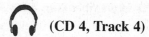 **(CD 4, Track 4)**

Topic One

Audio

Narrator 2:

Exercise 33, Topic One. Read a short passage and listen to a talk on the same topic. Then listen for a question about them. After you hear the question, you have 30 seconds to prepare and 60 seconds to record your answer.

Narrator 1:

The administration at City College is considering a proposal for an accelerated bachelor's degree program. Read the notice from a poster on campus. You have 45 seconds to complete it (refer to page 64). Please begin reading now.

[Reading Time: 45 seconds]

Narrator 1:

Now listen to a student who is speaking to an advisor. She is expressing her opinion about the new program.

Woman student:

First, I'd like you to know that I probably qualify for the accelerated program because I'm an honors student, but I'm not going to apply because I don't agree with the plan. You see, the idea is to select some students for special treatment, and I don't think that's fair. If you limit the classes to twenty students each, then the big lecture classes for the rest of the students will just have to get bigger and more impersonal than they already are. Look, I'm already accelerating my program by taking extra classes every term. Students don't need a new program to do that. Besides, it will cost money, and that always means higher tuition and fees.

Narrator 1:

The student expresses her opinion about the college's plans for an accelerated three-year degree program. Summarize her opinion and the reasons she gives for having that opinion.

Narrator 2:

Please prepare your answer after the beep.

Beep

[Preparation Time: 30 seconds]

Narrator 2:

Please begin speaking after the beep.

Beep

[Recording Time: 60 seconds]

Example Notes

special treatment unfair
   regular classes bigger to limit accelerated
not necessary
   take more courses every term
cost → higher tuition + fees

Example Speaking Answer

The woman feels that the accelerated program is unfair because the large lecture classes—the ones for the students who aren't admitted to the program, I mean the new program—those classes will probably be even larger in order to limit the number of students in the accelerated classes to twenty. She's also concerned that the accelerated program will be expensive to administer, and the additional cost could result in, uh, in an increase in tuition for all the students. Um . . . she also points out that it isn't necessary to create an accelerated program for students to complete their degrees in three years because . . . because she's already doing that by taking more than the usual number of classes every term.

Beep

Topic Two

Audio
Narrator 2:
Exercise 33, Topic Two. Read a short passage and listen to a talk on the same topic. Then listen for a question about them. After you hear the question, you have 30 seconds to prepare and 60 seconds to record your answer.

Narrator 1:
The administration at State University is considering a proposal to close the dorms during spring break. Read the notice from the campus newspaper. You have 45 seconds to complete it (refer to page 65). Please begin reading now.

[Reading Time: 45 seconds]

Narrator 1:
Now listen to a student who is speaking at the meeting. He is expressing his opinion about the new program.

Man student:
Well, I'm all for a plan that will help the university save money, but not like this. When we sign our dorm contracts, the university agrees to provide us with a home, and it isn't right to tell us that we can't stay in our home over the break if we choose to. Besides, we keep some valuable possessions in our rooms, like computers and audio equipment. I live in Norman Hall, and I don't want someone else living in my room. Do I have to move all my stuff out or do I just hope that the person who is staying there won't bother it? I don't think that the university has thought this through.

Narrator 1:
The student expresses his opinion about the proposal for closing the dorms over spring break. Summarize his opinion and the reasons he gives for having that opinion.

Narrator 2:
Please prepare your answer after the beep.

Beep

[Preparation Time: 30 seconds]

Narrator 2:
Please begin speaking after the beep.

Beep

[Recording Time: 60 seconds]

Example Notes
should be able to stay
   dorm contracts→home
   Norman Hall—valuable possessions = computers + audio

Example Speaking Answer
The man thinks that students should be able to stay in their dorm rooms over spring break if they choose to. He argues that the dorm students have a contract with the university. He also says that, um, the students consider the dorm their home, and . . . and they should be able to stay home during a break if they want to. Um, his strongest argument is probably that the students in Norman Hall would have to let strangers stay in their dorm rooms over the break, so um, they would either have to move their valuables out, or . . . or they would have to trust the person staying in their rooms not to damage their computers and audio equipment. So . . . he doesn't think that the university has considered all the potential problems.

Beep

Exercise 34: Campus Situations—More Connections

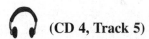 (CD 4, Track 5)

Topic One

Audio
Narrator 2:
Exercise 34, Topic One. Read a short passage and listen to a conversation on the same topic. Then listen for a question about them. After you hear the question, you have 30 seconds to prepare and 60 seconds to record your answer.

Narrator 1:
The administration at City College has decided to shorten the hours for on-site registration. Read the notice that students received. You have 45 seconds to complete it (refer to page 66). Please begin reading now.

[Reading Time: 45 seconds]

Narrator 1:
Now listen to a conversation between two students. The man is expressing his opinion about the change.

Man:	I think registration is going to be worse than ever.
Woman:	Oh, maybe not. A lot of people will just use the Internet to register online.
Man:	I won't. And a lot of other people won't either. For one thing, the web site keeps going down whenever there's heavy use, and there will be during registration week.
Woman:	That's true, but it's still better than standing around waiting your turn at all those tables in the gym.
Man:	Okay, but what about the problems that you can't work out online? Like the professor's signature for an override when there are too many students in the class? If you register on-site, the professor's right there to do it.
Woman:	That's true. And sometimes the advisors can help.
Man:	Right, they can keep you from taking the wrong course. But the real problem is going to be the long lines. If people have to register in three days instead of five, it's going to be more crowded than ever. It was just getting manageable because of the Internet option.

Narrrator 1:

The man expresses his opinion about the changes in the registration procedure. Report his opinion and explain the reasons he gives for having that opinion.

Narrator 2:

Please prepare your answer after the beep.

Beep

[Preparation Time: 30 seconds]

Narrator 2:

Please begin speaking after the beep.

Beep

[Recording Time: 60 seconds]

Example Notes

registration worse
   heavy use → web site goes down
   problems can't work out online
      professor's signature for override
      advisor for wrong course
   crowded
      long lines
      three days instead of five

Example Speaking Answer

The man thinks that the changes in registration will cause problems for the students. The university claims that students will be able to register online, but the man won't use that option because the web site is unreliable during peak use, um, like a registration period. He also maintains that there are problems that require a professor's signature, for example, when a student wants permission to register for a class that's already full. That can't be done on the computer. And he says that it's helpful for students to see their advisors to be sure they're signing up for the right courses. Um . . . but his biggest concern is that the three-day registration schedule on site is going to be even more crowded than in the past because the same number of people will be trying to register in a . . . a shorter time frame.

Beep

Topic Two

Audio

Narrator 2:

Exercise 34, Topic Two. Read a short passage and listen to a conversation on the same topic. Then listen for a question about them. After you hear the question, you have 30 seconds to prepare and 60 seconds to record your answer.

Narrator 1:

The fall career fair is being planned. Read the notice that appeared in the campus newspaper. You have 45 seconds to complete it (refer to page 67). Please begin reading now.

[Reading Time: 45 seconds]

Narrator 1:
Now listen to a conversation between two students. The woman is expressing her opinion about the fair.

Man: I can't decide whether to go to the career fair.

Woman: Well, I'm going to go. I missed it last year, but I was just a junior. Now that I'm a senior, I'm serious about finding a job.

Man: Yeah, but there will be so many other people trying to talk to the representatives, all at the same time. Maybe it's not worth it.

Woman: Look, you have to, you know, make an impression. I'm working really hard on my resume, and I'm going to wear a suit, even if it is Saturday. I think this is an opportunity to stand out from the crowd. And besides that, where else can you find people from 100 companies in the same room? I'm saving a lot of work later by deciding which companies *I* really want to work for.

Man: You mean, you won't send applications to companies that don't impress *you.*

Woman: Right. But probably the best reason to go is because my friend Carla got her job at a company that interviewed her at the career fair last year. It works.

Narrator 1:
The woman expresses her opinion about the career fair. Report her opinion and explain the reasons that she gives for having that opinion.

Narrator 2:
Please prepare your answer after the beep.

Beep

[Preparation Time: 30 seconds]

Narrator 2:
Please begin speaking after the beep.

Beep

[Recording Time: 60 seconds]

Example Notes
woman going to fair
   senior
   serious about job
make impression
   resume
   suit
100 companies
   deciding which companies
friend got job at fair last year

Example Speaking Answer
The woman has a very positive opinion about the career fair because she's a senior and she's a serious candidate for a position, and she thinks that by presenting a good resume and dressing well, she'll make a good impression on the recruiters, which will give her an edge on the competition. She also points out that it's a good opportunity to form opinions about the companies—the companies that participate in the fair. She mentions that there are 100 companies participating, and this will give her a chance to

talk to a lot of representatives. Um . . . after the fair, she'll only pursue positions with the companies that she chooses, based on her conversations. She says that her friend interviewed at the career fair last year, and was hired by one of the companies, so she knows that it's possible to get a job by attending the fair, and that's probably the best reason for her favorable opinion.

Beep

EXERCISE 35: Academic Content—Connections

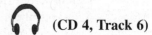 (CD 4, Track 6)

Topic One

Audio
Narrator 2:
Exercise 35, Topic One. Read a short passage and listen to a lecture on the same topic. Then listen for a question about them. After you hear the question, you have 30 seconds to prepare and 60 seconds to record your answer.

Narrator 1:
Now read the passage about a village. You have 45 seconds to complete it (refer to page 68).
Please begin reading now.

[Reading Time: 45 seconds]

Narrator 1:
Now listen to part of a lecture in an anthropology class. The professor is talking about an academic village.

Professor:
Thomas Jefferson was probably the first to refer to a college campus as an "academic village." This term seems appropriate because the campus that Jefferson created when he designed the University of Virginia included all of the qualities that are found in the definition of a traditional village. His plan was realized in the shape of a large rectangle. It featured a grassy lawn with the rotunda library at the center, and ten pavilions along two sides of the lawn, each to house the classrooms for one branch of learning. Behind the pavilions, he created formal gardens with another set of buildings on each side to serve as residences and dining halls. Quite soon, businesses grew up around the periphery of the rectangle to support all manner of basic services as well as to provide areas for social and educational exchange.

It is interesting to reflect on the impression that the classical architecture and the balanced pattern of the campus may have had on the self-concept of the students and faculty. Clearly, Jefferson had provided them with the outward structure of an organized, rational academic community.

Narrator 1:
Refer to Thomas Jefferson's definition of a college campus presented in the lecture, and explain how the information in the anthropology text supported Jefferson's view.

Narrator 2:
Please prepare your answer after the beep.

Beep

[Preparation Time: 30 seconds]

Narrator 2:
Please begin speaking after the beep.

Beep

[Recording Time: 60 seconds]

Example Notes
"academic village"
University of Virginia
 large rectangle—library center
 pavilions—classrooms
 gardens—residences + dining halls
 periphery—businesses for basic services + social
classical architecture
 balanced pattern
 organized + rational

Example Speaking Answer
Jefferson called a college campus an "academic village," and the definition of a traditional village in the anthropology text supports his view. First, a village is self-contained, and so is a campus because . . . because there are facilities for daily life—residences, dining halls, and classrooms. Second, a village can store most of the goods and services inside its limits, and so does a campus because businesses for basic services and social life . . . they spring up around the main area. Um . . . third, residents in a traditional village have common objectives, and so do the students and faculty of a college campus who are united by, um, educational goals. And um . . . last, a traditional village reflects the spirit of the community. By using classical architecture, Jefferson designed the University of Virginia to . . . to give the impression of a rational academic village.

Beep

Topic Two

Audio
Narrator 2:
Exercise 35, Topic Two. Read a short passage and listen to a lecture on the same topic. Then listen for a question about them. After you hear the question, you have 30 seconds to prepare and 60 seconds to record your answer.

Narrator 1:
Now read the passage about entrepreneurs. You have 45 seconds to complete it (refer to page 69). Please begin reading now.

[Reading Time: 45 seconds]

Narrator 1:
Now listen to part of a lecture in a business class. The professor is talking about Levi Strauss.

Professor:
Levi Strauss is a good example of the kind of entrepreneur that is described in your textbook. He came to the United States from Bavaria as a teenager. After selling clothing and dry goods from door to door for several years in New York, he made the journey to California with a supply of canvas. The gold rush was at its peak, and Strauss got the idea to sell tents to the gold miners. When he discovered that the miners were not very interested in purchasing tents, he wasted no time in recycling the brown canvas cloth into sturdy pants, a product in great demand in the mining camps. Later he began making work

pants in a blue cotton fabric imported from France, called "serge de Nimes" but known in America as "denim." Along with Jacob Davis, a tailor from Nevada, Strauss patented a pattern of copper rivets to strengthen the stress points on pants, especially the pockets. They first became known as "waist over-alls," then "levis." They became so popular that Strauss concentrated most of his effort on the manu-facture and sales of durable work pants.

Narrator 1:
Referring to both the lecture and the reading passage, explain why the experience of Levi Strauss is typical of small-business owners.

Narrator 2:
Please prepare your answer after the beep.

Beep

[Preparation Time: 30 seconds]

Narrator 2:
Please begin speaking after the beep.

Beep

[Recording Time: 60 seconds]

Example Notes
Strauss = entrepreneur
    teenager—sold clothing + dry goods
    California—canvas tents to miners
    miners not interested—wanted work pants
    recycled canvas into pants—later blue denim
    patent for copper rivets—strengthen stress points

Example Speaking Answer
Levi Strauss is representative of the small-business owners described in the reading passage. He was already employed full time as a teenager selling clothing and dry goods. He showed a strong desire for independence, uh, when he journeyed to California, and . . . and a high level of initiative when he fol-lowed through on his idea to sell tents to miners. Then, when he realized that the miners needed work pants more than they needed tents, he was quick to take advantage of the opportunity. First, he recy-cled the canvas fabric from his tents into sturdy pants, and later, uh, he made work pants in denim. The patent for the copper rivets to protect the stress points on pockets was very . . . uh . . . very innovative. Finally, like so many successful entrepreneurs, Strauss didn't follow a fixed business plan. He reacted to coincidence and, uh, he responded to opportunity.

Beep

EXERCISE 36: Academic Content—More Connections 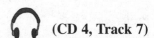 (CD 4, Track 7)

Topic One

Audio
Narrator 2:
Exercise 36, Topic One. Read a short passage and listen to a lecture on the same topic. Then listen for a question about them. After you hear the question, you have 30 seconds to prepare and 60 seconds to record your answer.

Narrator 1:
Now read the passage about color. You have 45 seconds to complete it (refer to page 70). Please begin reading now.

[Reading Time: 45 seconds]

Narrator 1:
Now listen to part of a lecture in an Earth science class. The professor is talking about the color of the sky.

Professor:
Let's look at a very practical application of the theory that you read about in the assignment. As you will recall, sunlight contains all of the colors, but when it is scattered, it is perceived by the human eye as having a specific color depending on the wavelength. Red light has the longest wavelength, for example, and blue light has about half that of red light. This difference in wavelength means that blue light will be scattered nearly ten times more than red light. Even without all the smoke and dust in the atmosphere that would cause light to scatter, the oxygen and nitrogen molecules would still cause the scattering of light. When blue light waves try to go through the oxygen and nitrogen molecules, light is scattered in all directions. All of the other colors are scattered too, but the shorter the wavelength of the color, the more that color gets scattered by the atmosphere. So, blue light's short wavelength causes it to be scattered the most, and we see blue from all directions in the sky.

Narrator 1:
Referring to both the lecture and the reading passage, explain why the sky is blue.

Narrator 2:
Please prepare your answer after the beep.

Beep

[Preparation Time: 30 seconds]

Narrator 2:
Please begin speaking after the beep.

Beep

[Recording Time: 60 seconds]

Example Notes
sunlight = all colors
scattered = wavelength → specific color
red = longest
blue = half red → scatters ten times red
scattering ← smoke, dust, oxygen + nitrogen molecules
shorter wavelength → scatters more
blue scatters most—all directions in sky

Example Speaking Answer
Color travels in light waves that emanate from a light source. When light is scattered, as for example, by a prism, white light is refracted into bands of color, and each has its individual wavelength. Um . . . blue light has a short wavelength as compared with, say, red light, which has the longest

wavelength. The result is that blue light is scattered about ten times more than red light. So, in the sky, the Sun is the light source, and when blue light waves go through the atmosphere, then oxygen and nitrogen molecules or even smoke and dust particles scatter the light in all directions. All of the colors are scattered, in fact, but because blue light has such a short wavelength, it gets scattered the most, and the human eye perceives the color blue from everywhere we look in the sky. That's why the sky's blue.

Beep

Topic Two

Audio
Narrator 2:
Exercise 36, Topic Two. Read a short passage and listen to a lecture on the same topic. Then listen for a question about them. After you hear the question, you have 30 seconds to prepare and 60 seconds to record your answer.

Narrator 1:
Now read the passage about polio. You have 45 seconds to complete it (refer to page 71).
Please begin reading now.

[Reading Time: 45 seconds]

Narrator 1:
Now listen to part of a lecture in a biology class. The professor is talking about polio.

Professor:
Epidemics of poliomyelitis have been referred to as the "plague of development." Ironically, major epidemics seem to occur after there's an improvement in sanitation. That's because when children are living in unsanitary conditions, such as a town with open sewage pipes, virtually all of them are exposed to the polio virus during infancy when the disease is least likely to cause symptoms. So the infants and small children who are exposed, well, they acquire a lifelong immunity to the disease, whereas older children or adults who become infected, uh, they more often suffer paralysis or death.

Okay. As a society improves its sanitation system, it's more probable that fewer babies will be exposed to the polio virus, and so, as they're exposed in later childhood, the disease begins to appear sporadically and spreads in the usual ways. Because the more wealthy members of society are the beneficiaries of all improvements, including sanitation, they're often the first victims of the polio epidemics. Of course, improvements may eliminate many other diseases. It's just that immunization for polio becomes more urgent in societies that have improved sanitation.

Narrator 1:
Referring to both the lecture and the reading passage, explain how polio is spread, and why the more developed societies tend to suffer more serious epidemics.

Narrator 2:
Please prepare your answer after the beep.

Beep

[Preparation Time: 30 seconds]

Narrator 2:

Please begin speaking after the beep.

Beep

[Recording Time: 60 seconds]

Example Notes
"plague of development"
   epidemic ← improvement in sanitation
   open sewage pipes → infants exposed to polio virus
   infants
      least likely symptoms
      lifelong immunity
   older children + adults
      paralysis + death
society improves sanitation → fewer babies exposed + more later childhood
wealthy society → improvements sanitation → victims

Example Speaking Answer
Polio is spread by drinking water that's contaminated by the virus. This often happens when sewage, uh, it pollutes the water supplies. The virus is swallowed in the water and, uh, passes into the digestive tract through the intestines and . . . back into the sewage system where it repeats the cycle. In infants, the disease doesn't usually cause serious symptoms, but among older children and adults, polio can result in paralysis or death. So . . . the more developed societies tend to suffer epidemics because, in communities without sewage treatment, babies are exposed to the polio virus early enough to acquire a lifelong immunity, but in wealthier communities with sanitation systems, well, fewer babies are exposed to the virus, and then if they are exposed when they are older, they suffer symptoms and contribute to an epidemic because the population isn't immune.

Beep

EXERCISE 37: Campus Situations—Problems

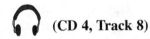 (CD 4, Track 8)

Topic One

Audio
Narrator 2:
Exercise 37, Topic One. Listen to a short conversation. Then listen for a question about it. After you hear the question, you have 20 seconds to prepare and 60 seconds to record your answer.

Narrator 1:
Now listen to a conversation between two students.

Woman: How's the paper coming along?
Man: Not very well.
Woman: Really? What's the problem?
Man: Well, I can't possibly get it done by ten o'clock tomorrow morning.
Woman: I see. . . . Maybe I could help you. I'm a really fast typist.
Man: Thanks. It's great of you to offer, but I don't know what I would ask you to do. I have the research done, and now I'm writing it on the computer . . . uh . . . I'm composing everything on the screen, so . . .
Woman: Um . . . I was thinking maybe you were writing it out on cards. Then I could have typed it for you while you were doing something else, you know, organizing the bibliography or something.
Man: I wish. But I guess I'll just have to go it alone.

Woman: Well then, why don't you ask the professor for an extension?

Man: I don't know. I thought about that, and he's really good about things like that, but it's so late now. I mean, it's the day before it's due.

Woman: I'd still try to talk with him if I were you. You don't have to ask for a week, just a couple of days. But listen, if you try to finish it instead, call me. Maybe there will be something I can do to help.

Narrator 1:

Describe the man's problem and the two suggestions that the woman makes about how to handle it. What do you think the man should do, and why?

Narrator 2:

Please prepare your answer after the beep.

Beep

[Preparation Time: 20 seconds]

Narrator 2:

Please begin speaking after the beep.

Beep

[Recording Time: 60 seconds]

Example Notes

P—can't get paper done tomorrow
S—help type (writing on computer)
   ask professor for extension (so late)
   couple of days

Example Speaking Answer

The man has a paper due the next morning, but he doesn't think he can complete it by the deadline. So the woman makes two suggestions. First, she offers to help him type the paper, but he's composing it on the computer, so . . . then she encourages him to ask the professor for an extension. But the man is reluctant to do that because he feels it's too late to work it out with the professor. Um . . . I think the man should try to talk with the professor, and . . . and he should ask for a few more days to finish the paper. He should be honest about it, and he should apologize for the late notice, and accept responsibility . . . The truth is usually the best approach, in my opinion . . . and if the professor refuses, well then the man can still work hard to finish on time.

Beep

Topic Two

Audio

Narrator 2:

Exercise 37, Topic Two. Listen to a short conversation. Then listen for a question about it. After you hear the question, you have 20 seconds to prepare and 60 seconds to record your answer.

Narrator 1:
Now listen to a conversation between two students.

Woman: You don't know anyone who's looking for a roommate, do you?
Man: Not really. But I thought you *had* a roommate.
Woman: I do. Or rather, I did. But she's getting married in the fall, so I have to find somebody else.
Man: Okay. Why don't you put an ad in the newspaper? The campus paper, I mean, not the city paper. Or, better yet, you could sign up at the housing office. They post notices on a big bulletin board, and there are always people looking for roommates.
Woman: Yeah. I could do that, but I just keep hoping I'll find out that one of my friends is looking for a roommate. I'd rather live with someone I know.
Man: I can understand that. Still, it's really expensive to keep an apartment on your own. . . . I know. How about the dorm?
Woman: What?
Man: Okay. It wouldn't be my first choice either, but it's inexpensive compared with an apartment, so you could save some money while you're there, and that way you could get a better apartment when you moved out. Besides, maybe you'll find someone you really want to share an apartment with who, well, who wants to move out of the dorm the next semester with you.

Narrator 1:
Describe the woman's problem and the three suggestions that the man makes about how to handle it. What do you think the woman should do, and why?

Narrator 2:
Please prepare your answer after the beep.

Beep

[Preparation Time: 20 seconds]

Narrator 2:

Please begin speaking after the beep.

Beep

[Recording Time: 60 seconds]

Example Notes
P—roommate getting married
S—ad in campus paper
   notice on bulletin board in housing office (rather live friends)
   dorm → save money for better apartment + find someone to share

Example Speaking Answer
Because the woman's roommate is getting married in the fall, she has to find another living situation. The man offers several suggestions. He mentions putting an ad in the school newspaper and posting a sign in the housing office. Um . . . he also suggests that she could move into the dormitory to save money until she finds another roommate. Well . . . I think the woman should use all of the man's ideas. She should advertise for a roommate, but she should also make preliminary arrangements to live in the

dorm if she isn't successful in locating someone who . . . someone she wants to share an apartment with . . . and if she's really lucky, she'll learn that one of her friends needs a roommate for the fall term . . . because that's what she'd really like to happen.

Beep

EXERCISE 38: Campus Situations—More Problems

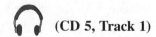 (CD 5, Track 1)

Topic One

Audio
Narrator 2:
Exercise 38, Topic One. Listen to a short conversation. Then listen for a question about it. After you hear the question, you have 20 seconds to prepare and 60 seconds to record your answer.

Narrator 1:
Now listen to a conversation between two students.

Woman: It doesn't seem right that I have to take Earth Science 100.
Man: Why not? I took it, and it's really an interesting course.
Woman: I know. It's just that I took so many science courses in high school, I don't think I'll learn anything new. But I have to take it because it's a prerequisite for Environmental Science 300, and that's a required course for my major. So you see my problem.
Man: Well, let's think about this. If you take the prerequisite, you'll get credit for it, and the course will be an easy A, right?
Woman: I guess so.
Man: Then, if I were you, I'd just take Earth Science 100 as a sort of review, then take Environmental Science 300 next semester. You could spend more time on your other classes.
Woman: Yeah. I could do that.
Man: Or, you could talk to the professor, the environmental science professor, I mean. You could just ask for an exception to the prerequisite. Tell him you'll take a test or something to prove that you already know the material.
Woman: Could the professor do that?
Man: Absolutely. It's his class, and he can allow anyone he wants to in it.

Narrator 1:
Describe the woman's problem and the two suggestions that the man makes about how to handle it. What do you think the woman should do, and why?

Narrator 2:
Please prepare your answer after the beep.

Beep

[Preparation Time: 20 seconds]

Narrator 2:
Please begin speaking after the beep.

Beep

[Recording Time: 60 seconds]

Example Notes
P—Earth Science 100 prerequisite
    Environmental Science 300 required for major
    science courses in high school → nothing new in 100
S—take prerequisite → easy A + more time for other courses
    ask professor for exception + take test

Example Speaking Answer
The woman has a lot of background in Earth science from high school courses, but she's being required to take an introductory Earth science course as a prerequisite for an environmental science course that's on her major program plan. The man suggests that she take the Earth science anyway because it'll be easy and she'll probably get an A in it. He points out that she can spend more time on other courses because she won't need to spend much time on the Earth science. But . . . when she seems reluctant to do that, he recommends that she speak with the professor to, uh, to request special permission to take Environmental Science 300 . . . without the prerequisite. She already understands the material, so he tells her that she could offer to take a test. I think the woman should speak with the professor because, if she gets permission, then she can take another course that will teach her something new instead of spending time and money on reviewing material she already knows.

Beep

Topic Two

Audio
Narrator 2:
Exercise 38, Topic Two. Listen to a short conversation. Then listen for a question about it. After you hear the question, you have 20 seconds to prepare and 60 seconds to record your answer.

Narrator 1:
Now listen to a conversation between two students.

Man: We have to make a group presentation in my economics class. And you know how I feel about standing up in front of a group.
Woman: Yeah, I know. You always do a great job though.
Man: Thanks. I but get so stressed out.
Woman: Well, have you tried relaxation techniques, like deep breathing, or closing your eyes and visualizing success? I used to go through my entire presentation in my head, and I even tried to imagine everyone applauding at the end.
Man: Oh, I don't know. I don't think I'd be very good at that. Maybe the deep breathing though.
Woman: Okay, then. You could just avoid being the presenter.
Man: That sounds good. How do I do that?
Woman: Easy. Just offer to do the preparation. You know, like the handouts and overheads. In an economics presentation, you must have at least one chart to present.
Man: Actually, we have four of them.
Woman: You see? Then, let someone else do the talking. There's got to be someone in your group who enjoys being up front and center. Just so the professor knows that you did your part, and you can take care of that by handing in a list of the presenters and their responsibilities.

Narrator 1:
Describe the man's problem and the two suggestions that the woman makes about how to handle it. What do you think the man should do, and why?

Narrator 2:
Please prepare your answer after the beep.

Beep

[Preparation Time: 20 seconds]

Narrator 2:
Please begin speaking after the beep.

Beep

[Recording Time: 60 seconds]

Example Notes
P—group presentation → stressed out
S—relaxation techniques = deep breathing + visualization
    avoid being presenter
        preparation handouts + overheads + charts
        someone else up front
        professor knows your part ← list presenters + responsibilities

Example Speaking Answer
The man's problem is that he's concerned about making a presentation in his economics class because of his fear of speaking in front of a group. One suggestion that the woman makes is for the man to try relaxation techniques like visualization and deep breathing before he makes the presentation. Um . . . another suggestion is to . . . to take responsibility for preparing the visual materials like handouts, charts, and overheads, and . . . and then ask another group member to speak in front of the class. But she tells him to be certain that the professor knows he's done his share of the work by including the names of the group members and their responsibilities as part of the material they submit. Well, I think that the man should try to overcome his problem by taking the opportunity to do some of the presenting in the class. By avoiding it, he isn't making much progress.

Beep

EXERCISE 39: Academic Content—Summaries

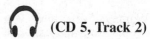 **(CD 5, Track 2)**

Topic One

Audio
Narrator 2:
Exercise 39, Topic One. Listen to part of a lecture. Then listen for a question about it. After you hear the question, you have 20 seconds to prepare, and 60 seconds to record your answer.

Narrator 1:
Now listen to part of a lecture in a botany class. The professor is discussing flowering plants.

Professor:
Flowering plants have traditionally been divided into two major classes—Dicots and Monocots. The actual basis for the distinction is the number of cotyledons. Remember cotyledons are the seed leaves that the embryo produces. In Monocots there is a single seed leaf, and in Dicots there are two seed leaves. Although there are a number of other characteristics that distinguish them, two are particularly

useful—the number of flower parts and the leaf vein patterns are different in the two classes. The petals of the flowers or other flower parts are divisible by three in Monocots, whereas they are divisible by four or five in Dicots. And a parallel leaf structure is usual in Monocots, but Dicots tend to have numerous auxiliary veins that connect the major veining.

That seems relatively straightforward then, right? Wrong. Botanists are not always in agreement regarding several families of flowering plants because they have a combination of characteristics that don't fit neatly into the classifications. For example, water lilies have leaf veining like Dicots, but it appears that there is only a single seed leaf as would be expected in a Monocot. So how can this happen? Well, we believe that the two groups may actually have a shared ancestor, a basic group probably more similar to the Dicots, from which the Monocots have evolved. This means that no one characteristic of a flowering plant—the number of flower parts, leaf veining, or even the number of seed leaves— is going to be sufficient to identify it as either a Monocot or a Dicot.

Narrator 1:
Referring to the main points and examples from the lecture, describe the two general groups of flowering plants. Then explain the problem for classification that the professor presents.

Narrator 2:
Please prepare your answer after the beep.

Beep

[Preparation Time: 20 seconds]

Narrator 2:
Please begin speaking after the beep.

Beep

[Recording Time: 60 seconds]

Example Notes
flowering plants

Dicots	Monocots
two seed leaves (cotyledons)	single seed leaf
petals /4 or 5	/3
parallel leaf structure	auxiliary veins

problem
   combination characteristics
   water lilies veining like Dicot + single seed leaf like Monocot
shared ancestor
   Dicots → Monocots
no one characteristic to identify

Example Speaking Answer
Dicots and Monocots are the two major classes of flowering plants. Basically, a Monocot has one seed leaf and a Dicot has two. In Monocots, the number of petals can be divided evenly by three, but in Dicots, the number can be divided evenly by four or five. Also, Monocots have parallel veins in their leaves, but Dicots have, um, numerous veins with connecting patterns. Now, the problem in classification is that sometimes the characteristics overlap. The professor's example is the . . . the water lily, which has characteristics from both the Monocot and the Dicot. The professor explains that the two classifi-

cations may have descended from a common ancestor, and that makes classification of a plant on the basis of any one characteristic . . . that one characteristic is insufficient to identify it as either a Monocot or a Dicot.

Beep

Topic Two

Audio
Narrator 2:
Exercise 39, Topic Two. Listen to part of a lecture. Then listen for a question about it. After you hear the question, you have 20 seconds to prepare, and 60 seconds to record your answer.

Narrator 1:
Now listen to part of a lecture in an engineering class. The professor is discussing bridge construction.

Professor:
Okay, let's talk about bridge construction, specifically, arch bridges and suspension bridges. Arch bridges have been a standard for bridge construction since ancient times because they are very stable structures. In an arch, the force of the load is carried outward from the top to the ends of the arch where abutments prevent the ends from pulling apart. So, you see, an arch bridge can be designed so that no part of it has to withstand tension. Another advantage of arch bridges is the fact that they can be constructed from such a wide variety of materials, including stone, brick, timber, cast iron, steel, or reinforced concrete. It's also adaptable. The deck can be propped above the arch or hung below the arch. One major disadvantage of the arch bridge though—the bridge is completely unstable until the two spans meet in the middle, so that can make an arch bridge a little tricky to build.

Now, a suspension bridge consists of a deck suspended from cables. The two largest cables or main cables are hung from towers with the cable ends buried in huge concrete blocks or rock called anchorages. The cables support the weight of the bridge and transfer the load to the anchorages and the towers. Suspension bridges are considered aesthetically beautiful, and because they are relatively light and strong, they can be used for the longest spans. The cables, usually of high tensile wire, can support an immense weight. But the design does have the disadvantage of potential bending in the roadway. And because suspension bridges are light and flexible, wind is always a serious concern.

Narrator 1:
Referring to the main points and examples from the lecture, describe the two types of bridge construction presented by the professor. Then explain the specific advantages and disadvantages of each type.

Narrator 2:
Please prepare your answer after the beep.

Beep

[Preparation Time: 20 seconds]

Narrator 2:
Please begin speaking after the beep.

Beep

[Recording Time: 60 seconds]

Example Notes

Arch bridge

advantages

stable—force load top to ends

　　　abutments prevent ends apart

materials—stone, brick, timber, iron, steel, concrete

adaptable—deck above or below

disadvantage

unstable until two spans meet middle

Suspension bridge

　deck suspended from cables

　cables hung from towers

　cables buried in anchorages

advantages

　beautiful

　light

　strong—support weight

disadvantage

　bending

　wind

Example Speaking Answer

The professor describes two types of bridges—the arch bridge and the suspension bridge. Arch bridges are very stable because the weight is distributed from the top to the ends of the arch where abutments keep the ends from separating. In addition to stability, an advantage of arch bridges is that they can be constructed from many different materials, like wood, steel, stone, brick, or concrete. The problem is that an arch is difficult to build because it's unstable until the middle span is complete. Now suspension bridges. They have a deck suspended from cables that are hung from towers. So the cables support the weight and distribute the load to anchorages of concrete or rock, and to the towers as well. Suspension bridges are beautiful, and they're light and strong, which makes them appropriate choices for the longest spans. The problem is that the deck of a suspension bridge may bend, and they're not appropriate for very windy areas.

Beep

EXERCISE 40: Academic Content—More Summaries (CD 5, Track 3)

Topic One

Audio

Narrator 2:

Exercise 40, Topic One. Listen to part of a lecture. Then listen for a question about it. After you hear the question, you have 20 seconds to prepare, and 60 seconds to record your answer.

Narrator 1:

Now listen to part of a lecture in an anatomy class. The professor is discussing the functions of the liver.

Professor:

So that brings us to our discussion of the liver, the largest internal organ in the human body. As you already know, it's part of the digestive system, and it performs more than 500 functions. Today, we'll talk about the three primary functions of the liver. First, the liver functions as a storage system. The liver stores energy in the form of *glycogen*, which is made from a type of sugar called *glucose*. When the glucose levels in the blood are high, the liver uses the glucose to create glycogen, and stores it as energy that can be used later. When the glucose level in the blood falls below the minimum level, the liver changes glycogen into glucose for energy. The liver also stores essential vitamins such as A, D, K, and the B vitamins, all of which are critical to maintain good health.

In addition to storing energy and vitamins, the liver produces essential chemicals, including important proteins like albumin which retains calcium and regulates the movement of water from the bloodstream to the tissues. And globin, which is key to maintaining the immune system. And, uh, cholesterol, an important part of the cell membrane which is used to transport fats in the blood to tissues in the body.

All right, the last crucial function of the liver is to help eliminate toxic substances such as alcohol and drugs from the bloodstream. To clear these harmful substances, the liver absorbs them, then chemically alters them, and finally, excretes them into bile. And the bile works its way out of the system through the small intestine of the digestive tract.

Narrator 1:
Referring to the main points and examples from the lecture, describe the three basic functions of the liver presented by the professor.

Narrator 2:
Please prepare your answer after the beep.

Beep

[Preparation Time: 20 seconds]

Narrator 2:

Please begin speaking after the beep.

Beep

[Recording Time: 60 seconds]

Example Notes
liver = largest internal organ
500 functions
primary functions
   stores energy
      glucose levels in blood high glucose→glycogen
      levels low glycogen→glucose energy
      stores vitamin A, D, K, B
   produces chemicals = proteins
      albumin—regulates water from blood to tissues
      globin—immune system
      cholesterol—transports fat from blood to tissues
   eliminates toxic from bloodstream—alcohol + drugs
      liver absorbs, alters, excretes into bile
      bile through small intestine

Example Speaking Answer
The liver has more than 500 functions, but the professor concentrates on three. First, the liver is used as a storage system. The liver regulates the glucose levels in the blood, and when it's too high, the liver converts glucose into glycogen and stores it as energy for later use. When the glucose level's too low, it changes the glycogen back into glucose for energy. The liver also stores vitamins A, B, D, and K. Second, the liver is a chemical system . . . it produces essential proteins, um, proteins that transport water and fats from the blood to, uh, tissues in the body, and they also support the immune system. Third, the liver eliminates toxic material from the blood, for example, drugs and alcohol. Um . . . the

liver absorbs them and changes their chemical composition, and excretes them into bile that gets eliminated through the small intestine.

Beep

Topic Two

Audio
Narrator 2:
Exercise 40, Topic Two. Listen to part of a lecture. Then listen for a question about it. After you hear the question, you have 20 seconds to prepare, and 60 seconds to record your answer.

Narrator 1:
Now listen to part of a lecture in a psychology class. The professor is discussing how behavior can be predicted.

Professor:
In addition to describing behavior, psychologists try to predict future performance. We do this by designing studies that determine relationships between the behavior that we expect with the behavior that we can actually record. We use a statistical measurement called a *correlation* to tell us whether two variables, like perhaps two test scores, whether they vary together in the same way. For example, studies have shown a positive correlation between a student's performance on the SAT, that's the Scholastic Aptitude Test, and the same student's performance in college courses. It's a *positive* correlation because the higher the score on the SAT, the better we can expect the college grades to be.

But what about a *negative* correlation? Well, other studies suggest that getting a lot of sleep the night before taking the SAT will result in fewer errors on the verbal section. So in a negative correlation like that, the variables move in the opposite direction. The more hours sleep, the fewer verbal errors.

Now, that's all well and good, but the problem occurs when we try to understand *why* correlations exist. That gets us into *causality*. You see, there are so many potentially uncontrolled or unknown factors, that the two variables we are studying may appear to be connected, but they may both be responding to a common third variable. Let's go back to the SAT verbal example. What if the students who slept well the night before the SAT were all very intelligent, or were more prepared for the verbal section, or by chance, many words that they already knew showed up on the exam? Then the real cause wouldn't be the sleep at all.

Narrator 1:
Referring to the main points and examples from the lecture, describe two types of research correlations that the professor presents. Then explain causality.

Narrator 2:
Please prepare your answer after the beep.

Beep

[Preparation Time: 20 seconds]

Narrator 2:
Please begin speaking after the beep.

Beep

[Recording Time: 60 seconds]

Example Notes

correlation = whether two variables vary together same way
positive correlation—SAT + college courses
    higher SAT → better grades
negative correlation—sleep + errors verbal section
    more sleep → fewer verbal errors
problem = why correlations exist = causality
    uncontrolled or unknown factors
    two variables appear connected but responding to common third variable
    students slept well ← all intelligent, more prepared, knew words
    (real cause wasn't sleep)

Example Speaking Answer

A correlation indicates whether two variables correspond—I mean whether they vary in the same way. The professor uses the example of students' scores on the SAT and their performances in college to demonstrate a positive correlation. If a student has a high SAT score, we can expect good grades in college. The variables move in the same direction. Um . . . the professor uses the example of getting a good night's sleep before taking the SAT and, uh, the number of incorrect answers on the verbal section . . . that's an example of a negative correlation. If a student gets a good night's sleep, we can expect fewer errors. The variables move in opposite directions. But . . . but even when a correlation can be shown, we don't know the cause. The two variables could be affected by a third factor they have in common. As an example, the students in the study might be more prepared for the verbal section and would have performed well whether they were rested or not.

Beep

Structure

EXERCISE 41: Sentences—Verbs

1. **(C)** The verb *fail* requires an infinitive in the complement. Choices (A) and (D) are *-ing* forms, not infinitives. Choice (B) is an infinitive, but it expresses a past time, and does not maintain the point of view established by the verb *fails*.

2. **(B)** Because the verb phrase *to get through* requires an *-ing* form in the complement, *to lay* should be *laying*.

3. **(A)** *If* is used before the noun *endangered species* and the present verb *are* followed by the infinitive *to be* to express the result of a condition with *must*. Choice (B) is a verb word, not a present verb. Choices (C) and (D) are modals.

4. **(C)** The infinitive *to complete* is used to express purpose. Choice (A) includes the unnecessary word *for*. Choice (B) is an *-ing* form, not an infinitive. Choice (D) expresses manner, not purpose.

5. **(B)** *Not* is used before the infinitive *to be* in the clause after the verb *agreed*. "Doctors agreed that they shouldn't be truthful" would also be correct. The verb *agree* requires an infinitive in the complement. Choice (A) is an infinitive, but the negative *don't* is used instead of *not*. The modal in Choice (C) requires a verb word, not the participle *been*. Choice (D) uses *not* as the negative, but *been* is a participle, not an infinitive.

6. **(A)** *In* is used after *interested*. The *-ing* form *establishing* is used after the preposition *in*. The preposition in Choice (B) is *for*, not *in*. Choice (C) does not have the correct preposition, *in*. Choice (D) is an infinitive, not a preposition with an *-ing* form.

7. **(C)** The infinitive *to communicate* is used to express purpose. Choice (A) is an *-ing* form after the preposition *to*, not an infinitive. In Choice (B), *for*, not *to*, is used. In Choice (D), *for* is used with a past verb.

8. **(C)** The subject *art* is used before the verb phrase *tends to be* followed by *worth* and the indefinite amount *more* to express value. The words in Choices (A), (B), and (D) are related in meaning to *worth*, but they are not idiomatic expressions with *to be*.

9. **(A)** *Let* is used as a causative to express permission before the complement *their offspring* followed by the verb word *build*. Choice (B) is a present verb, not a verb word. Choice (C) is an *-ing* form. Choice (D) is an infinitive.

10. **(C)** An infinitive is used to express purpose. *To reading* should be *to read*.

11. **(A)** A present verb in the condition requires a present modal such as *will* in the result. *Will* expresses future time. Choice (B) is a past form, not a present modal. Choice (C) is a past modal. Choice (D) is an *-ing* form.

12. **(C)** An infinitive is used to express purpose. *To understanding* should be *to understand*.

13. **(B)** Every English sentence must have a subject and a main verb. Choices (A), (C), and (D) do not include a main verb.

14. **(B)** In contrary-to-fact clauses, *were* is the only accepted form of the verb BE. *Was* should be *were*.

15. **(A)** The anticipatory clause *it is generally accepted that* introduces a subject and a verb, *schools are*. Choice (B) is a subject clause that requires a verb, not a subject and verb. The clauses in Choices (C) and (D) do not introduce a subject and verb.

16. **(A)** The word order for a passive sentence is a form of BE followed by a participle. *Found* should be *was founded*. *Found* means "discovered." *Founded* means "established."

17. **(D)** An infinitive that expresses purpose such as *to relieve pain* introduces a verb word that expresses a manner to accomplish that purpose. Choice (A) is an *-ing* form, not a verb word. Choice (B) is an infinitive. Choice (C) is a participle.

18. **(C)** For scientific results, a present form in the condition such as *mixes* requires a present or future form in the result, *will occur*. Choice (A) is a past, not a present, form. Choice (B) is *had* followed by a participle. Choice (D) is a noun.

19. **(A)** The verb *refuse* requires an infinitive in the complement. Choice (B) is an *-ing* form, not an infinitive. Choice (C) is a noun. Choice (D) is a verb word.

20. **(C)** A form of *make* with something such as *the vocal chords* [*them*] and a verb word expresses a causative. Choice (A) is an infinitive, not a verb word. Choice (B) is an *-ing* form. Choice (D) is a noun.

EXERCISE 42: Sentences— Auxiliary Verbs

1. **(B)** *Ought* is used before *to* to express obligation. *A healthy heart should pump* would also be correct. Choices (A), (C), and (D) are modals that are used before verb words, not before *to*.
2. **(B)** *Wrote* should be *written* because the auxiliary *had* requires a participle. *Wrote* is a past form. *Written* is a participle.
3. **(C)** *Will have* is used before the participle *decreased* to predict the future, *by the second year of production*. The modals in Choices (A) and (D) require a verb word, not past and present forms of the verb. Choice (B) expresses a past, not a future, point of view.
4. **(B)** A passive sentence is used to focus on the *structures* rather than on the *builders*. In a passive sentence, a form of *be* is followed by a participle. *Build* should be *built*.
5. **(A)** Every sentence must have a main verb. *Having* should be *has*.
6. **(B)** Every sentence must have a main verb. *Composed* should be *are composed*.
7. **(D)** *Won't* means will not. *Won't* is used before *be* followed by the participle *developed* in a passive to express the importance of the *cure*. "Scientists won't develop a cure until more funds are allocated" would also be correct to express the importance of the *scientists*. Choices (B) and (C) do not express future. Choice (A) is not a passive.
8. **(B)** The past form of the verb *to spend* is *spent*. *Spended* should be *spent*.
9. **(A)** *Had better* requires a verb word. Choice (B) is an *-ing* form, not a verb word. Choice (C) is a noun. Choice (D) is a past verb.
10. **(B)** The participle is used after a form of BE in a passive sentence. *Finding* should be *found* after *to be*.
11. **(C)** Every English sentence must have a subject and a main verb. Choice (A) is an infinitive, not a main verb. Choice (B) is an *-ing* form. Choice (D) is a main verb, but it does not agree with the plural subject *cones*.

12. **(A)** A verb word must be used in a clause after the verb *to require*. *Taken* should be *be taken*.
13. **(A)** A verb word must be used in a clause after an impersonal expression such as *it is important that*. *Is* should be *be*.
14. **(C)** *Had hoped that* introduces a clause with a subject and *would* followed by a verb word. Choice (A) is a verb word without *would*. Choice (B) is *had* followed by a participle. Choice (D) is an *-ing* form.
15. **(C)** *Used to* requires a verb word to express a custom in the past. *Was used to be carried* should be *used to be carried*.
16. **(C)** *Must* followed by *be* and an *-ing* form expresses a logical conclusion about an event that is happening now. *Save* should be *saving*.
17. **(D)** *Unless* introduces a clause with a subject and a main verb. *Be* should be *is* to maintain the point of view established by *is* in the previous clause, *jewelry is*.
18. **(B)** The modal *can* followed by a verb word expresses ability. The infinitive in Choice (A) the *-ing* form in Choice (C), and the verb word in Choice (D) do not express ability.
19. **(A)** A form of HAVE followed by a participle expresses a duration of time. The participle *been* is a form of BE used with the participle *caused* in a passive before the agent *by the aphids or pollution*. *Been caused* should be *has been caused*.
20. **(B)** A form of HAVE followed by a participle expresses a duration of time. The infinitive is *to have*. *Had been* should be *have been* after *to*.

EXERCISE 43: Sentences—Nouns

1. **(A)** Either an *-ing* form or an infinitive may be used as the subject of a sentence. *The understanding* should be *Understanding* or *To understand*. "The understanding of electricity" would also be correct.
2. **(B)** Singular and plural expressions of noncount nouns such as *mail* occur in idiomatic phrases, often *piece* or *pieces of*. *Mails* should be *pieces of mail*.
3. **(A)** *Kinds of* is used before the plural count noun *magnets* to express classification. *Kind* in Choices (B) and (C) is used before a singular count noun or a noncount noun, not a

plural count noun. In Choice (D), the preposition *of* does not follow *kinds*.

4. **(A)** *Ice* is a noncount noun because it is a natural substance that can change shape according to natural laws. Choices (B) and (D) are not noncount nouns. Choice (C) implies specific *ice*, but is incomplete without a qualifying phrase.

5. **(D)** No article before a plural count noun such as *dogs* has the same meaning as *all dogs*. Choice (A) is redundant and incorrect. *That* in Choice (B) introduces a subject clause before a main verb, but only the subject follows, *that dogs can live to be more than fifteen years old*. Choice (C) also provides a subject clause with no main verb.

6. **(B)** *Plant* should be *plants* to imply *one* of many.

7. **(B)** The plural of leaf is *leaves*. Choices (A), (C), and (D) do not provide the correct plural noun.

8. **(D)** *Fruit* is usually a noncount noun, and *vegetables* is a count noun. In Choices (A) and (B), *vegetable* is used as a noncount, not a count, noun. *The* in Choice (C) implies specific *fruit* and *vegetables*, but there is no qualifying phrase.

9. **(A)** Singular and plural expressions of noncount nouns such as *thunder* occur in idiomatic phrases. *Thunder* should be *a clap of thunder* to mean one, or *thunder* to mean *all thunder*.

10. **(B)** The determiner *an* is used before singular count nouns that begin with a vowel sound such as *a* in *area*. The determiner *a* in Choice (A) is used before singular count nouns that begin with consonant sounds, not vowel sounds. *The* in Choice (C) is incomplete without a specific qualifying phrase. Choice (D) requires a determiner because it is a count noun.

11. **(B)** No article before a plural count noun such as *beavers* has the same meaning as *all beavers*. Choices (A) and (C) do not agree with the plural verb *were* in the sentence. *That* in Choice (D) introduces a subject clause for a main verb, but only the subject follows, *that beavers were hunted for their pelts*.

12. **(D)** The noun *children* is the irregular plural form of *child*. *Childrens* should be *children*.

13. **(D)** It is logical to assume that there is more than one museum throughout the United States. *Museum* should be *museums*.

14. **(D)** *Types of* is used before plural count nouns to express classification. *Ten types* should be *ten types of*.

15. **(B)** An *-ing* form such as *spraying* may be used as a noun. *The* precedes the noun when a prepositional phrase such as *of designs on a wall* qualify the noun. Choice (A) is incomplete without *the*. Choices (C) and (D) are not *-ing* forms.

16. **(B)** No article before a plural count noun such as *novels* has the same meaning as *all novels*. The singular noun *novel* in Choices (A), (C), and (D) does not agree with the verb *are* in the sentence.

17. **(D)** The noun clause *that computers have made communications faster and easier through the use of e-mail and the Internet* is a very long subject of the main verb *is*. Choices (A), (B), and (C) cannot function as the subject of the main verb.

18. **(A)** Either an infinitive or an *-ing* form can be used as the subject of a sentence. *Provide* should be *to provide* or *providing*.

19. **(A)** Singular and plural expressions of noncount nouns such as *equipment* occur in idiomatic phrases, often *piece* or *pieces of*. *Equipments* should be *pieces of equipment*.

20. **(D)** Although *damage* is a count noun in many other languages, *damage* is a noncount noun in English. The article *a* in Choice (A) and the plural *-s* ending in Choice (B) are forms that are correct for singular and plural, but not for noncount nouns. Choice (C) implies specific *damage*, but is incomplete without a qualifying phrase.

EXERCISE 44: Sentences—Pronouns

1. **(D)** There must be agreement between pronoun and antecedent. Choices (A), (B), and (C) do not agree in number, gender, and case with the singular, neuter, objective antecedent *crime rate*. Choice (A) is plural. Choice (B) is masculine. Choice (C) is possessive.

2. **(B)** There must be agreement between pronoun and antecedent. *Its* should be *their* to agree with the plural antecedent *sloths*.

3. **(D)** Object pronouns are used after prepositions such as *from. Their* should be *them.*

4. **(B)** A reflexive pronoun is used when the subject and complement refer to the same person. Only *themselves* in Choice (B) is a reflexive pronoun. *Them* in Choice (A) is an object pronoun. *They* in Choice (C) is a subject pronoun. *Their* in Choice (D) is a possessive pronoun.

5. **(B)** *Him* should be *he* because it is part of the subject, with *Drs. Daniel Nathan* and *Hamilton Smith*, of the verb *were awarded. He* functions as a subject. *Him* functions as a complement.

6. **(C)** *Which* should be *who* because it refers to people, not things.

7. **(D)** *Each other* is used to express mutual acts such as *trade.* Choices (A), (B), and (C) are not idiomatic. "One another" would also be correct.

8. **(D)** There must be agreement between pronoun and antecedent. *Their* should be *our* to agree with the second person antecedent *those of us.*

9. **(C)** Object pronouns are used after prepositions such as *for.* Choices (A) and (B) are subject, not object, pronouns. Choice (D) is a possessive pronoun.

10. **(D)** *Each other* is used to express mutual acts. Choices (A), (B), and (C) are not idiomatic. "One another" would also be correct.

11. **(A)** There must be agreement between pronoun and antecedent. *Which* should be *who* to refer to the antecedent *George Herman Ruth. Which* refers to things. *Who* refers to persons.

12. **(B)** There must be agreement between pronoun and antecedent. Only *its* in Choice (B) agrees with the singular noun *the constellation.* Choice (A) would agree with *you,* not *the constellation.* Choice (C) would agree with a plural, not a singular, noun. Choice (D) would agree with *she.*

13. **(C)** *Whom* should be *whose,* a pronoun used as an adjective to modify *creative genius.*

14. **(B)** There must be agreement between pronoun and antecedent. *Themselves* refers to the plural antecedent *wolves.* Choices (A) and (C) would agree with a singular, not a plural, noun. Choice (D) is not a word in

standard English, although it does occur in some nonstandard dialects.

15. **(A)** There must be agreement between pronoun and antecedent. *Which* refers to the antecedent *very hardy plants. Which* refers to things. *What* and *where* in Choices (B) and (D) do not logically refer to *plants. Who* in Choice (C) refers to persons, not things, such as *plants.*

16. **(A)** Possessive pronouns are used before *-ing* nouns. *Result from* should be followed by a noun, not a clause with a subject and verb as in Choice (B). The infinitive in Choice (C) is not idiomatic after the preposition *from.* Choice (D) is an object pronoun, not a possessive pronoun.

17. **(D)** *Themself* should be *himself* to agree with the singular noun, *the patient.*

18. **(D)** Object pronouns are used after prepositions such as *for. They* should be *them.*

19. **(C)** There must be agreement between pronoun and antecedent. *Their eggs* should be *her eggs* to refer to the antecedent, a *female* sea horse.

20. **(B)** *Whom* is the complement of the subject *Cooper* and the verb *created.* Choice (A) is used as a subject, not a complement. Choice (C) refers to things, not to a person, like *Hawkeye.* Choice (D) is used as a possessive, not a complement.

EXERCISE 45: Sentences—Modifiers

1. **(C)** The *-ing* form adjective *interesting* is used to describe the noun *data.* Choice (A) is not logical since the *scientist,* not the *data,* would be *interested.* Choice (B) is a noun, not an adjective. Choice (D) would also be correct without the adverb *very.*

2. **(C)** *Any other* excludes all others. *The other* should be *other.*

3. **(B)** *Real* is an adjective used in colloquial speech as an adverb. *Real great* should be *very great* in standard, written English.

4. **(D)** *No* is used before the noun *earthquakes.* Choice (A) is a pronoun that would take the place of the noun, *serious earthquakes.* Choices (C) and (D) must be used with a verb such as *have not* before the participle *had.* "The New England states have not had any serious earthquakes" would also be correct.

5. **(B)** *Almost* is used before *all* to express approximation. Choices (A), (C), and (D) are not idiomatic. "Nearly all" would also be correct.

6. **(D)** *Others* is used consecutively with *some*. Choice (A) is not a word in English unless it has an apostrophe in it. Choice (B) is used consecutively with *one*, not *some*. Choice (C) is used before a noun.

7. **(B)** *So* is used before the adjective *great* to express cause. *As* should be *that* to introduce the clause of result.

8. **(B)** When two nouns occur together, the first noun functions as an adjective. Adjectives do not change form when the noun that follows is plural. *Light year* should be *light years* to agree with the plural number *500 million*.

9. **(C)** *A large number of* is used before the plural count noun *doctors*. Choice (A) is used before a noncount noun, not a plural count noun. In Choices (B) and (D), the article *a* is missing.

10. **(A)** *None of* should be *no*. *No* before a noun means *not any*.

11. **(A)** A cardinal number is used after a noun. *The* is used with an ordinal number before a noun. Choice (B) is incomplete because it does not include *the* before the ordinal number. Choice (C) is not used after a noun. Choice (D) is incomplete because it does not have a *-th* ending. "President four" would also be correct, but not as idiomatic.

12. **(B)** *As* should be *that* to introduce a clause of result after *so* and an adjective.

13. **(D)** Both *a few* and *a little* are used after *only*, but *a few* must be used with the count noun *nations*. "Few nations in the world" would also be correct.

14. **(A)** An adjective is used before *enough* to express sufficiency. In Choice (B), there is an adverb used after *enough*. In Choice (C), the adjective is used after, not before, *enough*, and the word *as* is unnecessary and incorrect. In Choice (D), the word *as* is unnecessary and incorrect.

15. **(B)** Most adverbs of manner are formed by adding *-ly* to adjectives. *Careful* should be *carefully* to qualify the manner in which *you must listen*.

16. **(D)** An adjective is used before *enough* to express sufficiency. *As* should be deleted.

17. **(D)** When two nouns occur together, the first noun functions as an adjective. Choice (A) is not logical because it implies ownership of the *restaurants* by a chain. In Choice (B), the adjective is plural, but adjectives in English do not change form to agree in number with the nouns they modify. In Choice (C), the singular noun *restaurant* does not agree with the two nouns, *McDonald's* and *Kentucky Fried Chicken*, to which it refers.

18. **(B)** *Too* means excessively. When an infinitive follows, *too* expresses cause, as in *too old*, and the infinitive expresses result, as in *to return*. Choice (A) would be followed by a clause with *that*, not an infinitive. Choices (C) and (D) would be used to compare *Glen* to others, but a comparison is not implied in the sentence.

19. **(A)** *The* can be used before a noncount noun that is followed by a qualifying phrase. *The art* is qualified by the phrase *that is known as Art Deco*. Choices (B) and (C) use plural and singular forms for the noncount noun *art*. The count noun *artist* in Choice (D) requires either *the* or *an* for singular or *-s* for plural.

20. **(A)** The number *second* appears as the first in a series of hyphenated adjectives. Choice (B) reverses the order of the number with the other adjective. Choice (C) is redundant and indirect. In Choice (D), the adjective *magnitude* had a plural form, but adjectives in English do not change form to agree in number with the nouns they modify.

EXERCISE 46: Sentences—Comparatives

1. **(C)** *As high as* is used before the amount of money *thirty-five thousand dollars* to establish a limit. None of the words after *high* in Choices (A), (B), and (D) is idiomatic.

2. **(B)** *The same* is used with a quality noun such as *color* followed by *as* in comparisons. *Than* should be *as*.

3. **(B)** The comparative adjective *better* is used for separate comparisons of two, including *images . . . and . . . signals*, and *images . . . and tapes*. *Best* should be *better*.

4. **(D)** *Much too much* is a phrase that is used to express excess. Choice (A) introduces a clause with *that*, not a phrase with *for*.

Choice (B) is incomplete. In Choice (C), *very* does not express excess. "The cost is too much for most businesses" would also be correct.

5. **(B)** *The most longest* should be *the longest*. Because *long* is a one-syllable adjective, the superlative is formed by adding *-est*. *Most* is used with two-syllable adjectives that do not end in *-y*.

6. **(D)** *The same* is used with a quality noun such as *age* followed by *as* in comparisons. *Old* is an adjective *Old* should be *age*.

7. **(A)** The comparative of a three-syllable adverb is formed by using *more* before the adverb and *than* after the adverb. Choice (B) is an adverb, but it is not a comparative with *more*. Choices (C) and (D) are an adjective comparative and superlative, not adverbs.

8. **(B)** *The larger* should be *the largest*. Because it is logical that there were more than two newspapers in the colonies, a superlative form with *-est* should be used to compare three or more.

9. **(D)** *Same* should be *the same as* between two comparable nouns, *the area where a microchip is manufactured* and *that* [the area] *of an operating room.*

10. **(C)** Multiple comparatives like *half* are expressed by the multiple number followed by the phrases *as . . . as.* Choice (A) is a multiple with an incomplete phrase. In Choices (B) and (D), the multiples are not first, and the phrases that follow are incomplete.

11. **(A)** The verb *differ* is used with *from* to express general difference. *Differ* should be *differ from.*

12. **(D)** When the degree of one quality, *the pulse*, is dependent upon the degree of another quality, *the heart rate*, two comparatives are required, each of which must be preceded by *the. Faster* should be *the faster.*

13. **(B)** A two-syllable adjective like *severe* forms the comparative by using *more* or *less* before the adjective form followed by *than.* In Choice (C), the adjective is after, not before, *than.* Choices (A) and (D) use the incorrect form *lesser.*

14. **(C)** Comparisons must be made with logically comparable nouns. *That of* is used instead of repeating a singular noun, and *those of* is used instead of repeating a plural noun. Choice (A) illogically compares *two*

stages of development with *marsupials.* Choice (B) would be correct for a singular, not a plural, noun like *stages.* In Choice (D), *of* is not used after *those.*

15. **(C)** *More than* is used before a specific number like *fifty* to express an estimate that exceeds the number. Choice (A) is incomplete without *than.* Choice (B) uses *as*, not *than*, with *more.* Choice (D) uses *most*, not *more*, with *than.*

16. **(B)** *As many as* is used before a count noun to express an estimate that does not exceed the number. *Much* in Choice (A) would be correct with a noncount noun, not a count noun with a number. Choices (C) and (D) are incomplete because *as* is used only once, before or after *many.*

17. **(A)** Comparatives require *than.* Choices (B) and (C) use *that* and *as* instead of *than.* Choice (D) is incomplete without *than.*

18. **(D)** *Better* is the comparative form of the irregular adjective *good*, used to compare two activities, *the fair* and *any other event.* Choices (A) and (B) are superlatives that would be used to compare more than two. Choice (C) does not have a comparative adjective before *than.*

19. **(A)** *Like* is a preposition. *Alike* should be *like.*

20. **(C)** Comparatives with adverbs like *strenuously* require *as* before and *as* after the adverb. In Choice (A), *as* appears before, but not after, the adverb. Choice (B) uses *more*, not *as*, before the adverb. Choice (D) uses *that*, not *as*, after the adverb.

Exercise 47: Sentences—Connectors

1. **(B)** The preposition *from* is used before the *-ing* form *watching* to express cause. Choices (A) and (D) express purpose, not cause. In Choice (C), there is a verb word, not an *-ing* form, after the preposition.

2. **(B)** The preposition *to* is used after the verb *prefer.* None of the words in Choices (A), (C), and (D) is idiomatic with *prefer.*

3. **(B)** *Such as* introduces an example. *Such* should be *such as* before the examples of metals.

4. **(B)** *When* is used before the subject *it* and the present verb *ages* to express a general truth. Choice (A) is a modal, not a present verb. Choice (C) expresses present time, but it is

not the simple present verb that is required in clauses after *when*. Choice (D) is a past, not a present, verb.

5. **(B)** *But* is used before the noun *smell* to express exception. The words in Choices (A), (C), and (D) do not mean *except*.

6. **(A)** *Because* introduces a clause with a subject and verb. *Because of* introduces a phrase. *Because* should be *because of* before the nouns *expense . . . and concern*. "Because traditional fuels were expensive, there was concern . . ." would also be correct.

7. **(B)** *Instead of* is used before a noun to indicate replacement. Choice (A) does not have the preposition *of*. The word *that* in Choice (C) introduces a clause with a subject and verb, but no verb follows. The word *instead* at the end of a sentence or clause as in Choice (D) would not include two options, in this case, both kinds of *current*. "The lights and appliances in most homes use alternating current instead" would also be correct.

8. **(A)** *In* is used between numbers to express a fraction. *On* should be *in*.

9. **(B)** *In* is used before the month *December*. Choice (A) is used before dates. Choice (C) is used before clock time. Choice (D) is used before duration of time.

10. **(D)** *By* is used before the *-ing* form *increasing* to express method. Choices (A) and (C), which express purpose, not method, are not logical in this sentence. Choice (B) has a verb word, not an *-ing* form, after the preposition *for*.

11. **(B)** *Among* refers to three or more nouns. *Between* refers to two nouns. *Among* should be *between* to refer to the two nouns *speed* and *pressure*.

12. **(B)** Subject-verb order is used in the clause after a question word connector such as *what*. In Choices (A) and (D), subject-verb order is reversed. In Choice (C), the auxiliary *did* is unnecessary and incorrect.

13. **(B)** *So* is commonly used as a purpose connector in spoken English, but *so that* should be used in written English.

14. **(C)** *In spite* should be *in spite of* because *in spite of* introduces a condition with an unexpected result. "Despite" would also be correct.

15. **(C)** Affirmative agreement with *so* requires verb-subject order and an affirmative

verb that refers to the verb in the main clause. Choices (A) and (B) have verb-subject order, but the verbs DO and HAVE do not refer to the verb BE in the main clause. In Choice (D), *so* is used at the end, not at the beginning, of the clause, and there is no verb.

16. **(A)** *Because* is used before a subject and verb to introduce cause. Choices (B) and (C) are not accepted for statements of cause. Choice (D) is used before a noun, not before a subject and verb.

17. **(C)** *On* is used before the street name *Beacon*. *In* is used before the city *Boston*. Choices (A), (B), and (D) all use inappropriate prepositions before the street name *Beacon*. Choices (B) and (D) use inappropriate prepositions before the city *Boston*.

18. **(B)** *Besides* means "in addition to." Choice (A) means "near," not "in addition." In Choice (C), *in addition* is used without *to*. *Also* in Choice (D) is used with verbs, not a noun like *the original document*.

19. **(C)** *But* should be *but also*, which is used in correlation with the inclusive *not only*.

20. **(C)** Negative agreement requires verb-subject order and an affirmative verb after *neither*, or subject-verb order and a negative verb before *either*. In Choices (A) and (D), there are no verbs. In Choice (B), the verb is affirmative, not negative, with *either*.

EXERCISE 48: Sentences—Sentences and Clauses

1. **(A)** *Are* is the main verb of the subject *some ancient units*. Choices (B), (C), and (D) are all part of subject classes that would require a main verb after *today*.

2. **(D)** *Was issued* is the main verb of the subject *paper money*. Choices (A) and (C) are part of subject clauses that would require a main verb after *American Revolution*. Choice (B) is an active verb before a passive agent.

3. **(C)** *That are* should be *are* to provide a main verb for the subject *the plastic arts*.

4. **(B)** *Is taken* is the main verb of the subject *The Scholastic Aptitude Text*. Choices (A) and (C) are part of subject clauses that would require a main verb after *many colleges*. Choice (D) is an active verb before a passive agent.

5. **(A)** *That* should be deleted to provide a main verb [*help*] for the subject *ocean currents*.

6. **(D)** *Is* is the main verb of the subject *Camp David*. Choice (A) is part of a subject clause that would require a main verb after *U.S. presidents*. Choices (B) and (C) are redundant because the subject pronoun *it* is used consecutively with the subject noun *Camp David*.

7. **(C)** *Forming* should be *form* to provide a main verb for the subject *gas and dust*.

8. **(A)** *Which* should be deleted to provide a main verb [*regulated*] for the subject *ordinances*.

9. **(B)** The subject *blue chip stock* and the verb *is* are simple and direct. In addition, *is considered* provides for parallelism with *is favored*. Choices (A), (C), and (D) are redundant.

10. **(B)** *That* introduces a subject and verb in the clause. *Exhibiting* in Choices (A) and (C) cannot be used as a verb without a form of BE. Choice (D) is redundant because the pronoun *they* is used consecutively with the noun *seed*.

11. **(D)** *Is named* is the main verb of the subject *La Guardia Airport*. Choices (A) and (B) are part of subject clauses that would require a main verb after *most popular mayors*. the active verb in Choice (C) is not logical because it implies that the *airport* did the *naming*.

12. **(D)** *Are valued* is the main verb of the subject *intelligence and ability*. Choices (A) and (C) are not logical because they imply that the *intelligence and ability* can *value* something or someone. Choice (B) is part of a subject clause that would require a main verb after *social position or wealth*.

13. **(B)** *Which it feed* should be *feeds* to provide a main verb for the subject *the larva*.

14. **(B)** *95 percent of them* is the subject, and *are filed* is the verb. The usual word order of subject and verb is not followed in Choice (A). Choices (C) and (D) are redundant, and the usual word order is not followed.

15. **(B)** Choice (B) is an example of a dependent clause. Choice (A) is incomplete without the verb *was written* in the clause. Choice (C) is incomplete without *which*, the subject of the clause. Choice (D) is a clause that is not connected to the main clause by a clause marker.

16. **(C)** *Cats and dogs* is the subject of the verb *are kept*. Choices (A) and (D) are part of a subject clause that would require a main verb after *in the world*. The word order in Choice (B) would be correct for a question, but not for a sentence with a period.

17. **(B)** *Which* should be *which are* to provide a verb for the clause.

18. **(D)** *Is* is the main verb of the subject *PTA*, and *a group* is the complement. Choice (A) is redundant because the subject pronoun *it* is used consecutively with the subject noun *PTA*. Choice (B) is part of a subject clause that would require a main verb after *other activities*. *Which* in Choice (C) requires a verb in the clause.

19. **(B)** *Appears* should be *which appears* to provide a subject for the clause. The sentence is also correct without the verb *appears*.

20. **(B)** Choice (B) is the main clause that introduces a dependent clause. Choice (A) is part of a subject clause that would require a main verb after *latitude*. The appositive in Choice (C) would be correct with a comma before it and a comma after it. Choice (D) is redundant because the subject pronoun *it* is used consecutively with the subject noun *the jet stream*.

EXERCISE 49: Sentences— Point of View

1. **(A)** The adverbial phrase *in 1970* establishes a point of view in the past. *Are* should be *were* to maintain the point of view.

2. **(B)** The verb *cannot make* establishes a point of view in the present. *Were* should be *are* to maintain the point of view.

3. **(A)** The reference to an activity before the subject's death establishes a point of view in the past. *Publishes* should be *published* to maintain the point of view.

4. **(B)** The adverbial phrase *seven o'clock in the morning when the sun comes up* establishes a point of view in the present. *Disappeared* should be *disappears* to maintain the point of view.

5. **(C)** The adverbial phrase *Before the 1800s* establishes a point of view in the past. The modal *could* in Choice (C) maintains the point of view. Choices (A) and (B) are present, not past. Choice (D) is a participle without a verb.

6. **(C)** The adverbial phrase *seven months before the stock market crashed in 1929*, and the verb *said* establish a point of view in the past. *Is* should be *was* to maintain the point of view.

7. **(C)** The adverbial phrase *In the Middle Ages* establishes a point of view in the past. The verb *was* in Choice (C) maintains the point of view. Choice (A) is also a past verb, but it is an active, not a passive, verb. A passive is required by the agent *by. a journeyman*. Choice (B) is a present, not a past, verb. Choice (D) is an active verb.

8. **(B)** The adverbial phrase *for about twelve thousand years* establishes a point of view that begins in the past. *Are living* should be *have been living* to maintain the point of view.

9. **(A)** The adverbial clause *although we once thought* establishes a point of view in the past. *Has* should be *had* to maintain the point of view.

10. **(D)** Activities of the dead logically establish a point of view in the past. Choice (D) maintains the point of view. Choices (A) and (C) are present, not past, verbs. Choice (B) is a past verb with a noun, not an adjective, to describe *Carver*.

11. **(D)** Activities of historical figures known to be dead logically establish a point of view in the past. The verb *reported* further establishes that point of view. Choices (A) and (C) are present, not past, verbs. Choice (B) is a past verb, but it is an active verb.

12. **(D)** The adverbial phrase *In 1975* establishes a point of view in the past. *Is* should be *was* to maintain the point of view.

13. **(C)** The adverbial phrase *in 1605* and the verb *founded* establish a point of view in the past. *Builds* should be *built* to maintain the point of view.

14. **(C)** The adverbial phrase *in 1991* establishes a point of view in the past. *Are passed* should be *were passed* to maintain the point of view.

15. **(B)** The adverbial phrase *on June 17, 1775* establishes a point of view in the past. *Occurs* should be *occurred* to maintain the point of view.

16. **(D)** The *development of language* is a historical event that logically establishes a point of view in the past. Choice (D) is a past verb that maintains the point of view. Choice (A) is an infinitive, not a past verb. Choice (B) is a present verb. Choice (C) is a noun.

17. **(B)** The adverb *originally* establishes a point of view in the past. *Is* should be *was* to maintain the point of view.

18. **(A)** Activities of the dead logically establish a point of view in the past. Choice (A) is a past verb. Choice (B) is an *-ing* form, not a past verb. Choice (C) is a present verb. Choice (D) is a verb word.

19. **(B)** The phrase *ancient cultures* establishes a point of view in the past. *Begin* should be *began* to maintain the point of view.

20. **(B)** The phrase *remember when* establishes a point of view in the past. Choice (B) is a past verb. Choice (A) is a present, not a past, verb. Choices (C) and (D) are *-ing* forms.

EXERCISE 50: Sentences—Agreement

1. **(B)** There must be agreement between subject and verb. *Is* should be *are* to agree with the plural subject *both a term paper and a final exam*.

2. **(A)** There must be agreement between subject and verb. *Were* should be *was* to agree with the singular subject *the popularity*.

3. **(D)** *Are* is used before *there* to refer to the noun *notes* at the specific place in the musical scale, and to maintain word order for questions. The singular verb *is* in Choices (A) and (B) does not agree with the plural phrase *many musical notes*. Choice (C) reverses the word order for questions.

4. **(B)** There must be agreement between subject and verb. *Develop* should be *develops* to agree with the singular subject *not one*.

5. **(D)** There must be agreement between subject and verb. *Live* in Choice (D) agrees with the plural subject *nine of every ten people*. Choice (A) is an *-ing* form, not a verb. Choice (B) is redundant because the noun subject is followed by the pronoun subject *they*. Choice (C) would agree with a singular, not a plural, subject.

6. **(D)** There must be agreement between pronoun and antecedent. *Their* should be *its* to agree with the third person singular neuter noun *the eagle*.

7. **(D)** There must be agreement between subject and verb. *Require* should be *requires* to agree with the singular subject *the Blue Spruce*.

8. **(A)** There must be agreement between subject and verb. *Is* should be *are* to agree with the plural subject *few airports*.

9. **(C)** *There* is used before *is* to refer to the noun *salt* at the specific place *in the ocean*.

10. **(B)** There must be agreement between subject and verb. *Were* should be *was* to agree with the singular subject *work*.

11. **(C)** There must be agreement between subject and verb. The verb *is* in Choice (C) agrees with the singular subject *the average temperature of rocks*. Choice (A) is a verb word, not a verb that can agree with a subject. Choice (B) is a verb that would agree with a plural, not a singular, subject. Choice (D) is a participle without an auxiliary verb that would agree with a subject.

12. **(B)** There must be agreement between pronoun and antecedent. *Their* should be *his* or *her* to agree with the singular subject *each voter*.

13. **(B)** There must be agreement between pronoun and antecedent. *They* should be *one* or *he* to agree with the impersonal antecedent *one*.

14. **(A)** There must be agreement between subject and verb. *Are* should be *is* to agree with the singular subject *a large percentage*.

15. **(B)** There must be agreement between subject and verb. The verb *has* in Choice (B) agrees with the singular subject *a mature grove*. The verbs in Choices (A) and (C) would agree with a plural, not a singular, subject. Choice (D) is an *-ing form*, not a verb that can agree with a subject.

16. **(D)** There must be agreement between subject and verb. *Is* should be *are* to agree with the plural subject *coins*.

17. **(C)** There must be agreement between subject and verb. *Are* should be *is* to agree with the inverted singular subject *evidence*.

18. **(D)** There must be agreement between subject and verb. *Are contained* should be *is contained* to agree with the plural subject *the urinary system*.

19. **(C)** There must be agreement between subject and verb. The verb *were* in Choice (C) agrees with the plural subject *flying dinosaurs*. Choice (A) does not contain a verb. The verb in Choice (B) would agree with a singular, not a plural, subject. Choice (D) agrees with the subject, but *have* with a participle does not express a completed past action or state. Since dinosaurs are extinct, the simple past verb correctly expresses completion.

20. **(D)** There must be agreement between subject and verb. *Were* should be *was* to agree with the singular subject *Art Deco*.

EXERCISE 51: Sentences— Introductory Verbal Modifiers

1. **(A)** An introductory verbal phrase followed by a comma should immediately precede the noun that it modifies. *After finishing Roots* is misplaced because it does not modify the noun it precedes, *author Alex Haley*.

2. **(A)** An introductory verbal phrase followed by a comma should immediately precede the noun that it modifies. *A competitive sport* is misplaced because it does not modify the noun it precedes, *gymnasts*.

3. **(B)** An introductory verbal phrase followed by a comma should immediately precede the noun that it modifies. *Carefully soaking* should be [*you*] *carefully soak them* to provide a noun and a verb for the introductory verbal phrase *to remove stains from permanent press clothing*.

4. **(C)** An introductory phrase should immediately precede the noun that it modifies. Only Choice (C) provides a noun that could be logically modified by the introductory phrase *An abstract painter and pioneer of Surrealism*. Neither *Miro's works,* nor *the works of Miro* nor *bright colors* could logically be *painters* as would be implied by Choices (A), (B), and (D).

5. **(A)** An introductory verbal phrase followed by a comma should immediately precede the noun that it modifies. *Found in Tanzania by Mary Leakey* is misplaced because it does not precede the noun it modifies, *the three-million-year-old fossils*.

6. **(D)** An introductory verbal phrase followed by a comma should immediately precede the noun that it modifies. *Columbus's final resting place* should be *Columbus is now buried* because the man, not the place, is modified by the verbal phrase *Originally having been buried in Spain*.

7. **(A)** An introductory phrase should immediately precede the noun that it modifies. Only Choice (A) provides a noun that could be logically modified by the introductory phrase *One of the largest hotels on Earth*. In Choice (C), *91 elevators* could not logically be a *hotel*. Choices (B) and (D) are sentences, not nouns.

8. **(B)** An introductory verbal phrase followed by a comma should immediately precede the noun that it modifies. *New York audiences received the new play* should be *the new play was received by New York audiences* because the play, not the audiences, is modified by the verbal phrase *written by Neil Simon*.

9. **(A)** An introductory verbal phrase followed by a comma should immediately precede the noun that it modifies. *Dental floss should be used* should be [*you*] *use dental floss* to provide a noun for the introductory verbal phrase *to prevent cavities*.

10. **(A)** An introductory verbal phrase followed by a comma should immediately precede the noun that it modifies. *The Senate committee's discovery* should be *The Senate committee discovered* because the *committee*, not the *discovery*, is modified by the verbal phrase *while researching the problem of violent crime*.

11. **(B)** An introductory phrase should immediately precede the noun that it modifies. Neither *one third of North America*, nor *North America*, nor *the water* could logically be a *river* as would be implied by Choices (A), (C), and (D).

12. **(A)** An introductory verbal phrase followed by a comma should immediately precede the noun that it modifies. *After reviewing the curriculum* is misplaced because it does not precede the noun it modifies, *faculty*.

13. **(D)** An introductory verbal phrase followed by a comma should immediately precede the noun that it modifies. *Hank Aaron's record* should be *Hank Aaron* because the *man*, not the *record*, is modified by the verbal phrase *having hit more home runs in one year than any other player in the history of baseball*.

14. **(A)** An introductory verbal phrase followed by a comma should immediately precede the noun that it modifies. *Banned in the U.S.* is misplaced because it does not precede the noun it modifies, *fluorocarbons*.

15. **(B)** An introductory verbal phrase should immediately precede the noun that it modifies. Only Choice (B) provides a noun that could logically be modified by the introductory phrase *while trying to build a tunnel*. Neither *coal* nor *the construction site* could logically *build a tunnel* as would be implied by Choices (A) and (C). Choice (D) is wordy and indirect.

16. **(A)** An introductory verbal phrase followed by a comma should immediately precede the noun that it modifies. *To avoid jet lag* is misplaced because it does not precede the noun it modifies, *patients*.

17. **(B)** An introductory verbal phrase followed by a comma should immediately precede the noun that it modifies. *Named for women* is misplaced because it does not precede the noun it modifies, *a hurricane*.

18. **(C)** An introductory verbal phrase should immediately precede the noun that it modifies. Only Choice (C) provides a noun that could logically be modified by the introductory verbal phrase, *published by Penguin Press*. *Ernest Hemingway* would not logically be *published* as would be implied by Choice (A). Choices (B) and (D) are wordy and indirect.

19. **(B)** An introductory verbal phrase should immediately precede the noun that it modifies. Only Choice (A) provides a noun that could logically be modified by the introductory phrase *born in 1892*. Neither *the library* nor *at the library* could logically *be born* as would be implied by Choices (A) and (D). Choice (C) is awkward because it has two introductory phrases used consecutively.

20. **(A)** An introductory verbal phrase followed by a comma should immediately precede the noun that it modifies. *Founded in 1919* is misplaced because it does not precede the noun it modifies, *the Institute for International Education*.

EXERCISE 52: Sentences—Parallel Structure

1. **(B)** Ideas after inclusives should be expressed by parallel structures. *Not only popular* should be *popular not only* to provide parallelism between the adverbial phrases *in the United States* and *abroad*.

2. **(A)** Ideas in a series should be expressed by parallel structures. *Making* should be *to make* to provide parallelism with the infinitive *to control*.

3. **(B)** Ideas after exclusives should be expressed by parallel structure. The correlative conjunction *neither* requires *nor*. Choice (B) has a verb word after *nor* to provide parallelism with the verb word *read* after *neither*. Choice (A) has a pronoun, not a verb word, after *nor*. The word *or* in Choice (C) and *neither* in Choice (D) are not the correct correlative conjunction for *neither*.

4. **(D)** Ideas in a series should be expressed by parallel structures. *Signing your name* should be *the signature* to provide parallelism with the nouns *the address*, *the inside address*, *the salutation*, *the body*, and *the closing*.

5. **(D)** Ideas in a series should be expressed by parallel structures. The noun *diagnosis* in Choice (D) provides parallelism with the nouns *cooking* and *telecommunications*. Choice (A) is an infinitive, not a noun. Choice (B) is an *-ing* form. Choice (C) is a past verb.

6. **(A)** Ideas in a series should be expressed by parallel structures. *Being introduced* should be *to be introduced* to provide parallelism with the infinitive *to read*.

7. **(A)** Ideas in a series should be expressed by parallel structures. *Ice skating* should be *to go ice skating* to provide parallelism with the infinitive *to go skiing*.

8. **(C)** Ideas in a series should be expressed by parallel structures. *Avoiding* should be *avoid* to provide parallelism with the verb words *drink* and *eat*.

9. **(A)** Ideas after exclusives should be expressed by parallel structures. The verb word *transmit* in Choice (A) provides parallelism with the verb word *conduct*. Choice (B) is an *-ing* form, not a verb word. Choices (C) and (D) are nouns.

10. **(D)** Ideas in a series should be expressed by parallel structures. *There are* should be deleted to provide parallelism among the nouns *the flag, the airplane*, and *the gowns*.

11. **(D)** Ideas after inclusives should be expressed by parallel structures. *The House of Representatives* should be *by the House of Representatives* to provide parallelism with the phrase *by the Senate*.

12. **(B)** Ideas in a series should be expressed by parallel structures. The noun phrase *the energy* in Choice (A) provides parallelism with the noun phrase *the heat*. Choice (A) is a question word conjunction, not a noun phrase. Choices (C) and (D) are nouns, but they are not noun phrases with the determiner *the*.

13. **(D)** Ideas in a series should be expressed by parallel structures. *With ease* should be *easily* to provide parallelism with the adverbs *safely* and *efficiently*.

14. **(C)** Ideas after exclusives should be expressed by parallel structures and exclusives should be used in coordinating pairs. *But also* should be *but* to coordinate with *not*.

15. **(C)** Ideas in a series should be expressed by parallel structures. The adjective *decorated* in Choice (C) provides parallelism with the adjectives *cast* and *carved*. Choice (A) is a noun, not an adjective. Choice (B) is an *-ing* form. Choice (D) is a verb word.

16. **(C)** Ideas in a series should be expressed by parallel structures. *Also they* should be deleted to provide parallelism among the verb words *stick out, move*, and *retract*.

17. **(C)** Ideas after inclusives should be expressed by parallel structures, and inclusives should be used in coordinating pairs. *Also* should be *but also* to coordinate with *not only*.

18. **(D)** Ideas in a series should be expressed by parallel structures. *Move* should be *the movement of* to provide parallelism with the noun phrase *the maintenance of*.

19. **(D)** Ideas in a series should be expressed by parallel structures. The verb *help* in Choice (D) provides parallelism with the verbs *report* and *give*. Choices (A) and (B) are *-ing* forms, not verbs. Choice (C) is a parallel verb, but when the verb *help* is used as a causative, it requires a verb word after it, not an *-ing* form.

20. **(D)** Ideas in a series should be expressed by parallel structures. *To control* should be *the control of* to provide parallelism with the nouns *techniques, capitalization*, and *specialization*.

EXERCISE 53: Sentences—Redundancy

1. **(D)** Repetition of a word by another word with the same meaning is redundant. *Again* should be deleted because it means *repeat*.
2. **(A)** Repetition of the subject by a subject pronoun is redundant. *It* should be deleted.
3. **(B)** Redundant, indirect phrases should be avoided. The adverb *uniformly* in Choice (B) is simple and more direct than the phrases in Choices (A) and (C). Choice (D) is not an adverb, and cannot describe the manner in which the *gas expands*.
4. **(D)** Indirect phrases instead of adverbs are redundant. *In an impartial manner* should be *impartially*.
5. **(C)** Repetition of the subject by the subject pronoun is redundant. *They* should be deleted.
6. **(D)** Repetition of a word by another word with the same meaning is redundant. *Bank* should be deleted because it means *return*.
7. **(B)** Redundant, indirect phrases should be avoided. Choice (B) is the simplest, most direct choice. Choice (A) is redundant because the pronoun *it* is used consecutively after the noun clause subject *that witches cause disasters and misfortunes*. Choice (C) is redundant because the phrase *in a wide way* is used instead of the simpler, more direct adverb *widely*. Choice (D) is an additional clause that does not provide a main verb for the noun clause subject that precedes it, *that witches cause disasters and misfortunes*.
8. **(B)** Repetition of a word by another word with the same meaning is redundant. *Enough* should be deleted because it means *sufficiently*.
9. **(B)** Words or phrases that do not add information are redundant. *In nature* should be deleted.
10. **(C)** Repetition of a subject by a subject pronoun is redundant. *They* should be deleted.
11. **(C)** Redundant, indirect phrases should be avoided. Choice (C) is the simplest, most direct choice. Choices (A), (B), and (D) are redundant because they all use the subject pronoun *it* along with the subject noun *Joshua tree*.
12. **(B)** Redundant, indirect phrases should be avoided. The adverb in Choice (B) is the simplest, most direct choice. Choices (A), (C), and (D) are all redundant phrases.
13. **(C)** Repetition of a word by another word with the same meaning is redundant. *New* should be deleted because it means *innovations*.
14. **(D)** Repetition of a word by another word with the same meaning is redundant. *By name* should be deleted
15. **(B)** Repetition of a word by another word with the same meaning is redundant. *Forward* should be deleted because it means *advances*.
16. **(B)** Repetition of the subject by a subject pronoun is redundant. *It* should be deleted.
17. **(D)** Indirect phrases instead of adverbs are redundant. *With rapidity* should be *rapidly*.
18. **(B)** Redundant, indirect phrases should be avoided. Choice (B) provides a verb and a modified adjective in the complement. Choice (A) is redundant because the subject pronoun *they* is used consecutively with the noun phrase subject *digital clocks*. Choice (C) requires a verb before *not*. Choice (D) requires a modal before *not*.
19. **(C)** Using words with the same meaning consecutively is repetitive. *Both, together*, and *with* in Choices (A), (B), and (D) all have the same meaning.
20. **(A)** Repetition of the subject by a subject pronoun is redundant. *It* should be deleted.

EXERCISE 54: Sentences— Word Choice

1. **(D)** *Equal to* is a prepositional idiom. *As* should be *to*.
2. **(B)** *Raise* means "to move to a higher place." *Is risen* should be *is raised*.
3. **(C)** *Compare with* is a prepositional idiom. *Comparing* should be *compared with*.
4. **(D)** The past verb *borrowed* is used to maintain the past point of view established by the past adverbial phrase *in 1620*. Choices (B) and (C) are not past verbs. Choice (A) is not logical since the Pilgrims received the money. To *borrow* means to "receive." To *lend* means "to give." "An English company lent the Pilgrims seven thousand dollars" would also be correct.

5. **(C)** *Effects on* is a prepositional idiom. *In* should be *on*.

6. **(C)** *Let* means "allow." *Leave* should be *let*.

7. **(A)** *Effective* is not the correct part of speech. *Effective* should be *effect* to provide a noun as the subject of *is*.

8. **(A)** *The cops* is a colloquial expression. *The cops* should be *the police*.

9. **(B)** In order to refer to *residue*, *leave* should be used. *To leave* means "to let something [*residue*] remain." *To let* in Choice (A) means "to allow." *Residue* in Choice (C) cannot be used as a verb. Choice (D) is not idiomatic.

10. **(A)** In order to refer to a range of *frequencies*, *lie* should be used. *To lie* means "to occupy a place" [within the range]. *To lay* in Choice (B) means "to put in a place." Choices (C) and (D) are *-ing* forms, not verbs to agree with the subject *the audible range*.

11. **(A)** *To suspicion* is not idiomatic. *Suspicions* should be *suspects*.

12. **(A)** *Menkind* is not idiomatic. *Menkind* should be *mankind* or *humankind*.

13. **(A)** *As a whole* means "generally." Choices (B) and (D) are not idiomatic. Choice (C) means "completely."

14. **(A)** *The classify* is not the correct part of speech. *Classify* should be *Classification* to provide a noun as the subject of *begins*.

15. **(A)** *The develop* is not the correct part of speech. *Develop* should be *development* to provide a noun as the object of the preposition *with*.

16. **(C)** Become *bored with* is a prepositional idiom. Choices (A), (B), and (D) are not idiomatic expressions with *bored*.

17. **(A)** *An understand* is not the correct part of speech. *Understand* should be *understanding* to provide a noun as the subject of the verb *is*.

18. **(B)** *Presided over* is a prepositional idiom. *Presided* should be *presided over*.

19. **(C)** *Next to* is a prepositional idiom. Choices (A) and (B) are not idiomatic. Choice (D) means "almost," not "beside." "Near" would also be correct.

20. **(B)** *Depends on* is a prepositional idiom. *Depends to* should be *depends on*.

EXERCISE 55: Sentences— Comprehensive Structures

1. **(C)** *Most* is used before a noncount noun to express a quantity that is larger than half the amount. A singular verb follows the noncount noun. Choice (A) does not have a verb. In Choice (B), the verb is before, not after the noun. In Choice (D), *the* is used before *most*.

2. **(B)** An adjective is used before *enough* to express sufficiency. In Choice (A), *goodly* is ungrammatical. The adverbial form of the adjective *good* is *well*. In Choice (C), *as* is unnecessary and incorrect. In Choice (D), the adjective is used after, not before *enough*.

3. **(A)** *The* can be used before a noncount noun that is followed by a qualifying phrase. *Population* should be *the population* before the qualifying phrase *of the Americas*.

4. **(C)** An adjective clause modifies a noun in the main clause. *That the earliest cultures evolved* modifies *the way*. Choice (A) is a clause marker *that* and a noun. Choice (B) is a verb and a noun. Choice (D) is a clause marker *which* and a noun.

5. **(C)** A sentence has a subject and a verb. Choice (A) is redundant because the subject pronoun *it* is used consecutively with the subject *calculus*. Choice (B) has the marker *that* to introduce a main clause. Choice (D) is redundant because it has a verb that replaces the main verb *can reduce*.

6. **(B)** Subject-verb order and a negative verb with *either* expresses negative agreement. Negative agreement with *neither* requires verb-subject order and an affirmative verb. In Choice (A), verb-subject order is reversed. In Choice (C), verb-subject order is reversed, and *neither* is used at the beginning, not at the end of the clause. In Choice (D) *either*, not *neither*, is used with verb-subject order and an affirmative verb. "Neither did Mexico" would also be correct.

7. **(D)** A sentence has a subject and a verb. Choice (A) does not have a verb. Choices (B) and (C) introduce a main clause subject and verb.

8. **(C)** The anticipatory clause *it is accepted that* introduces a subject and verb, *the*

formation . . . began. Choices (A), (B), and (D) are incomplete and ungrammatical.

9. **(A)** The word order for a passive sentence is a form of BE followed by a participle. Only Choice (A) has the correct word order. Choice (B) does not have a BE form. Choice (C) has a HAVE, not a BE form. Choice (D) is a present tense verb, not BE followed by a participle.

10. **(C)** Subject-verb order is used in the clause after a question word connector such as *how much*. In Choice (A), subject-verb order is reversed. In Choice (B), the auxiliary *does* is unnecessary and incorrect. In Choice (D), the verb *are* is repetitive. "The Consumer Price Index lists how much every car *is*" would also be correct.

11. **(C)** A logical conclusion about the past is expressed by *must have* and a participle. Choices (A), (B), and (D) are not logical because they imply that the *theater* will act to restore *itself*.

12. **(A)** The verb *to want* requires an infinitive complement. Choice (B) is an *-ing* form, not an infinitive. Choice (C) is a verb word. Choice (D) is ungrammatical.

13. **(C)** An introductory verbal phrase should immediately precede the noun that it modifies. Only Choice (C) provides a noun which could be logically modified by the introductory verbal phrase, *after seeing the movie.* Neither *the book* nor *the reading* could logically *see a movie* as would be implied by Choices (A), (B), and (D).

14. **(A)** An introductory phrase should immediately precede the subject noun that it modifies. It does not have a main verb. Choices (B) and (C) contain both subjects and verbs. Choice (D) does not modify the subject noun, *Carl Sandburg.*

15. **(B)** A form of *make* with someone such as *us* and a verb word expresses a causative. Choice (A) is an *-ing* form, not a verb word. Choice (C) is a past form. Choice (D) is an infinitive.

16. **(A)** *Responsible for* is a prepositional idiom. *Responsible the* should be *responsible for the.*

17. **(B)** A form of BE is used with the participle in passive sentences. *Practice* should be *practiced.*

18. **(C)** There must be agreement between pronoun and antecedent. *Their* should be *our* to agree with the second person antecedent *those of us.*

19. **(B)** *Wrote* should be *written* because the auxiliary *had* requires a participle. *Wrote* is a past form. *Written* is a participle.

20. **(A)** *Would have* and a participle in the result require *had* and a participle in the condition. Because *would have won* is used in the result, *would have* should be *had* in the condition.

21. **(B)** There must be agreement between pronoun and antecedent. *Which* should be *who* to refer to the antecedent *Shirley Temple Black. Which* refers to things. *Who* refers to persons.

22. **(D)** Comparative forms are usually followed by *than.* After the comparative *more reasonable, as* should be *than.*

23. **(D)** *To know* should be *to know how* before the infinitive *to use. To know* is used before nouns and noun clauses. *To know how* is used before infinitives.

24. **(C)** *There* introduces inverted order, but there must still be agreement between subject and verb. *Has been* should be *have been* to agree with the plural subject *two major factions.*

25. **(A)** In order to refer to occupying a place on the battlefields, *lain* should be used. *To lay* means "to put in a place," and the participle is *laid. To lie* means "to occupy a place," and the participle is *lain.*

26. **(B)** *Purposeful* should be *purposes. Purposeful* is an adjective. *Purposes* is a noun.

27. **(B)** *Large* should be *largest.* Because there were more than two ethnic groups, a superlative form must be used.

28. **(B)** The determiner *a* is used before a singular count noun. *Results* should be *result.*

29. **(B)** Most adverbs of manner are formed by adding *-ly* to adjectives. *Calm* should be *calmly* to qualify the manner in which the talking should be done.

30. **(B)** When the degree of one quality, *the heat*, is dependent upon the degree of another quality, *the humidity*, two comparatives are used, each preceded by *the. The worst* should be *the worse* because it is a comparative.

31. **(B)** A dependent clause modifies an independent clause. *Which are* should be *are* to provide a verb for the subject *statistical data*, of the independent clause.

32. **(D)** Ideas in a series should be expressed by parallel structures. *The Assassinate* should be *The Assassination of* to provide for parallelism with the nouns *Causes*, *Economy*, and *Strategies*.

33. **(A)** *Despite of* is a combination of *despite* and *in spite of*. Either *despite* or *in spite of* should be used.

34. **(A)** Because it is a prepositional phrase, in a comparison *as every nation* should be *like every nation*. *As* functions as a conjunction. *Like* functions as a preposition.

35. **(A)** A verb word must be used in a clause after the phrase *It is necessary*. *Met* should be *meet*. *Met* is a past form. *Meet* is a verb word.

36. **(D)** The verb *forbid* may be used with either an infinitive or an *-ing* complement. *From owning* should be *to own*. The *-ing* form *owning* would require the possessive pronoun modifier *their*.

37. **(C)** *More cheaper* should be *cheaper*. Because *cheap* is a one-syllable adjective, the comparative is formed by adding *-er*. *More* is used with two-syllable adjectives that do not end in *-y*.

38. **(A)** The verb *thought* establishes a point of view in the past. *Will* should be *would* in order to maintain the point of view.

39. **(D)** Because the verb *enjoy* requires an *-ing* form in the complement, *to play* should be *playing*.

40. **(D)** Ideas in a series should be expressed by parallel structures. *To plant* should be *planting* to provide parallelism with the *-ing* forms *plowing* and *rotating*.

Reading

EXERCISE 56: Narration/Sequence—Popular Culture

1. **(B)** The main idea is found in the concluding sentence, "Although he created the game of basketball . . ." Choices (A), (C), and (D) are major points that support the main idea, "the development of basketball."

2. **(D)** ". . . basketball was introduced as a demonstration sport in the 1904 Olympic Games . . ." Choice (A) refers to the date that Naismith organized the first basketball game, not to its introduction in the Olympics. Choice (C) refers to the date that five players became standard. Choice (B) is not mentioned and may not be concluded from information in the passage.

3. **(A)** In the context of this passage, *balk* means to "resist." Choices (B), (C), and (D) are not accepted meanings of the word *balk*.

4. **(C)** In the context of this passage, *fierce* means "extreme." Choices (A), (B), and (D) are not accepted meanings of the word *fierce*.

5. **(C)** "First he attempted to adapt outdoor games such as soccer and rugby to indoor play, but he soon found *them* [outdoor games] unsuitable for confined areas." The pronoun *them* does not refer to Choices (A), (B), or (D).

6. **(C)** "Five years later, a championship tournament was staged in New York City, which was won by the Brooklyn Central YMCA." The other lines do not discuss the winner of the first basketball championship tournament.

7. **(B)** Choice (B) is a paraphrase of the statement. The phrase to "quickly spread throughout the world" means to "become popular worldwide." Choices (A), (C), and (D) do not paraphrase what the author means.

8. **(C)** "Dr. Naismith noticed a lack of interest in exercise among students during the wintertime." Choice (A) is not correct because Dr. Naismith tried to adapt soccer and rugby. Choice (D) is not correct because basketball is played indoors. Choice (B) is not mentioned and may not be concluded from information in the passage.

9. **(B)** Choice (A) is mentioned in line 16. Choice (C) is mentioned in line 15. Choice (D) is mentioned in lines 17–18. Choice (B) is not correct because running with the ball was a violation.

10. **(C)** Because someone had to climb a ladder to retrieve the ball every time a goal was made, it may be concluded that the original baskets did not have a hole in the bottom. Choice (A) is not correct because someone had to climb a ladder to retrieve the ball. Choice (B) is not correct because a metal hoop was introduced in 1906. Choice (D) is not correct because the baskets were hung at either side of the gymnasium.

EXERCISE 57: Definition/Illustration—Popular Culture

1. **(A)** The main idea is found in the concluding sentence, "Mickey Mouse was not Walt Disney's first successful cartoon creation, but he is certainly his most famous one." Choices (B), (C), and (D) are major points that support the main idea, "the image of Mickey Mouse."

2. **(B)** "In the third short cartoon, *Steamboat Willie*, Mickey was whistling and singing through the miracle of the modern sound track" Choice (C) is not correct because Minnie was a co-star in the first cartoon, *Plane Crazy*. Choices (A) and (D) are not mentioned and may not be concluded from information in the passage.

3. **(B)** In the context of this passage, *pervasive* means "widespread." Choices (A), (C), and (D) are not accepted meanings of the word *pervasive*.

4. **(A)** In the context of this passage, *appealing* means "attractive" Choices (B), (C), and (D) are not accepted meanings of the word *appealing*.

5. **(A)** "Although he has received a few minor changes throughout his lifetime, most notably the addition of white gloves and the rounder forms of a more childish body, he has remained true to his nature since *those* [cartoons] first cartoons." The pronoun *those* does not refer to Choices (B), (C), or (D).

6. **(A)** "But we do know that Disney had intended to call him Mortimer until his wife Lillian intervened and christened him

Mickey Mouse." The other lines do not indicate Disney's first choice of a name for Mickey Mouse.

7. **(D)** Choice (D) is a paraphrase of the statement. "Nature" means "personality." Choices (A), (B), and (C) do not paraphrase what the author means.

8. **(C)** "Perhaps that was Disney's own image of himself." Choices (A) and (D) are true, but they are not what Disney means when he says that "There is a lot of the mouse in me." Choice (B) is not mentioned and may not be concluded from information in the passage.

9. **(D)** Choices (A) and (C) are mentioned in lines 7–8. Choice (B) is mentioned in line 4. Choice (D) is not correct because the gloves were added later.

10. **(B)** Because the last sentence of this passage mentions one image in popular culture, it may be concluded that the paragraph following the passage most probably discusses other images in popular culture. Choices (A) and (D) are referred to only as they relate to the Mickey Mouse image. Choice (C) is not mentioned and may not be concluded from information in the passage.

EXERCISE 58: Narration/Sequence— Social Sciences

1. **(C)** The main idea is found in the topic sentence, "Federal policy toward the Native Americans has a long history of inconsistency, reversal, and failure." Choice (A) contradicts the fact that the policies have been inconsistent. Choice (B) contradicts the fact that today, government policies are unclear. Choice (D) is a major point that supports the main idea, "inconsistent and unclear policies."

2. **(B)** ". . . expulsion of the major Southeastern tribes to . . . what is now Oklahoma . . . which the Cherokee Nation refers to as the 'Trail of Tears' . . ." Choice (A) refers to the Dawes Severalty Act, not to the "Trail of Tears." Choice (C) refers to policies before the "Trail of Tears." Choice (D) refers to policies in the 1950s.

3. **(B)** In the context of this passage, *ambivalent* means "experiencing contradictory feelings." Choices (A), (C), and (D) are not accepted meanings of the word *ambivalent*.

4. **(A)** In the context of this passage, *culminated* means "ended." Choices (B), (C), and (D) are not accepted meanings of the word *culminated*.

5. **(A)** "At the same time, the government supported missionary groups in their efforts to build churches, schools, and model farms for those tribes that permitted *them* [missionary groups] to live in their midst."

6. **(C)** "Congress passed the Dawes Severalty Act, and for the next forty years Indian agents and missionaries attempted to destroy the tribal system by separating the members. It was during this time that the government boarding schools were established to educate Native-American youth outside of the home environment." The other lines do not refer to the congressional act that allowed Native-American students to be sent to boarding schools.

7. **(D)** Choice (D) is a paraphrase of the statement. In both sentences, the president gives the order, but Congress and the Supreme Court oppose it. None of the other choices paraphrases what the author means.

8. **(A)** ". . . the government had discovered that some of the land allocated as permanent reservations for the Native Americans contained valuable resources. Congress passed the Dawes Severalty Act. . . ." Choice (B) refers to the plan that was put in place after the act was passed in order to break up the tribes. Choice (C) refers to a policy from the 1950s, not from the 1800s. Choice (D) refers to the attitude of some government officials today, not during the era of the Dawes Severalty Act.

9. **(C)** Choices (A) and (D) are mentioned in paragraph 1, sentence 1. Choice (B) is mentioned in paragraph 2, sentence 3.

10. **(A)** Because the last sentence of this passage mentions the ambivalence of the Native Americans about the role of the federal government in their affairs, it may be concluded that the paragraph following the passage most probably discusses the Native Americans' point of view regarding government policies today. Choices (B), (C), and (D) are not mentioned and may not be concluded from information in the passage.

EXERCISE 59: Narration/Sequence—Arts/Architecture

1. **(C)** The main idea is found in the concluding sentence, ". . . his work chronicled his life." Choice (A) contradicts the fact that the first six lines of the passage describe his life before he began writing. Choice (B) contradicts the fact that the last twelve lines of the passage describe his work. Choice (D) refers to the fact that his characters were portraits of himself and his family, not to the theme of the passage.

2. **(C)** "The play [*Beyond the Horizon*] won the Pulitzer prize for the best play of the year. O'Neill was to be awarded the prize again in 1922, 1928, and 1957." Choice (A) refers to the number of times that O'Neill won the Nobel, not the Pulitzer, prize. Choice (B) refers to the number of times that O'Neill won the Pulitzer prize in addition to the first time. Choice (D) refers to the total number of times that O'Neill was awarded the Pulitzer and Nobel prizes.

3. **(B)** In the context of this passage, *briefly* means "for a short time." Choices (A), (C), and (D) are not accepted meanings of the word *briefly*.

4. **(B)** In the context of this passage, *struggle* means "conflict." Choices (A), (C), and (D) are not accepted meanings of the word *struggle*.

5. **(B)** "It [the one-act *Bound East for Cardiff*] was produced on Cape Cod by the Province-town Players, an experimental theater group that was later to settle in the famous Greenwich Village theater district in New York."

6. **(B)** "Upon returning from voyages to South Africa and South America, he was hospitalized for six months to recuperate from tuberculosis." The other lines do not indicate the reason for O'Neill's hospitalization.

7. **(A)** Choice (A) is a paraphrase of the statement. In both Sentences, family members were characters in his plays. None of the other choices paraphrases what the author means.

8. **(D)** "Although he did not receive the Pulitzer Prize for it, *Mourning Becomes Electra*, produced in 1931, is arguably his most lasting contribution to the American theater." Choices (A), (B), and (C) refer to plays that were awarded the Pulizer Prize, not to the play that the author identified as the most important to the American theater.

9. **(A)** Choice (B) is mentioned in paragraph 1, sentence 5. Choices (C) and (D) are mentioned in paragraph 3, sentence 1.

10. **(C)** ". . . several themes emerge, including the ambivalence of family relationships, the struggle between the sexes, the conflict between spiritual and material desires, and the vision of modern man as a victim." Choice (A) contradicts the fact that the themes mentioned were controversial. Choice (B) contradicts the fact that most of the characters were portraits of himself and his family. Choice (D) contradicts the fact that O'Neill's plays won so many awards.

EXERCISE 60: Narration/Sequence—Humanities/Business

1. **(B)** The main topic is found in the title, "The Print Revolution," and is developed throughout the passage. Choices (A), (C), and (D) are major points that support the main topic, "A history of the printing process worldwide."

2. **(B)** "Once they [myths, songs, and histories] appeared in print, they could no longer be performed and refashioned, only recited." Choice (A) is not correct because print standardized popular culture, but the effect of oral tradition on print is not mentioned. Choice (D) is not correct because traditional performers would have been adept at oral history, not recitation. Choice (C) is not mentioned and may not be concluded from information in the passage.

3. **(B)** In the context of this passage, *crucial* means "very significant." Choices (A), (C), and (D) are not accepted meanings of the word *crucial*.

4. **(B)** In the context of this passage, *character* means "nature." Choices (A), (C), and (D) are not accepted meaning of the word *character*.

5. **(A)** "Molten metal was poured into *it* [the box], producing a single piece of type." The pronoun *it* does not refer to Choices (B), (C), or (D).

6. **(A)** "It appears that the Mongol armies brought examples of Chinese printing—the Venetian Marco Polo described seeing paper money during his travels—to western Asia and Europe at the end of the thirteenth

century." Choice (B) refers to the printing press, not to block printing. Choice (C) is not correct because the passage mentions that Europeans saw paper money in their travels, but the passage does not mention whether they printed paper money. Choice (D) is not mentioned and may not be concluded from information in the passage.

7. **(B)** Choice (B) is a paraphrase of the statement. Choices (A), (C), and (D) change the meaning of the statement.

8. **(D)** Choice (A) is mentioned in paragraph 7, sentence 5. Choice (B) is mentioned in paragraph 7, sentence 6. Choice (C) is mentioned in paragraph 6, sentence 3.

9. **(D)** Because Gutenberg engaged in years of costly experimentation, it may be concluded that he worked for a long time to perfect his printing process. Choice (B) is not correct because he was alive after the Bibles were printed. Choice (C) is not correct because he was a goldsmith, not a painter. Choice (A) is not mentioned and may not be concluded from information in the passage.

10. **(C)** Paraphrase is a transitional device that connects the inserted sentence with the previous sentence. The previous sentence indicates that Gutenberg "was forced to turn over his equipment and . . . Bibles," which implies that he did not benefit financially. In the inserted sentence, the paraphrase is ". . . he did not receive the financial remuneration that he deserved." Choices (A), (B), and (D) do not include transitional devices that connect with the sentences marked in the passage.

11. **(B)** *Egypt* is the place where scribes began to copy manuscripts. **(D) (G)** *China* and *Korea* are the places where block printing was devised. **(A)** *Germany* is the place where the Gutenberg Bible was published. **(C)** *Italy* is the place where smaller "octavo" books were popularized. **(F)** *England* is the place where native-language books appeared. Choice (E) is not mentioned in the passage.

12. **(A) (B) (E)** summarize the passage. Choice (C) is true, but it is a minor point that is mentioned in reference to the information and ideas made available throughout Europe. Choice (F) is true, but it is a minor point that is mentioned in the context of Gutenberg's invention. Choice (E) is not mentioned in the passage.

EXERCISE 61: Narration/Sequence— Natural Sciences

1. **(D)** The main topic is found in the title, "Glacial Movement." Choices (A), (B), and (C) are major points that support the main topic, "The movement of glaciers."

2. **(A)** ". . . a glacier's basal ice layer, which can extend tens of meters above its base, has a much greater debris content than the ice above." Choice (B) is not correct because a crevasse often contains a veneer of snow, not debris. Choice (C) is not correct because the ice above contains less debris. Choice (D) is not correct because the soft bed contains water and sediment, not debris.

3. **(B)** In the context of this passage, *brittle* means "fragile." Choices (A), (C), and (D) are not accepted meanings of the word *brittle*.

4. **(A)** In the context of this passage, *abrupt* means "unexpected." Choices (B), (C), and (D) are not accepted meanings of the word *abrupt*.

5. **(B)** "But glacial ice has different properties, depending on *its* [the glacial ice's] location in a glacier." The pronoun *its* does not refer to Choices (A), (C), or (D).

6. **(B)** "Some surge events result from a buildup of water pressure under the glacier. . . . Surges can occur in dry conditions . . . as the glacier . . . picks up rock from its bed and moves forward. Another cause of glacier surges is the presence of a water-saturated layer of sediment." Choice (A) is not correct because the rate of snow accumulation affects the pace of normal glacial movement, not glacial surges. Choice (C) refers to the rock that the glacier picks up, not to the cause of a surge. Choice (D) is not correct because the icequakes occur after the surge begins, not before.

7. **(B)** Choice (B) is a paraphrase of the statement. *To have or be different* means "to vary." Choices (A), (C), and (D) change the meaning of the statement.

8. **(A)** Choice (B) is mentioned in paragraph 1, sentence 1. Choice (C) is mentioned in paragraph 1, sentence 4, and paragraph 3, sentence 2. Choice (D) is mentioned in paragraph 5, sentence 3.

9. **(A)** Because normal rates are reported in inches or feet, it may be concluded that

glaciers move very slowly. Choice (B) is not correct because regelation facilitates down-slope movement. Choice (C) is not correct because icequakes occur at the beginning of a surge, but they have not been identified as a cause. Choice (D) is not mentioned and may not be concluded from information in the passage.

10. **(B)** "In other words" is a transitional phrase that connects the inserted sentence with the previous sentence. The two sentences are related by the restatement of "the rate of snow accumulation" in the previous sentence and "the heavier the snowfall" in the inserted sentence. Choices (A), (C), and (D) do not include transitional devices that connect with the sentences marked in the passage.

11. **(E)** and **(G)** are characteristic of *basal slip*. **(A)** and **(H)** are characteristic of *regelation*. **(C)** and **(I)** are characteristic of *glacier surge*. Choice (F) is not correct because it refers to crevasses. Choices (B) and (D) are not mentioned in the passage.

12. **(A) (C) (E)** summarize the passage. Choice (B) is true, but it is a minor point that is mentioned in reference to the movement of a glacier. Choice (D) is true, but it is a minor point that is mentioned as an example of a glacier surge. Choice (F) is not mentioned in the passage.

EXERCISE 62: Definition/Illustration—Humanities/Business

1. **(C)** The main idea is found in the topic sentence, "Canada is a constitutional monarchy with a parliamentary system of government modeled after that of Great Britain." Choices (A), (B), and (D) are major points that support the main idea, "the Canadian system of government."

2. **(B)** "When a government loses its majority support in a general election, a change of government occurs." Choices (A), (C), and (D) are not correct because the government is elected by the voters. In Choice (A), the governor-general represents the queen but he does not appoint the government. Choice (C) is not correct because the prime minister chooses a cabinet, not a government. Choice (D) is not correct because the House of Commons holds a great deal of power in the government, but does not choose the government.

3. **(D)** In the context of this passage, *dissolved* means "dismissed." Choices (A), (B), and (C) are not accepted meanings of the word *dissolved*.

4. **(B)** In the context of this passage, *varied* means "different." Choices (A), (C), and (D) are not accepted meanings of the word *varied*.

5. **(B)** "The system is referred to as responsible government, which means that the cabinet members sit in parliament and are directly responsible to *it* [parliament], holding power only as long as a majority of the House of Commons shows confidence by voting with them."

6. **(B)** "The actual head of government is the prime minister, who is responsible for choosing a cabinet." The other lines do not indicate whose responsibility it is to choose the cabinet.

7. **(C)** Choice (C) is a paraphrase of the statement. If the system of government is "modeled after that of Great Britain" then the two countries must have "very similar systems of government." None of the other choices paraphrases what the author means.

8. **(C)** "Although major and minor political parties were not created by law, they are recognized by law in Canada. The party that wins the largest number of seats in a general election forms the government, and its leader becomes the prime minister." Choice (A) is not correct because political parties are recognized by law. Choice (B) is not correct because the party that wins the general election forms the [official] government. Choice (D) may be true, but it is not mentioned and may not be concluded from information in the passage.

9. **(B)** Choices (A) and (C) are mentioned in paragraph 1, sentence 3. Choice (D) is mentioned in paragraph 3, sentence 1. Choice (B) contradicts the fact that the actual head of government is the prime minister.

10. **(D)** Because a change of government occurs when a government loses its majority support in a general election, it may be concluded that the voters in Canada determine when a change of government should occur. Choice (A) contradicts the fact that the prime

minister chooses the cabinet. Choice (C) contradicts the fact that the members of the House of Commons are elected directly by voters in general elections. Choice (B) is not mentioned and may not be concluded from information in the passage.

EXERCISE 63: Definition/Illustration— Natural Sciences

1. **(A)** The main idea is found in the topic sentence, "It [hydrogen] is among the ten most common elements on Earth as well and one of the most useful for industrial purposes." It is repeated in the first sentence in the second paragraph "hydrogen . . . has several properties that make it valuable for many industries." Choices (B), (C), and (D) are major ". . . points that support the main idea, "the industrial uses of hydrogen."

2. **(D)** ". . . hydrogen is used with oxygen for welding torches that produce temperatures as high as 4,000 degrees F and can be used in cutting steel." Choice (A) is not correct because the hydrogen is heated, and the steel is not cooled. Choice (B) is not correct because the hydrogen is heated, not cooled. Choice (C) is not correct because the hydrogen, not the temperature of the steel, is heated.

3. **(D)** In the context of this passage, *readily* means "easily." Choices (A), (B), and (C) are not accepted meanings of the word *readily*.

4. **(B)** In the context of this passage, *combining* means "adding." Choices (A), (C), and (D) are not accepted meanings of the word *combining*.

5. **(B)** "Hydrogen also serves to prevent metals from tarnishing during heat treatments by removing the oxygen from *them* [metals]."

6. **(D)** "Hydrogen is also one of the coolest refrigerants. [because] It does not become a liquid until it reaches temperatures of –425 degrees F." None of the other lines explains why hydrogen is used as a refrigerant.

7. **(D)** Choice (D) is a paraphrase of the statement. In both sentences, the oxygen and hydrogen are combined, and then heated. None of the other choices paraphrases what the author means.

8. **(B)** "Pure hydrogen seldom occurs naturally, but it exists in most organic compounds. . . .

Moreover, hydrgoen is found in inorganic compounds." Choices (A) and (C) are not correct because pure hydrogen seldom occurs naturally. Choice (D) is not correct because hydrogen is added, not released, during hydrogenation.

9. **(D)** Choice (A) is mentioned in paragraph 2, sentence 1. Choice (B) is mentioned in paragraph 4, sentence 4. Choice (C) is mentioned in paragraph 3, sentence 2. Choice (D) contradicts the fact that liquids are changed to semi-solids, not the reverse.

10. **(B)** Because several uses for hydrogen in a number of industries are mentioned in the passage, it may be concluded that hydrogen has many purposes in a variety of industries. Choices (A) and (D) contradict the fact that several industrial purposes are mentioned in the passage. Choice (C) contradicts the fact that hydrogen has several properties that make it valuable for many industries.

EXERCISE 64: Definition/Illustration— Social Sciences

1. **(B)** The main idea is found in the topic sentence, "Ritzer noticed that the principles that characterize fast-food organizations are increasingly coming to dominate more and more aspects of U.S. society, indeed, of societies around the world." Choices (A), (C), and (D) are major points that support the main topic, "The McDonald's organization is being copied in many aspects of society."

2. **(D)** "Calculability means that there is an emphasis on the quantitative aspects . . . everything has to be accounted for." Choice (A) is not correct because it refers to efficiency, not calculability. Choice (B) refers to predictability. Choice (C) is not mentioned and may not be concluded from information in the passage.

3. **(A)** In the context of this passage, *subject to* means "influenced by." Choices (B), (C), and (D) are not accepted meanings of the phrase *subject to*.

4. **(B)** In the context of this passage, *capacity* means "potential." Choices (A), (C), and (D) are not accepted meanings of the word *capacity*.

5. **(C)** "Ritzer argues that McDonald's has been such a successful model of business organi-

zation that other industries have adopted the same organizational characteristics, so much so that their nicknames associate *them* [other industries] with the McDonald's chain." The pronoun *them* does not refer to Choices (A), (B), or (D).

6. **(A)** "Control is the primary organizational principle that lies behind McDonaldization." Choices (B), (C), and (D) refer to other dimensions, but they are not identified as the most important.

7. **(C)** Choice (C) is a paraphrase of the statement. Choices (A), (B), and (D) change the meaning of the statement.

8. **(B)** Choices (A), (C), and (D) are mentioned in paragraph 4, sentence 2.

9. **(A)** Because Ritzer points out the danger of dehumanization in the McDonald's model and refers to its presence as "ubiquitous," it must be concluded that he does not support it. Choice (B) is not correct because Ritzer coined the term. Choices (C) and (D) are not mentioned and may not be concluded from information in the passage.

10. **(C)** Paraphrase is a transitional device that connects the inserted sentence with a previous sentence. The two sentences are related by the restatement of "exactly the same" in a previous sentence and "impossible to tell the difference" in the inserted sentence. In this case, the sentences are separated by an example. Choices (A), (B), and (D) do not include transitional devices that connect with the sentences marked in the passage.

11. **(F)** refers to *efficiency*. **(A)** and **(D)** refer to *calculability*. **(E)** refers to *predictability*. **(B)** refers to *control*. Choice (C) is not mentioned in the passage.

12. **(B) (C) (E)** summarize the passage. Choice (A) is true, but it is a minor point that is mentioned as an example of McDonaldization on a global scale. Choice (D) is true, but it is a minor point that is mentioned as an example of the association of an organization with the McDonald's business model. Choice (F) is not mentioned in the passage.

EXERCISE 65: Definition/Illustration—Arts/Architecture

1. **(B)** The main topic is found in the title, "The Audible Frequency Spectrum," and in the topic sentence, "Every musical culture of the world uses only a certain number of frequencies from the audible spectrum." Choice (C) is a major point that supports the main topic, "a definition of the audible spectrum." Choice (D) is a topic introduced at the end of the passage in anticipation of the next passage. Choice (A) is not mentioned in the passage.

2. **(B)** "In European-based music, the octave represents an eight-pitch structure, but if you count the number of white and black piano keys in an octave, you will count thirteen." Choice (A) is not correct because seven refers to the number of letters to label the pitches, not to the number of pitches themselves. Choice (C) is not correct because twelve refers to the number of half steps, not to the number of pitches. Choice (D) is not correct because thirteen refers to the number of keys.

3. **(B)** In the context of this passage, *particular* means "specific." Choices (A), (C), and (D) are not accepted meanings of the word *particular*.

4. **(A)** In the context of this passage, *adjacent* means "beside each other." Choices (B), (C), and (D) are not accepted meanings of the word *adjacent*.

5. **(D)** "Some cultures, such as *that* [the culture among some cultures] of Bali (Indonesia), use fewer pitches with wider distances between them; others use more pitches—twenty-two in Indian music, twenty-four in Arabic music." The pronoun *that* does not refer to Choices (A), (B), and (C).

6. **(A)** "Half steps and whole steps are examples of what are called *intervals*—specifiable distances between two pitches." Choice (B) refers to the term *register*. Choice (C) refers to the term *octave*. Choice (D) refers to the term *enharmonic*.

7. **(A)** Choice (A) is a paraphrase of the statement. *At least two* means "two or more." Choices (B), (C), and (D) change the meaning of the statement.

8. **(D)** Choice (A) is mentioned in paragraph 4, sentence 6. Choice (B) is mentioned in paragraph 5, sentence 4. Choice (C) is mentioned in paragraph 5, sentences 1 and 2.

9. **(C)** Because the author states that this discussion was "fundamental to understand-

ing its qualities" in reference to the qualities of "melody" and states that "we will discuss [melody] next," it may be concluded that the discussion will continue on the topic of melody. Choice (B) is not correct because it refers to the topic of the current passage, not to the topic of the next passage. Choices (A) and (D) are not mentioned and may not be concluded from information in the passage.

10. **(B)** "Thus" is a transitional word that connects the inserted sentence with the sentences in the previous paragraph. The key of "C" is used as an example of an "octave" in the paragraph. "Thus" introduces the insert sentence as a conclusion for the paragraph. Choices (A), (C), and (D) do not include transitional devices that connect with the sentences marked in the passage.

11. **(A) (C) (G)** are typical of *Western music*. **(B)** and **(E)** are typical of *non-Western music*. Choices (D) and (F) are not mentioned in the passage.

12. **(B) (D) (E)** summarize the passage. Choice (A) is true, but it is a minor point that is mentioned as an example of the term *enharmonic*. Choice (C) is true, but it is a minor point that is mentioned as an example of how one culture labels pitches. Choice (F) is not mentioned in the passage.

EXERCISE 66: Classification— Humanities/Business

1. **(C)** The main idea is found in the topic sentence, after the introduction, "There are four basic types of competition in business that form a continuum . . ." Choices (A) and (B) are major points that support the main idea, "the competition continuum." Choice (D) is not mentioned and may not be concluded from information in the passage.

2. **(D)** "The classic example of monopolistic competition is coffee and tea." Choice (A) is an example of pure competition, not monopolistic competition. Choice (B) is an example of a monopoly, not monopolistic competition. Choice (C) is an example of an oligopoly.

3. **(A)** In the context of this passage, *tolerate* means "permit." Choices (B), (C), and (D) are not accepted meanings of the word *tolerate*.

4. **(B)** In the context of this passage, *dominate* means "control." Choices (A), (C), and (D) are not accepted meanings of the word *dominate*.

5. **(A)** "In oligopoly, serious competition is not considered desirable because *it* [competition] would result in reduced revenue for every company in the group."

6. **(A)** "At one end of the continuum, pure competition results when every company has a similar product." The other lines do not explain pure competition.

7. **(A)** Choice (A) is a paraphrase of the statement. "Not unusual" means "usual." None of the other choices paraphrases what the author means.

8. **(A)** "In these cases [of monopolies], it is government control, rather than competition, that protects and influences sales." The chart that represents the competition continuum shows "monopoly" as the business with the least competition, and therefore, the most control. Choices (B), (C), and (D) are positioned on the continuum with increasingly more competition, and therefore less control.

9. **(A)** Choice (B) is mentioned in paragraph 4, sentence 3. Choice (C) is mentioned in paragraph 4, sentence 2. Choice (D) is mentioned in paragraph 4, sentence 1. Choice (A) refers to monopolistic competition, not to monopoly.

10. **(A)** Because the purpose of the passage is to teach the differences among the basic types of competition in business, it may be concluded that the passage was first printed in a business textbook. It is not as probable that an expository passage of this kind would be printed in any of the other choices—(B), (C), or (D).

EXERCISE 67: Classification— Social Sciences

1. **(C)** The main idea is developed in the first paragraph, "Whether one is awake or asleep, the brain emits electrical waves. During wakefulness . . . small waves. With . . . sleep, the waves become larger. . . ." Choices (A), (B), and (D) are major points that support the main idea, "two types of sleep."

2. **(B)** "In a period of eight hours, most sleepers experience from three to five instances of REM sleep." Choice (A) refers to the number of hours, not the times per night. Choice (C) refers to the number of minutes that each

instance of REM sleep lasts. Choice (D) refers to the number of minutes interval between instances of REM sleep.

3. **(B)** In the context of this passage, *vague* means indefinite. Choices (A), (C), and (D) are not accepted meanings of the word *vague*.

4. **(D)** In the context of this passage, *essential* means "necessary." Choices (A), (B), and (C) are not accepted meanings of the word *essential*.

5. **(C)** ". . . sleep is essential because in some way it [sleep] regenerates the brain and the nervous system."

6. **(D)** "Sleep is essential because it regenerates the brain and the nervous system." The other lines do not explain why sleep is essential.

7. **(D)** Choice (D) is a paraphrase of the statement. "Physical activity" is "muscle control." None of the other choices paraphrases what the author means.

8. **(C)** "REM sleep is emotionally charged. The heart beats irregularly, and blood pressure may be elevated. In contrast, the body is so still that the dreamer may appear to be paralyzed." Choices (A), (B), and (D) are all mentioned as typical of REM sleep. Choice (C) is not correct because the body is still.

9. **(A)** Choice (B) is mentioned in paragraph 2, sentence 1. Choice (C) is mentioned in paragraph 2, sentence 3. Choice (D) is mentioned in paragraph 2, sentence 4. Choice (A) refers to slow-wave sleep, not to REM sleep.

10. **(C)** Because REM sleep is important for mental activity, it may be concluded that students who are writing term papers need REM sleep to restore mental functioning. Choice (A) contradicts the fact that slow-wave sleep is helpful in restoring muscle control, not mental activity. Choice (B) contradicts the fact that one kind of sleep will not compensate for the lack of another kind of sleep. Choice (D) is not mentioned and may not be concluded from information in the passage.

Exercise 68: Classification— Arts/Architecture

1. **(A)** The main topic is found in the title, "Classical Architecture," and in the topic sentence, "There are three different types or styles of order (column) in Greek architecture." Choices (B) and (C) are major points that support the main topic, "classical columns in architecture." Choice (D) is not mentioned in the passage.

2. **(C)** ". . . the height of a Corinthian column [is] ten times the diameter of its base." Choice (A) is not correct because the formula refers to a Doric column, not to a Corinthian column. Choice (B) is not correct because the formula refers to an Ionic column. Choice (D) is not correct because it is not mentioned in reference to any of the columns in the passage.

3. **(C)** In the context of this passage, *passable* means "satisfactory." Choices (A), (B), and (D) are not accepted meanings of the word *passable*.

4. **(B)** In the context of this passage, *enormous* means "very large." Choices (A), (C), and (D) are not accepted meanings of the word *enormous*.

5. **(B)** "The only exception to this rule was to have one order for the exterior and *another* [order] for the interior." The pronoun *that* does not refer to Choices (A), (C), or (D).

6. **(B)** **(C)** "The two styles which the Romans added were Tuscan—an even simpler form of Doric, and Composite—a richer form of Corinthian." Choices (A) and (D) refer to Greek styles.

7. **(C)** Choice (C) is a paraphrase of the statement. *Never more than one* means "only one." Choices (A), (B), and (D) change the meaning of the statement.

8. **(C)** Choice (A) is mentioned in paragraph 9, sentence 3. Choice (B) is mentioned in paragraph 4, sentence 2. Choice (D) is mentioned in paragraph 10, sentence 3.

9. **(B)** Because the height of the Corinthian column is ten times the diameter of its base, as compared with smaller ratios for the other columns, it may be concluded that the Corinthian column is the slimmest. Choice (D) is not correct because the Tuscan column is even simpler than the Doric. Choices (A) and (C) are not mentioned and may not be concluded from information in the passage.

10. **(C)** Noun reference is a transitional device that connects the inserted sentence with the previous sentence. The two sentences are related by the reference to "Greek" orders and "Roman" orders in the previous sentence and by the reference to "both the Greek and

Roman orders" in the inserted sentence. Choices (A), (B), and (D) do not include transitional devices that connect with the sentences marked in the passage.

11. **(C)** and **(D)** refer to the *Doric order*. **(E)** and **(F)** refer to the *Ionic order*. **(A)** and **(G)** refer to the *Corinthian order*. Choice (B) is not mentioned in the passage.

12. **(A) (C) (F)** summarize the passage. Choice (B) is true, but it is a minor point that is mentioned in reference to the mathematical rules in Greek architecture. Choice (E) is true, but it is a minor point that is mentioned in reference to the Doric order. Choice (D) is not mentioned in the passage.

EXERCISE 69: Classification/Natural Sciences

1. **(B)** The main idea is found in the title, "Galaxies," and in the topic sentence: "Astronomers classify galaxies into three major categories." Choice (A) is a major point that supports the main topic, "the most important types of galaxies." Choice (C) is a minor point mentioned in several examples. Choice (D) is not mentioned in the passage.

2. **(D)** "The major difference between elliptical and spiral galaxies is that ellipticals lack a significant disk component." Choice (B) is not correct because elliptical galaxies have little gas and dust. Choice (C) is not correct because irregularly shaped galaxies are included in the irregular category, not in the elliptical category. Choice (A) is not correct because the size of the halo of the elliptical galaxy is not mentioned and may not be concluded from information in the passage.

3. **(B)** In the context of this passage, *devoid* means "empty." Choices (A), (C), and (D) are not accepted meanings of the word *devoid*.

4. **(A)** In the context of this passage, *remnant* means "remains." Choices (B), (C), and (D) are not accepted meanings of the word *remnants*.

5. **(C)** "Elliptical galaxies usually contain very little dust or cool gas, although they are not completely devoid of *either* [dust or cool gas]." The pronoun *either* does not refer to Choices (A), (B), or (D).

6. **(A)** "These are called *lenticular* galaxies because they look lens-shaped when seen edge-on (*lenticular* means "lens-shaped . . . like spiral galaxies without arms . . . an intermediate class between spirals and ellipticals." Choice (B) refers to an elliptical galaxy. Choice (C) refers to a barred spiral galaxy. Choice (D) refers to an irregular galaxy.

7. **(A)** Choice (A) is a paraphrase of the statement. If large bulges have less gas and dust, then small bulges have more gas and dust. Choices (B), (C), and (D) change the meaning of the statement.

8. **(D)** Choice (A) is mentioned in paragraph 9, sentence 3. Choice (B) is mentioned in paragraph 9, sentence 5. Choice (C) is mentioned in paragraph 9, sentence 3. Choice (D) refers to lenticular galaxies, not to irregular galaxies.

9. **(C)** Because the Milky Way is compared with "other spiral galaxies," it may be concluded that the Milky Way is a spiral galaxy. Choice (A) is not correct because astronomers classify galaxies into three major categories. Choice (B) is not correct because elliptical galaxies are more likely than spiral galaxies to be found in clusters. Choice (D) is not correct because the halo can extend to 100,000 light-years, but it is not identified as an average radius.

10. **(D)** Example is a transitional device that connects the insert sentence with the previous sentence. The two sentences are related by the reference to "dwarf elliptical galaxies" in the "Local Group" in the previous sentence and the specific example of "a dwarf elliptical galaxy: in the inserted sentence. Choices (A), (B), and (C) do not include transitional devices that connect with the sentences marked in the passage.

11. **(B)** and **(F)** are typical of *spiral galaxies*. **(A)** and **(G)** are typical of *elliptical galaxies*. **(D)** and **(H)** are typical of *irregular galaxies*. Choices (C) and (E) are not mentioned in the passage.

12. **(B) (D) (E)** summarize the passage. Choice (C) is true, but it is a minor point that is mentioned as an example of an elliptical galaxy. Choice (F) is true, but it is a minor point that is mentioned in reference to lenticular galaxies, a subcategory of the spiral

type. Choice (A) is not mentioned in the passage.

EXERCISE 70: Comparison/Contrast— Humanities/Business

1. **(C)** The main idea is found in the topic sentence, "Most languages have several levels of vocabulary that may be used by the same speakers." Choices (A), (B), and (D) are major points that support the main idea, "different types of usage."
2. **(D)** "Slang . . . refers to words and expressions understood by a large number of speakers but not accepted as good formal usage by the majority." Choice (A) refers to standard usage. Choice (B) is not correct because colloquial expressions and even slang may be found in standard dictionaries. Choice (C) is not correct because slang is understood by a large number of speakers.
3. **(A)** In the context of this passage, *obscurity* means "disappearance." Choices (B), (C), and (D) are not accepted meanings of the word *obscurity*.
4. **(C)** In the context of this passage, *appropriate* means "correct." Choices (A), (B), and (D) are not accepted meanings of the word *appropriate*.
5. **(B)** "In some cases, the majority never accepts certain slang phrases but nevertheless retains *them* [slang phrases] in their collective memories."
6. **(B)** "Both colloquial usage and slang are more common in speech than in writing." The other lines do not explain where one is more likely to find colloquial language and slang used.
7. **(C)** Choice (C) is a paraphrase of the statement. If colloquialisms are "not considered acceptable," then they are probably "not found" in more formal language. None of the other choices paraphrases what the author means.
8. **(A)** "Standard usage includes those words and expressions understood, used, and accepted by a majority of the speakers of a language in any situation regardless of the level of formality." Choice (B) is not correct because colloquial expressions and slang are more common in speech than in writing, but standard language is used in speech, espe-cially in formal settings. Choice (C) is not correct because standard usage is under-stood, used, and accepted by a majority of speakers, not esclusively by the upper classes. Choice (D) is true, but it is not men-tioned and may not be concluded from infor-mation in the passage.
9. **(D)** Choices (A) and (C) are mentioned in paragraph 3, sentence 2. Choice (B) is men-tioned in paragraph 2, sentence 4.
10. **(C)** Because the author states without judg-ment that most speakers of English will select and use standard, colloquial, and slang expressions in appropriate situations, it may be concluded that the author approves of slang and colloquial speech in appropriate situations. Choices (A), (B), and (D) contra-dict the fact that the author points out there are appropriate situations for slang and colloquial speech.

EXERCISE 71: Comparison/Contrast— Arts/Architecture

1. **(A)** The main idea is found in the conclud-ing sentences, "Chiefly through the efforts of Steiglitz, modern photography [the Photo-Secession Movement] had seceded from painting, and had emerged as a legitimate art form. In summary, the Aesthetic Movement rejected reality for beauty, but the Photo-Secessionists embraced realism as even more beautiful." Choices (B), (C), and (D) are major points that support the main idea, "The Photo-Secession Movement."
2. **(B)** ". . . they [earlier photographs] were cloudy. . . . In contrast, the straightforward photographers produced images that were sharp and clear." Choices (C) and (D) refer to modern, not earlier, photographs. Choice (A) is not mentioned and may not be con-cluded from information in the passage.
3. **(D)** In the context of this passage, a *defect* means an "imperfection." Choices (A), (B), and (C) are not accepted meanings of the word *defect*.
4. **(B)** In the context of this passage, *chiefly* means "mostly." Choices (A), (C), and (D) are not accepted meanings of the word *chiefly*.
5. **(B)** "Since *they* [aesthetic prints] were cloudy because of the gum bichromate plate

that allowed for manual intervention, the aesthetic prints were easily distinguished from the more modern prints, which came to be called straightforward photographs."

6. **(C)** "The subjects included nature in its undisturbed state and people in everyday situations." The other lines do not identify the subjects that modern photographers used.

7. **(B)** Choice (B) is a paraphrase of the statement. If "mechanical precision" was considered a defect by members of the Aesthetic Movement, then they must have engaged in "criticism" of it. None of the other choices paraphrases what the author means.

8. **(B)** "Founded by Alfred Steiglitz in New York City in 1902, Photo-Secession had as its proposition the promotion of straightforward photography through exhibits and publications. One of its publications, *Camera Work*, has been recognized among the most beautiful journals ever produced. . . . Photo-Secessionists embraced realism as even more beautiful." Choice (B) is not correct because the magazine encouraged Photo-Secessionists, not members of the older Aesthetic Movement.

9. **(D)** Choice (A) is mentioned in paragraph 2, sentence 2. Choice (B) is mentioned in paragraph 1, sentence 4. Choice (C) is mentioned in paragraph 1, sentence 4. Choice (D) refers to the Aesthetic Movement, not to the Photo-Secession Movement.

10. **(D)** Because the author credits Steiglitz with the establishment of modern photography and the publication of one of the most beautiful journals ever produced, it may be concluded that the author admired Alfred Steiglitz. Choices (B) and (C) contradict the fact that the author praises Steiglitz for his work. Choice (A) is not mentioned and may not be concluded from information in the passage.

Exercise 72: Comparison/Contrast— Social Sciences

1. **(A)** The main topic is found in the headings, "Functionalism" and "Behaviorism," and is developed in the passage. Choice (C) is a major point that supports the main topic, "Modern psychological approaches." Choices (B) and (D) are minor points that are mentioned in examples.

2. **(D)** ". . . North American psychologists worried more about the *function* of immediate experience. What is the purpose?" Choice (A) is not correct because evolutionists were influential in the development of functionalism, but they were more concerned with biology than with psychology. Choice (B) is not correct because behaviorists were interested in observable behavior, not the purposes of the behavior. Choice (C) is not correct because structuralists were interested in the content, not the purpose of experiences.

3. **(D)** In the context of this passage, *atypical* means "not usual." Choices (A), (B), and (C) are not accepted meanings of the word *atypical*.

4. **(C)** In the context of this passage, *expanded* means "enlarged." Choices (A), (B), and (D) are not accepted meanings of the word *expanded*.

5. **(D)** "Because *its* [behaviorism's] entire emphasis was on behavior, Watson called this new approach *behaviorism* (Watson, 1913, 1919)." The pronoun *its* does not refer to Choices (A), (B), or (C).

6. **(B)** "Not all psychologists were convinced that self-observation could produce valid scientific results. . . . It is difficult to determine whether the knowledge gained is accurate or representative. . . . Introspection might change the mental operations being observed. . . . Introspection also limited the range of populations and topics." Choice (A) is not correct because the method is being criticized, not advanced. Choices (C) and (D) are not mentioned and may not be concluded from information in the passage.

7. **(A)** Choice (A) is a paraphrase of the statement. *Influential* means "respected," and *no longer dominant* means "not primary." Choices (B), (C), and (D) change the meaning of the statement.

8. **(A)** Choice (B) is mentioned in paragraph 8, sentence 6. Choice (C) is mentioned in paragraph 2, sentence 4. Choice (D) is mentioned in paragraph 5, sentence 4.

9. **(A)** Because the first sentence of the passage refers to a structuralist approach advocated by European psychologists, it may be concluded that the previous page was a summary of structuralism in Europe. Choices (B), (C), and (D) are mentioned later in the passage

with no reference to previous information from the textbook.

10. **(A)** Paraphrase is a transitional device that connects the inserted sentence with a previous sentence. The two sentences are related by the restatement of "scientific results" in a previous sentence and "replicate the experiments scientifically" in the inserted sentence. Choices (B), (C), and (D) do not include transitional devices that connect with the sentences marked in the passage.

11. **(A) (C) (D)** are representative of *functionalism*. **(B)** and **(F)** are representative of *behaviorism*. Choice (E) is not mentioned in the passage.

12. **(B) (C) (F)** summarize the passage. Choice (A) is true, but it is a minor point that is mentioned as an example of behaviorism. Choice (D) is true, but it is a minor point that is mentioned in reference to functionalism. Choice (E) is not mentioned in the passage.

EXERCISE 73: Comparison/Contrast— Natural Sciences

1. **(B)** The main topic is found in the title, "Engineering and Science," and in the topic sentences under each heading, "To better understand what engineers do, let's contrast the roles of engineers with those of the closely related field of the scientist," and "Another profession closely related to engineering is engineering technology." Choice (A) is a major point that supports the main topic, "a comparison of careers in science and engineering." Choice (D) refers to several examples in the passage. Choice (C) is not mentioned in the passage.

2. **(D)** "Rather than being trained to use specific machines or processes [like engineering technologists], engineering students study additional mathematics and engineering science subjects." Choice (A) is not correct because scientists, not technologists, engage in basic technological research. Choice (B) is not correct because engineers apply research to create technology. Choice (C) is not correct because engineers make the new products.

3. **(D)** In the context of this passage, *roles* means "positions." Choices (A), (B), and (C) are not accepted meanings of the word *roles*.

4. **(C)** In the context of this passage, *phenomenon* means "occurrence." Choices (A), (B), and (D) are not accepted meanings of the word *phenomenon*.

5. **(B)** "Scientists study the planets in our solar system to understand *them* [the planets]; engineers study the planets so they can design a spacecraft to operate in the environment of that planet." The pronoun *them* does not refer to Choices (A), (C), or (D).

6. **(C)** "ABET, which accredits engineering technology programs as well as engineering programs, defines engineering technology as follows: *Engineering technology is that part of the technological field which requires the application of scientific and engineering knowledge and methods combined with technical skills in support of engineering activities*." Choices (A), (B), and (D) are not correct because the professor quotes from an accrediting organization.

7. **(C)** Choice (C) is a paraphrase of the statement. *Rather than* means "instead of." Choices (A), (B), and (D) change the meaning of the statement.

8. **(C)** Choice (A) is mentioned in paragraph 5, sentence 1. Choice (B) is mentioned in paragraph 5, sentence 2. Choice (D) is mentioned in paragraph 5, sentence 3.

9. **(B)** Because the author offers information about career choices, it may be concluded that this passage would be published in an orientation book. Choice (A) is not correct because the focus is not on mathematics. Choice (C) is not correct because the information is too basic for an advanced textbook. Choice (D) is not correct because engineering technology is only one of three career fields explained.

10. **(B)** Paraphrase is a transitional device that connects the inserted sentence with the previous sentence. The two sentences are related by the restatement of "determine . . . the right career" in the previous sentence and "make a good choice" in the insert sentence. The inserted sentence also introduces a new paragraph that explains the "main difference" between what "scientists and engineers do on the job." Choices (A), (C), and (D) do not include transitional devices that connect with the sentences marked in the passage.

11. **(A)** and **(F)** describe the work of a *scientist*. **(C)** and **(D)** describe the work of an *engineer*. **(B)** and **(E)** describe the work of a *technologist*.

12. **(A) (C) (E)** summarize the passage. Choice (B) is true, but it is a minor point that is mentioned to compare engineers and technologists. Choice (D) is true, but it is a minor point that is mentioned to introduce the main topic, the differences among career fields for engineers, scientists, and technologists. Choice (F) is not mentioned in the passage.

EXERCISE 74: Cause/Effect— Natural Sciences

1. **(A)** The main idea is found in the topic sentence, "Light from a living plant or animal is called bioluminescence or cold light. . . ." Choices (B), (C), and (D) are major points that support the main idea, "cold light."

2. **(B)** ". . . some primitive plants and animals continue to use the light for new functions such as mating or attracting prey." Choices (A) and (D) refer to the original purposes of bioluminescence, not to the reason it has continued in modern plants and animals. Choice (C) refers to incandescence, not to bioluminescence.

3. **(A)** In the context of this passage, *primitive* means "very old; at an early stage of development." Choices (B), (C), and (D) are not accepted meanings of the word *primitive*.

4. **(A)** In the context of this passage, *relatively* means "comparatively." Choices (B), (C), and (D) are not accepted meanings of the word *relatively*.

5. **(C)** "Light from a living plant or animal is called bioluminescence, or cold light, to distinguish *it* [bioluminescence, or cold light] from incandescence, or heat-generating light."

6. **(B)** "Living light occurs when luciferin and oxygen combine in the presence of luciferase." The other lines do not explain how living light occurs.

7. **(A)** Choice (A) is a paraphrase of the statement. The phrase "little or no measurable heat" means "without heat." None of the other choices paraphrases what the author means.

8. **(D)** "The earliest recorded experiments with bioluminescence in the late 1800s are attributed to Raphael Dubois, who extracted a luminous fluid from a clam, observing that it continued to glow in the test tube for several minutes. He named the substance *luciferin*. . . ." Choice (A) is not correct becuase *luciferin* was discovered in the late 1800s, not recently. Choice (C) is not correct

because *luciferase* was always present with *luciferin*. Choice (B) refers to oxygen, which may have been poisonous to life forms on early Earth.

9. **(D)** Choice (A) is mentioned in paragraph 1, sentence 4. Choice (B) is mentioned in paragraph 2, sentences 4 and 5. Choice (C) is mentioned in line 1. Choice (D) refers to oxygen in the earth's early atmosphere, not to bioluminescence.

10. **(D)** Because the last sentence of this passage mentions that some primitive plants and animals continue to use bioluminescence for new functions, it may be concluded that the paragraph following the passage most probably discusses bioluminescence in modern plants and animals. Choices (A), (B) and (C) have already been discussed earlier in the passage.

EXERCISE 75: Cause/Effect— Social Sciences

1. **(A)** The main idea is found in the concluding sentence of the paragraph, "This population trend has been referred to as the graying of America." Choices (B), (C), and (D) are major points that support the main idea, "the graying of America."

2. **(C)** "Among females, the life span increased from 78.3 years in 2000 . . ." Choice (A) refers to the average male life span in 2000. Choice (B) refers to the average male life span in 2005. Choice (D) refers to the average female life span in 2005, not 2000.

3. **(A)** In the context of this passage, a *pool* means a "group of people." Choices (B), (C), and (D) are not accepted meanings of the word *pool*.

4. **(D)** In the context of this passage, *trends* means "general directions." Choices (A), (B), and (C) are not accepted meanings of the word *trends*.

5. **(C)** "Because the birth rates among this specialized population were very high, *their* [this specialized population's] children, now among the elderly, are a significant segment of the older population."

6. **(B)** "Although the increase in the birth rate is the most dramatic factor, the decline in the death rate is also significant." The other lines do not explain what has influenced life expectancy.

7. **(A)** Choice (A) is a paraphrase of the statement. If the second factor is "also signifi-

cant," then they are "both . . . significant." None of the other choices paraphrases what the author means.

8. **(C)** ". . . and by 2025, there will be 59 million elderly Americans, representing 21 percent of the population in the United States." Choices (A) and (D) refer to the years when the "baby boom" will become the "senior boom." Choice (B) is not mentioned and may not be concluded from information in the passage.

9. **(D)** Choice (A) is mentioned in paragraph 2, sentence 3. Choice (B) is mentioned in paragraph 4, sentence 2. Choice (C) is mentioned in paragraph 3, sentence 2.

10. **(A)** Because older people tend to get gray hair, it may be concluded that the word *gray* is a reference to the hair color of older people. Choices (B), (C), and (D) are not mentioned and may not be concluded from information in the passage.

EXERCISE 76: Cause/Effect— Arts/Architecture

1. **(C)** The main idea is found in the topic sentence, "But researchers at the Chelsea and Westminster in England are exploring a different premise—that simply pleasing the eyes and the ears [with art and music] will help people recover." Choices (A) and (D) are major points that support the main topic, "Music and art in the hospital environment contributes to patient recovery." Choice (B) is a point that is made in the introduction before the main topic is presented.

2. **(C)** "Staricoff and her colleague Jane Duncan used a standard psychological questionnaire to assess anxiety and clinical depression in the patients." Choices (A), (B), and (D) are not mentioned in reference to the study by Staricoff and Duncan.

3. **(B)** In the context of this passage, *trivial* means "insignificant." Choices (A), (C), and (D) are not accepted meanings of the word *trivial*.

4. **(B)** In the context of this passage, *controversial* means "causing disagreement." Choices (A), (C), and (D) are not accepted meanings of the word *controversial*.

5. **(B)** "These were changed every week so that patients wouldn't see the same *ones* [pictures] week after week." The pronoun *ones* does not refer to Choices (A), (C), or (D).

6. **(C)** "Finally, a control group was treated in a standard ward, without any music or art." Choice (A) refers to the questionnaire to which both the experimental and the control groups responded. Choice (B) refers to the treatment for one of the experimental groups. Choice (D) is not mentioned and may not be concluded from information in the passage.

7. **(C)** Choice (C) is a paraphrase of the statement. Choices (A), (B), and (D) change the meaning of the statement.

8. **(A)** Choice (B) is mentioned in paragraph 2, sentence 7. Choice (C) is mentioned in paragraph 7, sentence 5. Choice (D) is mentioned in paragraph 2, sentence 7, paragraph 3, sentence 3, and paragraph 7, sentence 2.

9. **(B)** Because the tone of the quotations by researchers is optimistic, and "the results so far are almost all positive," it may be concluded that the researchers expect the final results to be positive. Choice (A) is not correct because the author makes a positive statement as a conclusion, "After all, if music or paintings can take the place of a course of antidepressants, it has to be better for everyone." Choice (C) is not correct because the King's Fund contributed £70,000. Choice (D) is not mentioned and may not be concluded from information in the passage.

10. **(C)** Addition is the transitional device that connects the insert sentence with the previous sentence. The previous sentence concludes the report of one study. In the inserted sentence, "four additional studies" are cited. Choices (A), (B), and (D) do not include transitional devices that connect with the sentences marked in the passage.

11. **(B)** and **(H)** refer to the Royal Adelaide Hospital study in South Australia. **(C)**, **(D)**, and **(G)** refer to the Chelsea and Westminster study in the U.K. **(A)** and **(E)** refer to the classic hospital study in the United States. Choice (F) is a statement made in the introduction to the passage, but it does not refer to any of the studies in the chart.

12. **(A) (B) (E)** summarize the passage. Choice (C) is true, but it is a minor point that is mentioned in reference to the current Chelsea and Westminster studies. Choice (D) is true, but it refers to the historical relationship between health and the arts. Choice (F) is not mentioned in the passage.

EXERCISE 77: Cause/Effect— Social Sciences

1. **(D)** The main idea is found in the topic sentence. "The dust storms were largely the consequence of years of stripping the landscape of its natural vegetation." Choice (A) is a minor point that is mentioned in the passage. Choice (C) is not correct because conservation succeeded for a few years until regular rainfall returned and World War II began. Choice (B) is not mentioned in the passage.

2. **(A)** "By 1940 the acreage subject to blowing in the Dust Bowl area of the southern Plains had been reduced from roughly 50 million acres to less than 4 million acres." Choice (C) is not correct because 8 million refers to the number of acres of public lands used for grazing under the Taylor Grazing Act, not to the number of acres affected by the Dust Bowl. The number in Choice (D) is not correct because 4 million refers to the number of acres affected after government policies had been implemented, not to the number at the height of the storms. Choice (B) is not mentioned and may not be concluded from information in the passage.

3. **(B)** In the context of this passage, *calamity* means "disaster." Choices (A), (C), and (D) are not accepted meanings of the word *calamity*.

4. **(D)** In the context of this passage, *alter* means "modify." Choices (A), (B), and (C) are not accepted meanings of the word *alter*.

5. **(A)** "But the return of regular rainfall and the outbreak of World War II led many farmers to abandon the techniques that the SCS had taught *them* [the farmers] to accept." The pronoun *them* does not refer to Choices (B), (C), or (D).

6. **(D)** "But the return of regular rainfall and the outbreak of World War II led many farmers to abandon the techniques that the SCS had taught them to accept. Wheat farming expanded and farms grew as farmers once again pursued commercial agriculture." Choices (A) and (B) refer to the practices after the Dust Bowl but before World War II. Choice (C) is not mentioned and may not be concluded from information in the passage.

7. **(B)** Choice (B) is a paraphrase of the statement. A government *subsidy* is a payment to farmers in exchange for "not growing crops." Choices (A), (C), and (D) change the meaning of the statement.

8. **(D)** Choice (A) is mentioned in paragraph 6, sentence 3. Choice (B) is mentioned in paragraph 5, sentence 3. Choice (C) is mentioned in paragraph 4, sentence 3.

9. **(C)** Because the increased demand for wheat during World War I encouraged farmers to plow and plant even wider areas in the Great Plains, it may be concluded that the Great Plains is a wheat-producing region in the United States. In the context of this passage, the word *buffalo* that appears in Choice (A) refers to a variety of grass, not to the animal. Choices (B) and (D) are not mentioned and may not be concluded from information in the passage.

10. **(C)** Elaboration is a transitional device that connects the inserted sentence with the previous sentence. The "losses" in the previous sentence are elaborated by the newspaper account in which "destroying possessions" and "provisions" is mentioned. Choices (A), (B), and (D) do not include transitional devices that connect with the sentences marked in the passage.

11. **(A) (D) (G)** are among the *causes* of the Dust Bowl. **(B) (E) (F) (H)** are among the *solutions* to the problem. Choice (C) is not mentioned in the passage.

12. **(B) (C) (F)** summarize the passage. Choice (A) is true, but it is a minor point that is mentioned as an example of how federal agencies intervened. Choice (E) is true, but it is a minor point that is mentioned as an example of the cause of soil erosion and dust storms. Choice (D) is not mentioned in the passage.

EXERCISE 78: Persuasion/ Justification—Natural Sciences

1. **(C)** The main topic is found in the title, "Endangered Species," and in the topic sentence: "There are three valid arguments to support the preservation of endangered species." Choices (A) and (B) are mentioned in reference to the major point, "aesthetic justification," one of the three arguments. Choice (D) is mentioned in reference to the major point, "ecological self-interest," one of the three arguments.

2. **(D)** "...proponents of a *moral justification* contend that all species have the right to exist." Choice (A) is not correct because it supports the experience of humankind, not that of animals. Choice (B) is not correct because it is an argument that supports protection of animals for their benefit to humans. Choice (C) is not correct because it is the same argument as the ecological argument, supporting the benefits to the human species, not animal rights.

3. **(D)** In the context of this passage, *perspective* means "view." Choices (A), (B), and (C) are not accepted meanings of the word *perspective*.

4. **(C)** In the context of this passage, *unique* means "special." Choices (A), (B), and (D) are not accepted meanings of the word *unique*.

5. **(C)** "Furthermore, if humankind views itself as the stewards of all the creatures on Earth, then it is incumbent upon human beings to protect *them* [the creatures], and to ensure the continued existence of all species."

6. **(C)** "Some advocates of the ecological argument contend that important chemical compounds derived from rare plants may contain the key to a cure for one of the diseases currently threatening human beings." The other lines do not explain how rare species contribute to the health of human beings.

7. **(D)** Choice (D) is a paraphrase of the statement. Choices (A), (B), and (C) change the meaning of the statement.

8. **(B)** "By preserving all species, we retain a balance of nature that is ultimately beneficial to humankind. Recent research on global ecosystems has been cited as evidence that every species contributes important or even essential functions that may be necessary to the survival of our own species." Choices (A), (C), and (D) are true, but they are not what is cited in the passage from research on global ecosystems.

9. **(C)** Choice (A) is mentioned in paragraph 2, sentence 4. Choice (B) is mentioned in paragraph 1, sentences 2 and 4. Choice (D) is mentioned in paragraph 3, sentence 1.

10. **(C)** Because the author states that there are three valid arguments to support the preservation of endangered species, it may be concluded that the author supports all of the arguments. Choice (A) is not correct because

the author refers to the members of deep ecology as "they," not "we." Choice (B) is not correct because the author included ecological self-interest as one of the three valid arguments. Choice (D) is not mentioned and may not be concluded from information in the passage.

EXERCISE 79: Persuasion/Justification—Social Sciences

1. **(A)** The main idea is found in the topic sentence in the second paragraph, after the introduction, "Although the stated objective of most prison systems ... is to rehabilitate the inmates ... the systems themselves do not support such a goal. ... If prisons are ... to achieve the goal ... then the prisons themselves will have to change." Choice (D) contradicts the fact that the goal is rehabilitation and reintegration. Choices (B) and (C) are major points that support the main idea, "that prisons must be restructured."

2. **(B)** "... only one-third of the inmates have vocational training opportunities or work release options." Choice (D) refers to the percentage rate for rearrest. Choices (A) and (C) are not mentioned and may not be concluded from information in the passage.

3. **(B)** In the context of this passage, *recidivism* refers to people who "return to a former activity," in this case to criminal activity that leads to prison after release. Choices (A), (C), and (D) are not accepted meanings of the word *recidivism*.

4. **(C)** In the context of this passage, *options* means "alternatives." Choices (A), (B), and (D) are not accepted meanings of the word *options*.

5. **(B)** "Although the stated goal of most prison systems, on both federal and state levels, is to rehabilitate the inmates and reintegrate *them* [the inmates] into society, the systems themselves do not support such a goal."

6. **(B)** "Even more shocking is the fact that the number and rate of imprisonment has more than doubled over the past twenty years, and the recidivism—that is, the rate for rearrest—is more than 60 percent." The other lines do not explain the rate of imprisonment over the past twenty years.

7. **(C)** Choice (C) is a paraphrase of the statement. The phrase "not support" means "not promote." None of the other choices paraphrases what the author means.

8. **(C)** "Second, *they* [prisons] will have to be built in or near population centers with community resources available for gradual reintegration into society." Choices (A), (B), and (D) are not mentioned and may not be concluded from information in the passage.

9. **(A)** Choice (B) is mentioned in paragraph 3, sentence 2. Choice (C) is mentioned in paragraph 3, sentence 4. Choice (D) is mentioned in paragraph 3, sentence 3.

10. **(C)** Because the last sentence of this passage mentions models for collaborative efforts between the criminal justice system and the community, it may be concluded that the paragraph following the passage most probably discusses examples of models for community collaboration. Choices (A) and (D) have already been discussed earlier in the passage. Choice (B) is not mentioned and may not be concluded from information in the passage.

EXERCISE 80: Persuasion/ Justification—Humanities/Business

1. **(D)** The main topic is found in the topic sentences: "Lexicostatistical glottochronology is an approach . . . which determines the rate at which a language has changed over the centuries. It aims to work out the length of time which has elapsed since two related languages (or two languages thought to be related) began to diverge." Choices (A) and (B) are major points that support the main topic, "Historical divergence of related languages." Choice (C) refers to an example of the vocabulary item for "father."

2. **(D)** "They found on average two languages would have 86% in common after 1,000 years of separation." Choice (A) is not correct because 12% refers to the percentage of cognates left after 70 centuries. Choice (B) is not correct because 60% refers to the percentage used as an example of more distant divergence. Choice (C) is not correct because 80% refers to the percentage used in an example of more recent divergence. The example was not for 1,000 years of separation.

3. **(C)** In the context of this passage, *ancillary* means "additional." Choices (A), (B), and (D) are not accepted meanings of the word *ancillary*.

4. **(A)** In the context of this passage, *limitations* means "weak points." Choices (B), (C), and (D) are not accepted meanings of the word *limitations*.

5. **(D)** "But he argued that there must be a balance between the forces which maintain uniformity in language and *those* [forces] which encourage fluctuation, and pointed out that it is possible to obtain ancillary evidence from the dating methods used in archaeology." The pronoun *those* does not refer to Choices (A), (B), or (C).

6. **(A)** "Lexicostatistical glottochronology is an approach . . . which determines the rate at which a language has changed over the centuries . . . the length of time which has elapsed since two related languages . . . began to diverge." Choices (B), (C), and (D) are not mentioned and may not be concluded from information in the passage.

7. **(C)** Choice (C) is a paraphrase of the statement. *The lower the number* means "fewer," and *the longer . . . separated* means "separated a long time ago." Choices (A), (B), and (D) change the meaning of the statement.

8. **(C)** Choice (A) is mentioned in paragraph 5, sentence 3. Choice (B) is mentioned in paragraph 5, sentence 4. Choice (D) is mentioned in paragraph 5, sentence 2. Choice (C) is true, but it is a justification for using the method, not a criticism of it.

9. **(D)** Because the passage includes criticisms as well as an unbiased presentation of the approach, it may be concluded that the author has a balanced view of the work. Choice (A) is not correct because there are no comments that would indicate a lack of interest. Choices (B) and (C) are not mentioned and may not be concluded from information in the passage.

10. **(B)** Paraphrase is a transitional device that connects the inserted sentence with the previous sentence. The two sentences are related by the restatement of "a table of historical divergence" in the previous sentence and the "scale in years" in the insert sentence. Choices (A), (C), and (D) do not include transitional devices that connect with the sentences marked in the passage.

11. **(B) (D) (E)** would be *acceptable* items for the basic word list. Choice **(A)** would be a *controversial* word because it may have religious significance in some cultures. Choices **(C)** and **(G)** would be *controversial* words because they are plants that may have geographical bias. Choice **(F)** would be *controversial* because it is an animal that may have geographical bias.

12. **(A) (D) (E)** summarize the passage. Choice (B) is true, but it is a minor point that is mentioned in reference to the criticisms of the method. Choice (C) is true, but it is a minor point that is mentioned as an example of cognate words. The precise nature of the word list in Choice (F) is not mentioned in the passage.

EXERCISE 81: Persuasion/Justification—Arts/Architecture

1. **(D)** The main idea is found in the title, "Looking at Art," and is developed in the passage. Choice (A) is a major point that contrasts science with art. Choice (B) is a major point that supports the main topic, "the appreciation of works of art." Choice (C) refers to an example.

2. **(C)** "Matisse . . . hoped that they would be familiar with . . . a long-ago sculptor." Choice (A) is not correct because it refers to the inspiration for the sculpture, not the painting. Choice (D) is not correct because the woman was a myth, not a historical personage. Choice (B) is not mentioned and may not be concluded from information in the passage.

3. **(B)** In the context of this passage, *bequeath* means "pass on." Choices (A), (C), and (D) are not accepted meanings of the word *bequeath*.

4. **(C)** In the context of this passage, *intrigued* means "very interested." Choices (A), (B), and (D) are not accepted meanings of the word *intrigued*.

5. **(D)** "The greatest of *them* [works of art] seem to speak anew to each generation and to each attentive observer." The pronoun *them* does not refer to Choices (A), (B), and (C).

6. **(B)** "In visual perception our eyes take in information in the form of light patterns; the brain processes these patterns to give them meaning." Choice (A) is not correct because

the process is the same but the interpretation is different. Choice (C) is not correct because the author says that science tells us about perception. Choice (D) refers to other types of perception, not to visual perception.

7. **(B)** Choice (B) is a paraphrase of the statement. *The same* means "similar," and to *not see the same things* means to "see images differently." Choices (A), (C), and (D) change the meaning of the statement.

8. **(C)** Choice (A) is mentioned in paragraph 4, sentence 1. Choice (B) is mentioned in paragraph 5, sentence 1. Choice (D) is implied in paragraph 6.

9. **(A)** Because the cypress symbolizes death and eternal life and because the artist believed that people journeyed to a star after death, Van Gogh might have painted the cypress to symbolize the journey of life after death. Choice (B), (C), and (D) are not mentioned and may not be concluded from information in the passage.

10. **(B)** Example is a transitional device that connects the inserted sentence with the previous sentence. The two sentences are related by the reference to the fact that we "do not all see the same things" in the previous sentence and the specific examples of "one person . . . another person" in the inserted sentence. Choices (A), (C), and (D) do not include transitional devices that connect with the sentences marked in the passage.

11. **(A)** refers to the study of *biography*. **(D)** and **(F)** refer to the study of *history*. **(C)** and **(G)** refer to the study of *media*. Choices (B) and (E) refer to scientific definitions of perception, not to a way to appreciate art.

12. **(B) (C) (E)** summarize the passage. Choice (A) is true, but it is a minor point that is mentioned as an example of how knowledge of the artist's life enhances art appreciation. Choice (D) is true, but it is a minor point that is mentioned in reference to the fact that sensory perception allows us to see art without confining us to seeing it in the same way. Choice (F) is not mentioned in the passage.

EXERCISE 82: Problem/Solution—Arts/Architecture

1. **(C)** The main idea is found in the topic sentence, "The practice of signing and numbering individual prints was introduced

by James Abbott McNeill Whistler ..."
Choices (A) and (B) are major points that
support the main idea, "the practice of
signing prints." Choice (D) is not mentioned
and may not be concluded from information
in the passage.

2. **(C)** "As soon as Whistler and Haden began
signing and numbering their prints, their
work began to increase in value." Choice (A)
is not correct because it is not mentioned as
a reason why Whistler's work was more
valuable. Choice (B) refers to Whistler's
best-known work, but not to the reason that
his work increased in value. Choice (D)
refers to the prints that were signed along
with those of Whistler.

3. **(A)** In the context of this passage, *speculate*
means "guess." Choices (B), (C), and (D)
are not accepted meanings of the word
speculate.

4. **(A)** In the context of this passage, *distinguish*
means "recognize differences." Choices (B),
(C), and (D) are not accepted meanings of the
word *distinguish*.

5. **(D)** "Wherever the artist elects to sign *it*
[the print], a signed print is still valued
above an unsigned one, even in the same
edition."

6. **(C)** "Although most prints are signed on the
right-hand side in the margin below the
image, the placement of the signature is a
matter of personal choice." The other lines
do not indicate where one might find an
artist's signature on his work.

7. **(A)** Choice (A) is a paraphrase of the statement. To "increase in value" means to be
"worth more." None of the other choices paraphrases what the author means.

8. **(B)** "... James Abbott McNeill Whistler ...
[was] best known for the painting of his
mother, called, 'Arrangement in Grey and
Black.' but known to most of us as
'Whistler's Mother.'" Choice (A) refers to
Whistler's brother-in-law, who, along with
Whistler, began the practice of signing and
numbering prints. Choices (C) and (D) are
not mentioned and may not be concluded
from information in the passage.

9. **(C)** Choices (A) and (B) are mentioned in
paragraph 1, sentence 3. Choice (D) is mentioned in paragraph 1, sentence 2. Choice (C)
is true, but it is not a reason why a collector
prefers a signed print.

10. **(B)** Because Whistler's brother-in-law
speculated that collectors would find prints
more attractive if there were only a limited
number of copies produced and an artist
could guarantee and personalize each print, it
may be concluded that artists number
their prints to guarantee a limited edition.
Choice (C) contradicts the fact that there
are a limited number. Choice (D) contradicts
the fact that the placement of the signature
and the number is a matter of personal choice.
Choice (A) is not mentioned and may not be
concluded from information in the passage.

EXERCISE 83: Problem/Solution—Humanities/Business

1. **(D)** The main idea is found in the topic
sentence, "For Americans to play a more effective role in international business negotiations,
they must put forth more effort to improve
cross-cultural understanding." Choices (A),
(B), and (C) are major points that support the
main idea, "that American negotiators need to
learn more about other cultures."

2. **(C)** "Negotiating is the process of communicating back and forth for the purpose of
reaching an agreement." Choice (B) refers to
the process, not to the purpose of negotiation.
Choice (D) refers to an important aspect of
international negotiations. Choice (A) is not
mentioned and may not be concluded from
information in the passage.

3. **(D)** In the context of this passage, *persuade*
means "convince." Choices (A), (B), and
(C) are not accepted meanings of the word
persuade.

4. **(D)** In the context of this passage, *undermining* means "making weak." Choices (B),
(C), and (D) are not accepted meanings of the
word *undermining*.

5. **(B)** "The American negotiator's role
becomes *that* [the role] of an impersonal purveyor of information and cash."

6. **(A)** "*It* [Negotiating] involves persuasion and
compromise, but in order to participate in
either one, the negotiators must understand the
ways in which people are persuaded and how
compromise is reached within the culture of
the negotiation." The other lines do not indicate the two criteria necessary for negotiation.

7. **(C)** Choice (C) is a paraphrase of the statement. The phrase to "not enjoy the same

level of success" means to be "less successful." None of the other choices paraphrases what the author means.

8. **(B)** "... American negotiators often insist on realizing short-term goals. Foreign negotiators, on the other hand, may value the relationship established between negotiators and may be willing to invest time in it for long-term benefits." Choices (A), (B), and (D) are true, but they are not mentioned and may not be concluded from information in the passage.

9. **(B)** Choice (A) is mentioned in paragraph 3, sentence 1. Choice (C) is mentioned in paragraph 4, sentence 2. Choice (D) is mentioned in paragraph 4, sentence 3. Choice (B) refers to foreign negotiators, not to the American negotiator.

10. **(A)** Because the last sentence of this passage mentions efforts to improve cross-cultural understanding, it may be concluded that the paragraph following the passage most probably discusses ways to increase cross-cultural understanding. Choices (B), (C), and (D) have already been discussed earlier in the passage.

EXERCISE 84: Problem/Solution— Social Sciences

1. **(B)** The main idea is found in the title, "School Children with Disabilities," and is developed in the passage. Choice (C) is a major point that supports the main idea, "providing educational services for children with disabilities." Choices (A) and (D) are minor points that are mentioned in the definition of terms.

2. **(B)** "Best practices in service delivery to children who are disabled or at risk for disabilities are moving toward a family-focused or family-centered approach. . . . This approach emphasizes the importance of partnerships between parents and disability professionals." Choice (A) is not correct because some experts believe that separate programs may be more effective. Choices (C) and (D) are not mentioned as being the most current views, and their recent acceptance may not be concluded from information in the passage.

3. **(B)** In the context of this passage, *broad* means "general." Choices (A), (C), and (D) are not accepted meanings of the word *broad*.

4. **(B)** In the context of this passage, *disruptive* means "causing confusion." Choices (A),

(C), and (D) are not accepted meanings of the word *disruptive*.

5. **(A)** "Among the explanations for this gender difference are a greater biological vulnerability of boys, as well as referral bias (boys are more likely than girls to be referred by teachers for treatment because of *their* [boys'] disruptive behavior." The pronoun *their* does not refer to Choices (B), (C), or (D).

6. **(C)** "Children with a learning disability (1) are of normal intelligence or above, (2) have difficulties in at least one academic area, ... (3) have a difficulty that is not attributable to any other diagnosed problem ... problems in listening, concentrating, speaking, thinking." The other paragraphs do not identify the characteristics of children with learning disabilities. Choice (A) is not correct because they may have a problem in one area. Choice (B) is not correct because they may be identified because their disability is not attributed to any other diagnosed problem. Choice (D) is not mentioned and may not be concluded from information in the passage.

7. **(A)** Choice (A) is a paraphrase of the statement. If more children receive services today, then fewer children received services in the past. Choices (B), (C), and (D) change the meaning of the statement.

8. **(C)** Choice (A) is mentioned in paragraph 8, sentence 3. Choice (B) is mentioned in paragraph 6, sentence 3. Choice (D) is mentioned in paragraph 6, sentence 3.

9. **(B)** Because 10 percent of all children in the United States receive special education and half of them have a learning disability, it may be concluded that 5 percent of the children in the United States have a learning disability. Choice (A) is not correct because children with a learning disability are of normal intelligence or above. Choices (C) and (D) are not mentioned and may not be concluded from information in the passage.

10. **(B)** Noun reference is a transitional device that connects the inserted sentence with the previous sentence. The two sentences are related by the reference to "a learning disability" in the previous sentence and "children with a learning disability" in the inserted sentence. Choices (A), (C), and (D) do not include transitional devices that connect with the sentences marked in the passage.

11. (**F**) is the definition of a *handicapping condition.* (**E**) is the definition of an *LRE* (least restrictive environment). (**B**) is the definition of *inclusion.* (**A**) is the definition of an *IEP* (individualized education plan). (**G**) is the definition of *IDEA* (Individuals with Disabilities Education Act). Choices (C) and (D) do not define terms that are mentioned in the passage.

12. (**C**) (**D**) (**F**) summarize the passage. Choice (A) is true, but it is a minor point that is mentioned in reference to children with learning disabilities. Choice (E) is true, but it is a minor point that is mentioned as part of the criteria for identifying a child with a learning disability. Choice (B) is not mentioned in the passage.

EXERCISE 85: Problem/Solution— Natural Sciences

1. (**B**) The main idea is found in the title, "Resistance to Antibiotics," and is developed in the passage. Choice (A) is a major point that supports the main topic, "drug-resistant bacteria." Choice (C) is mentioned as an example. Choice (D) is mentioned in contrast to the development of new antibiotics.

2. (**A**) ". . . a large number of antibiotics, each of which intervenes in the bacterial life cycle in a slightly different way." Choice (B) is not correct because antibiotics block the construction of the cell walls in bacteria, but they do not construct walls. Choice (C) is not correct because mitosis affects the explosion of cell walls, not enzymes. Choice (D) is not mentioned and may not be concluded from information in the passage.

3. (**C**) In the context of this passage, *complacency* means "lack of concern." Choices (A), (B), and (D) are not accepted meanings of the word *complacency.*

4. (**A**) In the context of this passage, *anticipated* means "predicted." Choices (B), (C), and (D) are not accepted meanings of the word *anticipated.*

5. (**B**) "It doesn't affect *them* [the resistant bacteria], but it does wipe out all of their competition." The pronoun *them* does not refer to Choices (A), (C), or (D).

6. (**A**) ". . . the introduction of the antibiotic . . . doesn't affect them [the resistant bacteria], but it does wipe out all of their competition. They are thus free to multiply." Choice

(B) is not correct because the resistant bacteria compete with other bacteria, not with the antibiotic. Choice (C) is not correct because the competition is wiped out. Choice (D) is not mentioned and may not be concluded from information in the passage.

7. (**D**) Choice (D) is a paraphrase of the statement. *A few* means "a small number," and *not affected* means "resistant." Choices (A), (B), and (C) change the meaning of the statement.

8. (**C**) Choice (A) is mentioned in paragraph 7, sentence 3. Choice (B) is mentioned in paragraph 3, sentence 2. Choice (D) is mentioned in paragraph 4, sentences 2 and 3.

9. (**D**) Because the problem was recognized in the early 1990s and drug companies began to develop new drugs that would be available early in the twenty-first century, ten years after they began working on them, it may be concluded that it takes years for a new drug to be made available. Choice (A) is not correct because the author states that the development of new antibiotics should remain a priority. Choice (B) is not correct because the appearance of drug-resistant bacteria should have been anticipated, but it wasn't. Choice (C) is not mentioned and may not be concluded from information in the passage.

10. (**A**) Paraphrase is a transitional device that connects the inserted sentence with the previous sentence. The two sentences are related by the restatement of "should have been anticipated" in the previous sentence and "should have alerted" in the inserted sentence. Choices (B), (C), and (D) do not include transitional devices that connect with the sentences marked in the passage.

11. (**E**) (**C**) (**D**) (**B**) (**A**) in that order are a chronology of the passage. *Genetic research* in Choice (F) is a promising future technology, but it has not solved the problem of bacterial resistance.

12. (**A**) (**C**) (**E**) summarize the passage. Choice (D) is true, but it is a minor point that is mentioned as an example of a strain of bacteria that is resistant to antibiotics. Choice (F) is true, but it is a minor point that is mentioned as an example of how doctors have traditionally handled the problem of resistance to antibiotics. Choice (B) is not mentioned in the passage.

Evaluation of Writing—General Topics

Essays on general topics can be evaluated by referring to the checklist printed below and the rubric on page 566. Examples of Level 5 essays for Exercises 86–91 follow.

NO	⇨	⇨	⇨	⇨	YES
0	1	2	3	4	5

✓ The essay answers the topic question.

✓ The point of view or position is clear.

✓ The essay is direct and well-organized.

✓ The sentences are logically connected to each other.

✓ Details and examples support the main idea.

✓ The writer expresses complete thoughts.

✓ The meaning is easy for the reader to understand.

✓ A wide range of vocabulary is used.

✓ Various types of sentences are included.

✓ There are only minor errors in grammar and idioms.

✓ The general essay is within a range of 300–350 words.

NOTE: Although a scale of 1–6 has traditionally been used for the Test of Written English (TWE) on the Paper-Based TOEFL and the essay on the Computer-Based TOEFL, this new 0–5 scale will be the best way to evaluate general topic essays on all versions of the TOEFL.

Writing

EXERCISE 86: General Topics—Agree or Disagree

Topic One
Example Notes

Outline

Smoking should not be permitted in restaurants.
- Health problems are caused by secondary smoke.
- Smoke affects the taste of food.
- Nonsmoking areas are ineffective.

The state law in California makes it easy for restaurant proprietors to do the right thing.

Map

Example Essay One

In my view, smoking should not be permitted in restaurants for a number of reasons. First, many health problems are caused by secondary smoke. Although smokers make a choice to endanger their health, the other people in their immediate area are not involved in that choice. For a long time, we have been informed about the dangers of smoke inhaled by nonsmokers. It is only responsible for restaurant owners to protect their nonsmoking customers.

Furthermore, smoke affects the taste of the food. Part of the pleasure of a meal is the aroma of the food with its unique blend of spices and flavorings. If it isn't possible to smell the dishes, the experience is diminished. Moreover, the senses of smell and taste are related. I would argue that with smoke permeating the restaurant, the food absorbs the taste of smoke, and the customers have a different meal than they would enjoy without the smoke-filled environment.

Finally, it is important to mention that nonsmoking areas are not effective in most restaurants. Although the hostess may seat diners in an area designated for nonsmoking customers, it is very difficult, if not impossible, to confine smoke. The smokers may be segregated in a different area, but the smoke itself drifts into the nonsmoking side of the restaurant. Besides the unpleasant experience of eating in a smoke-filled environment, the diners go home with the smell of smoke on their clothing and hair.

In short, the state law in California makes it easy for restaurant proprietors to do the right thing without directly offending their customers. I think it is a very good law.

Topic Two
Example Notes

Outline

College curriculum
- Increase knowledge
- Career possibilities
- More leisure time

Map

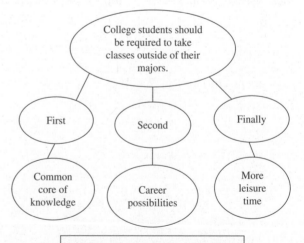

Example Essay Two

I agree that college students should be required to take classes outside of their major fields of study in order to graduate. Although it could be argued that these classes do not contribute to the career goals of students and, furthermore, require investments of additional time and tuition, I contend that there are three important reasons for the requirement.

First, exposure to a variety of subjects provides a common core of knowledge for all educated people. If students limited their courses to their major fields of study, they would not have a broad view of the world. Their perspective would be very narrow, and they would not be able to exchange views with others whose education had been limited to the study of a different field. Taking courses in many subjects allows the free flow of information and ideas among members of an educated society.

Second, many students entering college are unsure of their career goals. By selecting courses in a variety of fields during the first two years, students have an opportunity to experiment and learn about several career possibilities. Many students find their life's work in a class that they never would have taken if they had not been required to do so. Furthermore, many people change careers several times during their lives. Early exposure to many subjects in college can be valuable when a career ends, either by choice or by circumstance. Alternatives explored during college could be pursued long after graduation.

Finally, the amount of leisure time available is expanding. Past generations worked longer hours. Moreover, the life expectancy did not afford as many people with the possibility of a long retirement. Today, however, a large number of college graduates can expect to enjoy several decades of recreational activities after they have stopped working full-time. The interests that they may have developed during their college years as a result of taking a wide range of courses could be helpful in making choices for a happy retirement.

To summarize, there is more to education than merely training for a career. By taking courses outside of their major fields, students prepare not only for successful professions but also for lives that include intellectual exchange with other educated people, and the pursuit of interests outside of the work-place.

Topic Three
Example Notes

Outline
The motto "if at first you don't succeed, try, try again" is a saying that I agree with.

Examples of struggle to maintain a healthy weight
- Low-calorie plan
- Rigorous exercise plan
- The Zone

What is important is not to give up and to learn from each failure.

Map

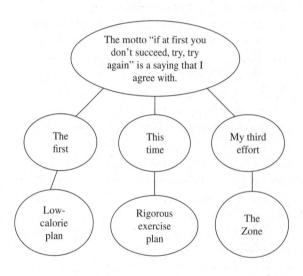

Example Essay Three

The motto "if at first you don't succeed, try, try again" is a saying that I agree with. In my life, I have made an effort to persevere, using several different approaches to a problem or goal in order to be successful. One example that comes to mind is a long-term struggle to maintain a healthy weight. Even as a child, I preferred sedentary activities like reading to sports. Truthfully, I would still rather have ice cream than an apple. Nevertheless, I have launched several campaigns to lose weight.

My first weight loss program was a low-calorie plan. For six weeks, I ate fewer than fifteen hundred calories a day, counting every calorie carefully. I learned to choose foods like lettuce because it did not add many calories to my total. At the end of six weeks, I had lost twelve pounds! The problem was I felt hungry and tired all the time, and I missed the foods that I had eliminated from my life. I gained the weight back almost as quickly as I had lost it.

Although I had failed in my first effort, I decided to try again. This time, I followed a rigorous exercise plan. I walked two miles every morning instead of sleeping in. I parked my car at the furthest end of the parking lot so that I would have to walk. I joined a gym and used machines to lift weights. Although I didn't lose as much weight as I had on the low-calorie plan, I began to receive compliments from friends on my appearance. Nevertheless, I found myself sleeping later, missing walks and workouts because I was "too busy." Parking the car so far from the door wasn't possible because I was arriving late. I gained weight again.

But I tried again. My third effort was a program called The Zone, a diet that balances food intake. Forty percent of each meal is from the carbohydrate group, including fruits, vegetables, and bread. Thirty percent is from the protein group, including meat, cheese, and eggs, and thirty percent is from good fats like olive oil, fish oil, and almonds. By limiting the portions, by walking three times a week, and by following this meal plan, I have slowly reached my goal. It has been two years since I started The Zone, and I feel confident that I can maintain this plan.

So, as you see, I tried and tried again, but at last I succeeded in finding a program that worked for me. What is important is not to give up and to learn from each failure.

EXERCISE 87: General Topics— Argue a Point of View

Topic Four
Example Notes

Outline

Advantages of American roommates:
- Practice and improve English
- Share and explain American culture
- Provide insights and advice for new situations at the university

Advantages of roommates from my country:
- Rest from the stress of speaking a foreign language
- Have a more familiar lifestyle—food

- Offer better suggestions for situations— experience

I view my home as a place to relax, not as an extension of my learning environment.

Map

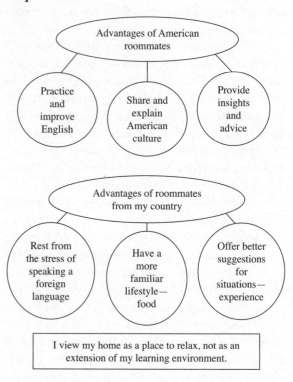

I view my home as a place to relax, not as an extension of my learning environment.

Example Essay Four

There are many advantages to living with American roommates. Perhaps the most obvious is the opportunity to practice and improve your English. By interacting all the time with your roommates and their friends in English, your language skills would naturally improve. In addition, American roommates would share and explain many aspects of American culture. I know of many international students who receive their degrees in the United States without ever being invited to an American home. American roommates would probably invite you to celebrate holidays with their families. Moreover, the culture of the campus itself can be confusing. It would be very helpful to have American roommates to provide their insights and advice when new situations occurred at the university.

On the other hand, the advantages of living with roommates from your own culture should be considered. Although speaking English all the time is beneficial, it is also very tiring. The opportunity to communicate in your own language at home would give you a much needed rest from the stress of speaking a foreign language. Even though sharing another culture is interesting and would contribute to your education, it is also more comfortable to have a more familiar lifestyle. For example, cooking and eating the food you are used to would be appealing, especially over a period of several years while you are in school. Finally, when situations arise on campus, American insights would certainly be helpful, but international students have many experiences that are unique, and most Americans don't have the knowledge to provide good advice in many cross-cultural situations. Other international students from your country may have gone through and solved the same problems and would therefore be able to offer better suggestions.

As for me, roommates from my own country would be a better choice because I view my home as a place to relax, not as an extension of my learning environment. However, I also think that it would be very important to make American friends in order to practice English, appreciate the culture more fully, and have some resources for friendly advice. By inviting American friends to my home, my roommates and I could have the best of both worlds.

Topic Five
Example Notes

Outline

Advantages of small colleges
- Professors have more interaction with their students
- The expense of a car can be saved
- Students make lifelong friendships

Advantages of a large university
- Professors have national, international reputations
- The library will offer greater resources
- Frequency and quality of cultural events would be greater

I consider cross-cultural exchange a major part of my education, and it would be more likely to occur in a small college atmosphere.

Map

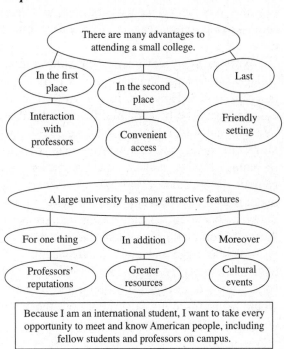

Example Essay Five

There are many advantages to attending a small college. In the first place, the professors at small colleges have more interaction with their students. Because the campus is small, you see each other more often in informal settings like the student union or the library. In such an environment, it is more likely that the professor will know your name and view you as a person, not just a number on a roster. In the second place, you can usually walk to all of the buildings on campus in a short time, and often, it is possible to walk downtown. The expense of a car can be saved, and the money can be used toward academic tuition, fees, and books. Last, a small college tends to be a more friendly setting. Students know each other by name and make lifelong friendships. Although these kinds of close relationships are possible on a larger campus, a smaller college encourages them through frequent contact and shared activities.

On the other hand, a large university has many attractive features. For one thing, on a large campus, you are more likely to find professors who have national or even international reputations for research. In addition, the library will probably offer greater resources for students. Moreover, the frequency and quality of cultural events on campus would be greater on a large campus because the facilities would accommodate a larger audience and would therefore provide more revenue to sponsor major events.

With so many advantages for both a small college and a large university, it is difficult to make a choice. However, in my view, a small college would be best for me. Because I am an international student, I want to take every opportunity to meet and know American people, including fellow students and professors on campus. I consider cross-cultural exchange a major part of my education, and it would be more likely to occur in a small college atmosphere. After I complete my undergraduate degree, perhaps the large university environment will have more appeal. As a graduate student, professors who are engaged in important research would be useful to my career. For now, the small college is better for me.

Topic Six
Example Notes

Outline

Advantages of working
- Friends would praise them for their initiative and perseverance
- Future employers might be impressed by their work records
- They might derive satisfaction from their personal investments

Advantages of family support
- Friends would praise them for efforts on behalf of their families
- Future employers would not expect a work record
- They might feel greater responsibility toward others in their families

For my part, I must argue in favor of family support. It is the way that my society rewards.

Map

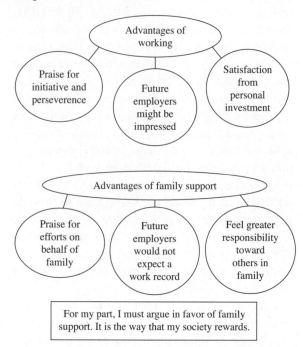

For my part, I must argue in favor of family support. It is the way that my society rewards.

Example Essay Six

Some students in the United States work while they are earning their degrees; others receive support from their families. Both approaches have advantages and disadvantages. In this essay, I will name some of the advantages of each approach, and I will argue in favor of family support.

In a society where independence and individual accomplishment are valued, students who have earned their degrees by working would be greatly admired. Friends would praise them for their initiative and perseverance. Future employers might be impressed by their work records. They might derive greater satisfaction from their personal investment.

On the other hand, in a society where cooperation and family dependence are valued, students who have received support would be better understood. Friends would praise them for their efforts on behalf of their families. Future employers would not expect a work record from students. They might feel greater responsibility toward others in their families because the accomplishment was shared. Thus, not one but every family member would be assured some opportunity or benefit.

For my part, I must argue in favor of family support. While I study at an American university, my older brother will send me money every month. Because I don't have to work, I can spend more time studying, and I can get better grades. My family is proud because I am on the dean's list of honor students. When I finish my degree and find a good job, I will send my younger sister to a school or university. I will repay my family by helping her. It may not be a better way, but it is the way that my society rewards.

EXERCISE 88: General Topics—Describe Characteristics

Topic Seven
Example Notes

Outline

In my opinion, good teachers must possess both excellent professional qualifications and a number of personal qualities that support their success.

Professional qualifications
• Thorough knowledge of the subject
• Skills and talent to communicate
• Excellent communication skills

Personal qualifications
• Enthusiasm
• Patience
• Kindness

The good teachers who have influenced us have probably insisted on high standards for themselves in both their professional and personal lives.

Map

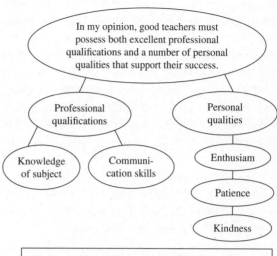

The good teachers who have influenced us have probably insisted on high standards for themselves in both their professional and personal lives.

Example Essay Seven

In my opinion, good teachers must possess both excellent professional qualifications and a number of personal qualities that support their success.

To be considered a highly qualified professional, a teacher should demonstrate a thorough knowledge of the subject. In addition to providing the best instruction, good teachers will stay current by reading the latest research. Nevertheless, I would argue that "knowing" is not "teaching." Besides understanding the subject themselves, good teachers must have the skills and talent to communicate the subject to their students. Unfortunately, many of us have been in classes with teachers who were quite brilliant in their fields, perhaps respected researchers who achieved their reputations through publications, however, they were incapable of basic instruction such as presenting information clearly or answering questions so that students could understand. In my opinion, without both knowledge and communication skills, teachers may not be regarded as highly qualified professionals.

Apart from the professional qualifications, the personal qualities of teachers seem to make a difference in the classroom and therefore distinguish good teachers from others. Teachers who are enthusiastic, patient, and kind possess characteristics that influence their students in positive ways. Teachers who are enthusiastic motivate their students and increase interest and participation. Teachers who are patient give students the time and confidence to continue studying until they have mastered the lesson. Teachers who are kind encourage interaction with their students and thereby create opportunities for learning. Moreover, the teachers who show kindness set an example for their students that transcends the subject.

We can all recall the good teachers who have influenced us. I submit that they probably insisted on high standards for themselves in both their professional and personal lives.

EXERCISE 89: General Topics— Imagine a Situation

Topic Eight
Example Notes

Outline

If I could meet one important person during my stay in the United States, I would meet the president.

- To evaluate him as a person
- To ask him about his foreign policy
- To provide him with information about international students

If I had the opportunity to meet the president, I would observe, listen, and offer my opinions.

Map

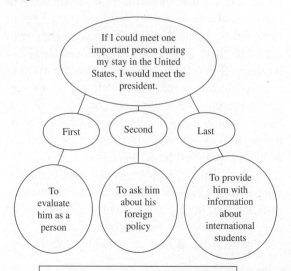

If I had the opportunity to meet the president, I would observe, listen, and offer my opinions.

Example Essay Eight

If I could meet one important person during my stay in the United States, I would meet the president. I would like to make his acquaintance for three reasons. First, I would like to evaluate him as a person. Although we have many opportunities to see the president in formal settings on television, in my opinion, the best way to judge character is by having a personal interview. In this way, it is possible to see into the person's eyes and take note of small mannerisms that indicate truthfulness and integrity. I would like to meet the president to know for myself what kind of man is the leader of the United States.

Second, I would like to have the chance to ask the president about his foreign policy. Of course, I am most interested in the plans for collaboration with leaders from my region as well as specific goals for peace. It would be very enlightening to be able to hear the president's own words instead of listening to a speech that had been written by others for him to deliver to the public.

Last, the opportunity to meet the president would allow me to provide him with information about international students in the United States. In spite of the many advisors that are constantly available to the president on cross-cultural affairs. I doubt that any of them could relate to the president the experience of an international student on an American campus. I would like him to know how important it is to work with other nations to provide scholarships for study in the United States and once students are living on American campuses, what a unique opportunity American people have to extend hospitality and friendship to them. The impression that international students gain of the United States may be more important to world peace than the technology that they learn to use in their college classes.

If I had the opportunity to meet the president, I would observe, listen, and offer my opinions. Then, I would take a photograph of the two of us in order to prove that it had happened.

EXERCISE 90: General Topics—Support or Oppose

Topic Nine
Example Notes

Outline

I support the construction of an airport in our local community.
• Economic opportunities
• The exchange of people

I support the building of an airport in our community for both the economic and the intellectual advantages that would occur as a result.

Map

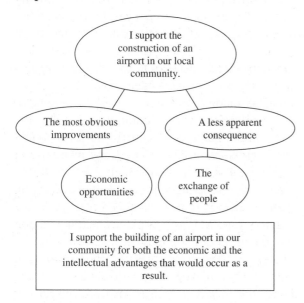

Example Essay Nine

I support the construction of an airport in our local community. Although I acknowledge that it would cause some problems, most notably noise in the adjacent neighborhoods, congestion on the highways, and possibly pollution from the jet fuel, I think that these problems would be more than compensated for by the progress that would occur in the area.

Perhaps the most obvious improvements in the community would be the economic opportunities. There would be many jobs created as a direct result of the airport. Construction of buildings, roads, and parking facilities would require workers. After the structures and infrastructures were completed, a large number of service personnel would need to be hired to handle the ticketing, baggage, and food service facilities. In addition, some businesses already established in the community would benefit from the new airport. For example, taxi and transportation services, hotels, and restaurants could expect to receive more visitors. Even the shops might experience an increase in revenue as a result of more tourists. Local artisans who sell their crafts on the streets might also benefit. The sum total of the financial influx could have a significant impact on the standard of living for people in our community.

A less apparent but potentially important consequence of an airport would be the exchange of people regionally, nationally, and even internationally. Previously, the community has been very isolated. Such provincialism encourages a very narrow perspective of life. By opening our community to different people, we could also expect to be exposed to new ideas that they would bring with them. Although some of the differences might be shocking and we might reject them for our own lifestyles, I suggest that it is worthwhile to know about different points of view and ways of living. The convenience of travel out of the community to other cities should also provide opportunities for observing and participating in different lifestyles as well as for communicating more regularly with other people in a global society. It can be argued that choices for life made in ignorance are not really choices at all.

In short, I support the building of an airport in our community for both the economic and the intellectual advantages that would occur as a result.

EXERCISE 91: General Topics—Defend a Choice

Topic Ten
Example Notes

Outline

The most significant achievement, in my opinion, is the Internet.
• Communications
• Business
• Politics
• Products

In my view, it is fair to say that the Internet is the most important achievement of the twentieth century for the effect that it has had on so many levels of our society.

Map

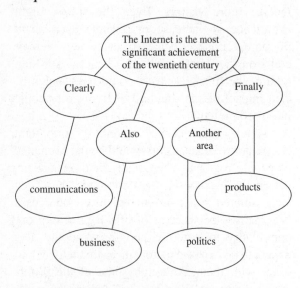

Example Essay Ten

Of all the inventions created in the twentieth century, the most significant achievement, in my opinion, is the Internet. Although it is true that advances in biomedical engineering and genome mapping have the potential to alleviate suffering from many diseases, I did not choose them because they will affect our futures. The Internet, on the other hand, is affecting all of us right now. I especially notice four areas in which the Internet has brought revolutionary change. Clearly, communications has been transformed by e-mail over the Internet. Messages across international boundaries can now be sent instantly at minimal cost. The convenience and cost effectiveness has encouraged global interaction and has contributed to the exchange of ideas at all levels of personal and professional communication.

Business has also been revolutionized by the Internet. Besides the obvious advantages of advertisement to a global consumer community by large companies, individual consumers have also found that shopping on E-Bay or other web sites offers them a wider selection of goods than their local stores. The success of business over the Internet is evidenced by the huge yearly increase in the number of shoppers using the Internet for purchases.

Another area that has shown fundamental change as a result of the Internet is the political arena. In the United States, politicians running for office are using web sites to contact constituents and speak to a large number of potential supporters. Politicians in other countries have noted the effectiveness of this model, and are also beginning to take advantage of the Internet for political action.

Finally, it is worth mentioning that all of the technology that was crucial to the invention of the Internet has been used to create many useful products. The microchip, which was key to the information superhighway, is found in everything from microwaves in the kitchen to toys in the playroom, as well as cell phones and navigation equipment in our vehicles. In my view, it is fair to say that the Internet is the most important achievement of the twentieth century for the effect that it has had on so many levels of our society.

Evaluation of Writing—Academic Topics

Essays on academic topics can be evaluated by referring to the checklist printed below and the rubric on page 566. Examples of Level 5 essays for Exercises 92–100 follow.

NO	⇨	⇨	⇨	⇨	YES
0	1	2	3	4	5

✓ The essay answers the topic question.

✓ There are only minor inaccuracies in the content.

✓ The essay is direct and well-organized for the topic.

✓ The sentences are logically connected to each other.

✓ Details and examples support the main idea.

✓ The writer expresses complete thoughts.

✓ The meaning is easy for the reader to comprehend.

✓ A wide range of vocabulary is used.

✓ The writer paraphrases, using his or her own words.

✓ The writer credits the author with wording when necessary.

✓ There are only minor errors in grammar and idioms.

✓ The academic essay is within a range of 150–225 words.

EXERCISE 92: Academic Topics—Summaries of Textbooks and Lectures

 (CD 5, Track 4)

Audio

Narrator: Now listen to a professor's response to the textbook passage.

Professor:

Today we're going to talk about the Rosenhan study, which is probably the classic example of the effect that labeling has on the diagnosis and treatment of psychiatric disorders. The purpose of the study was to determine how the initial diagnosis of schizophrenia . . . how that label would affect the treatment of patients who were not suffering from the disorder.

Rosenhan and his team were admitted separately to several different psychiatric hospitals with the, uh, reported symptom of hearing voices. In reality, all of the investigators were completely normal, but because . . . because of the reported symptom, they were identified and labeled as schizophrenic. After their admission, all of the investigators behaved normally. Nevertheless, their behavior was interpreted by the health care professionals as symptomatic of the disorder in their original diagnosis. So it was . . . it had to be the expectation that influenced the staff.

Investigators remained in the hospitals for as long as two months without being detected. Interestingly enough, the other patients seemed to sense that the investigators were not really ill. In fact, several patients confronted them, they asked whether they might be journalists or professors. But the hospital staff did not question the original diagnosis, and discharged the investigators with a diagnosis of schizophrenia in remission, that is, not active at the moment.

The Rosenhan study is important because it suggests that labels can create expectations, and expectations can influence treatment, even in the absence of symptoms.

Example Notes

Textbook—Deviant behavior
   1950s—consensus theory/structural functionalism
      standard social norms
      deviant form of behavior
   recently—labeling theory
     label
     social expectations
     consider social context
     environment supports

Lecture—Rosenhan study
   effect labeling on diagnosis, treatment
   psychiatric disorders
   patients not suffering disorder
purpose = how initial diagnosis schizophrenia affected treatment
method
   investigators normal, reported symptom, labeled
   behaved normally, interpreted symptomatic, two months
result
   expectation influenced staff
   other patients questioning
conclusion
   labels create expectations, influence treatment in absence of symptoms

Example Writing Answer

The textbook details the history of abnormal psychology, beginning with consensus theory and structural functionalism in the 1950s in which deviant behavior was measured against standard social norms.

In contrast, a more modern theory known as labeling theory was explained. Labeling theory contends that the social expectations of others and the physical environment will influence behavior on the part of those people who are labeled.

The purpose of the Rosenhan study was to discover the effect of a false diagnosis on the treatment of patients in a psychiatric hospital. Investigators who were not suffering from schizophrenia reported symptoms typical of the disorder and were labeled at intake as schizophrenic. Although they behaved normally during the period of their confinement, the hospital staff continued to interpret their behavior as abnormal. Rosenhan's study suggests that the expectations established by the label can determine the treatment of patients even when symptoms do not support the original diagnosis.

EXERCISE 93: Academic Topics—Summaries of Textbooks and Lectures

 (CD 5, Track 5)

Audio

Narrator: Now listen to a professor's response to the textbook passage.

Professor:

Using the basic technique pioneered by Fantz, Dr. Elizabeth Spelke, a professor at Harvard University, has developed a large number of experiments with preferential staring. Remember, that's the tendency of infants to look at something that's new or surprising for a longer period of time. So, she uses preferential staring to assess the general knowledge that infants have without benefit of prior experience, and she generalizes her conclusions to speculate about the basic cognitive skills with which humans are born—those which distinguish humans as a species. According to Spelke, neuronal modules must be in place at birth, and their presence must allow babies to quickly build mental representations of people, familiar objects, spatial and numerical relationships. This innate core knowledge explains how children are able to learn and organize their world at such a rapid rate. According to Spelke, the foundation for human learning is part of the nature of human beings. As you might imagine, Spelke's work is used as an argument for heredity in the continuing discussion about the relative importance of heredity and environment. She asserts that the origin of human knowledge is a fundamentally human legacy.

Example Notes

Textbook—infant preference = studies rely on inference
Robert Fantz technique
   two visual choices
   look at one visual longer
   same choices, change position, track same visual
Johnson
   three choices = human face, features scrambled, blank
   moved visuals, recorded head + eye movements
   babies 1 day old tracked correctly drawn face

Lecture—Spelke/Harvard
   preferential staring
   general knowledge infants
   innate cognitive skills
   "core knowledge"
   explains rapid learning
   supports heredity

Example Writing Answer

In order to determine preferences by infants, Robert Fantz developed a technique for inferring choices. Researchers show two visuals to a baby, recording the length of time that each visual holds its attention. Repeating the presentation and changing the position of the visuals allow the researcher to identify whether the baby is tracking a visual consistently. Using this technique, Johnson showed babies three visuals, including a normal human face, a face with the features misplaced, and a blank. By moving the visuals and recording the degree to which babies tracked them, Johnson determined that even very young babies preferred the normal face.

Building on the work by Fantz, Spelke developed a number of experiments with infants in an effort to determine their general knowledge. Using preferential staring to determine their responses, Spelke posited that babies are born with "core knowledge," which explains their rapid learning curve. With innate cognitive skills that are available from birth, infants are able to respond quickly to their environment. The results support the claim that heredity is an important factor in development.

EXERCISE 94: Academic Topics—Summaries of Textbooks and Lectures

 (CD 5, Track 6)

Audio

Narrator: Now listen to a professor's response to the textbook passage.

Professor:

Whales and other mammals who inhabit the ocean have been problematic in the context of evolutionary theories. Since they breathe air, we can't classify them as fish, but they have adapted themselves to life in the ocean. So how did that happen? The most widely accepted explanation has been that they . . . that whales must have evolved from land animals that migrated into the water for some pressing environmental reason.

This was highly speculative until the discovery of fossils that chronicled a number of, uh, of intermediary stages from land animals to whales, including whale-like creatures with tiny appendages similar to legs and feet. It's now generally agreed that whales must have descended from mammals, and furthermore, that these mammals lived about 50 million years ago. And I think that's pretty amazing.

Now, the question is which mammals were the ancestors of the whale? So . . . using DNA analysis, we see that segments of non-coding DNA are shared by the whale and the hippopotamus but not by the whale and other close relatives of the hippo like giraffes, camels, and pigs. Although the premise still needs further study, there's quite a bit of support for the "whippo" hypothesis. Although they may not look like cousins, whales and hippos may be closely related.

Example Notes

Textbook—classification of species

Linnaeus—18 C *System of Nature* naming

Darwin—100 yrs *Origin of Species* genealogy
   evolutionary relationships
   comparison anatomy, fossils

Today—tree branches
   2 species diverge
   orders/families—similarities evident
   Ex-Cetaceans
      fish-shaped bodies
      paddles for arms, no legs
      blubber

Lecture—whales problematic
   breathe air, not fish
   adapted life in ocean
widely accepted
   whales evolved from land animals
   environmental reason → migrated water

fossils
  intermediary stages
  tiny legs, feet
  descended land animals 50 million years
DNA
  shared whale + hippo, not giraffes, camels, pigs = "whippo" hypothesis

Example Writing Answer

According to the textbook, the Linnaeus system, which is used to name species, and Darwin's theory, which identifies evolutionary relationships among species, are supported by a comparison of anatomical structures and their fossil remains. The similarities are evident at the level of orders and families, as for example, that of Cetaceans with fish-shaped bodies, paddles for arms, no legs, and a layer of insulating blubber.

It is difficult to classify whales because they breathe air like mammals but they live in water like fish. One generally accepted theory is that whales evolved from mammals on land, adapting themselves to life in the ocean as a result of an environmental change. Fossilized remains of a number of sea creatures with legs and feet in various stages of development seem to prove the theory that whales are the descendants of land mammals, and that they probably diverged about 50 million years ago. Furthermore, DNA testing suggests that the hippopotamus may be the closest relative of the whale, a possibility referred to as the "whippo" hypothesis.

EXERCISE 95: Academic Topics—Summaries of Textbooks and Lectures

 (CD 5, Track 7)

Audio

Narrator: Now listen to a professor's response to the textbook passage.

Professor:

Of course, we must give credit to Daniel Coleman for his valuable contribution to the field of psychology. Clearly, it is a good service to popularize concepts so that the general public can understand and use what we're learning in the field of psychology. In the case of emotional intelligence, companies have taken a hard look at IQ testing as a basis for hiring employees, and schools have begun to rethink the emphasis that has been place on standardized testing. However, there are three areas in Coleman's work that trouble me. First, very little credit is given to the original psychologists who put forward the notion of emotional intelligence. I do not, by the way, blame Coleman for this oversight. Rather, the media seems to have been responsible for identifying the term almost exclusively with Coleman at the expense of such early psychologists as Peter Salovey and Jack Mayer. Okay . . . another concern is that Coleman has used the term so broadly, um . . . interchanging it with related but not...identical terms, such as emotional literacy, emotional skills, emotional health, and even emotional competency. Finally, and this is probably the most serious criticism, Coleman fails to refer to and cite research over many years in the area of personality studies. Instead, he appears to uphold personal beliefs about what constitutes emotional intelligence, ignoring the large body of empirical research available to support or . . . or refute some of the specific claims he makes about the relative importance of EI . . . as compared with IQ or other measures.

Example Notes

Textbook—emotional intelligence
  capacity to understand own emotions
  make judgments others
  respond emotionally charged situations
measures EI
  discriminating feeling, actions
  managing, expressing emotions
  interpreting
  participating relationships

Emotional Intelligence
    Daniel Coleman
    IQ tests not as helpful as EI tests predicting success career, social
employers
    recruit teams
    screen applicants
parents traditionally taught EI, children → deficiencies basic life skills
schools EI curricula as significant as subjects
    listening
    conflict resolution
    life skills—responsibility, dependability

Lecture—Coleman
    + popularize concepts
    + reconsider IQ standardized tests employment/school
    – failed credit to Salovey/Mayer (media)
    – extended term to literacy, skills, health, competency
    – neglected empirical research personality studies
    – specific claims based on belief

Example Writing Answer

    Emotional intelligence is the capacity to understand one's own emotions and to make judgments about the way that others are responding emotionally to situations and events, as well as to respond to emotionally charged situations in socially acceptable ways. Measures of emotional intelligence consist of discriminating between feelings and actions, managing emotions and expressing them appropriately, interpreting the emotions that others express, and successfully initiating and participating in relationships.

    In his book, *Emotional Intelligence*, Daniel Coleman claimed that standardized intelligence tests were not as helpful in predicting success in a career or in social settings as tests of emotional intelligence. Employers in business and industry who need to recruit people for positions on teams have shown interest in emotional intelligence scores to assist them in screening applicants. Furthermore, some educators think that the skills associated with emotional intelligence are as significant as the subjects traditionally taught in school.

    Although the professor acknowledges Coleman's contribution to applied psychology in the workplace and school, she identifies three problems in the research. First, Coleman failed to give credit to previous researchers, especially to Salovey and Mayer, who first used the term "emotional intelligence." In fairness, the professor concedes that the media may be responsible for this oversight. Second, Coleman uses the term to refer to a number of related but different concepts, including literacy, skills, health, and competency. The reference to emotional intelligence in so many different contexts is confusing. Finally, Coleman neglects to use the empirical research on personality studies to support specific claims, using his belief structure instead. According to the professor, Coleman simply didn't meet the standards for scientific research.

EXERCISE 96: Academic Topics—Summaries of Textbooks and Lectures

 (CD 5, Track 8)

Audio
Narrator: Now listen to a professor's response to the textbook passage.

Professor:
    Although I agree for the most part with the information found in your textbook, I am disturbed by the fact that the authors focus almost exclusively on the geographical and geological changes brought about by shifting sea levels. In addition to these, and arguably, of equal or more importance, are the

serious effects on the organisms that live in the littoral zone and adapt to the fluctuating sea levels. Whether the changes are abrupt or gradual, organisms must adjust to new conditions as the water recedes and exposes their habitat to the air, or creates turbulence in the water where, uh, rough waves can dislodge them and even carry them out of the habitat in which they can survive. Water temperature and the levels of salinity in tide pools also vary with the changes in the littoral zone . . . and this is serious when we consider that even a few degrees or a slight change in the salt content can mean that an entire species will be extinguished. So, uh, I invite you to think about the repercussions of the various geographical changes on the total environment, including the millions of species that inhabit the littoral zones throughout the world.

Example Notes
Textbook—littoral zone = coastal environment
    water line highest
    200 feet below water, storm waves cannot disturb sediment
coast = general term land high tide to change landscape
shoreline = point land sea meet, shifting tides, weather
changes sea level → littoral zone fluctuates
    falls → exposing land
    rises → submerging coastal areas
factors = currents, temperatures, barometric pressure, gravity
mean sea level
    average hourly
    forty sites US coast
sea levels up 100 years
    sudden changes—volcanic
    gradual changes—erosion

Lecture—basic agreement
Textbook—geography/geology
    also affects marine life
        exposes habitat to air
        disrupts area out to sea
        changes temperature/salt content—extinction

Example Writing Answer
    The "littoral zone" is a term that is used to refer to the coastal environment. The zone spans the area from the place on land where the water line appears at its highest point to about 200 feet below the water where it is so deep that the storm waves cannot disturb the sediment on the sea floor. The littoral zone may be distinguished from the coast which is a general term for the land that can be seen at high tide to the first major change in the geographical landscape, for example, a mountain range. In contrast, the shoreline is the point where the land and the sea meet, a shifting line that responds to variations in the tides and weather conditions.

    In fact, changes in sea level can cause the littoral zone to fluctuate, exposing land as the sea level falls, and submerging coastal areas under the ocean as the sea level rises. Many factors can produce changes in sea level, including currents, temperatures, barometric pressure, and gravity. In order to standardize such a relative measure, a "mean sea level" is averaged for a particular site, using hourly sea levels to compute it.

    Although the professor is in basic agreement with the information presented in the textbook, he objects to the emphasis placed on geography and geology at the expense of biology. He claims that the changes in the littoral zone are equally significant for the marine life that inhabits it, citing several significant disruptions to habitats. Exposure to air, turbulence in the coastal waters, and changes in temperature or salt content can all cause serious problems for plants and animals. Even minor changes can result in the extinction of a species.

EXERCISE 97: Academic Topics—Summaries of Textbooks and Lectures

 (CD 5, Track 9)

Audio

Narrator: Now listen to a professor's response to the textbook passage.

Professor:

Although the ecological and the societal interpretations of *The Pearl* are interesting, I think that Steinbeck had a more personal reason for writing it. Remember that he wrote this novella after he had been awarded the Pulitzer Prize for fiction and had achieved both fame and fortune as a writer. Like Kino, the protagonist of *The Pearl*, Steinbeck is trying to reconcile his new position in society with his previous life as an impoverished artist. Although the fisherman had dreamed that peace and happiness could be bought with the pearl, he realizes that these spiritual gifts are beyond price. They cannot be purchased. Perhaps Steinbeck is somewhat autobiographical when he depicts Kino's rise to prominence and prosperity, and the disillusionment that follows. Success had provided material wealth and luxury, but it had come with a price. Steinbeck was struggling with disappointing relationships and alcoholism. His spiritual life had declined as his material wealth increased. So I think the work can be interpreted as an allegory of human desires, the vanity of material wealth, and the struggle between good and evil that Steinbeck himself was facing. As he writes in the introduction, "If this story is a parable, perhaps everyone takes his own meaning from it and reads his own life into it." Precisely this latitude for personal interpretation within the universal themes gives *The Pearl* such enduring appeal and permits us to speculate about Steinbeck himself.

Example Notes

Textbook—Interpretation *The Pearl*—John Steinbeck
   ecological—exploring Gulf CA
     not to disturb balance nature
     returning pearl to sea reestablishes balance
   social justice—relationships between classes
     priest, doctor—upper, fishermen—lower
     rich ignore, take advantage—priest, doctor expected financial reward for interest
   parable—evil vs good
     pearl can buy material comfort
     spiritual peace more precious

Lecture—autobiographical Steinbeck
   wrote *The Pearl* after famous/Pulitzer Prize
   Kino/Steinbeck material possessions disillusioned
   ruined relationships/alcoholism
   both spiritual deterioration

Example Writing Answer

There are a number of interpretations of *The Pearl*, a legend about a poor fisherman retold by John Steinbeck. The critics who promote an ecological interpretation point out that Steinbeck heard the story when he was exploring the Gulf of California as part of an expedition to research the marine life there. To them, the book issues a warning not to disturb the balance of nature. By returning the pearl to the sea, the fisherman reestablishes a balance of nature. Another interpretation focuses on social justice. The way that the pearl merchants exploit the fishermen supports this explanation. The relationships between the upper class as represented by the priest and the doctor and the lower class personified by the fishermen demonstrate how the rich either ignore or take advantage of the poor. It is only when they can expect to be rewarded financially that the priest and the doctor show any interest in the poor fisherman. A third interpretation is that *The Pearl* is a parable of the battle between evil and good, symbolically exemplified by the material comfort that the pearl can buy and the spiritual peace and satisfaction that are more precious than any price.

In the lecture, the professor suggests that Steinbeck may have written *The Pearl* as an autobiographical account. He points out that the novella was published after he had achieved fame and financial independence. The Pulitzer Prize provided Steinbeck with attention and allowed him to indulge himself by purchasing material possessions; however, he became disillusioned. Like Kino, his spiritual life suffered. Steinbeck spiraled into alcoholism, leaving a trail of ruined relationships behind. Perhaps Steinbeck longed for the past, when he was a struggling artist, before he found his prize.

EXERCISE 98: Academic Topics—Summaries of Textbooks and Lectures

 (CD 5, Track 10)

Audio

Narrator: Now listen to a professor's response to the textbook passage.

Professor:

So why did the humans in the Allen experiment actually increase the level of stress on the part of the subjects? Well, several ideas come to mind. For one thing, the, uh, human companions may actually have felt stress for the subjects, and . . . and may have transmitted their higher stress levels to the subjects. A friend might want the subject to succeed at the task, and the subject might sense that, so . . . so their presence might increase the stress already present in the situation. In other words, the subject may have felt more pressure to do well instead of feeling support for completing the task.

Or, it's possible that the subjects were embarrassed because, uh, because they feared that their performance might be evaluated by their friends, and failure . . . I mean not completing the task correctly . . . that could cause them to risk losing some of the respect that had been built into their relationship. Clearly, a pet is nonjudgmental about mathematical ability whereas a human friend might register disappointment or criticism or the subject might perceive criticism, even when none existed.

In a related follow-up study in which the subjects were asked to respond to the stress that they had felt during the task, several women mentioned the fact that . . . here, let me read this . . . that "dogs don't get angry, dogs don't trade in their owners for new friends, and dogs don't stop loving their owners if they aren't successful." According to Allen, the data doesn't reveal exactly why the dogs provided greater support, but it's persuasive as to the value of pets in the lives of their owners when it's necessary to cope with stressful situations.

Example Notes

Textbook—Karen Allen experiment
    pets effective emotional support in stressful situations, more effective than human
    procedure
        women dog owners solve difficult math problem
        pet, no one, human friend present
        fluctuations in blood pressure, heart rate measured stress
    results
        negative effect friend in room
        pulse 115 humans, 100 no one, 80 dog

Lecture—explanations for increased stress with friend
    friend's stress transmitted to subject
    desire for friend to succeed → tension room → increased pressure
    fear losing face
    follow up study—dogs not critical, friends might pass judgment

Example Writing Answer

According to a study by Karen Allen and reported in the textbook, pets are very effective in providing emotional support to their owners when stressful situations occur. In fact, the study suggested that pets were more effective than human friends. Women who owned dogs were selected to participate in the experiment. When confronted with the task of solving a difficult math problem, the group that was allowed to keep their dogs nearby experienced lower levels of stress as measured by fluctuations in blood pressure and heart rate than the groups that were alone in the room or those that had taken a good friend with them. The surprisingly negative effect of a friend in the room was documented by an average pulse rate of 115 for subjects with humans present, compared with 100 without support, and 80 for subjects with dogs present.

Several explanations for the increased level of stress when friends were in the room were explored in the lecture. If human friends felt stress themselves, they could have transmitted those feelings to the subjects, or the desire for a friend to succeed may have contributed to general tension in the room, thereby increasing the pressure to solve the problem correctly. Another possibility is that fear of losing face in front of a friend caused stress. In a follow-up survey, several participants remarked that a dog doesn't withhold its affection or abandon its owners if they aren't successful. In short, the fact that dogs are not perceived as critical may make them more supportive in certain stressful situations than human friends who might pass judgment on one's ability to cope.

EXERCISE 99: Academic Topics—Summaries of Textbooks and Lectures

 (CD 5, Track 11)

Audio

Narrator: Now listen to a professor's response to the textbook passage.

Professor:

Well, you've read about some of the perceived disadvantages of telecommuting. Now let's look at some of the advantages that one company found when they surveyed employees who had elected to work from their computers at home for two hours at the beginning of every day. After trying a partial telecommuting schedule for four months, participating employees at International Box Corporation reported a marked decrease in job-related stress due to traditional commuting. By working at home from eight in the morning until ten o'clock mid-morning, employees noticed that they were able to avoid the overcrowded buses and trains at peak hours of use, and they didn't have to drive on the freeways at rush hour. A significant segment of the employees responding to the survey cited worrying about being late to work as a primary concern before the telecommuting option. According to those who expressed this concern, driving home during rush hour is less stressful than driving to work in the morning because there's an element of choice about when to leave and less pressure to arrive punctually. Some participants mentioned the cost of commuting by car as a reason to use a full-time telecommuting option, should the company decide to implement one.

Another finding was that telecommuting, even part-time, seemed to influence the degree of job satisfaction on the part of participating employees. Why? Because they felt that they had more control over their time than they had experienced before the telecommuting schedule was instituted. And even though some of the employees actually worked longer than the required two hours from their home computers, they still reported a more positive attitude about their work. One reason that appeared frequently in the responses was that they enjoyed the quiet environment, and the opportunity to dress casually during the early morning hours.

Finally, the company discovered that the telecommuters were actually more productive as compared with a similar group of employees who worked on the regular eight-to-five schedule at the office. Employees cited the advantage of an extended period of time to focus on projects that required concentration without the usual interruptions that usually occurred in the office, such as telephones ringing and colleagues appearing at the door. In fact, the most commonly mentioned activity for the telecommuting hours seemed to be report writing and special projects. Any questions?

Example Notes

Textbook—reasons telecommuting not popular
　　new system takes time
　　managers reluctant, employees not concentrated
　　employees
　　　　value social, professional interaction
　　　　fear forgotten when promotions
　　　　work longer hours, never separating life + work

Lecture—positive perspective
　　employees International Box Corp—partial schedule
　　less stress to work on time—avoid rush hours, full time save money for car
job satisfaction—independence time
higher productivity—quieter + fewer interruptions → concentrate on projects, reports

Example Writing Answer

　　The textbook passage presents several reasons why telecommuting has not been as popular as predicted in early news publications. In addition to the fact that the implementation of new systems requires time, some managers have been reluctant to participate in the management of employees who are not concentrated in one location. Besides that, employees themselves have shown less interest than had been anticipated. The value of social and professional interaction with colleagues appears to be valued by employees, and there are concerns about being forgotten when supervisors are making decisions about promotions. Furthermore, working from home can encourage employees to work longer hours, never really separating their life from their work.

　　In contrast, the lecture provides a more positive perspective. Employees at International Box Corporation who participated in a partial schedule of telecommuting reported that they felt less stress about getting to work on time because they could avoid the rush hours for public transportation and freeway use. The possibility of saving money for maintaining and operating a car made full-time telecommuting more attractive than traditional commuting. Job satisfaction, independence in scheduling work time, and higher levels of productivity were also uncovered among telecommuters at International Box. A quieter environment with fewer interruptions gave employees an opportunity to concentrate on projects and reports.

EXERCISE 100: Academic Topics—Summaries of Textbooks and Lectures

 (CD 5, Track 12)

Audio

Narrator: Now listen to a professor's response to the textbook passage.

Professor:

　　Let's consider the question about whether gifts can ever be considered voluntary and without compensation like the definition that we find in an English language dictionary. Although we claim that in mainstream American culture, gift giving is devalued when there are obligations attached to the gift, let's look more closely at that assumption. Are gifts really voluntary in modern American society, or ultimately, do all gifts originate as social obligations with the potential for reciprocity? If we look at major social events in the United States, the kind to which invitations are sent, say a child's birthday party or a wedding, doesn't the invitation imply that a gift is required, and if so, is the act truly voluntary? For example, if your child receives an invitation to a birthday party at a classmate's home, and if you send a nice gift, well, isn't it likely that when the time comes for a birthday party for your child, you'll send an invitation to that classmate, and isn't it true that you'll expect a gift of more or less equal value? And what if the classmate isn't able to attend your child's party? Won't you expect a gift to be delivered anyway? Why would you feel this way if gift giving were voluntary, with no obligation attached?

Instead of buying into public declarations and published definitions, we need to study our own culture as closely as we study what anthropologists have traditionally considered the more . . . more exotic cultures. By scrutinizing our history and literature, and by questioning the assumptions behind our own social actions, we . . . we position ourselves for a more honest appraisal of who we are, and . . . and how our values intersect with the activities of our daily lives. In other words, we begin to understand our own culture.

Ask yourself, why are you embarrassed by an expensive gift? Why do you feel uncomfortable accepting it? Is it because you know that along with the gift is the expectation that a gift should be reciprocated? Do you feel obligated to return an equally impressive gift? And what if your circumstances don't permit you to do so? In that case, is the gift a problem? If so, then it isn't only reciprocity that defines gift giving in America, but also parity, I mean, keeping an accounting of the value of gifts so that equal exchanges are given at the appropriate times.

Now, consider this. Recognition can also be traded, as sociologist Warren Hagstrom has pointed out. Among my own subculture, academics . . . we pay careful attention to citations and acknowledgments of each other's works in an effort to extend and benefit from our gift-giving networks. I mean, the citation is our gift, and if it's a highly regarded colleague in the field, how different are these citations from the kula gifts in New Guinea?

Example Notes
Textbook—significance of gifts in other cultures
anthropologists presented gifts
social significance
   negative—humiliation, aggression
   positive—appreciation, goodwill
way, time reciprocated—friendship or rejection
example island culture near New Guinea—kula
   sending shell necklace—expectation reciprocity
   arm band reciprocated—months, years later
   value—properties shells, importance of previous owners

Lecture—gift giving American society
presumed voluntary, gift devalued if obligation implied
reality—reciprocity expected invited occasions, parties, weddings
students encouraged to question responses—cost, obligation to respond, equal value
Hagstrom compares academic culture to kula—reciprocity, prestige by association

Example Writing Answer
By presenting gifts to members of the cultures that they were studying, anthropologists have learned about the social significance of gift giving in other cultures. According to the textbook, the gift can be used to convey negative intentions such as humiliation or aggression as well as appreciation or goodwill. The time and way that a gift is reciprocated is also a signal of friendship or rejection. For example, island culture near New Guinea practices a system of gift giving referred to as the "kula," which consists of sending a shell necklace with the expectation that an armband will be reciprocated several months or years later. The properties of the shells and their connection with an important person who may have owned it previously influence the value.

In the lecture, the professor points out that gift giving in American society is presumed to be voluntary and that the gift is devalued if a social obligation is implied. However, the case is made that reciprocity is expected when gifts are exchanged for invited occasions like parties and weddings. Students are encouraged to probe their own responses to gift giving and the expectations associated with receiving a gift, especially as regards the cost of a gift and the obligation to respond with a gift of equal value. Hagstrom compares the academic subculture that requires the acknowledgement of works through citations to the island culture that exchanges kula gifts with the expectation of reciprocity and prestige by association.

MODEL TESTS

PBT Model Test Answer Sheet

—————————————————— **Section 1** ——————————————————

1 2 3 4 5 6 7 8 9 10 11 12 13 14 15 16 17 18 19 20 21 22 23 24 25 26 27 28 29 30
Ⓐ Ⓑ Ⓒ Ⓓ

31 32 33 34 35 36 37 38 39 40 41 42 43 44 45 46 47 48 49 50
Ⓐ Ⓑ Ⓒ Ⓓ

—————————————————— **Section 2** ——————————————————

1 2 3 4 5 6 7 8 9 10 11 12 13 14 15 16 17 18 19 20 21 22 23 24 25 26 27 28 29 30
Ⓐ Ⓑ Ⓒ Ⓓ

31 32 33 34 35 36 37 38 39 40
Ⓐ Ⓑ Ⓒ Ⓓ

—————————————————— **Section 3** ——————————————————

1 2 3 4 5 6 7 8 9 10 11 12 13 14 15 16 17 18 19 20 21 22 23 24 25 26 27 28 29 30
Ⓐ Ⓑ Ⓒ Ⓓ

31 32 33 34 35 36 37 38 39 40 41 42 43 44 45 46 47 48 49 50
Ⓐ Ⓑ Ⓒ Ⓓ

Cut here to remove answer sheet.

$$1 \quad 1 \quad 1 \quad 1 \quad 1 \quad 1 \quad 1 \quad 1 \quad 1 \quad 1 \quad 1 \quad 1$$

PBT Model Test

Section 1: Listening Comprehension   (CD 5, Track 13)

50 QUESTIONS 40 MINUTES

In this section of the test, you will have an opportunity to demonstrate your ability to understand conversations and talks in English. There are three parts to this section with special directions for each part. Answer all the questions on the basis of what is stated or implied by the speakers in this test. When you take the actual TOEFL test, you will not be allowed to take notes or write in your test book. Try to work on this Model Test in the same way.

Part A

Directions: In Part A, you will hear short conversations between two people. After each conversation, you will hear a question about the conversation. The conversations and questions will not be repeated. After you hear a question, read the four possible answers in your book and choose the best answer. Then, on your Answer Sheet, find the number of the question and fill in the space that corresponds to the letter of the answer you have chosen.

1. (A) Car repairs should be done at a garage.
   (B) The price was not too high.
   (C) The garage took advantage of the woman.
   (D) The car had serious problems.

2. (A) Have a party.
   (B) Attend the International Students' Association.
   (C) Go to work.
   (D) Get some rest.

3. (A) Leave immediately.
   (B) Watch the game on TV.
   (C) Start to play.
   (D) Eat a sandwich.

4. (A) He went to see the foreign student advisor.
   (B) He went to Washington.
   (C) He wrote to the Passport Office.
   (D) He reported it to the Passport Office.

5. (A) It is the policy of the bank.
   (B) The man was not helpful at all.
   (C) Her account at the bank is in order.
   (D) The check should be cashed.

6. (A) Ask Dr. Tyler to clarify the assignment.
   (B) Show a preliminary version to Dr. Tyler.
   (C) Let her see the first draft before Dr. Tyler sees it.
   (D) Talk to some of the other students in Dr. Tyler's class.

7. (A) Dr. Clark is a good teacher.
   (B) Statistics is a boring class.
   (C) Two semesters of statistics are required.
   (D) The students do not like Dr. Clark.

8. (A) He cannot do them.
   (B) They are finished.
   (C) It will be a difficult job.
   (D) They will be ready Saturday afternoon.

GO ON TO THE NEXT PAGE

1 1 1 1 1 1 1 1 1 1 1

9. (A) A concert.
   (B) An art museum.
   (C) A flower shop.
   (D) A restaurant.

10. (A) He is at lunch.
    (B) He is at the office.
    (C) He is in class.
    (D) He is at home.

11. (A) Take the ten o'clock bus.
    (B) Come back in five minutes.
    (C) Go to New York another day.
    (D) Call the airport.

12. (A) A teacher.
    (B) A textbook.
    (C) An assignment.
    (D) A movie.

13. (A) Make corrections on the original.
    (B) Make copies.
    (C) Deliver the copies to Mr. Brown.
    (D) Find the original.

14. (A) She was Sally Harrison's cousin.
    (B) She was Sally Harrison's sister.
    (C) She was Sally Harrison's friend.
    (D) She was Sally Harrison.

15. (A) The desk drawer won't open.
    (B) The pen is out of ink.
    (C) She cannot find her pen.
    (D) She is angry with the man.

16. (A) John is usually late.
    (B) John will be there at eight-thirty.
    (C) John will not show up.
    (D) John is usually on time.

17. (A) She does not agree with the man.
    (B) She needs a larger home.
    (C) She regrets the cost of their vacation.
    (D) She thinks that houses are very
        expensive.

18. (A) He did not make a presentation.
    (B) He got confused during the
        presentation.
    (C) He should have spoken more loudly.
    (D) He did a very complete job.

19. (A) He has decided not to mail the
        invitations.
    (B) He wants to get Janet's opinion.
    (C) He is waiting for Janet to answer the
        phone.
    (D) He does not want to invite Janet.

20. (A) The baby is asleep.
    (B) The baby is very active.
    (C) The baby is not staying with the
        woman.
    (D) The baby is just about to start walking.

21. (A) The results of the tests are not
        available.
    (B) The experiment had unexpected results.
    (C) He has not completed the experiment
        yet.
    (D) It is taking a lot of time to do the
        experiment.

22. (A) She does not put much effort in her
        studies.
    (B) She is very likable.
    (C) She prefers talking to the woman.
    (D) She has a telephone.

23. (A) See the doctor.
    (B) Get another job.
    (C) Go to the counter.
    (D) Buy some medicine.

24. (A) She will try her best.
    (B) She has to save her money.
    (C) She is still undecided.
    (D) She needs an application.

GO ON TO THE NEXT PAGE →

1 1 1 1 1 1 1 1 1 1 1 1

25. (A) She is glad to meet Robert.
    (B) She is surprised to hear from Robert.
    (C) She does not enjoy talking with Robert.
    (D) She was ready to call Robert.

26. (A) The man must stop working.
    (B) There is a little more time.
    (C) The test is important.
    (D) It is time for the test.

27. (A) The woman's roommate took a
        different class.
    (B) The book is very expensive.
    (C) The textbook may have been changed.
    (D) The course is not offered this semester.

28. (A) Sally may get a bike for Christmas.
    (B) Sally already has a bike like that one.
    (C) Sally likes riding a bike.
    (D) Sally may prefer a different gift.

29. (A) He does not want to give Carol a ride.
    (B) He does not have a car.
    (C) He cannot hear well.
    (D) He does not know Carol.

30. (A) Take a break.
    (B) Go to work.
    (C) Do the other problems.
    (D) Keep trying.

Part B

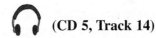 (CD 5, Track 14)

Directions: In this part of the test, you will hear longer conversations. After each conversation, you will hear several questions. The conversations and questions will not be repeated.

After you hear a question, read the four possible answers in your book and choose the best answer. Then, on your Answer Sheet, find the number of the question and fill in the space that corresponds to the letter of the answer you have chosen.

Remember, you are **not** allowed to take notes or write on your test pages.

31. (A) Whether to introduce the metric system
        in the United States.
    (B) How the metric system should be
        introduced in the United States.
    (C) Which system is better—the English
        system or the metric system.
    (D) How to convert measurements from the
        English system to the metric system.

32. (A) Now the weather on radio and TV is
        reported exclusively in metrics.
    (B) Road signs have miles marked on them,
        but not kilometers.
    (C) Both the English system and the metric
        system are being used on signs,
        packages, and weather reports.
    (D) Grocery stores use only metrics for
        their packaging.

33. (A) He thought that a gradual adoption
        would be better for everyone.
    (B) He thought that only metrics should
        be used.
    (C) He thought that only the English
        system should be used.
    (D) He thought that adults should use both
        systems, but that children should be
        taught only the metric system.

34. (A) Unfriendly.
    (B) Patronizing.
    (C) Uninterested.
    (D) Cooperative.

GO ON TO THE NEXT PAGE ➡

1 1 1 1 1 1 1 1 1 1 1

35. (A) To change his travel plans.
    (B) To arrange a time to pick up his tickets.
    (C) To reserve a hotel room.
    (D) To make a plane reservation.

36. (A) The man can save money by staying an extra night.
    (B) The man should have called earlier.
    (C) She needs the man to come into the office.
    (D) She will mail the tickets to the man.

37. (A) Travel on May 19 as planned.
    (B) Wait for a cheaper fare.
    (C) Stay an extra day in Atlanta.
    (D) Return on Sunday.

38. (A) Go back to his hotel.
    (B) Pack his suitcase.
    (C) Call a different travel agent.
    (D) Go to the travel agent's office in the afternoon.

Part C

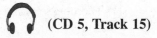 (CD 5, Track 15)

Directions: In this part of the test, you will hear several short talks. After each talk, you will hear some questions. The talks and questions will not be repeated.

After you hear a question, read the four possible answers in your book and choose the best answer. Then, on your Answer Sheet, find the number of the question and fill in the space that corresponds to the letter of the answer you have chosen.

39. (A) Private industry.
    (B) Advances in medicine.
    (C) Space missions.
    (D) Technological developments.

40. (A) Contact lenses.
    (B) Cordless tools.
    (C) Food packaging.
    (D) Ultrasound.

41. (A) To monitor the condition of astronauts in spacecraft.
    (B) To evaluate candidates who wanted to join the space program.
    (C) To check the health of astronauts when they returned from space.
    (D) To test spacecraft and equipment for imperfections.

42. (A) Archaeologists and astronauts were compared.
    (B) Astronauts made photographs of the Earth later used by archaeologists.
    (C) Archaeologists have used advances in medical technology developed for astronauts.
    (D) Space missions and underwater missions are very similar.

43. (A) Transportation on the Pacific Coast.
    (B) History of California.
    (C) Orientation to San Francisco.
    (D) Specifications of the Golden Gate Bridge.

44. (A) Golden Gate.
    (B) San Francisco de Asis Mission.
    (C) Military Post Seventy-six.
    (D) Yerba Buena.

GO ON TO THE NEXT PAGE ➡

1 1 1 1 1 1 1 1 1 1 1 1

45. (A) Gold was discovered.
    (B) The Transcontinental Railroad was completed.
    (C) The Golden Gate Bridge was constructed.
    (D) Telegraph communications were established with the East.

46. (A) Eighteen miles.
    (B) 938 feet.
    (C) One mile.
    (D) Between five and six miles.

47. (A) The term "essay."
    (B) Prose writing.
    (C) Personal viewpoint.
    (D) Brainstorming.

48. (A) The work of Alexander Pope.
    (B) The difference between prose and poetry.
    (C) The general characteristics of essays.
    (D) The reason that the phrase "personal essay" is redundant.

49. (A) It is usually short.
    (B) It can be either prose or poetry.
    (C) It expresses a personal point of view.
    (D) It discusses one topic.

50. (A) They will prepare for a quiz.
    (B) They will write their first essay.
    (C) They will read works by Pope.
    (D) They will review their notes.

THIS IS THE END OF THE LISTENING COMPREHENSION SECTION.

DO NOT READ OR WORK ON ANY OTHER SECTION OF THE TEST.

   STOP

2   2   2   2   2   2   2   2   2   2   2

Section 2: Structure and Written Expression

40 QUESTIONS 25 MINUTES

This section is designed to measure your ability to recognize language that is appropriate for standard written English. There are two types of questions in this section, with special directions for each type.

Structure

Directions: Questions 1–15 are incomplete sentences. Beneath each sentence you will see four words or phrases, marked (A), (B), (C), and (D). Choose the **one** word or phrase that best completes the sentence. Then, on your Answer Sheet, find the number of the question and fill in the space that corresponds to the letter of the answer you have chosen. Fill in the space so that the letter inside the oval cannot be seen.

1. Based on the premise that light was composed of color, the Impressionists came to the conclusion ---------- not really black.

    (A) which was that shadows
    (B) was shadows which
    (C) were shadows
    (D) that shadows were

2. ---------- a parliamentary system, the prime minister must be appointed on the basis of the distribution of power in the parliament.

    (A) The considered
    (B) To be considered
    (C) Considering
    (D) Considers

3. ---------- of the play *Mourning Becomes Electra* introduces the cast of characters and hints at the plot.

    (A) The act first
    (B) Act one
    (C) Act first
    (D) First act

4. As soon as -------- with an acid, salt, and sometimes water, is formed.

    (A) a base will react
    (B) a base reacts
    (C) a base is reacting
    (D) the reaction of a base

5. The Internal Revenue Service ------- their tax forms by April 15 every year.

    (A) makes all Americans file
    (B) makes all Americans to file
    (C) makes the filing of all Americans
    (D) makes all Americans filing

6. Although one of his ships succeeded in sailing all the way back to Spain past the Cape of Good Hope, Magellan never completed the first circumnavigation of the world, and ---------- .

    (A) most of his crew didn't too
    (B) neither most of his crew did
    (C) neither did most of his crew
    (D) most of his crew didn't also

7. To answer accurately is more important than ---------- .

    (A) a quick finish
    (B) to finish quickly
    (C) finishing quickly
    (D) you finish quickly

GO ON TO THE NEXT PAGE

2 **2** **2** **2** **2** **2** **2** **2** **2** **2**

8. Weathering ---------- the action whereby surface rock is disintegrated or decomposed.

   (A) it is
   (B) is that
   (C) is
   (D) being

9. A telephone recording tells callers ---------.

   (A) what time the movie starts
   (B) what time starts the movie
   (C) what time does the movie start
   (D) the movie starts what time

10. The people of Western Canada have been considering ---------- themselves from the rest of the provinces.

    (A) to separate
    (B) separated
    (C) separate
    (D) separating

11. It costs about ninety dollars to have a tooth ---------- .

    (A) filling
    (B) to fill
    (C) filled
    (D) fill

12. Not until a student has mastered algebra ---------- the principles of geometry, trigonometry, and physics.

    (A) he can begin to understand
    (B) can he begin to understand
    (C) he begins to understand
    (D) begins to understand

13. Although Margaret Mead had several assistants during her long investigations of Samoa, the bulk of the research was done by ---------- alone.

    (A) herself
    (B) she
    (C) her
    (D) hers

14. ---------- war correspondent, Hemingway used his experiences for some of his most powerful novels.

    (A) But a
    (B) It is a
    (C) While
    (D) A

15. Thirty-eight national sites are known as parks, another eighty-two as monuments, and ---------- .

    (A) the another one hundred seventy-eight as historical sites
    (B) the other one hundred seventy-eight as historical sites
    (C) seventy-eight plus one hundred more as historical sites
    (D) as historical sites one hundred seventy-eight

GO ON TO THE NEXT PAGE ➤

2 2 2 2 2 2 2 2 2 2 2

Written Expression

Directions: In questions 16–40, each sentence has four underlined words or phrases. The four underlined parts of the sentence are marked (A), (B), (C), and (D). Identify the **one** underlined word or phrase that must be changed in order for the sentence to be correct. Then, on your Answer Sheet, find the number of the question and fill in the space that corresponds to the letter of the answer you have chosen.

16. Interest <u>in</u> automatic data processing has <u>grown</u> <u>rapid</u> <u>since</u> the first large calculators were
     (A)   (B) (C) (D)
introduced in 1950.

17. Vaslav Nijinsky <u>achieved</u> world recognition <u>as</u> both <u>a dancer</u> <u>as well as</u> a choreographer.
                 (A)   (B)   (C)   (D)

18. Airports must <u>be located</u> <u>near to</u> major population centers for the advantage of <u>air transportation</u>
             (A)   (B)   (C)
<u>to be retained</u>.
   (D)

19. <u>It is said</u> that Einstein felt <u>very</u> <u>badly</u> about the application of his theories <u>to</u> the creation of
  (A)   (B) (C)   (D)
weapons of war.

20. The plants that <u>they</u> <u>belong to</u> the family of ferns <u>are</u> quite varied in <u>their</u> size and structure.
            (A)   (B)   (C)   (D)

21. <u>Despite of</u> the increase in air fares, most people <u>still</u> <u>prefer</u> <u>to travel</u> by plane.
  (A)   (B) (C)   (D)

22. All of <u>we</u> students must <u>have</u> an identification card in order to check books <u>out</u> <u>of</u> the library.
      (A)   (B)   (C)(D)

23. Columbus Day <u>is celebrated</u> <u>on</u> the <u>twelve</u> of October <u>because</u> on that day in 1492, Christopher
              (A)   (B)   (C)   (D)
Columbus first landed in the Americas.

24. One of <u>the most</u> <u>influence</u> newspapers in the U.S. <u>is</u> *The New York Times,* which is <u>widely distributed</u>
      (A)   (B)   (C)   (D)
throughout the world.

25. An unexpected <u>raise</u> in the cost of living <u>as well as</u> a decline in employment opportunities
            (A)   (B)
<u>resulted in</u> the <u>rapid</u> creation by Congress of new government programs for the unemployed.
  (C)   (D)

GO ON TO THE NEXT PAGE ➡

2 2 2 2 2 2 2 2 2 2 2

26. It is imperative that a graduate student maintains a grade point average of "B" in his major field.
    (A)   (B)   (C)   (D)

27. Coastal and inland waters are inhabited not only by fish but also by such sea creature as shrimps
                              (A)   (B)   (C)   (D)
    and clams.

28. Economists have tried to discourage the use of the phrase "underdeveloped nation" and
                        (A)   (B)
    encouraging the more accurate phrase "developing nation" in order to suggest an ongoing process.
    (C)   (D)

29. A gas like propane will combination with water molecules in a saline solution to form a solid
          (A)   (B)   (C)
    called a hydrate.
    (D)

30. Although it cannot be proven, presumable the expansion of the universe will slow down as
              (A)   (B)   (C)
    it approaches a critical radius.
    (D)

31. Regardless of your teaching method, the objective of any conversation class should be for the
    (A)   (B)
    students to practice speaking words.
              (C)   (D)

32. A City University professor reported that he discovers a vaccine that has been 80 percent effective
                                            (A)   (B)
    in reducing the instances of tooth decay among small children.
    (C)   (D)

33. American baseball teams, once the only contenders for the world championship, are now being
                              (A)   (B)
    challenged by either Japanese teams and Venezuelan teams.
              (C) (D)

34. When they have been frightened, as, for example, by an electrical storm, dairy cows may refuse
              (A)   (B)   (C)
    giving milk.
    (D)

35. Miami, Florida is among the few cities in the United States that has been awarded official status
                        (A)   (B)   (C)
    as bilingual municipalities.
    (D)

GO ON TO THE NEXT PAGE

2 2 2 2 2 2 2 2 2 2 2

36. No other quality is more important for a scientist to acquire as to observe carefully.
    (A)   (B)   (C)   (D)

37. After the police try unsuccessfully to determine to who the stolen property belongs, they
          (A)   (B)   (C)
    auction it locally or online.
            (D)

38. Fertilizers are used primarily to enrich soil and increasing yield.
               (A)   (B)   (C)   (D)

39. If the ozone gases of the atmosphere did not filter out the ultraviolet rays of the sun, life as we
                                          (A)   (B)
    know it would not have evolved on Earth.
         (C)   (D)

40. The regulation requires that everyone who holds a nonimmigrant visa reports an address to the
                                             (A) (B)   (C) (D)
    federal government in January of each year.

THIS IS THE END OF THE STRUCTURE AND WRITTEN EXPRESSION SECTION.

IF YOU FINISH BEFORE 25 MINUTES HAS ENDED, CHECK YOUR WORK ON SECTION 2 ONLY.

DO NOT READ OR WORK ON ANY OTHER SECTION OF THE TEST.

3 3 3 3 3 3 3 3 3 3 3

Section 3: Reading Comprehension

50 QUESTIONS 55 MINUTES

Directions: In this section, you will read several passages. Each one is followed by a number of questions about it. For questions 1–50, you are to choose the **one** best answer, (A), (B), (C), or (D), to each question. Then, on your Answer Sheet, find the number of the question and fill in the space that corresponds to the letter of the answer you have chosen.

Answer all questions about the information in a passage on the basis of what is **stated** or **implied** in that passage.

Questions 1–10

Precipitation, commonly referred to as rainfall, is a measure of the quantity of water in the form of either rain, hail, or snow which reaches the ground. The average annual precipitation over the whole of the United States is thirty-six inches. It should be understood

Line however, that a foot of snow is not equal to a foot of precipitation. A general formula for
(5) computing the precipitation of snowfall is that ten inches of snow is equal to one inch of precipitation. In New York State, for example, twenty inches of snow in one year would be recorded as only two inches of precipitation. Forty inches of rain would be recorded as forty inches of precipitation. The total annual precipitation would be recorded as forty-two inches.

The amount of precipitation is a combined result of several factors, including location,
(10) altitude, proximity to the sea, and the direction of prevailing winds. Most of the precipitation in the United States is brought originally by prevailing winds from the Pacific Ocean, the Gulf of Mexico, the Atlantic Ocean, and the Great Lakes. Because these prevailing winds generally come from the West, the Pacific Coast receives more annual precipitation than the Atlantic Coast. Along the Pacific Coast itself, however, altitude causes some diversity in rain-
(15) fall. The mountain ranges of the United States, especially the Rocky Mountain Range and the Appalachian Mountain Range, influence the amount of precipitation in their areas. East of the Rocky Mountains, the annual precipitation decreases substantially from that west of the Rocky Mountains. The precipitation north of the Appalachian Mountains is about 40 percent less than that south of the Appalachian Mountains.

1. What does this passage mainly discuss?

   (A) Precipitation
   (B) Snowfall
   (C) New York State
   (D) A general formula

2. Which of the following is another word that is often used in place of *precipitation*?

   (A) Humidity
   (B) Wetness
   (C) Rainfall
   (D) Rain-snow

3. The term *precipitation* includes

   (A) only rainfall
   (B) rain, hail, and snow
   (C) rain, snow, and humidity
   (D) rain, hail, and humidity

GO ON TO THE NEXT PAGE

4. What is the average annual rainfall in inches in the United States?

(A) Thirty-six inches
(B) Thirty-eight inches
(C) Forty inches
(D) Forty-two inches

5. If a state has 40 inches of snow in a year, by how much does this increase the annual precipitation?

(A) By two feet
(B) By four inches
(C) By four feet
(D) By 40 inches

6. The phrase "proximity to" in line 10 is closest in meaning to

(A) communication with
(B) dependence on
(C) nearness to
(D) similarity to

7. Where is the annual precipitation highest?

(A) The Atlantic Coast
(B) The Great Lakes
(C) The Gulf of Mexico
(D) The Pacific Coast

8. Which of the following was NOT mentioned as a factor in determining the amount of precipitation that an area will receive?

(A) Mountains
(B) Latitude
(C) The sea
(D) Wind

9. The word "substantially" in line 17 could best be replaced by

(A) fundamentally
(B) slightly
(C) completely
(D) apparently

10. The word "that" in line 19 refers to

(A) decreases
(B) precipitation
(C) areas
(D) mountain ranges

Questions 11–20

Course numbers are an indication of which courses are open to various categories of students at the University. Undergraduate courses with the numbers 100 or 200 are generally introductory courses appropriate for freshmen or sophomores, whereas courses with the numbers
Line 300 or 400 often have prerequisites and are open to juniors and seniors only. Courses with the
(5) numbers 800 or above are open only to graduate students. Certain graduate courses, generally those devoted to introductory material, are numbered 400 for undergraduate students who qualify to take them and 600 for graduate students. Courses designed for students seeking a professional degree carry a 500 number for undergraduate students and a 700 number for graduate students. Courses numbered 99 or below are special interest courses that do not carry
(10) academic credit. If students elect to take a special interest course, it will not count toward the number of hours needed to complete graduation requirements.

A full-time undergraduate student is expected to take courses that total twelve to eighteen credit hours. A full-time graduate student is expected to take courses that total ten to sixteen credit hours. Students holding assistantships are expected to enroll for proportionately
(15) fewer hours. A part-time graduate student may register for a minimum of three credit hours.

GO ON TO THE NEXT PAGE ➡

An overload, that is, more than the maximum number of hours, may be taken with the approval of an academic advisor. To register for an overload, students must submit the appropriate approval form when registering. Overloads above 24 hours will not be approved under any circumstances.

11. Where would this passage most likely be found?

   (A) In a syllabus
   (B) In a college catalog
   (C) In an undergraduate course
   (D) In a graduate course

12. What is the purpose of the passage?

   (A) To inform
   (B) To persuade
   (C) To criticize
   (D) To apologize

13. The word "prerequisites" in line 4 is closest in meaning to

   (A) courses required before enrolling
   (B) courses needed for graduation
   (C) courses that include additional charges
   (D) courses that do not carry academic credit

14. The word "those" in line 6 refers to

   (A) graduate students
   (B) graduate courses
   (C) introductory courses
   (D) course numbers

15. Which classification of students would be eligible to enroll in Mechanical Engineering 850?

   (A) A graduate student
   (B) A part-time student
   (C) A full-time student
   (D) An undergraduate student

16. If an undergraduate student uses the number 520 to register for an accounting course, what number would a graduate student probably use to register for the same course?

   (A) Accounting 520
   (B) Accounting 620
   (C) Accounting 720
   (D) Accounting 820

17. How is a student who registers for eight credit hours classified?

   (A) Full-time student
   (B) Graduate student
   (C) Part-time student
   (D) Non-degree student

18. Which of the following courses would not be included in the list of courses for graduation?

   (A) English 90
   (B) English 100
   (C) English 300
   (D) English 400

19. A graduate student may NOT

   (A) enroll in a course numbered 610
   (B) register for only one one-hour course
   (C) register for courses if he has an assistantship
   (D) enroll in an introductory course

20. The phrase "under any circumstances" in lines 18 is closest in meaning to

   (A) without cause
   (B) without permission
   (C) without exception
   (D) without a good reason

GO ON TO THE NEXT PAGE

3 3 3 3 3 3 3 3 3 3 3

Questions 21–30

During the nineteenth century, women in the United States organized and participated in a large number of reform movements, including movements to reorganize the prison system, improve education, ban the sale of alcohol, and, most importantly, to free the slaves. Some *Line* women saw similarities in the social status of women and slaves. Women like Elizabeth Cady (5) Stanton and Lucy Stone were feminists and abolitionists who supported the rights of both women and blacks. A number of male abolitionists, including William Lloyd Garrison and Wendell Philips, also supported the rights of women to speak and participate equally with men in antislavery activities. Probably more than any other movement, abolitionism offered women a previously denied entry into politics. They became involved primarily in order to (10) better their living conditions and the conditions of others.

When the Civil War ended in 1865, the Fourteenth and Fifteenth Amendments to the Constitution adopted in 1868 and 1870 granted citizenship and suffrage to blacks but not to women. Discouraged but resolved, feminists influenced more and more women to demand the right to vote. In 1869, the Wyoming Territory had yielded to demands by feminists, but (15) eastern states resisted more stubbornly than before. A women's suffrage bill had been presented to every Congress since 1878 but it continually failed to pass until 1920, when the Nineteenth Amendment granted women the right to vote.

21. With what topic is the passage primarily concerned?

(A) The Wyoming Territory
(B) The Fourteenth and Fifteenth Amendments
(C) Abolitionists
(D) Women's suffrage

22. The word "ban" in line 3 most nearly means to

(A) encourage
(B) publish
(C) prohibit
(D) limit

23. The word "supported" in line 5 could best be replaced by

(A) disregarded
(B) acknowledged
(C) contested
(D) promoted

24. According to the passage, why did women become active in politics?

(A) To improve the conditions of life that existed at the time
(B) To support Elizabeth Cady Stanton for president
(C) To be elected to public office
(D) To amend the Declaration of Independence

25. The word "primarily" in line 9 is closest in meaning to

(A) above all
(B) somewhat
(C) finally
(D) always

GO ON TO THE NEXT PAGE ➤

26. What had occurred shortly after the Civil War?

   (A) The Wyoming Territory was admitted to the Union.
   (B) A women's suffrage bill was introduced in Congress.
   (C) The eastern states resisted the end of the war.
   (D) Black people were granted the right to vote.

27. The word "suffrage" in line 12 could best be replaced by which of the following?

   (A) pain
   (B) citizenship
   (C) freedom from bondage
   (D) the right to vote

28. What does the Nineteenth Amendment guarantee?

   (A) Voting rights for blacks
   (B) Citizenship for blacks
   (C) Voting rights for women
   (D) Citizenship for women

29. The word "it" in line 16 refers to

   (A) bill
   (B) Congress
   (C) Nineteenth Amendment
   (D) vote

30. When were women allowed to vote throughout the United States?

   (A) After 1866
   (B) After 1870
   (C) After 1878
   (D) After 1920

Questions 31–40

Fertilizer is any substance that can be added to the soil to provide chemical elements essential for plant nutrition. Natural substances such as animal droppings and straw have been used as fertilizers for thousands of years, and lime has been used since the Romans intro-
Line duced it during the Empire. It was not until the nineteenth century, in fact, that chemical fer-
(5) tilizers became popular. Today, both natural and synthetic fertilizers are available in a variety of forms.

A complete fertilizer is usually marked with a formula consisting of three numbers, such as 4-8-2 or 3-6-4, which designate the percentage content of nitrogen, phosphoric acid, and potash in the order stated.

(10) Synthetic fertilizers are available in either solid or liquid form. Solids, in the shape of chemical granules are popular because they are easy to store and apply. Recently, liquids have shown an increase in popularity, accounting for about 20 percent of the nitrogen fertilizer used throughout the world. Formerly, powders were also used, but these were found to be less convenient than either solids or liquids.

(15) Fertilizers have no harmful effects on the soil, the crop, or the consumer as long as they are used according to recommendations based on the results of local research. Occasionally, however, farmers may use more fertilizer than necessary, damaging not only the crop but also the animals or humans that eat it. Accumulations of fertilizer in the water supply accelerate the growth of algae and, consequently, may disturb the natural cycle of life, contributing to the
(20) death of fish. Too much fertilizer on grass can cause digestive disorders in cattle and in infants who drink cow's milk.

GO ON TO THE NEXT PAGE

3 3 3 3 3 3 3 3 3 3 3

31. With which of the following topics is the passage primarily concerned?

    (A) Local research and harmful effects of fertilizer
    (B) Advantages and disadvantages of liquid fertilizer
    (C) A formula for the production of fertilizer
    (D) Content, form, and effects of fertilizer

32. The word "essential" in line 2 could best be replaced by which of the following?

    (A) limited
    (B) preferred
    (C) anticipated
    (D) required

33. In the formula 3-6-4

    (A) the content of nitrogen is greater than that of potash
    (B) the content of potash is greater than that of phosphoric acid
    (C) the content of phosphoric acid is less than that of nitrogen
    (D) the content of nitrogen is less than that of phosphoric acid

34. Which of the following has the smallest percentage content in the formula 4-8-2?

    (A) Nitrogen
    (B) Phosphorus
    (C) Acid
    (D) Potash

35. What is the percentage of nitrogen in a 5-8-7 formula fertilizer?

    (A) 3 percent
    (B) 5 percent
    (C) 7 percent
    (D) 8 percent

36. The word "designate" in line 8 could be replaced by

    (A) modify
    (B) specify
    (C) limit
    (D) increase

37. Which of the following statements about fertilizer is true?

    (A) Powders are more popular than ever.
    (B) Solids are difficult to store.
    (C) Liquids are increasing in popularity.
    (D) Chemical granules are difficult to apply.

38. The word "these" in line 13 refers to

    (A) powders
    (B) solids
    (C) liquids
    (D) fertilizer

39. The word "convenient" in line 14 is closest in meaning to

    (A) effective
    (B) plentiful
    (C) easy to use
    (D) cheap to produce

40. What happens when too much fertilizer is used?

    (A) Local research teams provide recommendations.
    (B) Algae in the water supplies begin to die.
    (C) Animals and humans may become ill.
    (D) Crops have no harmful effects.

GO ON TO THE NEXT PAGE

3 3 3 3 3 3 3 3 3 3 3

Questions 41–50

In 1626, Peter Minuit, governor of the Dutch settlements in North America known as New Amsterdam, negotiated with Canarsee Indian chiefs for the purchase of Manhattan Island for merchandise valued at sixty guilders or about $24.12. He purchased the island for the Dutch
Line West India Company.
(5)   The next year, Fort Amsterdam was built by the company at the extreme southern tip of the island. Because attempts to encourage Dutch immigration were not immediately successful, offers, generous by the standards of the era, were extended throughout Europe. Consequently, the settlement became the most heterogeneous of the North American colonies. By 1637, the fort had expanded into the village of New Amsterdam, and other small communities had
(10) grown up around it, including New Haarlem and Stuyvesant's Bouwery, and New Amsterdam began to prosper, developing characteristics of religious and linguistic tolerance unusual for the times. By 1643, it was reported that eighteen different languages were heard in New Amsterdam alone.
     Among the multilingual settlers was a large group of English colonists from Connecticut
(15) and Massachusetts who supported the English King's claim to all of New Netherlands set out in a charter that gave the territory to his brother James, the Duke of York. In 1664, when the English sent a formidable fleet of warships into the New Amsterdam harbor, Dutch governor Peter Stuyvesant surrendered without resistance.
     When the English acquired the island, the village of New Amsterdam was renamed New
(20) York in honor of the Duke. By the onset of the Revolution, New York City was already a bustling commercial center. After the war, it was selected as the first capital of the United States. Although the government was eventually moved, first to Philadelphia and then to Washington, D.C., New York City has remained the unofficial commercial capital.
     During the 1690s, New York became a haven for pirates who conspired with leading mer-
(25) chants to exchange supplies for their ships in return for a share in the plunder. As a colony, New York exchanged many agricultural products for English manufactured goods. In addition, trade with the West Indies prospered. Three centuries after his initial trade with the Indians, Minuit's tiny investment was worth more than seven billion dollars.

41. Which of the following would be the best title for this passage?

(A) A History of New York City
(B) An Account of the Dutch Colonies
(C) A Biography of Peter Minuit
(D) The First Capital of the United States

42. What did the Indians receive in exchange for their island?

(A) Sixty Dutch guilders
(B) $24.12 U.S.
(C) Goods and supplies
(D) Land in New Amsterdam

43. Where was New Amsterdam located?

(A) In Holland
(B) In North America
(C) On the island of Manhattan
(D) In India

44. The word "heterogeneous" in line 8 could best be replaced by

(A) liberal
(B) renowned
(C) diverse
(D) prosperous

GO ON TO THE NEXT PAGE ➡

45. Why were so many languages spoken in New Amsterdam?

(A) The Dutch West India Company was owned by England.
(B) The Dutch West India Company allowed freedom of speech.
(C) The Dutch West India Company recruited settlers from many different countries in Europe.
(D) The Indians who lived there before the Dutch West India Company purchase spoke many languages.

46. The word "formidable" in line 17 is closest in meaning to

(A) powerful
(B) modern
(C) expensive
(D) unexpected

47. The name of New Amsterdam was changed

(A) to avoid a war with England
(B) to honor the Duke of York
(C) to attract more English colonists
(D) to encourage trade during the 1690s

48. The word "it" in line 21 refers to

(A) Revolution
(B) New York City
(C) the island
(D) the first capital

49. Which city was the first capital of the new United States?

(A) New Amsterdam
(B) New York
(C) Philadelphia
(D) Washington

50. On what date was Manhattan valued at $7 billion?

(A) 1626
(B) 1726
(C) 1656
(D) 1926

THIS IS THE END OF THE READING COMPREHENSION SECTION.

IF YOU FINISH BEFORE 55 MINUTES HAS ENDED, CHECK YOUR WORK ON SECTION 3 ONLY.

DO NOT READ OR WORK ON ANY OTHER SECTION OF THE TEST.

To check your answers for the PBT Model Test, refer to the Answer Key on page 505.

THE TEST OF WRITTEN ENGLISH (TWE) FOLLOWS.

Test of Written English (TWE)

When you take this Model Test, you should use one sheet of paper, both sides. Time the Model Test carefully. After you have read the topic, you should spend 30 minutes writing. For results that would be closest to the actual testing situation, it is recommended that an English teacher score your test, using the guidelines on page 453 of this book.

In your opinion, what is the best way to choose a marriage partner? Use specific reasons and examples why you think this approach is best.

Notes

PBT Model Test Scripts for the Listening Section

Section 1

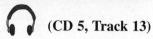 (CD 5, Track 13)

50 QUESTIONS 40 MINUTES

In this section of the test, you will have an opportunity to demonstrate your ability to understand conversations and talks in English. There are three parts to this section with special directions for each part. Answer all the questions on the basis of what is stated or implied by the speakers in this test. When you take the actual TOEFL test, you will not be allowed to take notes or write in your test book. Try to work on this Model Test in the same way.

Part A

Directions: In Part A, you will hear short conversations between two people. After each conversation, you will hear a question about the conversation. The conversations and questions will not be repeated. After you hear a question, read the four possible answers in your book and choose the best answer. Then, on your Answer Sheet, find the number of the question and fill in the space that corresponds to the letter of the answer you have chosen.

1. Woman: You'd better take the car to the garage from now on. They charged me seventy-five dollars for a few minor repairs.
   Man: That's not too bad.
   Narrator: What does the man mean?

(Note: There should be a 12-second pause after each test question in this section.)

2. Man: The International Students' Association is having a party Saturday night. Can you come or do you have to work at the hospital?
   Woman: I wish I could.
   Narrator: What will the woman probably do?

3. Woman: I think that the game starts at eight.
   Man: Good. We have just enough time to get there.
   Narrator: What will the speakers probably do?

4. Woman: What did you do after you lost your passport?
   Man: I went to see the foreign student advisor, and he reported it to the Passport Office in Washington.
   Narrator: What did the man do after he lost his passport?

5. Man: If you don't have an account here, I can't cash your check. I'm sorry, but that's the way it is.
   Woman: Well, thanks a lot! You're a big help!
   Narrator: What does the woman mean?

6. Man: I'm not sure what Dr. Tyler wants us to do.
   Woman: If I were you, I'd write a rough draft and ask Dr. Tyler to look at it.
   Narrator: What does the woman suggest the man do?

7.   Man: Dr. Clark is the only one teaching statistics this term.
     Woman: You mean we have to put up with her for another semester?
     Narrator: What does the woman mean?

8.   Man: Do you think that you can have these shirts finished by Friday morning?
     Woman: I'm sorry. I couldn't possibly get them done by then. Saturday afternoon would be the earliest that you could have them.
     Narrator: What does the woman say about the shirts?

9.   Woman: The music and the flowers are lovely.
     Man: Yes. I hope that the food is good.
     Narrator: What kind of place are the speakers probably talking about?

10. Man: Hello, Anne. This is Larry at the office. Is Fred at home?
     Woman: No, Larry, He's in class now. He'll be home for lunch though.
     Narrator: What do we know about Fred?

11. Man: When does the next bus leave for New York?
     Woman: Buses leave for New York every half-hour. You just missed the nine-thirty bus by five minutes.
     Narrator: What will the man probably do?

12. Woman: Did we have an assignment for Monday? I don's have anything written down.
     Man: Nothing to read in the textbook, but we have to see a movie and write a paragraph about it.
     Narrator: What are the speakers discussing?

13. Man: Make thirty copies for me and twenty copies for Mr. Brown.
     Woman: As soon as I make the final corrections on the original.
     Narrator: What is the woman probably going to do?

14. Man: Excuse me. Are you Sally Harrison's sister?
     Woman: No, I'm not. I'm her cousin.
     Narrator: What had the man assumed about the woman?

15. Woman: I can't find my pen. It was right here on the desk yesterday and now it's gone. Have you seen it?
     Man: Yes. I put it in the desk drawer.
     Narrator: What is the woman's problem?

16. Woman: When is John coming?
     Man: Well, he said he'd be here at eight-thirty, but if I know him, it will be at least nine o'clock.
     Narrator: What does the man imply about John?

17. Man: I suppose we should look for a bigger house, but I don't see how we can afford one right now.
     Woman: If only we hadn't spent so much money on our vacation this year.
     Narrator: What does the woman mean?

18.   Man: Did you see Jack's presentation?
        Woman: Yes. What happened? He didn't seem to know up from down.
        Narrator: What does the woman imply about Jack?

19.   Woman: Shall I send out the invitations?
        Man: Let's hold off on that until I can talk to Janet.
        Narrator: What does the man mean?

20.   Man: How's the baby? Is she walking yet?
        Woman: Oh, yes. I can't keep up with her!
        Narrator: What does the woman mean?

21.   Woman: How is your experiment coming along?
        Man: It's finished, but it didn't turn out quite like I thought it would.
        Narrator: What does the man mean?

22.   Woman: Barbara sure likes to talk on the phone.
        Man: If only she liked her classes as well!
        Narrator: What does the man imply about Barbara?

23.   Woman: My allergies are really bothering me. I guess I'll have to go to the doctor.
        Man: If I were you, I'd try some over-the-counter medications first. They usually
                    do the job.
        Narrator: What does the man suggest the woman do?

24.   Man: What did you decide about the scholarship? Did you fill out the application?
        Woman: I'm going to give it all I've got.
        Narrator: What does the woman mean?

25.   Man: Hello, Anne. This is Robert.
        Woman: Oh, hi, Robert. I was just about to call you.
        Narrator: What does the woman mean?

26.   Man: Could I have a few more minutes to finish?
        Woman: I'm afraid not. It's a timed test.
        Narrator: What does the woman mean?

27.   Woman: The best part is I can use my roommate's book.
        Man: I'm not so sure about that. I think they're using a different book this semester.
        Narrator: What does the man imply?

28.   Man: I'm going to get Sally a bike for Christmas.
        Woman: Are you sure she'd like one?
        Narrator: What does the woman imply?

29.   Woman: Carol needs a ride downtown, and I said you'd take her.
        Man: Oh no. Please say you didn't!
        Narrator: What can be inferred about the man?

30.   Man: I just can't get the answer to this problem. I've been working on it for three
                           hours.
         Women: Maybe you should get some rest and try it again later.
         Narrator: What does the woman suggest that the man do?

Part B

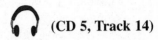 **(CD 5, Track 14)**

Directions: In this part of the test, you will hear longer conversations. After each conversation, you will
hear several questions. The conversations and questions will not be repeated.

After you hear a question, read the four possible answers in your book and choose the best answer.
Then, on your Answer Sheet, find the number of the question and fill in the space that corresponds to
the letter of the answer you have chosen.

Remember, you are **not** allowed to take notes or write on your test pages.

Questions 31–34. Listen to a class discussion.

         Baker: It seems to me that the question is not whether the metric system should be introduced
                           in the United States, but rather, how it should be introduced.
         Woman: I think that it should be done gradually to give everyone enough time to adjust.
         Man: Yes. Perhaps we could even have two systems for a while. I mean, we could keep the
                           English system and use metrics as an optional system.
         Woman: That's what they seem to be doing. When you go to the grocery store, look at the labels
                           on the cans and packages. They are marked in both ounces and grams.
         Man: Right. I've noticed that too. And the weather reporters on radio and TV give the
                           temperature readings in both degrees Fahrenheit and degrees Celsius now.
         Woman: Some road signs have the distances marked in both miles and kilometers, especially on
                           the interstate highways. What do you think, Professor Baker?
         Baker: Well, I agree that a gradual adoption is better for those of us who have already been
                           exposed to the English system of measurement. But I would favor teaching only metrics
                           in the elementary schools.
         Man: I see your point. It might be confusing to introduce two systems at the same time.

Narrator: 31.   What is the topic under discussion?

(Note: There should be a 12-second pause after each test question in this section.)

                   32.   What changes in measurement in the United States have the students observed?

                   33.   What was Professor Baker's opinion?

                   34.   Which word best describes Professor Baker's attitude toward his students?

Questions 35–38. Listen to a telephone call to a travel agent.

         Man: Hi. This is Roger Jackson. I'm calling to make a reservation for a flight from Houston
                           to Atlanta.
         Woman: Yes, Mr. Jackson. And what day would you like to travel?
         Man: Oh, not until next month. I want to leave on May 15th and return on May 19th. I thought
                           maybe if I called in advance I could get a better fare.
         Woman: Yes, you can. But if you stay over Saturday night and return on Sunday, May 20th, the
                           ticket will be even cheaper.

Man:	Really? How much cheaper?
Woman:	Almost fifty dollars.
Man:	Hmnn. but I would have an extra night in a hotel. No. That's okay. I'll just keep it for May 19th.
Woman:	All right. Do you have a seating preference?
Man:	I'd rather have a window seat.
Woman:	Good. There is one available. And do you want me to mail these tickets or will you pick them up?
Man:	I'll pick them up. When can I have them?
Woman:	Any time after two o'clock.
Man:	Great!

Narrator: 35. What is the main purpose of the telephone call?

36. What does the woman suggest?

37. What does the man decide to do?

38. What will the man probably do?

Part C

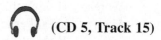 **(CD 5, Track 15)**

Directions: In this part of the test, you will hear several short talks. After each talk, you will hear some questions. The talks and questions will not be repeated.

After you hear a question, read the four possible answers in your book and choose the best answer. Then, on your Answer Sheet, find the number of the question and fill in the space that corresponds to the letter of the answer you have chosen.

[Remember, you are **not** allowed to take notes or write on your test pages.]

Questions 39–42. Listen to "Breakthroughs in Science," a weekly radio program.

Since the National Aeronautical and Space Administration was established in 1961, NASA has been engaged in an extensive research effort, which, in cooperation with private industry, has transferred technology to the international marketplace. Hundreds of everyday products can be traced back to the space mission, including cordless electrical tools, airtight food packaging, water purification systems, and even scratch coating for eye glasses.

In addition, may advances in medical technology can be traced back to NASA laboratories. First used to detect flaws in spacecraft, ultrasound is now standard equipment in almost every hospital for diagnosis and assessment of injuries and disease; equipment first used by NASA to transmit images from space to Earth is used to assist in cardiac imaging, and lasers first used to test satellites are now used in surgical procedures. Under-the-skin implants for the continuous infusion of drugs, and small pacemakers to regulate the heart were originally designed to monitor the physical condition of astronauts in space.

Finally, with the help of images that were obtained during space missions, and NASA technology, archaeologists have been able to explore the Earth. Cities lost under desert sands have been located and rediscovered, and the sea floor has been mapped using photographs from outer space.

Narrator: 39. What is the talk mainly about?

(Note: There should be a 12-second pause after each test question in this section.)

40. Which of the products listed are NOT mentioned as part of the technology development for space missions?

41. According to the speaker, why did NASA develop medical equipment?

42. Why does the speaker mention archaeology?

Questions 43–46. Listen to a talk by a tour guide on a bus.

The first permanent settlement was made at this site in 1776, when a Spanish military post was established on the end of that peninsula. During the same year, some Franciscan Fathers founded the Mission San Francisco de Asis on a hill above the post. A trail was cleared from the military post to the mission, and about halfway between the two, a station was established for travelers called *Yerba Buena*, which means "good herbs."

For thirteen years the village had fewer than one hundred inhabitants. But in 1848, with the discovery of gold, the population grew to ten thousand. That same year, the name was changed from Yerba Buena to San Francisco.

By 1862, telegraph communications linked San Francisco with eastern cities, and by 1869, the first transcontinental railroad connected the Pacific coast with the Atlantic seaboard. Today San Francisco has a population of almost seven million. It is the financial center of the West, and serves as the terminus for trans-Pacific steamship lines and air traffic. The port of San Francisco, which is almost eighteen miles long, handles between five and six million tons of cargo annually.

And now, if you will look to your right, you should just be able to see the Golden Gate Bridge. The bridge, which is more than one mile long, spans the harbor from San Francisco to Marin County and the Redwood Highway. It was completed in 1937 at a cost of thirty-two million dollars and is still one of the largest suspension bridges in the world.

Narrator: 43. What is the main purpose of this talk?

44. According to the tour guide, what was the settlement called before it was renamed San Francisco?

45. According to the tour guide, what happened in 1848?

46. How long is the Golden Gate Bridge?

<u>Questions 47–50</u>. Listen to a talk by a college instructor in an English class.

So many different kinds of writing have been called essays, it is difficult to define exactly what an essay is. Perhaps the best way is to point out four characteristics that are true of most essays. First, an essay is about one topic. It does not start with one subject and digress to another and another. Second, although a few essays are long enough to be considered a small book, most essays are short. Five hundred words is the most common length for an essay. Third, an essay is written in prose, not poetry. True, Alexander Pope did call two of his poems essays, but that word is part of a title, and after all, the "Essay on Man" and the "Essay on Criticism" really are not essays at all. They are long poems. Fourth, and probably most important, an essay is personal. It is the work of one person whose purpose is to share a thought, idea, or point of view. Let me also state here that since an essay is always personal, the term "personal essay" is redundant. Now, taking into consideration all of these characteristics, perhaps we can now define an essay as a short, prose composition with a personal viewpoint that discusses one topic. With that in mind, let's brainstorm some topics for your first essay assignment.

Narrator: 47.   What is the instructor defining?

48.   What is the main point of the talk?

49.   According to the talk, which of the characteristics are NOT true of an essay?

50.   What will the students probably do as an assignment?

Answer Key—PBT

Section 1: Listening Comprehension

1. (B)	11. (A)	21. (B)	31. (B)	41. (D)
2. (C)	12. (C)	22. (A)	32. (C)	42. (B)
3. (A)	13. (A)	23. (D)	33. (D)	43. (C)
4. (A)	14. (B)	24. (A)	34. (D)	44. (D)
5. (B)	15. (C)	25. (D)	35. (D)	45. (A)
6. (B)	16. (A)	26. (A)	36. (A)	46. (C)
7. (D)	17. (C)	27. (C)	37. (A)	47. (A)
8. (D)	18. (B)	28. (D)	38. (D)	48. (C)
9. (D)	19. (B)	29. (A)	39. (D)	49. (B)
10. (C)	20. (B)	30. (A)	40. (A)	50. (B)

Section 2: Structure and Written Expression

1. (D)	11. (C)	21. (A)	31. (D)
2. (B)	12. (B)	22. (A)	32. (A)
3. (B)	13. (C)	23. (C)	33. (D)
4. (B)	14. (D)	24. (B)	34. (D)
5. (A)	15. (B)	25. (A)	35. (C)
6. (C)	16. (C)	26. (B)	36. (C)
7. (B)	17. (D)	27. (D)	37. (C)
8. (C)	18. (B)	28. (C)	38. (D)
9. (A)	19. (C)	29. (B)	39. (A)
10. (D)	20. (A)	30. (C)	40. (C)

Section 3: Reading Comprehension

1. (A)	11. (B)	21. (D)	31. (D)	41. (A)
2. (C)	12. (A)	22. (C)	32. (D)	42. (C)
3. (B)	13. (A)	23. (D)	33. (D)	43. (B)
4. (A)	14. (B)	24. (A)	34. (D)	44. (C)
5. (B)	15. (A)	25. (A)	35. (B)	45. (C)
6. (C)	16. (C)	26. (D)	36. (B)	46. (A)
7. (D)	17. (C)	27. (D)	37. (C)	47. (B)
8. (B)	18. (A)	28. (C)	38. (A)	48. (B)
9. (A)	19. (B)	29. (A)	39. (C)	49. (B)
10. (B)	20. (C)	30. (D)	40. (C)	50. (D)

iBT® Model Test

Reading Section

This section tests your ability to understand reading passages like those in college textbooks. After each passage, you will answer questions about it. You will have 25 minutes to read each passage and answer the comprehension questions. You may use notes to answer. There are two types of reading comprehension questions. The multiple-choice questions require that you choose the best of four possible answers. The computer-assisted questions require that you follow directions on the screen. You may return to previous questions in the same reading passage, but after you go to the next passage, you may not return to a previous passage.

Independent Reading 1: "Norms"

Directions: Choose the best answer for multiple-choice questions. Follow the directions on the page for computer-assisted questions.

Norms are social rules that specify appropriate and inappropriate behavior in given situations. They tell us what we "should," "ought," and "must" do, as well as what we "should not," "ought not," and "must not" do. In all cultures the great body of these social rules deal with matters involving sex, property, and safety.

But norms are not just moral rules. They provide guidance so that we can align our actions with those of others when situations are unclear or ambiguous, and they provide standards by which we judge other people and make decisions about how we will interact with them. People riding the subway provide an example. Appropriate behaviors might include reading the newspaper, gazing at the advertisements, or commenting briefly on the weather. Someone not following these "rules" by chatting too much would probably be identified by other riders as an out-of-town visitor and not a serious danger; someone not following these "rules" by punching and kicking another rider would probably be identified as a danger to other riders, who might react by calling for help or trying to subdue the "norm-breaker."

Though norms are subjective human creations, we experience them as objective and independent features of our social environment (Reno, Cialdini, and Kallgren, 1993). People attach a good deal of importance to some norms, called **mores**, and they mete out harsh punishment to violators. Other norms, called **folkways**, people deem to be of less importance, and they exact less stringent conformity to them (Sumner, 1906). Some norms are formalized and are enforced by special political organizations. These we refer to as **laws**. Folkways, mores, and laws are discussed below.

Folkways

Folkways have to do with the customary ways and ordinary conventions by which we carry out our daily activities. We bathe, brush our teeth, groom our hair, wear shoes or sandals, wave greetings to friends, mow our lawns, and sleep in beds. We view people who violate folkways, especially those who violate a good number of them, as somehow "different" and even "strange." However, ordinarily we do not attach moral significance to folkways. For example, we may regard people who wear soiled clothing as crude but not as sinful, and people who are late for appointments as thoughtless but not evil. Gossip and ridicule are important mechanisms for enforcing folkways.

Mores

Members of a culture or society are more concerned about violations of mores. Murder, theft, rape, treason, and child molestation bring strong disapproval and severe punishment in the United States. Mores are seen as vital to a society's well-being and survival. People usually attach moral significance to mores, and they define people who violate them as sinful and evil. Consequently, the punishment for violators of a society's mores is severe; they may be put to death, imprisoned, cast out, mutilated, or tortured.

Folkways and mores are distinguished by the fact that they are usually enforced by people acting in a spontaneous and often collective manner. On contemporary Pitcairn Island, for example, islanders are afraid that if they do or say something against someone, that person will get back at them at some later date (Birkett, 1997). When one Pitcairner cut down another's banana tree, he was greeted the next morning with 3-inch nails planted in the mud path outside his house. Social censure also is achieved through the ancient formidable weapon of gossip. Sometimes rumors will reach the culprit within hours, and once accused, a person is as good as guilty (Birkett, 1997).

These efforts at social control involve not only individual interests but also group interests. Because you are a member of numerous groups, other people—your family members, friends, neighbors, and coworkers—may also benefit or suffer from your conduct. If you are arrested or fired, others may experience spillover effects. Indeed, group members are often held accountable for one another's actions. Some U.S. corporations link their employees through group incentive plans, and military boot camps punish everyone in the barracks for one recruit's misconduct. Such spillover effects give group members a stake in regulating one another's behavior. However, in the case of some groups (e.g., criminal and revolutionary organizations) a person's peers often have a stake in helping the violator avoid detection and punishment (Heckathorn, 1990).

Laws

Some norms are formalized into laws, rules that are enforced by a special political organization composed of individuals who have the right to use force. As anthropologist E. A. Hoebel (1958: 470–471) observes: "The essentials of legal coercion are general acceptance of the application of physical power, in threat or in fact, by a privileged party, for a legitimate cause, in a legitimate way, and at a legitimate time." The people who administer laws may make use of physical force with a low probability of retaliation by a third party (Collins, 1975). Laws tend to be the result of conscious thought, deliberate planning, and formal declaration. They can be changed more readily than folkways and mores.

Glossary:
Incentive plans: benefits that encourage employees to increase production
Boot camp: a military training program

"Norms" (Question References)

Paragraph 1 [A] Norms are social rules that specify appropriate and inappropriate behavior in given situations. They tell us what we "should," "ought," and "must" do, as well as what we "should not," "ought not," and "must not" do. In all cultures the great body of these social rules deal with matters involving sex, property, and safety. [B]

2 But norms are not just moral rules. [C] They provide guidance so that we can align our actions with those of others when situations are unclear or ambiguous, and they provide standards by which we judge other people and make decisions about how we will interact with them. People riding the subway provide an example. [D] Appropriate behaviors might include reading the newspaper, gazing at the advertisements, or commenting briefly on the weather. Someone not following these "rules" by chatting too much would probably be identified by other riders as an out-of-town visitor and not a serious danger; someone not following these "rules" by punching and kicking another rider would probably be identified as a danger to other riders, who might react by calling for help or trying to subdue the "norm-breaker."

3 Though norms are subjective human creations, we experience them as objective and independent features of our social environment (Reno, Cialdini, and Kallgren, 1993). People attach a good deal of importance to some norms, called **mores**, and they mete out harsh punishment to violators. Other norms, called **folkways**, people deem to be of less importance, and they exact less stringent conformity to them (Sumner, 1906). Some norms are formalized and are enforced by special political organizations. These we refer to as **laws**. Folkways, mores, and laws are discussed below.

Folkways

4 Folkways have to do with the customary ways and ordinary conventions by which we carry out our daily activities. We bathe, brush our teeth, groom our hair, wear shoes or sandals, wave greetings to friends, mow our lawns, and sleep in beds. We view people who violate folkways, especially those who violate a good number of them, as somehow "different" and even "strange." However, ordinarily we do not attach moral significance to folkways. For example, we may regard people who wear soiled clothing as crude but not as sinful, and people who are late for appointments as thoughtless but not evil. Gossip and ridicule are important mechanisms for enforcing folkways.

Mores

5   Members of a culture or society are more concerned about violations of mores. Murder, theft, rape, treason, and child molestation bring strong disapproval and severe punishment in the United States. Mores are seen as vital to a society's well-being and survival. People usually attach moral significance to mores, and they define people who violate them as sinful and evil. Consequently, the punishment for violators of a society's mores is severe; they may be put to death, imprisoned, cast out, mutilated, or tortured.

6   Folkways and mores are distinguished by the fact that they are usually enforced by people acting in a spontaneous and often collective manner. On contemporary Pitcairn Island, for example, islanders are afraid that if they do or say something against someone, that person will get back at them at some later date (Birkett, 1997). When one Pitcairner cut down another's banana tree, he was greeted the next morning with 3-inch nails planted in the mud path outside his house. Social censure also is achieved through the ancient formidable weapon of gossip. Sometimes rumors will reach the culprit within hours, and once accused, a person is as good as guilty (Birkett, 1997).

7   These efforts at social control involve not only individual interests but also group interests. Because you are a member of numerous groups, other people—your family members, friends, neighbors, and coworkers—may also benefit or suffer from your conduct. If you are arrested or fired, others may experience spillover effects. Indeed, group members are often held accountable for one another's actions. Some U.S. corporations link their employees through group incentive plans, and military boot camps punish everyone in the barracks for one recruit's misconduct. Such spillover effects give group members a stake in regulating one another's behavior. However, in the case of some groups (e.g., criminal and revolutionary organizations) a person's peers often have a stake in helping the violator avoid detection and punishment (Heckathorn, 1990).

Laws

8   Some norms are formalized into laws, rules that are enforced by a special political organization composed of individuals who have the right to use force. As anthropologist E. A. Hoebel (1958: 470–471) observes: "the essentials of legal coercion are general acceptance of the application of physical power, in threat or in fact, by a privileged party, for a legitimate cause, in a legitimate way, and at a legitimate time." The people who administer laws may make use of physical force with a low probability of retaliation by a third party (Collins, 1975). Laws tend to be the result of conscious thought, deliberate planning, and formal declaration. They can be changed more readily than folkways and mores.

1. The word they in the passage refers to
   - (A) norms
   - (B) actions
   - (C) others
   - (D) situations

2. The author uses the example of people riding in a subway in paragraph 2 in order to
   - (A) explain moral rules that deal with sex, property, and safety
   - (B) contrast social rules as they are practiced in various cultures
   - (C) demonstrate appropriate behaviors for a social situation
   - (D) illustrate how social control occurs when norms are broken

3. According to paragraph 3, what do folkways, mores, and laws have in common?
   - (A) They are experienced subjectively.
   - (B) They are all viewed as equally important.
   - (C) They are formalized and enforceable.
   - (D) They are all considered norms.

4. According to paragraph 4, people who do not observe folkways are considered
   - (A) dangerous
   - (B) odd
   - (C) sinful
   - (D) uneducated

5. The word spontaneous in the passage is closest in meaning to
   - (A) unplanned
   - (B) incomplete
   - (C) unimportant
   - (D) abnormal

6. Why does the author mention the example of Pitcairn Island?
   - (A) To demonstrate the effects of gossip
   - (B) To show what can happen without norms
   - (C) To discuss the enforcement of mores
   - (D) To explain ancient customs in one culture

7. The word formidable in the passage is closest in meaning to
   - (A) powerful
   - (B) regular
   - (C) new
   - (D) changing

8. All of the following are mentioned as ways to enforce mores EXCEPT
   - (A) gossip
   - (B) death
   - (C) imprisonment
   - (D) education

9. Which of the following sentences best expresses the essential information in the highlighted sentence in the passage? *Incorrect* answer choices change the meaning or leave out information.
   - Ⓐ Both group and individual interests are included.
   - Ⓑ Individual interests are not included, but group interests are.
   - Ⓒ Individual and group interests are not included.
   - Ⓓ Individual interests are not included in group interests.

10. According to paragraph 8, what is true of laws?
   - Ⓐ They cannot be easily modified once they are passed.
   - Ⓑ They are enforced by politics instead of by physical force.
   - Ⓒ They often involve third parties who take revenge.
   - Ⓓ They are formalized norms subject to legitimate enforcement.

11. The word readily in the passage is closest in meaning to
   - Ⓐ clearly
   - Ⓑ routinely
   - Ⓒ easily
   - Ⓓ initially

12. Look at the four squares [☐] that indicate where the following sentence can be added to the passage. Choose the best place to insert the sentence.

   However, the specific moral restrictions vary greatly from one culture to another.
   - Ａ
   - Ｂ
   - Ｃ
   - Ｄ

13. Complete the summary by choosing THREE answer choices that express the most important ideas in the passage. The other answer choices do not belong in the summary because they express ideas that are not in the passage or they do not refer to the major points.
   This question is worth two points.

   Norms are social rules that specify appropriate and inappropriate behavior in given situations.
   - Ⓐ Folkways provide conventional standards for daily activities such as grooming.
   - Ⓑ People who violate mores are usually subject to harsh punishment for their behavior.
   - Ⓒ Beliefs are the basis for many of the norms and values of a given culture.
   - Ⓓ Group members may experience either advantage or harm from the actions of associates.
   - Ⓔ Laws are rules that are enforced by a political organization with legitimate authority.
   - Ⓕ Strict norms that control moral and ethical behavior are referred to as mores.

Independent Reading 2: "The Death of Stars"

Sometime in the future, the core of the Sun will run out of hydrogen; indeed, every star must eventually deplete its fuel. In order to understand the spectacular events that occur when a star dies, we have to understand a little more about the lives of stars.

One way to look at the life of a star like the Sun is to think of it as a continual battle against the force of gravity. From the moment when the Sun's original gas cloud started to contract, the force of gravity acted on every particle, forcing it inward and trying to make the entire structure collapse on itself. When the nuclear fires ignited in the core of the Sun 4.5 billion years ago, gravity was held at bay. The increase in temperature in the center raised the pressure in the star's interior and balanced the inward pull of gravity. But, in the long view of things, this balance can be only a temporary state of affairs. The Sun can stave off the inward tug of gravity only as long as it has hydrogen to burn. When hydrogen fuel in the core is depleted, the amount of energy generated in the core will decrease, and gravity will begin to take over. The Sun will begin to contract and heat up.

This dramatic situation will have two effects. First, the temperature in the region immediately surrounding the core will begin to rise. Any remaining hydrogen in that region, which had not burned because it had been at too low a temperature, will begin to burn. Thus a hydrogen-burning shell will begin to form around the extinguished core. The second effect is that the temperature in the core will rise until helium, the "ash" of hydrogen burning, will begin to undergo nuclear fusion reactions. The net reaction will be a process called *helium burning*, in which the helium in the core burns to make carbon. The Sun will then resemble an onion, with a helium-burning core surrounded by a layer where hydrogen is being burned.

This notion, that the ashes of one nuclear fire serve as fuel for the next, is central to an understanding of what goes on in stars. In stars like the Sun, the temperature never gets high enough to ignite the carbon, so helium burning is the final energy-producing stage. In more massive stars, this process of successive burning cycles can go on for quite a while, as we shall see.

The Death of the Sun

The Sun will burn at more or less its present size and temperature for billions of years more. But, in its final stages, our star will undergo dramatic changes. When the core burns out, the hydrogen-burning shells surrounding the central region are pulled in. This temporary collapse increases the amount of energy generated by fusion, and the increased energy causes the surface of the Sun to balloon out. At its maximum expansion, the dying Sun extends out past the orbit of Venus. Because the solar wind also increases during this period, however, the Sun's mass drops and the planets move outward. In the end, only Mercury is actually swallowed. During this phase of its life, the Sun will emit its energy through a much larger surface than it does now, and that surface will appear to be very cool—red hot to our eyes. In fact, our Sun will become a red giant, and the helium in the Sun's core will burn to produce an inner core primarily of carbon.

As carbon accumulates in the core, a slow collapse will ensue until some other force intervenes. In the case of the Sun, that force will come from the Pauli principle—the principle that tells us that no two electrons can occupy the same state. As the core starts to collapse, its electrons are compressed into a smaller and smaller volume. They reach the point (what we call the "full parking lot") where they can no longer be pushed together. At this point, the Pauli principle takes over and the collapse stops for the simple reason that the electrons can't be pushed together any closer than they already are. A permanent outward force is exerted on every element in the star—an outward force that cancels the inward force of gravity. Astronomers call this force "degeneracy pressure."

When the Sun reaches this stage, it will be rather small— probably about the size of the Earth (though still hundreds of thousands of times more massive than Earth)—and it will no longer be generating energy through nuclear reactions. It will be very hot and will take a long time to cool off. During this phase, the temperature of each part of the Sun's surface will be very high, but, because the Sun will be so small, the total amount of radiation coming from it will not be very large. It will be, in other words, a white dwarf. Most of the carbon that is the end product of helium burning will remain locked in the white dwarf, and will not be returned to the cosmos.

"The Death of Stars" (Question References)

Paragraph 1   Sometime in the future, the core of the Sun will run out of hydrogen; indeed, every star must eventually deplete its fuel. In order to understand the spectacular events that occur when a star dies, we have to understand a little more about the lives of stars.

2   One way to look at the life of a star like the Sun is to think of it as a continual battle against the force of gravity. From the moment when the Sun's original gas cloud started to contract, the force of gravity acted on every particle, forcing it inward and trying to make the entire structure collapse on itself. When the nuclear fires ignited in the core of the Sun 4.5 billion years ago, gravity was held at bay. The increase in temperature in the center raised the pressure in the star's interior and balanced the inward pull of gravity. But, in the long view of things, this balance can be only a temporary state of affairs. The Sun can stave off the inward tug of gravity only as long as it has hydrogen to burn. When hydrogen fuel in the core is depleted, the amount of energy generated in the core will decrease, and gravity will begin to take over. The Sun will begin to contract and heat up.

3   This dramatic situation will have two effects. First, the temperature in the region immediately surrounding the core will begin to rise. Any remaining hydrogen in that region, which had not burned because it had been at too low a temperature, will begin to burn. Thus a hydrogen-burning shell will begin to form around the extinguished core. The second effect is that the temperature in the core will rise until helium, the "ash" of hydrogen burning, will begin to undergo nuclear fusion reactions. The net reaction will be a process called *helium burning*, in which the helium in the core burns to make carbon. The Sun will then resemble an onion, with a helium-burning core surrounded by a layer where hydrogen is being burned.

4   This notion, that the ashes of one nuclear fire serve as fuel for the next, is central to an understanding of what goes on in stars. In stars like the Sun, the temperature never gets high enough to ignite the carbon, so helium burning is the final energy-producing stage. In more massive stars, this process of successive burning cycles can go on for quite a while, as we shall see.

The Death of the Sun

5   The Sun will burn at more or less its present size and temperature for billions of years more. But, in its final stages, our star will undergo dramatic changes. When the core burns out, the hydrogen-burning shells surrounding the central region are pulled in. [A] This temporary collapse increases the amount of energy generated by fusion, and the increased energy causes the surface of the Sun to balloon out. [B] At its maximum expansion, the dying Sun extends out past the orbit of Venus. Because the solar wind also increases during this period, however, the Sun's mass drops and the planets move outward. In the end, only Mercury is actually swallowed. During this phase of its life, the Sun will emit its energy through a much larger surface than it does now, and that surface will appear to be very cool—red hot to our eyes. [C] In fact, our Sun will become a red giant, and the helium in the Sun's core will burn to produce an inner core primarily of carbon. [D]

6   As carbon accumulates in the core, a slow collapse will ensue until some other force intervenes. In the case of the Sun, that force will come from the Pauli principle—the principle that tells us that no two electrons can occupy the same state. As the core starts to collapse, its electrons are compressed into a smaller and smaller volume. They reach the point (what we call the "full parking lot") where they can no longer be pushed together. At this point, the Pauli principle takes over and the collapse stops for the simple reason that the electrons can't be pushed together any closer than they already are. A permanent outward force is exerted on every element in the star—an outward force that cancels the inward force of gravity. Astronomers call this force "degeneracy pressure."

7   When the Sun reaches this stage, it will be rather small—probably about the size of the Earth (though still hundreds of thousands of times more massive than Earth)—and it will no longer be generating energy through nuclear reactions. It will be very hot and will take a long time to cool off. During this phase, the temperature of each part of the Sun's surface will be very high, but, because the Sun will be so small, the total amount of radiation coming from it will not be very large. It will be, in other words, a white dwarf. Most of the carbon that is the end product of helium burning will remain locked in the white dwarf, and will not be returned to the cosmos.

14. The word deplete in the passage is closest in meaning to
  Ⓐ scatter
  Ⓑ consume
  Ⓒ propel
  Ⓓ expose

15. The word particle in the passage is closest in meaning to
  Ⓐ minor movement
  Ⓑ stage of a process
  Ⓒ very small piece
  Ⓓ change in temperature

16. Which of the following sentences best expresses the essential information in the highlighted sentence in the passage? *Incorrect* answer choices change the meaning or leave out information.
  Ⓐ The Sun burns hydrogen because of gravity.
  Ⓑ The force of gravity pulls the Sun's hydrogen in.
  Ⓒ While the Sun is burning hydrogen, it can resist gravity.
  Ⓓ Hydrogen will burn for a long time before gravity affects it.

17. According to paragraph 3, what happens in *helium burning*?
  Ⓐ Carbon creates ashes that heat and burn the helium.
  Ⓑ Nuclear reactions ignite the hydrogen around the helium shell.
  Ⓒ Hydrogen and helium combine to raise the temperatures.
  Ⓓ The heat in the core causes helium to experience nuclear reactions.

18. The word it in the passage refers to
  Ⓐ core
  Ⓑ region
  Ⓒ hydrogen
  Ⓓ shell

19. The word massive in the passage is closest in meaning to
  Ⓐ hotter
  Ⓑ brighter
  Ⓒ larger
  Ⓓ older

20. According to paragraph 5, all of the following are true of the final stages of the Sun EXCEPT
  Ⓐ the solar winds accelerate
  Ⓑ the surface of the Sun expands
  Ⓒ Mercury is consumed by the Sun
  Ⓓ the carbon core turns the Sun black

21. Why does the author refer to a "full parking lot" in paragraph 6?
  Ⓐ To explain the Pauli principle
  Ⓑ To give an example of degeneracy pressure
  Ⓒ To refer to nuclear reactions
  Ⓓ To demonstrate how carbon is trapped

22. According to paragraph 7, what happens when the Sun becomes a white dwarf?
    - Ⓐ The temperature is high. ✓
    - Ⓑ The radiation is intense.
    - Ⓒ The carbon is released.
    - Ⓓ The helium is cool.

23. According to the passage, what is the last stage in the death of a star like the Sun?
    - Ⓐ It becomes very light.
    - Ⓑ It decreases in size.
    - Ⓒ It disappears from sight.
    - Ⓓ It loses its orbit.

24. According to information in the passage, what can be inferred about the Sun?
    - Ⓐ Solar winds are probably beginning to increase now.
    - Ⓑ The age of the Sun is estimated at 4.5 billion years.
    - Ⓒ The Sun is about halfway through its natural cycle.
    - Ⓓ The Sun will destroy three planets when it expands.

25. Look at the four squares [☐] that indicate where the following sentence can be added to the passage. Choose the best place to insert the sentence.

    In about one hundred million years, the helium is completely exhausted.

    Ⓐ

    Ⓑ

    Ⓒ

    Ⓓ

26. Complete the summary by choosing THREE answer choices that express the most important ideas in the passage. The other answer choices do not belong in the summary because they express ideas that are not in the passage or they do not refer to the major points. *This question is worth two points.*

    The life of a star is a continual battle against the forces of gravity.
    - Ⓐ A helium flash dumps enormous amounts of thermal energy into the core.
    - Ⓑ An increase in temperature in the core balances the inward pull of gravity.
    - Ⓒ When the core burns out, a temporary collapse creates a red giant.
    - Ⓓ A permanent outward force overcomes gravity in the white dwarf stage.
    - Ⓔ Two electrons cannot occupy the same space in a star.
    - Ⓕ The carbon that results from helium burning is retained in the white dwarf.

Independent Reading 3:
"The Methods and Materials of Sculpture"

Modeling

For sculpture, the most common modeling material is clay, an earth substance found in most parts of the world. Wet clay is wonderfully pliable; few can resist the temptation to squeeze and shape it. As long as clay remains wet, the sculptor can do almost anything with it—add on more and more clay to build up the form, gouge away sections, pinch it outward, scratch into it with a sharp tool, smooth it with the hands. But when a clay form has dried and been fired (heated to a very high temperature), it becomes hard. Fired clay, sometimes called by the Italian name *terra cotta*, is surprisingly durable. Much of the ancient art that has survived was formed from this material.

In some ways modeling is the most direct of sculpture methods. The workable material responds to every touch, light or heavy, of the sculptor's fingers. Sculptors often use clay modeling in the same way that painters traditionally have used drawing, to test ideas before committing themselves to the finished work. As long as the clay is kept damp, it can be worked and reworked almost indefinitely. Even the terminology is the same; we sometimes call a clay test piece a "sketch."

Casting

In contrast to modeling, casting seems like a very *indirect* method of creating a sculpture. Sometimes the sculptor never touches the final piece at all. Metal, and specifically bronze, is the material we think of most readily in relation to casting. Bronze can be superheated until it flows, will pour freely into the tiniest crevices and forms, and then hardens to extreme durability.

The most common method for casting metal is called the **lost-wax** process, sometimes known by its French name, *cire perdue*. Dating back to the third millennium B.C.E., the basic concept is simple and ingenious. We describe it here as it was practiced by the African sculptors of ancient Ife.

First, a core is built up of specially prepared clay. Over this core, the sculptor models the finished form in a layer of wax. When the sculpture is complete, wax rods and a wax cup are attached to it to form a sort of "arterial system," and the metal pins are driven through the wax sculpture to the core inside. The whole is encased in specially prepared clay. When the clay has dried, it is heated so that the wax melts and runs out (hence "lost wax") and the clay hardens. The lost wax leaves a shaped void inside the block. Where the wax rods and block were, channels and a depression called a pouring cup remain. The pins hold the core in place, preserving the space where the wax was. Next, the mold is righted, and molten metal is poured into the pouring cup. The metal enters the mold through the channels, driving the air before it. When the metal bubbles up through the air channels, it is a sign that the mold is probably filled. Metal, therefore, has *replaced* the wax, which is why casting is known as a replacement method. When the metal has cooled, the mold is broken apart, freeing the form. The channels, now cast in metal as well, are cut away, the clay core is removed (if desired), holes or other flaws are patched or repaired, and the form is ready for smoothing and polishing.

A sculpture cast in this way is unique, for the wax original is destroyed in the process. Standard practice today is a variation called indirect or investment casting, which allows multiples to be made. In this method, the artist finishes the sculpture completely in clay, plaster, or other material. A mold is formed around the solid sculpture (today's foundries use synthetic rubber for this mold). The mold is removed from the sculpture in sections, then reassembled. Melted wax is painted or "slushed" inside the mold to build up an inner layer about 3/16" thick. After it has hardened, this wax casting is removed from the mold and checked against the original sculpture for accuracy; it should be an exact duplicate, but hollow. The wax casting is fitted with wax rods, pierced with pins, then encased in solid plaster, which both fills and surrounds it. This plaster is called the investment. From this point on, the process is the same: the investment is heated so that the wax melts and runs out, metal is poured into the resulting void, and the investment is broken away to free the casting. The key difference is that the mold that makes the wax casting is reusable, thus multiple wax versions of an original can be prepared and multiple bronzes of a sculpture cast.

Carving

Carving is more aggressive than modeling, more direct than casting. In this process the sculptor begins with a block of material and cuts, chips, and gouges away until the form of the sculpture emerges. Wood and stone are the principal materials for carving, and both tend to resist the sculptor's tools. When approaching the block to be carved, the sculptor must study the grain of the material—its fibrous or crystalline structure—so as to work *with* that material. Any attempt to violate the grain could result in a failed sculpture.

Types of wood and stone vary considerably in their suitability for carving. Jade, for example, is too hard to be carved at all and can be shaped only through abrasion—patient rubbing with an even harder stone such as quartzite or diamond. Artists throughout history have learned to work with the natural properties of available materials and to master the capabilities of available tools.

"The Methods and Materials of Sculpture" (Question References)

Modeling

Paragraph 1   For sculpture, the most common modeling material is clay, an earth substance found in most parts of the world. Wet clay is wonderfully pliable; few can resist the temptation to squeeze and shape it. As long as clay remains wet, the sculptor can do almost anything with it—add on more and more clay to build up the form, gouge away sections, pinch it outward, scratch into it with a sharp tool, smooth it with the hands. But when a clay form has dried and been fired (heated to a very high temperature), it becomes hard. Fired clay, sometimes called by the Italian name *terra cotta*, is surprisingly durable. Much of the ancient art that has survived was formed from this material.

2   In some ways modeling is the most direct of sculpture methods. The workable material responds to every touch, light or heavy, of the sculptor's fingers. Sculptors often use clay modeling in the same way that painters traditionally have used drawing, to test ideas before committing themselves to the finished work. As long as the clay is kept damp, it can be worked and reworked almost indefinitely. Even the terminology is the same; we sometimes call a clay test piece a "sketch."

Casting

3   In contrast to modeling, casting seems like a very *indirect method of creating a sculpture.* Sometimes the sculptor never touches the final piece at all. Metal, and specifically bronze, is the material we think of most readily in relation to casting. Bronze can be superheated until it flows, will pour freely into the tiniest crevices and forms, and then hardens to extreme durability.

4   The most common method for casting metal is called the **lost-wax** process, sometimes known by its French name, *cire perdue*. Dating back to the third millennium B.C.E., the basic concept is simple and ingenious. We describe it here as it was practiced by the African sculptors of ancient Ife.

5   First, a core is built up of specially prepared clay. Over this core, the sculptor models the finished form in a layer of wax. When the sculpture is complete, wax rods and a wax cup are attached to it to form a sort of "arterial system," and the metal pins are driven through the wax sculpture to the core inside. The whole is encased in specially prepared clay. When the clay has dried, it is heated so that the wax melts and runs out (hence "lost wax") and the clay hardens. [A] The lost wax leaves a shaped void inside the block. Where the wax rods and block were, channels and a depression called a pouring cup remain. The pins hold the core in place, preserving the space where the wax was. [B] Next, the mold is righted, and molten metal is poured into the pouring cup. The metal enters the mold through the channels, driving the air before it. When the metal bubbles up through the air channels, it is a sign that the mold is probably filled. [C] Metal, therefore, has *replaced* the wax, which is why casting is known as a replacement method. When the metal has cooled, the mold is broken apart, freeing the form. The channels, now cast in metal as well, are cut away, the clay core is removed (if desired), holes or other flaws are patched or repaired, and the form is ready for smoothing and polishing. [D]

6   A sculpture cast in this way is unique, for the wax original is destroyed in the process. Standard practice today is a variation called indirect or investment casting, which allows multiples to be made. In this method, the artist finishes the sculpture completely in clay, plaster, or other material. A mold is formed around the solid sculpture (today's foundries use synthetic rubber for this mold). The mold is removed from the sculpture in sections, then reassembled. Melted wax is painted or "slushed" inside the mold to build up an inner layer about 3/16" thick. After it has hardened, this wax casting is removed from the mold and checked against the original sculpture for accuracy; it should be an exact duplicate, but hollow. The wax casting is fitted with wax rods, pierced with pins, then encased in solid plaster, which both fills and surrounds it. This plaster is called the investment. From this point on, the process is the same: the investment is heated so that the wax melts and runs out, metal is poured into the resulting void, and the investment is broken away to free the casting. The key difference is that the mold that makes the wax casting is reusable, thus multiple wax versions of an original can be prepared and multiple bronzes of a sculpture cast.

Carving

7   Carving is more aggressive than modeling, more direct than casting. In this process the sculptor begins with a block of material and cuts, chips, and gouges away until the form of the sculpture emerges. Wood and stone are the principal materials for carving, and both tend to resist the sculptor's tools. When approaching the block to be carved, the sculptor must study the grain of the material—it's fibrous or crystalline structure—so as to work *with* that material. Any attempt to violate the grain could result in a failed sculpture.

8   Types of wood and stone vary considerably in their suitability for carving. Jade, for example, is too hard to be carved at all and can be shaped only through abrasion—patient rubbing with an even harder stone such as quartzite or diamond. Artists throughout history have learned to work with the natural properties of available materials and to master the capabilities of available tools.

27. It can be inferred from the passage that
    Ⓐ carving is an older method of sculpture than modeling
    Ⓑ clay modeling was popular because the material was easy to find
    Ⓒ drawings must be made before beginning to create a sculpture
    Ⓓ casting was developed because clay sculptures did not last

28. The word durable in the passage is closest in meaning to
    Ⓐ strong
    Ⓑ fine
    Ⓒ practical
    Ⓓ smooth

29. Which of the following can be inferred from paragraph 2?
    Ⓐ The author prefers modeling to all of the other methods of sculpture.
    Ⓑ A sculptor might experiment with a clay sculpture before creating it in marble.
    Ⓒ Clay is not easy to work with because it can get hard before the piece is finished.
    Ⓓ Artists who are talented at drawing often create sculptures as well as paintings.

30. Which of the following sentences best expresses the essential information in the highlighted sentence in the passage? *Incorrect* answer choices change the meaning or leave out information.
    Ⓐ Casting a sculpture is an indirect method of modeling.
    Ⓑ Modeling is a more direct method than casting.
    Ⓒ Both casting and modeling are indirect methods.
    Ⓓ Indirect methods provide contrasts in sculptures.

31. The word core in the passage is closest in meaning to
    Ⓐ center
    Ⓑ surface
    Ⓒ shell
    Ⓓ mold

32. According to paragraph 5, what is the purpose of the channels in the "lost-wax" process?
    Ⓐ To hold the wax core in place.
    Ⓑ To break the metal mold apart.
    Ⓒ To keep the clay from hardening too fast.
    Ⓓ To allow the metal to replace the wax.

33. The word flaws in the passage is closest in meaning to
    Ⓐ enhancements
    Ⓑ hazards
    Ⓒ defects
    Ⓓ innovations

34. According to paragraph 5, what replaces the wax in the "lost wax" process?
    Ⓐ plaster
    Ⓑ bronze
    Ⓒ rubber
    Ⓓ clay

35. The word unique in the passage is closest in meaning to
    Ⓐ fragile
    Ⓑ attractive
    Ⓒ superior
    Ⓓ rare

36. What is the advantage of investment casting?
    Ⓐ The sculpture is stronger because it is solid.
    Ⓑ Copies of the sculpture may be made.
    Ⓒ The method is faster than regular casting.
    Ⓓ Rubber is easier to work with than clay.

37. According to the passage, all of the following considerations are important in carving EXCEPT
    Ⓐ the type of stone
    Ⓑ the grain of the wood
    Ⓒ the nature of the tools
    Ⓓ the age of the material

38. Look at the four squares [□] that indicate where the following sentence can be added to the passage. Choose the best place to insert the sentence.

    All but the simplest sculptures are cast in two pieces and then welded together.
    Ⓐ
    Ⓑ
    Ⓒ
    Ⓓ

39. Complete the summary by choosing THREE answer choices that express the most important ideas in the passage. The other answer choices do not belong in the summary because they express ideas that are not in the passage or they do not refer to the major points. *This question is worth two points.*

    There are three methods that are still used for sculpture.
    Ⓐ The lost wax process is the most common method for casting metal sculptures.
    Ⓑ The qualities of bronze make it a popular material for casting sculptures.
    Ⓒ Many ancient sculptures have survived because they were buried in wet clay.
    Ⓓ Modeling is the most direct and probably the oldest method for sculpture.
    Ⓔ In carving, the sculptor must work aggressively with the materials.
    Ⓕ Rubber molds have improved the casting method because they can be reused.

Listening Section

This section tests your ability to understand campus conversations and academic lectures in English. You will hear each conversation and lecture one time. You may take notes while you listen. After each conversation or lecture, you will answer questions about it. You may use your notes to answer. There are two types of listening comprehension questions. The multiple-choice questions require that you choose the best of four possible answers. The computer-assisted questions require that you follow directions on the screen. You must answer each question in order to go to the next question. You cannot return to previous questions.

Independent Listening 1: "Talking About Professors"

 (CD 6, Track 1)

Directions: Choose the best answer for multiple-choice questions. Follow the directions on the page for computer-assisted questions.

1. What are the students mainly discussing?
   Ⓐ The textbook for Dr. Peterson's course.
   Ⓑ The lecture notes for their psychology class.
   Ⓒ The professors that they are taking classes with.
   Ⓓ The courses that they will take next term.

2. What kind of lecture does the woman prefer?
   Click on 2 answers.
   Ⓐ A linear presentation.
   Ⓑ Pictures and videos.
   Ⓒ Stories and anecdotes.
   Ⓓ Handouts with lists.

3. Why does the man criticize Dr. Woods?
   Ⓐ He isn't very well prepared for his lectures.
   Ⓑ Sometimes he has his teaching assistant give the class.
   Ⓒ His research is not very interesting.
   Ⓓ The way he responds to questions is confusing.

4. What is the woman's attitude toward Dr. Woods?
   Ⓐ She is not very interested in his lectures.
   Ⓑ She thinks that he is very handsome.
   Ⓒ She does not like his choice of teaching assistant.
   Ⓓ She enjoys his class because of his teaching style.

5. What will the woman most probably do?
   Ⓐ Register for Dr. Peterson's class next semester.
   Ⓑ Take child psychology with Dr. Woods.
   Ⓒ Change her major to psychology.
   Ⓓ Read the book instead of attending class.

Independent Listening 2: "Internet Connections"

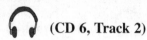

(CD 6, Track 2)

6. What is the purpose of this lecture?
   Ⓐ To discuss the effect of the Internet on social interaction.
   Ⓑ To prove that computers have had a positive influence on life.
   Ⓒ To report that almost all college students use the Internet.
   Ⓓ To design an experiment that will measure Internet use by the class.

7. Listen again to part of the lecture. Then answer the question.
   "What do *you* think?"
   "Disappointment maybe."
   "Go on."
   "Well, maybe they expected too much from their Internet friends. I mean, if you think that a person you meet on the Internet is going to be your special someone, that probably isn't going to happen."

   Why does the professor say this:
   "Go on."
   Ⓐ He wants to give someone else a turn to speak.
   Ⓑ He is asking the student to give a more complete answer.
   Ⓒ He disagrees with the student's answer to the question.
   Ⓓ He is telling the student to try another answer.

8. What were the results of the research study?
   Click on 2 answers.
   Ⓐ People who used the Internet were less likely to feel lonely.
   Ⓑ Internet users had less communication with family who lived nearby.
   Ⓒ More depression was reported by those who used the Internet.
   Ⓓ Mental health improved when people used the Internet more.

9. The professor gives an example of a person who exchanges recipes with someone on the Internet. What does this example demonstrate?
   Ⓐ Who is likely to make friends on the Internet.
   Ⓑ Why the Internet is good for someone in a rural area.
   Ⓒ How to get good advice on the Internet.
   Ⓓ What to expect from an Internet friend.

10. Why does the professor question the results of the research?
    Ⓐ Because the study lasted only a few months.
    Ⓑ Because there were very few subjects in the study.
    Ⓒ Because there was only one study done.
    Ⓓ Because the findings were not conclusive.

11. What is the attitude of the professor toward the students?
    Ⓐ He wants them to wait for him to call on them.
    Ⓑ He expects them to agree with him about the research.
    Ⓒ He respects their opinions on the topic of discussion.
    Ⓓ He does not like them to ask many questions.

Independent Listening 3: "Managing Failure"

 (CD 6, Track 3)

12. What is the class mainly discussing?
    - Ⓐ A class project in a business course.
    - Ⓑ A business in the community.
    - Ⓒ A case study from their book.
    - Ⓓ A hypothetical situation.

13. Listen again to part of the discussion. Then answer the question.
    "Right. And why did they underbid? Anyone?"

    Why does the professor say this:
    "Anyone?"
    - Ⓐ She wants the students to continue speaking.
    - Ⓑ She wants a volunteer to lead the discussion.
    - Ⓒ She wants a student to answer the question.
    - Ⓓ She wants the students to pay attention.

14. What does the professor mean when she says this:
    "That's it in a nutshell."
    - Ⓐ It is not a complete answer.
    - Ⓑ It is a good summary.
    - Ⓒ It is an estimate of the cost.
    - Ⓓ It is not very logical.

15. How did the mistake occur?
    - Ⓐ The salesperson made an error in writing up the order.
    - Ⓑ The workers forgot to assemble the furniture.
    - Ⓒ The account supervisor did not include assembly in the bid.
    - Ⓓ The warehouse delivered the wrong furniture.

16. Based on information in the lecture, indicate whether the statements refer to the way that the manager responded to the error.
    For each sentence, click in the YES or NO column.

	YES	NO
Ⓐ He was angry because no one took responsibility for the error.		
Ⓑ His position was that the procedures needed to be changed.		
Ⓒ He reprimanded the employee who made the mistake.		
Ⓓ He remained calm while he chaired the open meeting.		

17. What conclusion did the students make about the management style?
    - Ⓐ They agreed that he should have acted differently when the employees concealed the error.
    - Ⓑ They thought that he turned the problem into an opportunity to improve the company.
    - Ⓒ They were surprised that he admitted the mistake in a meeting of all his employees.
    - Ⓓ They felt that he was willing to accept too many excuses when the problem was discovered.

Independent Listening 4: "Application for a Scholarship"

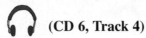 **(CD 6, Track 4)**

18. Why does the student go to see the professor?
    Ⓐ To make an appointment for tomorrow.
    Ⓑ To interview with him for a scholarship.
    Ⓒ To get advice about her scholarship application.
    Ⓓ To turn in her essay before the due date.

19. What information is required in the essay?
    Click on 2 answers.
    Ⓐ The applicant's financial situation.
    Ⓑ The educational background of the applicant.
    Ⓒ The goals that the applicant has set.
    Ⓓ The names of professors who support the applicant.

20. When does the woman need to turn in her application to the committee?
    Ⓐ Today.
    Ⓑ Tomorrow.
    Ⓒ This Friday.
    Ⓓ Next week.

21. Listen again to part of the conversation. Then answer the question.
    "Your grade point average is what . . . a 4.0?"
    "So far I have all As."
    "See what I'm saying?"

    Why does the professor say this:
    "Your grade point average is what . . . a 4.0?"
    Ⓐ To determine whether she would qualify for the scholarship.
    Ⓑ To verify the number that she has written on the application.
    Ⓒ To encourage her and give her more self-confidence.
    Ⓓ To ask her to think about the advice that he has given her.

22. Why does Professor Walters tell the woman to pretend she is writing about her friend Kathy?
    Ⓐ Because she needs to practice writing an essay.
    Ⓑ Because Kathy is a good candidate for a scholarship.
    Ⓒ Because she is embarrassed to write about herself.
    Ⓓ Because she is Kathy's best friend.

Independent Listening 5: "Pest Management"

 (CD 6, Track 5)

23. What is this lecture mainly about?
    - Ⓐ Manipulation of the reproductive cycles of pests.
    - Ⓑ The use of new pesticides to kill pests.
    - Ⓒ The genetic modification of plants to manage pests.
    - Ⓓ Integrated strategies to control pests.

24. According to the professor, what are *pheromones*?
    - Ⓐ A technical term for a female moth.
    - Ⓑ A sterilization process for male moths.
    - Ⓒ A chemical that attracts male moths.
    - Ⓓ A predator that controls the moth population.

25. Why does the professor mention the example of ladybugs?
    - Ⓐ To prove that all insects are not harmful.
    - Ⓑ To show how a predator can control pests.
    - Ⓒ To demonstrate how to control weeds.
    - Ⓓ To explain why pest management is necessary.

26. Which changes in farming practices support pest management?
    Click on 2 answers.
    - Ⓐ Planting crops that contain natural pesticides near other crops.
    - Ⓑ Plowing under habitats where pests usually survive the winter.
    - Ⓒ Planting the same crop to repeat and strengthen the same pest control.
    - Ⓓ Leaving weeds in the field to attract the pests away from the crop.

27. Listen again to part of the lecture. Then answer the question.
    "Although this is a simplification, in general, generic engineering . . . did I say generic? . . .
    genetic engineering, that's genetic engineering . . . involves the insertion of genes from other
    species into crop plants in order to develop beneficial traits."

    Why does the professor ask the following question:
    "Did I say generic?"
    - Ⓐ To emphasize the importance of the concept.
    - Ⓑ To determine whether students have understood.
    - Ⓒ To correct the misuse of a word in the lecture.
    - Ⓓ To include information that he forgot to mention.

28. What does the professor imply about genetic modification of plants?
    - Ⓐ It is a very cost effective way to manage pests.
    - Ⓑ It may have serious consequences for the ecosystem.
    - Ⓒ It could be a major export to other countries.
    - Ⓓ It results in a lower yield when plants are modified.

Independent Listening 6: "Arts and Crafts"

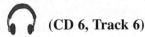 (CD 6, Track 6)

29. What is the professor mainly discussing?
    Ⓐ Victorian designs and decorations.
    Ⓑ The Arts and Crafts style.
    Ⓒ Mass production in the industrial age.
    Ⓓ The East Aurora Workshop.

30. Listen again to part of the lecture. Then answer the question.
"As you'll recall from our study of the Victorians, theirs was an age of quantity. That is to say, every surface was covered with pictures, ornaments, and objects. Also, the Victorians were noted for extravagance, and uh . . . even excess in decoration."

    Why does the professor say this:
    "As you will recall from our study of the Victorians, theirs was an age of quantity."
    Ⓐ To introduce the class to the Victorian period.
    Ⓑ To criticize the Victorian style of decoration.
    Ⓒ To refer to a previous lecture about the Victorian age.
    Ⓓ To give an example of the Victorian style.

31. What are two design elements of Arts and Crafts chairs?
    Click on 2 answers.
    Ⓐ Comfortable cushions.
    Ⓑ Carved legs and arms.
    Ⓒ Large proportions.
    Ⓓ Rich fabrics.

32. What did the motto "hand, head, and heart" mean?
    Ⓐ Craftsmen should love their work.
    Ⓑ Artisans should live together.
    Ⓒ Tradition is important for artists.
    Ⓓ No machines should be used.

33. According to the professor, why did the Arts and Crafts bungalows become so popular?
    Ⓐ They had front porches that could be used as outdoor rooms.
    Ⓑ They were not as expensive as the homes of the Victorian era.
    Ⓒ The workmanship on the bungalows impressed the neighbors.
    Ⓓ They were like the farm homes that the middle class had moved from.

34. Why did the professor use the example of the Van Briggle Pottery Works?
    Ⓐ To prove her point about the continuing popularity of the Arts and Crafts style.
    Ⓑ To demonstrate one of the advantages of the matte glazing process.
    Ⓒ To give an example of highly prized antique Arts and Crafts sculptures.
    Ⓓ To show how the Van Briggle Pottery designs changed over time.

Speaking Section

This section tests your ability to communicate in English in an academic context. The directions are both spoken and written. There are two types of speaking questions. The independent speaking questions require that you talk about personal experiences or preferences related to topics presented in the questions. You may take notes as you prepare. In the independent speaking questions, you should express your opinions. The integrated speaking questions require that you respond to an academic reading, a lecture, or a campus-related conversation. You may take notes as you read and listen. In the integrated questions, you should NOT express opinions. Your response should be based on the information in the reading and lecture material.

Independent Speaking 1: "A Good Neighbor"

 (CD 6, Track 7)

Question:

What are the qualities of a good neighbor? Why do you think these qualities are important? Be sure to include specific examples and details in your answer.

Preparation Time: 15 seconds
Recording Time: 45 seconds

Independent Speaking 2: "On Time"

 (CD 6, Track 8)

Question:

Some people feel that it is important to be on time for every meeting, whether it is a business appointment or a party with friends. Other people feel that being on time is important only for business and professional appointments, but social occasions do not require that the participants arrive on time. Which approach do you think is better and why?

Preparation Time: 15 seconds
Recording Time: 45 seconds

Integrated Speaking 3: "Parking Problems"

 (CD 6, Track 9)

Reading Time: 45 seconds

Question:

Notice Concerning Parking Proposal

State University administration is discussing how to improve the parking situation for students who commute to the campus. Although there are more than 5,000 students who live off campus, only 1,000 parking spaces are available in the student parking lots. The university is considering a plan that would link a campus bus system to the city bus lines in an effort to solve the problem. This plan will be discussed at a meeting in the student union on Saturday, May 2, at 9:30 a.m.

The student expresses his opinion about the university's plans for improving the parking situation at State University. Report his opinion and explain the reasons that he gives for having that opinion.

Preparation Time: 30 seconds
Recording Time: 60 seconds

Integrated Speaking 4: "Land-Use Planning"

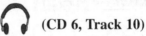 **(CD 6, Track 10)**

Reading Time: 45 seconds

Question:

Land-Use Planning

Land-use planning is a system of evaluation that attempts to balance the needs and desires of the population with the characteristics and value of a particular land resource. An evaluation includes the exploration of alternatives for the use of a particular piece of land before changes are made to it. The problem inherent in any land-use decision is that competing uses may all be important, but it may not be possible to serve all interests in the final plan. A basic premise of land-use planning is to make as few changes as possible in order to accommodate the economic or recreational needs of the population.

Explain what the land-use committee believed to be the problem in their area, and what they recommended to solve it. Explain how their decision reflects the fundamental principles of land-use planning.

Preparation Time: 30 seconds
Recording Time: 60 seconds

Integrated Speaking 5: "Scholarships"

 (CD 6, Track 11)

Question:
Describe the woman's problem and the two suggestions that the man makes about how to handle it. What do you think the woman should do and why?

Preparation Time: 20 seconds
Recording Time: 60 seconds

Integrated Speaking 6: "X-Rays"

 (CD 6, Track 12)

Question:
Using the main points and examples from the lecture, explain how x-rays work, and then describe the two functions of x-rays explained by the professor.

Preparation Time: 20 seconds
Recording Time: 60 seconds

Writing Section

This section tests your ability to write essays in English. There are two types of essay questions. The independent essay requires that you state and support your opinion about a topic presented in the question. The integrated essay requires that you respond to an academic reading passage, a lecture or both. You may take notes as you read and listen. In the integrated essay, you should NOT express opinions. Your response should be based on the information in the reading and lecture material.

Independent Writing: "Technology in Education"

Directions:

You have 30 minutes to plan, write, and revise your essay. Typically, a good response will require that you write a minimum of 300 words.

Question:

Some students enjoy taking distance-learning courses on the computer or by television. Other students would rather take all of their courses with a teacher in a classroom. Which of these options do you think is better? Use specific reasons and examples in support of your opinion.

Notes

Use this space for essay notes only. Work done on this work sheet will *not* be scored.

Essay

Integrated Writing: "The Mozart Effect"

Directions:
You have 20 minutes to plan, write and revise your response to a reading passage and a lecture on the same topic. First, read the passage below and take notes. Then, listen to the lecture and take notes. Finally, write your response to the writing question. Typically, a good response will require that you write 200–250 words.

The popular press has reported a number of studies documenting the positive effect of classical music on cognitive tasks. In one of the earlier experiments, Shaw and Rauscher tested the performance of three groups of college students. In preparation for a series of reasoning problems, the first group listened to 10 minutes of *Mozart's Sonata for Two Pianos in D Major*, the second group spent the same amount of time listening to relaxation tapes, and the third group sat in silence for 10 minutes. All three groups were given the same tasks to perform after the ten-minute preparatory phase. The students who listened to the classical music scored significantly higher than the students in the other two groups, leading researchers to conclude that at least some measures of cognitive ability may be influenced positively by the introduction of classical music as a preparatory strategy. Furthermore, Rauscher speculated that Mozart's music, known for its complex and creative structure, could be activating portions of the brain that are important to spatial reasoning. Although it was disappointing that the beneficial results lasted only a few minutes, listening to classical music was still considered a promising approach in preparation for a cognitively challenging task. The results were referred to as the "Mozart Effect."

In a more comprehensive investigation by the same researchers, children from three California preschools were tested for cognitive ability, and then divided into four groups. One group took private piano lessons while another group received singing lessons, and a third group participated in computer training. The control group did not have any special interventions. Unlike the research with the college students, all of the children were tested six to eight months later to determine whether there were any long-term results. By the end of the experiment, the children who had taken piano lessons had improved their scores by 34 percent on a task that required them to put together a jigsaw puzzle, a grade-appropriate measure of spatial reasoning.

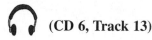 **(CD 6, Track 13)**

Now listen to a lecture on the same topic as the passage that you have just read.

Writing Question:
Summarize the main points in the lecture, referring to the way that they cast doubt on the research presented in the reading.

Notes

Use this space for essay notes only. Work done on this work sheet will *not* be scored.

Essay

iBT® Model Test Scripts for the Listening Section

Independent Listening 1: "Talking About Professors"

 (CD 6, Track 1)

Narrator: Listen to a conversation between two students. They are talking after class.

Joe: So, how did you like the lecture?

Alice: It was okay, I guess.

Joe: That doesn't sound very enthusiastic.

Alice: Well, to tell the truth, Dr. Peterson's lectures usually leave me cold.

Joe: Really? That surprises me. I mean, she's so organized.

Alice: That's just it. My outline's perfect. No digressions, no interesting asides. Just the facts. I might as well read the book and skip the class. What about you?

Joe: Hmmn. That's why I like her lectures, actually. I read the book before class, then her lecture gives me a really good review of the chapter. In fact, sometimes, when I don't have time to read the chapter, I just listen and take notes, then I, uh, study from . . .

Alice: Oh, I see. You . . .

Joe: No, no. I usually read the chapters, too. I said sometimes. . . . What kind of lecture *do* you like?

Alice: Well, something that adds value. I like stories, examples, you know, the kind of thing that makes the material seem more real. Like Professor . . .

Joe: Woods.

Alice: Exactly. Now, I could listen to his lectures anytime.

Joe: Not to mention the fact that he looks so good.

Alice: That doesn't have anything to do with it.

Joe: Come on, you know that half the class is . . . half the class has a crush on him.

Alice: No, no, what I like is how interesting he makes the material. He always brings in pictures and videos, and . . . and that gets me interested. Dr. Peterson might as well read from the book.

Joe: That's not fair. She's very well prepared. Like today.

Alice: Okay, I'll give you that. She *is* organized. But Woods is organized, too . . . it's just that . . . that . . . he's more flexible.

Joe: Hey, professors just have different presentation styles.

Alice: True, and students have different learning styles, too. So, uh, naturally, a student is going to prefer a professor whose presentation style is, well, more compatible with that student's learning style. Don't you think?

Joe: That does make sense. I know I'm a linear thinker, so. . . .

Alice: No kidding!

Joe: And you . . . aren't.

Alice: No, I'm more holistic, I'd say. Probably more . . . well, more of a visual learner.

Joe: Right. So that proves your theory. Peterson certainly has a linear presentation style — everything's laid out in lists on the handouts. And Woods does bring in all those visuals.

Alice: Umhum. I like Professor Jones, too.

Joe: And probably Stanley and Green as well.

Alice: Yeah, I do. You don't?

Joe: Too much extra stuff. I don't know. I get confused with all that. I relate to the professors who summarize the material. Like Peterson or, uh, Baker. And another thing, don't forget that Peterson shows up for every lecture, not like some professors who send their TAs to teach their classes.

Alice: That's not fair. Woods doesn't do that very often. Besides the TA isn't that bad.

Joe: No, but . . . but a lot of professors do, especially the ones who are doing a lot of research. But when you sign up for Peterson's class, you know that *she's* going to teach it.

Alice: I'll give her that. She does do her own lecturing. But on the other hand, Woods brings his research into the class, and you know, that just makes it more interesting, in my opinion. Even if he does have his TA do some of the lectures.

Joe: Um, actually his TA's pretty good. Better than Woods in some ways.

Alice: Well, to each his own, but even you have to admit that Woods is better than Peterson about answering questions.

Joe: He's good on his feet. But with Peterson, I don't have that many questions to ask. It's so . . . so straightforward. Like today, no one asked any questions because it was so, uh, clear.

Alice: And, besides you can just look in the book.

Joe: Which I like.

Alice: I know. So are you going to take any more courses with her?

Joe: Sure. Next semester I'm going to sign up for the course . . . her class in child psychology.

Alice: I probably will, too.

Joe: Really?

Alice: Yeah, even though I complain about her, I do learn a lot in her classes, and child psychology would be an interesting elective for my major. And um . . . and I think she's the only one who teaches it.

Joe: Great. Then we can study together again, if you want to.

Alice: Okay. That sounds good.

> Now get ready to answer the questions.

1. What are the students mainly discussing?
2. What kind of lecture does the woman prefer?
3. Why does the man criticize Dr. Woods?
4. What is the woman's attitude toward Dr. Woods?
5. What will the woman most probably do?

Independent Listening 2: "Internet Connections"

 (CD 6, Track 2)

Narrator:	Listen to part of a discussion in a sociology class. The professor is talking about the Internet.
Professor:	I'm sure if I asked you, everyone present would respond positively to the question, "Do you use the Internet?" I know this because the use of the Internet among college students is almost 100 percent. We shop on the computer, we learn on the computer, we're entertained on the computer. And more and more we use the computer as a primary means of communication not only with, uh, business associates but also with friends and family. Chat rooms are becoming more and more popular, and, uh, . . . and list-serves connect people from around the world with the information that's important to their group. We even find our prospective mates by using the Internet. So the question is: what effect does the Internet have on social interaction? Any ideas?
Student 1:	Well, from what you said, I think it would be a very positive influence.
Student 2:	Me, too. I mean, in my case, I write e-mails to my family 'cause it's just so easy to jump from what I'm doing at school, a paper or something, to the e-mail program, and you know, write a few lines to my sister. I'd never take the time to write her a letter, buy a stamp, take it to the post office. You know.
Student 1:	Right.
Student 3:	Maybe, but a lot of people aren't using the Net to talk to family or friends. It's a more superficial thing. Well, more of a way to communicate anonymously with uh . . . with strangers. Half the time they aren't even using their real names.
Student 4:	That's true. Besides, what about all the time people spend playing computer games alone instead of doing something with another person?
Professor:	Good observations on both sides. And basically, you've brought out the arguments that have been made for and against Internet use. Some people think that the computer facilitates social interaction, and others feel that it impedes it. So, to find the answer, to investigate how Internet use affects social relationships, a team of psychologists at Carnegie Mellon University . . . they conducted a longitudinal study of Internet users. More than 150 people were monitored for one to two years. The subjects were recruited from among people who hadn't used the Internet previously. In exchange for their participation, they received a computer, free software, a free phone line, and Internet hookup. Before they began using their computers, they were assessed for mental health and, uh, social well-being. After an extended period of Internet use, the team found that time on the computer was, uh, it was detrimental to both mental health and social well-being. In fact, increased use of the Internet correlated with less communication among family members and friends in the local area. Also interesting was the incidence of . . . the highest users . . . reported increased loneliness and a higher degree of depression.
Student 1:	Hmnn. So why did that happen, did they think?
Professor:	What do *you* think?
Student 1:	Disappointment maybe.
Professor:	Go on.
Student 1:	Well, maybe they expected too much from their Internet friends. I mean, if you think that a person you meet on the Internet is going to be your special someone, that probably isn't going to happen. Someone who has Internet friends probably enjoys that, and probably has a lot of . . . of relationships on the Net.

Student 3:	Or, they may be neglecting important friendships while they spend time online, and later, well they may find that they are damaging those . . . those relationships.
Professor:	Both of those ideas sound reasonable. The researchers put it this way: the relationships on the Internet were weak. Example: you might exchange recipes with someone online through a web site, but that person won't probably . . . won't offer help and support when you need it, at least not like some of the friends that you might make at school, work, church, or in your community. So . . . when you say you shouldn't expect too much from an Internet friend, that's uh . . . that's good advice, Nancy. And Rob, when you say that important friendships could be neglected, that's part of the picture, too. But, do you see anything about the findings that we should question?
Student 2:	Well, everybody doesn't use the Internet for the same purposes. So, uh, maybe how the Internet is being used . . . they should probably look at that.
Professor:	Good point. Anything else?
Students 1:	Some people aren't going to make those other kinds of friendships anyway, so, you know, the Internet at least allows them to have some social interaction.
Professor:	That seems reasonable, too, especially in the case of isolated living situations, like, uh, rural areas where there might not be many face-to-face resources. I'd also like to point out that we need more research to draw conclusions. Because this was only one study.

Now get ready to answer the questions.

6. What is the purpose of this lecture?
7. Listen again to part of the lecture. Then answer the question.
   "What do *you* think?" "Disappointment maybe." "Go on." "Well, maybe they expected too much from their Internet friends. I mean, if you think that a person you meet on the Internet is going to be your special someone, that probably isn't going to happen."
   Why does the professor say this: "Go on."
8. What were the results of the research study?
9. The professor gives an example of a person who exchanges recipes with someone on the Internet. What does this example demonstrate?
10. Why does the professor question the results of the research?
11. What is the attitude of the professor toward the students?

Independent Listening 3: "Managing Failure"

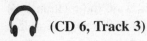 (CD 6, Track 3)

Narrator: Listen to part of a class discussion in a business management class.

Professor: First, let me say that managing success requires a certain set of managing skills, and we're usually focusing on how to be successful managers, but it's also, uh, inevitable that all managers will have to deal with failure—their own or their staff's, or the people they have delegated responsibility to. I assume that you've all read the case study for the Anderson Company. That's on page 347 of your textbook. So, let's summarize that study and use it for the . . . uh . . . our discussion on how to manage failure. Because, believe me, as a manager, you must be able to identify and intervene when mistakes occur. Okay. Back to the Anderson Company. What happened?

Student 1:   Well, first of all, the Anderson Company was a distributor for office supplies, and they lost money because they . . . they underbid a job for a client . . . an important client. So that was the mistake they made.

Professor: Right. And why did they underbid? Anyone?

Student 2:   I don't have my book here, but I think I remember it. There was a large order for furniture . . . wasn't it office furniture? So there was a large order, which was good, but somehow there wasn't any charge in the estimate for assembly of the furniture, so the client expected delivery of desks and chairs, and I think filing cabinets, ready to go, completely assembled, but uh . . . there wasn't any cost figured in for the labor. It was a fairly large figure, too, maybe three thousand dollars.

Professor: Thanks, Anne. That's it in a nutshell. So what was the manager's response when the problem became known?

Student 1:   Well, at first, everybody started pointing fingers at everybody else. And no one was taking responsibility. But, then, uh, the manager called a meeting, and . . . and he said he wanted explanations, not excuses. I remembered that line because I wrote it down. I thought it was really good. And he said that the problem wasn't that something had gone wrong. It was that the cause . . . um . . . the reason why the mistake happened . . . that was what was important . . . because that meant that they could make the same mistake twice.

Professor: So how did the manager handle the meeting? Do you recall?

Student 1:   Oh yeah. That was good, too. He was really calm and not angry at all. And um . . . he said that every mistake was the result of an error in the company, not the employees . . . so the company needed to be modified so the mistake wouldn't happen again, and he told everyone at the meeting that it wasn't his intention to punish anyone for the mistake unless there was an effort to cover it up.

Professor: So the manager's position was to depersonalize the failure and try to prevent it from happening again.

Student 1:   Exactly.

Professor: Okay. Then what happened? Joe?

Student 3:   Um, well, the salesperson who sold the furniture recognized that he forgot to mention the uh . . . the agreement to assemble the furniture before delivery . . . he forgot that when he gave the order to the account supervisor, but it was written on the order. Anyway, he ended up taking some responsibility because it was an unusual request, and he thought he should have maybe pointed it out. Then, the account supervisor admitted that she'd gone through the order very quickly, and . . . and she hadn't seen the word "assembled" on the order, so she didn't figure in the cost when she sent the bid.

Professor: So, once the guilty parties were found, what did the manager do?

Student 2:   I remember that part. He didn't focus on the error at all. He went directly to brainstorming a procedure that would prevent the same error from being made in the future, and they came up with asking the sales team to identify each furniture order as "assembly required" or "no assembly required" after each item, and the account supervisor . . . she was asked to be alert to the instruction on each order so . . . so she could factor in the cost on the bids.

Professor: Okay. What do you think about the manager's style?

Student 1:   Well, I was surprised that he called . . . that it was an open meeting, I mean to resolve the problem. I would have thought that he might have just talked with the people who made the mistake, you know, privately.

Student 2:   That occurred to me, too, when I read the case study, but then I was thinking he was probably running into so many excuses that he needed to just bring it out into the open.

Student 1:   Oh, okay. That makes sense.

Student 3:   I think he was also trying to demonstrate that the company procedures were the problem, not just the employees who had made the error.

Professor: Do you think that the employees should have been reprimanded? After all, the mistake could have been avoided, couldn't it?

Student 2:   Sure, sure, the mistake shouldn't have happened, but I think the manager . . . I think he probably gained more in terms of . . . what do you call it? . . . team building. Probably there was more of a willingness on the part of the employees to come up with positive changes in the procedure too, I mean, I think that was more valuable than the three thousand dollars, and he wouldn't have accomplished that by calling in employees privately to give them a reprimand.

Professor: Okay. And it turned out fine because the people responsible stepped up and accepted their responsibility. But what if they hadn't done that? What do you think the manager would have done . . . in that case?

Student 2:   I think he would have been very firm about concealing the mistake, and he . . . I think he probably would have acted very differently.

Professor: You mean he would have reprimanded them in some way?

Student 2:   I think he would have.

Now get ready to answer the questions.

---

12. What is the class mainly discussing?

13. Listen again to part of the discussion. Then answer the question.
   "Right. And why did they underbid? Anyone?"
   Why does the professor say this: "Anyone?"

14. What does the professor mean when she says this: "That's it in a nutshell."

15. How did the mistake occur?

16. Based on information in the lecture, indicate whether the statements refer to the way that the manager responded to the error.

17. What conclusion did the students make about the management style?

Independent Listening 4: "Application for a Scholarship"

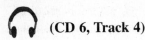 **(CD 6, Track 4)**

Narrator: Listen to a conversation between a student and a professor.

Student:	Hi, Professor Walters.
Walters:	Hi, Jan. How are you doing?
Student:	Great, thanks. How are you?
Walters:	Just fine. What can I do for you?
Student:	Well, um . . . I'd really appreciate your help with my scholarship application.
Walters:	Oh, good. I'm glad you applied. Oh, wait, that deadline is the end of next week, isn't it?
Student:	It's . . . it's this Friday. But I have everything done on the computer, so, uh, any changes will be easy to fix. And, uh, it shouldn't take long to finish it up.
Walters:	Okay.
Student:	Actually, the main problem I'm having is with . . . I'm not sure my essay is what they're looking for. You know, I find it a little embarrassing to, well, to tell them what a great person I am, if you know what I mean.
Walters:	Have you written anything yet?
Student:	Just an outline. Here it is.
Walters:	Okay. But before I look at this, do you have the directions for the application, or better yet, for the essay?
Student:	Yeah, right here. I have the, um, instructions for the application right here.
Walters:	Let me see that first, because the committee usually wants . . . has some specific points that they're looking for. This is sponsored by a private donor as I recall, and it's open only to women who are seniors in the college of business.
Student:	Right. And I'll be a senior next year, so it's . . . it would be perfect.
Walters:	But there have to be some more, uh, more specific requirements here . . . somewhere. . . . Oh, here we are. Look at this. They want to know about your personal background, then they want you to tell them about, uh, the first three years of your college education, and . . . and last, they want specifics about your goals.
Student:	Uh-oh. Well, I didn't do this right then. Hmmn. I just wrote why I needed the scholarship.
Walters:	And that may be okay for the part about your college education, or, uh, you might even be able to put it in with the part about your goals . . . uh . . . but I can assure you that you'll lose points if you don't follow these directions and write . . . it appears to me they want a three-part essay—personal background, college education, and goals. Listen, I've been involved in quite a few scholarship committees, and in order to be as . . . as fair as possible, we all read the applications and assign points to them—usually one hundred—just because it's easy to figure up, but anyway, there will be a certain number of points for the essay, and because this almost has to be a three-part essay, um . . . you'll probably get one-third of the points for each part. So . . . if you don't write about your personal background, for example, uh . . . you'll lose one-third of the points for the essay, and that, uh, that could mean the difference between being in the final group that gets called in for an interview or not moving into the final group at all.
Student:	Wow. I almost blew it. I'd better go back and rewrite this. Professor Walters, uh . . . could you possibly give me another appointment . . . before Friday? I mean, so I can show you my essay? My new essay?

Walters:	Sure, Jan. But, the sooner the better. Even if the committee doesn't meet for a month, what usually happens is the secretary will stamp a date on every application packet. And uh . . . any packets with dates after the deadline . . . those will be eliminated first. There will probably be over a hundred applications. I'm just guessing here, but there will be a lot of them, and using the date as the first screening is . . . is pretty common.
Student:	Well, it's only three paragraphs, so I could have that done by tomorrow, but . . . but I don't know if you could see me then?
Walters:	Tomorrow's fine. I'll be here between one and three.
Student:	Great. When. . . .
Walters:	You don't need an appointment. I'll see you when you get here.
Student:	Thanks so much, Dr. Walters. That's so great.
Walters:	No problem. I can see from the way that you have your application prepared that . . . I can tell you've taken a lot of time to work on this. Besides that, Jan, you're an excellent student. Your grade point average is what . . . a 4.0?
Student:	So far I have all As.
Walters:	See what I'm saying? I think you're a good candidate for this scholarship, and I'd like to see you give it your best shot.
Student:	Thanks.
Walters:	And Jan, that part about being embarrassed to tell the committee how good you are? Pretend you're writing this essay about your best friend. You're good friends with Kathy, right?
Student:	She's my best friend for sure.
Walters:	Well then, pretend you're writing this essay about her. Just use the information about *you* when you do it. Okay?
Student:	Okay. Like you said, I'm going to give it my best shot.

> Now get ready to answer the questions.

18. Why does the student go to see the professor?
19. What information is required in the essay?
20. When does the woman need to turn in her application to the committee?
21. Listen again to part of the conversation. Then answer the question.
    "Your grade point average is what . . . a 4.0?"
    "So far I have all As."
    "See what I'm saying?"
    Why does the professor say this: "Your grade point average is what . . . a 4.0?"
22. Why does Professor Walters tell the woman to pretend she is writing about her friend Kathy?

Independent Listening 5: "Pest Management"

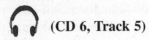 **(CD 6, Track 5)**

Narrator: Listen to part of a lecture in an environmental science class.

Professor:

Today I'd like to introduce the topic of integrated pest management. Now unlike the previous methods that uh relied on . . . on pesticides alone, integrated pest management requires a complete analysis of the . . . ecology of the crop—which pests it might be susceptible to, how the pests interact with parasites or predators, how the climate affects the pests, and . . . and how beneficial insects can be, uh, encouraged. It's also important to . . . to understand the points of vulnerability in the life cycles of pests. Now reproduction is especially important, as you can imagine, because . . . because if you can reduce the number of new pests, then the population will be dramatically affected . . . I'm talking about during the next crop season. For example, during the mating stage of some species of moths, a chemical called a pheromone . . . pheromone spelled with a p-h . . . so a pheromone is released by females to attract males. Believe it or not, the males can detect pheromones from, well, as far away as two miles—that's nearly three kilometers. So spraying an area with a pheromone or something synthetic like a pheromone . . . that confuses the males, that makes them . . . they are unsuccessful finding females to mate with, and . . . and the moth population the following year is greatly reduced. So, there are fewer pests to deal with. Of course, another option is to . . . is male sterilization, which has been very effective, especially with certain varieties of flies. The screwworm fly can actually kill large grazing animals like cattle or goats, but since the female mates only once in her life cycle, the population can be controlled by, uh, developing sterile males . . . and they do this in . . . in lab settings and then they release them into the environment. So, as you can see, manipulating the reproductive cycles is one very good way to manage pests.

Now another management strategy is to use a predator to control the pests. Most of you are familiar with the ladybug, but you may not know that the ladybug is a natural predator of aphids and aphids attack citrus trees and reduce crop yields. So by increasing the ladybug population, the aphid population . . . it naturally decreases. And ladybugs aren't harmful to other plants. Okay, I should mention that the definition of a pest extends to vegetation. Weeds are pests too, and they can be controlled effectively by introducing predators as well. Uh, the criteria are a little bit tricky though, since weeds are plants, and uh . . . it's important to find a predator that attacks the weeds but it doesn't like the crop, so it leaves the plant crop alone. But, it can be done, like the case of several species of beetles that feed on a wetlands weed called purple loosestrife. The problem is the loosestrife crowds out cattails and other native vegetation in the wetlands ecosystem. So, the beetles are introduced, and they reduce the loosestrife . . . don't quote me on this, but I think it is as much as 90 percent in some areas.

So, that brings us to the use of bacteria to kill pests, which I'll just mention briefly. One example of an effective intervention is the introduction of *Bacillus thuringiensis* . . . let me write that on the board for you . . . *Bacillus thuringiensis* . . . which releases a toxin that destroys large populations of mosquitoes and caterpillars and is especially efficient in ridding crop areas of the caterpillars that become adult leaf-eating moths.

Actually, the modification of farming practices can make a . . . a huge difference in pest management. For one thing, there are some naturally occurring pesticides in plants. Marigolds control soil nematodes, and, uh, garlic controls some species of beetles, so you see, planting these crops along with another crop that needs protection can, uh, really help. Another thing . . . destroying crop residues by plowing them under . . . that eliminates an environment where pests may live during the winter, and they die out so there aren't as many and that reduces the need for insecticides in the spring. Oh yes, the old practice of crop rotation has become popular again too, because it prevents a buildup of the same pests year after year.

But uh . . . the latest strategy in pest management involves the genetic modification of the plants themselves. Now in the next decade, we hope to be able to . . . to engineer high-yield plant varieties, and uh . . . they'll be much more resistant to insects and diseases. Although this is a simplification, in general, generic engineering . . . did I say generic? . . . genetic engineering, that's genetic engineering . . . involves the insertion of genes from other species into crop plants in order to develop beneficial traits. One example that is very exciting is the insertion of bacterial genes, and these genes will . . . support the plant's production of a natural, uh, pesticide that . . . the pesticide will protect it against its primary pest. And in another successful project, genes are being inserted to . . . to protect the crop from the pesticides that are used to control weeds. So that could be a real breakthrough. Of course, there are ethical considerations, and cost effectiveness issues. In fact, uh, some countries won't import genetically engineered plants because there are still so many unknowns. Can we really know the result to the total ecosystem that the introduction of a biotechnologically engineered plant will cause?

In any case, you can see that there are a number of alternatives for integrated pest management, including pesticides, but also using intervention in the reproductive cycle, the introduction of natural predators, substitution of bacteria for pesticides, modification of farming practices, and . . . and even genetic modification of the plants themselves. Most management plans will, in fact, use a number of these strategies for uh . . . in a complete plan.

Now get ready to answer the questions.

23. What is this lecture mainly about?
24. According to the professor, what are *pheromones*?
25. Why does the professor mention the example of ladybugs?
26. Which changes in farming practices support pest management?
27. Listen again to part of the lecture. Then answer the question.
    "Although this is a simplification, in general, generic engineering . . . Did I say generic? . . . genetic engineering, that's genetic engineering . . . involves the insertion of genes from other species into crop plants in order to develop beneficial traits."
    Why does the professor ask the following question: "Did I say generic?"
28. What does the professor imply about genetic modification of plants?

Independent Listening 6: "Arts and Crafts"

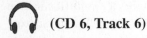 (CD 6, Track 6)

Narrator: Listen to part of a lecture in an art history class.

Professor:

The Arts and Crafts movement was a reaction to the mass production of the industrial period. It began at the very end of the nineteenth century, but it's generally considered a twentieth-century movement, and really, there's no clear end to it. In fact, arguably, there's still evidence of an Arts and Crafts school today. So, what identifies Arts and Crafts? I'm going to talk about four characteristics: quality, simplicity, comfort, and hand craftsmanship. But to . . . to really understand the philosophy, and it is a philosophy, we should compare all of those characteristics with the qualities from the Victorian age that preceded the Arts and Crafts movement. As you'll recall from our study of the Victorians, theirs was an age of quantity. That is to say, every surface was covered with pictures, ornaments, and objects. Also, the Victorians were noted for extravagance, and uh . . . even excess in decoration. And, they were impressed by the new machine reproductions that were being mass-produced, uh, at reasonable prices. Finally, don't forget that style and show were more important to them than comfort, and by that I mean the Victorians were more interested in . . . in impressing the guests that came to call than uh, than uh, than making them comfortable.

Now, with that in mind, let's go back and compare the Victorians with the Arts and Crafts artisans that came after them. 1. Quality instead of quantity. In other words, the Arts and Crafts artisans thought that it was better to have a few fine objects than . . . than a clutter of objects that were less valuable. 2. Simplicity instead of excess. A room decorated in the Arts and Crafts style would have looked . . . well, people who were accustomed to Victorian opulence would probably have thought it was quite bare. Simple lines replaced the carvings that . . . that seemed to cover every inch of furniture and architectural ornamentation in Victorian homes. 3. Comfort instead of display. And this was especially evident in the Arts and Crafts chairs that were uh . . . uh . . . softly padded with leather cushions and rounded edges. The Victorian chairs were more like, well, really like tiny thrones and were built for people to perch on, but the Arts and Crafts chairs were practical, big, and roomy. You could sink into the chairs. And the rest of the furniture was also practical, with . . . with clean lines and comfort built in. The, uh, Eastwood chair comes to mind, although Gustav Stickley was also producing chairs in a Mission style that's still popular today. And . . . and that's what I meant about not having a clear end to the movement since it's still an alternative for decorative arts today.

Okay. How did the movement begin? Well, the industrial age caused a reaction among artists in many places, but William Morris in England was certainly in the forefront, along with Elbert Hubbard who . . . Hubbard founded the East Aurora Workshop. The East Aurora motto was "hand, head, and heart" which probably sums up the movement as well and . . . and concisely as anything. Originally the workshop was a group of fifty artisans living in a community, and they followed the tradition of medieval craftsmen, although they used machines as tools for their crafts. I think they were probably best known for hand-bound books, but the East Aurora Workshop also produced, uh . . . pieces of hammered metalwork and . . . and furniture, primarily oak and chestnut furniture. Remember that motto, "hand, head, and heart." Well, according to Hubbard, if you love the work and work with integrity, the rest will follow. So that was his way of living the motto. In 1914 . . . sorry . . . 1915 . . . that was the date when Hubbard died, and the community dispersed, but almost one hundred years later, the pieces of Roycroft furniture that they produced there are highly prized.

So, let's see . . . what was happening in the outside world? Farmers were moving to the cities to work in factories, and there was an . . . an expansion of the middle class. The Victorian homes were too expensive, too ornate, and the Arts and Crafts bungalow home emerged as the affordable, well-constructed alternative to, uh, the castle-like mansions of the Victorian era. Bungalows were charming, homey, and affordable. They often had open living and dining areas that gave a more spacious feel to a smaller space, and built-in cabinets that, uh, reduced the need to buy furniture. The front porches became outdoor rooms with simple, comfortable tables and chairs. Instead of the Victorian facade that was built to impress the neighbors, the porch was . . . was unadorned but welcoming. In many ways, these bungalows became the standard for middle-class neighborhoods. But when we look at them today, they're impressive in their own way. The workmanship, in many cases, is just superb. The wood beams and natural wood floors, the fireplaces, and the cabinetry are . . . let's say . . . unpretentious but exquisitely crafted. And the tile work should also be mentioned. The name to remember for tile is Henry Chapman Mercer, who founded the Moravian Pottery and Tile Works in Pennsylvania. While working with apprentices, he supervised every piece and they decorated them all by hand. The maker was part of the product and often signed the tiles.

I guess what strikes me as an art historian about the Arts and Crafts movement is the fact that the designs are so timeless. Van Briggle Pottery, for example, was founded in Colorado Springs almost one hundred years ago by Artis Van Briggle, who demanded that the function of pottery . . . uh . . . the utility . . . be combined with the art. Van Briggle created designs that were shaped to resemble sculptures, and then he developed a unique glaze that came out of the firing with a matte finish, which was really new since the pottery of the time was, uh, very highly polished. But my point is that the Van Briggle Pottery Works continues to operate today, using those original designs. That's what I mean by timeless.

> Now get ready to answer the questions.

29. What is the professor mainly discussing?
30. Listen again to part of the lecture. Then answer the question.
    "As you'll recall from our study of the Victorians, theirs was an age of quantity. That is to say, every surface was covered with pictures, ornaments, and objects. Also, the Victorians were noted for extravagance, and uh . . . even excess in decoration."
    Why does the professor say this: "As you'll recall from our study of the Victorians, theirs was an age of quantity."
31. What are two design elements of Arts and Crafts chairs?
32. What did the motto "hand, head, and heart" mean?
33. According to the professor, why did the Arts and Crafts bungalows become so popular?
34. Why did the professor use the example of the Van Briggle Pottery Works?

iBT® Model Test Scripts for the Speaking Section

Narrator 2: This is the speaking section of the TOEFL Model Test. During the test, you will respond to six speaking questions. You may take notes as you listen. The reading passages and the questions are printed in the book, but most of the directions will be spoken.

Independent Speaking 1: "A Good Neighbor"

 (CD 6, Track 7)

Narrator 2:
Number 1. Listen for a question about a familiar topic. After you hear the question, you have 15 seconds to prepare and 45 seconds to record your answer.

Narrator 1:
What are the qualities of a good neighbor? Explain why you think these qualities are important. Be sure to include specific examples and details in your answer.

Narrator 2:
Please prepare your answer after the beep.

Beep

[Preparation Time: 15 seconds]

Narrator 2:
Please begin speaking after the beep.

Beep

[Recording Time: 45 seconds]

Beep

Independent Speaking 2: "On Time"

 (CD 6, Track 8)

Narrator 2:
Number 2. Listen for a question that asks your opinion about a familiar topic. After you hear the question, you have 15 seconds to prepare and 45 seconds to record your answer.

Narrator 1:
Some people feel that it is important to be on time for every meeting, whether it is a business appointment or a party with friends. Other people feel that being on time is important only for business and professional appointments, but social occasions do not require that the participants arrive on time. Which approach do you think is better, and why? Be sure to use specific reasons and examples to support your opinion.

Narrator 2:
Please prepare your answer after the beep.

Beep

[Preparation Time: 15 seconds]

Narrator 2:
Please begin speaking after the beep.

Beep

[Recording Time: 45 seconds]

Beep

Integrated Speaking 3: "Parking Problems"

 (CD 6, Track 9)

Narrator 2:
Number 3. Read a short passage and then listen to a talk on the same topic. Then listen for a question about them. After you hear the question, you have 30 seconds to prepare and 60 seconds to record your answer.

Narrator 1:
The administration at State University recognizes that there are not enough parking spaces for commuter students. Read the notice from a poster on campus. You have 45 seconds to complete it (refer to page 533). Please begin reading now.

[Reading Time: 45 seconds]

Narrator 1:
Now listen to a student who is speaking at the open meeting. He is expressing his opinion about the parking problem.

Student:
    I understand that there are good reasons to use public transportation, but for many of us, it just isn't practical. If you look at the number of married students with children, you'll see that there are quite a few who have to take children to school, go to work, and then come to campus, and it wouldn't be very convenient to try to do all that by bus. Besides, a lot of times, I stay really late at the library, but the public buses stop running at nine. And to tell the truth, I don't think students will use the buses, so the parking problem won't be solved anyway.

Narrator 1:
The student expresses his opinion about the university's plans for improving the parking situation at State University. Report his opinion and explain the reasons that he gives for having that opinion.

Narrator 2:
Please prepare your answer after the beep.

Beep

[Preparation Time: 30 seconds]

Narrator 2:
Please begin speaking after the beep.

Beep

[Recording Time: 60 seconds]

Beep

Integrated Speaking 4: "Land-Use Planning"

 (CD 6, Track 10)

Narrator 2:
Number 4. Read a short passage and then listen to a lecture on the same topic. Then listen for a question about them. After you hear the question, you have 30 seconds to prepare and 60 seconds to record your answer.

Narrator 1:
Now read the passage about land-use planning. You have 45 seconds to complete it (refer to page 533). Please begin reading now.

[Reading Time: 45 seconds]

Narrator 1:
Now listen to part of a lecture in an environmental science class. The professor is talking about a land-use problem.

Professor:
Recently, there was an opportunity for a recreational area to be established on public land in Arizona, with funding from a large private benefactor, but the area had traditionally been used for ranching. It seems that a special use permit had been granted to several large ranchers who had been grazing cattle on the land for years. So the problem for the land-use committee was how to resolve the dispute. On the one hand, public sentiment favored using public land for recreation that would benefit the community. On the other hand, the permits had been issued, and the ranchers were influential and politically well-connected.

One obvious solution was to designate the public land for a particular type of use, and to locate a similar area nearby for the other purpose. But the committee decided to allow the recreational area to be established on the rangeland, and to continue to grant range rights to the ranchers. Although the ranchers resented the intrusion of the hikers and campers, and the people who participated in recreational activities were not happy about the herds of cattle on what they considered a wilderness area, the committee was firm about the shared use.

Narrator 1:
Explain what the land-use committee believed to be the problem in their area, and what they recommended to solve it. Explain how their decision reflects the fundamental principles of land-use planning.

Narrator 2:
Please prepare your answer after the beep.

Beep

[Preparation Time: 30 seconds]

Narrator 2:
Please begin speaking after the beep.

Beep

[Recording Time: 60 seconds]

Beep

Integrated Speaking 5: "Scholarships"

 (CD 6, Track 11)

Narrator 2:
Number 5. Listen to a short conversation. Then listen for a question about it. After you hear the question, you have 20 seconds to prepare and 60 seconds to record your answer.

Narrator 1:
Now listen to a conversation between a student and her advisor.

Student: I've been looking for information about scholarships, but so far I haven't found anything for foreign students. You see, I'm from Canada.

Advisor: Well, I'm not surprised about the scholarship situation. Unfortunately, the university offers very little in the way of financial support for nonresident students. I would say that about 80 percent of the scholarships go to in-state residents. You know, students who graduated from high schools in this state.

Student: What about the other 20 percent?

Advisor: Scholarships for specific fields of study. But most of them are restricted to citizens of the U.S. [pause] What's your major?

Student: It's engineering.

Advisor: Engineering. Well, you might qualify for the Williams Memorial Scholarship. Mr. Williams was a successful engineer in Chicago and his family arranged for a scholarship in his name. It's highly competitive, but there are no restrictions on nationality. How are your grades?

Student: I have a 3.9.

Advisor: Well, that's good enough to try for it. But, if that doesn't work out, have you considered work-study? You could work twenty hours a week. It's usually office work, although occasionally there are jobs in the library.

Student: Can I do that on a student visa? I don't have a work permit.

Advisor: That's okay. You're allowed to work part time, as long as it's on campus.

Narrator 1:
Describe the woman's problem, and the two suggestions that her advisor makes about how to handle it. What do you think the woman should do, and why?

Narrator 2:
Please prepare your answer after the beep.

Beep

[Preparation Time: 20 seconds]

Narrator 2:
Please begin speaking after the beep.

Beep

[Recording Time: 60 seconds]

Beep

Integrated Speaking 6: "X-Rays"

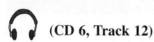 **(CD 6, Track 12)**

Narrator 2:
Number 6. Listen to part of a lecture. Then listen for a question about it. After you hear the question, you have 20 seconds to prepare, and 60 seconds to record your answer.

Narrator 1:
Now listen to part of a lecture in a science class. The professor is discussing x-rays.

Professor:
Okay, let's review what we talked about yesterday, about x-rays, I mean. Remember, x-rays are electromagnetic waves that range in wavelength from as large as 100 nanometers to as small as 0.1 nanometers. That's smaller than an atom. But, these waves, though small, have a very high frequency and consequently, a very high-energy output. So x-rays can penetrate several centimeters into most objects.

But what makes x-rays really important is the fact that they are absorbed by varying degrees, right? This property is why x-rays are commonly used in medical science—to capture visual images of the skeleton and organs in the human body—because bones and teeth absorb x-rays more efficiently than soft tissues like skin or muscle, and well, a detailed picture of the internal organs can be formed in an image. Another very important function of x-rays is to make images of manufactured structures in industries where welded parts are joined. Using x-rays, it's possible to locate defects and correct them as part of the inspection process, again because materials will absorb the x-rays in varying degrees. The transportation industry relies heavily on this technology to inspect automobiles and aircraft. And x-ray scanners are standard equipment for security, as for example, in the machines at airports that check the contents of baggage. Other possibilities for x-rays are being explored in atomic research. As more powerful x-rays are developed, we believe that it'll be possible to use beams to study the exact position of atoms in something as small and delicate as a crystal. Then we'll be able to explore the properties of matter with much greater precision.

Narrator 1:
Referring to the main points and examples from the lecture, describe the properties that make x-rays useful. Then describe the specific purposes of x-rays that the professor presents.

Narrator 2:
Please prepare your answer after the beep.

Beep

[Preparation Time: 20 seconds]

Narrator 2:
Please begin speaking after the beep.

Beep

[Recording Time: 60 seconds]

Beep

iBT® Model Test Scripts for the Writing Section

Integrated Writing: "The Mozart Effect"

 (CD 6, Track 13)

Narrator: Now listen to a lecture on the same topic as the passage that you have just read.

Professor:

Now that you've read the article on the "Mozart Effect," here are a few thoughts for your consideration. Let me say that although the research on the effect of exposure to music or actual training in music is very interesting, and, uh, I agree that this line of investigation should be continued, I think that we need to look more closely at . . . at three aspects of these studies. First, it's being conducted by a limited number of researchers, and I understand that this is happening in part because it takes a degree of musical expertise to accomplish and interpret these kinds of studies, but it would be much more convincing if a larger number of researchers were making contributions to the work. That way, the studies wouldn't cite previous studies by the same investigators.

Second, the research has been used to . . . to make a case for music education in schools. As you probably already know, both music and art have been removed from the curriculum in many schools because of budget cuts. And um, the way that the research has been presented outside of the academic community has often been less than scientific. I mean, even if you agree that music is important to children, as I do, it doesn't follow that the results of these studies conclude that the music programs should be reinstated. In defense of the researchers, let me mention that some of the general interest magazines and newspapers summed up their reports with conclusions that the original researchers did not put forward.

Okay, third, an entire industry has grown up around the "Mozart Effect." Children's publishers have come out with a number of products that claim to make babies smarter. Audio tapes and toys with classical music cues are becoming popular among parents who want to give their children an intellectual advantage before they begin school. So it seems to me that the rush to sell the idea to parents muddies the water because the toy companies interject the research into advertising copy in such a way that the ad itself appears to be a legitimate conclusion of the studies cited. You see, we just don't have very much information about the way the brain processes music. We may be able to conclude that there's some benefit, the so-called "Mozart Effect," but how does that happen? We do know quite a lot about the way that the human brain processes language, and . . . and when we get to that point in our understanding of music, then the explanations that are currently so speculative in the music research will be more convincing, and then any programs and products developed will be more valuable.

Answer Key—iBT®

Reading

1. (A)	9. (A)	17. (D)	25. (D)	33. (C)
2. (C)	10. (D)	18. (C)	26. (B) (C) (D)	34. (B)
3. (D)	11. (C)	19. (C)	27. (B)	35. (D)
4. (B)	12. (B)	20. (D)	28. (A)	36. (B)
5. (A)	13. (A) (E) (F)	21. (A)	29. (B)	37. (D)
6. (C)	14. (B)	22. (B)	30. (B)	38. (D)
7. (A)	15. (C)	23. (B)	31. (A)	39. (A) (D) (E)
8. (D)	16. (C)	24. (B)	32. (D)	

Listening

1. (C)	8. (B) (C)	15. (C)	22. (C)	29. (B)
2. (B) (C)	9. (D)	16. (B) (D) YES (A) (C) NO	23. (D)	30. (C)
3. (B)	10. (C)	17. (B)	24. (C)	31. (A) (C)
4. (D)	11. (C)	18. (C)	25. (B)	32. (A)
5. (B)	12. (C)	19. (B) (C)	26. (A) (B)	33. (B)
6. (A)	13. (C)	20. (C)	27. (C)	34. (A)
7. (B)	14. (B)	21. (C)	28. (B)	

Speaking

For evaluation of this section, refer to checklists and rubrics on pages 387, 392, and 566.

Writing

For evaluation of this section, refer to checklists and rubrics on pages 453, 463, and 566.

SCORE ESTIMATES

Score Scales for Paper-Based Model Test

Section 1 Listening Comprehension

Correct Answers	Scaled Score
48–50	65
45–47	60
42–44	58
39–41	56
36–38	54
33–35	42
30–32	50
27–29	48
24–26	47
21–23	45
18–20	42
15–17	40
12–14	33
9–11	30

Section 2 Structure and Written Expression

Correct Answers	Scaled Score
38–40	65
36–38	62
33–35	60
30–32	55
27–29	52
24–26	50
21–23	47
18–20	44
15–17	40
12–14	34
9–11	30

Section 3 Reading Comprehension

Correct Answers	Scaled Score
48–50	65
45–47	60
42–44	58
39–41	56
36–38	54
33–35	52
30–32	50
27–29	48
24–26	46
21–23	43
18–20	40
15–17	36
12–14	30
9–11	25

How to Calculate the Estimated Score

1. Add the number of items correct for Section 1 on the Paper-Based Model Test, and locate the scaled score in the chart that corresponds to it. For example, if you have 10 items correct, your scaled score for Section 1 is 30.
2. Use the same procedure for Sections 2 and 3.
3. Now add all three numbers from Sections 1, 2, and 3.
4. Multiply the total by 10, and divide that number by 3.

Example of Estimated Score

Section 1:   40 items correct = 56
Section 2:   36 items correct = 62
Section 3:   43 items correct = 58

$$\text{TOTAL} = 176$$

$176 \times 10 = 1760 \div 3 = 586.66 \text{ or } 587$

Score Scales for Internet-Based iBT Model Test

Section 1 Reading

Correct Answers	Scaled Score
39	30
38	29
37	29
36	28
35	27
34	27
33	26
32	25
31	24
30	23
29	23
28	22
27	22
26	21
25	20
24	20
23	19
22	19
21	18
20	18
19	17
18	17
17	16
16	16
15	15
14	15
13	14
12	13
11	12
10	11
9	10
8	9
7	8
6	6
5	5
4	4
3	3
2	2
1	1
0	0

Section 2 Listening

Correct Answers	Scaled Score
34	30
33	29
32	28
31	28
30	27
29	26
28	25
27	25
26	24
25	23
24	22
23	22
22	21
21	21
20	20
19	19
18	19
17	18
16	17
15	17
14	16
13	15
12	15
11	14
10	13
9	13
8	12
7	11
6	9
5	8
4	6
3	5
2	4
1	2
0	0

Section 3 Speaking

Rubric Score	Scaled Score
4.0	30
3.5	27
3.0	23
2.5	19
2.0	15
1.5	11
1.0	8

Rubrics for Speaking

Good   3.5–4.0
Very comprehensible pronunciation
Accurate content
Fluent speech
Wide range of vocabulary
Few errors in grammar
Well-organized ideas
Logical progression
Easy to understand

Fair   2.5–3.0
Mostly comprehensible pronunciation
Some hesitation in speech
Somewhat limited vocabulary
Errors in grammar
Content not fully developed
Fairly logical progression
Able to communicate

Limited   1.5–2.0
Pronunciation that interferes with
    comprehension
Frequent hesitation in speech
Very limited vocabulary
Errors in grammar that confuse meaning
Partial response

Weak   0–1.0
Incomplete response
Difficult to understand

Section 4 Writing

Rubric Score	Scaled Score
5.0	30
4.5	28
4.0	25
3.5	22
3.0	20
2.5	17
2.0	14
1.5	11
1.0	8

Rubrics for Writing

Good   4.0–5.0
Very comprehensible essay
Accurate content (integrated essay)
Clear relationship between reading and
    lecture (integrated essay)
Wide range of vocabulary
Few errors in grammar
Well-organized ideas
Logical progression
Easy to understand

Fair   2.5–3.5
Mostly comprehensible essay
Some important ideas that are unclear
Partial relationship between reading and
    lecture (integrated essay)
Incorrect word usage
Grammatical errors that interfere with
    comprehension
Communicates general idea

Limited   1.0–2.0
Partially comprehensible essay
Comprehension of content not demonstrated
    (integrated essay)
Unclear relationship between reading and
    lecture (integrated essay)
Very limited vocabulary
Errors in grammar that confuse meaning
Requires interpretation to understand

Weak   0
Incomplete response
Different topic

How to Calculate the Estimated iBT® Score

1. Add the number of items correct for Section 1 on the iBT® Model Test, and locate the scaled score in the chart that corresponds to it. For example, if you have 39 items correct, your scaled score for Section 1 is 30.
2. Use the same procedure for Section 2.
3. Now use the rubrics to score Section 3. Locate the scaled score in the chart that corresponds to your rubric score. For example, if your rubric score is 3.0, your scaled score for Section 3 is 23.
4. Use the same procedure for Section 4.
5. Now add all four numbers from Sections 1, 2, 3, and 4.

Example of Estimated Score

Section 1:   35 items correct = 27
Section 2:   25 items correct = 23
Section 3:   3.5 rubric score = 27
Section 4:   4.0 rubric score = 25

TOTAL = 102

Acknowledgments

I am fortunate to have been associated with so many talented collaborators. Heartfelt thanks to

Lillie Sharpe, my mother
for the lifelong example of positive thinking that inspired chapter one of this book;

Robert Sharpe, my dad
for wise counsel and a good laugh at just the right times;

Marcy Rosenbaum, Senior Editor at Barron's Educational Series, Inc.
for managing the production of the previous editions with intelligence, kindness, creativity, and extraordinary skill;

Pat Hunter, Senior Editor at Barron's Educational Series, Inc.
for bringing a new perspective to the *7th Edition* and for coordinating the production with enthusiasm, patience, and outstanding professionalism;

Debby Becak, Senior Production Manager at Barron's Educational Series, Inc.
for making insightful suggestions and creating designs that greatly enhanced the content;

Michele Sandifer, Copy Editor
for marking the manuscript clearly and constructively;

Bob O'Sullivan, Publisher, Testing Division at Barron's Educational Series, Inc.
for providing exceptional leadership and making the tough decisions with wit and wisdom;

John T. Osterman, my husband
for making countless cups of tea, supplying a copy machine, and living without complaint among the paper storms that I created while completing the manuscript. Life with John continues to be the best chapter in my life story.

Permissions